The Addison-Wesley Series in Finance

SECOND EDITION

FINANCIAL MARKETS AND INSTITUTIONS

FREDERIC S. MISHKIN
Graduate School of Business, Columbia University

CONTRIBUTING AUTHOR
STANLEY G. EAKINS
East Carolina University

ADDISON-WESLEY

An Imprint of Addison Wesley Longman, Inc.

Reading, Massachusetts • Menlo Park, California • New York • Harlow, England
Don Mills, Ontario • Sydney • Mexico City • Madrid • Amsterdam

Senior Editor: Denise Clinton
Associate Editor: Julie Zasloff
Developmental Editor: Jane Tufts
Production Supervisor: Heather Garrison
Supplements Editor: Joan Twining
Marketing Manager: Jodi Fazio
Cover Designer: Larry DiDona
Text Designer: Lesiak/Crampton Design, Inc.
Art Editor: Dale Horn
Cover Photos: Howard Bjornson/Photonica and Photodisc, Inc.
Part and Chapter Opener Photos: Superstock

Financial Markets and Institutions

Library of Congress Cataloging-in-Publication Data

Mishkin, Frederic S.
    Financial markets and institutions / Frederic S. Mishkin, Stanley G. Eakins—2nd ed.
        p.   cm.
Previously published: Financial markets, institutions, and money.
ISBN: 0-321-01465-0
    1. Financial institutions—United States. 2. Money—United States.   3. Money
market—United States.   4. Banks and banking—United States.   I. Eakins, Stanley G.
II. Mishkin, Frederic S. Financial markets, institutions, and money.   III. Title.
HG181.M558   1997
332.1'0973—dc21   97-19647
                                                                           CIP

10 9 8 7 6 5 4 3 2 1—RNT—02 01 00 99 98

■ TO MY DAD

Contents in Brief

Contents

---

*Summary, Key Terms, and Questions and Problems occur at the end of each chapter.

PREFACE

The second edition of *Financial Markets and Institutions* is such a substantial revision that it is almost an entirely new book. Other textbooks in this field are almost entirely descriptive. As such, they do not adequately prepare students either for jobs in the financial services industry or for successful interaction with financial institutions, whatever their jobs. In contrast, this revised edition takes the study of financial markets and institutions in an entirely new direction by emphasizing a practitioner's approach.

This approach has been stimulated by my experience in the Federal Reserve System, which has deepened my understanding of the practical aspects of financial markets and institutions. Also, a new contributing author, Stanley G. Eakins, has been brought on board to provide a more in-depth look at financial markets and institutions. Now a finance professor at East Carolina University, Stan was once a practitioner, serving as vice president and comptroller at the First National Bank of Fairbanks. He has also had firsthand experience as a commercial and real estate loan officer and ran the operations side of the bank.

■ A PRACTITIONER'S APPROACH TO FINANCIAL MARKETS AND INSTITUTIONS

This textbook is a major departure from the traditional descriptive approach. Six basic features distinguish it from its competitors: (1) a unifying analytic framework, (2) complete but not overwhelming institutional detail, (3) an applied managerial perspective, (4) full integration of an international perspective, (5) flexibility, and (6) supplementary materials that facilitate teaching.

Unifying Analytic Framework

Focusing on a mass of dull facts that will soon become obsolete is a poor way to prepare students for the real world. Instead, this textbook develops a unifying analytic framework to organize students' thinking so that they will be better able to interact with or operate in financial markets and institutions in the future. The book's framework enables students to make sense of key facts about our financial system. The framework does more than keep their knowledge from becoming obsolete and make the material inherently interesting; it also relieves students from having to memorize a mass of facts that they will forget soon after the final exam. The unifying analytic framework also provides students with the tools to understand trends in the financial marketplace and in variables such as interest rates and exchange rates.

The analytic framework employs a few basic principles that students can use to organize their thinking about the structure of financial markets and financial innovation, about changes in interest rates and foreign exchange rates over time, and about the management of financial institutions. These principles include portfolio choice, an asset market approach to understanding behavior in financial markets, the theory of efficient capital markets, a theory of financial structure based on transaction costs and asymmetric information, and the measurement and management of interest-rate risk.

To help students apply these basic principles, the text adopts an approach found in the best business and finance textbooks: Models are constructed in which the variables held constant are carefully delineated; then the models are used to explain various phenomena by focusing on changes in one variable at a time, holding all other variables constant. This method discourages rote memorization and encourages students to approach financial markets and institutions using clear, analytic thinking, not an abstract collection of facts. In a field characterized by rapid change, the use of basic analytic models helps students not only understand the current operation of financial institutions and financial markets but also see how these institutions and markets might respond to future changes in the economic and regulatory environment.

To reinforce the models' usefulness, this text emphasizes the interaction of theoretical analysis and empirical data. Throughout the text and in special-interest boxes, evidence is presented that supports or cast doubts on the theories being discussed. This exposure to real-life events and data should dissuade students from thinking that finance professors just make abstract assumptions and develop theories that have nothing to do with actual behavior.

An additional benefit of teaching financial markets and institutions with unifying analytic models is that this method enables the instructor to take a modern approach based on the latest research. For example, the model used to analyze interest-rate and exchange rate determination is based on a modern asset market approach. In contrast, other textbooks rely on older approaches that stress flows rather than stocks of assets. Because the modern asset market approach is much better suited to explaining the volatility we see in asset prices such as interest rates, exchange rates, and stock prices, the finance industry has adopted it in the professional literature.

The unifying analytic framework also incorporates the literature on asymmetric information and financial structure. This framework, unique to this book, provides a modern understanding of financial markets and institutions and allows in-depth analysis of current problems in banking regulation. In addition, it enables students to understand how financial institutions affect the state of economy. For example, the theory is used to show how the capital crunch for the banking industry might have led to the credit crunch that produced a sluggish recovery from the 1990–1991 recession.

Complete but Not Overwhelming Institutional Detail

Comments from instructors and from reviewers of the first edition indicated that they wanted more institutional detail on specific financial markets and institutions. We have responded to this challenge by adding seven entirely new chapters, written by Stan Eakins, which cover money markets, capital markets, mortgage markets, the thrift industry, contractual savings institutions (insurance companies and pension funds), finance companies, and securities market institutions. Combined with updated chapters on foreign exchange markets, derivatives, the banking industry, banking regulation, and the structure of central banks, this edition provides complete institutional detail but avoids overwhelming students with facts that may bore or confuse them.

Applied Managerial Perspective

In teaching a course in financial markets and institutions at Columbia Business School over the past ten years, I have found that students get more out of the course if it is applications-oriented. Accordingly, this edition strongly emphasizes the applications orientation by integrating into the body of the text applications that explain many real-world situations and by increasing the number of applications to more than 50.

I have also found that today's financial markets and institutions students often seek a managerial slant to the course. Many are considering a future in the financial services industry and want to know what kinds of problems managers of financial institutions face in their day-to-day jobs. Others realize that even if they enter the business world in the nonfinancial sector, they still need to understand how financial institutions are managed so that they can interact with them knowledgeably and get a good deal.

This book takes a unique approach to teaching financial markets and institutions by including nearly 20 special applications called "The Practicing Financial Institutions Manager." These applications introduce students to real-world problems that managers of financial institutions have to solve. For example, how does a financial institution manager measure interest-rate risk? How does a manager use interest-rate and foreign exchange rate forecasts to increase profits? How does the manager come up with a new financial product that will be profitable or manage the risk his or her institution faces from potential loan defaults or from fluctuations in interest rates, stock prices, or foreign exchange rates? How should the manager of a financial institution use information about what the Federal Reserve is doing to improve profits?

To provide an additional managerial perspective, we have included short "cases" at the end of many chapters that take students through real-world situations in which the managerial tools they have learned in the chapter can be applied. These cases, along with the "Practicing Financial Institutions Manager" applications, make the course both relevant and exciting for students. They are not meant to prepare students fully for jobs in financial institutions—it is up to more specialized courses such as bank or financial institutions management to do that—but these cases and applications teach them some of the special analytic tools that they will need when they enter the business world.

The treatment of financial derivatives markets (forwards, futures, options, and swaps) in this book differs from that in other books. Financial derivatives are approached from the perspective of managers of financial institutions, and that is why this material is placed in the financial institutions part of the book. Rather than spotlighting a lot of facts about these different markets, the two chapters on financial derivatives focus on how the markets work and how they can be used to hedge the risk that financial institutions face. This approach makes sense to students because it demonstrates why studying these markets and their operation is relevant.

To succeed in the business world, students must be able to follow the financial news that appears in leading financial publications such as the *Wall Street Journal.* Encouraging students to read the financial section of the newspaper helps them understand and apply the material covered in the financial markets and institutions course. To this end, this book contains two special features.

The first is a set of special boxes titled "Following the Financial News," which feature columns and data from the *Wall Street Journal* that typically appear daily or periodically. In addition, these self-contained boxes give students the detailed information and definitions they need to evaluate the data.

The second feature, a set of special applications titled "Reading the *Wall Street Journal,*" expands on the "Following the Financial News" boxes. These applications show students how they can use the analytic framework of the book to understand the daily columns in the United States' leading financial newspaper. They include reading the bond page (Chapter 3), the credit markets column (Chapter 5), the commodities column (Appendix to Chapter 5), and the foreign exchange column (Chapter 8). Once students see how to use the analytic framework by working through these applications in the textbook, they can do this analysis every day when they read the newspaper. In my own course, I bring the previous day's *Wall Street Journal* columns into class and use them to conduct a discussion along the lines of the "Reading the *Wall Street Journal*" applications in the text.

One important characteristic of the "Following the Financial News" boxes and the "Reading the *Wall Street Journal*" applications is that they never go out of date. Because the columns or data analyzed in these two special features typically appear daily or periodically, the information and analysis provided will continue to prove useful to students well into the future.

In addition to these applications, this book contains 400 end-of-chapter problems that ask students to apply the economic concepts covered in the text to other real-world issues. Particularly relevant to students are a special class of problems titled "Predicting the Future." The problems, half of which are answered at the back of the book, should further stimulate students' interest. A collection of Case Studies have also been added to selected chapters in this edition. Written by James F. Buck at East Carolina University, the cases provide further practical application of the subject matter.

Full Integration of an International Perspective

In the course of my work in academia and at the Federal Reserve Bank of New York, I have been continually exposed to international issues, have written many research papers with an international orientation, and have traveled extensively to foreign countries. Furthermore, both professors and students have suggested to me that they want to see the study of financial markets and institutions thoroughly internationalized. Comments by users of the book and my work experience have thus led me to take the internationalization of the text well beyond that of other texts (and the previous edition of this book). Indeed, instead of relegating the international material to separate chapters or boxes, I have completely integrated it into the body of the text, starting with the first chapter.

The extensive international material of the previous edition remains in this edition: for example, the foreign exchange market (Chapters 1 and 8), growing internationalization of financial markets (Chapters 2 and 21), puzzles in financial structure throughout the world (Chapter 12), international banking (Chapters 14 and 16), the woes of Lloyd's of London (Chapter 17), and the September 1992 foreign exchange crisis (Chapter 25). I also have included substantial additional international material in this edition in new sections on financial development and economic growth (Chapter 12), the Mexican foreign exchange and financial crisis of 1994 (Chapters 12 and 25), banking crises throughout the world (Chapter 16), separation of the banking and securities industries in other countries (Chapter 16), the decline of traditional banking throughout the world (Chapter 14), the structure and independence of foreign central banks (Chapter 23), and monetary and inflation targeting in other countries (Chapter 24).

Flexibility

There are as many ways to teach financial markets and institutions as there are instructors. Thus there is a great need to make a textbook flexible in order to satisfy the diverse needs of instructors, and that has been a primary objective in writing this book. This textbook achieves this flexibility in the following ways:

- Core chapters provide the basic analysis used throughout the book, and other chapters or sections of chapters can be assigned or omitted according to instructor preferences. For example, Chapter 2 introduces the financial system and basic concepts such as transaction costs, adverse selection, and moral hazard. After covering Chapter 2, an instructor can decide to teach a more detailed treatment of financial structure in Chapter 12, or can skip this chapter or take any of a number of different paths.
- The approach to internationalizing the text using separate, marked international sections within chapters and separate chapters on the foreign exchange market and the international monetary system is comprehensive yet flexible. Although many instructors will teach all the international material, others will choose not to. Instructors who want less emphasis on international topics can easily skip Chapter 8 (on the foreign exchange market) and Chapter 25 (on the international financial system). Instructors who would like to teach material on the foreign exchange market later in the course can easily teach Chapter 8 just before Chapter 25.
- The "Practicing Financial Institutions Manager" applications, as well as Part V on the management of financial institutions, are self-contained and so can be skipped without loss of continuity. Thus an instructor wishing to teach a less managerially oriented course, who might want to focus instead on more public policy–oriented issues, will have no trouble doing so.

The course outlines listed next for a semester teaching schedule illustrate how this book can be used for courses with a different emphasis. More detailed information about how the text can be used flexibly in your course is available in the *Instructor's Manual.*

Financial Markets and Institutions Emphasis: Chapters 1–6, 9–11, 13–19, and four other chapters
Financial Markets and Institutions with International Emphasis: Chapters 1–6, 8–11, 13–19, 25, and two other chapters
Managerial Emphasis: Chapters 1–6, 13–14, 16, 20–22, and eight other chapters
Public Policy Emphasis: Chapters 1–6, 13–16, 23–24, and eight other chapters

Supplementary Materials That Facilitate Teaching

The demands for good teaching at business schools have increased dramatically in recent years. To meet these demands for the previous edition and this edition alike, I have provided the instructor with supplementary materials, unavailable with any competing text, that should make teaching this course substantially easier.

This edition of the book comes with over 100 full-color overhead transparencies of figures and tables in the book. Furthermore, the *Instructor's Manual* contains transparency masters of the lecture notes, perforated so they can be easily detached for class use.

The lecture notes are comprehensive and outline all the major points covered in the text. They have been class-tested successfully—they are the ones that I use in my own course—and they should help other instructors prepare their lectures as they have aided me. Some instructors might use these lecture notes as their own class notes and prefer to teach with a blackboard. But for those who prefer to teach with visual aids, the lecture notes on transparency masters, in combination with the full-color transparencies of the figures and tables, provide the flexibility to do so.

I am also aware that in their lectures, many instructors want to depart somewhat from material covered in the text. For their convenience, the entire set of lecture notes has been put on diskette using the WordPerfect and Word word processing languages, and the diskette is included with the *Instructor's Manual.* Instructors can modify the lecture notes as they see fit for their own use, for class handouts, or for transparencies to be used with an overhead projector.

The diskette also contains the entire contents of the *Instructor's Manual,* which includes chapter outlines, overviews, and teaching tips; answers to the end-of-chapter problems that are not included in the text; and discussion questions. Using this handy supplement, instructors can prepare student handouts such as solutions to problem sets made up of end-of-chapter problems, the outline of the lecture that day, or essay questions for homework. I have used handouts of this type in my teaching and have found them to be very effective. Instructors have my permission and are encouraged to photocopy all of the materials on the diskette and use them as they see fit in class.

■ SUPPLEMENTARY MATERIALS

Financial Markets and Institutions, Second Edition, includes the most comprehensive program of supplementary materials of any financial markets and institutions textbook. These items are available to qualified domestic adopters but in some cases may not be available to international adopters. These include the following items:

1. **Study Guide and Workbook,** prepared by Frederick Schadler of East Carolina University, which includes chapter synopses and completions, exercises, self-tests, and answers to the exercises and self-tests
2. ***Instructor's Resource Manual,*** prepared by Stanley Eakins and myself, which includes sample course outlines, chapter outlines, answers to questions and problems in the text, and transparency masters for the lecture notes
3. **Diskette with Entire Contents of the *Instructor's Resource Manual*** (including the lecture notes), featuring WordPerfect and Word files that can be modified to fit any particular course
4. **Full-Color Transparencies,** numbering over 100, for key figures, tables, and summary tables
5. **Power Point Electronic Transparencies,** numbering over 300, which include all the book's figures and tables in full color, plus the lecture notes.
6. **Test Bank,** available both in print form and on diskettes, which comprises over 2500 multiple-choice, true-false, and essay test items. The test bank is computerized so that the instructor can easily produce exams automatically

■ PEDAGOGICAL AIDS

A textbook must be a solid motivational tool. To this end, I have incorporated a wide variety of pedagogical features.

1. **Chapter Previews** at the beginning of each chapter tell students where the chapter is heading, why specific topics are important, and how they relate to other topics in the book.
2. **Applications** demonstrate how the analysis in the book can be used to explain many important real-world situations. A special set of applications called "Reading the *Wall Street Journal*" shows students how to read daily columns in this leading financial newspaper.
3. **"The Practicing Financial Institutions Manager"** is a set of special applications that introduce students to real-world problems that managers of financial institutions have to solve.
4. **"Following the Financial News" Boxes** introduce students to relevant news articles and data that are reported daily in the press and explain how to read them.
5. **"Inside the Fed" Boxes** give students a feel for what is important in the operation and structure of the Federal Reserve System.

6. **Special-Interest Boxes** highlight dramatic historical episodes, interesting ideas, and intriguing facts related to the subject matter.
7. **Study Guides** are highlighted statements scattered throughout the text that provide hints on how to think about or approach a topic as students work their way through it.
8. **Summary Tables** are useful study aids for reviewing material.
9. **Key Statements** are important points that are set in boldfaced type so that the students can easily find them for later reference.
10. **Graphs** with captions, numbering over 60, help students understand the interrelationship of the variables plotted and the principles of analysis.
11. **Summary** at the end of each chapter lists the main points.
12. **Key Terms** are important words or phrases that appear in boldfaced type when they are defined for the first time and are listed at the end of the chapter.
13. **End-of-Chapter Questions and Problems,** numbering 400, help students learn the subject matter by applying economic concepts and feature a special class of problems that students find particularly relevant, titled "Predicting the Future."
14. **Glossary** at the back of the book defines all the key terms.
15. **Solutions to Problems** at the back of the book provide the solutions to about half the questions and problems, indicated in the text by an asterisk (*).

■ ACKNOWLEDGMENTS

As always in so large a project, there are many people to thank. My special gratitude goes to Bruce Kaplan, former economics editor at HarperCollins; Julie Zasloff, finance editor at Addison Wesley Longman; and Jane Tufts, development editor, who is the best in the business. I also have been assisted by comments from my colleagues at Columbia and from my students.

In addition, I have been guided in this edition and its predecessor by the thoughtful comments of outside reviewers and correspondents. Their feedback has made this a better book. In particular, I thank:

Ibrahim J. Affanen, Indiana University of Pennsylvania
Ronald Anderson, University of Nevada—Las Vegas
Bala G. Arshanapalli, Indiana University Northwest
James C. Baker, Kent State University
Dallas R. Blevins, University of Montevallo
Paul J. Bolster, Northeastern University
Yea-Mow Chen, San Francisco State University
N.K. Chidambaran, Tulane University
Jeffrey A. Clark, Florida State University
Robert Bruce Cochran, San Jose State University
William Colclough, University of Wisconsin—La Crosse
Elizabeth Cooperman, University of Baltimore
Carl Davison, Mississippi State University

Franklin R. Edwards, Columbia University
Marty Eichenbaum, Northwestern University
Elyas Elyasiani, Temple University
E. Bruce Fredrikson, Syracuse University
James Gatti, University of Vermont
Paul Girma, SUNY—New Paltz
Beverly L. Hadaway, University of Texas
John A. Halloran, University of Notre Dame
Billie J. Hamilton, East Carolina University
John H. Hand, Auburn University
Don P. Holdren, Marshall University
Adora Holstein, Robert Morris College
Sylvia C. Hudgins, Old Dominion University
Jerry G. Hunt, East Carolina University
William E. Jackson, University of North Carolina—Chapel Hill
Melvin H. Jameson, University of Nevada—Las Vegas
Kurt Jessewein, Texas A&M International University
Jack Jordan, Seton Hall University
Taeho Kim, American Graduate School of International Management
Glen A. Larsen Jr., University of Tulsa
James E. Larsen, Wright State University
Rick LeCompte, Wichita State University
Boyden E. Lee, New Mexico State University
John Litvan, Southwest Missouri State
Richard A. Lord, Georgia College
Robert L. Losey, American University
Anthony Loviscek, Seton Hall University
James Lynch, Robert Morris College
Judy E. Maese, New Mexico State
William Marcum, Wake Forest University
David A. Martin, Albright College
Khalid Metabdin, College of St. Rose
A. H. Moini, University of Wisconsin—Whitewater
Terry Nixon, Indiana University
William E. O'Connell, Jr., The College of William and Mary
Masao Ogaki, Ohio State University
Coleen C. Pantalone, Northeastern University
Scott Pardee, University of Chicago
James Peters, Fairleigh Dickinson University
Fred Puritz, SUNY—Oneonta
Mahmud Rahman, Eastern Michigan University
Anoop Rai, Hofstra University
David Reps, Pace University—Westchester
Jack Rubens, Bryant College
William Sackley, University of Southern Mississippi
Kevin Salyer, University of California—Davis
Siamack Shojai, Manhattan College

Sonya Williams Stanton, Ohio State University
Anjan Thackor, University of Michigan
Janet M. Todd, University of Delaware
James Tripp, Western Illinois University
Carlos Ulibarri, Washington State University
John Wagster, Wayne State University
David A. Whidbee, California State University—Sacramento
Arthur J. Wilson, George Washington University
Shee Q. Wong, University of Minnesota—Duluth
Criss G. Woodruff, Radford University

Finally, I want to thank my wife, Sally; my son, Matthew; and my daughter, Laura, who provide me with a warm and happy environment that enables me to do my work, and my father, Sydney, now deceased, who a long time ago put me on the path that led to this book.

Frederic S. Mishkin

ABOUT THE AUTHOR

*F*rederic S. Mishkin is the A. Barton Hepburn Professor in the Division of Finance and Economics at the Graduate School of Business, Columbia University. He is also a research associate at the National Bureau of Economic Research. Since receiving his Ph.D. from the Massachusetts Institute of Technology in 1976, he has taught at the University of Chicago, Northwestern University, Princeton University, and Columbia. From 1994 until 1997 he was executive vice president and director of research at the Federal Reserve Bank of New York and was an associate economist to the Federal Open Market Committee of the Federal Reserve System.

Professor Mishkin's research focuses on monetary policy and its impact on financial markets and the aggregate economy. He is the author of *A Rational Expectations Approach to Macroeconometrics: Testing Policy Ineffectiveness and Efficient Markets Models* (Chicago: University of Chicago Press, 1983); *Money, Interest Rates, and Inflation* (London: Edward Elgar, 1993); and *The Economics of Money, Banking, and Financial Markets* (Reading, Mass.: Addison Wesley Longman, 1998). In addition, he has published nearly one hundred articles in such journals as the *American Economic Review,* the *Journal of Political Economy, Econometrica,* the *Quarterly Journal of Economics,* the *Journal of Finance,* the *Journal of Financial Economics,* and the *Journal of Monetary Economics.*

Professor Mishkin has served on the editorial board of the *American Economic Review,* has been an associate editor at the *Journal of Business and Economic Statistics,* and was the editor of the Federal Reserve Bank of New York's *Economic Policy Review.* He is currently an associate editor at the *Journal of Applied Econometrics,* the *Journal of International Money and Finance,* the *Journal of Money, Credit and Banking,* and the *Journal of Economic Perspectives.* He has been an academic consultant to the Board of Governors of the Federal Reserve System, on the Academic Advisory Panel of the Federal Reserve Bank of New York, and a visiting scholar at the Ministry of Finance in Japan and the Reserve Bank of Australia.

PART I

INTRODUCTION

WHY STUDY FINANCIAL MARKETS AND INSTITUTIONS?

PREVIEW On the evening news you have just heard that the bond market has been booming. Does this mean that interest rates will fall so that it is easier for you to finance the purchase of a new computer system for your small retail business? Will the economy improve in the future so that it is a good time to build a new building or add to the one you are in? Should you try to raise funds by issuing stocks or bonds or instead go to the bank for a loan? If you import goods from abroad, should you be concerned that they will become more expensive?

This book provides answers to these questions by examining how financial markets (such as those for bonds, stocks, and foreign exchange) and financial institutions (banks, insurance companies, mutual funds, and so on) work. Financial markets and institutions not only affect your everyday life but also involve huge flows of funds (trillions of dollars) throughout our economy, which in turn affect business profits, the production of goods and services, and even the economic well-being of countries other than the United States. What happens to financial markets and institutions is of great concern to our politicians and can even have a major impact on our elections. The study of financial markets and institutions will reward you with an understanding of many exciting issues. In this chapter we provide a road map of the book by outlining these exciting issues and exploring why they are worth studying.

WHY STUDY FINANCIAL MARKETS?

Parts II and III of this book focus on **financial markets,** markets in which funds are transferred from people who have an excess of available funds to people who have a shortage. Financial markets such as the bond and stock markets are important in channeling funds from people who do not have a productive use for them to those who do, resulting in greater economic efficiency. Activities in financial markets also have direct effects on personal wealth, the behavior of businesses and consumers, and the overall performance of the economy.

Debt Markets and Interest Rates

A **security** (also called a *financial instrument*) is a claim on the issuer's future income or **assets** (any financial claim or piece of property that is subject to ownership), and a **bond** is a debt security that promises to make payments periodically for a specified period of time.[1] Debt markets, also often referred to generically as the *bond market,* are especially important to economic activity because they enable corporations or governments to borrow to finance their activities and because it is where interest rates are determined. An **interest rate** is the cost of borrowing or the price paid for the rental of funds (usually expressed as a percentage of the rental of $100 per year). There are many interest rates in the economy—mortgage interest rates, car loan rates, and interest rates on many different types of bonds.

Interest rates are important on a number of levels. On a personal level, high interest rates could deter you from buying a house or a car because the cost of financing it would be high. Conversely, high interest rates could encourage you to save because you can earn more interest income by putting aside some of your earnings as savings. On a more general level, interest rates have an impact on the overall health of the economy because they affect not only consumers' willingness to spend or save but also businesses' investment decisions. High interest rates, for example, may cause a corporation to postpone building a new plant that would ensure more jobs.

The level of interest rates is especially important to financial institutions. A rise in interest rates raises the cost of acquiring funds for financial institutions such as banks and raises the income on assets such as loans. In addition, changes in interest rates affect the prices of securities such as stocks and bonds that are held by financial institutions. Changes in interest rates thus directly affect the profitability and value of financial institutions.

Because changes in interest rates have important effects on individuals, financial institutions, businesses, and the overall economy, it is important to explain fluctuations in interest rates, which have been substantial in the past 30 years. As a matter of fact, in no other 30-year period of United States history have interest-rate fluctuations been as great. For example, the interest rate on long-term U.S. Treasury bonds was about 5% in 1963, rose to close to 15% in 1981, and was below 6% for a short time in 1996. In the preceding 30-year period, from 1936 to 1966, the rate fluctuated between 2% and 5%.

---

[1]The definition of *bond* used throughout this book is the broad one in common use by academics, which covers short- as well as long-term debt instruments. However, some practitioners in financial markets use the word *bond* only to describe specific long-term debt instruments such as corporate bonds or U.S. Treasury bonds.

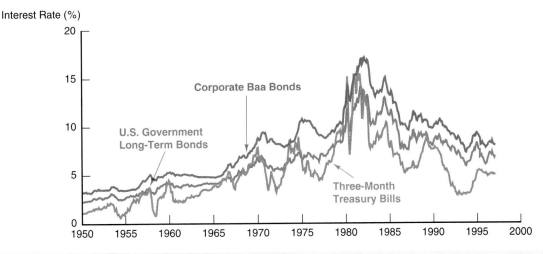

■ FIGURE 1 Interest Rates on Selected Bonds, 1950–1996

Sources: Federal Reserve *Bulletin*; Citibase databank.

Because different interest rates have a tendency to move in unison, economists frequently lump interest rates together and refer to "the" interest rate. As
Figure 1 shows, however, interest rates on several types of bonds can differ substantially. The interest rate on three-month Treasury bills, for example, fluctuates
more than the other interest rates and is lower, on average. The interest rate on
Baa (medium-quality) corporate bonds is higher, on average, than the other interest rates, and the spread between it and the other rates became larger in the
1970s.

In Chapters 2 and 9 through 11 we study the role of debt markets in the economy, and in Chapters 3 through 6 we examine what an interest rate is, how the
common movements in interest rates come about, and why interest rates on different securities vary.

The Stock Market

A **stock** is a security that is a claim on the earnings and assets of a corporation.
Issuing stock and selling it to the public is a way for corporations to raise funds to
finance their activities. The stock market, in which claims on the earnings of corporations (shares of stock) are traded, is the most widely followed financial market in America (that's why it is often called simply "the market"). A big swing in
the prices of shares in the stock market is always a big story on the evening news.
People often express their opinion on where the market is heading and will frequently tell you about their latest "big killing" (although you seldom hear about
their latest "big loss"!). The attention that the market receives can probably be
best explained by one simple fact: It is a place where people can get rich quickly.

As Figure 2 indicates, stock prices have been extremely volatile. They
climbed steadily in the 1950s, reached a peak in 1966 and then fluctuated up and

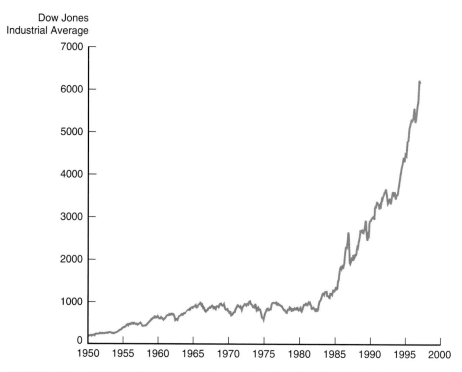

■ FIGURE 2 Stock Prices As Measured by the Dow Jones Industrial
Average, 1950–1996

Sources: Citibase databank.

down until 1973, when they fell sharply. Stock prices had recovered substantially
by the early 1980s when a major stock market boom began, sending the Dow Jones
Industrial Average (DJIA) to a peak of 2722 on August 25, 1987. After a 17%
decline over the next month and a half, the stock market experienced the worst
one-day drop in its entire history on "Black Monday," October 19, 1987, when the
DJIA fell by more than 500 points, a 22% decline. The stock market then recovered, climbing above the 7000 level in 1997. These considerable fluctuations in
stock prices affect the size of people's wealth and as a result may affect their willingness to spend.

The stock market is also an important factor in business investment decisions
because the price of shares affects the amount of funds that can be raised by selling newly issued stock to finance investment spending. A higher price for a firm's
shares means that it can raise a larger amount of funds, which can be used to buy
production facilities and equipment.

In Chapter 2 we examine the role that the stock market plays in the financial
system, and we return to the issue of how stock prices behave and respond to information in the marketplace in Chapter 7. Stocks are also covered in Chapter 10.

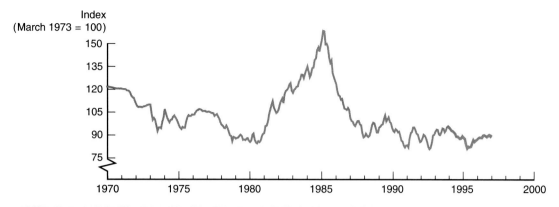

■ FIGURE 3 Exchange Rate of the U.S. Dollar, 1970–1996

Source: Federal Reserve *Bulletin;* Citibase databank.

The Foreign Exchange Market

For funds to be transferred from one country to another, they have to be converted from the currency in the country of origin (say, dollars) into the currency of the country they are going to (say, francs). The **foreign exchange market** is where this conversion takes place, and so it is instrumental in moving funds between countries. It is also important because it is where the **foreign exchange rate,** the price of one country's currency in terms of another's, is determined.

Figure 3 shows the exchange rate for the U.S. dollar from 1970 to 1996 (measured as the value of the American dollar in terms of a basket of foreign currencies). The fluctuations in prices in this market have also been substantial: The dollar weakened considerably from 1971 to 1973, rose slightly in value until 1976, and then reached a low point in the 1978–1980 period. From 1980 to early 1985, the dollar appreciated dramatically in value, but since then it has fallen substantially.

What have these fluctuations in the exchange rate meant to the American public and businesses? A change in the exchange rate has a direct effect on American consumers because it affects the cost of foreign goods. In 1985, when the British currency, the pound sterling, cost approximately $1.30, £100 of British goods (say, Shetland sweaters) would cost $130. When a weaker dollar raised the cost of a pound to $1.60 in 1997, the same £100 of Shetland sweaters cost $160. Thus a weaker dollar leads to more expensive foreign goods, makes vacationing abroad more expensive, and raises the cost of indulging your yen for imported delicacies. When the value of the dollar drops, Americans will decrease their purchases of foreign goods and increase their consumption of domestic goods (such as travel in the United States or American-made sweaters).

Conversely, a strong dollar means that U.S. goods exported abroad will cost more in foreign countries, and hence foreigners will buy fewer of them. Exports of steel, for example, declined sharply when the dollar strengthened in the 1980–1985 period. A strong dollar benefited American consumers by making foreign goods cheaper but hurt American businesses and eliminated some jobs by cutting both domestic and foreign sales of their products. The decline in the value of the dollar since 1985 has had the opposite effect: It has made foreign goods more expensive but has made American businesses more competitive. Fluctuations in the foreign exchange markets have major consequences for the American economy.

In Chapter 8 we study how exchange rates are determined in the foreign exchange market in which dollars are bought and sold for foreign currencies.

■ WHY STUDY FINANCIAL INSTITUTIONS?

The second major focus of this book is financial institutions. Financial institutions are what make financial markets work. Without them, financial markets would not be able to move funds from people who save to people who have productive investment opportunities. They thus also have important effects on the performance of the aggregate economy as a whole.

Structure of the Financial System

The financial system is complex, comprising many different types of financial institutions, including banks, insurance companies, mutual funds, finance companies, and investment banks, all of which are heavily regulated by the government. If you wanted to make a loan to IBM or General Motors, for example, you would not go directly to the president of the company and offer a loan. Instead, you would lend to such companies indirectly through **financial intermediaries,** institutions such as commercial banks, savings and loan associations, mutual savings banks, credit unions, insurance companies, mutual funds, pension funds, and finance companies that borrow funds from people who have saved and in turn make loans to others.

Why are financial intermediaries so crucial to well-functioning financial markets? Why do they give credit to one party but not to another? Why do they usually write complicated legal documents when they extend loans? Why are they the most heavily regulated businesses in the economy?

We answer these questions by developing a coherent framework for analyzing financial structure both in the United States and in the rest of the world in Chapter 12.

Banks and Other Financial Institutions

Banks are financial institutions that accept deposits and make loans. Included under the term *banks* are firms such as commercial banks, savings and loan associations, mutual savings banks, and credit unions. Banks are the financial intermediaries that the average person interacts with most frequently. A person who needs a loan to buy a house or a car usually obtains it from a local bank. Most Americans keep a large proportion of their financial wealth in banks in the form of checking accounts, savings accounts, or other types of bank deposits. Because banks are the largest financial intermediaries in our economy, they deserve careful study. However, banks are not the only important financial institutions. Indeed, in recent years, other financial institutions such as insurance companies, finance companies, pension funds, mutual funds, and investment banks have been growing at the expense of banks, and so we need to study them as well. We study banks and all these other institutions in Parts IV and V.

Financial Innovation

In the good old days, when you took cash out of the bank or wanted to check your account balance, you got to say hello to the friendly teller. Nowadays you are more likely to interact with an automatic teller machine when withdrawing cash and can get your account balance from your home computer. To see why these options have been developed, we study why and how financial innovation takes place in Chapters 13, 14, and 16. We also study financial innovation because it shows us how creative thinking on the part of financial institutions can lead to higher profits. By seeing how and why financial institutions have been creative in the past, we obtain a better grasp of how they may be creative in the future. This knowledge provides us with useful clues about how the financial system may change over time and will help keep our knowledge about banks and other financial institutions from becoming obsolete.

Managing Risk in Financial Institutions

In recent years, the economic environment has become an increasingly risky place. Interest rates fluctuate wildly, stock markets have crashed both here and abroad, speculative crises have occurred in the foreign exchange markets, and failures of financial institutions have reached levels unprecedented since the Great Depression. To avoid wild swings in profitability (and even possibly failure) resulting from this environment, financial institutions must be concerned with how to cope with increased risk. We look at techniques that these institutions use when they engage in risk management in Chapter 20. Then in Chapters 21 and 22 we look at how these institutions make use of new financial instruments, such as financial futures, options, and swaps, to manage risk.

■ WHY STUDY MONETARY POLICY?

The final topic in the book is **monetary policy,** the management of interest rates and the quantity of **money,** also referred to as the **money supply** (defined as anything that is generally accepted in payment for goods and services or in the repayment of debt). The organization responsible for the conduct of monetary policy is the **central bank,** the government agency responsible for the conduct of monetary policy, which in the United States is the **Federal Reserve System** (also called the **Fed**). Because monetary policy affects interest rates, inflation, and business cycles, all of which have an important impact on financial markets and institutions, we study how monetary policy is conducted by central banks in both the United States and abroad in Chapters 23 through 25.

■ APPLIED MANAGERIAL PERSPECTIVE

Another reason for studying financial institutions is that they are among the largest employers in the country and frequently pay very high salaries. Hence some of you have a very practical reason for studying financial institutions: It may help you get a good job in the financial sector. Even if your interests lie elsewhere, you should still care about how financial institutions are run because there will be many times in your life, as an individual, an employee, or the owner of a business, when you will interact with these institutions. Knowing how financial institutions are managed may help you get a better deal when you need to borrow from them or if you decide to supply them with funds.

This book emphasizes an applied managerial perspective in teaching you about financial markets and institutions by including special applications headed "The Practicing Financial Institution Manager." These applications introduce you to the real-world problems that managers of financial institutions commonly face and need to solve in their day-to-day jobs. For example, how does the manager of a financial institution come up with a new financial product that will be profitable? How does a financial institution manager manage the risk that the institution faces from fluctuations in interest rates, stock prices, or foreign exchange rates? Should a manager hire an expert on Federal Reserve policymaking, referred to as a "Fed watcher," to help the institution discern where monetary policy might be going in the future?

Not only do the "Practicing Financial Institution Manager" applications, which answer these questions and others like them, provide you with some special analytic tools that you will need if you make your career at a financial institution, but they also give you a feel for what a job as the manager of a financial institution is all about.

■ HOW WE WILL STUDY FINANCIAL MARKETS AND INSTITUTIONS

Instead of focusing on a mass of dull facts that will soon become obsolete, this textbook stresses a unifying, analytic framework to study financial markets and institutions. This framework uses a few basic concepts to help organize your thinking about the determination of asset prices, the structure of financial markets, bank management, and the role of monetary policy in the economy. The basic concepts are a simplified approach to portfolio choice, the concept of equilibrium, basic supply and demand analysis to explain behavior in financial markets, the search for profits, and an approach to financial structure based on transaction cost and asymmetric information.

The unifying framework used in this book will not only keep your knowledge from becoming obsolete and make the material more interesting but also discourage you from memorizing a mass of facts that will be forgotten soon after the final exam. The framework also provides the tools you need to understand trends in the financial marketplace and in variables such as interest rates and exchange rates. To help you understand and apply the unifying analytic framework, simple models are constructed in which the variables held constant are carefully delineated, each step in the derivation of the model is clearly and carefully laid out, and the models are then used to explain various phenomena by focusing on changes in one variable at a time, holding all other variables constant. To reinforce the models' usefulness, this text also emphasizes the interaction of theoretical analysis and empirical data in order to expose you to real-life events and data. To make the study of financial markets and institutions even more relevant and to help you learn the material, the book contains, besides the "Practicing Financial Institution Manager" applications, numerous additional applications that demonstrate how the analysis in the book can be used to explain many real-world situations.

To function better in the real world outside the classroom, you must have the tools to follow the financial news that appear in leading financial publications such as the *Wall Street Journal*. To help and encourage you to read the financial section of the newspaper, this book contains two special features. The first is a set of special boxed inserts titled "Following the Financial News" that contain actual columns and data from the *Wall Street Journal* that typically appear daily or periodically. These boxes give you the detailed information and definitions you need to evaluate the data being presented. The second feature is a set of special applications titled "Reading the *Wall Street Journal*" that expand on the "Following the Financial News" boxes. These applications show you how the analytic framework in the book can be used directly to make sense of the daily columns in the United States' leading financial newspaper. In addition to these applications, this book also contains 400 end-of-chapter problems that ask you to apply the analytic concepts you have learned to other real-world issues. Particularly relevant are a special class of problems headed "Predicting the Future." So that you can work on many of these problems on your own, answers to half of them are found at the end of the book. You will also find Case Studies following several of the chapters in this book. These give you an opportunity to review and apply many of the important financial concepts and tools presented throughout the book.

■ CONCLUDING REMARKS

The field of financial markets and institutions is an exciting one. Not only will you learn material that affects your life directly—for example, gaining skills that would be valuable in your career—but you will also gain a clearer understanding of events in financial markets and institutions you frequently hear about in the news media. Our study of financial markets and institutions will also introduce you to many of the controversies that are currently the subject of hot debate in the political arena.

SUMMARY

1. Activities in financial markets have direct effects on individuals' wealth, the behavior of businesses, and the efficiency of our economy. Three financial markets deserve particular attention: the bond market (debt markets), where interest rates are determined; the stock market, which has a major effect on people's wealth and on firms' investment decisions; and the foreign exchange market, because fluctuations in the foreign exchange rate have major consequences for the American economy.

2. Banks and other financial institutions channel funds from people who might not put them to productive use to people who can do so and thus play a crucial role in improving the efficiency of the economy.

3. Because monetary policy affects interest rates, inflation, and business cycles, all of which have an important impact on financial markets and institutions, we need to understand how monetary policy is conducted by central banks in the United States and abroad.

4. Understanding how financial institutions are managed is important because there will be many times in your life, as an individual, an employee, or the owner of a business, when you will interact with them. The "Practicing Financial Institution Manager" applications provide special analytic tools that are useful if you make your career at a financial institution and also give you a feel for what a job as the manager of a financial institution is all about.

5. This textbook stresses an analytic way of thinking by developing a unifying framework for the study of financial markets and institutions using a few basic principles. This textbook also emphasizes the interaction of theoretical analysis and empirical data.

KEY TERMS

asset, p. 4
banks, p. 8
bond, p. 4
central bank, p. 9
Federal Reserve System (the Fed), p. 9

financial intermediaries, p. 8
financial markets, p. 3
foreign exchange market, p. 7
foreign exchange rate, p. 7
interest rate, p. 4
monetary policy, p. 9

money (money supply), p. 9
security, p. 4
stock, p. 5

QUESTIONS AND PROBLEMS

1. Why are financial markets important to the health of the economy?

*2. When interest rates rise, how might businesses and consumers change their economic behavior?

3. How can a change in interest rates affect the profitability of financial institutions?

*4. Is everybody worse off when interest rates rise?

5. What effect might a fall in stock prices have on business investment?

*6. What effect might a rise in stock prices have on consumers' decisions to spend?

7. How does a decline in the value of the pound sterling affect British consumers?

*8. How does an increase in the value of the pound sterling affect American businesses?

9. How can changes in foreign exchange rates affect the profitability of financial institutions?

*10. Looking at Figure 3, in what years would you have chosen to visit the Grand Canyon in Arizona rather than the Tower of London?

11. What is the basic activity of banks?

*12. What are the other important financial intermediaries in the economy besides banks?

13. Can you think of any financial innovation in the past ten years that has affected you personally? Has it made you better or worse off? In what way?

*14. What types of risks do financial institutions face?

15. Why do managers of financial institutions care so much about the activities of the Federal Reserve System?

CHAPTER 2

OVERVIEW OF THE FINANCIAL SYSTEM

■ **PREVIEW** Suppose that you want to start a business that manufactures a recently invented low-cost robot that cleans house (even does windows), mows the lawn, and washes the car, but you have no funds to put this wonderful invention into production. Walter has plenty of savings that he has inherited. If you and Walter could get together so that he could provide you with the funds, your company's robot would see the light of day, and you, Walter, and the economy would all be better off: Walter could earn a high return on his investment, you would get rich from producing the robot, and we would have cleaner houses, shinier cars, and more beautiful lawns.

Financial markets (bond and stock markets) and financial intermediaries (banks, insurance companies, pension funds) have the basic function of getting people such as you and Walter together by moving funds from those who have a surplus of funds (Walter) to those who have a shortage of funds (you). More realistically, when IBM invents a better computer, it may need funds to bring it to market, or a local government may need funds to build a road or a school. Well-functioning financial markets and financial intermediaries are needed to improve our economic well-being and are crucial to our economic health.

To study the effects of financial markets and financial intermediaries on the economy, we must first acquire an understanding of their general structure and operation. In this chapter we learn about the major financial intermediaries and the instruments that are traded in financial markets.

This chapter offers a preliminary overview of the fascinating study of financial markets and institutions. We return to a more detailed treatment of the regulation, structure, and evolution of financial markets and institutions in Parts III through V.

■ FUNCTION OF FINANCIAL MARKETS

Financial markets perform the essential economic function of channeling funds from people who have saved surplus funds by spending less than their income to people who have a shortage of funds because they wish to spend more than their income. This function is shown schematically in Figure 1. Those who have saved and are lending funds, the lender-savers, are at the left, and those who must borrow funds to finance their spending, the borrower-spenders, are at the right. The principal lender-savers are households, but business enterprises and the government (particularly state and local government), as well as foreigners and their governments, sometimes also find themselves with excess funds and so lend them out. The most important borrower-spenders are businesses and the government (particularly the federal government), but households and foreigners also borrow to finance their purchases of cars, furniture, and houses. The arrows show that funds flow from lender-savers to borrower-spenders via two routes.

In *direct finance* (the route at the bottom of Figure 1), borrowers borrow funds directly from lenders in financial markets by selling them *securities* (also called *financial instruments*), which are claims on the borrower's future income or assets. Securities are assets for the person who buys them but **liabilities** (IOUs or debts) for the individual or firm that sells (issues) them. For example, if General Motors needs to borrow funds to pay for a new factory to manufacture

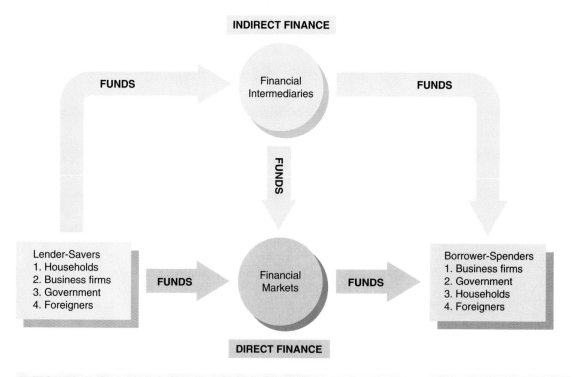

■ **FIGURE 1** Flows of Funds Through the Financial System

computerized cars, it might borrow the funds from a saver by selling the saver a *bond,* a debt security that promises to make payments periodically for a specified period of time.

Why is this channeling of funds from savers to spenders so important to the economy? The answer is that the people who save are frequently not the same people who have profitable investment opportunities available to them, the entrepreneurs. Let's first think about this on a personal level. Suppose that you have saved $1000 this year, but no borrowing or lending is possible because there are no financial markets. If you do not have an investment opportunity that will permit you to earn income with your savings, you will just hold on to the $1000 and will earn no interest. However, Carl the Carpenter has a productive use for your $1000: He can use it to purchase a new tool that will shorten the time it takes him to build a house, thereby earning an extra $200 per year. If you could get in touch with Carl, you could lend him the $1000 at a rental fee (interest) of $100 per year, and both of you would be better off. You would earn $100 per year on your $1000, instead of the zero amount that you would earn otherwise, while Carl would earn $100 more income per year (the $200 extra earnings per year minus the $100 rental fee for the use of the funds).

In the absence of financial markets, you and Carl the Carpenter might never get together. Without financial markets, it is hard to transfer funds from a person who has no investment opportunities to one who has them; you would both be stuck with the status quo, and both of you would be worse off. Financial markets are thus essential to promoting economic efficiency.

The existence of financial markets is also beneficial even if someone borrows for a purpose other than increasing production in a business. Say that you are recently married, have a good job, and want to buy a house. You earn a good salary, but because you have just started to work, you have not yet saved much. Over time you would have no problem saving enough to buy the house of your dreams, but by then you would be too old to get full enjoyment from it. Without financial markets, you are stuck; you cannot buy the house and will continue to live in your tiny apartment.

If a financial market were set up so that people who had built up savings could lend you the money to buy the house, you would be more than happy to pay them some interest in order to own a home while you are still young enough to enjoy it. Then, when you had saved up enough funds, you would pay back your loan. The overall outcome would be such that you would be better off, as would the persons who made you the loan. They would now earn some interest, whereas they would not if the financial market did not exist.

Now we can see why financial markets have such an important function in the economy. They allow funds to move from people who lack productive investment opportunities to people who have such opportunities. By so doing, financial markets contribute to higher production and efficiency in the overall economy. They also directly improve the well-being of consumers by allowing them to time their purchases better. They provide funds to young people to buy what they need and can eventually afford without forcing them to wait until they have saved up the entire purchase price. Financial markets that are operating efficiently improve the economic welfare of everyone in the society.

■ STRUCTURE OF FINANCIAL MARKETS

Now that we understand the basic function of financial markets, let's look at their structure. The following descriptions of several categorizations of financial markets illustrate essential features of these markets.

Debt and Equity Markets

A firm or an individual can obtain funds in a financial market in two ways. The most common method is to issue a debt instrument, such as a bond or a mortgage, which is a contractual agreement by the borrower to pay the holder of the instrument fixed dollar amounts at regular intervals (interest and principal payments) until a specified date (the maturity date), when a final payment is made. The **maturity** of a debt instrument is the time (term) to that instrument's expiration date. A debt instrument is **short-term** if its maturity is less than a year and **long-term** if its maturity is ten years or longer. Debt instruments with a maturity between one and ten years are said to be **intermediate-term.**

The second method of raising funds is by issuing **equities,** such as common stock, which are claims to share in the net income (income after expenses and taxes) and the assets of a business. If you own one share of common stock in a company that has issued one million shares, you are entitled to 1 one-millionth of the firm's net income and 1 one-millionth of the firm's assets. Equities usually make periodic payments (**dividends**) to their holders and are considered long-term securities because they have no maturity date.

The main disadvantage of owning a corporation's equities rather than its debt is that an equity holder is a *residual claimant;* that is, the corporation must pay all its debt holders before it pays its equity holders. The advantage of holding equities is that equity holders benefit directly from any increases in the corporation's profitability or asset value because equities confer ownership rights on the equity holders. Debt holders do not share in this benefit because their dollar payments are fixed. We examine the pros and cons of debt versus equity instruments in more detail in Chapter 12, which provides an analytical framework for understanding financial structure.

The total value of equities in the United States has typically fluctuated between $1 and $10 trillion since the early 1970s, depending on the prices of shares. Although the average person is more aware of the stock market than any other financial market, the size of the debt market greatly exceeds that of the equities market: The value of debt instruments ($15 trillion at the end of 1996) is more than 50% larger than the value of equities ($10 trillion at the end of 1996).

Primary and Secondary Markets

A **primary market** is a financial market in which new issues of a security, such as a bond or a stock, are sold to initial buyers by the corporation or government agency borrowing the funds. A **secondary market** is a financial market in which securities that have been previously issued (and are thus secondhand) can be resold.

The primary markets for securities are not well known to the public because the selling of securities to initial buyers takes place behind closed doors. An important financial institution that assists in the initial sale of securities in the primary market is the **investment bank.** It does this by **underwriting** securities: It guarantees a price for a corporation's securities and then sells them to the public.

The New York and American stock exchanges, in which previously issued stocks are traded, are the best-known examples of secondary markets, although the bond markets, in which previously issued bonds of major corporations and the U.S. government are bought and sold, actually have a larger trading volume. Other examples of secondary markets are foreign exchange markets, futures markets, and options markets. Securities brokers and dealers are crucial to a well-functioning secondary market. **Brokers** are agents of investors who match buyers with sellers of securities; **dealers** link buyers and sellers by buying and selling securities at stated prices.

When an individual buys a security in the secondary market, the person who has sold the security receives money in exchange for the security, but the corporation that issued the security acquires no new funds. A corporation acquires new funds only when its securities are first sold in the primary market. Nonetheless, secondary markets serve two important functions. First, they make it easier to sell these financial instruments to raise cash; that is, they make the financial instruments more **liquid.** The increased liquidity of these instruments then makes them more desirable and thus easier for the issuing firm to sell in the primary market. Second, they determine the price of the security that the issuing firm sells in the primary market. The firms that buy securities in the primary market will pay the issuing corporation no more than the price that they think the secondary market will set for this security. The higher the security's price in the secondary market, the higher will be the price that the issuing firm will receive for a new security in the primary market and hence the greater the amount of capital it can raise. Conditions in the secondary market are therefore the most relevant to corporations issuing securities. It is for this reason that books like this one, which deal with financial markets, focus on the behavior of secondary markets rather than primary markets.

Exchanges and Over-the-Counter Markets

Secondary markets can be organized in two ways. One is to organize **exchanges,** where buyers and sellers of securities (or their agents or brokers) meet in one central location to conduct trades. The New York and American stock exchanges for stocks and the Chicago Board of Trade for commodities (wheat, corn, silver, and other raw materials) are examples of organized exchanges.

The other method of organizing a secondary market is to have an **over-the-counter (OTC) market,** in which dealers at different locations who have an inventory of securities stand ready to buy and sell securities "over the counter" to anyone who comes to them and is willing to accept their prices. Because over-the-counter dealers are in computer contact and know the prices set by one another, the OTC market is very competitive and not very different from a market with an organized exchange.

Many common stocks are traded over-the-counter, although the largest corporations have their shares traded at organized stock exchanges such as the New York Stock Exchange. The U.S. government bond market, with a larger trading volume than the New York Stock Exchange, is set up as an over-the-counter market. Forty or so dealers establish a "market" in these securities by standing ready to buy and sell U.S. government bonds. Other over-the-counter markets include those that trade other types of financial instruments such as negotiable certificates of deposit, federal funds, banker's acceptances, and foreign exchange.

Money and Capital Markets

Another way of distinguishing between markets is on the basis of the maturity of the securities traded in each market. The **money market** is a financial market in which only short-term debt instruments (maturity of less than one year) are traded; the **capital market** is the market in which longer-term debt (maturity of one year or greater) and equity instruments are traded. Money market securities are usually more widely traded than longer-term securities and so tend to be more liquid. In addition, as we will see in Chapter 3, short-term securities have smaller fluctuations in prices than long-term securities, making them safer investments. As a result, corporations and banks actively use this market to earn interest on surplus funds that they expect to have only temporarily. Capital market securities, such as stocks and long-term bonds, are often held by financial intermediaries such as insurance companies and pension funds, which have little uncertainty about the amount of funds they will have available in the future.

■ FINANCIAL MARKET INSTRUMENTS

To complete our understanding of how financial markets perform the important role of channeling funds from lender-savers to borrower-spenders, we need to examine the securities (instruments) traded in financial markets. We first focus on the instruments traded in the money market and then turn to those traded in the capital market.

Money Market Instruments

Because of their short terms to maturity, the debt instruments traded in the money market undergo the least price fluctuations and so are the least risky investments. The money market has undergone great changes in the past three decades, with the amount of some financial instruments growing at a far more rapid rate than others.

The principal money market instruments are listed in Table 1 along with the amount outstanding at the end of 1970, 1980, 1990, and 1996.

United States Treasury Bills These short-term debt instruments of the U.S. government are issued in 3-, 6-, and 12-month maturities to finance the deficits of the federal government. They pay a set amount at maturity and have no interest payments, but they effectively pay interest by initially selling at a discount, that is, at a price lower than the set amount paid at maturity. For instance, you might buy in May 1998 for $9000 a one-year Treasury bill that can be redeemed in May 1999 for $10,000.

U.S. Treasury bills are the most liquid of all the money market instruments because they are the most actively traded. They are also the safest of all money market instruments because there is no possibility of **default,** a situation in which the party issuing the debt instrument (the federal government in this case) is unable to make interest payments or pay off the amount owed when the instrument matures. The federal government is always able to meet its debt obligations because it can raise taxes or issue **currency** (paper money or coins) to pay off its debts. Treasury bills are held mainly by banks, although small amounts are held by households, corporations, and other financial intermediaries.

Negotiable Bank Certificates of Deposit A *certificate of deposit (CD)* is a debt instrument sold by a bank to depositors that pays annual interest of a given amount and at maturity pays back the original purchase price. Before 1961, CDs were nonnegotiable; that is, they could not be sold to someone else and could not be redeemed from the bank before maturity without paying a substantial penalty. In 1961, to make CDs more liquid and more attractive to investors, Citibank introduced the first negotiable CD in large denominations (over $100,000) that could be resold in a secondary market. This instrument is now issued by almost all the major commercial banks and has been extremely successful, with the amount

■ TABLE 1 Principal Money Market Instruments

Type of Instrument	Amount Outstanding ($ billions, end of year)			
	1970	1980	1990	1996
U.S. Treasury bills	81	216	527	777
Negotiable bank certificates of deposit (large denominations)	55	317	543	494
Commercial paper	33	122	557	779
Banker's acceptances	7	42	52	24
Repurchase agreements	3	57	144	191
Federal funds*	16	18	61	92
Eurodollars	2	55	92	110

*Figures after 1970 are for large banks only.

Sources: Federal Reserve Flow of Funds Accounts; Federal Reserve *Bulletin; Banking and Monetary Statistics, 1945–1970; Annual Statistical Digest, 1971–1975; Economic Report of the President;* Board of Governors of the Federal Reserve System, Statistical Release H. 6, April 1997.

outstanding currently around $500 billion. CDs are an extremely important source of funds for commercial banks, from corporations, money market mutual funds, charitable institutions, and government agencies.

Commercial Paper *Commercial paper* is a short-term debt instrument issued by large banks and well-known corporations, such as General Motors or AT&T. Before the 1960s, corporations usually borrowed their short-term funds from banks, but since then they have come to rely more heavily on selling commercial paper to other financial intermediaries and corporations for their immediate borrowing needs; in other words, they engage in direct finance. Growth of the commercial paper market has been substantial: The amount of commercial paper outstanding has increased by over 2000% (from $33 billion to $779 billion) in the period 1970–1996. We will discuss why the commercial paper market has had such tremendous growth in Chapter 9.

Banker's Acceptances These money market instruments are created in the course of carrying out international trade and have been in use for hundreds of years. A *banker's acceptance* is a bank draft (a promise of payment similar to a check) issued by a firm, payable at some future date, and guaranteed for a fee by the bank that stamps it "accepted." The firm issuing the instrument is required to deposit the required funds into its account to cover the draft. If the firm fails to do so, the bank's guarantee means that it is obligated to make good on the draft. The advantage to the firm is that the draft is more likely to be accepted when purchasing goods abroad because the foreign exporter knows that even if the company purchasing the goods goes bankrupt, the bank draft will still be paid off. These "accepted" drafts are often resold in a secondary market at a discount and so are similar in function to Treasury bills. Typically, they are held by many of the same parties that hold Treasury bills, and the amount outstanding has also experienced growth, rising by 250% ($7 billion to $24 billion) from 1970 to 1996.

Repurchase Agreements *Repurchase agreements (repos)* are effectively short-term loans (usually with a maturity of less than two weeks) in which Treasury bills serve as *collateral,* an asset that the lender receives if the borrower does not pay back the loan. Repos are made as follows: A large corporation, such as General Motors, may have some idle funds in its bank account, say, $1 million, which it would like to lend for a week. GM uses this excess $1 million to buy Treasury bills from a bank, which agrees to repurchase them the next week at a price slightly above GM's purchase price. The effect of this agreement is that GM makes a loan of $1 million to the bank and holds $1 million of the bank's Treasury bills until the bank repurchases the bills to pay off the loan. Repurchase agreements are a fairly recent innovation in financial markets, having been introduced in 1969. They are now an important source of bank funds (near $200 billion), and the most important lenders in this market are large corporations.

Federal (Fed) Funds These are typically overnight loans between banks of their deposits at the Federal Reserve. The *federal funds* designation is somewhat confusing because these loans are not made by the federal government or by the Federal Reserve but rather by banks to other banks. One reason why a bank might borrow in the federal funds market is that it might find that it does not have enough deposits at the Fed to meet the amount required by regulators. It can then borrow these deposits from another bank, which transfers them to the borrowing bank using the Fed's wire transfer system. This market is very sensitive to the credit needs of the banks, so the interest rate on these loans, called the **federal funds rate,** is a closely watched barometer of the tightness of credit market conditions in the banking system and the stance of monetary policy; when it is high, it indicates that the banks are strapped for funds, whereas when it is low, banks' credit needs are low.

Eurodollars   U.S. dollars deposited in foreign banks outside the United States or in foreign branches of U.S. banks are called **Eurodollars.** American banks can borrow these deposits from other banks or from their own foreign branches when they need funds. Eurodollars have become an important source of funds for banks (over $100 billion).

Capital Market Instruments

Capital market instruments are debt and equity instruments with maturities of greater than one year. They have far wider price fluctuations than money market instruments and are considered to be fairly risky investments. The principal capital market instruments are listed in Table 2, which shows the amount outstanding at the end of 1970, 1980, 1990, and 1996.

Stocks   *Stocks* are equity claims on the net income and assets of a corporation. Their value of over $10 trillion at the end of 1996 exceeds that of any other type

■ **TABLE 2** Principal Capital Market Instruments

Type of Instrument	Amount Outstanding ($ billions, end of year)			
	1970	1980	1990	1996
Corporate stocks (market value)	906	1,601	4,146	10,090
Residential mortgages	355	1,106	2,886	4,221
Corporate bonds	167	366	1,008	1,399
U.S. government securities (marketable long-term)	160	407	1,653	2,667
State and local government bonds	146	310	870	1,087
U.S. government agency securities	51	193	435	924
Bank commercial loans	152	459	818	789
Consumer loans	134	355	813	1,226
Commercial and farm mortgages	116	352	829	833

Sources: Federal Reserve Flow of Funds Accounts; Federal Reserve *Bulletin; Banking and Monetary Statistics, 1941–1970.*

of security in the capital market. The amount of new stock issues in any given year is typically quite small, less than 1% of the total value of shares outstanding. Individuals hold around half of the value of stocks; the rest are held by pension funds, mutual funds, and insurance companies.

Mortgages *Mortgages* are loans to households or firms to purchase housing, land, or other real structures, where the structure or land itself serves as collateral for the loans. The mortgage market is the largest debt market in the United States, with the amount of residential mortgages (used to purchase residential housing) outstanding more than quadruple the amount of commercial and farm mortgages. Savings and loan associations and mutual savings banks have been the primary lenders in the residential mortgage market, although commercial banks have started to enter this market more aggressively. The majority of commercial and farm mortgages are made by commercial banks and life insurance companies. The federal government plays an active role in the mortgage market via the three government agencies—the Federal National Mortgage Association (FNMA, "Fannie Mae"), the Government National Mortgage Association (GNMA, "Ginnie Mae"), and the Federal Home Loan Mortgage Corporation (FHLMC, "Freddie Mac")—that provide funds to the mortgage market by selling bonds and using the proceeds to buy mortgages. An important development in the residential mortgage market in recent years is the mortgage-backed security which is discussed in Chapter 11.

Corporate Bonds These are long-term bonds issued by corporations with very strong credit ratings. The typical *corporate bond* sends the holder an interest payment twice a year and pays off the face value when the bond matures. Some corporate bonds, called *convertible bonds,* have the additional feature of allowing the holder to convert them into a specified number of shares of stock at any time up to the maturity date. This feature makes these convertible bonds more desirable to prospective purchasers than bonds without it and allows the corporation to reduce its interest payments because these bonds can increase in value if the price of the stock appreciates sufficiently. Because the outstanding amount of both convertible and nonconvertible bonds for any given corporation is small, they are not nearly as liquid as other securities such as U.S. government bonds.

Although the size of the corporate bond market is substantially smaller than that of the stock market, with the amount of corporate bonds outstanding less than one-fifth that of stocks, the volume of new corporate bonds issued each year is substantially greater than the volume of new stock issues. Thus the behavior of the corporate bond market is probably far more important to a firm's financing decisions than the behavior of the stock market. The principal buyers of corporate bonds are life insurance companies; pension funds and households are other large holders.

U.S. Government Securities These long-term debt instruments are issued by the U.S. Treasury to finance the deficits of the federal government. Because they are the most widely traded bonds in the United States (the volume of transactions on average exceeds $100 billion daily), they are the most liquid security traded in the capital market. They are held by the Federal Reserve, banks, households, and foreigners.

U.S. Government Agency Securities   These are long-term bonds issued by various government agencies such as Ginnie Mae, the Federal Farm Credit Bank, or the Tennessee Valley Authority in order to finance such items as mortgages, farm loans, or power-generating equipment. Many of these securities are guaranteed by the federal government. They function much like U.S. government bonds and are held by similar parties.

State and Local Government Bonds   State and local bonds, also called *municipal bonds,* are long-term debt instruments issued by state and local governments to finance expenditures on schools, roads, and other large programs. An important feature of these bonds is that their interest payments are exempt from federal income tax and generally from state taxes in the issuing state. Commercial banks, with their high income tax rate, are the biggest buyers of these securities, owning over half the total amount outstanding. The next biggest group of holders consists of wealthy individuals in high income brackets, followed by insurance companies.

Consumer and Bank Commercial Loans   These are loans to consumers and businesses made principally by banks but, in the case of consumer loans, also by finance companies. There are often no secondary markets in these loans, which makes them the least liquid of the capital market instruments listed in Table 2. However, secondary markets are developing.

 # INTERNATIONALIZATION OF FINANCIAL MARKETS

The growing internationalization of financial markets has become an important trend. Before the 1980s, U.S. financial markets were much larger than financial markets outside the United States, but in recent years the dominance of U.S. markets has been disappearing. The extraordinary growth of foreign financial markets has been the result of both large increases in the pool of savings in foreign countries such as Japan and the deregulation of foreign financial markets, which has enabled them to expand their activities. American corporations and banks are now more likely to tap international capital markets to raise needed funds, and American investors often seek investment opportunities abroad. Similarly, foreign corporations and banks raise funds from Americans, and foreigners are becoming important investors in the United States. A look at international bond markets and world stock markets will give us a picture of how this globalization of financial markets is taking place.

International Bond Market and Eurobonds

The traditional instruments in the international bond market are known as **foreign bonds.** Foreign bonds are sold in a foreign country and are denominated in that country's currency. For example, if the Swedish automaker Volvo sells a bond in the United States denominated in U.S. dollars, it is classified as a foreign bond. Foreign bonds have been an important instrument in the international capital market for centuries. In fact, a large percentage of U.S. railroads built in the nineteenth century were financed by sales of foreign bonds in Britain.

A more recent innovation in the international bond market is the **Eurobond,** a bond denominated in a currency other than that of the country in which it is sold—for example, a bond denominated in U.S. dollars sold in London. Currently, over 80% of the new issues in the international bond market are Eurobonds, and the market for these securities has grown very rapidly. As a result, the Eurobond market has passed the U.S. corporate bond market as a source of new funds.

World Stock Markets

Until recently, the U.S. stock market was by far the largest in the world, but foreign stock markets have been growing in importance. Now the United States is not always number one: Since the mid-1980s, the value of stocks traded in Japan has at times exceeded the value of stocks traded in the United States. The increased interest in foreign stocks has prompted the development in the United States of mutual funds specializing in trading in foreign stock markets. American investors now pay attention not only to the Dow Jones Industrial Average but also to stock price indexes for foreign stock markets such as the Nikkei 225 Average (Tokyo) and the Financial Times–Stock Exchange 100-Share Index (London).

The internationalization of financial markets is having profound effects on the United States. Foreigners, particularly the Japanese, are not only providing funds to corporations in the United States but are also helping finance a significant fraction of the federal government's huge budget deficit. Without these foreign funds, the U.S. economy would have grown far less rapidly in the 1980s and 1990s. The internationalization of financial markets is also leading the way to a more integrated world economy in which flows of goods and technology between countries are more commonplace. In later chapters we will encounter many examples of the important roles that international factors play in our economy.

■ FUNCTION OF FINANCIAL INTERMEDIARIES

As shown in Figure 1, funds can move from lenders to borrowers by a second route, called *indirect finance* because it involves a financial intermediary that stands between the lender-savers and the borrower-spenders and helps transfer funds from one to the other. A financial intermediary does this by borrowing funds from the lender-savers and then uses these funds to make loans to borrower-spenders. For example, a bank might acquire funds by issuing a liability to the public in the form of savings deposits. It might then use the funds to acquire an asset by making a loan to General Motors or by buying a GM bond in the financial market. The ultimate result is that funds have been transferred from the public (the lender-savers) to GM (the borrower-spender) with the help of the financial intermediary (the bank).

FOLLOWING THE FINANCIAL NEWS

Foreign Stock Market Indexes

STOCK MARKET INDEXES

Exchange	01/30/97 Close	Net Chg	Pct Chg
Amsterdam AEX Index	675.09 +	2.46 +	0.37
Argentina Merval Index	689.21 +	12.32 +	1.82
Australia All Ordinaries	2417.7 +	3.5 +	0.14
Bombay Sensex	3511.08 −	11.5 −	0.33
Brazil Sao Paulo Bovespa	77888 +	519 +	0.67
Brussels Bel-20 Index	2045.87 +	14.2 +	0.70
Dow Jones China 88	122.47 +	0.47 +	0.39
Dow Jones Shanghai	121.73 −	0.12 −	0.10
Dow Jones Shenzhen	146.28 +	1.14 +	0.79
Euro, Aust, Far East MSCI-p	1128.2 +	0 +	0.00
Frankfurt DAX	3017.32 +	18.12 +	0.60
Frankfurt IBIS DAX	3018.58 +	20.63 +	0.69
Hong Kong Hang Seng	13288.4 +	2.97 +	0.02
Johannesburg J'burg Gold	1365 −	20 −	1.44
London FT 100-share	4228.4 +	20.9 +	0.50
London FT 250-share	4572.6 +	6.1 +	0.13
Madrid General Index	459.49 −	1.51 −	0.33
Mexico I.P.C.	3672.92 +	41.30 +	1.14
Milan Mibtel Index	12246 +	47 +	0.39
Paris CAC 40	2503.06 +	38.05 +	1.54
Singapore Straits Times	2216.71 −	3.41 −	0.15
S. Korea Composite	676.52 +	12.96 +	1.95
Stockholm Affaersvaerlden	2544.32 +	14.76 +	0.58
Taiwan Weighted	7221.98 +	72.44 +	1.01
Tokyo Nikkei 225 Average	17864.04 −	471.26 −	2.57
Tokyo Nikkei 300 Index	255.85 −	3.94 −	1.52
Tokyo Topix Index	1345.70 −	20.74 −	1.52
Toronto 300 Composite	6085.1 +	13.82 +	0.23
Zurich Swiss Market	4109.1 +	39.4 +	0.94

p-Preliminary
na-Not available

Foreign stock market indexes are published daily in the *Wall Street Journal* next to the "World Markets" column, which reports developments in foreign stock markets.

The first column identifies the foreign stock exchange and the market index; for example, the colored entry is for the Nikkei 225 Average for the Tokyo Stock Exchange. The second column, "CLOSE," gives the closing value of the index, which was 17,864.04 for the Nikkei 225 Average on January 30, 1997. The "NET CHG" column indicates the change in the index from the previous trading day, −471.26, and the "PCT CHG" column indicates the percentage change in the index, −2.57%.

Source: Wall Street Journal, January 31, 1997, p. C12.

The process of indirect finance using financial intermediaries, called **financial intermediation,** is the primary route for moving funds from lenders to borrowers. Indeed, although the media focus much of their attention on securities markets, particularly the stock market, financial intermediaries are a far more important source of financing for corporations than securities markets are. This is true not only for the United States but for other industrialized countries as well (see Box 1). Why are financial intermediaries and indirect finance so important in financial markets? To answer this question, we need to understand the role of transaction costs and information costs in financial markets.

Transaction Costs

Transaction costs, the time and money spent in carrying out financial transactions, are a major problem for people who have excess funds to lend. As we have seen, Carl the Carpenter needs $1000 for his new tool, and you know that it is an excellent investment opportunity. You have the cash and would like to lend him the money, but to protect your investment, you have to hire a lawyer to write

BOX 1   A GLOBAL PERSPECTIVE

The Importance of Financial Intermediaries to Securities Markets: An International Comparison

 Patterns of financing corporations differ across countries, but one key fact emerges. Studies of the major developed countries, including the United States, Canada, Great Britain, Japan, Italy, Germany, and France, show that when businesses go looking for funds to finance their activities, they usually obtain them indirectly through financial intermediaries and not directly from securities markets.* Even in the United States and Canada, which have the most developed securities markets in the world, loans from financial intermediaries are far more important for corporate finance than securities markets are. The countries that have made the least use of securities markets are Germany and Japan; in these two countries, financing from financial intermediaries has been almost ten times greater than that from securities markets. However, with the deregulation of Japanese securities markets in

recent years, the share of corporate financing by financial intermediaries has been declining relative to the use of securities markets.

Although the dominance of financial intermediaries over securities markets is clear in all countries, the relative importance of bond versus stock markets differs widely across countries. In the United States, the bond market is far more important as a source of corporate finance: On average, the amount of new financing raised using bonds is ten times the amount using stocks. By contrast, countries such as France and Italy make use of equities markets more than the bond market to raise capital.

*See, for example, Colin Mayer, "Financial Systems, Corporate Finance, and Economic Development," in *Asymmetric Information, Corporate Finance, and Investment*, ed. R. Glenn Hubbard (Chicago: University of Chicago Press, 1990), pp. 307–332.

---

up the loan contract that specifies how much interest Carl will pay you, when he will make these interest payments, and when he will repay you the $1000. Obtaining the contract will cost you $500. When you figure in this transaction cost for making the loan, you realize that you can't earn enough from the deal (you spend $500 to make perhaps $100) and reluctantly tell Carl that he will have to look elsewhere.

This example illustrates that small savers like you or potential borrowers like Carl might be frozen out of financial markets and thus be unable to benefit from them. Can anyone come to the rescue? Financial intermediaries can.

Financial intermediaries can substantially reduce transaction costs because they have developed expertise in lowering them and because their large size allows them to take advantage of **economies of scale,** the reduction in transaction costs per dollar of transactions as the size (scale) of transactions increases. For example, a bank knows how to find a good lawyer to produce an airtight loan contract, and this contract can be used over and over again in its loan transactions, thus lowering the legal cost per transaction. Instead of a loan contract (which may not be all that well written) costing $500, a bank can hire a topflight lawyer for $5000 to draw up an airtight loan contract that can be used for 2000 loans at a cost of $2.50 per loan. At a cost of $2.50 per loan, it now becomes profitable for the financial intermediary to loan Carl the $1000.

Because financial intermediaries are able to reduce transaction costs substantially, they make it possible for you to provide funds indirectly to people with productive investment opportunities like Carl. In addition, a financial intermediary's low transaction costs mean that it can provide its customers with liquidity services, services that make it easier for customers to conduct transactions. For example, banks provide depositors with checking accounts that enable them to pay their bills easily. In addition, depositors can earn interest on checking and savings accounts and yet still convert them into goods and services whenever necessary.

Asymmetric Information: Adverse Selection and Moral Hazard

The presence of transaction costs in financial markets explains, in part, why financial intermediaries and indirect finance play such an important role in financial markets. An additional reason is that in financial markets, one party often does not know enough about the other party to make accurate decisions. This inequality is called **asymmetric information.** For example, a borrower who takes out a loan usually has better information about the potential returns and risk associated with the investment projects for which the funds are earmarked than the lender does. Lack of information creates problems in the financial system on two fronts: before the transaction is entered into and after.

Adverse selection is the problem created by asymmetric information *before* the transaction occurs. Adverse selection in financial markets occurs when the potential borrowers who are the most likely to produce an undesirable *(adverse)* outcome—the bad credit risks—are the ones who most actively seek out a loan and are thus most likely to be selected. Because adverse selection makes it more likely that loans might be made to bad credit risks, lenders may decide not to make any loans even though there are good credit risks in the marketplace.

To understand why adverse selection occurs, suppose that you have two aunts to whom you might make a loan—Aunt Sheila and Aunt Louise. Aunt Louise is a conservative type who borrows only when she has an investment that she is quite sure will pay off. Aunt Sheila, by contrast, is an inveterate gambler who has just come across a get-rich-quick scheme that will make her a millionaire if she can just borrow $1000 to invest in it. Unfortunately, as with most get-rich-quick schemes, there is a high probability that the investment won't pay off and that Aunt Sheila will lose the $1000.

Which of your aunts is more likely to call you to ask for a loan? Aunt Sheila, of course, because she has so much to gain if the investment pays off. You, however, would not want to make a loan to her because there is a high probability that her investment will turn sour and she will be unable to pay you back.

If you knew both your aunts very well—that is, if information was not asymmetric—you wouldn't have a problem because you would know that Aunt Sheila is a bad risk and so you would not lend to her. Suppose, though, that you don't know your aunts well. You are more likely to lend to Aunt Sheila than to Aunt Louise because Aunt Sheila would be hounding you for the loan. Because of the possibility of adverse selection, you might decide not to lend to either of your aunts, even though there are times when Aunt Louise, who is an excellent credit risk, might need a loan for a worthwhile investment.

Moral hazard is the problem created by asymmetric information *after* the transaction occurs. Moral hazard in financial markets is the risk *(hazard)* that the borrower might engage in activities that are undesirable *(immoral)* from the lender's point of view because they make it less likely that the loan will be paid back. Because moral hazard lowers the probability that the loan will be repaid, lenders may decide that they would rather not make a loan.

As an example of moral hazard, suppose that you made a $1000 loan to another relative, Uncle Melvin, who needs the money to purchase a word processor so that he can set up a business typing students' term papers. Once you have made the loan, however, Uncle Melvin is more likely to slip off to the track and play the horses. If he bets on a 20-to-1 long shot and wins with your money, he is able to pay you back your $1000 and live high on the hog with the remaining $19,000. But if he loses, as is likely, you don't get paid back, and all he has lost is his reputation as a reliable, upstanding uncle. Uncle Melvin therefore has an incentive to go to the track because his gains ($19,000) if he bets correctly may be much greater than the cost to him (his reputation) if he bets incorrectly. If you knew what Uncle Melvin was up to, you would prevent him from going to the track, and he would not be able to increase the moral hazard. However, because it is hard for you to keep informed about his whereabouts—that is, because information is asymmetric—there is a good chance that Uncle Melvin will go to the track and you will not get paid back. The risk of moral hazard might therefore discourage you from making the $1000 loan to Uncle Melvin, even if you were sure that you would be paid back if he used it to set up his business.

■**S T U D Y   G U I D E**   Because the concepts of adverse selection and moral hazard are extremely useful in understanding the behavior we examine in this and many of the later chapters (and in life in general), you must understand them fully. One way to distinguish between them is to remember that adverse selection is a problem of asymmetric information *before* entering into a transaction, whereas moral hazard is a problem of asymmetric information *after* the transaction has occurred. A helpful way to nail down these concepts is to think of other examples, for financial or other types of transactions, in which adverse selection or moral hazard plays a role. Several problems at the end of the chapter provide additional examples of situations involving adverse selection and moral hazard.

The problems created by adverse selection and moral hazard are an important impediment to well-functioning financial markets. Again, financial intermediaries can alleviate these problems.

With financial intermediaries in the economy, small savers can provide their funds to the financial markets by lending these funds to a trustworthy intermediary, say, the Honest John Bank, which in turn lends the funds out either by making loans or by buying securities such as stocks or bonds. Successful financial intermediaries have higher earnings on their investments because they are better equipped than individuals to screen out good from bad credit risks, thereby reducing losses due to adverse selection. In addition, financial intermediaries have high earnings because they develop expertise in monitoring the parties they lend to, thus reducing losses due to moral hazard. The result is that financial intermediaries can afford to pay lender-savers interest or provide substantial services and still earn a profit.

The success of financial intermediaries is evidenced by the fact that most Americans invest their savings with them and also obtain their loans from them. Financial intermediaries play a key role in improving economic efficiency because they help financial markets channel funds from lender-savers to people with productive investment opportunities. Without a well-functioning set of financial intermediaries, it is very hard for an economy to reach its full potential. We will explore further the role of financial intermediaries in the economy in Part IV.

■ FINANCIAL INTERMEDIARIES

We have seen why financial intermediaries play such an important role in the economy. Now we look at the principal financial intermediaries and how they perform the intermediation function. They fall into three categories: depository institutions (banks), contractual savings institutions, and investment intermediaries. Table 3 provides a guide to the discussion of the financial intermediaries that fit into these three categories by describing their primary liabilities (sources of funds) and assets (uses of funds). The relative size of these intermediaries in the United States is indicated in Table 4, which lists the amount of their assets at the end of 1970, 1980, 1990, and 1996.

■ TABLE 3 Primary Assets and Liabilities of Financial Intermediaries

Type of Intermediary	Primary Liabilities (Sources of Funds)	Primary Assets (Uses of Funds)
Depository institutions (banks)		
Commercial banks	Deposits	Business and consumer loans, mortgages, U.S. government securities and municipal bonds
Savings and loan associations	Deposits	Mortgages
Mutual savings banks	Deposits	Mortgages
Credit unions	Deposits	Consumer loans
Contractual savings institutions		
Life insurance companies	Premiums from policies	Corporate bonds and mortgages
Fire and casualty insurance companies	Premiums from policies	Municipal bonds, corporate bonds and stock, U.S. government securities
Pension funds, government retirement funds	Employer and employee contributions	Corporate bonds and stock
Investment intermediaries		
Finance companies	Commercial paper, stocks, bonds	Consumer and business loans
Mutual funds	Shares	Stocks, bonds
Money market mutual funds	Shares	Money market instruments

Source: Federal Reserve Flow of Funds Accounts.

■ **TABLE 4** Principal Financial Intermediaries

Type of Intermediary	Value of Assets ($ billions, end of year)			
	1970	1980	1990	1996
Depository institutions (banks)				
Commercial banks	517	1481	3334	4710
Savings and loan associations and mutual savings banks	250	792	1365	1035
Credit unions	18	67	215	327
Contractual savings institutions				
Life insurance companies	201	464	1367	2239
Fire and casualty insurance companies	50	182	533	804
Pension funds (private)	112	504	1629	3031
State and local government retirement funds	60	197	737	1735
Investment intermediaries				
Finance companies	64	205	610	897
Mutual funds	47	70	654	2349
Money market mutual funds	0	76	498	891

Source: Federal Reserve Flow of Funds Accounts.

Depository Institutions

Depository institutions (which for simplicity we refer to as *banks* throughout this text) are financial intermediaries that accept deposits from individuals and institutions and make loans. These institutions include commercial banks and the so-called **thrift institutions (thrifts):** savings and loan associations, mutual savings banks, and credit unions.

Commercial Banks These financial intermediaries raise funds primarily by issuing checkable deposits (deposits on which checks can be written), savings deposits (deposits that are payable on demand but do not allow their owner to write checks), and time deposits (deposits with fixed terms to maturity). They then use these funds to make commercial, consumer, and mortgage loans and to buy U.S. government securities and municipal bonds. There are approximately 10,000 commercial banks in the United States, and as a group, they are the largest financial intermediary and have the most diversified portfolios (collections) of assets.

Savings and Loan Associations Savings and loan associations (S&Ls) obtain funds primarily through savings deposits (often called shares) and time and checkable deposits. The acquired funds have traditionally been used to make mortgage loans. S&Ls are the second-largest group of financial intermediaries, numbering around 1500. In the 1950s and 1960s, S&Ls grew much more rapidly than commercial banks, but when interest rates climbed sharply from the late 1960s to the early 1980s, S&Ls encountered difficulties that slowed their rapid growth. Because most mortgages are long-term loans, with maturities in excess of 25 years, many were made years earlier when interest rates were substantially lower. When interest rates rose, S&Ls frequently found that the income from their mortgages was well below the cost of acquiring funds. Many of them suffered large losses, and many went out of business.

Until 1980, savings and loans were restricted to making mortgage loans and could not establish checking accounts. Their troubles encouraged Congress to pass legislation in the early 1980s allowing them to offer checking accounts, make consumer loans, and pursue many activities previously restricted to commercial banks. In addition, they are now subject to the same requirements as the commercial banks regarding deposits with the Federal Reserve. The net result of this legislation is that the distinction between savings and loans and commercial banks has blurred, and these intermediaries have become more alike and much more competitive with each other.

Mutual Savings Banks Mutual savings banks are very similar to savings and loans. They raise funds by accepting deposits (often called shares) and use them primarily to make mortgage loans. Their corporate structure is somewhat different from that of S&Ls in that they are always structured as "mutuals," or cooperatives: The depositors own the bank. There are around 500 of these institutions, located primarily in the Northeast. Like savings and loans, until 1980 they were restricted to making mortgage loans, and they suffered similar problems when interest rates rose from the late 1960s to the early 1980s. They were similarly affected by the banking legislation in the 1980s and can now issue checkable deposits and make loans other than mortgages.

Credit Unions These financial institutions, numbering about 12,000, are very small cooperative lending institutions organized around a particular group: union members, employees of a particular firm, and so forth. They acquire funds from deposits called shares and primarily make consumer loans. Thanks to the banking legislation in the 1980s, credit unions are also allowed to issue checkable deposits and can make mortgage loans in addition to consumer loans.

Contractual Savings Institutions

Contractual savings institutions, such as insurance companies and pension funds, are financial intermediaries that acquire funds at periodic intervals on a contractual basis. Because they can predict with reasonable accuracy how much they will have to pay out in benefits in the coming years, they do not have to worry as much as depository institutions about losing funds. As a result, the liquidity of assets is not as important a consideration for them as it is for depository institutions, and they tend to invest their funds primarily in long-term securities such as corporate bonds, stocks, and mortgages.

Life Insurance Companies Life insurance companies insure people against financial hazards following a death and sell annuities (annual income payments upon retirement). They acquire funds from the premiums that people pay to keep their policies in force and use them mainly to buy corporate bonds and mortgages. They also purchase stocks but are restricted in the amount that they can hold.

Currently, with $2.2 trillion in assets, they are among the largest of the contractual savings institutions.

Fire and Casualty Insurance Companies These companies insure their policy-holders against loss from theft, fire, and accidents. They are very much like life insurance companies, receiving funds through premiums for their policies, but they have a greater possibility of loss of funds if major disasters occur. For this reason, they use their funds to buy more liquid assets than life insurance companies do. Their largest holding of assets is municipal bonds; they also hold corporate bonds and stocks and U.S. government securities.

Pension Funds and Government Retirement Funds Private pension funds and state and local government retirement funds provide retirement income in the form of annuities to employees who are covered by a pension plan. Funds are acquired by contributions from employers or from employees, who either have a contribution automatically deducted from their paychecks or contribute voluntarily. The largest asset holdings of pension funds are corporate bonds and stocks. The establishment of pension funds has been actively encouraged by the federal government both through legislation requiring pension plans and through tax incentives to encourage contributions.

Investment Intermediaries

This category of financial intermediaries includes finance companies, mutual funds, and money market mutual funds.

Finance Companies Finance companies raise funds by selling commercial paper (a short-term debt instrument) and by issuing stocks and bonds. They lend these funds to consumers, who make purchases of such items as furniture, automobiles, and home improvements, and to small businesses. Some finance companies are organized by a parent corporation to help sell its product. For example, Ford Motor Credit Company makes loans to consumers who purchase Ford automobiles.

Mutual Funds These financial intermediaries acquire funds by selling shares to many individuals and use the proceeds to purchase diversified portfolios of stocks and bonds. Mutual funds allow shareholders to pool their resources so that they can take advantage of lower transaction costs when buying large blocks of stocks or bonds. In addition, mutual funds allow shareholders to hold more diversified portfolios than they otherwise would. Shareholders can sell (redeem) shares at any time, but the value of these shares will be determined by the value of the mutual fund's holdings of securities. Because these fluctuate greatly, the value of mutual fund shares will too; therefore, investments in mutual funds can be risky.

Money Market Mutual Funds These relatively new financial institutions have the characteristics of a mutual fund but also function to some extent as a depository institution because they offer deposit-type accounts. Like most mutual funds, they sell shares to acquire funds that are then used to buy money market instruments that are both safe and very liquid. The interest on these assets is then paid out to the shareholders.

A key feature of these funds is that shareholders can write checks against the value of their shareholdings. There are generally restrictions on the use of the check-writing privilege, however; checks frequently cannot be written for amounts less than a set minimum, such as $500, and a substantial amount of money is required initially to open an account. In effect, shares in a money market mutual fund function like checking account deposits that pay interest, but with some restrictions on the check-writing privilege. Money market mutual funds have experienced extraordinary growth since 1971, when they first appeared. By 1996, their assets had climbed to nearly $900 billion.

■ REGULATION OF THE FINANCIAL SYSTEM

The financial system is among the most heavily regulated sectors of the American economy. The government regulates financial markets for three main reasons: to increase the information available to investors, to ensure the soundness of the financial system, and to improve control of monetary policy. We will examine how these three reasons have led to the present regulatory environment. As a study aid, the principal regulatory agencies of the U.S. financial system are listed in Table 5.

Increasing Information Available to Investors

Asymmetric information in financial markets means that investors may be subject to adverse selection and moral hazard problems that may hinder the efficient operation of financial markets. Risky firms or outright crooks may be the most eager to sell securities to unwary investors, and the resulting adverse selection problem may keep investors out of financial markets. Furthermore, once an investor has bought a security, thereby lending money to a firm, the borrower may have incentives to engage in risky activities or to commit outright fraud. The presence of this moral hazard problem may also keep investors away from financial markets. Government regulation can reduce adverse selection and moral hazard problems in financial markets and increase their efficiency by increasing the amount of information available to investors.

As a result of the stock market crash in 1929 and revelations of widespread fraud in the aftermath, political demands for regulation culminated in the Securities Act of 1933 and the establishment of the Securities and Exchange Commission (SEC). The SEC requires corporations issuing securities to disclose certain information about their sales, assets, and earnings to the public and restricts trading by the largest stockholders (known as insiders) in the corporation. By requiring disclosure of this information and by discouraging insider trading, which could be used to manipulate security prices, the SEC hopes that

■ TABLE 5 Principal Regulatory Agencies of the U.S. Financial System

Regulatory Agency	Subject of Regulation	Nature of Regulations
Securities and Exchange Commission (SEC)	Organized exchanges and financial markets	Requires disclosure of information, restricts insider trading
Commodities Futures Trading Commission (CFTC)	Futures market exchanges	Regulates procedures for trading in futures markets
Office of the Comptroller of the Currency	Federally-chartered commercial banks	Charters and examines the books of federally chartered commercial banks and imposes restrictions on assets they can hold
National Credit Union Administration (NCUA)	Federally-chartered credit unions	Charters and examines the books of federally chartered credit unions and imposes restrictions on assets they can hold
State banking and insurance commissions	State-chartered depository institutions	Charter and examine the books of state-chartered banks and insurance companies, impose restrictions on assets they can hold, and impose restrictions on branching
Federal Deposit Insurance Corporation (FDIC)	Commercial banks, mutual savings banks, savings and loan associations	Provides insurance of up to $100,000 for each depositor at a bank, examines the books of insured banks, and imposes restrictions on assets they can hold
Federal Reserve System	All depository institutions	Examines the books of commercial banks that are members of the system, sets reserve requirements for all banks
Office of Thrift Supervision	Savings and loan associations	Examines the books of savings and loan associations, imposes restrictions on assets they can hold

investors will be better informed and be protected from some of the abuses in financial markets that occurred before 1933. Indeed, in recent years, the SEC has been particularly active in prosecuting people involved in insider trading.

Ensuring the Soundness of Financial Intermediaries

Asymmetric information can also lead to widespread collapse of financial intermediaries, referred to as a **financial panic.** Because providers of funds to financial intermediaries may not be able to assess whether the institutions holding their funds are sound or not, if they have doubts about the overall health of financial intermediaries, they may want to pull their funds out of both sound and unsound institutions. The possible outcome is a financial panic that produces large losses for the public and causes serious damage to the economy. To protect the public and the economy from financial panics, the government has implemented six types of regulations.

1. State banking and insurance commissions, as well as the Office of the Comptroller of the Currency (an agency of the federal government), have created very tight regulations as to who is allowed to set up a financial intermediary. Individuals or groups that want to establish a financial intermediary, such as a bank or an insurance company, must obtain a charter from the state or the federal government. Only if they are upstanding citizens with impeccable credentials and a large amount of initial funds will they be given a charter.

2. There are stringent reporting requirements for financial intermediaries. Their bookkeeping must follow certain strict principles, their books are subject to periodic inspection, and they must make certain information available to the public.

3. There are restrictions on what financial intermediaries are allowed to do and what assets they can hold. Before you put your funds into a bank or some other such institution, you would want to know that your funds are safe and that the bank or other financial intermediary will be able to meet its obligations to you. One way of doing this is to restrict the financial intermediary from engaging in certain risky activities. Legislation passed in 1933 separates commercial banking from the securities industry so that banks do not engage in risky ventures associated with this industry. Another way is to restrict financial intermediaries from holding certain risky assets, or at least from holding a greater quantity of these risky assets than is prudent. For example, commercial banks and other depository institutions are not allowed to hold common stock because stock prices experience substantial fluctuations. Insurance companies are allowed to hold common stock, but their holdings cannot exceed a certain fraction of their total assets.

4. The government can insure people providing funds to a financial intermediary from any financial loss if the financial intermediary should fail. The most important government agency that provides this type of insurance is the Federal Deposit Insurance Corporation (FDIC), which insures each depositor at a commercial bank or mutual savings bank up to a loss of $100,000 per account. All commercial and mutual savings banks, with a few minor exceptions, make contributions into the FDIC's Bank Insurance Fund, which are used to pay off depositors in the case of a bank's failure. The FDIC was created in 1934 after the massive bank failures of 1930–1933 in which the savings of many depositors at commercial banks were wiped out. Similar government agencies exist for other depository institutions: The Savings Association Insurance Fund (part of the FDIC) provides deposit insurance for savings and loan associations, and the National Credit Union Share Insurance Fund (NCUSIF) does the same for credit unions.

5. Politicians have often declared that unbridled competition among financial intermediaries promotes failures that will harm the public. Although the evidence that competition does this is extremely weak, it has not stopped the state and federal governments from imposing many restrictive regulations. These regulations have taken two forms. First are the restrictions on the opening of additional locations (branches). In the past, banks were not allowed to open up branches in other states, and in some states banks were restricted from opening additional locations.

6. Competition has also been inhibited by regulations that impose restrictions on interest rates that can be paid on deposits. For decades after 1933, banks were prohibited from paying interest on checking accounts. In addition, until 1986, the Federal Reserve System had the power under **Regulation Q** to set maximum interest rates that banks could pay on savings deposits. These regulations were instituted because of the widespread belief that unrestricted interest-rate competition helped encourage bank failures during the Great Depression. Later evidence does not seem to support this view, and restrictions like Regulation Q have been abolished.

Improving Control of Monetary Policy

Because banks play a very important role in determining the supply of money (which in turn affects many aspects of the economy), much regulation of these financial intermediaries is intended to improve control over the money supply. One such regulation is **reserve requirements,** which make it obligatory for all depository institutions to keep a certain fraction of their deposits in accounts with the Federal Reserve System (the Fed), the central bank in the United States. Reserve requirements help the Fed exercise more precise control over the money supply. Deposit insurance regulation can also be rationalized along these lines: The FDIC gives depositors confidence in the banking system and eliminates widespread bank failures, which can in turn cause large, uncontrollable fluctuations in the quantity of money.

In later chapters we will look more closely at government regulation of financial markets and will see whether it has improved the functioning of financial markets.

 ## Financial Regulation Abroad

Not surprisingly, given the similarity of the economic system here and in Japan, Canada, and the nations of Western Europe, financial regulation in these countries is similar to financial regulation in the United States. The provision of information is improved by requiring corporations issuing securities to report details about assets and liabilities, earnings, and sales of stock and by prohibiting insider trading. The soundness of intermediaries is ensured by licensing, periodic inspection of financial intermediaries' books, and the provision of deposit insurance (although its coverage is smaller and its existence is often intentionally not advertised).

The major differences between financial regulation in the United States and abroad relate to bank regulation. In the past, the United States was the only industrialized country to subject banks to restrictions on branching, which limited banks' size and restricted them to certain geographic regions. U.S. banks are also the most restricted in the range of financial services they may provide and the assets they may hold. Banks abroad frequently hold shares in commercial firms; in Japan and Germany, those stakes can be sizable.

SUMMARY

1. The basic function of financial markets is to channel funds from savers who have an excess of funds to spenders who have a shortage of funds. Financial markets can do this either through direct finance, in which borrowers borrow funds directly from lenders by selling them securities, or through indirect finance, which involves a financial intermediary who stands between the lender-savers and the borrower-spenders and helps transfer funds from one to the other. This channeling of funds improves the economic welfare of everyone in the society because it allows funds to move from people who have no productive investment opportunities to those who have such opportunities, thereby contributing to increased efficiency in the economy. In addition, it directly benefits consumers by allowing them to make purchases when they need them most.

2. Financial markets can be classified as debt and equity markets, primary and secondary markets, exchanges and over-the-counter markets, and money and capital markets.

3. The principal money market instruments (debt instruments with maturities of less than one year) are U.S. Treasury bills, negotiable bank certificates of deposit, commercial paper, banker's acceptances, repurchase agreements, federal funds, and Eurodollars. The principal capital market instruments (debt and equity instruments with maturities greater than one year) are stocks, mortgages, corporate bonds, U.S. government securities, U.S. government agency securities, state and local government bonds, and consumer and bank commercial loans.

4. An important trend in recent years is the growing internationalization of financial markets. Eurobonds, which are denominated in a currency other than that of the country in which they are sold, are now the dominant security in the international bond market and have surpassed U.S. corporate bonds as a source of new funds.

5. Financial intermediaries are financial institutions that acquire funds by issuing liabilities and in turn use those funds to acquire assets by purchasing securities or making loans. Financial intermediaries play such an important role in the financial system because they reduce transaction costs and solve problems created by adverse selection and moral hazard. As a result, financial intermediaries allow small savers and borrowers to benefit from the existence of financial markets, thereby increasing the efficiency of the economy.

6. The principal financial intermediaries fall into three categories: (a) banks—commercial banks, savings and loan associations, mutual savings banks, and credit unions; (b) contractual savings institutions—life insurance companies, fire and casualty insurance companies, and pension funds; and (c) investment intermediaries—finance companies, mutual funds, and money market mutual funds.

7. The government regulates financial markets and financial intermediaries for three main reasons: to increase the information available to investors, to ensure the soundness of the financial system, and to improve control of monetary policy. Regulations include requiring disclosure of information to the public, restrictions on who can set up a financial intermediary, restrictions on what assets financial intermediaries can hold, the provision of deposit insurance, reserve requirements, and the setting of maximum interest rates that can be paid on checking accounts and savings deposits.

KEY TERMS

adverse selection, p. 27
asymmetric information, p. 27
brokers, p. 17
capital market, p. 18
currency, p. 19
dealers, p. 17
default, p. 19
dividends, p. 16

economies of scale, p. 26
equities, p. 16
Eurobonds, p. 24
Eurodollars, p. 21
exchanges, p. 17
federal funds rate, p. 21
financial intermediation, p. 25
financial panic, p. 34

foreign bonds, p. 23
intermediate-term, p. 16
investment banks, p. 17
liabilities, p. 14
liquid, p. 17
long-term, p. 16
maturity, p. 16
money market, p. 18

moral hazard, p. 28
over-the-counter (OTC)
   market, p. 17
primary market, p. 16

Regulation Q, p. 36
reserve requirements, p. 36
secondary market, p. 17
short-term, p. 16

thrift institutions (thrifts),
   p. 30
transaction costs, p. 25
underwriting, p. 17

QUESTIONS AND PROBLEMS

*1. Why is a share of IBM common stock an asset for its owner and a liability for IBM?

2. If I can buy a car today for $5000 and it is worth $10,000 in extra income next year to me because it enables me to get a job as a traveling anvil seller, should I take out a loan from Larry the Loan Shark at a 90% interest rate if no one else will give me a loan? Will I be better or worse off as a result of taking out this loan? Can you make a case for legalizing loan-sharking?

*3. Some economists suspect that one of the reasons that economies in developing countries grow so slowly is that they do not have well-developed financial markets. Does this argument make sense?

4. The U.S. economy borrowed heavily from the British in the nineteenth century to build a railroad system. What was the principal debt instrument used? Why did this make both countries better off?

*5. "Because corporations do not actually raise any funds in secondary markets, they are less important to the economy than primary markets." Comment.

6. If you suspect that a company will go bankrupt next year, which would you rather hold, bonds issued by the company or equities issued by the company? Why?

*7. How can the adverse selection problem explain why you are more likely to make a loan to a family member than to a stranger?

8. Think of one example in which you have had to deal with the adverse selection problem.

*9. Why do loan sharks worry less about moral hazard in connection with their borrowers than some other lenders do?

10. If you are an employer, what kinds of moral hazard problems might you worry about with your employees?

*11. If there were no asymmetry in the information that a borrower and a lender had, could there still be a moral hazard problem?

12. "In a world without information and transaction costs, financial intermediaries would not exist." Is this statement true, false, or uncertain? Explain your answer.

*13. Why might you be willing to make a loan to your neighbor by putting funds in a savings account earning a 5% interest rate at the bank and having the bank loan her the funds at a 10% interest rate, rather than loan her the funds yourself?

14. In two lists, rank the following money market instruments in terms of their liquidity and their safety:
   a. U.S. Treasury bills
   b. Negotiable CDs
   c. Repurchase agreements
   d. Commercial paper

15. Discuss some of the manifestations of the globalization of world capital markets.

PART II

Principles of Financial Markets

CHAPTER 3

UNDERSTANDING INTEREST RATES

■ **PREVIEW** Interest rates are among the most closely watched variables in the economy. Their movements are reported almost daily by the news media because they directly affect our everyday lives and have important consequences for the health of the economy. They affect personal decisions such as whether to consume or save, whether to buy a house, and whether to purchase bonds or put funds into a savings account. Interest rates also affect the economic decisions of businesses and households, such as whether to use their funds to invest in new equipment for factories or to save their money in a bank.

Before we can go on with the study of financial markets, we must understand exactly what the phrase *interest rates* means. In this chapter we see that a concept known as the *yield to maturity* is the most accurate measure of interest rates; the yield to maturity is what financial economists mean when they use the term *interest rate*. We discuss how the yield to maturity is measured on many of the credit market instruments mentioned in Chapter 2 and examine alternative (but less accurate) ways in which interest rates are quoted. We also see that a bond's interest rate does not necessarily indicate how good an investment the bond is because what it earns (its rate of return) can differ from its interest rate. Finally, we explore the distinction between real interest rates, which are adjusted for changes in the price level, and nominal interest rates, which are not.

Although learning definitions is not always the most exciting of pursuits, it is important to read carefully and understand the concepts presented in this chapter. Not only are they continually used throughout the remainder of this text, but a firm grasp of these terms will give you a clearer understanding of the role that interest rates play in your life as well as in the general economy.

MEASURING INTEREST RATES

In Chapter 2 you were introduced to a number of debt market instruments, which fall into four types:

1. A **simple loan** provides the borrower with an amount of funds (principal) that must be repaid to the lender at the maturity date along with an additional amount known as an *interest* payment. For example, if a bank made you a simple loan of $100 for one year, you would have to repay the principal of $100 in one year's time along with an additional interest payment of, say, $10. Commercial loans to businesses are often of this type.

2. A **fixed-payment loan** provides a borrower with an amount of funds that is to be repaid by making the same payment every month, consisting of part of the principal and interest for a set number of years. For example, if you borrowed $1000, a fixed-payment loan might require you to pay $126 every year for 25 years. Installment loans (such as auto loans) and mortgages are frequently of the fixed-payment type.

3. A **coupon bond** pays the owner of the bond a fixed interest payment (coupon payment) every year until the maturity date, when a specified final amount **(face value** or **par value)** is repaid. The coupon payment is so named because the bondholder used to obtain payment by clipping a coupon off the bond and sending it to the bond issuer, who then sent the payment to the holder. Nowadays, for most coupon bonds it is no longer necessary to send in coupons to receive these payments. A coupon bond with $1000 face value, for example, might pay you a coupon payment of $100 per year for ten years and at the maturity date repay you the face value amount of $1000. (The face value of a bond is usually in $1000 increments.)

A coupon bond is identified by three pieces of information. First is the corporation or government agency that issues the bond. Second is the maturity date of the bond. Third is the bond's **coupon rate,** the dollar amount of the yearly coupon payment expressed as a percentage of the face value of the bond. In our example, the coupon bond has a yearly coupon payment of $100 and a face value of $1000. The coupon rate is then $100/$1000 = 0.10, or 10%. Treasury bonds and notes and corporate bonds are examples of coupon bonds.

4. A **discount bond** (also called a **zero-coupon bond**) is bought at a price below its face value (at a discount), and the face value is repaid at the maturity date. Unlike a coupon bond, a discount bond does not make any interest payments; it just pays off the face value. For example, a discount bond with a face value of $1000 might be bought for $900 and in a year's time the owner would be repaid the face value of $1000. U.S. Treasury bills, U.S. savings bonds, and long-term zero-coupon bonds are examples of discount bonds.

These four types of instruments require payments at different times: Simple loans and discount bonds make payment only at their maturity dates, whereas fixed-payment loans and coupon bonds have payments periodically until maturity. How would you decide which of these instruments provides you with more income? They all seem so different because they make payments at different times. To solve this problem, we use the concept of *present value* to provide us with a procedure for measuring interest rates on these different types of instruments.

Present Value

The concept of **present value** is based on the commonsense notion that a dollar paid to you one year from now is less valuable to you than a dollar paid to you today; this notion is true because you can deposit the dollar in a savings account that earns interest and have more than a dollar in one year. We will now define this concept more formally.

In the case of a simple loan, the interest payment divided by the amount of the loan is a natural and sensible way to measure the cost of borrowing funds: The measure of the cost is the *simple interest rate*. In the example we used to describe the simple loan, a loan of $100 today requires the borrower to repay the $100 a year from now and to make an additional interest payment of $10. Hence, using the definition just given, the simple interest rate i is

$$i = \frac{\$10}{\$100} = 0.10 = 10\%$$

If you make this $100 loan, at the end of the year you would receive $110, which can be rewritten as

$$\$100 \times (1 + 0.10) = \$110$$

If you then loaned out the $110, at the end of the second year you would receive

$$\$110 \times (1 + 0.10) = \$121$$

or, equivalently,

$$\$100 \times (1 + 0.10) \times (1 + 0.10) = \$100 \times (1 + 0.10)^2 = \$121$$

Continuing with the loan again, you would receive at the end of the third year

$$\$121 \times (1 + 0.10) = \$100 \times (1 + 0.10)^3 = \$133.10$$

These calculations of the proceeds from a simple loan can be generalized as follows: If the simple interest rate i is expressed as a decimal fraction (such as 0.10 for the 10% interest rate in our example), then after making these loans for n years, you will receive a total payment of

$$\$100 \times (1 + i)^n$$

We can also work these calculations backward. Because $100 today will turn into $110 next year when the simple interest rate is 10%, we could say that $110 next year is worth only $100 today. Or we could say that no one would pay more than $100 to get $110 next year. Similarly, we could say that $121 two years from now or $133.10 three years from now is worth $100 today. This process of calculating what dollars received in the future are worth today is called *discounting the future.* We have been implicitly solving our forward-looking equations for today's value of a future dollar amount. For example, in the case of the $133.10 received three years from now, when $i = 0.10$,

$$\underset{\$100 \times (1 + i)^3}{\overset{\text{Current}}{}} = \underset{\$133.10}{\overset{\text{Future}}{}}$$

so that

$$\$100 = \frac{\$133.10}{(1 + i)^3}$$

More generally, we can solve this equation to tell us the **present value** *(PV),* or **present discounted value,** of the future $1, that is, today's value of a $1 payment received n years from now when the simple interest rate is i:

$$PV \text{ of future } \$1 = \frac{\$1}{(1 + i)^n} \qquad (1)$$

Intuitively, what Equation 1 tells us is that if you are promised $1 for certain ten years from now, this dollar would not be as valuable to you as $1 is today because you can earn interest on the dollar.

The concept of present value is extremely useful because it allows us to figure out today's value of a credit market instrument at a given simple interest rate i by just adding up the present value of all the future payments received. This information allows us to compare the value of two instruments with very different timing of their payments, such as a discount bond and a coupon bond. As we will see, this concept also allows us to obtain an equivalent measure of the interest rate on all four types of credit market instruments discussed here.

APPLICATION   **COST OF THE S&L BAILOUT: WAS IT REALLY $500 BILLION?**

The government bailout of the savings and loan industry in 1989 was one of the major news stories of the past decade. Statements frequently appeared in the press that the cost of the bailout to taxpayers would exceed $500 billion—more than $2000 for every man, woman, and child in the United States. The $500 billion–plus figure made for wonderful political rhetoric, but was the cost really this high?

The answer is no, and the concept of present value tells us why. The $500 billion figure includes bond payments over the next 40 years. The present value concept tells us that to figure out the cost of these payments in today's dollars, we have to discount them back to the present. When we do this, the present value of these payments is on the order of $150 billion, not $500 billion. It is still true that a present value of the bailout of $150 billion is nothing to sneeze at, but it is not quite as scary as a figure more than three times that size. (Chapter 15 contains an extensive discussion of the S&L crisis and bailout.)

Yield to Maturity

Of the several common ways of calculating interest rates, the most important is the **yield to maturity,** the interest rate that equates the present value of payments received from a debt instrument with its value today. Because the concept behind the calculation of the yield to maturity makes good economic sense, financial economists consider it the most accurate measure of interest rates.

To understand the yield to maturity better, we now look at how it is calculated for the four types of credit market instruments.

Simple Loan   Using the concept of present value, the yield to maturity on a simple loan is easy to calculate. For the one-year loan we discussed, today's value is $100, and the payments in one year's time would be $110 (the repayment of $100 plus the interest payment of $10). We can use this information to solve for the yield to maturity i by recognizing that the present value of the future payments must equal today's value of a loan. Making today's value of the loan ($100) equal to the present value of the $110 payment in a year (using Equation 1) gives us

$$\$100 = \frac{\$110}{1 + i}$$

Solving for i,

$$i = \frac{\$110 - \$100}{\$100} = \frac{\$10}{\$100} = 0.10 = 10\%$$

This calculation of the yield to maturity should look familiar because it equals the interest payment of $10 divided by the loan amount of $100; that is, it equals the simple interest rate on the loan. An important point to recognize is that *for simple loans, the simple interest rate equals the yield to maturity.* Hence the same term i is used to denote both the yield to maturity and the simple interest rate.

■ **STUDY GUIDE**   The key to understanding the calculation of the yield to maturity is equating today's value of the debt instrument with the present value of all of its future payments. The best way to learn this principle is to apply it to other specific examples of the four types of credit market instruments in addition to those we discuss here. See if you can develop the equations that would allow you to solve for the yield to maturity in each case.

Fixed-Payment Loan   Recall that this type of loan has the same payment every year throughout the life of the loan. On a fixed-rate mortgage, for example, the borrower makes the same payment to the bank every month until the maturity date, when the loan will be completely paid off. To calculate the yield to maturity for a fixed-payment loan, we follow the same strategy we used for the simple loan—we equate today's value of the loan with its present value. Because the fixed-payment loan involves more than one payment, the present value of the fixed-payment loan is calculated as the sum of the present values of all payments (using Equation 1).

In the case of our earlier example, the loan is $1000 and the yearly payment is $126 for the next 25 years. The present value is calculated as follows: At the end of one year, there is a $126 payment with a *PV* of $126/(1 + i)$; at the end of two years, there is another $126 payment with a *PV* of $126/(1 + i)^2$; and so on until at the end of the twenty-fifth year, the last payment of $126 with a PV of $\$126/(1 + i)^{25}$ is made. Making today's value of the loan ($1000) equal to the sum of the present values of all the yearly payments gives us

$$\$1000 = \frac{\$126}{1 + i} + \frac{\$126}{(1 + i)^2} + \frac{\$126}{(1 + i)^3} + \cdots + \frac{\$126}{(1 + i)^{25}}$$

More generally, for any fixed-payment loan,

$$LV = \frac{FP}{1 + i} + \frac{FP}{(1 + i)^2} + \frac{FP}{(1 + i)^3} + \cdots + \frac{FP}{(1 + i)^N} \qquad (2)$$

where

$$LV = \text{loan value}$$
$$FP = \text{fixed yearly payment}$$
$$N = \text{number of years until maturity}$$

For a fixed-payment loan amount, the fixed yearly payment and the number of years until maturity are known quantities, and only the yield to maturity is not. So we can solve this equation for the yield to maturity i. Because this calculation is not easy, tables have been created that allow you to find i given the loan's numbers for LV, FP, and N. For example, in the case of the 25-year loan with yearly payments of $126, the yield to maturity taken from the table that solves Equation 2 is 12%. Real estate brokers always have such a table handy (or a pocket calculator that can solve such equations) so that they can immediately tell the prospective house buyer exactly what the yearly (or monthly) payments will be if the house purchase is financed by taking out a mortgage (see Figure 1).[1]

Coupon Bond To calculate the yield to maturity for a coupon bond, follow the same strategy used for the fixed-payment loan: Equate today's value of the bond with its present value. Because coupon bonds also have more than one payment, the present value of the bond is calculated as the sum of the present values of all the coupon payments plus the present value of the final payment of the face value of the bond.

The present value of a $1000-face-value bond with ten years to maturity and yearly coupon payments of $100 (a 10% coupon rate) can be calculated as follows: At the end of one year, there is a $100 coupon payment with a PV of $\$100/(1 + i)$; at the end of the second year, there is another $100 coupon payment with a PV of $\$100/(1 + i)^2$; and so on until at maturity, there is a $100 coupon payment with a PV of $\$100/(1 + i)^{10}$ plus the repayment of the $1000 face value with a PV of $\$1000/(1 + i)^{10}$. Setting today's value of the bond (its current price, denoted by P_b) equal to the sum of the present values of all the payments for this bond gives

$$P_b = \frac{\$100}{1 + i} + \frac{\$100}{(1 + i)^2} + \frac{\$100}{(1 + i)^3} + \cdots + \frac{\$100}{(1 + i)^{10}} + \frac{\$1000}{(1 + i)^{10}}$$

---

[1]The calculation with a pocket calculator programmed for this purpose requires simply that you enter the value of the loan LV, the number of years to maturity N, and the interest rate i and then run the program.

12%			Monthly Payment Necessary to Amortize a Loan				
			Term (years)				
Amount($)	19	20	21	22	23	24	25
25	.28	.28	.28	.27	.27	.27	.27
50	.56	.56	.55	.54	.54	.54	.53
75	.84	.83	.82	.81	.81	.80	.79
100	1.12	1.11	1.09	1.08	1.07	1.07	1.06
200	2.24	2.21	2.18	2.16	2.14	2.13	2.11
300	3.35	3.31	3.27	3.24	3.21	3.19	3.16
400	4.47	4.41	4.36	4.32	4.28	4.25	4.22
500	5.58	5.51	5.45	5.39	5.35	5.31	5.27
600	6.70	6.61	6.54	6.47	6.42	6.37	6.32
700	7.81	7.71	7.63	7.55	7.48	7.43	7.38
800	8.93	8.81	8.71	8.63	8.55	8.49	8.43
900	10.04	9.91	9.80	9.71	9.62	9.55	9.48
1000	11.16	11.02	10.89	10.78	10.69	10.61	10.54
2000	22.31	22.03	21.78	21.56	21.38	21.21	21.07
3000	33.47	33.04	32.67	32.34	32.06	31.82	31.60
4000	44.62	44.05	43.55	43.12	42.75	42.42	42.13
5000	55.77	55.06	54.44	53.90	53.43	53.02	52.67

■FIGURE 1 A Mortgage Payment Table

This table is for loans with a 12% interest rate. To find the monthly payment for the loan, pick out the amount of the loan in the first column and then follow that row across to the entry in the column with the number of years to maturity of the loan. For a $1000, 25-year fixed-payment loan with a 12% interest rate, following this procedure indicates that the monthly payment is $10.54 ($126 per year).

More generally, for any coupon bond,[2]

$$P_b = \frac{C}{1+i} + \frac{C}{(1+i)^2} + \frac{C}{(1+i)^3} + \cdots + \frac{C}{(1+i)^N} + \frac{F}{(1+i)^N} \qquad (3)$$

where
$$P_b = \text{price of coupon bond}$$
$$C = \text{yearly coupon payment}$$
$$F = \text{face value of the bond}$$
$$N = \text{years to maturity date}$$

In Equation 3, the coupon payment, the face value, the years to maturity, and the price of the bond are known quantities, and only the yield to maturity is not. Hence we can solve this equation for the yield to maturity i.[3] Just as in the case of the fixed-payment loan, this calculation is not easy, so bond tables (see Figure 2) have been created that allow you to read off the yield to maturity for a bond given

---

[2]Most coupon bonds actually make coupon payments on a semiannual basis rather than once a year as assumed here. The effect on the calculations is only very slight and will be ignored here.

[3]In other contexts, it is also called the *internal rate of return.*

10.00%   Bond Values per $100 of Face Value

Yield (%)	Years to Maturity									
	1	2	3	4	5	6	7	8	9	10
10.00	100.00	100.00	100.00	100.00	100.00	100.00	100.00	100.00	100.00	100.00
10.25	99.77	99.56	99.37	99.20	99.04	98.90	98.77	98.66	98.55	98.46
10.50	99.54	99.12	98.74	98.40	98.09	97.82	97.56	97.34	97.13	96.95
10.75	99.31	98.68	98.12	97.61	97.16	96.75	96.38	96.04	95.74	95.47
11.00	99.08	98.25	97.50	96.83	96.23	95.69	95.21	94.77	94.38	94.02
11.25	98.85	97.82	96.89	96.06	95.32	94.65	94.05	93.52	93.04	92.61
11.50	98.62	97.39	96.28	95.30	94.41	93.63	92.92	92.29	91.72	91.22
11.75	98.39	96.96	95.68	94.54	93.52	92.61	91.80	91.08	90.44	89.86
12.00	98.17	96.53	95.08	93.79	92.64	91.62	90.71	89.89	89.17	88.53
12.25	97.94	96.11	94.49	93.05	91.77	90.63	89.62	88.73	87.93	87.23
12.50	97.72	95.69	93.90	92.31	90.91	89.66	88.56	87.58	86.72	85.95
12.75	97.49	95.28	93.32	91.59	90.06	88.71	87.51	86.46	85.52	84.70

■**FIGURE 2** A Bond Table

This table is for bonds with a 10% coupon rate. To find the price of the bond, pick out its yield to maturity in the first column and then follow that row across to the entry in the column with the number of years to maturity for the bond. For a ten-year, 10%-coupon-rate bond with a yield to maturity of 11.75%, following this procedure indicates that the price of the bond is $89.86 per $100 of face value (which means that a $1000-face-value bond sells for approximately $900).

its coupon rate, its years to maturity, and its price. Some business-oriented pocket calculators have built-in programs that solve this equation for you.[4]

Let's look at some examples of the solution for the yield to maturity on our 10%-coupon-rate bond that matures in ten years. If the purchase price of the bond is $1000, then either using a pocket calculator with the built-in program or looking at a bond table, we will find that the yield to maturity is 10%. If the price is $900, we find that the yield to maturity is 11.75%. Table 1 shows the yields to maturity calculated for several bond prices.

Three interesting facts are illustrated by Table 1:

1. When the coupon bond is priced at its face value, the yield to maturity equals the coupon rate.
2. The price of a coupon bond and the yield to maturity are negatively related; that is, as the yield to maturity rises, the price of the bond falls. If the yield to maturity falls, the price of the bond rises.
3. The yield to maturity is greater than the coupon rate when the bond price is below its face value.

These three facts are true for any coupon bond and are really not surprising if you think about the reasoning behind the calculation of the yield to maturity.

---

[4]The calculation of a bond's yield to maturity with the programmed pocket calculator requires simply that you enter the amount of the yearly coupon payment C, the face value F, the number of years to maturity N, and the price of the bond P_b and then run the program.

■ **TABLE 1** Yields to Maturity on a 10%-Coupon-Rate Bond Maturing in Ten Years
                (Face Value = $1000)

Price of Bond ($)	Yield to Maturity (%)
1200	7.13
1100	8.48
1000	10.00
900	11.75
800	13.81

When you put $1000 in a bank account with an interest rate of 10%, you can take out $100 every year and you will be left with the $1000 at the end of ten years. This is similar to buying the $1000 bond with a 10% coupon rate analyzed in Table 1, which pays a $100 coupon payment every year and then repays $1000 at the end of ten years. If the bond is purchased at the par value of $1000, its yield to maturity must equal the interest rate of 10%, which is also equal to the coupon rate of 10%. The same reasoning applied to any coupon bond demonstrates that if the coupon bond is purchased at its par value, the yield to maturity and the coupon rate must be equal.

It is straightforward to show that the bond price and the yield to maturity are negatively related. As i, the yield to maturity, rises, all denominators in the bond price formula must necessarily rise. Hence a rise in the interest rate as measured by the yield to maturity means that the price of the bond must fall. Another way to explain why the bond price falls when the interest rises is that a higher interest rate implies that the future coupon payments and final payment are worth less when discounted back to the present; hence the price of the bond must be lower.

There is one special case of a coupon bond that is worth discussing because its yield to maturity is particularly easy to calculate. This bond is called a **consol;** it is a perpetual bond with no maturity date and no repayment of principal that makes fixed coupon payments of C forever. Consols were first sold by the British Treasury during the Napoleonic Wars and are still traded today; however, they are quite rare in American capital markets. The formula in Equation 3 for the price of the consol P_c simplifies to the following[5]:

---

[5]The bond price formula for a consol is

$$P_c = \frac{C}{1+i} + \frac{C}{(1+i)^2} + \frac{C}{(1+i)^3} + \cdots$$

which can be written as

$$P_c = C(x + x^2 + x^3 + \cdots)$$

in which $x = 1/(1+i)$. From your high school algebra you might remember the formula for an infinite sum:

$$1 + x + x^2 + x^3 + \cdots = \frac{1}{1-x} \quad \text{for} \quad x < 1$$

and so

$$P_c = C\left(\frac{1}{1-x} - 1\right) = C\left[\frac{1}{1 - 1/(1+i)} - 1\right]$$

which by suitable algebraic manipulation becomes

$$P_c = C\left(\frac{1+i}{i} - \frac{i}{i}\right) = \frac{C}{i}$$

$$P_c = \frac{C}{i} \tag{4}$$

One nice feature of consols is that you can immediately see that as i goes up, the price of the bond falls. For example, if a consol pays $100 per year forever and the interest rate is 10%, its price will be $1000 = $100/0.10. If the interest rate rises to 20%, its price will fall to $500 = $100/0.20. We can also rewrite this formula as

$$i = \frac{C}{P_c} \tag{5}$$

We see then that it is also easy to calculate the yield to maturity for the consol (despite the fact that it never matures). For example, with a consol that pays $100 yearly and has a price of $2000, the yield to maturity is easily calculated to be 5% (= $100/$2000).

Discount Bond The yield-to-maturity calculation for a discount bond is similar to that for the simple loan. Let us consider a discount bond such as a one-year U.S. Treasury bill, which pays off a face value of $1000 in one year's time. If the current purchase price of this bill is $900, then equating this price to the present value of the $1000 received in one year, using Equation 1, gives

$$\$900 = \frac{\$1000}{1 + i}$$

and solving for i,

$$i = \frac{\$1000 - \$900}{\$900} = 0.111 = 11.1\%$$

More generally, for any one-year discount bond, the yield to maturity can be written as

$$i = \frac{F - P_d}{P_d} \tag{6}$$

where F = face value of the discount bond
                         P_d = current price of the discount bond

In other words, the yield to maturity equals the increase in price over the year $F - P_d$ divided by the initial price P_d.

An important feature of this equation is that it indicates that for a discount bond, the yield to maturity is negatively related to the current bond price. This is the same conclusion that we reached for a coupon bond. For example, Equation 6 shows that a rise in the bond price from $900 to $950 means that the bond will have a smaller increase in its price over its lifetime, and the yield to maturity falls from 11.1% to 5.3%. Similarly, a fall in the yield to maturity means that the price of the discount bond has risen.

Summary The concept of present value tells you that a dollar in the future is not as valuable to you as a dollar today because you can earn interest on this dollar.

Specifically, a dollar received n years from now is worth only $\$1/(1 + i)^n$ today. The present value of a set of future payments on a debt instrument equals the sum of the present values of each of the future payments. The yield to maturity for an instrument is the interest rate that equates the present value of the future payments on that instrument to its value today. Because the procedure for calculating the yield to maturity is based on sound economic principles, this is the measure that financial economists think most accurately describes the interest rate.

Our calculations of the yield to maturity for a variety of bonds reveal the important fact that ***current bond prices and interest rates are negatively related: When the interest rate rises, the price of the bond falls, and vice versa.***

OTHER MEASURES OF INTEREST RATES

The yield to maturity is the most accurate measure of interest rates and is what financial economists mean when they use the term *interest rate.* Unless otherwise specified, the terms *interest rate* and *yield to maturity* are used synonymously in this book. However, because the yield to maturity is sometimes difficult to calculate, other, less accurate measures of interest rates have come into common use in bond markets. You will frequently encounter two of these measures, the *current yield* and the *yield on a discount basis,* when reading the newspaper, and it is important for you to understand what they mean and how they differ from the more accurate measure of interest rates, the yield to maturity.

Current Yield

The **current yield** is an approximation of the yield to maturity on coupon bonds that is often reported because in contrast to the yield to maturity, it is easily calculated. It is defined as the yearly coupon payment divided by the price of the security,

$$i_c = \frac{C}{P_b} \qquad (7)$$

where

$$i_c = \text{current yield}$$
$$P_b = \text{price of the coupon bond}$$
$$C = \text{yearly coupon payment}$$

This formula is identical to the formula in Equation 5, which describes the calculation of the yield to maturity for a consol. Hence, for a consol, the current yield is an exact measure of the yield to maturity. When a coupon bond has a long term to maturity (say, 20 years or more), it is very much like a consol, which pays coupon payments forever. Thus you would expect the current yield to be a rather close approximation of the yield to maturity for a long-term coupon bond, and you can safely use the current-yield calculation instead of looking up the yield to maturity in a bond table. However, as the time to maturity of the coupon bond shortens (say, it becomes less than five years), it behaves less and less like a consol and so the approximation afforded by the current yield becomes worse and worse.

We have also seen that when the bond price equals the par value of the bond, the yield to maturity is equal to the coupon rate (the coupon payment divided by the par value of the bond). Because the current yield equals the coupon payment divided by the bond price, the current yield is also equal to the coupon rate when the bond price is at par. This logic leads us to the conclusion that when the bond price is at par, the current yield equals the yield to maturity. This means that the nearer the bond price is to the bond's par value, the better the current yield will approximate the yield to maturity.

The current yield is negatively related to the price of the bond. In the case of our 10%-coupon-rate bond, when the price rises from $1000 to $1100, the current yield falls from 10% (= $100/$1000) to 9.09% (= $100/$1100). As Table 1 indicates, the yield to maturity is also negatively related to the price of the bond; when the price rises from $1000 to $1100, the yield to maturity falls from 10% to 8.48%. In this we see an important fact: The current yield and the yield to maturity always move together; a rise in the current yield always signals that the yield to maturity has also risen.

The general characteristics of the current yield (the yearly coupon payment divided by the bond price) can be summarized as follows: The current yield better approximates the yield to maturity when the bond's price is nearer to the bond's par value and the maturity of the bond is longer. It becomes a worse approximation when the bond's price is further from the bond's par value and the bond's maturity is shorter. Regardless of whether the current yield is a good approximation of the yield to maturity, a change in the current yield *always* signals a change in the same direction of the yield to maturity.

Yield on a Discount Basis

Before the advent of calculators and computers, dealers in U.S. Treasury bills found it difficult to calculate interest rates as a yield to maturity. Instead, they quoted the interest rate on bills as a **yield on a discount basis** (or **discount yield**), and they still do so today. Formally, the yield on a discount basis is defined by the following formula:

$$i_{db} = \frac{F - P_d}{F} \times \frac{360}{\text{days to maturity}} \tag{8}$$

where

i_{db} = yield on a discount basis
F = face value of the discount bond
P_d = purchase price of the discount bond

This method for calculating interest rates has two peculiarities. First, it uses the percentage gain on the face value of the bill $(F - P_d)/F$ rather than the percentage gain on the purchase price of the bill $(F - P_d)/P_d$ used in calculating the yield to maturity. Second, it puts the yield on an annual basis by taking the year to be 360 days long rather than 365 days.

Because of these peculiarities, the discount yield understates the interest rate on bills as measured by the yield to maturity. On our one-year bill, which is selling for $900 and has a face value of $1000, the yield on a discount basis would be as follows:

$$i_{db} = \frac{\$1000 - \$900}{\$1000} \times \frac{360}{365} = 0.099 = 9.9\%$$

whereas the yield to maturity for this bill, which we calculated before, is 11.1%. The discount yield understates the yield to maturity by a factor of over 10%. A little more than 1% can be attributed to the understatement of the length of the year: When the bill has one year to maturity, the second term on the right-hand side of the formula is 360/365 = 0.986 rather than 1.0, as it should be.

The more serious source of the understatement, however, is the use of the percentage gain on the face value rather than on the purchase price. Because, by definition, the purchase price of a discount bond is always less than the face value, the percentage gain on the face value is necessarily smaller than the percentage gain on the purchase price. The greater the difference between the purchase price and the face value of the discount bond, the more the discount yield understates the yield to maturity. Because the difference between the purchase price and the face value gets larger as maturity gets longer, we can draw the following conclusion about the relationship of the yield on a discount basis to the yield to maturity: The yield on a discount basis always understates the yield to maturity, and this understatement becomes more severe the longer the maturity of the discount bond.

Another important feature of the discount yield is that, like the yield to maturity, it is negatively related to the price of the bond. For example, when the price of the bond rises from $900 to $950, the formula indicates that the yield on a discount basis declines from 9.9% to 4.9%. At the same time, the yield to maturity declines from 11.1% to 5.3%. Here we see another important factor about the relationship of yield on a discount basis to yield to maturity: They always move together; that is, a rise in the discount yield always means that the yield to maturity has risen, and a decline in the discount yield means that the yield to maturity has declined as well.

The characteristics of the yield on a discount basis can be summarized as follows: Yield on a discount basis understates the more accurate measure of the interest rate, the yield to maturity; and the longer the maturity of the discount bond, the greater this understatement becomes. Even though the discount yield is a somewhat misleading measure of the interest rates, however, a change in the discount yield always indicates a change in the same direction for the yield to maturity.

APPLICATION | **THE BOND PAGE**

READING THE *WALL STREET JOURNAL*

Now that we understand the different interest-rate definitions, let's apply our knowledge and take a look at what kind of information appears on the bond page of a typical newspaper, in this case the *Wall Street Journal.* The "Following the Financial News" box contains the *Journal*'s listing for three different types of

FOLLOWING THE FINANCIAL NEWS

Bond Prices and Interest Rates

Bond prices and interest rates are published daily. In the *Wall Street Journal* they can be found in the "NYSE/AMEX Bonds" and "Treasury/Agency Issues" section of the paper. Three basic formats for quoting bond prices and yields are illustrated here.

Monday, October 7, 1996
Representative Over-the-Counter quotations based on transactions of $1 million or more.

Treasury bond, note and bill quotes are as of mid-afternoon. Colons in bid-and-asked quotes represent 32nds; 101:01 means $101\frac{1}{32}$. Net changes in 32nds. n-Treasury note. Treasury bill quotes in hundredths, quoted on terms of a rate of discount. Days to maturity calculated from settlement date. All yields are to maturity and based on the asked quote. Latest 13-week and 26-week bills are boldfaced. For bonds callable prior to maturity, yields are computed to the earliest call date for issues quoted above par and to the maturity date for issues below par.
*-When issued.
Source: Federal Reserve Bank of New York.

U.S. Treasury strips as of 3 p.m. Eastern time, also based on transactions of $1 million or more. Colons in bid-and-asked quotes represent 32nds; 99:01 means $99\frac{1}{32}$. Net changes in 32nds. Yields calculated on the asked quotation. ci-stripped coupon interest. bp-Treasury bond, stripped principal. np-Treasury note, stripped principal. For bonds callable prior to maturity, yields are computed to the earliest call date for issues quoted above par and to the maturity date for issues below par.
Source: Beer, Stearns & Co. via Street Software Technology, Inc.

(a) Treasury bonds and notes

GOVT. BONDS & NOTES

	Rate	Maturity Mo/Yr	Bid	Asked	Chg.	Ask Yld.	
T-bond 1—	4³/₈	Nov 96n	99:29	99:31	. . . .	4.61	— Current Yield = 4.38%
	7¹/₄	Nov 96n	100:07	100:09	. . . .	4.32	
	6¹/₂	Nov 96n	100:06	100:08	. . . .	4.62	
T-bond 2—	7¹/₄	Nov 96n	100:08	100:10	— 1	4.91	— Current Yield = 7.22%
T-bond 3—	7⁵/₈	Feb 25	109:16	109:18	—19	6.86	— Current Yield = 6.96%
	6⁷/₈	Aug 25	100:16	100:18	—17	6.83	
	6	Feb 26	89:22	89:24	—17	6.81	
T-bond 4—	6³/₄	Aug 26	99:18	99:20	—19	6.78	— Current Yield = 6.78%

(b) Treasury Bills

TREASURY BILLS

Maturity	Days to Mat.	Bid	Asked	Chg.	Ask Yld.	Maturity	Days to Mat.	Bid	Asked	Chg.	Ask Yld.
Oct 10 '96	0	5.04	4.94	−0.01	0.00	Feb 06 '97	119	5.04	5.02	+0.02	5.19
Oct 17 '96	7	4.89	4.79	+0.06	4.87	Feb 13 '97	126	5.04	5.02	+0.01	5.18
Oct 24 '96	14	4.85	4.75	. . . .	4.82	Feb 20 '97	133	5.04	5.02	+0.02	5.19
Oct 31 '96	21	4.83	4.73	. . . .	4.81	Feb 27 '97	140	5.05	5.03	+0.01	5.20
Nov 07 '96	28	4.79	4.69	+0.01	4.77	Mar 06 '97	147	5.05	5.03	. . . .	5.21
Nov 14 '96	35	4.85	4.81	−0.02	4.91	Mar 13 '97	154	5.06	5.04	+0.01	5.22
Nov 21 '96	42	4.84	4.80	. . . .	4.89	Mar 20 '97	161	5.05	5.03	+0.01	5.22
Nov 29 '96	50	4.81	4.77	−0.03	4.87	Mar 27 '97	168	4.99	4.97	+0.01	5.16
Dec 05 '96	56	4.84	4.80	. . . .	4.90	Apr 03 '97	175	5.09	5.07	. . . .	5.27
Dec 12 '96	63	4.89	4.87	−0.01	4.99	Apr 10 '97	182	5.09	5.07	+0.02	5.28
Dec 19 '96	70	4.87	4.85	. . . .	4.96	May 01 '97	203	5.12	5.10	. . . .	5.31
Dec 26 '96	77	4.84	4.82	−0.01	4.94	May 29 '97	231	5.16	5.14	−0.01	5.36
Jan 02 '97	84	4.92	4.90	−0.01	5.03	Jun 26 '97	259	5.17	5.15	. . . .	5.38
Jan 09 '97	91	4.99	4.97	+0.01	5.12	Jul 24 '97	287	5.21	5.19	. . . .	5.44
Jan 16 '97	98	4.99	4.97	+0.01	5.11	Aug 21 '97	315	5.23	5.21	+0.01	5.47
Jan 23 '97	105	4.99	4.97	+0.01	5.11	Sep 18 '97	343	5.23	5.21	. . . .	5.49
Jan 30 '97	112	4.98	4.96	. . . .	5.11						

(c) New York Stock Exchange bonds

CORPORATION BONDS

Volume, $18,261,000

	Bonds	Cur Yld	Vol	Close	Net Chg.	
Bond 1—	ATT 4³/₄ 98	4.8	27	98 ¹/₈	+ ¹/₄	— Yield to Maturity = 5.76%
	ATT 6s00	6.1	154	98 ¹/₂	+ ¹/₈	
	ATT 5 ¹/₈ 01	5.4	3	94 ³/₈	− ³/₈	
	ATT 7 ¹/₈ 02	7.0	90	102 ¹/₂	+ ¹/₂	
	ATT 6 ³/₄ 04	6.8	22	100	+ ³/₈	
	ATT 7s05	6.9	25	100 ⁷/₈	+ ³/₄	
	ATT 7 ¹/₂ 06	7.2	15	104	+ ¹/₈	
	ATT 8 ¹/₈ 22	7.8	158	103 ⁵/₈	. . . .	
	ATT 8 ¹/₈ 24	7.9	4	103 ¹/₈	+ ¹/₈	
Bond 2—	ATT 8 ⁵/₈ 31	8.2	15	105 ¹/₈	− 1 ⁷/₈	— Yield to Maturity = 8.18%

bonds on Monday, October 7, 1996. Panel (a) contains the information on U.S. Treasury bonds and notes. Both are coupon bonds, the only difference being their time to maturity from when they were originally issued: Notes have a time to maturity of less than ten years; bonds have a time to maturity of more than ten years.

The information found in the "Rate" and "Maturity" columns identifies the bond by coupon rate and maturity date. For example, T-bond 1 has a coupon rate of $4\frac{3}{8}$%, indicating that it pays out $43.75 per year on a $1000-face-value bond and matures in November 1996. In bond market parlance, it is referred to as the Treasury's $4\frac{3}{8}$s of 1996. The next three columns tell us about the bond's price. By convention, all prices in the bond market are quoted per $100 of face value. Furthermore, the numbers after the colon represent thirty-seconds. In the case of T-bond 1, the first price of 99:29 represents $99\frac{29}{32} = 99.906$, or an actual price of $999.06 for a $1000-face-value bond. The bid price tells you what price you will receive if you sell the bond, and the asked price tells you what you must pay for the bond. (You might want to think of the bid price as the "wholesale" price and the asked price as the "retail" price.) The "Chg." column indicates how much the bid price has changed in 32nds (in this case, no change) from the previous trading day.

Notice that for all the bonds and notes, the asked price is more than the bid price. Can you guess why this is so? The difference between the two (the *spread*) provides the bond dealer who trades these securities with a profit. For T-bond 1, the dealer who buys it at $99\frac{29}{32}$ and sells it for $99\frac{31}{32}$ makes a profit of $\frac{2}{32}$. This profit is what enables the dealer to make a living and provide the service of allowing you to buy and sell bonds at will.

The "Ask Yld." column provides the yield to maturity, which is 4.61% for T-bond 1. It is calculated with the method described earlier in this chapter using the asked price as the price of the bond. The asked price is used in the calculation because the yield to maturity is most relevant to a person who is going to buy and hold the security and thus earn the yield. The person selling the security is not going to be holding it and hence is less concerned with the yield.

The figure for the current yield is not usually included in the newspaper's quotations for Treasury securities, but it has been added in panel (a) to give you some real-world examples of how well the current yield approximates the yield to maturity. Our previous discussion provided us with some rules for deciding when the current yield is likely to be a good approximation and when it is not.

T-bonds 3 and 4 mature in more than 20 years, meaning that their characteristics are like those of a consol. The current yields should then be a good approximation of the yields to maturity, and they are: The current yields are within two-tenths of a percentage point of the values for the yields to maturity. This approximation is reasonable even for T-bond 3, which has a price nearly 10% above its face value.

Now let's take a look at T-bonds 1 and 2, which have a much shorter time to maturity. The current yield is a good approximation when the price is very near the par price of 100, as it is for T-bond 1. However, the price of T-bond 2 differs by less than 1% from the par value, and look how poor an approximation the current yield is for the yield to maturity; it overstates the yield to maturity by more than

2 percentage points. This bears out what we learned earlier about the current yield: It can be a very misleading guide to the value of the yield to maturity for a short-term bond if the bond price is not very close to par.

Two other categories of bonds are reported much like the Treasury bonds and notes in the newspaper. Government agency and miscellaneous securities include securities issued by U.S. government agencies such as the Government National Mortgage Association, which makes loans to savings and loan institutions, and international agencies such as the World Bank. Tax-exempt bonds are the other category reported in a manner similar to panel (a), except that yield-to-maturity calculations are not usually provided. Tax-exempt bonds include bonds issued by local government and public authorities whose interest payments are exempt from federal income taxes.

Panel (b) quotes yields on U.S. Treasury bills, which, as we have seen, are discount bonds. Since there is no coupon, these securities are identified solely by their maturity dates, which you can see in the first column. The next column, "Days to Mat.," provides the number of days to maturity of the bill. Dealers in these markets always refer to prices by quoting the yield on a discount basis. The "Bid" column gives the discount yield for people selling the bills to dealers, and the "Asked" column gives the discount yield for people buying the bills from dealers. As with bonds and notes, the dealers' profits are made by the asked price being higher than the bid price, leading to the asked discount yield being lower than the bid discount yield.

The "Chg." column indicates how much the asked discount yield changed from the previous day. When financial analysts talk about changes in the yield, they frequently describe the changes in terms of **basis points,** which are hundredths of a percentage point. For example, a financial analyst would describe the + 0.06 change in the asked discount yield for the October 17, 1996, T-bill by saying that it had risen by 6 basis points.

As we learned earlier, the yield on a discount basis understates the yield to maturity, which is reported in the column of panel (b) headed "Ask Yld." This is evident from a comparison of the "Ask Yld." and "Asked" columns. As we would also expect from our discussion of the calculation of yields on a discount basis, the understatement grows as the maturity of the bill lengthens.

Panel (c) has quotations for corporate bonds traded on the New York Stock Exchange. Corporate bonds traded on the American Stock Exchange are reported in like manner. The first column identifies the bond by indicating the corporation that issued it. The bonds we are looking at have all been issued by American Telephone and Telegraph (AT&T). The next column tells the coupon rate and the maturity date ($4\frac{3}{4}$ and 1998 for Bond 1). The "Cur. Yld." column reports the current yield (4.8), and "Vol." gives the volume of trading in that bond (27 bonds of $1000 face value traded that day). The "Close" price is the last traded price that day per $100 of face value. The price of $98\frac{1}{8}$ represents $981.25 for a $1000-face-value bond. The "Net Chg." is the change in the closing price from the previous trading day.

The yield to maturity is also given for two bonds. This information is not usually provided in the newspaper, but it is included here because it shows how misleading the current yield can be for a bond with a short maturity such as the $4\frac{3}{4}$s of 1998. The current yield of 4.8% is a misleading measure of the interest rate because the yield to maturity is actually 5.76%. By contrast, for the $8\frac{5}{8}$s of 2031, with over 30 years to maturity, the current yield and the yield to maturity are almost exactly equal.

■ THE DISTINCTION BETWEEN INTEREST RATES AND RETURNS

Many people think that the interest rate on a bond tells them all they need to know about how well off they are as a result of owning it. If Irving the Investor thinks he is better off when he owns a long-term bond yielding a 10% interest rate and the interest rate rises to 20%, he will have a rude awakening: As we will shortly see, Irving has lost his shirt! How well a person does by holding a bond or any other security over a particular time period is accurately measured by the **return** or, in more precise terminology, the **rate of return.** For any security, the rate of return is defined as the payments to the owner plus the change in its value, expressed as a fraction of its purchase price. To make this definition clearer, let us see what the return would look like for a $1000-face-value coupon bond with a coupon rate of 10% that is bought for $1000, held for one year, and then sold for $1200. The payments to the owner are the yearly coupon payments of $100, and the change in its value is $1200 − $1000 = $200. Adding these together and expressing them as a fraction of the purchase price of $1000 gives us the one-year holding-period return for this bond:

$$\frac{\$100 + \$200}{\$1000} = \frac{\$300}{\$1000} = 0.30 = 30\%$$

You may have noticed something quite surprising about the return that we have just calculated: It equals 30%, yet as Table 1 indicates, initially the yield to maturity was only 10%. This demonstrates that **the return on a bond will not necessarily equal the interest rate on that bond.** We now see that the distinction between interest rate and return can be important, although for many securities the two may be closely related.

■ **S T U D Y   G U I D E**   The concept of return discussed here is extremely important because it is used continually throughout the book. Make sure that you understand how a return is calculated and why it can differ from the interest rate. This understanding will make the material presented later in the book easier to follow.

More generally, the return on a bond held from time t to time $t + 1$ can be written as

$$RET = \frac{C + P_{t+1} - P_t}{P_t} \tag{9}$$

where RET = return from holding the bond from time t to time $t + 1$
           P_t = price of the bond at time t
         P_{t+1} = price of the bond at time $t + 1$
           C = coupon payment

A convenient way to rewrite the return formula in Equation 9 is to recognize that it can be split up into two separate terms. The first is the current yield i_c (the coupon payment over the purchase price):

$$\frac{C}{P_t} = i_c$$

The second term is the **rate of capital gain,** or the change in the bond's price relative to the initial purchase price:

$$\frac{P_{t+1} - P_t}{P_t} = g$$

where g = rate of capital gain. Equation 9 can then be rewritten as

$$RET = i_c + g \tag{10}$$

which shows that the return on a bond is the current yield i_c plus the rate of capital gain g. This rewritten formula illustrates the point we just discovered. Even for a bond for which the current yield i_c is an accurate measure of the yield to maturity, the return can differ substantially from the interest rate. Returns will differ from the interest rate especially if there are sizable fluctuations in the price of the bond that produce substantial capital gains or losses.

To explore this point even further, let's look at what happens to the returns on bonds of different maturities when interest rates rise. Table 2 calculates the one-year return on several 10%-coupon-rate bonds all purchased at par when interest rates on all these bonds rise from 10% to 20%. Several key findings in this table are generally true of all bonds:

- The only bond whose return equals the initial yield to maturity is one whose time to maturity is the same as the holding period (see the last bond in Table 2).
- A rise in interest rates is associated with a fall in bond prices, resulting in capital losses on bonds whose terms to maturity are longer than the holding period.
- The more distant a bond's maturity, the greater the size of the price change associated with an interest-rate change.

■ **TABLE 2** One-Year Returns on Different-Maturity 10%-Coupon-Rate Bonds When Interest Rates Rise

(1) Years to Maturity When Bond Is Purchased	(2) Initial Yield to Maturity (%)	(3) Initial Price ($)	(4) Yield to Maturity Next Year (%)	(5) Price Next Year* ($)	(6) Initial Current Yield (%)	(7) Rate of Capital Gain (%)	(8) Rate of Return (6 + 7) (%)
30	10	1000	20	503	10	−49.7	−39.7
20	10	1000	20	516	10	−48.4	−38.4
10	10	1000	20	597	10	−40.3	−30.3
5	10	1000	20	741	10	−25.9	−15.9
2	10	1000	20	917	10	− 8.3	+1.7
1	10	1000	20	1000	10	0.0	+10.0

*Calculated using Equation 3.

- The more distant a bond's maturity, the lower the rate of return that occurs as a result of the increase in the interest rate.
- Even though a bond has a substantial initial interest rate, its return can turn out to be negative if interest rates rise.

At first it frequently puzzles students that a rise in interest rates can mean that a bond has been a poor investment (as it puzzles poor Irving the Investor). The trick to understanding this is to recognize that a rise in the interest rate means that the price of a bond has fallen. A rise in interest rates therefore means that a capital loss has occurred, and if this loss is large enough, the bond can be a poor investment indeed.[6] For example, we see in Table 2 that the bond that has 30 years to maturity when purchased has a capital loss of 49.7% when the interest rate rises from 10% to 20%. This loss is so large that it exceeds the current yield of 10%, resulting in a negative return (loss) of −39.7%.

Maturity and the Volatility of Bond Returns: Interest-Rate Risk

The finding that the prices of longer-maturity bonds respond more dramatically to changes in interest rates helps explain an important fact about the behavior of bond markets: ***Prices and returns for long-term bonds are more volatile than those for shorter-term bonds.*** Price changes of + 20% and −20% within a year, with corresponding variations in returns, are common for bonds more than 20 years away from maturity.

We now see that changes in interest rates make investments in long-term bonds quite risky. Indeed, the riskiness of an asset's return that results from interest-rate changes is so important that it has been given a special name, **interest-rate risk.** Dealing with interest-rate risk is a major concern of managers of financial institutions, as we will see in later chapters.

Although long-term debt instruments have substantial interest-rate risk, short-term debt instruments do not. Indeed, bonds with a maturity that is as short as the holding period have no interest-rate risk.[7] We see this for the coupon bond at the bottom of Table 2, which has no uncertainty about the rate of return because it equals the yield to maturity, which is known at the time the bond is purchased. The key to understanding why there is no interest-rate risk for *any* bond whose time to maturity matches the holding period is to recognize that (in this case) the price at the end of the holding period is already fixed at the face value. The change in interest rates can then have no effect on the price at the end of the

---

[6]If Irving does not sell the bond, his capital loss is often referred to as a "paper loss." This is a loss nonetheless because if he had not bought this bond and had instead put his money in the bank, he would now be able to buy more bonds at their lower price than he presently owns.

[7]The statement that there is no interest-rate risk for any bond whose time to maturity matches the holding period is literally true only for discount bonds and zero-coupon bonds that make no intermediate cash payments before the holding period is over. A coupon bond that makes an intermediate cash payment before the holding period is over requires that this payment be reinvested at some future date. Because the interest rate at which this payment can be reinvested is uncertain, there is some uncertainty about the return on this coupon bond even when the time to maturity equals the holding period. However, the riskiness of the return on a coupon bond from reinvesting the coupon payments is typically quite small, and so the basic point that a coupon bond with a time to maturity equaling the holding period has very little risk still holds true.

holding period for these bonds, and the return will therefore be equal to the yield to maturity known at the time the bond is purchased.

Reinvestment Risk

Up to now, we have been assuming that all holding periods are as short as the maturity on short-term bonds and are thus not subject to interest-rate risk. However, if an investor's holding period is longer than the term to maturity of the bond, the investor is exposed to a type of interest-rate risk called **reinvestment risk.** Reinvestment risk occurs because the proceeds from the short-term bond need to be reinvested at a future interest rate that is uncertain.

To understand reinvestment risk, suppose that Irving the Investor has a holding period of two years and decides to purchase a $1000 one-year bond at face value and will then purchase another one at the end of the first year. If the initial interest rate is 10%, Irving will have $1100 at the end of the year. If the interest rate on one-year bonds rises to 20% at the end of the year, as in Table 2, Irving will find that buying $1100 worth of another one-year bond will leave him at the end of the second year with $1100 × (1 + 0.20) = $1320. Thus Irving's two-year return will be ($1320 − $1000)/$1000 = 0.32 = 32%, which equals 14.9% at an annual rate. In this case, Irving has earned more by buying the one-year bonds than if he had initially purchased the two-year bond with an interest rate of 10%. Thus when Irving has a holding period that is longer than the term to maturity of the bonds he purchases, he benefits from a rise in interest rates. Conversely, if interest rates on one-year bonds fall to 5% at the end of the year, Irving will have only $1155 at the end of two years: $1100 × (1 + 0.05). Thus his two-year return will be ($1155 − $1000)/$1000 = 0.155 = 15.5%, which is 7.2% at an annual rate. With a holding period greater than the term to maturity of the bond, Irving now loses from a fall in interest rates.

We have thus seen that when the holding period is longer than the term to maturity of a bond, the return is uncertain because the future interest rate when reinvestment occurs is also uncertain—in short, there is reinvestment risk. We also see that if the holding period is longer than the term to maturity of the bond, the investor benefits from a rise in interest rates and is hurt by a fall in interest rates.

Summary

The return on a bond, which tells you how good an investment it has been over the holding period, is equal to the yield to maturity in only one special case: when the holding period and the maturity of the bond are identical. Bonds whose term to maturity is longer than the holding period are subject to interest-rate risk: Changes in interest rates lead to capital gains and losses that produce substantial differences between the return and the yield to maturity known at the time the bond is purchased. Interest-rate risk is especially important for long-term bonds, where the capital gains and losses can be substantial. This is why long-term bonds are not considered to be safe assets with a sure return over short holding periods. Bonds whose term to maturity is shorter than the holding period are also subject

■ **TABLE 3** Prices and One-Year Returns on U.S. Treasury $11\frac{1}{4}$s of 2015, 1985–1996

Year	Price at End of Year	Return (%)
1985	117 $^{29}/_{32}$	
1986	138 $^{4}/_{32}$	+26.7
1987	121 $^{31}/_{32}$	−3.6
1988	121 $^{31}/_{32}$	+9.2
1989	133 $^{26}/_{32}$	+18.9
1990	129 $^{24}/_{32}$	+5.4
1991	141 $^{27}/_{32}$	+18.0
1992	141 $^{14}/_{32}$	+7.6
1993	154 $^{6}/_{32}$	+17.0
1994	132 $^{3}/_{32}$	−7.0
1995	160	+29.6
1996	149 $^{12}/_{32}$	+0.5

to reinvestment risk. Reinvestment risk occurs because the proceeds from the short-term bond need to be reinvested at a future interest rate that is uncertain.

APPLICATION   **SHOULD RETIREES INVEST IN "GILT-EDGED" LONG-TERM BONDS?**

A common bit of conventional wisdom is that retirees should invest their money in "gilt-edged" securities like long-term U.S Treasury bonds because this will provide them with a safe return. Is this good advice given today's financial markets?

The concept of interest-rate risk indicates that the answer is no because long-term bonds have very volatile returns. To see this, let's examine the returns on a long-term Treasury bond such as the Treasury $11\frac{1}{4}$s of 2015 (a coupon bond with a coupon rate of $11\frac{1}{4}$%, maturing in 2015). Table 3 provides the prices and one-year returns for this bond from 1985 to 1996. (To make sure you understand the concepts of a return and a coupon bond, you might try to calculate these returns yourself using the formula in Equation 9.)

As you can see, there have been big swings in the returns on this supposedly safe investment, with low returns and even losses occurring in some years. If retirees at times need to sell bonds to pay bills so that they might only hold bonds for periods as short as a year, they may find themselves in financial difficulties when the bonds decline in value. Conclusion: Retirees beware!

■ **THE PRACTICING FINANCIAL INSTITUTION MANAGER**
Calculating Duration to Measure Interest-Rate Risk

Earlier in our discussion of interest-rate risk, we saw that when interest rates change, a bond with a longer term to maturity has a larger change in its price and hence more interest-rate risk than a bond with a shorter term to maturity. Although this is a useful general fact, in order to measure interest-rate risk, the manager of a financial institution needs more precise information on the actual capital gain or loss that occurs when the interest rate changes by a certain amount. To do this, the manager needs to make use of the concept of **duration,** the average lifetime of a debt security's stream of payments.

The fact that two bonds have the same term to maturity does not mean that they have the same interest-rate risk. A long-term discount bond with ten years to maturity, a so-called zero-coupon bond, makes all of its payments at the end of the ten years, whereas a 10% coupon bond with ten years to maturity makes substantial cash payments before the maturity date. Since the coupon bond makes payments earlier than the zero-coupon bond, we might intuitively guess that the coupon bond's *effective maturity*, the term to maturity that accurately measures interest-rate risk, is shorter than it is for the zero-coupon discount bond.

That is exactly what we find. To see this, let's calculate the rate of capital gain on the ten-year zero-coupon bond when interest rates rise from the current 10% to 20% next year. If the zero-coupon bond has a face value of $1000, which it pays at the end of ten years' time, its initial price when the interest rate is 10% is just the present value of the $1000 paid in ten years: $1000/ $(1 + 0.10)^{10}$ = $385.54. When the interest rate rises to 20% next year, the price of the zero-coupon bond will be the present value of the $1000 paid nine years later, equal to $1000/$(1 + 0.20)^9$ = $193.81. The rate of capital gain is then

$$g = \frac{P_{t+1} - P_t}{P_t} = \frac{\$193.81 - \$385.54}{\$385.54} = -0.497 = -49.7\%$$

But, as we have already calculated in Table 2, the capital gain on the 10% ten-year coupon bond is -40.3%. We see that interest-rate risk for the ten-year coupon bond is less than for the ten-year zero-coupon bond, so the effective maturity on the coupon bond (which measures interest-rate risk) is, as expected, shorter than the effective maturity on the zero-coupon bond.

Calculating Duration

To calculate the duration or effective maturity on any debt security, Frederick Macaulay, a researcher at the National Bureau of Economic Research, invented the concept of duration more than half a century ago. Because a zero-coupon bond makes no cash payments before the bond matures, it makes sense to define its effective maturity as equal to its actual term to maturity. Macaulay then realized that he could measure the effective maturity of a coupon bond by recognizing that a coupon bond is equivalent to a set of zero-coupon discount bonds. A ten-year 10% coupon bond with $1000 face value has cash payments identical to the following set of zero-coupon bonds: a $100 one-year zero-coupon bond (which pays the equivalent of the $100 coupon payment made by the $1000 ten-year 10% coupon bond at the end of one year), a $100 two-year zero-coupon bond (which pays the equivalent of the $100 coupon payment at the end of two years), . . . , a $100 ten-year zero-coupon bond (which pays the equivalent of the $100 coupon payment at the end of ten years), and a $1000 ten-year zero-coupon bond (which pays back the equivalent of the coupon bond's $1000 face value). This set of zero-coupon bonds is listed in column (2) of Table 4, which calculates the duration on the ten-year coupon bond when its interest rate is 10%.

■ TABLE 4 Calculating Duration on a $1000, Ten-Year 10% Coupon Bond When Its Interest Rate Is 10%

(1)	(2)	(3)	(4)	(5)
Year	Cash Payments (Zero-Coupon Bonds) ($)	Present Value (PV) of Cash Payments (i = 10%) ($)	Weights (% of total PV = PV/$1000) (%)	Weighted Maturity (1 × 4)/100 (years)
1	100	90.91	9.091	0.09091
2	100	82.64	8.264	0.16528
3	100	75.13	7.513	0.22539
4	100	68.30	6.830	0.27320
5	100	62.09	6.209	0.31045
6	100	56.44	5.644	0.33864
7	100	51.32	5.132	0.35924
8	100	46.65	4.665	0.37320
9	100	42.41	4.241	0.38169
10	100	38.55	3.855	0.38550
10	1000	385.54	38.554	3.85500
Total		1000.00	100.000	6.75850

To get the effective maturity of this set of zero-coupon bonds, we would want to sum up the effective maturity of each zero-coupon bond, weighting it by the percentage of the total value of all the bonds that it represents. In other words, the duration of this set of zero-coupon bonds is the weighted average of the effective maturities of the individual zero-coupon bonds, with the weights equaling the proportion of the total value represented by each zero-coupon bond. We do this in several steps in Table 4. First we calculate the present value of each of the zero-coupon bonds when the interest rate is 10% in column (3). Then in column (4) we divide each of these present values by $1000, the total present value of the set of zero-coupon bonds, to get the percentage of the total value of all the bonds that each bond represents. Note that the sum of the weights in column (4) must total 100%, as shown at the bottom of the column.

To get the effective maturity of the set of zero-coupon bonds, we add up the weighted maturities in column (5) and obtain the figure of 6.76 years. This figure for the effective maturity of the set of zero-coupon bonds is the duration of the 10% ten-year coupon bond because the bond is equivalent to this set of zero-coupon bonds.

The duration calculation done in Table 4 can be written as follows:

$$DUR = \sum_{t=1}^{N} t\frac{CP_t}{(1 + i)^t} \bigg/ \sum_{t=1}^{N} \frac{CP_t}{(1 + i)^t} \qquad (11)$$

where DUR = duration
t = years until cash payment is made
CP_t = cash payment (interest plus principal) at time t
i = interest rate
N = years to maturity of the security

This formula is not as intuitive as the calculation done in Table 4, but it does have the advantage that it can easily be programmed into a computer, making duration calculations very easy.

If we calculate the duration for an 11-year 10% coupon bond when the interest rate is again 10%, we find that it equals 7.14 years, which is greater than the 6.76 years for the ten-year bond. Thus we have reached the expected conclusion: ***All else being equal, the longer the term to maturity of a bond, the longer its duration.***

You might think that knowing the maturity of a coupon bond is enough to tell you what its duration is. However, that is not the case. To see this and to give you more practice in calculating duration, in Table 5 we again calculate the duration for the ten-year 10% coupon bond, but when the current interest rate is 20% rather than 10% as in Table 4. The calculation in Table 5 reveals that the duration of the coupon bond at this higher interest rate has fallen from 6.76 years to 5.72 years. The explanation is fairly straightforward. When the interest rate is higher, the cash payments in the future are discounted more heavily and become less important in present-value terms relative to the total present value of all the payments. The relative weight for these cash payments drops as we see in Table 5, and so the effective maturity of the bond falls. We have come to an important conclusion: ***All else being equal, when interest rates rise, the duration of a coupon bond falls.***

The duration of a coupon bond is also affected by its coupon rate. For example, consider a ten-year 20% coupon bond when the interest rate is 10%. Using the same procedure, we find that its duration at the higher 20% coupon rate is 5.98 years versus 6.76 years when the coupon rate is 10%. The explanation is that a higher coupon rate means that a relatively greater amount of the cash payments are made earlier in the life of the bond, and so the effective maturity of the bond must fall. We have thus established a third fact about

■ TABLE 5 Calculating Duration on a $1000, Ten-Year 10% Coupon Bond When Its Interest Rate Is 20%

(1)	(2)	(3)	(4)	(5)
Year	Cash Payments (Zero-Coupon Bonds) ($)	Present Value (PV) of Cash Payments ($i = 20\%$) ($)	Weights (% of total $PV = PV/\$580.76$) (%)	Weighted Maturity $(1 \times 4)/100$ (years)
1	100	83.33	14.348	0.14348
2	100	69.44	11.957	0.23914
3	100	57.87	9.965	0.29895
4	100	48.23	8.305	0.33220
5	100	40.19	6.920	0.34600
6	100	33.49	5.767	0.34602
7	100	27.91	4.806	0.33642
8	100	23.26	4.005	0.32040
9	100	19.38	3.337	0.30033
10	100	16.15	2.781	0.27810
10	$1000	161.51	27.808	2.78100
Total		580.76	100.000	5.72204

duration: ***All else being equal, the higher the coupon rate on the bond, the shorter the bond's duration.***

■ S T U D Y   G U I D E To make certain that you understand how to calculate duration, practice doing the calculations in Tables 4 and 5. Try to produce the tables for calculating duration in the case of an 11-year 10% coupon bond and also for the ten-year 20% coupon bond mentioned in the text when the current interest rate is 10%. Make sure your calculations produce the same results found in the text. You can get more practice by doing some of the problems involving duration calculations at the end of the chapter.

One additional fact about duration makes this concept useful when applied to a portfolio of securities. Our examples have shown that duration is equal to the weighted average of the durations of the cash payments (the effective maturities of the corresponding zero-coupon bonds). So if we calculate the duration for two different securities, it should be easy to see that the duration of a portfolio of the two securities is just the weighted average of the durations of the two securities, with the weights reflecting the proportion of the portfolio invested in each. For example, if the manager of a financial institution is holding 25% of a portfolio in a bond with a five-year duration and 75% in a bond with a ten-year duration, the duration of the portfolio is $(0.25 \times 5) + (0.75 \times 10) = 8.75$ years. We describe this fact about duration as follows: ***The duration of a portfolio of securities is the weighted-average of the durations of the individual securities, with the weights reflecting the proportion of the portfolio invested in each.*** This fact about duration is often referred to as the *additive property of duration,* and it is extremely useful because it means that the duration of a portfolio of securities is easy to calculate from the durations of the individual securities.

To summarize, our calculations of duration for coupon bonds have revealed four facts:

1. The longer the term to maturity of a bond, everything else being equal, the greater its duration.

2. When interest rates rise, everything else being equal, the duration of a coupon bond falls.

3. The higher the coupon rate on the bond, everything else being equal, the shorter the bond's duration.

4. Duration is additive: The duration of a portfolio of securities is the weighted average of the durations of the individual securities, with the weights reflecting the proportion of the portfolio invested in each.

Duration and Interest-Rate Risk

Now that we understand how duration is calculated, we want to see how it can be used by the practicing financial institution manager to measure interest-rate risk. As the following formula shows, the duration of a security indicates how much the security price changes for a given change in interest rates:

$$\%\Delta P \approx -DUR \times \frac{\Delta i}{1+i} \qquad (12)$$

where $\%\Delta P = (P_{t+1} - P_t)/P_t$ = percent change in the price of the security from t to $t + 1$ = rate of capital gain

$\qquad$ DUR = duration

$\qquad$ i = interest rate

If a pension fund manager is holding a ten-year 10% coupon bond in the fund's portfolio and the interest rate is currently 10%, the manager can use Equation 12 to see how much risk the fund would be exposed to if the interest rate rises to 11% tomorrow.

$\qquad$ The pension fund manager has already gone through the calculation in Table 4 and so knows that the duration of the ten-year 10% coupon bond is 6.76 years. Using the values of 6.76 for DUR, 0.01 for Δi, and 0.10 for i in the equation, the manager calculates the approximate percentage change in the bond's price to be

$$\%\Delta P = -DUR \times \frac{\Delta i}{1+i} = -6.76 \times \frac{0.01}{1+0.10} = -0.0615 = -6.15\%$$

The actual decline in the bond's price is 5.89%, which is quite close to that estimated by this calculation.

$\qquad$ The pension fund manager has the alternative of holding a ten-year coupon bond with a coupon rate of 20% rather than 10%. As mentioned earlier, the duration of this 20% coupon bond is 5.98 years when the current interest rate is 10%. The manager again calculates what happens when the interest rate rises from 10% to 11% by plugging the 5.98 figure in for DUR in the formula and finds that the approximate change in the bond's price is

$$\%\Delta P = -DUR \times \frac{\Delta i}{1+i} = -5.98 \times \frac{0.01}{1+0.10} = -0.054 = -5.4\%$$

The −5.4% change in the bond's price is smaller than for the higher-duration coupon bond. The pension fund manager realizes that the interest-rate risk on the 20% coupon bond is less than that on the 10% coupon bond and so switches the fund out of the 10% coupon bond into the 20% coupon bond.

$\qquad$ Using Equation 12, the pension fund manager has recognized an essential conclusion about the relationship of duration and interest-rate risk: ***The greater the duration of a security, the greater the percentage change in the market value of the security for a given change in interest rates. Therefore, the greater the duration of a security, the greater its interest-rate risk.***

$\qquad$ This reasoning applies equally to a portfolio of securities. So by calculating the duration of the fund's portfolio of securities using the methods outlined here, a pension fund manager can easily ascertain the amount of interest-rate risk the entire fund is exposed to. As we will see in Chapter 14, duration is a highly useful concept for the management of interest-rate risk that is widely used by managers of banks and other financial institutions.

■ THE DISTINCTION BETWEEN REAL AND NOMINAL INTEREST RATES

So far in our discussion of interest rates, we have ignored the effects of inflation on the cost of borrowing. What we have up to now been calling the interest rate makes no allowance for inflation, and it is more precisely referred to as the **nominal interest rate,** which is to distinguish it from the **real interest rate,** the interest rate that is adjusted for expected changes in the price level so that it more accurately reflects the true cost of borrowing.[8] The real interest rate is more accurately defined by the *Fisher equation,* named for Irving Fisher, one of the great monetary economists of the twentieth century. The Fisher equation states that the nominal interest rate i equals the real interest rate i_r plus the expected rate of inflation π^e.[9]

$$i = i_r + \pi^e \tag{13}$$

Rearranging terms, we find that the real interest rate equals the nominal interest rate minus the expected inflation rate:

$$i_r = i - \pi^e \tag{14}$$

To see why this definition makes sense, let us first consider a situation in which you have made a one-year simple loan with a 5% interest rate ($i = 5\%$) and you expect the price level to rise by 3% over the course of the year ($\pi^e = 3\%$). As a result of making the loan, at the end of the year you will have 2% more in **real terms,** that is, in terms of real goods and services you can buy. In this case, the interest rate you have earned in terms of real goods and services is 2%; that is,

$$i_r = 5\% - 3\% = 2\%$$

as indicated by the Fisher definition.

Now what if the interest rate rises to 8%, but you expect the inflation rate to be 10% over the course of the year? Although you will have 8% more dollars at the end of the year, you will be paying 10% more for goods; the result is that you will

---

[8]The real interest rate defined in the text is more precisely referred to as the *ex ante real interest rate* because it is adjusted for *expected* changes in the price level. This is the real interest rate that is most important to economic decisions, and typically it is what financial economists mean when they make reference to the "real" interest rate. The interest rate that is adjusted for *actual* changes in the price level is called the *ex post real interest rate.* It describes how well a lender has done in real terms *after the fact.*

[9]A more precise formulation of the Fisher equation is

$$i = i_r + \pi^e + (i_r \times \pi^e)$$

because

$$1 + i = (1 + i_r)(1 + \pi^e) = 1 + i_r + \pi^e + (i_r \times \pi^e)$$

and subtracting 1 from both sides gives us the first equation. For small values of i_r and π^e, the term $i_r \times \pi^e$ is so small that we ignore it, as in the text.

be able to buy 2% fewer goods at the end of the year and you are 2% worse off *in real terms*. This is also exactly what the Fisher definition tells us because

$$i_r = 8\% - 10\% = -2\%$$

As a lender, you are clearly less eager to make a loan in this case because in terms of real goods and services you have actually earned a negative interest rate of 2%. By contrast, as the borrower, you fare quite well because at the end of the year, the amounts you will have to pay back will be worth 2% less in terms of goods and services—you as the borrower will be ahead by 2% in real terms. ***When the real interest rate is low, there are greater incentives to borrow and fewer incentives to lend.***

A similar distinction can be made between nominal returns and real returns. Nominal returns, which do not allow for inflation, are what we have been referring to as simply "returns." When inflation is subtracted from a nominal return, we have the real return, which indicates the amount of extra goods and services that can be purchased as a result of holding the security.

The distinction between real and nominal interest rates is important because the real interest rate, which reflects the real cost of borrowing, is likely to be a better indicator of the incentives to borrow and lend. It appears to be a better guide to how people will be affected by what is happening in credit markets. Figure 3, which presents estimates from 1953 to 1996 of the real and nominal interest rates on three-month U.S. Treasury bills, shows us that nominal and real rates often do not move together. (This is also true for nominal and real interest rates in the rest

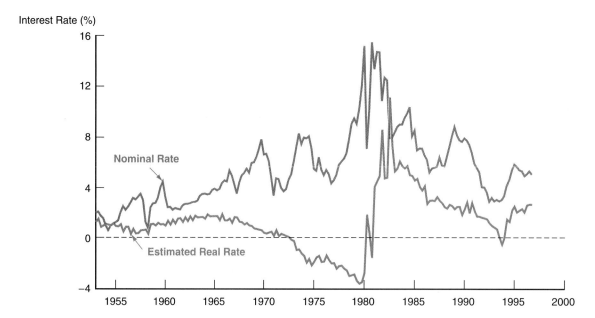

■FIGURE 3 Real and Nominal Interest Rates (Three-Month Treasury Bill), 1953–1996

SOURCES: Nominal rates from the Citibase databank. The real rate is constructed using the procedure outlined in Frederic S. Mishkin, "The Real Interest Rate: An Empirical Investigation," *Carnegie-Rochester Conference Series on Public Policy* 15 (1981): 151–200. This involves estimating expected inflation as a function of past interest rates, inflation, and time trends and then subtracting the expected inflation measure from the nominal interest rate.

of the world.) In particular, when nominal rates in the United States were high in the 1970s, real rates were actually extremely low, often negative. By the standard of nominal interest rates, you would have thought that credit market conditions were tight in this period because it was expensive to borrow. However, the estimates of the real rates indicate that you would have been mistaken. In real terms, the cost of borrowing was actually quite low.[10]

In future years, we will have more direct measures of real interest rates in the United States. In January 1997, the U.S. Treasury began to issue **indexed bonds,** bonds whose interest and principal payments are adjusted for changes in the price level and whose interest rate thus provides a direct measure of a real interest rate. Indexed bonds have been issued by the governments of countries such as the United Kingdom, Canada, Australia, and Sweden. Not only have they acquired a successful niche in the bond market in these countries, but they are also useful to policymakers, especially monetary policymakers, because by subtracting their interest rate from a nominal interest rate, they generate more direct information on expected inflation, a valuable piece of information.

SUMMARY

1. The yield to maturity, which is the measure that most accurately reflects the interest rate, is the interest rate that equates the present value of future payments of a debt instrument with its value today. Application of this principle reveals that bond prices and interest rates are negatively related: When the interest rate rises, the price of the bond must fall, and vice versa.

2. Two less accurate measures of interest rates are commonly used to quote interest rates on coupon and discount bonds. The current yield, which equals the coupon payment divided by the price of a coupon bond, is a less accurate measure of the yield to maturity the shorter the maturity of the bond and the greater the gap between the price and the par value. The yield on a discount basis (also called the

---

[10]Because most interest income in the United States is subject to federal income taxes, the true earnings in real terms from holding a debt instrument are not reflected by the real interest rate defined by the Fisher equation but rather by the *after-tax real interest rate,* which equals the nominal interest rate *after income tax payments have been subtracted,* minus the expected inflation rate. For a person facing a 30% tax rate, the after-tax interest rate earned on a bond yielding 10% is only 7% because 30% of the interest income must be paid to the Internal Revenue Service. Thus the after-tax real interest rate on this bond when expected inflation is 20% equals -13% ($= 7\% - 20\%$). More generally, the after-tax real interest rate can be expressed as

$$i(1 - \tau) - \pi^e$$

where $\tau = $ the income tax rate.

This formula for the after-tax real interest rate also provides a better measure of the effective cost of borrowing for many corporations and individuals in the United States because in calculating income taxes, they can deduct interest payments on loans from their income. Thus if you face a 30% tax rate and take out a mortgage loan with a 10% interest rate, you are able to deduct the 10% interest payment and thus lower your taxes by 30% of this amount. Your after-tax nominal cost of borrowing is then 7% (10% minus 30% of the 10% interest payment), and when the expected inflation rate is 20%, the effective cost of borrowing in real terms is again -13% ($= 7\% - 20\%$).

As the example (and the formula) indicates, after-tax real interest rates are always below the real interest rate defined by the Fisher equation. For a further discussion of measures of after-tax real interest rates, see Frederic S. Mishkin, "The Real Interest Rate: An Empirical Investigation," *Carnegie-Rochester Conference Series on Public Policy* 15 (1981): 151–200.

discount yield) understates the yield to maturity on a discount bond, and the understatement worsens the more distant the maturity of the discount security. Even though these measures are misleading guides to the size of the interest rate, a change in them always signals a change in the same direction for the yield to maturity.

3. The return on a security, which tells you how well you have done by holding this security over a stated period of time, can differ substantially from the interest rate as measured by the yield to maturity. Long-term bond prices have substantial fluctuations when interest rates change and thus bear interest-rate risk. The resulting capital gains and losses can be large, which is why long-term bonds are not considered to be safe assets with a sure return. Bonds whose maturity is shorter than the holding period are also subject to reinvestment risk, which occurs because the proceeds from the short-term bond need to be reinvested at a future interest rate that is uncertain.

4. Duration, the average lifetime of a debt security's stream of payments, is a measure of effective maturity, the term to maturity that accurately measures interest-rate risk. Everything else being equal, the duration of a bond is greater the longer the maturity of a bond, when interest rates fall, or when the coupon rate of a coupon bond falls. Duration is additive: The duration of a portfolio of securities is the weighted average of the durations of the individual securities, with the weights reflecting the proportion of the portfolio invested in each. The greater the duration of a security, the greater the percentage change in the market value of the security for a given change in interest rates. Therefore, the greater the duration of a security, the greater its interest-rate risk.

5. The real interest rate is defined as the nominal interest rate minus the expected rate of inflation. It is a better measure of the incentives to borrow and lend than the nominal interest rate, and it is a more accurate indicator of the tightness of credit market conditions than the nominal interest rate.

KEY TERMS

basis point, p. 56
consol, p. 49
coupon bond, p. 42
coupon rate, p. 42
current yield, p. 51
discount bond (zero-coupon
 bond), p. 42
duration, p. 61

face value (par value), p. 42
fixed-payment loan, p. 42
indexed bond, p. 69
interest-rate risk, p. 59
nominal interest rate, p. 67
present value (present
 discounted value), p. 43
rate of capital gain, p. 58

real interest rate, p. 67
real terms, p. 67
reinvestment risk, p. 60
return (rate of return), p. 57
simple loan, p. 42
yield on a discount basis
 (discount yield), p. 52
yield to maturity, p. 44

QUESTIONS AND PROBLEMS

*1. Would a dollar tomorrow be worth more or less to you today when the interest rate is 20% or when it is 10%?

2. You have just won $20 million in the state lottery, which promises to pay you $1 million (tax free) every year for the next 20 years. Have you really won $20 million?

*3. If the interest rate is 10%, what is the present value of a security that pays you $1100 next year, $1210 the year after, and $1331 the year after that?

4. If the security in Problem 3 sold for $4000, is the yield to maturity greater or less than 10%? Why?

*5. Write down the formula that is used to calculate the yield to maturity on a 20-year 10% coupon bond with $1000 face value that sells for $2000.

6. What is the yield to maturity on a $1000-face-value discount bond maturing in one year that sells for $800?

*7. What is the yield to maturity on a simple loan for $1 million that requires a repayment of $2 million in five years' time?

8. To pay for college, you have just taken out a $1000 government loan that makes you pay $126 per year for 25 years. However, you don't have to start making these payments until you graduate from col-

lege two years from now. Why is the yield to maturity necessarily less than 12%, the yield to maturity on a normal $1000 fixed-payment loan in which you pay $126 per year for 25 years?

*9. Which $1000 bond has the higher yield to maturity, a 20-year bond selling for $800 with a current yield of 15% or a one-year bond selling for $800 with a current yield of 5%?

10. Pick five U.S. Treasury bonds from the bond page of the newspaper, and calculate the current yield. Note when the current yield is a good approximation of the yield to maturity.

*11. You are offered two bonds, a one-year U.S. Treasury bond with a yield to maturity of 9% and a one-year U.S. Treasury bill with a yield on a discount basis of 8.9%. Which would you rather own?

12. If there is a decline in interest rates, which would you rather be holding, long-term bonds or short-term bonds? Why? Which type of bond has the greater interest-rate risk?

*13. A financial adviser has just given you the following advice: "Long-term bonds are a great investment because their interest rate is over 20%." Is the financial adviser necessarily right?

14. If mortgage rates rise from 5% to 10% but the expected rate of increase in housing prices rises from 2% to 9%, are people more or less likely to buy houses?

*15. Interest rates were lower in the mid-1980s than they were in the late 1970s, yet many observers have commented that real interest rates were actually much higher in the mid-1980s than in the late 1970s. Does this make sense? Do you think that these observers are right?

16. When interest rates rise, would you rather be holding a ten-year coupon bond with a 5% coupon rate or one with a 10% coupon rate?

*17. Calculate the duration on a five-year 8% coupon bond when the interest rate is 3%.

18. Calculate the duration on a five-year 5% coupon bond when the interest rate is 3%. Compare your answer to the answer to Problem 17 given at the back of the book. What is the intuition behind the difference in the answers?

*19. If a bond has a duration of eight years and interest rates rise from 7% to 8%, what will be the approximate percentage change in the price of the bond?

20. Calculate the approximate price change of two bonds, one with a three-year duration and the other with a five-year duration, when interest rates rise from 4% to 5%. Which of the bonds would you rather hold? Does this accord with your intuition?

■ CASE STUDY

■ Interest Rates, Bond Yields, and Duration

CONCEPTS IN THIS CASE

simple loans
fixed-payment loans
coupon bonds
present value
yield-to-maturity
current yield
nominal and real interest rates
rate of return
capital gain
interest-rate and reinvestment risk
duration

You have been hired to analyze the debt securities of your organization. The firm has outstanding loans and bonds. A quick review of the balance sheet shows the following:

	Liability Amount($)	Nominal Interest (coupon) Rate	Years to Maturity
Selected Liabilities of the firm			
Simple Loans	800	5%	1
Fixed-Payment Loans	5,000	12%	19
Long-term Bonds #1	500,000	10%	4
Long-term Bonds #2	1,080,000	10%	10
Liabilities Total	1,585,800		
Market Price for Bond #1	930.50		
Market Price for Bond #2	859.50		
Face Value of Each Bond	1,000.00		
Selected Current Assets of the firm			
Marketable Securities: Treasury Bills	100,000		

Note: Treasury Bills have a $10,000 face value, which matures in one year. Each Treasury Bill has a cost of $9,580.00

1. How much interest would the firm pay each year on the simple-interest loan?

2. How much would you write a check for to pay off the loan in one year?

3. What is the monthly payment needed to pay off the fixed-payment loans?

4. What is the current yield for each bond if the current price is:
   a. $930.50 for Bond #1?
   b. $859.50 for Bond #2?

5. What is the expected yield to maturity for each bond?
   a. Bond #1 selling for $930.50?
   b. Bond #2 selling for $859.50

6. What is the rate of capital gain if both bonds sell for $900.00 in one year?
   a. Bond #1 selling for $930.50 today?
   b. Bond #2 selling for $859.50 today?

7. If the Yield to Maturity expected by investors changes to 11%:
   a. What will be the market price of Bond #1?
   b. What will be the market price for Bond #2?
   c. What will be the dollar change in price for Bond #1?
   d. What will be the dollar change in price for Bond #2?
   e. What will be the percent change in price for Bond #1?
   f. What will be the percent change in price for Bond #2?
   g. Since the change in expected yield to maturity is the same, why is the amount of change different between the bonds?

8. If investors holding our 4-year bonds (Bond #1) receive interest income annually for four years, plus the face value of the bonds at maturity,

a. What will be the total interest earned on the bond over the next four years?
   b. What will be the face value received at maturity?

Given the following projected income stream for Bond #1:

Year	Coupon Interest ($)	Face Value ($)	Projected Reinvestment Rates	
			10%	5%
1	100			
2	100		10.00	5.00
3	100		21.00	10.25
4	100	1000	33.10	15.76
Total Income	400	1000	64.10	31.01

c. What is the total cash available over the next four years to the bond holder earning
   i. 10%
   ii. 15%
   d. What is the average annual rate of return for the bond holder earning
   i. 10%
   ii. 15%
   e. Why does the reinvestment rate affect the annual rate of return for the same bond?
   f. If the expected rate of return on our bonds is 10%, what is the duration of Bond #1?
   g. If interest rates change from 10% to 12%, what is the expected approximate change in the price of Bond #1?

9. What is the yield to maturity on the Treasury Bills (a discount bond)?

10. What is the real rate of interest if the nominal rate is 10% and the inflation rate is 3%?

CHAPTER 4

PORTFOLIO CHOICE

PREVIEW Suppose that your product takes off and the resulting profits leave your company with a lot of excess cash or that thanks to your astute management, the financial institution you work at has a huge inflow of funds. There are a lot of things you might want to do with these newly acquired funds: You might invest them in Treasury bills or purchase land, new computer equipment, gold coins, or AT&T stock. How will you decide what portfolio of assets your company should hold to store its newfound wealth? What criteria should you use to decide among these various stores of wealth? Should you buy only one type of asset or several different types?

This chapter helps answer these questions by developing a financial theory known as the *theory of portfolio choice*. This theory outlines criteria that are important when deciding which assets are worth buying. In addition, it gives us an idea why it is good to diversify and not to put all our eggs in one basket.

The theory of portfolio choice plays a pivotal role in the study of financial markets and institutions and is a building block for much of the analysis in the remainder of the text. In later chapters, for example, we use the theory of portfolio choice to understand the behavior of interest rates and foreign exchange rates, theories of financial market behavior, financial innovation, bank management, and the evolution of the financial system.

■ DETERMINANTS OF ASSET DEMAND

An **asset** is a piece of property that is a store of value. Items such as money, bonds, stocks, art, land, houses, farm equipment, and manufacturing machinery are all assets. Facing the question of whether to buy and hold an asset or whether to buy one asset rather than another, an individual must consider the following factors:

1. **Wealth,** the total resources owned by the individual, including all assets
2. **Expected return** (the return expected over the next period) on one asset relative to alternative assets
3. **Risk** (the degree of uncertainty associated with the return) on one asset relative to alternative assets
4. **Liquidity** (the ease and speed with which an asset can be turned into cash) relative to alternative assets

■ **S T U D Y G U I D E** As we discuss each factor that influences asset demand, remember that we are always holding all the other factors constant. Also, think of additional examples of how changes in each factor would influence your decision to purchase a particular asset, say, a house or a share of common stock. This intuitive approach will help you understand how the theory works in practice.

Wealth

When we find that our wealth has increased, we have more resources available with which to purchase assets and so, not surprisingly, the quantity of assets we demand increases.[1] The demand for different assets responds differently to changes in wealth, however; the quantity demanded of some assets grows more rapidly with a rise in wealth than the quantity demanded of others. The degree of this response is measured by a concept known as the **wealth elasticity of demand** (which is similar to the concept of income elasticity of demand, which you might have learned in an earlier economics course). The wealth elasticity of demand measures how much, with everything else unchanged, the quantity demanded of an asset changes in percentage terms in response to a percentage change in wealth:

$$\frac{\% \text{ change in quantity demanded}}{\% \text{ change in wealth}} = \text{wealth elasticity of demand}$$

If, for example, the quantity of currency demanded increases only by 50% when wealth increases by 100%, we say that currency has a wealth elasticity of demand of $\frac{1}{2}$. If, for a common stock, the quantity demanded increases by 200% when wealth increases by 100%, the wealth elasticity of demand equals 2.

Assets can be sorted into two categories, depending on the value of their wealth elasticity of demand. An asset is a **necessity** if there is only so much that people want to hold, so that as wealth grows, the percentage increase in the quantity demanded of the asset is less than the percentage increase in wealth—in other words, its wealth elasticity is less than 1. Because the quantity demanded of a necessity does not grow proportionally with wealth, the amount of this asset

---

[1]Although it is possible that some assets (called *inferior assets*) might have the property that the quantity demanded does not increase as wealth increases, such assets are rare. Hence we will always assume that demand for an asset increases as wealth increases.

that people want to hold relative to their wealth falls as wealth grows. An asset is a **luxury** if its wealth elasticity is greater than 1; as wealth grows, the quantity demanded of this asset grows more than proportionally, and the amount that people hold relative to their wealth grows. Common stocks and municipal bonds are examples of luxury assets, and currency and checking account deposits are necessities.

The effect of changes in wealth on the quantity demanded of an asset can be summarized in this way: ***Holding everything else constant, an increase in wealth raises the quantity demanded of an asset, and the percentage increase in the quantity demanded is greater if the asset is a luxury than if it is a necessity.***

Expected Returns

In Chapter 3 we saw that the return on an asset (such as a bond) measures how much we gain from holding that asset. When we make a decision to buy an asset, we are influenced by what we expect the return on that asset to be. If a Mobil Oil Corporation bond, for example, has a return of 15% half of the time and 5% the other half of the time, its expected return (which you can think of as the average return) is 10%. If the expected return on the Mobil Oil bond rises relative to expected returns on alternative assets, holding everything else constant, then it becomes more desirable to purchase it, and the quantity demanded increases. This can occur in either of two ways: (1) when the expected return on the Mobil Oil bond rises while the return on an alternative asset—say, stock in IBM— remains unchanged or (2) when the return on the alternative asset, the IBM stock, falls while the return on the Mobil Oil bond remains unchanged. To summarize, ***an increase in an asset's expected return relative to that of an alternative asset, holding everything else unchanged, raises the quantity demanded of the asset.***

Risk

The degree of risk or uncertainty of an asset's returns also affects the demand for the asset. Consider two assets, stock in Fly-by-Night Airlines and stock in Feet-on-the-Ground Bus Company. Suppose that Fly-by-Night stock has a return of 15% half of the time and 5% the other half of the time, making its expected return 10%, while stock in Feet-on-the-Ground has a fixed return of 10%. Fly-by-Night stock has uncertainty associated with its returns and so has greater risk than stock in Feet-on-the-Ground, whose return is a sure thing.

A *risk-averse* person prefers stock in Feet-on-the-Ground (the sure thing) to Fly-by-Night stock (the riskier asset), even though the stocks have the same expected return, 10%. By contrast, a person who prefers risk is a *risk preferrer* or *risk lover.* Most people are risk-averse: Everything else being equal, they prefer to hold the less risky asset. Hence, ***holding everything else constant, if an asset's risk rises relative to that of alternative assets, its quantity demanded will fall.***

| SUMMARY TABLE 1 | Response of the Quantity of an Asset Demanded to Changes in Income or Wealth, Expected Returns, Risk, and Liquidity |

Variable	Change in Variable	Change in Quantity Demanded
Income or wealth	↑	↑
Expected return relative to other assets	↑	↑
Risk relative to other assets	↑	↓
Liquidity relative to other assets	↑	↑

Note: Only increases (↑) in the variables are shown. The effect of decreases in the variables on the change in demand would be the opposite of those indicated in the rightmost column.

Liquidity

Another factor that affects the demand for an asset is how quickly it can be converted into cash without incurring large costs—its liquidity. An asset is liquid if the market in which it is traded has depth and breadth, that is, if the market has many buyers and sellers. A house is not a very liquid asset because it may be hard to find a buyer quickly; if a house must be sold to pay off bills, it might have to be sold for a much lower price. And the transaction costs in selling a house (broker's commissions, lawyer's fees, and so on) are substantial. A U.S. Treasury bill, by contrast, is a highly liquid asset. It can be sold in a well-organized market where there are many buyers, so it can be sold quickly at low cost. ***The more liquid an asset is relative to alternative assets, holding everything else unchanged, the more desirable it is, and the greater will be the quantity demanded.***

Theory of Portfolio Choice

All the determining factors we have just discussed can be assembled into the **theory of portfolio choice,** which states that, holding all of the other factors constant:

1. The quantity demanded of an asset is usually positively related to wealth, with the response being greater if the asset is a luxury than if it is a necessity.
2. The quantity demanded of an asset is positively related to its expected return relative to alternative assets.
3. The quantity demanded of an asset is negatively related to the risk of its returns relative to alternative assets.
4. The quantity demanded of an asset is positively related to its liquidity relative to alternative assets.

These results are summarized in Table 1.

■ BENEFITS OF DIVERSIFICATION

Our discussion of the theory of portfolio choice indicates that most people like to avoid risk; that is, they are risk-averse. Why, then, do many investors hold many risky assets rather than just one? Doesn't holding many risky assets expose the investor to more risk?

The old warning about not putting all your eggs in one basket holds the key to the answer: Because holding many risky assets (called **diversification**) reduces the overall risk an investor faces, diversification is beneficial. To see why this is so, let's look at some specific examples of how an investor fares when holding two risky securities.

Consider two assets, common stock of Frivolous Luxuries, Inc., and common stock of Bad Times Products, Unlimited. When the economy is strong, which we'll assume is half of the time, Frivolous Luxuries has high sales and the return on the stock is 15%; when the economy is weak, the other half of the time, sales are low and the return on the stock is 5%. In contrast, suppose that Bad Times Products thrives when the economy is weak so that its stock has a return of 15%, but it earns less when the economy is strong and has a return on the stock of 5%. Both stocks have a return of 15% half of the time and 5% the other half of the time, and both have an expected return of 10%. However, both stocks carry a fair amount of risk because there is uncertainty about their actual returns.

Suppose now that instead of buying one stock or the other, Irving the Investor puts half his savings in Frivolous Luxuries stock and the other half in Bad Times Products stock. When the economy is strong, Frivolous Luxuries stock has a return of 15% and Bad Times Products has a return of 5%. The result is that Irving earns a return of 10% (the average of 5% and 15%) on his holdings of the two stocks. When the economy is weak, Frivolous Luxuries has a return of only 5% and Bad Times Products has a return of 15%, so Irving still earns a return of 10%. If Irving diversifies by buying both stocks, he earns a return of 10% regardless of whether the economy is strong or weak. Irving is better off from this strategy of diversification because his expected return is 10%, the same as from holding either Frivolous Luxuries or Bad Times Products alone, yet he is not exposed to *any* risk.

Although the case we have described demonstrates the benefits of diversification, it is somewhat unrealistic. It is hard to find two securities with the characteristic that when the return of one is low, the return of the other is always high.[2] In the real world, we are more likely to find at best returns on securities that are independent of each other; that is, when one is low, the other is just as likely to be high as to be low.

Suppose that both securities have an expected return of 10%, with a return of 5% half of the time and 15% the other half of the time. Sometimes both securities will earn the higher return, and sometimes both will earn the lower return. In this case, if Irving holds equal amounts of each security, he will on average earn the same return as if he had just put all his savings into one of the securities. However, because the returns on these two securities are independent, it is just as likely that when one earns the high 15% return, the other earns the low 5% return, and vice versa, giving Irving a return of 10% (equal to the expected return). Because Irving is more likely to earn what he expected to earn when he holds both securities instead of just one, we can see that Irving has again reduced his risk through diversification.

---

[2]Such a case is described by saying that the returns on the two securities are perfectly *negatively* correlated.

The one case in which Irving will not benefit from diversifying occurs when the returns on the two securities move perfectly together. In this case, when the first security has a return of 15%, the other also has a return of 15%, and holding both securities results in a return of 15%. When the first security has a return of 5%, the other has a return of 5%, and holding both results in a return of 5%. The result of diversifying by holding both securities is a return of 15% half of the time and 5% the other half of the time, which is exactly the same returns that are earned by holding only one of the securities. Consequently, diversification in this case does not lead to any reduction of risk.

The examples we have just examined illustrate the following important points about diversification:

1. Diversification is almost always beneficial to the risk-averse investor because it reduces risk except in the extremely rare case where returns on securities move perfectly together.
2. The less the returns on two securities move together, the more benefit (risk reduction) there is from diversification.

■ SYSTEMATIC RISK

Given the benefits of diversification, you might think that by holding enough different securities in a portfolio, you could eliminate risk entirely. Unfortunately, this is not possible because securities have **systematic risk,** risk that cannot be eliminated through diversification. In other words, no matter how many different securities you hold in your portfolio, you will still be stuck with some unavoidable risk, and this is the systematic risk. To understand systematic risk better, we need to recognize that we can divide the risk of an asset into two components, systematic risk and **nonsystematic risk,** the risk unique to an asset that can be diversified away by holding enough different securities in your portfolio:

$$\text{Asset risk} = \text{systematic risk} + \text{nonsystematic risk}$$

Nonsystematic risk is unique to an asset because it is related to the part of an asset's return that does not vary with returns on other assets. With many assets in a portfolio, nonsystematic risk becomes less important because when the nonsystematic part of one asset's return goes up, it is likely that the nonsystematic part of another asset's return has gone down, movements that cancel each other out. Hence with enough diversification as a result of a portfolio containing a large number of different assets, the nonsystematic risk contributes nothing to the total risk of the portfolio. In other words, *the risk of a well-diversified portfolio is due solely to the systematic risk of assets in the portfolio.*

This fact is very important because it tells us that if we diversify sufficiently, the only component of an asset's risk that we have to worry about is its systematic risk. Systematic risk of an asset is measured by a concept called **beta,** a measure of the sensitivity of an asset's return to changes in the value of the entire market of assets. When on average a 1% rise in the value of the market portfolio leads to a 2% rise in the value of an asset, the beta for this asset is calculated to be 2.0. If, conversely, the value of the asset on average rises by only 0.5% when the market rises by 1%, the asset's beta is 0.5.

The first asset, with a beta of 2.0, has much more systematic risk than the asset with a beta of 0.5. To see this, we first recognize that the portfolio made up of the entire market is a completely diversified portfolio and hence has only systematic risk. When the value of the market fluctuates by a certain amount, the asset with a beta of 2.0 fluctuates twice as much. Therefore, its return has twice as much systematic risk. By contrast, the asset with a beta of 0.5 fluctuates less than the market and so has less systematic risk. Because an asset with a higher beta has more systematic risk, this asset is less desirable because the systematic risk cannot be diversified away. Thus, holding everything else constant, an asset with a higher beta has a lower quantity demanded. We have reached the following conclusion, which is of great importance to participants in financial markets: ***The greater an asset's beta, the greater the asset's systematic risk and the less desirable the asset.***

■ RISK PREMIUMS: CAPITAL ASSET PRICING MODEL AND ARBITRAGE PRICING THEORY

Our recognition that greater systematic risk makes an asset less desirable can be used to understand the *capital asset pricing model (CAPM),* a widely used theory developed by William Sharpe, John Litner, and Jack Treynor. The CAPM is useful because it provides an explanation for the magnitude of an asset's *risk premium,* the difference between the asset's expected return and the risk-free interest rate (the interest rate on a security that has no possibility of default).

We have seen that an asset contributes risk to a well-diversified portfolio in the amount of its systematic risk as measured by beta. When an asset has a high beta, meaning that it has a large amount of systematic risk and is therefore less desirable, we would expect that investors would be willing to hold this asset only if it yielded a higher expected return. This is exactly what the CAPM tells us in the equation

$$\text{Risk premium} = RET^e - RET_f = \beta(RET^e_m - RET_f) \tag{1}$$

where

$$RET^e = \text{expected return for the asset}$$
$$RET_f = \text{risk-free interest rate}$$
$$\beta = \text{beta of the asset}$$
$$RET^e_m = \text{expected return for the market portfolio}$$

The CAPM equation provides the commonsense result that when an asset's beta is zero, meaning that it has no systematic risk, its risk premium will be zero. If its beta is 1.0, meaning that it has the same systematic risk as the entire market, it will have the same risk premium as the market, $RET^e_m - RET_f$. If the asset has an even higher beta, say, 2.0, its risk premium will be greater than that of the market. For example, if the expected return on the market is 8% and the risk-free rate is 2%, the risk premium for the market is 6%. The asset with the beta of 2.0 would then be expected to have a risk premium of 12% (= 2 × 6%).

Although the capital asset pricing model has proved to be useful in real-world applications, it assumes that there is only one source of systematic risk, that found in the market portfolio. However, an alternative theory, the *arbitrage pricing theory (APT)*, developed by Stephen Ross of Yale University, takes the view that there are several sources of risk in the economy that cannot be eliminated by diversification. These sources of risk can be thought of as related to economywide factors such as inflation and changes in aggregate output. Instead of calculating a single beta, like the CAPM, arbitrage pricing theory calculates many betas by estimating the sensitivity of an asset's return to changes in each factor. The arbitrage pricing theory equation is

$$\text{Risk premium} = RET^e - RET_f$$
$$= \beta_1 (RET^e_{\text{factor 1}} - RET_f) + \beta_2 (RET^e_{\text{factor 2}} - RET_f) \qquad (2)$$
$$+ \cdots + \beta_k (RET^e_{\text{factor } k} - RET_f)$$

Arbitrage pricing theory thus indicates that the risk premium for an asset is related to the risk premium for each factor and that as the asset's sensitivity to each factor increases, its risk premium will increase as well.

Which of these theories provides a better explanation of risk premiums is still uncertain. Both agree that an asset has a higher risk premium when it has higher systematic risk, and both are considered valuable tools for explaining risk premiums.

■ THE PRACTICING FINANCIAL INSTITUTION MANAGER
Calculating the Gains from Diversification

Our discussion in this chapter has emphasized that risk can be substantially reduced through diversification. However, it is not enough for the manager of a financial institution to know that diversification is a good thing: He or she must also be able to quantify the gains from diversification. If the manager adds another security to the portfolio, how much will it reduce the total risk the institution faces? Would the organization be better off reducing its risk by purchasing this particular security rather than another?

To start the analysis that will answer these questions, we need to define more formally the expected return for an asset, the weighted sum of each possible realized return multiplied by the probability of its occurring:

$$RET^e = \sum_{i=1}^{n} p_i RET_i = p_1 RET_1 + p_2 RET_2 + \cdots + p_n RET_n \qquad (3)$$

where RET^e = expected return
             p_i = probability of getting the realization RET_i
             RET_i = realization of the return

For example, if Security 1 has the probabilities and returns given in Table 2, the expected return is

$$RET^e = 0.1(-5\%) + 0.2(0\%) + 0.2(5\%) + 0.2(10\%) + 0.2(15\%) +$$
$$0.1(20\%) = 7.5\%$$

■ TABLE 2 Probabilities and Returns for Three Securities

	Return (%)		
Probabilities	Security 1	Security 2	Security 3
0.1	− 5	+20	− 5
0.2	0	+ 5	+10
0.2	+ 5	+15	+15
0.2	+10	+10	+ 5
0.2	+15	0	0
0.1	+20	− 5	+20

Risk is typically measured by the *variance* or *standard deviation* of the returns, both of which indicate how volatile the return is. The variance of the return σ^2 equals

$$\sigma^2 = \sum_{i=1}^{n} p_i(RET_i - RET^e)^2 + p_1(RET_1 - RET^e)^2 + p_2(RET_2 - RET^e)^2$$
$$+ \cdots + p_n(RET_n - RET^e)^2 \qquad (4)$$

The standard deviation, the more commonly cited measure of risk, is the square root of the variance:

$$\sigma = \sqrt{\sigma^2} \qquad (5)$$

For Security 1 in Table 2, the standard deviation of the return is calculated as follows:

$$\sigma = [0.1(-5\% - 7.5\%)^2 + 0.2(0\% - 7.5\%)^2 + 0.2(5\% - 7.5\%)^2$$
$$+ 0.2(10\% - 7.5\%)^2 + 0.2(15\% - 7.5\%)^2 + 0.1(20\% - 7.5\%)^2]^{1/2}$$
$$= 7.5\%$$

Those of you who have taken statistics know that 95% of the time, a variable will be within two standard deviations of its mean. Thus in our case with an expected return (mean) of 7.5% and a standard deviation of 7.5%, we would expect 95% of the time to find the return between 22.5% [= 7.5% + (2 × 7.5%)] and −7.5% (= 7.5% − (2 × 7.5%)].

Doing the same calculations for Security 2 in Table 2 should verify that, just as for Security 1, its expected return is 7.5% and the standard deviation of its return is 7.5%. So 95% of the time, the return for Security 2 should also be between 22.5% and −7.5%.

Now that we understand how to calculate the expected return and standard deviation of the return for one asset, let's look at what happens to these measures when there are two assets in the portfolio.

The return on the portfolio RET_p is the weighted average of the returns on the individual assets, with the weights x_i reflecting the proportion of the portfolio invested in each asset:

$$RET_p = \sum_{i=1}^{n} x_i RET_i = x_1 RET_1 + x_2 RET_2 + \cdots + x_n RET_n \qquad (6)$$

The expected return for this portfolio RET^e_p is

$$RET^e_p = \sum_{i=1}^{n} x_i RET^e_i = x_1 RET^e_1 + x_2 RET^e_2 + \cdots + x_n RET^e_n \qquad (7)$$

If we invest equally in Securities 1 and 2 so that $x_1 = x_2 = 0.5$, we can calculate the expected return on the portfolio

$$RET^e_p = (0.5 \times 7.5\%) + (0.5 \times 7.5\%) = 7.5\%$$

Not surprisingly, the expected return for the portfolio is the same 7.5% that we found for each security.

Calculating the standard deviation for the portfolio's return involves a new concept, the *covariance* of returns between two assets, which measures the degree to which the returns on different assets move together. The covariance between returns on two assets A and B, denoted as σ_{ab}, is defined as

$$\sigma_{ab} = \sum_{i=1}^{n} p_i (RET_{ai} - RET^e_a)(RET_{bi} - RET^e_b)$$
$$= p_1(RET_{a1} - RET^e_a)(RET_{b1} - RET^e_b) + p_2(RET_{a2} - RET^e_a) \qquad (8)$$
$$(RET_{b2} - RET^e_b) + \cdots + p_n(RET_{an} - RET^e_a)(RET_{bn} - RET^e_b)$$

For Securities 1 and 2, the covariance σ_{12} is calculated as

$$\begin{aligned}
\sigma_{12} = {} & 0.1(-5\% - 7.5\%)(20\% - 7.5\%) + 0.2(0\% - 7.5\%)(5\% - 7.5\%) \\
& + 0.2(5\% - 7.5\%)(15\% - 7.5\%) + 0.2(10\% - 7.5\%)(10\% - 7.5\%) \\
& + 0.2(15\% - 7.5\%)(0\% - 7.5\%) + 0.1(20\% - 7.5\%)(-5\% - 7.5\%) \\
= {} & -41.25\%
\end{aligned}$$

The fact that Securities 1 and 2 have a negative covariance of their returns indicates that, on average, the returns on the two securities move in opposite directions. As we saw earlier in the chapter, the less the returns on two securities move together, the greater will be the risk-reducing benefit from diversification. That is exactly what we find.

The formula for the variance of a portfolio's returns σ^2_p involves both variances and covariances and equals

$$\sigma^2_p = \sum_{i=1}^{n} \sum_{j=1}^{n} x_i x_j \sigma_{ij} \qquad (9)$$

For our portfolio of two assets, this works out to be

$$\sigma^2_p = x^2_1 \sigma^2_1 + x^2_2 \sigma^2_2 + 2x_1 x_2 \sigma_{12} \qquad (10)$$

Recall that for our portfolio, which has an equal amount of Securities 1 and 2, $x_1 = x_2 = 0.5$, and the standard deviation and covariance are $\sigma_1 = \sigma_2 = 7.5\%$ and $\sigma_{12} = -41.25\%$, respectively. Using this information and noting that the standard deviation is the square root of the variance, we can calculate the standard deviation of the portfolio's returns as

$$\sigma_p = \sqrt{(0.5)^2(7.5\%)^2 + (0.5)^2(7.5\%)^2 + 2(0.5)(0.5)(-41.25\%)^2}$$
$$= \sqrt{7.5\%} = 2.7\%$$

Because the mean (expected) return on this portfolio is 7.5% and the portfolio's return should be within two standard deviations of the mean 95% of the time, the portfolio's return should fall between 12.9% and 2.1%. This much smaller range of the portfolio's return indicates the tremendous risk reduction that can be achieved with diversification, particularly when the returns on securities in the portfolio do not move together, as in the example here.

Suppose that a pension fund manager wonders whether the fund will be better off if it holds 25% of its portfolio in Security 1 and 75% in Security 2 rather than split its holdings 50/50, as in the example. First the manager calculates the expected return for the portfolio using Equation 7:

$$RET_p^e = (0.25 \times 7.5\%) + (0.75 \times 7.5\%) = 7.5\%$$

Since the expected return on the portfolio is the same as the equally split portfolio, on the basis of expected return the manager is just as happy holding either portfolio.

However, the pension fund manager knows to compare the risk of the two portfolios before coming to a final decision about which portfolio to hold. Having already calculated the covariance of Securities 1 and 2's returns to be -41.25%, as shown, the manager calculates the standard deviation of the return on the portfolio made up of 25% of Security 1 and 75% of Security 2:

$$\sigma_p = \sqrt{(0.25)^2(7.5\%)^2 + (0.75)^2(7.5\%)^2 + 2(0.25)(0.75)(-41.25\%)}$$
$$= \sqrt{19.69\%} = 4.4\%$$

The pension fund manager notes that the 4.4% standard deviation of the portfolio's return in this case is larger than the 2.7% standard deviation when the portfolio was equally split between Securities 1 and 2. The manager realizes that the fund will have less risk and thus be better off if it sticks with the equally split portfolio.

A new security, Security 3, comes on the market, and the pension fund manager now wants to know if it would be wise to replace Security 2 with Security 3 in the fund's portfolio. Using the information on Security 3 in Table 2, the manager calculates its expected return to be 7.5%, the standard deviation of its return also to be 7.5%, and the covariance between it and Security 1 to be 11.25%. Since Security 2 made up half the portfolio, this would be the case for Security 3 in the new portfolio, and so this portfolio has equal weights of 0.5 for both Security 1 and Security 3. Plugging in the appropriate numbers in Equations 7 and 10, the manager finds that the new portfolio has an expected return of 7.5% and that the standard deviation of the return is 5.8%. The expected return is thus identical to the portfolio with Security 2, but its return has a larger standard deviation (5.8% versus 2.7%). This result is not surprising because, as we learned earlier in the chapter, the less that the returns on two securities move together, the more risk reduction there is from diversification. Because Security 1's returns have a lower covariance with Security 2's returns than with Security 3's, Securities 1 and 2's returns move together less and so risk reduction is greater from combining them in a portfolio. Having discovered this fact from the calculations, the pension fund manager realizes that it is better to have Security 2 in the portfolio than Security 3 and so again decides to stick with the portfolio with equal amounts of Security 1 and Security 2.

■ **STUDY GUIDE** To test your understanding of how to calculate the gains from diversification, use the information on Security 3 in Table 2 to calculate its expected return, the standard deviation of its return, and the covariance of its return against Security 1's. Then use these numbers to calculate the expected return and standard deviation of the return for the portfolio with equal amounts of Securities 1 and 3. You should get the results for this portfolio reported here.

So far, we have been acting as if a portfolio can only have two assets, but typically a financial institution manager keeps many more assets in a portfolio. The complexity of the calculations increases greatly, however, as we increase the number of assets in the portfolio. For example, in the case with three assets, the calculation of the variance of the portfolio's return involves six terms rather than the three for a portfolio with only two assets. Although it is a good exercise to tackle this three-asset case, the statistical calculations outlined here can be cumbersome, so we leave them to the ambitious to pursue. However, if you are so inclined, you should be able to see that a portfolio made up of equal amounts of Securities 1, 2, and 3 will have the lowest risk of all.

Luckily, you do not have to be a math whiz to calculate the standard deviation of a portfolio's return, even when it contains hundreds of assets, because high-speed computers come to the rescue. Managers of financial institutions use computer programs that do these calculations for them easily and quickly. Our analysis here has shown the kind of information we need to supply these programs with, and once this information has been obtained, measuring the gains from diversification is straightforward.   ■

SUMMARY

1. The theory of portfolio choice tells us that the quantity demanded of an asset is (a) positively related to wealth, (b) positively related to the expected return on the asset relative to alternative assets, (c) negatively related to the riskiness of the asset relative to alternative assets, and (d) positively related to the liquidity of the asset relative to alternative assets.

2. Diversification (the holding of more than one asset) benefits investors because it reduces the risk they face, and the benefits are greater the less returns on securities move together.

3. An asset's risk is made up of two components: systematic risk, which cannot be diversified away, and nonsystematic risk, which can. An asset's systematic risk is measured by beta, and the higher an asset's beta and hence its systematic risk, the less desirable the asset.

4. Both the capital asset pricing model and arbitrage pricing theory provide an explanation for an asset's risk premium, the difference between the asset's expected return and the risk-free interest rate. The capital asset pricing model indicates that an asset's risk premium is positively related to the asset's beta, the sensitivity to the market return; arbitrage pricing theory indicates that an asset's risk premium is positively related to the asset's sensitivity to many factors that represent sources of nondiversifiable risk in the economy.

KEY TERMS

asset, p. 73
beta, p. 78
diversification, p. 77
expected return, p. 74
liquidity, p. 74

luxury, p. 75
necessity, p. 74
nonsystematic risk, p. 78
risk, p. 74
systematic risk, p. 78

theory of portfolio choice,
    p. 76
wealth, p. 74
wealth elasticity of demand,
    p. 74

QUESTIONS AND PROBLEMS

1. In terms of the theory of portfolio choice, explain why you would be more or less willing to buy a share of Polaroid stock in the following situations:
   a. Your wealth falls.
   b. You expect it to appreciate in value.
   c. The bond market becomes more liquid.
   d. You expect gold to appreciate in value.
   e. Prices in the bond market become more volatile.

*2. In terms of the theory of portfolio choice, explain why you would be more or less willing to buy a house under the following circumstances:
   a. You just inherited $100,000.
   b. Real estate commissions fall from 6% of the sales price to 4% of the sales price.
   c. You expect Polaroid stock to double in value next year.
   d. Prices in the stock market become more volatile.
   e. You expect housing prices to fall.

3. In terms of the theory of portfolio choice, explain why you would be more or less willing to buy gold under the following circumstances:
   a. Gold again becomes acceptable as a medium of exchange.
   b. Prices in the gold market become more volatile.
   c. You expect inflation to rise, and gold prices tend to move with the aggregate price level.
   d. You expect interest rates to rise.

*4. In terms of the theory of portfolio choice, explain why you would be more or less willing to buy AT&T bonds under the following circumstances:
   a. Trading in these bonds increases, making them easier to sell.
   b. You expect a bear market in stocks (stock prices are expected to decline).
   c. Brokerage commissions on stocks fall.
   d. You expect interest rates to rise.
   e. Brokerage commissions on bonds fall.

5. "The more risk-averse people are, the more likely they are to diversify." Is this statement true, false, or uncertain? Explain your answer.

*6. I own a professional football team, and I plan to diversify by purchasing shares in either a company that owns a pro basketball team or a pharmaceutical company. Which of these two investments is more likely to reduce the overall risk I face? Why?

7. "No one who is risk-averse will ever buy a security that has a lower expected return, more risk, and less liquidity than another security." Is this statement true, false, or uncertain? Explain your answer.

*8. "The demand for an asset will be lower, everything else being equal, if its beta is higher." Is this statement true, false, or uncertain? Explain your answer.

9. If on average a stock falls by 3% when the market rises by 2%, what is its beta?

*10. Which stock would you prefer to hold, everything else being equal: a stock that on average rises by 0.5% when the market rises by 1% or a stock that on average rises by 1% when the market rises by 2%?

11. "The higher a security's beta, the lower its risk premium." Is this statement true, false, or uncertain? Explain your answer.

*12. If the expected return for the market portfolio is 8% and the risk-free rate is 5%, what does the capital asset pricing model predict the expected return on a security with a beta of 3.0 to be?

13. What is the basic difference between arbitrage pricing theory and the capital asset pricing model?

*14. Given the probabilities and returns in Table 2, calculate the expected return and the standard deviation of the return on a portfolio made up equally of Securities 2 and 3. Would you rather hold this portfolio than the portfolio described in the text made up equally of Securities 1 and 2? Why or why not?

15. Given the probabilities and returns in Table 2, calculate the expected return and the standard deviation of the return on a portfolio made up equally of Securities 1, 2, and 3. Would you rather hold this portfolio than the portfolio described in the text made up equally of Securities 1 and 2? Why or why not?

■ CASE STUDY

■ Calculating the Gains from Portfolio Diversification

CONCEPTS IN THIS CASE

expected return
risk
portfolio choice
diversification
systematic risk
nonsystematic risk
beta
capital asset pricing model
arbitrage pricing

Your supervisor has asked that you quantify the effects of diversification using three potential portfolios. The information given regarding each portfolio is as follows:

Probability	Return (%) on Security A	Return (%) on Security B	Return (%) on Security C
.20	8	24	16
.30	10	16	10
.30	12	12	12
.20	14	17	6

1. Using the information above, calculate the following for each individual security:
   a. What is the expected return for security A?
   b. What is the expected return for security B ?
   c. What is the expected return for security C ?
   d. What is the variance of the return for security A?
   e. What is the variance of the return for security B?
   f. What is the variance of the return for security C?

2. Using the information above, calculate the following for each pair of securities:
   a. What is the covariance of securities A and B?
   b. What is the covariance of securities A and C?
   c. What is the covariance of securities B and C?

3. If your firm makes equal investments in securities A and B (50% in each):

a. What is the expected return of the portfolio that combines A and B?
   b. What is the variance of the portfolio that combines A and B?

4. If your firm makes equal investments in securities A and C (50% in each):
   a. What is the expected return of the portfolio that combines A and C?
   b. What is the variance of the portfolio that combines A and C?

5. If your firm makes equal investment in securities B and C (50% in each):
   a. What is the expected return of the portfolio that combines B and C?
   b. What is the expected variance of the portfolio that combines B and C?

6. Given the results of your work in questions 3, 4, and 5 above, which portfolio would you recommend to your supervisor? Explain.

7. You have searched online resources and found the BETA of each security. Security A has a BETA of 1.0, security B has a BETA of .50 and security C has a BETA of 1.50. If the risk-free interest rate is 5% and the expected return for the market portfolio is 12%:
   a. What is the CAPM risk premium for security A?
   b. What is the CAPM risk premium for security B?
   c. What is the CAPM risk premium for security C?

8. How would your definition of the risk premium change if you used the Arbitrage Pricing Theory (APT) equation?

MODELS OF CAPITAL MARKET ASSET PRICING

In Chapter 4 we demonstrated the benefits of diversification and provided a brief introduction to the capital asset pricing model (CAPM) and arbitrage pricing theory (APT). In this appendix we provide a more detailed derivation of these models.

DIVERSIFICATION AND BETA

We start our analysis by considering a portfolio of n assets whose return is

$$RET_p = x_1 RET_1 + x_2 RET_2 + \cdots + x_n RET_n \tag{1}$$

where
$\quad RET_p$ = return on the portfolio of n assets
$\quad RET_i$ = return on asset i
$\quad x_i$ = proportion of the portfolio held in asset i

Using E (. . .) to denote the expected values, the expected return on this portfolio $E(RET_p)$ equals

$$
\begin{aligned}
E(RET_p) &= E(x_1 RET_1) + E(x_2 RET_2) + \cdots + E(x_n RET_n) \\
&= x_1 E(RET_1) + x_2 E(RET_2) + \cdots + x_n E(RET_n)
\end{aligned}
\tag{2}
$$

An appropriate measure of the risk for this portfolio is the standard deviation of the portfolio's return (σ_p) or its squared value, the variance of the portfolio's return (σ_p^2), which can be written as

$$
\begin{aligned}
\sigma_p^2 &= E[RET_p - E(RET_p)]^2 = E\{[x_1 RET_1 + \cdots + x_n RET_n] - [x_1 E(RET_1) \\
&\qquad + \cdots + x_n E(RET_n)]\}^2 \\
&= E\{x_1[RET_1 - E(RET_1)] + \cdots + x_n[RET_n - E(RET_n)]\}^2
\end{aligned}
$$

This expression can be rewritten as

$$\sigma_p^2 = E(\{x_1[RET_1 - E(RET_1)] + \cdots + x_n[RET_n - E(RET_n)]\}$$
$$\times [RET_p - E(RET_p)])$$
$$= x_1 E\{[RET_1 - E(RET_1)] \times [RET_p - E(RET_p)]\} + \cdots +$$
$$x_n E\{[RET_n - E(RET_n)] \times [RET_p - E(RET_p)]\}$$

This gives us the following expression for the variance of the portfolio's return:

$$\sigma_p^2 = x_1\sigma_{1p} + x_2\sigma_{2p} + \cdots + x_n\sigma_{np} \tag{3}$$

where σ_{ip} = the covariance of the return on asset i with the portfolio's return
= $E\{[RET_i - E(RET_i)] \times [RET_p - E(RET_p)]\}$.

Equation 3 tells us that the contribution to risk of asset i to the portfolio is $x_i\sigma_{ip}$. By dividing this contribution to risk by the total portfolio risk σ_p^2, we have the proportionate contribution of asset i to the portfolio risk:

$$\frac{x_i\sigma_{ip}}{\sigma_p^2}$$

The ratio σ_{ip}/σ_p^2 tells us about the sensitivity of asset i's return to the portfolio's return. The higher the ratio, the more the value of the asset moves with changes in the value of the portfolio and the more asset i contributes to portfolio risk. Our algebraic manipulations have thus led to the following important conclusion: ***The marginal contribution of an asset to the risk of a portfolio depends not on the risk of the asset in isolation but rather on the sensitivity of that asset's return to changes in the value of the portfolio.***

If the total of all risky assets in the market is included in the portfolio, it is called the **market portfolio.** If we suppose that the portfolio p is the market portfolio m, the ratio σ_{im}/σ_m^2 is called the asset i's *beta;* that is,

$$\beta_i = \frac{\sigma_{im}}{\sigma_m^2} \tag{4}$$

where β_i = the beta of asset i. An asset's beta, then, is a measure of the asset's marginal contribution to the risk of the market portfolio. A higher beta means that an asset's return is more sensitive to changes in the value of the market portfolio and that the asset contributes more to the risk of the portfolio.

Another way to understand beta is to recognize that the return on asset i can be considered as being made up of two components—one, RET_m, that moves with the market's return and the other, ϵ_i, a random factor with an expected value of zero that is unique to the asset and so is uncorrelated with the market return:

$$RET_i = \alpha_i + \beta_i RET_m + \epsilon_i \tag{5}$$

The expected return of asset i can then be written as

$$E(RET_i) = \alpha_i + \beta_i E(RET_m)$$

It is easy to show that β_i in this expression is the beta of asset i we defined before by calculating the covariance of asset i's return with the market return using the two earlier equations:

$$\sigma_{im} = E\{[RET_i - E(RET_i)] \times [RET_m - E(RET_m)]\}$$
$$= E(\{\beta_i[RET_m - E(RET_m)] + \epsilon_i\} \times [RET_m - E(RET_m)])$$

However, because ϵ_i is uncorrelated with RET_m, $E\{\epsilon_i \times [RET_m - E(RET_m)]\} = 0$. Therefore,

$$\sigma_{im} = \beta_i \sigma_m^2$$

Dividing through by σ_m^2 gives us the following expression for β_i:

$$\beta_i = \frac{\sigma_{im}}{\sigma_m^2}$$

which is the same definition for beta we found in Equation 4.

The reason for demonstrating that the β_i in Equation 5 is the same as the one we defined before is that Equation 5 provides better intuition about how an asset's beta measures its sensitivity to changes in the market return. Equation 5 tells us that when the beta of an asset is 1, its return on average increases by 1 percentage point when the market return increases by 1 percentage point; when the beta is 2, the asset's return on average increases by 2 percentage points when the market return increases by 1 percentage point; and when the beta is 0.5, the asset's return only increases by 0.5 percentage point on average when the market return increases by 1 percentage point.

Equation 5 also tells us that we can get estimates of beta by comparing the average return on an asset with the average market return. For those of you who know a little econometrics, this estimate of beta is just an ordinary least-squares regression of the asset's return on the market return. Indeed, the formula for the ordinary least-squares estimate of $\beta_i = \sigma_{im}/\sigma_m^2$ is exactly the same as the definition of β_i given here.

■ SYSTEMATIC AND NONSYSTEMATIC RISK

We can derive another important idea about the riskiness of an asset using Equation 5. The variance of asset i's return can be calculated from Equation 5 as

$$\sigma_i^2 = E[RET_i - E(RET_i)]^2 = E\{\beta_i[RET_m - E(RET_m)] + \epsilon_i\}^2$$

and since ϵ_i is uncorrelated with the market return,

$$\sigma_i^2 = \beta_i^2 \sigma_m^2 + \sigma_\epsilon^2$$

the total variance of the asset's return can thus be broken up into a component that is related to market risk, $\beta_i^2 \sigma_m^2$, and a component that is unique to the asset,

σ_ϵ^2. The $\beta_i^2 \sigma_m^2$ component related to market risk is referred to as *systematic risk,* and the σ_ϵ^2 component unique to the asset is called *nonsystematic risk.* We can thus write the total risk of an asset as being made up of systematic risk and non-systematic risk:

$$\text{Total asset risk} = \text{systematic risk} + \text{nonsystematic risk}$$

Systematic and nonsystematic risk each have another feature that makes the distinction between these two types of risk important. Systematic risk is the part of an asset's risk that cannot be eliminated by holding the asset as part of a diver-sified portfolio, whereas nonsystematic risk is the part of an asset's risk that can be eliminated in a diversified portfolio. Understanding these features of system-atic and nonsystematic risk leads to the following important conclusion: ***The risk of a well-diversified portfolio depends only on the systematic risk of the assets in the portfolio.***

We can see that this conclusion is true by considering a portfolio of n assets, each of which has the same weight in the portfolio of $(1/n)$. Using Equation 5, the return on this portfolio is

$$RET_p = \frac{1}{n} \sum_{i=1}^n \alpha_i + \frac{1}{n} \sum_{i=1}^n \beta_i RET_m + \frac{1}{n} \sum_{i=1}^n \epsilon_i$$

which can be rewritten as

$$RET_p = \alpha + \beta RET_m + \frac{1}{n} \sum_{i=1}^n \epsilon_i$$

where

$$\overline{\alpha} = \text{average of all } \alpha_i = \frac{1}{n} \sum_{i=1}^n \alpha_i$$

$$\overline{\beta} = \text{average of all } \beta_i = \frac{1}{n} \sum_{i=1}^n \beta_i$$

If the portfolio is well diversified so that all ϵ_i are uncorrelated with each other, then using this fact and the fact that all ϵ_i are uncorrelated with the market return, the variance of the portfolio's return is calculated as

$$\sigma_p^2 = \overline{\beta}^2 \sigma_m^2 + \frac{1}{n} (\text{average variance of } \epsilon_i)$$

As n gets large, $(1/n)$ (average variance of ϵ_i) becomes very small, so a well-diversified portfolio has a risk of $\beta^2 \sigma_m^2$, which is only related to systematic risk. As the previous conclusion indicated, nonsystematic risk can be eliminated in a well-diversified portfolio. This reasoning also tells us that the risk of a well-diversified portfolio is greater than the risk of the market portfolio if the average beta of the assets in the portfolio is greater than 1; however, the portfolio's risk is less than the market portfolio if the average beta of the assets is less than 1.

■ CAPITAL ASSET PRICING MODEL (CAPM)

We can now use the ideas we developed about systematic and nonsystematic risk and beta to derive one of the most widely used models of asset pricing, the capital asset pricing model (CAPM) developed by William Sharpe, John Litner, and Jack Treynor.

Each cross in Figure 1 shows the standard deviation and expected return for each risky asset. By putting different proportions of these assets into portfolios, we can generate a standard deviation and an expected return for each of the portfolios using Equations 2 and 3. The shaded area in the figure shows these combinations of standard deviation and expected return for these portfolios. Because risk-averse investors always prefer to have a higher expected return and a lower standard deviation of the return, the most attractive standard deviation–expected return combinations are the ones that lie along the heavy line, which is called the **efficient portfolio frontier.** These are the standard deviation–expected return combinations that risk-averse investors would always prefer.

The CAPM assumes that investors can borrow and lend as much as they want at a risk-free rate of interest RET_f. By lending at the risk-free rate, the investor

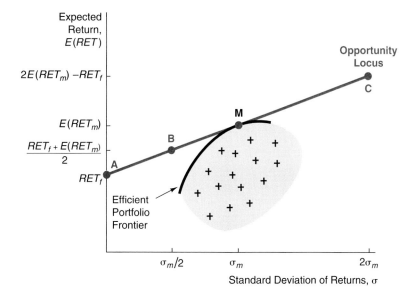

■FIGURE 1 Risk–Expected Return Trade-Off

The crosses show the combination of standard deviation and expected return for each risky asset. The efficient portfolio frontier indicates the most preferable standard deviation–expected return combinations that can be achieved by putting risky assets into portfolios. By borrowing and lending at the risk-free rate and investing in Portfolio M, the investor can obtain standard deviation–expected return combinations that lie along the line connecting A, B, M, and C. This line, the opportunity locus, contains the best combinations of standard deviations and expected returns available to the investor; hence the opportunity locus shows the trade-off between expected returns and risk for the investor.

earns an expected return of RET_f, and the investment has a standard deviation of zero because it is risk-free. The standard deviation–expected return combination for this risk-free investment is marked as point A in Figure 1. Suppose that Irving the Investor decides to put half of his total wealth in the risk-free loan and the other half in the portfolio on the efficient portfolio frontier with a standard deviation–expected return combination marked as point M in the figure. Using Equation 2, you should be able to verify that the expected return on this new portfolio is halfway between RET_f and $E(RET_m)$, that is, $[RET_f + E(RET_m)]/2$. Similarly, because the covariance between the risk-free return and the return on Portfolio M must necessarily be zero since there is no uncertainty about the return on the risk-free loan, you should also be able to verify, using Equation 3, that the standard deviation of the return on the new portfolio is halfway between zero and σ_m, that is, $\sigma_m/2$. The standard deviation–expected return combination for this new portfolio is marked as point B in the figure, and as you can see, it lies on the line between point A and point M. Similarly, if Inga the Investor borrows the total amount of her wealth at the risk-free rate of RET_f and invests the proceeds plus her wealth (that is, twice her wealth) in Portfolio M, the standard deviation of this new portfolio will be twice the standard deviation of return on portfolio M, $2\sigma_m$. However, using Equation 2, the expected return on this new portfolio is $E(RET_m) + E(RET_m) - RET_f = 2E(RET_m) - RET_f$. This standard deviation–expected return combination is plotted as point C in the figure.

You should now be able to see that both points B and C are on the line connecting points A and M. Indeed, by choosing different amounts of borrowing and lending, an investor can form a portfolio with a standard deviation–expected return combination that lies anywhere on the line connecting points A and M. You may have noticed that point M has been chosen so that the line connecting points A and M is tangent to the efficient portfolio frontier. The reason for choosing point M in this way is that it leads to standard deviation–expected return combinations along the line that are the most desirable for a risk-averse investor. This line can be thought of as the *opportunity locus,* which shows the best combinations of standard deviations and expected returns available to the investor.

The CAPM makes another assumption: All investors have the same assessment of the expected returns and standard deviations of all assets. In this case, Portfolio M is the same for all investors. Thus when all investors' holdings of Portfolio M are added together, they must equal all of the risky assets in the market, which is just the market portfolio. The assumption that all investors have the same assessment of risk and return for all assets thus means that Portfolio M is the market portfolio. Therefore, RET_m and σ_m in Figure 1 are identical to the market return RET_m and the standard deviation of this return σ_m referred to earlier in this appendix.

The conclusion that the market portfolio and Portfolio M are one and the same means that the opportunity locus in Figure 1 can be thought of as showing the trade-off between expected returns and increased risk for the investor. This trade-off is given by the slope of the opportunity locus, $[E(RET_m) - RET_f]/\sigma_m$, and it tells us that an investor who is willing to increase the risk of the portfolio by σ_m can earn an additional expected return of $E(RET_m) - RET_f$. The market price of a unit of market risk, σ_m, is $E(RET_m) - RET_f$. $E(RET_m) - RET_f$ is therefore referred to as the **market price of risk.**

We now know that market price of risk is $E(RET_m) - RET_f$ and have also learned that an asset's beta tells us about systematic risk because it is the marginal contribution of that asset to a portfolio's risk. Therefore, the amount by which an asset's expected return exceeds the risk-free rate $E(RET_i - RET_f)$ should equal the market price of risk times the marginal contribution of that asset to portfolio risk, $[E(RET_m) - RET_f]\beta_i$. This reasoning yields the CAPM asset pricing relationship:

$$E(RET_i) = RET_f + \beta_i[E(RET_m) - RET_f] \tag{6}$$

This CAPM asset pricing equation is represented by the upward-sloping line in Figure 2, which is called the **security market line.** It tells us the expected return that the market sets for a security, given its beta. For example, it tells us that if a security has a beta of 1 so that its marginal contribution to a portfolio's risk is the same as the market portfolio, it should be priced to have the same expected return as the market portfolio $E(RET_m)$.

To see that securities should be priced so that their expected return–beta combination should lie on the security market line, consider a security like S in the figure, which is below the security market line. If an investor makes an investment in which half is put into the market portfolio and half into a risk-free loan, the beta of this investment will be 0.5, the same as for Security S. However, this investment will have an expected return on the security market line, which is greater than that for Security S. Hence investors will not want to hold Security S, and its current price will fall, thus raising its expected return until it equals the amount indicated on the security market line. Now suppose that there is a security like T, which has a beta of 0.5 but whose expected return is above the security market

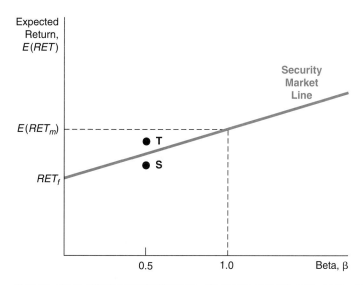

■FIGURE 2 Security Market Line

The security market line derived from the capital asset pricing model describes the relationship between an asset's beta and its expected return.

line. By including this security in a well-diversified portfolio with other assets with a beta of 0.5, none of which can have an expected return less than that indicated by the security line (as we have shown), investors can obtain a portfolio with a higher expected return than that obtained by putting half into a risk-free loan and half into the market portfolio. This would mean that all investors would want to hold more of Security T, and so its price would rise, thus lowering its expected return until it equaled the amount indicated on the security market line.

The capital asset pricing model formalizes the following important idea: ***An asset should be priced so that it has a higher expected return not when it has a greater risk in isolation but rather when its systematic risk is greater.***

■ ARBITRAGE PRICING THEORY

Although the capital asset pricing model has proved useful in practice, deriving it does require the adoption of some unrealistic assumptions, for example, that investors can borrow and lend freely at the risk-free rate or that all investors have the same assessment of expected returns and standard deviations of returns for all assets. An important alternative to the capital asset pricing model is arbitrage pricing theory (APT), developed by Stephen Ross of Yale University.

In contrast to the CAPM, which has only one source of systematic risk, the market return, APT takes the view that there can be several sources of systematic risk in the economy that cannot be eliminated through diversification. These sources of risk can be thought of as factors that may be related to such items as inflation, aggregate output, default risk premiums, or the term structure of interest rates. The return on an asset i can thus be written as being made up of components that move with these factors and a random component ϵ_i that is unique to the asset:

$$RET_i = \beta_{1i} \text{ (factor 1)} + \beta_{2i} \text{ (factor 2)} + \cdots + \beta_{ki} \text{ (factor } k) + \epsilon_i \qquad (7)$$

Since there are k factors, this model is called a k-factor model. The $b_{1i}, \cdots, b_{ki}$ describe the sensitivity of the asset i's return to each of these factors.

Just as in the capital asset pricing model, these systematic sources of risk should be priced. The market price for each factor j can be thought of as being $E(RET_{\text{factor } j}) - RET_f$, and hence the expected return on a security can be written as

$$E(RET_i) = RET_f + \beta_{1i}[E(RET_{\text{factor 1}}) - RET_f + \cdots + \beta_{ki}[E(RET_{\text{factor } k}) - RET_f \qquad (8)$$

This asset pricing equation indicates that all the securities should have the same market price for the risk contributed by each factor. If the expected return for a security were above the amount indicated by the APT pricing equation, it would provide a higher expected return than a portfolio of other securities with the same average sensitivity to each factor. Hence investors would want to hold more of this security and its price would rise until the expected return fell to the value indicated by the APT pricing equation. Conversely, if the security's expected return were less than the amount indicated by the APT pricing equation, no one would want to hold this security because a higher expected return could be obtained with a portfolio of securities with the same average sensitivity to each factor. As a result, the price of the security would fall until its expected return fell to the value indicated by the APT pricing equation.

As this brief outline of arbitrage pricing theory indicates, the theory supports a basic conclusion from the capital asset pricing model: An asset should be priced so that it has a higher expected return not when it has a greater risk in isolation but rather when its systematic risk is greater. There is still substantial controversy about whether a variant of the CAPM or APT is a better description of reality. At present, both are considered valuable tools for understanding how risk affects the prices of assets.

CHAPTER 5

THE BEHAVIOR OF INTEREST RATES

■ **PREVIEW** In the early 1950s, nominal interest rates on three-month Treasury bills were about 1% at an annual rate; by 1981, they had reached over 15%, then fell to 3% in 1993 and rose above 5% by the mid-1990s. What explains these substantial fluctuations in interest rates? One reason why we study financial markets and institutions is to provide some answers to this question.

In this chapter we examine how the overall level of *nominal* interest rates (which we refer to as simply "interest rates") is determined and the factors that influence their behavior. We learned in Chapter 3 that interest rates are negatively related to the price of bonds, so if we can explain why bond prices change, we can also explain why interest rates fluctuate. Here we will apply supply and demand analysis to examine how bond prices and interest rates change.

■ LOANABLE FUNDS FRAMEWORK: SUPPLY AND DEMAND IN THE BOND MARKET

We first approach the analysis of interest-rate determination by studying the supply of and demand for bonds. Because interest rates on different securities tend to move together, in this chapter we will act as if there is only one type of security and a single interest rate in the entire economy. In the following chapter, we will expand our analysis to look at why interest rates on different securities differ.

The first step in the analysis is to use the theory of portfolio choice discussed in Chapter 4 to obtain a **demand curve,** which shows the relationship between the quantity demanded and the price when all other economic variables are held constant (that is, values of other variables are taken as given). You may recall from previous finance and economics courses that the assumption that all other economic variables are held constant is called *ceteris paribus,* which means "other things being equal" in Latin.

Demand Curve

To clarify our analysis, let us consider the demand for one-year discount bonds, which make no coupon payments but pay the owner the $1000 face value in a year. If the holding period is one year, then as we have seen in Chapter 3, the return on the bonds is known absolutely and is equal to the interest rate as measured by the yield to maturity. This means that the expected return on this bond is equal to the interest rate i, which, using Equation 6 in Chapter 3, is

$$i = RET^e = \frac{F - P_d}{P_d}$$

where
$$i = \text{interest rate} = \text{yield to maturity}$$
$$RET^e = \text{expected return}$$
$$F = \text{face value of the discount bond}$$
$$P_d = \text{initial purchase price of the discount bond}$$

This formula shows that a particular value of the interest rate corresponds to each bond price. If the bond sells for $950, the interest rate and expected return is

$$\frac{(\$1000 - \$950)}{\$950} = 0.053 = 5.3\%$$

At this 5.3% interest rate and expected return corresponding to a bond price of $950, let us assume that the quantity of bonds demanded is $100 billion, which is plotted as point A in Figure 1. To display both the bond price and the corresponding interest rate, Figure 1 has two vertical axes. The left vertical axis shows the bond price, with the price of bonds increasing from $750 near the bottom of the axis toward $1000 at the top. The right vertical axis shows the interest rate, which increases in the *opposite* direction from 0% at the top of the axis to 33% near the bottom. The right and left vertical axes run in opposite directions because, as we learned in Chapter 3, bond price and interest rate are always negatively related: As the price of the bond rises, the interest rate on the bond necessarily falls.

At a price of $900, the interest rate and expected return equals

$$\frac{(\$1000 - \$900)}{\$900} = 0.111 = 11.1\%$$

Because the expected return on these bonds is higher, with all other economic variables (such as income, expected returns on other assets, risk, and liquidity) held constant, the quantity demanded of bonds will be higher as predicted by the theory of portfolio choice. Point B in Figure 1 shows that the quantity of bonds demanded at the price of $900 has risen to $200 billion. Continuing with this reasoning, if the bond price is $850 (interest rate and expected return = 17.6%), the quantity of bonds demanded (point C) will be greater than

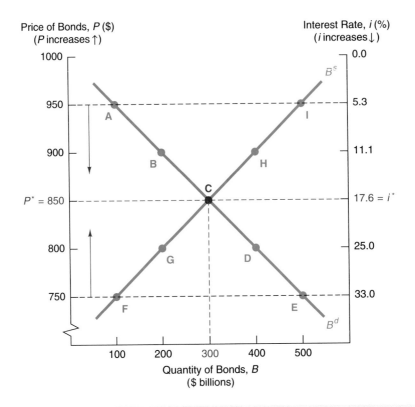

■FIGURE 1 Supply and Demand for Bonds

Equilibrium in the bond market occurs at point C, the intersection of the bond demand curve B^d and the bond supply curve B^s. The equilibrium price is $P^* = \$850$, and the equilibrium interest rate is $i^* = 17.6\%$. (*Note*: P and i increase in opposite directions. P on the left vertical axis increases as we go up the axis from \$750 near the bottom to \$1000 at the top, while i on the right vertical axis increases as we go down the axis from 0% at the top to 33% near the bottom.)

at point B. Similarly, at the lower prices of \$800 (interest rate = 25%) and \$750 (interest rate = 33.3%), the quantity of bonds demanded will be even higher (points D and E). The curve B^d, which connects these points, is the demand curve for bonds. It has the usual downward slope, indicating that at lower prices of the bond (everything else being equal), the quantity demanded is higher.[1]

Supply Curve

An important assumption behind the demand curve for bonds in Figure 1 is that all other economic variables besides the bond's price and interest rate are held constant. We use the same assumption in deriving a **supply curve,** which shows

---

[1]Note that although our analysis indicates that the demand curve is downward-sloping, it does not imply that the curve is a straight line. For ease of exposition, however, we will draw demand curves and supply curves as straight lines.

the relationship between the quantity supplied and the price when all other economic variables are held constant.

When the price of the bonds is $750 (interest rate = 33.3%), point F shows that the quantity of bonds supplied is $100 billion for the example we are considering. If the price is $800, the interest rate is the lower rate of 25%. Because at this interest rate it is now less costly to borrow by issuing bonds, firms will be willing to borrow more through bond issues, and the quantity of bonds supplied is at the higher level of $200 billion (point G). An even higher price of $850, corresponding to a lower interest rate of 17.6%, results in a larger quantity of bonds supplied of $300 billion (point C). Higher prices of $900 and $950 result in even greater quantities of bonds supplied (points H and I). The B^s curve, which connects these points, is the supply curve for bonds. It has the usual upward slope found in supply curves, indicating that as the price increases (everything else being equal), the quantity supplied increases.

Market Equilibrium

In finance and economics, **market equilibrium** occurs when the amount that people are willing to buy (*demand*) equals the amount that people are willing to sell (*supply*) at a given price. In the bond market, this is achieved when the quantity of bonds demanded equals the quantity of bonds supplied:

$$B^d = B^s \qquad\qquad (1)$$

In Figure 1, equilibrium occurs at point C, where the demand and supply curves intersect at a bond price of $850 (interest rate of 17.6%) and a quantity of bonds of $300 billion. The price of $P^* = 850$, where the quantity demanded equals the quantity supplied, is called the *equilibrium* or *market-clearing* price. Similarly, the interest rate of $i^* = 17.6\%$ that corresponds to this price is called the equilibrium or market-clearing interest rate.

The concepts of market equilibrium and equilibrium price or interest rate are useful because there is a tendency for the market to head toward them. We can see that it does in Figure 1 by first looking at what happens when we have a bond price that is above the equilibrium price. When the price of bonds is set too high, at, say, $950, the quantity of bonds supplied at point I is greater than the quantity of bonds demanded at point A. A situation like this, in which the quantity of bonds supplied exceeds the quantity of bonds demanded, is called a condition of **excess supply.** Because people want to sell more bonds than others want to buy, the price of the bonds will fall, and this is why the downward arrow is drawn in the figure at the bond price of $950. As long as the bond price remains above the equilibrium price, there will continue to be an excess supply of bonds, and the price will continue to fall. This will stop only when the price has reached the equilibrium price of $850, where the excess supply of bonds has been eliminated.

Now let's look at what happens when the price of bonds is below the equilibrium price. If the price of the bonds is set too low, at, say, $750, the quantity demanded at point E is greater than the quantity supplied at point F. This is called a condition of **excess demand.** People now want to buy more bonds than others are willing to sell, and so the price of bonds will be driven up. This is illustrated by the upward arrow drawn in the figure at the bond price of $750. Only when the excess demand for bonds is eliminated by the price rising to the equilibrium level of $850 is there no further tendency for the price to rise.

We can see that the concept of equilibrium price is a useful one because it indicates where the market will settle. Because each price on the left vertical axis of Figure 1 corresponds to a value of the interest rate on the right vertical axis, the same diagram also shows that the interest rate will head toward the equilibrium interest rate of 17.6%. When the interest rate is below the equilibrium interest rate, as it is when it is at 5.3%, the price of the bond is above the equilibrium price, and there will be an excess supply of bonds. The price of the bond then falls, leading to a rise in the interest rate toward the equilibrium level. Similarly, when the interest rate is above the equilibrium level, as it is when it is at 33.3%, there is excess demand for bonds, and the bond price will rise, driving the interest rate back down to the equilibrium level of 17.6%.

Supply and Demand Analysis

Our Figure 1 is a conventional supply and demand diagram with price on the left vertical axis and quantity on the horizontal axis. Because the interest rate that corresponds to each bond price is also marked on the right vertical axis, this diagram allows us to read the equilibrium interest rate, giving us a model that describes the determination of interest rates. It is important to recognize that a supply and demand diagram like Figure 1 can be drawn for *any* type of bond because the interest rate and price of a bond are *always* negatively related for any type of bond, be it a discount bond or a coupon bond.

One disadvantage of the diagram in Figure 1 is that interest rates run in an unusual direction on the right vertical axis: As we go up the right axis, interest rates fall. Because financial economists are typically more concerned with the value of interest rates rather than the price of bonds, we could plot the supply of and demand for bonds on a diagram that has only a left vertical axis that provides the values of the interest rates running in the usual direction, rising as we go up the axis. Figure 2 is such a diagram, in which points A through I match the corresponding points in Figure 1.

However, making interest rates run the "usual" direction on the vertical axis presents us with a problem. Our demand curve for bonds, points A through E, now looks peculiar because it has an upward slope. This upward slope is, however, completely consistent with our usual demand analysis, which produces a negative relationship between price and quantity. The inverse relationship between bond prices and interest rates means that in moving from point A to point B to point C, bond prices are falling and, consistent with usual demand analysis, the quantity demanded is rising. Similarly, our supply curve for bonds, points F through I, has an unusual-looking downward slope but is completely consistent with the usual view that price and the quantity supplied are positively related.

One way to give the demand curve the usual downward slope and the supply curve the usual upward slope is to rename the horizontal axis and the demand and

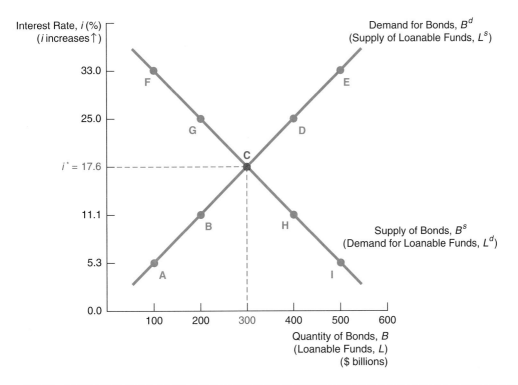

■FIGURE 2 A Comparison of Terminology: Loanable Funds and Supply and Demand for Bonds

The demand for bonds is equivalent to the supply of loanable funds, and the supply of bonds is equivalent to the demand for loanable funds. (*Note: i* increases as we go up the vertical axis, in contrast to Figure 1, in which the opposite occurs.)

supply curves. Because a firm supplying bonds is in fact taking out a loan from a person buying a bond, "supplying a bond" is equivalent to "demanding a loan." Thus the supply curve for bonds can be reinterpreted as indicating the *quantity of loans demanded* for each value of the interest rate. If we rename the horizontal axis **loanable funds,** defined as the quantity of loans, the supply of bonds can be reinterpreted as the *demand for loanable funds.* Similarly, the demand curve for bonds can be reidentified as the *supply of loanable funds* because buying (demanding) a bond is equivalent to supplying a loan. Figure 2 relabels the curves and the horizontal axis using the loanable funds terminology in parentheses, and now the renamed loanable funds demand curve has the usual downward slope and the renamed loanable funds supply curve the usual upward slope.

Because supply and demand diagrams that explain how interest rates are determined in the bond market most commonly use the loanable funds terminology, this analysis is frequently referred to as the **loanable funds framework.** However, because in later chapters describing the conduct of monetary policy we focus on how the demand for and supply of bonds is affected, we will continue to conduct supply and demand analysis in terms of bonds, as in Figure 1, rather than loanable funds. Whether the analysis is done in terms of loanable funds or in terms of the demand for and supply of bonds, the results are the same; the two ways of analyzing the determination of interest rates are equivalent.

An important feature of the analysis here is that supply and demand are always in terms of *stocks* (amounts at a given point in time) of assets, not in terms of *flows*. This approach is somewhat different from certain loanable funds analyses, which are conducted in terms of flows (loans per year). The **asset market approach** for understanding behavior in financial markets—which emphasizes stocks of assets rather than flows in determining asset prices—is now the dominant methodology used by financial economists because correctly conducting analyses in terms of flows is very tricky, especially when we encounter inflation. (See the appendix to this chapter for an application of the asset market approach to another market.)

◾ CHANGES IN EQUILIBRIUM INTEREST RATES

We will now use the supply and demand framework for bonds to analyze why interest rates change. To avoid confusion, it is important to make the distinction between *movements along* a demand (or supply) curve and *shifts in* a demand (or supply) curve. When quantity demanded (or supplied) changes as a result of a change in the price of the bond (or, equivalently, a change in the interest rate), we have a *movement along* the demand (or supply) curve. The change in the quantity demanded when we move from point A to B to C in Figure 1 or Figure 2, for example, is a movement along a demand curve. A *shift in* the demand (or supply) curve, by contrast, occurs when the quantity demanded (or supplied) changes *at each given price (or interest rate)* of the bond in response to a change in some other factor besides the bond's price or interest rate. When one of these factors changes, causing a shift in the demand or supply curve, there will be a new equilibrium value for the interest rate.

In the following pages we will look at how the supply and demand curves shift in response to changes in variables, such as expected inflation and wealth, and what effects these changes have on the equilibrium value of interest rates.

Shifts in the Demand for Bonds

The theory of portfolio choice developed in Chapter 4 provides a framework for deciding what factors cause the demand curve for bonds to shift. These factors include changes in four parameters:

1. Wealth
2. Expected returns on bonds relative to alternative assets
3. Risk of bonds relative to alternative assets
4. Liquidity of bonds relative to alternative assets

To see how a change in each of these factors (holding all other factors constant) can shift the demand curve, let us look at some examples. (As a study aid, Table 1 summarizes the effects of changes in these factors on the bond demand curve.)

■ TABLE 1 Factors That Shift the Demand Curve for Bonds

Variable	Change in Variable	Change in Quantity Demanded	Shift in Demand Curve		
Wealth	↑	↑	P (increases ↑)		i (increases ↓)
Expected interest rate	↑	↓	P (increases ↑)		i (increases ↓)
Expected inflation	↑	↓	P (increases ↑)		i (increases ↓)
Riskiness of bonds relative to other assets	↑	↓	P (increases ↑)		i (increases ↓)
Liquidity of bonds relative to other assets	↑	↑	P (increases ↑)		i (increases ↓)

NOTE: Only increases (↑) in the variables are shown. The effect of decreases in the variables on the change in demand would be the opposite of those indicated in the remaining columns.

Wealth When the economy is growing rapidly in a business cycle expansion and wealth is increasing, the quantity of bonds demanded at each bond price (or interest rate) increases as shown in Figure 3. To see how this works, consider point B on the initial demand curve for bonds B_1^d. It tells us that at a bond price of $900 and an interest rate of 11.1%, the quantity of bonds demanded is $200 billion. With

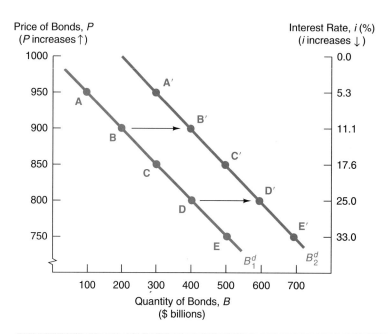

■FIGURE 3 Shift in the Demand Curve for Bonds

When the demand for bonds increases, the demand curve shifts to the right as shown. (*Note: P* and *i* increase in opposite directions. *P* on the left vertical axis increases as we go up the axis, while *i* on the right vertical axis increases as we go down the axis.)

higher wealth, the quantity of bonds demanded at the same interest rate must rise, say, to $400 billion (point B'). Similarly, the higher wealth causes the quantity demanded at a bond price of $800 and an interest rate of 25% to rise from $400 billion to $600 billion (point D to D'). Continuing with this reasoning for every point on the initial demand curve B^d_1, we can see that the demand curve shifts to the right from B^d_1 to B^d_2 as is indicated by the arrows.

The conclusion we have reached is that ***in a business cycle expansion with growing wealth, the demand for bonds rises and the demand curve for bonds shifts to the right.*** However, how much demand will shift (increase) will depend on the extent to which bonds are luxuries rather than necessities. Using the same reasoning, ***in a recession, when income and wealth are falling, the demand for bonds falls, and the demand curve shifts to the left.***

Another factor that affects wealth is the public's propensity to save. If households save more, wealth increases and, as we have seen, the demand for bonds rises and the demand curve for bonds shifts to the right. Conversely, if people save less, wealth and the demand for bonds will fall and the demand curve shifts to the left.

Expected Returns For a one-year discount bond and a one-year holding period, the expected return and the interest rate are identical. No component of the expected return is unrelated to the bond price or the interest rate.

For bonds with maturities of greater than one year, the expected return may differ from the interest rate. For example, we saw in Chapter 3, Table 2, that a rise in the interest rate on a long-term bond from 10% to 20% would lead to a sharp decline in price and a very negative return. Hence if people begin to think that interest rates will be higher next year than they had originally anticipated, the expected return today on long-term bonds would fall, and the quantity demanded would fall at each interest rate. ***Higher expected interest rates in the future decrease the demand for long-term bonds and shift the demand curve to the left.***

By contrast, a revision downward of expectations of future interest rates would mean that long-term bond prices would be expected to rise more than originally anticipated, and the resulting higher expected return today would raise the quantity demanded at each bond price and interest rate. ***Lower expected interest rates in the future increase the demand for long-term bonds and shift the demand curve to the right*** (as in Figure 3).

Changes in expected returns on other assets can also shift the demand curve for bonds. If people suddenly became more optimistic about the stock market and began to expect higher stock prices in the future, both expected capital gains and expected returns on stocks would rise. With the expected return on bonds held constant, the expected return on bonds today relative to stocks would fall, lowering the demand for bonds and shifting the demand curve to the left.

A change in expected inflation is likely to alter expected returns on physical assets (also called *real assets*) such as automobiles and houses, which affect the demand for bonds. An increase in expected inflation, say, from 5% to 10%, will lead to higher prices on cars and houses in the future and hence higher nominal capital gains. The resulting rise in the expected returns today on these real assets will lead to a fall in the expected return on bonds relative to the expected return on real assets today and thus cause the demand for bonds to fall. Alternatively, we can think of the rise in expected inflation as lowering the real interest rate on bonds, and the resulting decline in the relative expected return on bonds causes the demand for bonds to fall. ***An increase in the expected rate of inflation will cause the demand for bonds to decline and the demand curve to shift to the left.***

Risk If prices in the bond market become more volatile, the risk associated with bonds increases, and bonds become a less attractive asset. ***An increase in the riskiness of bonds causes the demand for bonds to fall and the demand curve to shift to the left.***

Conversely, an increase in the volatility of prices in another asset market, such as the stock market, would make bonds more attractive. ***An increase in the riskiness of alternative assets causes the demand for bonds to rise and the demand curve to shift to the right*** (as in Figure 3).

Liquidity If more people started trading in the bond market and as a result it became easier to sell bonds quickly, the increase in their liquidity would cause the quantity of bonds demanded at each interest rate to rise. ***Increased liquidity of bonds results in an increased demand for bonds, and the demand curve***

shifts to the right (see Figure 3). ***Similarly, increased liquidity of alternative assets lowers the demand for bonds and shifts the demand curve to the left.*** The reduction of brokerage commissions for trading common stocks that occurred when the fixed-rate commission structure was abolished in 1975, for example, increased the liquidity of stocks relative to bonds, and the resulting lower demand for bonds shifted the demand curve to the left.

Shifts in the Supply of Bonds

Certain factors can cause the supply curve for bonds to shift, among them these:

1. Expected profitability of investment opportunities
2. Expected inflation
3. Government activities

We will look at how the supply curve shifts when each of these factors changes (when all others remain constant). (As a study aid, Table 2 summarizes the effects of changes in these factors on the bond supply curve.)

■ **TABLE 2** Factors That Shift the Supply of Bonds

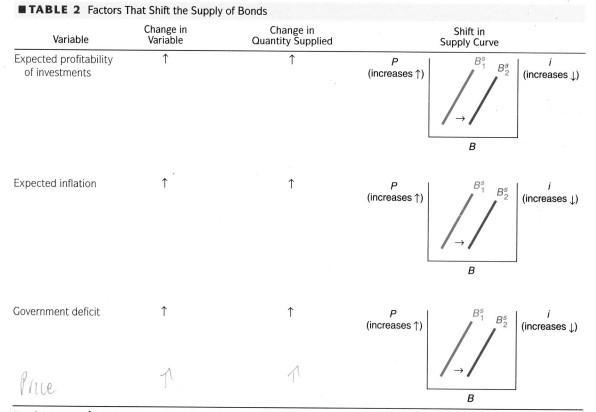

Variable	Change in Variable	Change in Quantity Supplied	Shift in Supply Curve		
Expected profitability of investments	↑	↑	P (increases ↑)	B^s_1 B^s_2	i (increases ↓)
Expected inflation	↑	↑	P (increases ↑)	B^s_1 B^s_2	i (increases ↓)
Government deficit	↑	↑	P (increases ↑)	B^s_1 B^s_2	i (increases ↓)

Price   ↑   ↑

NOTE: Only increases (↑) in the variables are shown. The effect of decreases in the variables on the change in supply would be the opposite of those indicated in the remaining columns.

Expected Profitability of Investment Opportunities The more profitable investments that a firm expects it can make, the more willing it will be to borrow and increase the amount of its outstanding debt in order to finance these investments. When the economy is growing rapidly, as in a business cycle expansion, investment opportunities that are expected to be profitable abound, and the quantity of bonds supplied at any given bond price and interest rate will increase (see Figure 4). Therefore, *in a business cycle expansion, the supply of bonds increases, and the supply curve shifts to the right. Likewise, in a recession, when there are far fewer expected profitable investment opportunities, the supply of bonds falls, and the supply curve shifts to the left.*

Expected Inflation As we saw in Chapter 3, the real cost of borrowing is more accurately measured by the real interest rate, which equals the (nominal) interest rate minus the expected inflation rate. For a given interest rate, when expected inflation increases, the real cost of borrowing falls; hence the quantity of bonds supplied increases at any given bond price and interest rate. *An increase in expected inflation causes the supply of bonds to increase and the supply curve to shift to the right* (see Figure 4).

Government Activities The activities of the government can influence the supply of bonds in several ways. The U.S. Treasury issues bonds to finance govern-

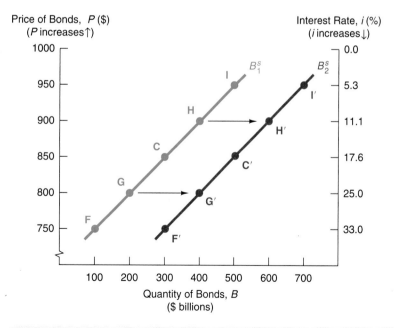

■FIGURE 4 Shift in the Supply Curve for Bonds

When the supply of bonds increases, the supply curve shifts to the right. (*Note: P* and *i* increase in opposite directions. *P* on the left vertical axis increases as we go up the axis, while *i* on the right vertical axis increases as we go down the axis.)

ment deficits, the gap between the government's expenditures and its revenues. When these deficits are large, as they have been recently, the Treasury sells more bonds, and the quantity of bonds supplied at each bond price and interest rate increases. *Higher government deficits increase the supply of bonds and shift the supply curve to the right* (see Figure 4).

State and local governments and other government agencies also issue bonds to finance their expenditures, and this can also affect the supply of bonds. We will see in later chapters that the conduct of monetary policy involves the purchase and sale of bonds, which in turn influences the supply of bonds.

APPLICATION	CHANGES IN THE EQUILIBRIUM INTEREST RATE DUE TO EXPECTED INFLATION OR BUSINESS CYCLE EXPANSIONS

We can now use our knowledge of how supply and demand curves shift to analyze how the equilibrium interest rate can change. The best way to do this is to pursue several applications that are particularly relevant to our understanding of how monetary policy affects interest rates.

■ **STUDY GUIDE** Supply and demand analysis for the bond market is best learned by practicing applications. When there is an application in the text and we look at how the interest rate changes because some economic variable increases, see if you can draw the appropriate shifts in the supply and demand curves when this same economic variable decreases. While you are practicing applications, keep two things in mind:

1. When you examine the effect of a variable change, remember that we are assuming that all other variables are unchanged; that is, we are making use of the *ceteris paribus* assumption.
2. Remember that the interest rate is negatively related to the bond price, so when the equilibrium bond price rises, the equilibrium interest rate falls. Conversely, if the equilibrium bond price moves downward, the equilibrium interest rate rises.

Changes in Expected Inflation: The Fisher Effect

We have already done most of the work to evaluate how a change in expected inflation affects the nominal interest rate in that we have already analyzed how a change in expected inflation shifts the supply and demand curves. Figure 5 shows the effect on the equilibrium interest rate of an increase in expected inflation.

Suppose that expected inflation is initially 5% and the initial supply and demand curves B_1^s and B_1^d intersect at point 1, where the equilibrium bond price is P_1 and the equilibrium interest rate is i_1. If expected inflation rises to 10%, the expected return on bonds relative to real assets falls for any given bond price and interest rate. As a result, the demand for bonds falls, and the demand curve shifts to the left from B_1^d to B_2^d. The rise in expected inflation also shifts the supply curve.

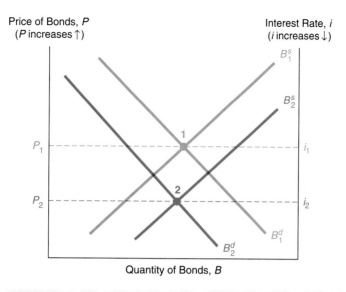

Price of Bonds, P
(P increases ↑)

Interest Rate, i
(i increases ↓)

Quantity of Bonds, B

■FIGURE 5 Response to a Change in Expected Inflation

When expected inflation rises, the supply curve shifts from B_1^s to B_2^s, and the demand curve shifts from B_1^d to B_2^d. The equilibrium moves from point 1 to point 2, with the result that the equilibrium bond price (left axis) falls from P_1 to P_2 and the equilibrium interest rate (right axis) rises from i_1 to i_2. (*Note*: P and i increase in opposite directions. P on the left vertical axis increases as we go up the axis, while i on the right vertical axis increases as we go down the axis.)

At any given bond price and interest rate, the real cost of borrowing has declined, causing the quantity of bonds supplied to increase, and the supply curve shifts to the right from B_1^s to B_2^s.

When the demand and supply curves shift in response to the change in expected inflation, the equilibrium moves from point 1 to point 2, which is the intersection of B_2^d and B_2^s. The equilibrium bond price has fallen from P_1 to P_2, and because the bond price is negatively related to the interest rate (as is indicated by the interest rate rising as we go down the right vertical axis), this means that the interest rate has risen from i_1 to i_2. Note that Figure 5 has been drawn so that the equilibrium quantity of bonds remains the same for both point 1 and point 2. However, depending on the size of the shifts in the supply and demand curves, the equilibrium quantity of bonds could either rise or fall when expected inflation rises.

Our supply and demand analysis has led us to an important observation: ***When expected inflation rises, interest rates will rise.*** This result has been named the **Fisher effect,** after Irving Fisher, the economist who first pointed out the relationship of expected inflation to interest rates. The accuracy of this prediction is shown in Figure 6. The interest rate on three-month Treasury bills has usually moved along with the expected inflation rate. Consequently, it is understandable that many economists recommend that the fight against inflation must be won if we want to lower interest rates.

Annual Rate (%)

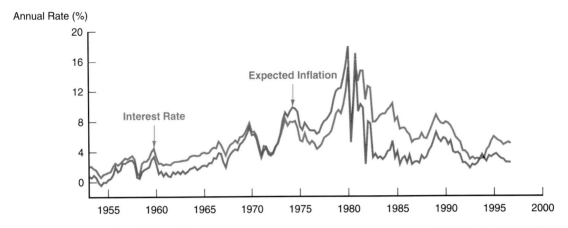

■FIGURE 6 Expected Inflation and Interest Rates (Three-Month Treasury Bills), 1953–1996

Source: Expected inflation calculated using procedures outlined in Frederic S. Mishkin, "The Real Interest Rate: An Empirical Investigation," *Carnegie-Rochester Conference Series on Public Policy* 15 (1981): 151–200. This involves estimating expected inflation as a function of past interest rates, inflation, and time trends.

Business Cycle Expansion

Figure 7 analyzes the effects of a business cycle expansion on interest rates. In a business cycle expansion, the amount of goods and services being produced in the economy rises, so national income increases. When this occurs, businesses will be more willing to borrow because they are likely to have many profitable investment opportunities for which they need financing. Hence at a given bond price and interest rate, the quantity of bonds that firms want to sell (that is, the supply of bonds) will increase. This means that in a business cycle expansion, the supply curve for bonds shifts to the right (see Figure 7) from B_1^s to B_2^s.

The expanding economy will also affect the demand for bonds. The theory of portfolio choice tells us that as the economy expands and wealth increases, the demand for bonds will rise as well. We see this in Figure 7, where the demand curve has shifted to the right from B_1^d to B_2^d.

Given that both the supply and demand curves have shifted to the right, we know that the new equilibrium reached at the intersection of B_2^d and B_2^s must also move to the right. However, depending on whether the supply curve shifts more than the demand curve or vice versa, the new equilibrium interest rate can either rise or fall.

The supply and demand analysis used here gives us an ambiguous answer to the question of what will happen to interest rates in a business cycle expansion. The figure has been drawn so that the shift in the supply curve is greater than the shift in the demand curve, causing the equilibrium bond price to fall to P_2, leading to a rise in the equilibrium interest rate to i_2. The reason the figure has been drawn so that a business cycle expansion and a rise in income lead to a higher interest rate is that this is the outcome we actually see in the data. Figure 8 plots the movement of the interest rate on three-month U.S. Treasury bills from 1951 to 1996 and indicates when the business cycle is undergoing recessions (shaded areas). As

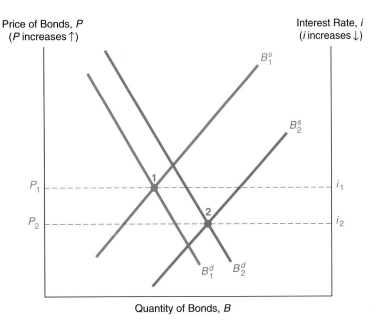

Price of Bonds, P
(P increases ↑)

Interest Rate, i
(i increases ↓)

Quantity of Bonds, B

■FIGURE 7 Response to a Business Cycle Expansion

In a business cycle expansion, when income and wealth are rising, the demand curve shifts rightward from B_1^d to B_2^d, and the supply curve shifts rightward from B_1^s to B_2^s. If the supply curve shifts to the right more than the demand curve, as in this figure, the equilibrium bond price (left axis) moves down from P_1 to P_2, and the equilibrium interest rate (right axis) rises from i_1 to i_2. (*Note:* P and i increase in opposite directions. P on the left vertical axis increases as we go up the axis, while i on the right vertical axis increases as we go down the axis.)

you can see, the interest rate rises during business cycle expansions and falls during recessions, which is what the supply and demand diagram indicates.

APPLICATION | **THE "CREDIT MARKETS" COLUMN**

READING THE *WALL STREET JOURNAL*

Now that we have an understanding of how supply and demand determines prices and interest rates in the bond market, we can use our analysis to understand discussions about bond prices and interest rates appearing in the financial press. Every day, the *Wall Street Journal* reports on developments in the bond market on the previous business day in its "Credit Markets" column, an example of which is found in the "Following the Financial News" box. Let's see how statements in the "Credit Markets" column can be explained using our supply and demand framework.

The column opens by stating that bond prices jumped on signs that the manufacturing sector grew moderately last month and on remarks by Federal Reserve Chairman Alan Greenspan suggesting that he was optimistic about the inflation outlook. This is exactly what our supply and demand analysis predicts would happen.

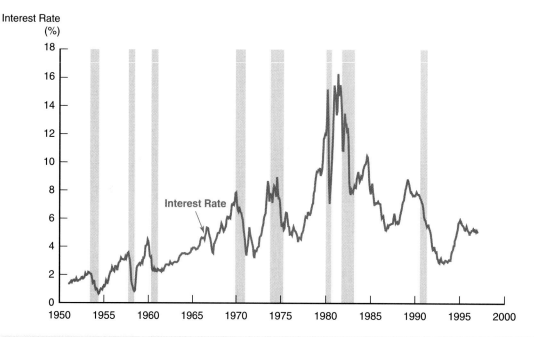

■FIGURE 8 Business Cycle and Interest Rates (Three-Month Treasury Bills), 1951–1996
Shaded areas indicate periods of recession. The figure shows that interest rates rise during business cycle expansions and fall during contractions, which is what Figure 7 suggests would happen. *Sources:* Federal Reserve *Bulletin;* Citibase databank.

The National Association of Purchasing Managers composite index, a gauge of manufacturing activity, which came in lower than forecast, suggests a downward revision in the strength of the economy. As we have seen in the text, this would indicate that investment opportunities are shrinking and so businesses are less likely to issue bonds, with the result that the quantity of bonds supplied decreases at each interest rate and the supply curve shifts to the left. Meanwhile, the weaker economy suggests that wealth is decreasing and hence the quantity of bonds demanded at each interest rate falls, shifting the demand curve to the left. Because, as discussed earlier, the leftward shift in the supply curve is likely to be greater than the leftward shift in the demand curve, equilibrium bond prices rise and their interest rates fall.

Greenspan's reported remarks that he is optimistic about the inflation outlook caused bond investors to revise their assessment of expected inflation. As we have seen in this chapter, the decline in expected inflation causes the expected return on bonds relative to real assets to rise, which shifts the demand curve to the right. In addition, the lower expected inflation raises the real cost of borrowing at any given interest rate, which decreases the quantity of bonds supplied at each interest rate and shifts the supply curve to the left. The outcome is a rise in bond prices and a drop in interest rates. Our analysis thus shows why both Greenspan's inflation optimism and the weaker than expected manufacturing activity contributed to the upward jump in bond prices.

The "Credit Markets" Column

The "Credit Markets" column appears daily in the *Wall Street Journal;* an example is presented here. It is found   in the third section, "Money and Investing."

CREDIT MARKETS

Bond Prices Are Lifted by Manufacturing Data, Remarks on Inflation Attributed to Greenspan

By CHARLENE LEE
AND VICTORIA M. ZUNITCH
Dow Jones News Services

NEW YORK—Bond prices jumped on signs that the manufacturing sector grew moderately last month. The market also drew support from remarks attributed to Federal Reserve Chairman Alan Greenspan suggesting that he is optimistic about the U.S. inflation outlook.

A business publication, the Australian Financial Review, reported that Mr. Greenspan made the comments Monday during a meeting in Washington with Australian Treasurer Peter Costello. A Fed spokesman confirmed that the two had

met, but declined to say whether the report was accurate.

But later, when read a portion of the report, Mr. Costello said the account was "fanciful." He was reluctant to address specifics of the report, adding, "I don't comment on U.S. interest rates."

Late yesterday, the benchmark 30-year Treasury bond was up 21/32 point in price, or $6.56 for a bond with $1,000 face value, at 98 13/32. Its yield, which moves in the opposite direction as prices, fell to 6.87% from 6.92% late Monday.

Bonds got an early boost when the National Association of Purchasing Management said its composite index

stood at 51.7 in September. The index, a closely monitored gauge of manufacturing activity, had been forecast by economists to be higher. "It failed to live up to the market's worst fears," said Kevin Flanagan, an economist at Dean Witter Reynolds Inc.

The Australian official was in Washington for meetings of the International Monetary Fund and the World Bank.

Traders, noting that technical factors also aided the bond market's rise, said many traders seized upon the report as an excuse to take the market higher.

Source: Wall Street Journal, October 2, 1996, p. C21.

APPLICATION | **HAVE LOW SAVINGS RATES IN THE UNITED STATES LED TO HIGHER INTEREST RATES?**

Since 1980, the United States has experienced a sharp drop in personal savings rates, falling from 8% of personal income to around the 5% level today. Many commentators, including high officials of the Federal Reserve System, have blamed the profligate behavior of the American public for high interest rates. Are they right?

Our supply and demand analysis of the bond market indicates that they could be. The decline in savings means that the wealth of American households is lower than would otherwise be the case. This smaller amount of wealth decreases the demand for bonds and shifts the demand curve to the left from B_1^d to B_2^d in Figure 9. The result is that the equilibrium bond price drops from P_1 to P_2 and the interest rate rises from i_1 to i_2. Low savings can thus raise interest rates, and the higher rates may retard investment in capital goods. The profligacy of Americans may therefore lead to a less productive economy and is of serious concern to both economists and policymakers. Suggested remedies for the problem range from

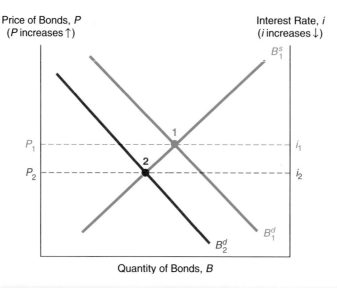

■FIGURE 9 Response to a Lower Savings Rate

With a lower savings rate, wealth decreases, and the demand curve shifts in from B_1^d to B_2^d. The equilibrium moves from point 1 to point 2, with the result that the equilibrium bond price (left axis) drops from P_1 to P_2 and the equilibrium interest rate (right axis) rises from i_1 to i_2. (*Note:* P and i increase in opposite directions. P on the left vertical axis increases as we go up the axis, while i on the right vertical axis increases as we go down the axis.)

changing the tax code to encourage saving to forcing Americans to save more by mandating increased contributions into retirement plans.

■ LIQUIDITY PREFERENCE FRAMEWORK: SUPPLY AND DEMAND IN THE MARKET FOR MONEY

Whereas the loanable funds framework determines the equilibrium interest rate using the supply of and demand for bonds, an alternative model developed by John Maynard Keynes, known as the **liquidity preference framework,** determines the equilibrium interest rate in terms of the supply of and demand for money. Although the two frameworks look different, the liquidity preference analysis of the market for money is closely related to the loanable funds framework of the bond market.[2]

The starting point of Keynes's analysis is his assumption that there are two main categories of assets that people use to store their wealth: money and bonds. Therefore, total wealth in the economy must equal the total quantity of bonds plus money in the economy, which equals the quantity of bonds supplied B^s plus the quantity of money supplied M^s. The quantity of bonds B^d and money M^d that peo-

---

[2]Note that the term *market for money* refers to the market for the medium of exchange, money. This market differs from the *money market* referred to by finance practitioners, which is the financial market in which short-term debt instruments are traded.

ple want to hold and thus demand must also equal the total amount of wealth because people cannot purchase more assets than their available resources allow. The conclusion is that the quantity of bonds and money supplied must equal the quantity of bonds and money demanded:

$$B^s + M^s = B^d + M^d \qquad (2)$$

Collecting the bond terms on one side of the equation and the money terms on the other, this equation can be rewritten as

$$B^s - B^d = M^d - M^s \qquad (3)$$

The rewritten equation tells us that if the market for money is in equilibrium ($M^s = M^d$), the right-hand side of Equation 3 equals zero, implying that $B^s = B^d$, meaning that the bond market is also in equilibrium.

Thus it is the same to think about determining the equilibrium interest rate by equating the supply and demand for bonds or by equating the supply and demand for money. In this sense, the liquidity preference framework, which analyzes the market for money, is equivalent to the loanable funds framework, which analyzes the bond market. In practice, the approaches differ because by assuming that there are only two kinds of assets, money and bonds, the liquidity preference approach implicitly ignores any effects on interest rates that arise from changes in the expected returns on real assets such as automobiles and houses. In most instances, both frameworks yield the same predictions.

The reason that we approach the determination of interest rates with both frameworks is that the loanable funds framework is easier to use when analyzing the effects from changes in expected inflation, whereas the liquidity preference framework provides a simpler analysis of the effects from changes in income, the price level, and the supply of money.

Because the definition of money that Keynes used includes currency (which earns no interest) and checking account deposits (which in his time typically earned little or no interest), he assumed that money has a zero rate of return. Bonds, the only alternative asset to money in Keynes's framework, have an expected return equal to the interest rate i.[3] As this interest rate rises (holding everything else unchanged), the expected return on money falls relative to the expected return on bonds, and as the theory of portfolio choice tells us, this causes the demand for money to fall.

We can also see that the demand for money and the interest rate should be negatively related by using the concept of **opportunity cost,** the amount of interest (expected return) sacrificed by not holding the alternative asset—in this case, a bond. As the interest rate on bonds i rises, the opportunity cost of holding money rises, and so money is less desirable and the quantity of money demanded must fall.

Figure 10 shows the quantity of money demanded at a number of interest rates, with all other economic variables, such as income and the price level, held

---

[3]Keynes did not actually assume that the expected returns on bonds equaled the interest rate but rather argued that they were closely related. This distinction makes no appreciable difference in our analysis.

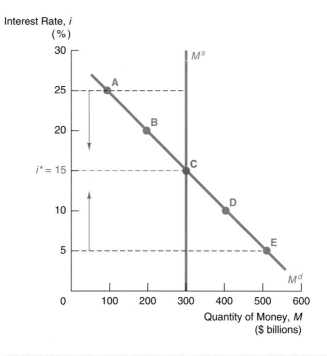

■FIGURE 10 Equilibrium in the Market for Money

constant. At an interest rate of 25%, point A shows that the quantity of money demanded is $100 billion. If the interest rate is at the lower rate of 20%, the opportunity cost of money is lower, and the quantity of money demanded rises to $200 billion, as indicated by the move from point A to point B. If the interest rate is even lower, the quantity of money demanded is even higher, as is indicated by points C, D, and E. The curve M^d connecting these points is the demand curve for money, and it slopes downward.

At this point in our analysis, we will assume that a central bank controls the amount of money supplied at a fixed quantity of $300 billion, so the supply curve for money M^s in the figure is a vertical line at $300 billion. The equilibrium where the quantity of money demanded equals the quantity of money supplied occurs at the intersection of the supply and demand curves at point C, where

$$M^d = M^s \tag{4}$$

The resulting equilibrium interest rate is at $i^* = 15\%$.

We can again see that there is a tendency to approach this equilibrium by first looking at the relationship of money demand and supply when the interest rate is above the equilibrium interest rate. When the interest rate is 25%, the quantity of money demanded at point A is $100 billion, yet the quantity of money supplied is $300 billion. The excess supply of money means that people are holding more money than they desire, so they will try to get rid of their excess money balances by trying to buy bonds. Accordingly, they will bid up the price of bonds, and as the bond price rises, the interest rate will fall toward the equilibrium interest rate of 15%. This tendency is shown by the downward arrow drawn at the interest rate of 25%.

Likewise, if the interest rate is 5%, the quantity of money demanded at point E is $500 billion, but the quantity of money supplied is only $300 billion. There is now an excess demand for money because people want to hold more money than they currently have. To try to get the money, they will sell their only other asset—bonds—and the price will fall. As the price of bonds falls, the interest rate will rise toward the equilibrium rate of 15%. Only when the interest rate is at its equilibrium value will there be no tendency for it to move further, and the interest rate will settle to its equilibrium value.

■ CHANGES IN EQUILIBRIUM INTEREST RATES

Analyzing how the equilibrium interest rate changes using the liquidity preference framework requires that we understand what causes the demand and supply curves for money to shift.

■ **S T U D Y G U I D E** Learning the liquidity preference framework also requires practicing applications. When there is an application in the text to examine how the interest rate changes because some economic variable increases, see if you can draw the appropriate shifts in the supply and demand curves when this same economic variable decreases. And remember to use the *ceteris paribus* assumption: When examining the effect of a change in one variable, hold all other variables constant.

Shifts in the Demand for Money

In Keynes's liquidity preference analysis, two factors cause the demand curve for money to shift: income and the price level.

Income Effect In Keynes's view, there were two reasons why income would affect the demand for money. First, as an economy expands and income rises, wealth increases and people will want to hold more money as a store of value. Second, as the economy expands and income rises, people will want to carry out more transactions using money, with the result that they will also want to hold more money. The conclusion is that **a higher level of income causes the demand for money to increase and the demand curve to shift to the right.**

Price-Level Effect Keynes took the view that people care about the amount of money they hold in real terms, that is, in terms of the goods and services that it can buy. When the price level rises, the same nominal quantity of money is no longer as valuable; it cannot be used to purchase as many real goods or services. To restore their holdings of money in real terms to its former level, people will want to hold a greater nominal quantity of money, so **a rise in the price level causes the demand for money to increase and the demand curve to shift to the right.**

Shifts in the Supply of Money

We will assume that the supply of money is completely controlled by the central bank, which in the United States is the Federal Reserve. (Actually, the process that determines the money supply is substantially more complicated and involves banks, depositors, and borrowers from banks. We will study it in more detail later in the book.) For now, all we need to know is that **an increase in the money supply engineered by the Federal Reserve will shift the supply curve for money to the right.**

APPLICATION | **CHANGES IN THE EQUILIBRIUM INTEREST RATE DUE TO CHANGES IN INCOME, THE PRICE LEVEL, OR THE MONEY SUPPLY**

To see how the liquidity preference framework can be used to analyze the movement of interest rates, we will again look at several applications that will be useful in evaluating the effect of monetary policy on interest rates. (As a study aid, Table 3 summarizes the shifts in the demand and supply curves for money.)

Changes in Income

When income is rising during a business cycle expansion, we have seen that the demand for money will rise. It is shown in Figure 11 by the shift rightward in the demand curve from M_1^d to M_2^d. The new equilibrium is reached at point 2 at the

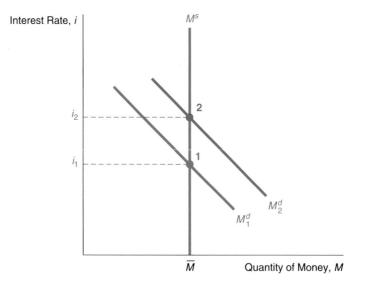

■FIGURE 11 Response to a Change in Income

In a business cycle expansion, when income is rising, the demand curve shifts from M_1^d to M_2^d. The supply curve is fixed at $M^s = \overline{M}$. The equilibrium interest rate rises from i_1 to i_2.

■ TABLE 3 Factors That Shift the Demand for and Supply of Money

Variable	Change in Variable	Change in Money Demand (M^d) or Supply (M^s)	Change in Interest Rate	
Income	↑	M^d↑	↑	
Price level	↑	M^d↑	↑	
Money supply	↑	M^s↑	↓	

NOTE: Only increases (↑) in the variables are shown. The effect of decreases in the variables on the change in demand or supply would be the opposite of those indicated in the remaining columns.

intersection of the M^d_2 curve with the money supply curve M^s. As you can see, the equilibrium interest rate rises from i_1 to i_2. The liquidity preference framework thus generates the conclusion that **when income is rising during a business cycle expansion (holding other economic variables constant), interest rates will rise.** This conclusion is unambiguous when contrasted to the conclusion reached about the effects of a change in income on interest rates using the loanable funds framework.

Changes in the Price Level

When the price level rises, the value of money in terms of what it can purchase is lower. To restore their purchasing power in real terms to its former level, people

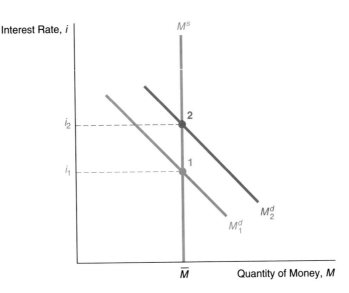

■FIGURE 12 Response to a Change in the Price Level

An increase in price level shifts the money demand curve from M_1^d to M_2^d, and the equilibrium interest rate rises from i_1 to i_2.

---

will want to hold a greater nominal quantity of money. A higher price level shifts the demand curve for money to the right from M_1^d to M_2^d (see Figure 12). The equilibrium moves from point 1 to point 2, where the equilibrium interest rate has risen from i_1 to i_2, illustrating that **when the price level increases, with the supply of money and other economic variables held constant, interest rates will rise.**

Changes in the Money Supply

An increase in the money supply due to expansionary monetary policy by the Federal Reserve implies that the supply curve for money shifts to the right. As is shown in Figure 13 by the movement of the supply curve from M_1^s to M_2^s, the equilibrium moves from point 1 down to point 2, where the M_2^s supply curve intersects with the demand curve M^d and the equilibrium interest rate has fallen from i_1 to i_2. **When the money supply increases (everything else remaining equal), interest rates will decline.**[4]

---

[4]This same result can be generated using the loanable funds framework. The primary way that a central bank produces an increase in the money supply is by buying bonds and thereby decreasing the supply of bonds to the public. The resulting shift to the left of the supply curve for bonds will lead to a decline in the equilibrium interest rate.

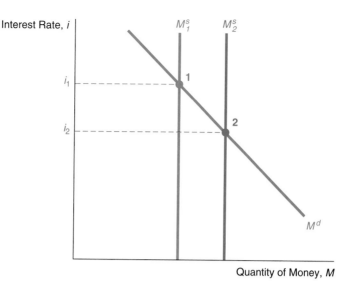

■FIGURE 13 Response to a Change in the Money Supply

When the money supply increases, the supply curve shifts from M_1^s to M_2^s, and the equilibrium interest rate falls from i_1 to i_2.

APPLICATION | **MONEY AND INTEREST RATES**

The liquidity preference analysis in Figure 13 seems to lead to the conclusion that an increase in the money supply will lower interest rates. This conclusion has important policy implications because it has frequently caused politicians to call for a more rapid growth of the money supply in order to drive down interest rates.

But is this conclusion that money and interest rates should be negatively related correct? Might there be other important factors left out of the liquidity preference analysis in Figure 13 that would reverse this conclusion? We will provide answers to these questions by applying the supply and demand analysis we have learned in this chapter to obtain a deeper understanding of the relationship between money and interest rates.

An important criticism of the conclusion that a rise in the money supply lowers interest rates has been raised by Milton Friedman, a Nobel laureate in economics. He acknowledges that the liquidity preference analysis is correct and calls the result—that an increase in the money supply (*everything else remaining equal*) lowers interest rates—the *liquidity effect*. However, he views the liquidity effect as merely part of the story: An increase in the money supply might not leave "everything else equal" and will have other effects on the economy that may make interest rates rise. If these effects are substantial, it is entirely possible that when the money supply rises, interest rates too may rise.

We have already laid the groundwork to discuss these other effects because we have shown how changes in income, the price level, and expected inflation affect the equilibrium interest rate.

■ **STUDY GUIDE** To get further practice with the loanable funds and liquidity preference frameworks, show how the effects discussed here work by drawing the
supply and demand diagrams that explain each effect. This exercise will also improve
your understanding of the effect of money on interest rates.

1. *Income Effect.* Because an increasing money supply is an expansionary influence on the economy, it should raise national income and wealth.
Both the liquidity preference and loanable funds frameworks indicate that
interest rates will then rise (see Figures 7 and 11). Thus **the income effect
of an increase in the money supply is a rise in interest rates in
response to the higher level of income.**

2. *Price-Level Effect.* An increase in the money supply can also cause
the overall price level in the economy to rise. The liquidity preference framework predicts that this will lead to a rise in interest rates. So **the price-level
effect from an increase in the money supply is a rise in interest
rates in response to the rise in the price level.**

3. *Expected-Inflation Effect.* The rising price level (the higher inflation
rate) that results from an increase in the money supply also affects interest
rates by affecting the expected inflation rate. Specifically, an increase in the
money supply may lead people to expect a higher price level in the future—
hence the expected inflation rate will be higher. The loanable funds framework has shown us that this increase in expected inflation will lead to a higher
level of interest rates. Therefore, **the expected-inflation effect of an
increase in the money supply is a rise in interest rates in response
to the rise in the expected inflation rate.**

At first glance it might appear that the price-level effect and the expected-
inflation effect are the same thing. They both indicate that increases in the price
level induced by an increase in the money supply will raise interest rates.
However, there is a subtle difference between the two, and this is why they are
discussed as two separate effects.

Suppose that there is a onetime increase in the money supply today that leads
to a rise in prices to a permanently higher level by next year. As the price level
rises over the course of this year, the interest rate will rise via the price-level
effect. Only at the end of the year, when the price level has risen to its peak, will
the price-level effect be at a maximum.

The rising price level will also raise interest rates via the expected-inflation
effect because people will expect that inflation will be higher over the course of
the year. However, when the price level stops rising next year, inflation and the
expected inflation rate will fall back down to zero. Any rise in interest rates as a
result of the earlier rise in expected inflation will then be reversed. We thus see
that in contrast to the price-level effect, which reaches its greatest impact next
year, the expected-inflation effect will have its smallest impact (zero impact) next
year. The basic difference between the two effects, then, is that the price-level
effect remains even after prices have stopped rising, whereas the expected-inflation effect disappears.

An important point is that the expected-inflation effect will persist only as long as the price level continues to rise. A onetime increase in the money supply will not produce a continually rising price level; only a higher rate of money supply growth will. Thus a higher rate of money supply growth is needed if the expected-inflation effect is to persist.

Does a Higher Rate of Growth of the Money Supply Lower Interest Rates?

We can now put together all the effects we have discussed to help us decide whether our analysis supports the politicians who advocate a greater rate of growth of the money supply when they feel that interest rates are too high. Of all the effects, only the liquidity effect indicates that a higher rate of money growth will cause a decline in interest rates. In contrast, the income, price-level, and expected-inflation effects indicate that interest rates will rise when money growth is higher. Which of these effects are largest, and how quickly do they take effect? The answers are critical in determining whether interest rates will rise or fall when money supply growth is increased.

Generally, the liquidity effect from the greater money growth takes effect immediately because the rising money supply leads to an immediate decline in the equilibrium interest rate. The income and price-level effects take time to work because the increasing money supply takes time to raise the price level and income, which in turn raise interest rates. The expected-inflation effect, which also raises interest rates, can be slow or fast, depending on whether people adjust their expectations of inflation slowly or quickly when the money growth rate is increased.

Three possibilities are outlined in Figure 14; each shows how interest rates respond over time to an increased rate of money supply growth starting at time T. Panel (a) shows a case in which the liquidity effect dominates the other effects so that the interest rate falls from i_1 at time T to a final level of i_2. The liquidity effect operates quickly to lower the interest rate, but as time goes by, the other effects start to reverse some of the decline. Because the liquidity effect is larger than the others, however, the interest rate never rises back to its initial level.

Panel (b) has a lesser liquidity effect than the other effects, with the expected-inflation effect operating slowly because expectations of inflation are slow to adjust upward. Initially, the liquidity effect drives down the interest rate. Then the income, price-level, and expected-inflation effects begin to raise it. Because these effects are dominant, the interest rate eventually rises above its initial level to i_2. In the short run, lower interest rates result from increased money growth, but eventually they end up climbing above the initial level.

Panel (c) has the expected-inflation effect dominating as well as operating rapidly because people quickly raise their expectation of inflation when the rate of money growth increases. The expected-inflation effect begins immediately to overpower the liquidity effect, and the interest rate immediately starts to climb. Over time, as the income and price-level effects start to take hold, the interest rate rises even higher, and the eventual outcome is an interest rate that is substantially above the initial interest rate. The result shows clearly that increasing money

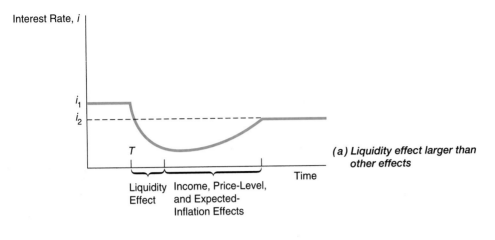

(a) *Liquidity effect larger than other effects*

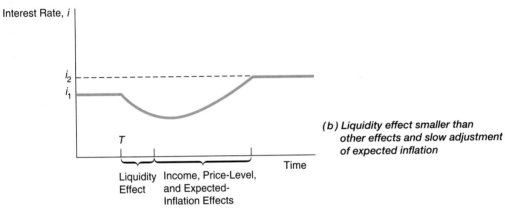

(b) *Liquidity effect smaller than other effects and slow adjustment of expected inflation*

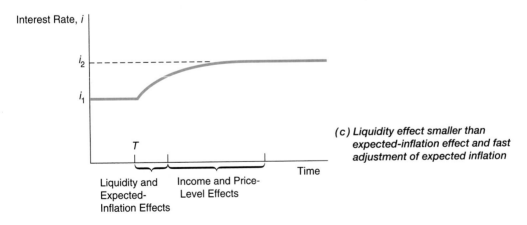

(c) *Liquidity effect smaller than expected-inflation effect and fast adjustment of expected inflation*

■FIGURE 14 Response over Time to an Increase in Money Supply Growth

supply growth is not the answer to reducing interest rates but rather that money growth should be reduced in order to lower interest rates!

An important issue for economic policymakers is which of these three scenarios is closest to reality. If a decline in interest rates is desired, then an increase in money supply growth is called for when the liquidity effect dominates the other effects, as in panel (a). A decrease in money growth is appropriate if the other effects dominate the liquidity effect and expectations of inflation adjust rapidly, as in panel (c). If the other effects dominate the liquidity effect but expectations of inflation adjust only slowly, as in panel (b), then whether you want to increase or decrease money growth depends on whether you care more about what happens in the short run or the long run.

Which scenario is supported by the evidence? The relationship of interest rates and money growth from 1951 to 1996 is plotted in Figure 15. When the rate of money supply growth began to climb in the mid-1960s, interest rates rose, indicating that the liquidity effect was dominated by the price-level, income, and expected-inflation effects. By the 1970s, interest rates reached levels unprecedented in the period after World War II, as did the rate of money supply growth.

The scenario depicted in panel (a) of Figure 14 seems doubtful, and the case for lowering interest rates by raising the rate of money growth is much weakened. Looking back at Figure 6, which shows the relationship between interest rates and expected inflation, you should not find this too surprising. The rise in the rate of

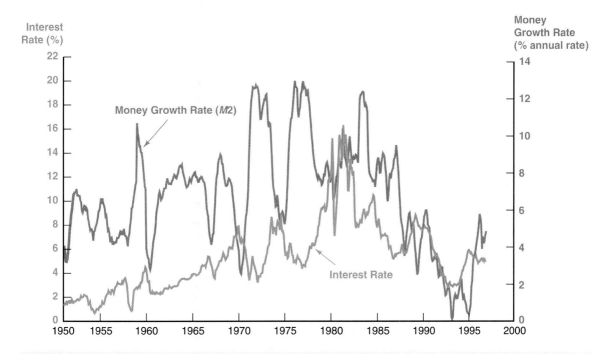

■FIGURE 15 Money Growth (M2, Annual Rate) and Interest Rates (Three-Month Treasury Bills), 1950–1996

Sources: Federal Reserve *Bulletin;* Citibase databank.

money supply growth in the 1960s and 1970s is matched by a large rise in expected inflation, which would lead us to predict that the expected-inflation effect would be dominant. It is the most plausible explanation for why interest rates rose in the face of higher money growth. However, Figure 15 does not really tell us which one of the two scenarios, panel (b) or panel (c) of Figure 14, is more accurate. It depends critically on how fast people's expectations about inflation adjust. However, recent research using more sophisticated methods than just looking at a graph like Figure 15 do indicate that increased money growth temporarily lowers short-term interest rates.[5]

THE PRACTICING FINANCIAL INSTITUTION MANAGER
Profiting from Interest-Rate Forecasts

Given the importance of interest rates, the media frequently report interest-rate forecasts, as the "Following the Financial News" box indicates. Because changes in interest rates have a major impact on the profitability of financial institutions, financial managers care a great deal about the path of future interest rates. Managers of financial institutions obtain interest-rate forecasts either by hiring their own staff economists to generate forecasts or by purchasing forecasts from other financial institutions or economic forecasting firms.

Several methods are used to produce interest-rate forecasts. One of the most popular is based on the loanable funds framework described earlier in the chapter, and it is used by financial institutions such as Salomon Brothers, Morgan Guaranty Trust Company, and the Prudential Insurance Company. Using the loanable funds framework, analysts predict what will happen to the factors that affect the supply of and demand for bonds—factors such as the strength of the economy, the profitability of investment opportunities, the expected inflation rate, and the size of government deficits and borrowing. They then use the supply and demand analysis outlined in the chapter to come up with their interest-rate forecasts. A variation of this approach makes use of the *Flow of Funds Accounts* produced by the Federal Reserve. These data show the sources and uses of funds by different sectors of the American economy. By looking at how well the supply of credit and the demand for credit by different sectors match up, forecasters attempt to predict future changes in interest rates.

Forecasting done with the loanable funds framework often does not make use of formal economic models but rather depends on the judgment or "feel" of the forecaster. An alternative method of forecasting interest rates makes use of

---

[5]See Lawrence J. Christiano and Martin Eichenbaum, "Identification and the Liquidity Effect of a Monetary Policy Shock," in *Business Cycles, Growth, and Political Economy,* ed. Alex Cukierman, Zvi Hercowitz, and Leonardo Leiderman (Cambridge, Mass.: MIT Press, 1992), pp. 335–370; Eric M. Leeper and David B. Gordon, "In Search of the Liquidity Effect," *Journal of Monetary Economics* 29 (1992): 341–370; Steven Strongin, "The Identification of Monetary Policy Disturbances: Explaining the Liquidity Puzzle," *Journal of Monetary Economics* 35 (1995): 463–497; and Adrian Pagan and John C. Robertson, "Resolving the Liquidity Effect," *Federal Reserve Bank of St. Louis Review* 77 (May-June 1995): 33–54.

Forecasting Interest Rates

Forecasting interest rates is a time-honored profession. Economists are hired (sometimes at very high salaries) to forecast interest rates because businesses need to know what the rates will be in order to plan their future spending, and banks and investors require interest-rate forecasts in order to decide which assets to buy. Interest-rate forecasters predict what will happen to the factors that affect the supply and demand for bonds and for money—factors such as the strength of the economy, the profitability of investment opportunities, the expected inflation rate, and the size of government budget deficits and borrowing. They then use the supply and demand analysis we have outlined in this chapter to come up with their interest-rate forecasts.

The *Wall Street Journal* reports interest-rate forecasts by leading prognosticators twice a year (early January and July) in its "Economy" column or in its "Credit Markets" column, which surveys developments in the bond market daily. Forecasting interest rates is a perilous business. To their embarrassment, even the top experts are frequently far off in their forecasts.

A SAMPLING OF INTEREST-RATE, ECONOMIC AND CURRENCY FORECASTS

In percent except for dollar vs. yen

GDP	JUNE 1996 SURVEY					NEW FORECASTS FOR 1997									
	3-MO. TREASURY BILLS-a 12/31	30-YR. BONDS 12/31	GDP-b 2nd HALF 1996	CPI-c NOV. 1996	DLR. vs. YEN 12/96	3-MO. TREASURY BILLS-a 6/30	3-MO. TREASURY BILLS-a 12/31	30-YR. TREASURY BONDS 6/30	30-YR. TREASURY BONDS 12/31	GDP-b 1st HALF 1997	GDP-b 2nd HALF 1997	CPI-c MAY	CPI-c NOV.	DOLLAR vs. YEN 6/30	DOLLAR vs. YEN 12/31
Maureen Allyn, Scudder Stevens & Clark	5.00	7.10	1.5	3.1	112	4.80	4.25	6.00	6.00	0.0	0.4	2.6	2.8	116	119
Wayne Angell, Bear Stearns	5.75	7.40	2.7	3.0	110	5.30	5.30	6.70	6.50	2.5	2.4	3.3	3.2	113	113
Richard B. Berner, Mellon Bank	5.85	7.10	2.8	2.9	110	5.60	6.00	7.20	6.50	3.1	1.7	2.7	3.0	112	105
David Berson, Fannie Mae	5.30	7.00	2.3	2.9	110	5.10	5.10	6.50	6.40	2.2	1.9	2.6	2.9	114	117
David Blitzer, S&P	5.65	7.55	2.7	3.0	110	5.25	5.45	6.65	6.75	2.6	1.8	3.1	2.8	115	110
Paul W. Boltz, T. Rowe Price	5.70	7.20	2.7	3.2	107	5.50	5.88	7.00	7.25	2.3	2.5	3.3	3.5	110	105
David Bostian, Herzog, Heine, Geduld	4.75	6.25	1.2	2.9	112	4.75	4.25	6.00	5.75	-0.9	-0.4	2.4	1.6	116	114
Phillip Braverman, DKB Securities	5.00	6.50	2.0	3.0	110	4.75	4.50	6.00	5.75	1.5	2.0	3.0	3.0	115	117
William Brown, J.P. Morgan	5.75	7.35	3.1	3.3	108	5.60	5.85	7.10	7.20	3.0	2.3	2.8	2.9	113	105
Rosanne Cahn, CS First Boston	5.06	6.25	2.3	3.1	110	5.75	5.75	7.25	6.25	3.0	1.6	2.8	2.7	110	115
James Coons, Huntington Natl Bank	5.10	6.75	1.7	3.2	112	4.77	4.54	6.69	6.64	1.6	2.0	3.0	2.9	117	121
Michael Cosgrove, The Econoclast	5.60	6.70	2.2	3.2	110	5.40	4.80	6.90	6.00	2.6	1.0	3.3	3.0	110	100
Robert Crow, Bechtel Group	N.A.	N.A.	N.A.	N.A.	N.A.	4.80	4.80	6.30	6.10	2.0	2.2	2.8	2.7	114	116
Dewey Daane, Vanderbilt Univ.	5.75	7.50	2.7	3.4	110	5.25	5.45	7.00	7.25	2.1	2.1	3.1	3.3	114	112
William Dudley, Goldman Sachs	6.30	7.40	3.1	3.4	116	5.60	6.20	7.20	7.40	3.2	2.3	3.0	3.4	106	105
Michael Englund, MMS Int'l.	5.60	6.75	2.7	3.2	110	5.40	5.00	6.50	6.00	2.9	2.1	3.3	3.4	110	108
Gail Fosler, Conference Board	5.50	7.65	3.2	3.5	98	5.70	5.80	7.60	7.00	3.0	1.6	3.3	3.9	100	96
Maury Harris, PaineWebber	5.25	6.50	1.75	2.75	110	5.00	5.00	6.50	6.10	2.4	1.7	2.9	2.9	115	115
Mitchell J. Held, Smith Barney	N.A.	N.A.	N.A.	N.A.	N.A.	5.35	5.10	6.50	6.25	2.3	2.6	2.9	2.8	115	115
Tracy Herrick, Jefferies	5.30	7.10	3.1	3.2	110	6.00	7.00	6.60	6.70	3.5	2.3	3.4	3.9	115	200
Stuart Hoffman, PNC Bank	5.60	6.95	2.3	3.1	113	5.10	4.80	6.60	6.40	2.0	1.0	3.1	2.8	115	108
William B. Hummer, Wayne Hummer	5.56	7.25	3.0	2.9	112	5.30	5.50	7.12	7.25	2.4	2.3	3.1	3.0	110	108
Edward Hyman, ISI Group	4.90	6.20	2.2	2.8	112	4.40	4.40	5.70	5.90	1.0	2.7	2.5	2.5	115	117
Saul Hymans, Univ. of Michigan	5.24	6.85	2.3	2.7	N.A.	5.12	5.14	6.47	6.46	2.5	2.5	2.1	1.9	110	108
Mieczyslaw Karczmar, Deutsche Bank AG	5.25	7.50	2.7	2.8	105	5.20	5.20	7.00	7.20	2.3	1.9	3.3	3.5	110	102
Kurt Karl, WEFA Group	4.90	6.20	1.9	2.6	108	4.90	4.80	6.40	6.30	1.8	2.2	2.5	2.5	114	113
Irwin L. Kellner, Chase Regional Bank	5.25	7.10	1.0	2.6	110	5.00	4.95	6.20	6.00	2.3	3.0	2.2	2.1	115	120
Daniel Laufenberg, Amer. Exp. Finl. Adv.	5.10	6.50	2.1	3.2	115	5.50	6.00	6.90	7.20	2.3	2.7	3.1	3.4	110	105
Carol A. Leisenring, CoreStates Finl.	5.00	6.80	2.5	2.7	105	4.90	4.60	6.20	5.90	2.0	2.5	2.7	2.6	118	121
Mickey D. Levy, NationsBank	5.20	6.90	2.4	2.6	110	5.00	4.80	6.30	6.20	2.0	2.0	2.8	2.5	114	114
David L. Littmann, Comerica	5.20	6.90	2.6	3.1	112	5.15	5.15	6.50	6.50	2.2	2.1	3.0	3.0	115	118
John Lonski, Moody's Investors Svc	5.70	7.00	2.8	3.3	110	5.60	5.30	7.00	6.60	2.5	2.2	3.5	3.2	112	110
Paul McCulley, UBS Securities	5.20	6.90	1.3	3.0	114	4.70	4.50	6.30	6.30	1.5	2.2	2.7	2.7	120	116
John McDevitt, 3M	5.00	6.20	2.0	2.6	105	5.10	5.00	6.30	6.20	2.1	2.0	2.7	2.8	112	109
Arnold Moskowitz, Moskowitz Capital	5.60	7.28	2.7	3.1	113	5.10	5.40	6.20	6.50	2.4	2.7	3.0	3.1	110	115
John Mueller, LBMC	4.50	6.25	-1.6	3.2	98	4.50	3.50	6.25	6.50	-1.3	0.3	3.0	2.8	110	105
David Munro, High Frequency Econ.	5.40	6.75	2.5	3.0	115	5.10	5.20	6.30	6.50	1.9	2.5	2.8	2.6	N.A.	N.A
Carl Palash, MCM Money Watch	5.50	7.00	2.5	3.0	108	6.00	5.75	7.25	6.50	3.0	2.0	3.5	3.5	120	115

continued

FOLLOWING THE FINANCIAL NEWS

Forecasting Interest Rates (cont.)

Nicholas S. Perna, Fleet Finl. Group	5.19	6.83	2.3	3.3	108	5.30	5.20	6.60	6.50	2.2	2.1	3.1	3.3	116	118
Elliott Platt, Donaldson Lufkin & Jenrette	5.10	6.00	1.5	2.8	110	4.45	3.94	5.75	5.50	1.3	0.9	2.8	2.3	108	108
Maria F. Ramirez, MF Ramirez	5.40	7.00	2.3	3.0	104	5.10	5.25	6.40	6.50	1.8	2.0	2.9	2.5	115	108
Donald Ratajczak, George State Univ.	5.63	7.11	2.8	3.0	108.5	5.05	5.12	6.55	6.30	2.6	2.1	3.2	3.3	113	110
David Rester, Nomura Securities Int'l.	4.95	6.67	1.6	2.9	112	5.00	4.75	6.25	6.10	2.1	2.4	2.7	2.7	115	115
Allan Reynolds, Hudson Institute	4.80	6.80	1.4	3.3	107	4.80	5.20	6.30	6.90	1.6	1.2	3.1	3.6	108	104
Richard D. Rippe, Prudential Securities	5.65	7.25	2.0	3.1	110	5.30	5.15	6.30	6.00	2.3	1.2	3.0	3.2	112	105
A. Gary Shilling, Shilling & Co.	5.00	6.50	2.8	3.0	115	6.50	6.00	7.50	7.00	2.0	1.5	2.5	2.5	119	125
Allen Sinai, Lehman Brothers	5.71	7.28	2.5	3.2	115.3	5.37	5.10	6.98	6.33	2.6	2.3	3.3	3.1	120	118
James F. Smith, Univ. Of N.C.	4.18	5.45	2.4	2.1	119	4.55	3.95	5.65	4.75	2.6	2.8	2.4	2.2	122	125
Susan M. Sterne, Economic Analysis Assoc.	4.50	6.00	1.0	2.5	N.A.	4.75	4.75	5.00	6.00	0.0	3.0	2.8	3.0	N.A.	N.A
Donald Straszhelm, Merrill Lynch	5.10	6.40	2.0	2.7	108	5.00	5.25	6.50	6.90	1.8	2.2	2.7	2.9	118	120
Thomas Synott 3rd, U.S. Trust	4.90	6.50	2.3	3.3	116	4.70	4.90	6.00	6.25	0.8	2.5	3.3	3.0	115	115
John Walter, Dow Corning	N.A.	N.A.	N.A.	N.A.	N.A.	4.60	4.20	5.50	5.00	1.3	2.6	2.8	2.4	114	112
John Williams, Bankers Trust	5.60	6.80	2.0	3.0	120	5.45	5.60	7.05	6.80	2.4	2.2	3.2	3.3	120	118
Raymond Worseck, A.G. Edwards	5.40	7.70	1.5	3.6	104	5.25	5.25	6.80	7.20	1.3	1.8	3.3	3.5	107	102
David Wyss, DRI/McGraw-Hill	5.50	7.10	2.2	3.0	110	5.20	5.00	6.70	6.70	2.1	2.4	2.8	2.9	110	105
Edward Yardeni, Deutsche Morgan Grenfell	5.00	6.25	1.5	2.2	112	4.75	4.75	5.50	5.00	1.7	2.5	3.0	2.2	120	128
Mark Zandi, Regional Finl. Associates	5.78	7.29	2.7	3.0	105.4	5.50	5.50	7.10	6.70	2.7	2.0	3.0	3.2	108	104
AVERAGE-d	**5.31**	**6.86**	**2.3**	**3.0**	**110**	**5.16**	**5.10**	**6.52**	**6.39**	**2.0**	**2.0**	**2.9**	**2.9**	**113**	**112**
CLOSING RATES as of 12/31/96	5.19	6.64	N.A.	3.2	116										

N.A. Not Available; a Treasury bill rates are on a bond-equivalent basis; b Real gross domestic product, annualized rate vs. prior six months; c Year-to-Year change in the consumer price index; d Averages for the June survey are for the analysts polled at that time.

Source: Wall Street Journal, January 2, 1997, p. C2.

econometric models, models whose equations are estimated with statistical procedures using past data. These models involve interlocking equations that, once input variables such as the behavior of government spending and monetary policy are plugged in, produce simultaneous forecasts of many variables including interest rates. The basic assumption of these forecasting models is that the estimated relationships between variables will continue to hold up in the future. Given this assumption, the forecaster makes predictions of the expected path of the input variables and then lets the model generate forecasts of variables such as interest rates.

Many of these econometric models are quite large, involving hundreds and sometimes over a thousand equations, and consequently require computers to produce their forecasts. In addition, many of these models rely heavily on the liquidity preference framework to produce their interest-rate forecasts and so are particularly concerned with developments in the market for money along lines we have discussed in the text. Prominent examples of these large-scale econometric models used by the private sector include those developed by Wharton Econometric Forecasting Associates, Chase Econometric Associates, and Data Resources, Inc. To generate its interest-rate forecasts, the Board of Governors of the Federal Reserve System makes use of its own large-scale econometric model, although it makes use of judgmental forecasts as well.

Managers of financial institutions rely on these forecasts to make decisions about which assets they should hold. A manager who believes that the forecast that long-term interest rates will fall in the future is reliable would seek to purchase long-term bonds for the asset account because, as we have seen in Chapter 3, the drop in interest rates will produce large capital gains.

Conversely, if forecasts say that interest rates are likely to rise in the future, the manager will prefer to hold short-term bonds or loans in the portfolio in order to avoid potential capital losses on long-term securities.

Forecasts of interest rates also help managers decide whether to borrow long-term or short-term. If interest rates are forecast to rise in the future, the financial institution manager will want to lock in the low interest rates by borrowing long-term; if the forecasts say that interest rates will fall, the manager will seek to borrow short-term in order to take advantage of low interest-rate costs in the future.

Clearly, good forecasts of future interest rates are extremely valuable to the financial institution manager, who, not surprisingly, would be willing to pay a lot for accurate forecasts. Unfortunately, interest-rate forecasting is a perilous business, and even the top forecasters, to their embarrassment, are frequently far off in their forecasts.

SUMMARY

1. The supply and demand analysis for bonds, known as the loanable funds framework, provides one theory of how interest rates are determined. It predicts that interest rates will change when there is a change in demand because of changes in income (or wealth), expected returns, risk, or liquidity, or when there is a change in supply because of changes in the attractiveness of investment opportunities, the real cost of borrowing, or government activities.

2. An alternative theory of how interest rates are determined is provided by the liquidity preference framework, which analyzes the supply of and demand for money. It shows that interest rates will change when there is a change in the demand for money because of changes in income or the price level or when there is a change in the supply of money.

3. There are four possible effects of an increase in the money supply on interest rates: the liquidity effect, the income effect, the price-level effect, and the expected-inflation effect. The liquidity effect indicates that a rise in money supply growth will lead to a decline in interest rates; the other effects work in the opposite direction. The evidence seems to indicate that the income, price-level, and expected-inflation effects dominate the liquidity effect such that an increase in money supply growth leads to higher rather than lower interest rates.

KEY TERMS

asset market approach, p. 102
demand curve, p. 96
econometric model, p. 126
excess demand, p. 99
excess supply, p. 99

Fisher effect, p. 109
liquidity preference framework,
 p. 114
loanable funds, p. 101

loanable funds framework,
 p. 101
market equilibrium, p. 99
opportunity cost, p. 115
supply curve, p. 98

QUESTIONS AND PROBLEMS

Answer each question by drawing the appropriate supply and demand diagrams.

*1. An important way in which the Federal Reserve decreases the money supply is by selling bonds to the public. Using the loanable funds framework, show what effect this action has on interest rates.

Is your answer consistent with what you would expect to find with the liquidity preference framework?

2. Using both the liquidity preference and loanable funds frameworks, show why interest rates are procyclical (rising when the economy is expanding and falling during recessions).

*3. Why should a rise in the price level (but not in expected inflation) cause interest rates to rise when the nominal money supply is fixed?

4. Find the "Credit Markets" column in the *Wall Street Journal*. Underline the statements in the column that explain bond price movements, and draw the appropriate supply and demand diagrams that support these statements.

5. What effect will a sudden increase in the volatility of gold prices have on interest rates?

*6. How might a sudden increase in people's expectations of future real estate prices affect interest rates?

7. Explain what effect a large federal deficit might have on interest rates.

*8. Using both the loanable funds and liquidity preference frameworks, show what the effect is on interest rates when the riskiness of bonds rises. Are the results the same in the two frameworks?

9. If the price level falls next year, remaining fixed thereafter, and the money supply is fixed, what is likely to happen to interest rates over the next two years? (Hint: Take account of both the price-level effect and the expected-inflation effect.)

*10. Will there be an effect on interest rates if brokerage commissions on stocks fall? Explain your answer.

Predicting the Future

11. The president of the United States announces in a press conference that he will fight the higher inflation rate with a new anti-inflation program. Predict what will happen to interest rates if the public believes him.

*12. The chairman of the Fed announces that interest rates will rise sharply next year, and the market believes him. What will happen to today's interest rate on AT&T bonds, such as the $8\frac{1}{8}$s of 2022?

13. Predict what will happen to interest rates if the public suddenly expects a large increase in stock prices.

14. Predict what will happen to interest rates if prices in the bond market become more volatile.

*15. If the next chair of the Federal Reserve Board has a reputation for advocating an even slower rate of money growth than the current chair, what will happen to interest rates? Discuss the possible resulting situations.

■ **CASE STUDY**
■
■ **The Behavior of Interest Rates**

CONCEPTS IN THIS CASE

effect of interest-rate changes,
Fisher effect
bond values
return equation
market equilibrium
loanable funds framework
asset market approach
liquidity preference framework
demand and supply curves

Your company is interested in analyzing the behavior of interest rates and the models used to predict interest rates in the future. As an initial project in this area, you have been assigned the task of creating a presentation that will show the top management team assigned this project the basics of what affects interest rates and how

equilibrium prices change over time. The better your presentation to this group, the more likely you are to become a voting member of the team. To begin your work, you have decided to identify a series of questions that you think this team will ask, including tables and graphs that will satisfy their concerns about the final presentation to the CFO. You decide to start by answering the following questions, assuming that the face value of a discount bond is $1,000 and the time to maturity is one year.

1. What is the expected return for this bond if the market price is
a. $800?
b. $850?
c. $900?
d. $950?
e. $1000?

2. If the market-clearing price (market equilibrium) of this bond has a return of 20% what is the market price where the quantity demanded equals the quantity supplied? (Hint: Use the same expected return equation, solve for P_d)

3. Which factors would cause the demand curve for bonds to shift?

4. Which factors would cause the supply curve for bonds to shift?

5. Explain what the Fisher effect is and how it would be reflected in rising interest rates.

6. Explain the meaning and differences between the loanable funds framework and the liquidity preference framework in estimating the equilibrium interest rate. (Include the effects of changes in income, price levels, and expected inflation.)

7. Predict the supply and demand changes for bonds and money that usually occur with the following events:

Bonds:
a. business cycle expansion with growing wealth
b. expected rise in interest rates
c. increase in expected rate of inflation
d. increased risk for bonds
e. increased liquidity for bonds
f. higher government deficits

Money:
g. increase in level of income
h. rise in the price level
i. income rising during an expansion
j. price level increases

APPLYING THE ASSET MARKET APPROACH TO A COMMODITY MARKET: THE CASE OF GOLD

Both models of interest-rate determination in Chapter 5 make use of an asset market approach in which supply and demand are always considered in terms of stocks of assets (amounts at a given point in time). The asset market approach is useful in understanding not only why interest rates fluctuate but also how any asset's price is determined.

One asset that has fascinated people for thousands of years is gold. It has been a driving force in history: The conquest of the Americas by Europeans was to a great extent the result of the quest for gold, to cite just one example. The fascination with gold continues to the present day, and developments in the gold market are followed closely by financial analysts and the media. This appendix shows how the asset market approach can be applied to understanding the behavior of commodity markets, in particular the gold market. (The analysis in this appendix can also be used to understand behavior in many other asset markets.)

■ SUPPLY AND DEMAND IN THE GOLD MARKET

The analysis of a commodity market, such as the gold market, proceeds in a similar fashion to the analysis of the bond market by examining the supply of and demand for the commodity. We again use the theory of portfolio choice to obtain a demand curve for gold, which shows the relationship between the quantity of gold demanded and the price when all other economic variables are held constant.

Demand Curve

To derive the relationship between the quantity of gold demanded and its price, we again recognize that an important determinant of the quantity demanded is its expected return:

$$RET^e = \frac{P^e_{t+1} - P_t}{P_t} = g^e$$

where

$$RET^e = \text{expected return}$$
$$P_t = \text{price of gold today}$$
$$P^e_{t+1} = \text{expected price of gold next year}$$
$$g^e = \text{expected capital gain}$$

In deriving the demand curve, we hold all other variables constant, particularly the expected price of gold next year P^e_{t+1}. With a given value of the expected price of gold next year P^e_{t+1}, a lower price of gold today P_t means that there will be a greater appreciation in the price of gold over the coming year. The result is that a lower price of gold today implies a higher expected capital gain over the coming year and hence a higher expected return: $RET^e = (P^e_{t+1} - P_t)/P_t$. Thus because the price of gold today (which for simplicity we will denote as P) is lower, the expected return on gold is higher, and the quantity demanded is higher. Consequently, the demand curve G^d_1 slopes downward in Figure A1.

Supply Curve

To derive the supply curve, expressing the relationship between the quantity supplied and the price, we again assume that all other economic variables are held constant. A higher price of gold will induce producers to mine for extra gold and also possibly induce governments to sell some of their gold stocks to the public, thus increasing the quantity supplied. Hence the supply curve G^s_1 in Figure A1 slopes upward. Notice that the supply curve in the figure is drawn to be very steep. The reason for this is that the actual amount of gold produced in any year is only a tiny fraction of the outstanding stock of gold that has been accumulated over hundreds of years. Thus the increase in the quantity of the gold supplied in response to a higher price is only a small fraction of the stock of gold, resulting in a very steep supply curve.

Market Equilibrium

Market equilibrium in the gold market occurs when the quantity of gold demanded equals the quantity of gold supplied:

$$G^d = G^s$$

With the initial demand and supply curves of G^d_1 and G^s_1, equilibrium occurs at point 1, where these curves intersect at a gold price of P_1. At a price above this

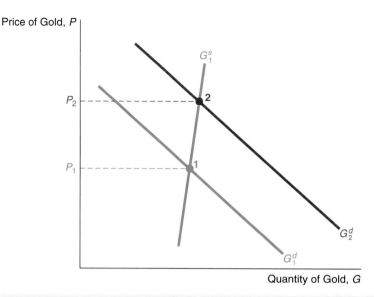

■FIGURE A1 A Change in the Equilibrium Price of Gold

When the demand curve shifts rightward from G_1^d to G_2^d, say, because expected inflation rises, equilibrium moves from point 1 to point 2, and the equilibrium price of gold rises from P_1 to P_2.

equilibrium, the amount of gold supplied exceeds the amount demanded, and this condition of excess supply leads to a decline in the gold price until it reaches P_1, the equilibrium price. Similarly, if the price is below P_1, there is excess demand for gold, which drives the price upward until it settles at the equilibrium price P_1.

■ CHANGES IN THE EQUILIBRIUM PRICE OF GOLD

Changes in the equilibrium price of gold occur when there is a shift in either the supply curve or the demand curve, that is, when the quantity demanded or supplied changes at each given price of gold in response to a change in some factor other than today's gold price.

Shift in the Demand Curve for Gold

The theory of portfolio choice provides the factors that shift the demand curve for gold: wealth, expected return on gold relative to alternative assets, riskiness of gold relative to alternative assets, and liquidity of gold relative to alternative assets. The analysis of how changes in each of these factors shift the demand curve for gold is the same as that found in the chapter.

When wealth rises, at a given price of gold, the quantity demanded increases, and the demand curve shifts to the right, as in Figure A1. When the expected return on gold relative to other assets rises—either because speculators think that the future price of gold will be higher or because the expected return on other assets declines—gold becomes more desirable; the quantity demanded therefore increases at any given price of gold, and the demand curve shifts to the right, as in Figure A1. When the relative riskiness of gold declines, either because gold prices become less volatile or because returns on other assets become more volatile, gold becomes more desirable, the quantity demanded at every given price rises, and the demand curve again shifts to the right. When the gold market becomes relatively more liquid and gold therefore becomes more desirable, the quantity demanded at any given price rises, and the demand curve also shifts to the right, as in Figure A1.

Shifts in the Supply Curve for Gold

The supply curve for gold shifts when there are changes in technology that make gold mining more efficient or when governments at any given price of gold decide to increase sales of their holdings of gold. In these cases, the quantity of gold supplied at any given price increases, and the supply curve shifts to the right.

APPLICATION **CHANGES IN THE EQUILIBRIUM PRICE OF GOLD DUE TO A RISE IN EXPECTED INFLATION**

To illustrate how changes in the equilibrium price of gold occur when supply and demand curves shift, let's look at what happens when there is a change in expected inflation.

Suppose that expected inflation is 5% and the initial supply and demand curves are at G_1^s and G_1^d so that the equilibrium price of gold is at P_1 in Figure A1. If expected inflation now rises to 10%, prices of goods and commodities next year will be expected to be higher than they otherwise would have been, and the price of gold next year P_{t+1}^e will also be expected to be higher than otherwise. Now at any given price of gold today, gold is expected to have a greater rate of appreciation over the coming year and hence a higher expected capital gain and return. The greater expected return means that the quantity of gold demanded increases at any given price, thus shifting the demand curve from G_1^d to G_2^d. Equilibrium therefore moves from point 1 to point 2, and the price of gold rises from P_1 to P_2.

By using a supply and demand diagram like that in Figure A1, you should be able to see that if the expected rate of inflation falls, the price of gold today will also fall. We thus reach the following conclusion: ***The price of gold should be positively related to the expected inflation rate.***

Because the gold market responds immediately to any changes in expected inflation, it is considered a good barometer of the trend of inflation in the future. Indeed, Alan Greenspan, the chairman of the Board of Governors of the Federal Reserve System, has advocated using the price of gold as an indicator of inflationary pressures in the economy. Not surprisingly, then, the gold market is followed closely by financial analysts and monetary policymakers.

■ **STUDY GUIDE** To give yourself practice with supply and demand analysis in the gold market, see if you can analyze what happens to the price of gold for the following situations, remembering that all other things are held constant: (1) Interest rates rise, (2) the gold market becomes more liquid, (3) the volatility of gold prices increases, (4) the stock market is expected to turn bullish in the near future, (5) investors suddenly become fearful that there will be a collapse in real estate prices, and (6) Russia sells a lot of gold in the open market to raise hard currency to feed its people.

The analysis in this appendix can also be applied to many other asset markets. See if you can apply the analysis here to understand fluctuations in the prices of classic comic books, old baseball cards, oil, Rembrandt paintings, or other commodities mentioned in the following application.

| APPLICATION | THE "COMMODITIES" COLUMN |

READING THE *WALL STREET JOURNAL*

The supply and demand analysis in this appendix can help you evaluate events in commodity markets that are reported in the media. Every day, the *Wall Street Journal* reports on developments in the commodities markets on the previous business day in its "Commodities" column, an example of which is found in the "Following the Financial News" box.

The column focuses on the fall in crude oil prices because of rumors that the U.S. government asked Saudi Arabia to increase its oil production. Our supply and demand analysis explains why this development would cause the price of oil to fall.

Increased oil production in the future would lead to a shift in the supply curve to the right, producing a future fall in oil prices. The lower future oil prices imply that P_{t+1}^e has fallen, so the expected return on holding oil has declined. Thus the quantity demanded of oil today also declines, shifting the demand curve today to the left and causing oil prices to decline today. The decline in corn and soybeans prices because of the prospect of a good fall harvest can be explained with a similar argument.

The "Commodities" Column

The "Commodities" column appears daily in the *Wall Street Journal;* an example is presented here. It is typ-ically found in the third section, "Money and Investing."

COMMODITIES

Crude Oil Prices Plunge Amid Rumors U.S. Urged Saudis to Boost Production

Dow Jones News Services

Crude oil futures plunged on reports that the Clinton administration has asked Saudi Arabia to boost its oil output in case U.S.-Iraqi tensions cause disruptions in oil deliveries from the Persian Gulf region.

Saudi Arabian officials denied the report after trading had ended, and Clinton administration officials weren't immediately available to comment.

But that didn't change the reaction on the New York Mercantile Exchange, where crude oil for October delivery fell $1.32 to $23.19 a barrel; October heating oil fell 2.65 cents to 65.29 cents a gallon and October unleaded gasoline fell 1.73 cents to 62.87 cents a gallon.

Crude and crude products faced heavy selling pressure throughout the day. The concern among traders is that Saudi Arabia will increase its production but that the flow of oil from Iraq won't be affected.

The result, traders fear, will be a glut, albeit a temporary one, of oil on the world market.

"The market is nervous enough about Iraq right now to react to any rumor that could be legitimate," said Tim Evans, an analyst at Pegasus Econometric Group. Saudi Arabia is the largest exporter of the Organization of Petroleum Exporting Countries. While many nations in the oil cartel exceed their quotas, Saudi Arabia has the best reputation for staying below its output ceiling despite ample capacity to export more.

Iraqi leader Saddam Hussein late last week said his military will stop firing on U.S. warplanes in American-enforced no-fly zones in the north and south of his country. Mr. Clinton said yesterday that the deployment of at

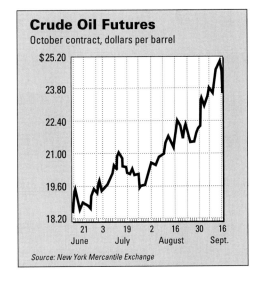

Crude Oil Futures
October contract, dollars per barrel

Source: New York Mercantile Exchange

least 3,000 troops to Kuwait doesn't indicate the U.S. is seeking a military confrontation with Iraq.

In other commodity markets:

GRAINS: Corn and soybean futures prices fell on the Chicago Board of Trade on forecasts calling for moderate temperatures through the end of the month. Moderate temperatures—as distinct from those that are below freezing—will help ensure a good fall harvest.

CHAPTER 6

THE RISK AND TERM STRUCTURE OF INTEREST RATES

■ **PREVIEW** In our supply and demand analysis of interest-rate behavior in Chapter 5, we examined the determination of just one interest rate. Yet we saw earlier that there are enormous numbers of bonds on which the interest rates can and do differ. In this chapter we complete the interest-rate picture by examining the relationship of the various interest rates to one another. Understanding why they differ from bond to bond can help businesses, banks, insurance companies, and private investors decide which bonds to purchase as investments or which ones to sell.

We first look at why bonds with the same term to maturity have different interest rates. The relationship among these interest rates is called the **risk structure of interest rates,** although risk, liquidity, and income tax rules all play a role in determining the risk structure. A bond's term to maturity also affects its interest rate, and the relationship among interest rates on bonds with different terms to maturity is called the **term structure of interest rates.** In this chapter we examine the sources and causes of fluctuations in interest rates relative to one another and look at a number of theories that explain these fluctuations.

■ RISK STRUCTURE OF INTEREST RATES

Figure 1 shows the yields to maturity for several categories of long-term bonds from 1919 to 1996. It shows us two important features of interest-rate behavior for bonds of the same maturity: Interest rates on different categories of bonds differ from one another in any given year, and the spread (or difference) between the interest rates varies over time. The interest rates on municipal bonds, for example, are above those on U.S. government (Treasury) bonds in the late 1930s but

■FIGURE 1 Long-Term Bond Yields, 1919–1996

Sources: Board of Governors of the Federal Reserve System, *Banking and Monetary Statistics, 1941–1970;* Federal Reserve *Bulletin.*

lower thereafter. In addition, the spread between the interest rates on Baa corporate bonds (riskier than Aaa corporate bonds) and U.S. government bonds is very large during the Great Depression years 1930–1933, is smaller during the 1940s–1960s, and then widens again in the 1970s–1990s. What factors are responsible for these phenomena?

Default Risk

One attribute of a bond that influences its interest rate is its **default risk,** the chance that the issuer of the bond will default, that is, be unable to make interest payments or pay off the face value when the bond matures. A corporation suffering big losses, such as Chrysler Corporation did in the 1970s, might be more likely to suspend interest payments on its bonds.[1] The default risk on its bonds would therefore be quite high. By contrast, U.S. Treasury bonds have usually been considered to have no default risk because the federal government can always increase taxes or even print money to pay off its obligations. Bonds like these with no default risk are called **default-free bonds.** (However, during the budget negotiations in Congress in 1995 and 1996, the Republicans threatened to let Treasury bonds default, and this had an impact on the bond market, as the application following this section indicates.) The spread between the interest rates on bonds with default risk and default-free bonds, called the **risk premium,** indicates how

---

[1]Chrysler did not default on its loans in this period, but it would have were it not for a government bailout plan intended to preserve jobs that in effect provided Chrysler with funds that were used to pay off creditors.

much additional interest people must earn in order to be willing to hold a risky bond. Our supply and demand analysis of the bond market in Chapter 5 can be used to explain why a bond with default risk always has a positive risk premium and why the higher the default risk is, the larger the risk premium will be.

■ **STUDY GUIDE** Two exercises will help you gain a better understanding of the risk structure:

1. Put yourself in the shoes of an investor—see how your purchase decision would be affected by changes in risk and liquidity.
2. Practice drawing the appropriate shifts in the supply and demand curves when risk and liquidity change. For example, see if you can draw the appropriate shifts in the supply and demand curves when, in contrast to the examples in the text, a corporate bond has a decline in default risk or an improvement in its liquidity.

To examine the effect of default risk on interest rates, let us look at the supply and demand diagrams for the default-free (U.S. Treasury) and corporate long-term bond markets in Figure 2. To make the diagrams somewhat easier to read, let's assume that initially there is no possibility of default on the corporate bonds, so they are default-free like U.S. Treasury bonds. In this case, these two bonds have the same attributes (identical risk and maturity); their equilibrium prices

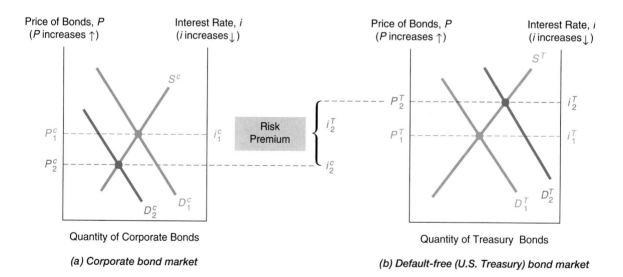

(a) Corporate bond market   **(b) Default-free (U.S. Treasury) bond market**

■**FIGURE 2** Response to an Increase in Default Risk on Corporate Bonds

An increase in default risk on corporate bonds shifts the demand curve from D_1^c to D_2^c. Simultaneously, it shifts the demand curve for Treasury bonds from D_1^T to D_2^T. The equilibrium price for corporate bonds (left axis) falls from P_1^c to P_2^c, and the equilibrium interest rate on corporate bonds (right axis) rises from i_1^c to i_2^c. In the Treasury market, the equilibrium bond price rises from P_1^T to P_2^T, and the equilibrium interest rate falls from i_1^T to i_2^T. The brace indicates the difference between i_2^c and i_2^T, the risk premium on corporate bonds. (*Note: P* and *i* increase in opposite directions. *P* on the left vertical axis increases as we go up the axis, while *i* on the right vertical axis increases as we go down the axis.)

and interest rates will initially be equal ($P^c_1 = P^T_1$ and $i^c_1 = i^T_1$), and the risk premium on corporate bonds ($i^c_1 - i^T_1$) will be zero.

If the possibility of a default increases because a corporation begins to suffer large losses, the default risk on corporate bonds will increase, and the expected return on these bonds will decrease. In addition, the corporate bond's return will be more uncertain as well. The theory of portfolio choice predicts that because the expected return on the corporate bond falls relative to the expected return on the default-free Treasury bond while its relative riskiness rises, the corporate bond is less desirable (holding everything else equal), and demand for it will fall. The demand curve for corporate bonds in panel (a) of Figure 2 then shifts to the left from D^c_1 to D^c_2.

At the same time, the expected return on default-free Treasury bonds increases relative to the expected return on corporate bonds while their relative riskiness declines. The Treasury bonds thus become more desirable, and demand rises, as shown in panel (b) by the rightward shift in the demand curve for these bonds from D^T_1 to D^T_2.

As we can see in Figure 2, the equilibrium price for corporate bonds (left axis) falls from P^c_1 to P^c_2, and since the bond price is negatively related to the interest rate, the equilibrium interest rate on corporate bonds (right axis) rises from i^c_1 to i^c_2. At the same time, however, the equilibrium price for the Treasury bonds rises from P^T_1 to P^T_2, and the equilibrium interest rate falls from i^T_1 to i^T_2. The spread between the interest rates on corporate and default-free bonds—that is, the risk premium on corporate bonds—has risen from zero to $i^c_2 - i^T_2$. We can now conclude that ***a bond with default risk will always have a positive risk premium, and an increase in its default risk will raise the risk premium.***

Because default risk is so important to the size of the risk premium, purchasers of bonds need to know whether a corporation is likely to default on its bonds. Two major investment advisory firms, Moody's Investors Service and Standard and Poor's Corporation, provide default risk information by rating the quality of corporate and municipal bonds in terms of the probability of default. The ratings and their description are contained in Table 1. Bonds with relatively low risk of default are called *investment-grade* securities and have a rating of Baa (or BBB) and above. Bonds with ratings below Baa (or BBB) have higher default risk and have been aptly dubbed **junk bonds.**

Next let's look back at Figure 1 and see if we can explain the relationship between interest rates on corporate and U.S. Treasury bonds. Corporate bonds always have higher interest rates than U.S. Treasury bonds because they always have some risk of default, whereas U.S. Treasury bonds do not. Because Baa-rated corporate bonds have a greater default risk than the higher-rated Aaa bonds, their risk premium is greater, and the Baa rate therefore always exceeds the Aaa rate.

We can use the same analysis to explain the huge jump in the risk premium on Baa corporate bond rates during the Great Depression years 1930–1933 and the rise in the risk premium in the 1970s, 1980s, and 1990s (see Figure 1). The depression period saw a very high rate of business failures and defaults. As we would expect, these factors led to a substantial increase in default risk for bonds issued by vulnerable corporations, and the risk premium for Baa bonds reached unprecedentedly high levels. The 1970s, 1980s, and 1990s again saw higher levels

■ TABLE 1 Bond Ratings by Moody's and Standard and Poor's

Rating			
Moody's	Standard and Poor's	Description	Examples of Corporations with Bonds Outstanding in 1997
Aaa	AAA	Highest quality (lowest default risk)	General Electric, Johnson and Johnson, Wisconsin Bell
Aa	AA	High quality	McDonalds, Mobil Oil, Wal-Mart
A	A	Upper medium grade	Anheuser-Busch, Ford Motor, Xerox
Baa	BBB	Medium grade	Chrysler, General Motors, Wendy's
Ba	BB	Lower medium grade	McDonnell Douglas, RJR-Nabisco, Time-Warner
B	B	Speculative	Marriott, Revlon, Turner Broadcasting
Caa	CCC, CC	Poor (high default risk)	
Ca	C	Highly speculative	
C	D	Lowest grade	

of business failures and defaults, although they were still well below Great Depression levels. Again, as expected, default risks and risk premiums for corporate bonds rose, widening the spread between interest rates on corporate bonds and Treasury bonds.

APPLICATION **THE STOCK MARKET CRASH OF 1987 AND THE JUNK BOND–TREASURY SPREAD**

The stock market crash on "Black Monday," October 19, 1987, when the Dow Jones Industrial Average fell more than 500 points, had a major impact not only on prices of stocks but on the bond market as well. Let's see how our supply and demand analysis explains the behavior of the spread between interest rates on junk bonds and Treasury securities in the aftermath of the crash using Figure 2.

As a consequence of the Black Monday crash, many investors began to doubt the financial health of corporations with lower credit ratings that had issued junk bonds. The increase in default risk for junk bonds made them less desirable at any given interest rate, decreased the quantity demanded, and shifted the demand curve for junk bonds to the left. As shown in panel (a) of Figure 2, the interest rate on junk bonds should have risen, which is indeed what happened: Interest rates on junk bonds shot up by about one percentage point. But the increase in the perceived default risk for junk bonds after the crash made default-free U.S. Treasury bonds relatively more attractive and shifted the demand curve for these securities to the right—an outcome described by some analysts as a "flight to quality." Just as our analysis predicts in Figure 2, interest rates on Treasury securities fell by about one percentage point. The overall outcome was that the spread between interest rates on junk bonds and government bonds rose by two percentage points, from 4% before the crash to 6% immediately after.

APPLICATION   **WHAT IF TREASURY SECURITIES WERE NO LONGER DEFAULT-FREE?**

Throughout our history, the U.S. Treasury has never defaulted on its securities. However, in late 1995 and early 1996, the budget battle between congressional Republicans and President Clinton almost led to an unprecedented default. In an attempt to get their way in the budget negotiations, the Republicans threatened to refuse to raise the federal government debt ceiling. If the threat had been carried out, the Treasury would have missed interest payments on its debt because it would not have been able to issue new debt to cover its interest outlays and other expenditures when the debt ceiling was reached. Default was averted when a budget compromise was finally reached and the debt ceiling was raised after several shutdowns of the federal government in which "nonessential" government workers were sent home. What would have been the impact of a Treasury default?

Our analysis in Figure 2 provides the answer. Default on Treasury bonds would mean that they would no longer be considered default-free and would now have the attributes of corporate bonds in panel (a) of Figure 2. The increase in default risk would decrease the quantity of Treasury bonds demanded at any given interest rate and would thus cause their demand curve to shift to the left. As we see in panel (a), this would result in a fall in their bond price and a rise in their interest rate. Indeed, just as our analysis predicts, when budget talks stalled on December 18, 1995, and fear of a possible government default rose, the Treasury bond market slumped: Bond prices fell, and the interest rate on 30-year Treasury bonds rose by 11/100s of a percentage point, the largest one-day rise in more than six months.

Liquidity

Another attribute of a bond that influences its interest rate is its liquidity. As we learned in Chapter 4, a liquid asset is one that can be quickly and cheaply converted into cash if the need arises. The more liquid an asset is, the more desirable it is (holding everything else constant). U.S. Treasury bonds are the most liquid of all long-term bonds because they are so widely traded that they are the easiest to sell quickly and the cost of selling them is low. Corporate bonds are not as liquid because fewer bonds for any one corporation are traded; thus it can be costly to sell these bonds in an emergency because it may be hard to find buyers quickly.

How does the reduced liquidity of the corporate bonds affect their interest rates relative to the interest rate on Treasury bonds? We can use supply and demand analysis with the same figure that was used to analyze the effect of default risk, Figure 2, to show that the lower liquidity of corporate bonds relative to Treasury bonds increases the spread between the interest rates on these two bonds. Let us start the analysis by assuming that initially corporate and Treasury bonds are equally liquid and all their other attributes are the same. As shown in

Figure 2, their equilibrium prices and interest rates will initially be equal: $P^c_1 = P^T_1$ and $i^c_1 = i^T_1$. If the corporate bond becomes less liquid than the Treasury bond because it is less widely traded, then as the theory of portfolio choice indicates, its demand will fall, shifting its demand curve from D^c_1 to D^c_2 as in panel (a). The Treasury bond now becomes relatively more liquid in comparison with the corporate bond, so its demand curve shifts rightward from D^T_1 to D^T_2 as in panel (b). The shifts in the curves in Figure 2 show that the price of the less liquid corporate bond falls and its interest rate rises, while the price of the more liquid Treasury bond rises and its interest rate falls.

The result is that the spread between the interest rates on the two bond types has risen. Therefore, the differences between interest rates on corporate bonds and Treasury bonds (that is, the risk premiums) reflect not only the corporate bond's default risk but its liquidity too. This is why a risk premium is sometimes called a *liquidity premium.* Most accurately, it should be called a "risk and liquidity premium," but convention dictates that it be called a *risk premium.*

Income Tax Considerations

Returning to Figure 1, we are still left with one puzzle—the behavior of municipal bond rates. Municipal bonds are certainly not default-free: State and local governments have defaulted on the municipal bonds they have issued in the past, particularly during the Great Depression and even more recently in the case of Orange County, California, in 1994 (more on this in Chapter 15). Also, municipal bonds are not as liquid as U.S. Treasury bonds.

Why is it, then, that these bonds have had lower interest rates than U.S. Treasury bonds for at least 40 years, as indicated in Figure 1? The explanation lies in the fact that interest payments on municipal bonds are exempt from federal income taxes, a factor that has the same effect on the demand for municipal bonds as an increase in their expected return.

Let us imagine that you have a high enough income to put you in the 40% income tax bracket, where for every extra dollar of income you have to pay 40 cents to the government. If you own a $1000-face-value U.S. Treasury bond that sells for $1000 and has a coupon payment of $100, you get to keep only $60 of the payment after taxes. Although the bond has a 10% interest rate, you actually earn only 6% after taxes.

Suppose, however, that you put your savings into a $1000-face-value municipal bond that sells for $1000 and pays only $80 in coupon payments. Its interest rate is only 8%, but because it is a tax-exempt security, you pay no taxes on the $80 coupon payment, so you earn 8% after taxes. Clearly, you earn more on the municipal bond after taxes, so you are willing to hold the riskier and less liquid municipal bond even though it has a lower interest rate than the U.S. Treasury bond. (This was not true before World War II, when the tax-exempt status of municipal bonds did not convey much of an advantage because income tax rates were extremely low.)

Another way of understanding why municipal bonds have lower interest rates than Treasury bonds is to use the supply and demand analysis displayed in Figure

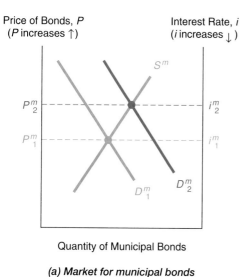

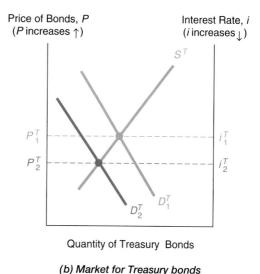

(a) Market for municipal bonds   *(b) Market for Treasury bonds*

■FIGURE 3 Interest Rates on Municipal and Treasury Bonds

When the municipal bond is given tax-free status, demand for the municipal bond shifts rightward from D_1^m to D_2^m and demand for the Treasury bond shifts leftward from D_1^T to D_2^T. The equilibrium price of the municipal bond (left axis) rises from P_1^m to P_2^m, so its interest rate (right axis) falls from i_1^m to i_2^m while the equilibrium price of the Treasury bond falls from P_1^T to P_2^T and its interest rate rises from i_1^T to i_2^T. The result is that municipal bonds end up with lower interest rates than those on Treasury bonds. (*Note: P* and *i* increase in opposite directions. *P* on the left vertical axis increases as we go up the axis, while *i* on the right vertical axis increases as we go down the axis.)

3. To begin with, we assume that municipal and Treasury bonds have identical attributes and so have the same bond prices and interest rates as drawn in the figure: $P_1^m = P_1^T$ and $i_1^m = i_1^T$. Once the municipal bonds are given a tax advantage that raises their after-tax expected return relative to Treasury bonds and makes them more desirable, demand for them rises, and their demand curve shifts to the right from D_1^m to D_2^m. The result is that their equilibrium bond price rises from P_1^m to P_2^m, and their equilibrium interest rate falls from i_1^m to i_2^m. By contrast, Treasury bonds have now become less desirable relative to municipal bonds, demand for Treasury bonds decreases, and D_1^T shifts to D_2^T. The Treasury bond price falls from P_1^T to P_2^T, and the interest rate rises from i_1^T to i_2^T. The resulting lower interest rates for municipal bonds and higher interest rates for Treasury bonds explains why municipal bonds can have interest rates below those of Treasury bonds.[2]

Summary

The risk structure of interest rates (the relationship among interest rates on bonds with the same maturity) is explained by three factors: default risk,

---

[2]In contrast to corporate bonds, Treasury bonds are exempt from state and local income taxes. Using the analysis in the text, you should be able to show that this feature of Treasury bonds provides an additional reason why interest rates on corporate bonds are higher than those on Treasury bonds.

liquidity, and the income tax treatment of the bond's interest payments. As a bond's default risk increases, the risk premium on that bond (the spread between its interest rate and the interest rate on a default-free Treasury bond) rises. The greater liquidity of Treasury bonds also explains why their interest rates are lower than interest rates on less liquid bonds. If a bond has a favorable tax treatment, as do municipal bonds, whose interest payments are exempt from federal income taxes, its interest rate will be lower.

APPLICATION	**EFFECTS OF THE CLINTON TAX INCREASE ON BOND INTEREST RATES**

As part of the Clinton administration's 1993 deficit reduction plan, the top income tax bracket was raised from 31% to 40% and the corporate income tax rate was raised from 34% to 35%. What was the effect of this income tax increase on interest rates in the municipal bond market relative to those in the Treasury bond market?

The supply and demand analysis in Figure 3 provides the answer. An increased income tax rate for rich people and corporations means that the tax-free status of municipal bonds raises their after-tax expected return relative to that on Treasury bonds because the interest on Treasury bonds is now taxed at a higher rate. Because municipal bonds now become more desirable, their demand increases, shifting the demand curve to the right as in Figure 3, which raises their price and lowers their interest rate. Conversely, the higher income tax rate makes Treasury bonds less desirable; that shifts their demand curve to the left, lowers their price, and raises their interest rates, as in Figure 3.

Our analysis thus shows that the Clinton tax increase lowered the interest rates on municipal bonds relative to interest rates on Treasury bonds.

■ TERM STRUCTURE OF INTEREST RATES

We have seen how risk, liquidity, and tax considerations (collectively embedded in the risk structure) can influence interest rates. Another factor that influences the interest rate on a bond is its term to maturity: Bonds with identical risk, liquidity, and tax characteristics may have different interest rates because the time remaining to maturity is different. A plot of the yields on bonds with differing terms to maturity but the same risk, liquidity, and tax considerations is called a **yield curve,** and it describes the term structure of interest rates for particular types of bonds, such as government bonds. The "Following the Financial News" box shows several yield curves for Treasury securities that were published in the *Wall Street Journal.* Yield curves can be classified as upward-sloping, flat, and downward-sloping (the last sort is often referred to as an **inverted yield curve**). When yield curves slope upward, as in the "Following the Financial News" box, the long-term interest rates are above the short-term interest rates; when yield curves are flat, short- and long-term interest rates are the same; and when yield curves are inverted, long-term interest rates are below short-term interest rates. Yield curves can also have more complicated shapes in which they first slope up and

FOLLOWING THE FINANCIAL NEWS

Yield Curves

The *Wall Street Journal* publishes a daily plot of the yield curves for Treasury securities, an example of which is presented here. It is typically found next to the "Credit Markets" column.

The numbers on the vertical axis indicate the interest rate for the Treasury security, with the maturity given by the numbers on the horizontal axis. For example, the yield curve marked "Yesterday" indicates that the interest rate on the three-month Treasury bill yesterday was 5.20%, while the one-year bill had an interest rate of 5.55% and the ten-year bond had an interest rate of 6.60%. As you can see, the yield curves in the plot have the typical upward slope.

Source: Wall Street Journal, January 31, 1997, p. C17.

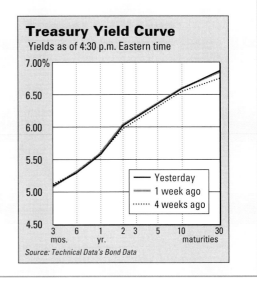

Treasury Yield Curve
Yields as of 4:30 p.m. Eastern time

— Yesterday
— 1 week ago
⋯⋯ 4 weeks ago

Source: Technical Data's Bond Data

then down, or vice versa. Why do we usually see upward slopes of the yield curve as in the "Following the Financial News" box but sometimes other shapes?

Besides explaining why yield curves take on different shapes at different times, a good theory of the term structure of interest rates must explain the following three important empirical facts.

1. As we see in Figure 4, interest rates on bonds of different maturities move together over time.
2. When short-term interest rates are low, yield curves are more likely to have an upward slope; when short-term interest rates are high, yield curves are more likely to slope downward and be inverted.
3. Yield curves almost always slope upward, as in the "Following the Financial News" box.

Three theories have been put forward to explain the term structure of interest rates, that is, the relationship among interest rates on bonds of different maturities reflected in yield curve patterns: (1) the expectations hypothesis, (2) the segmented markets theory, and (3) the preferred habitat theory (which is closely related to the liquidity premium theory). The expectations hypothesis does a good job of explaining the first two facts on our list but not the third. The segmented markets theory can explain fact 3 but not the other two facts, which are well explained by the expectations hypothesis. Because each theory explains facts that the other cannot, a natural way to seek a better understanding of the term structure is to combine features of both theories, which leads us to the preferred habitat theory and the closely related liquidity premium theory, which can explain all three facts.

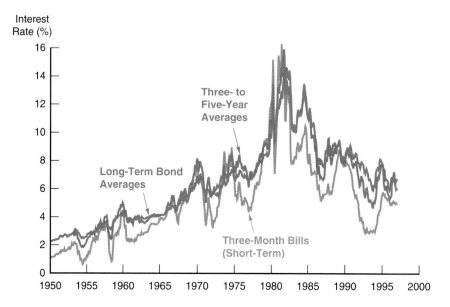

■**FIGURE 4** Movements over Time of Interest Rates on U.S. Government Bonds with
                 Different Maturities

Sources: Board of Governors of the Federal Reserve System, *Banking and Monetary Statistics, 1941–1970;* Federal Reserve
Bulletin; Citibase databank.

If the preferred habitat and liquidity premium theories do a better job of explaining the facts and are hence the most widely accepted theories, why do we spend time discussing the other two theories? There are two reasons. First, the ideas in these two theories provide the groundwork for the preferred habitat and liquidity premium theories. Second, it is important to see how financial economists modify theories to improve them when they find that the predicted results are inconsistent with the empirical evidence.

Expectations Hypothesis

The **expectations hypothesis** of the term structure states the following commonsense proposition: The interest rate on a long-term bond will equal an average of short-term interest rates that people expect to occur over the life of the long-term bond. For example, if people expect that short-term interest rates will be 10% on average over the coming five years, the expectations hypothesis predicts that the interest rate on bonds with five years to maturity will be 10% too. If short-term interest rates were expected to rise even higher after this five-year period so that the average short-term interest rate over the coming 20 years is 11%, then the interest rate on 20-year bonds would equal 11% and would be higher than the interest rate on five-year bonds. We can see that the explanation provided by the expectations hypothesis for why interest rates on bonds of different maturities differ is that short-term interest rates are expected to have different values at future dates.

The key assumption behind this theory is that buyers of bonds do not prefer bonds of one maturity over another, so they will not hold any quantity of a bond if its expected return is less than that of another bond with a different maturity. Bonds that have this characteristic are said to be *perfect substitutes*. What this means in practice is that if bonds with different maturities are perfect substitutes, the expected return on these bonds must be equal.

To see how the assumption that bonds with different maturities are perfect substitutes leads to the expectations hypothesis, let us consider the following two investment strategies:

1. Purchase a one-year bond, and when it matures in one year, purchase another one-year bond.
2. Purchase a two-year bond and hold it until maturity.

Because both strategies must have the same expected return if people are holding both one- and two-year bonds, the interest rate on the two-year bond must equal the average of the two one-year interest rates. For example, let's say that the current interest rate on the one-year bond is 9% and you expect the interest rate on the one-year bond next year to be 11%. If you pursue the first strategy of buying the two one-year bonds, the expected return over the two years will average out to be $(9\% + 11\%)/2 = 10\%$ per year. You will be willing to hold both the one- and two-year bonds only if the expected return per year of the two-year bond equals this. Therefore, the interest rate on the two-year bond must equal 10%, the average interest rate on the two one-year bonds.

We can make this argument more general. For an investment of $1, consider the choice of holding, for two periods, a two-period bond or two one-period bonds. Using the definitions

i_t = today's (time t) interest rate on a one-period bond
i^e_{t+1} = interest rate on a one-period bond expected for next period (time $t + 1$)
i_{2t} = today's (time t) interest rate on the two-period bond

the expected return over the two periods from investing $1 in the two-period bond and holding it for the two periods can be calculated as

$$(1 + i_{2t})(1 + i_{2t}) - 1 = 1 + 2i_{2t} + (i_{2t})^2 - 1$$

After the second period, the $1 investment is worth $(1 + i_{2t})(1 + i_{2t})$. Subtracting the $1 initial investment from this amount and dividing by the initial $1 investment gives the rate of return calculated in the first equation. Because $(i_{2t})^2$ is extremely small—if $i_{2t} = 10\% = 0.10$, then $(i_{2t})^2 = 0.01$—we can simplify the expected return for holding the two-period bond for the two periods to

$$2i_{2t}$$

With the other strategy, in which one-period bonds are bought, the expected return on the $1 investment over the two periods is

$$(1 + i_t)(1 + i^e_{t+1}) - 1$$

After the first period, the $1 investment becomes $1 + i_t$, and this is reinvested in the one-period bond for the next period, yielding an amount $(1 + i_t)(1 + i^e_{t+1})$. Subtracting the $1 initial investment from this amount and dividing by the initial investment of $1 gives the expected return for the strategy of holding one-period bonds for the two periods. Because $i_t(i^e_{t+1})$ is also extremely small—if $i_t = i^e_{t+1} = 0.10$, then $i_t(i^e_{t+1}) = 0.01$—we can simplify this to

$$i_t + i^e_{t+1}$$

Both bonds will be held only if these expected returns are equal, that is, when

$$2i_{2t} = i_t + i^e_{t+1}$$

Solving for i_{2t} in terms of the one-period rates, we have

$$i_{2t} = \frac{i_t + i^e_{t+1}}{2} \tag{1}$$

which tells us that the two-period rate must equal the average of the two one-period rates. We can conduct the same steps for bonds with a longer maturity so that we can examine the whole term structure of interest rates. Doing so, we will find that the interest rate of i_{nt} on an n-period bond must equal

$$i_{nt} = \frac{i_t + i^e_{t+1} + i^e_{t+2} + \cdots + i^e_{t+(n-1)}}{n} \tag{2}$$

Equation 2 states that the n-period interest rate equals the average of the one-period interest rates expected to occur over the n-period life of the bond. This is a restatement of the expectations hypothesis in more precise terms.[3]

A simple numerical example might clarify what the expectations theory in Equation 2 is saying. If the one-year interest rate over the next five years is expected to be 5%, 6%, 7%, 8%, and 9%, Equation 2 indicates that the interest rate on the two-year bond would be

$$\frac{5\% + 6\%}{2} = 5.5\%$$

while for the five-year bond it would be

$$\frac{5\% + 6\% + 7\% + 8\% + 9\%}{5} = 7\%$$

Doing a similar calculation for the one-, three-, and four-year interest rates, you should be able to verify that the one- to five-year interest rates are 5.0%, 5.5%, 6.0%, 6.5%, and 7.0%, respectively. Thus we see that the rising trend in short-term interest rates produces an upward-sloping yield curve along which interest rates rise as maturity lengthens.

The expectations hypothesis is an elegant theory that provides an explanation of why the term structure of interest rates (as represented by yield curves) changes at different times. When the yield curve is upward-sloping, the expectations hypoth-

---

[3]The analysis here has been conducted for discount bonds. Formulas for interest rates on coupon bonds would differ slightly from those used here but would convey the same principle.

esis suggests that short-term interest rates are expected to rise in the future, as we have seen in our numerical example. In this situation, in which the long-term rate is currently above the short-term rate, the average of future short-term rates is expected to be higher than the current short-term rate, which can occur only if short-term interest rates are expected to rise. This is what we see in our numerical example. When the yield curve slopes downward and is inverted, the average of future short-term interest rates is expected to be below the current short-term rate, implying that short-term interest rates are expected to fall, on average, in the future. Only when the yield curve is flat does the expectations hypothesis suggest that short-term interest rates are not expected to change, on average, in the future.

The expectations hypothesis also explains fact 1 that interest rates on bonds with different maturities move together over time. Historically, short-term interest rates have had the characteristic that if they increase today, they will tend to be higher in the future. Hence a rise in short-term rates will raise people's expectations of future short-term rates. Because long-term rates are related to the average of expected future short-term rates, a rise in short-term rates will also raise long-term rates, causing short- and long-term rates to move together.

The expectations hypothesis also explains fact 2 that yield curves tend to have an upward slope when short-term interest rates are low and are inverted when short-term rates are high. When short-term rates are low, people generally expect them to rise to some normal level in the future, and the average of future expected short-term rates is high relative to the current short-term rate. Therefore, long-term interest rates will be substantially above current short-term rates, and the yield curve would then have an upward slope. Conversely, if short-term rates are high, people usually expect them to come back down. Long-term rates would then drop below short-term rates because the average of expected future short-term rates would be below current short-term rates and the yield curve would slope downward and become inverted.[4]

The expectations hypothesis is an attractive theory because it provides a simple explanation of the behavior of the term structure, but unfortunately it has a major shortcoming: It cannot explain fact 3 that yield curves usually slope upward. The typical upward slope of yield curves implies that short-term interest rates are usually expected to rise in the future. In practice, short-term interest rates are just as likely to fall as they are to rise, and so the expectations hypothesis suggests that the typical yield curve should be flat rather than upward-sloping.

Segmented Markets Theory

As the name suggests, the **segmented markets theory** of the term structure sees markets for different-maturity bonds as completely separate and segmented.

---

[4]The expectations hypothesis explains another important fact about the relationship between short-term and long-term interest rates. As you can see looking back at Figure 4, short-term interest rates are more volatile than long-term rates. If interest rates are mean-reverting—that is, if they tend to head back down after they are at unusually high levels or go back up when they are at unusually low levels—then an average of these short-term rates must necessarily have lower volatility than the short-term rates themselves. Because the expectations hypothesis suggests that the long-term rate will be an average of future short-term rates, it implies that the long-term rate will have lower volatility than short-term rates.

The interest rate for each bond with a different maturity is then determined by the supply of and demand for that bond with no effects from expected returns on other bonds with other maturities.

The key assumption in the segmented markets theory is that bonds of different maturities are not substitutes at all, so the expected return from holding a bond of one maturity has no effect on the demand for a bond of another maturity. This theory of the term structure is at the opposite extreme to the expectations hypothesis, which assumes that bonds of different maturities are perfect substitutes.

The argument for why bonds of different maturities are not substitutes is that investors have strong preferences for bonds of one maturity but not for another, so they will be concerned with the expected returns only for bonds of the maturity they prefer. This might occur because they have a particular holding period in mind, and if they match the maturity of the bond to the desired holding period, they can obtain a certain return with no risk at all.[5] (We have seen in Chapter 3 that if the term to maturity equals the holding period, the return is known for certain because it equals the yield exactly, and there is no interest-rate risk.) For example, people who have a short holding period would prefer to hold short-term bonds. Conversely, if you were putting funds away for your young child to go to college, your desired holding period might be much longer, and you would want to hold longer-term bonds.

In the segmented markets theory, differing yield curve patterns are accounted for by supply and demand differences associated with bonds of different maturities. If, as seems sensible, investors generally prefer bonds with shorter maturities that have less interest-rate risk, the segmented markets theory can explain fact 3 that yield curves typically slope upward. Because the demand for long-term bonds is relatively lower than that for short-term bonds in the typical situation, long-term bonds will have lower prices and higher interest rates, and hence the yield curve will typically slope upward.

Although the segmented markets theory can explain why yield curves usually tend to slope upward, it has a major flaw in that it cannot explain facts 1 and 2. Because it views the market for bonds of different maturities as completely segmented, there is no reason for a rise in interest rates on a bond of one maturity to affect the interest rate on a bond of another maturity. Therefore, it cannot explain why interest rates on bonds of different maturities tend to move together (fact 1). Second, because it is not clear how demand and supply for short- versus long-term bonds changes with the level of short-term interest rates, the theory cannot explain why yield curves tend to slope upward when short-term interest rates are low and to be inverted when short-term interest rates are high (fact 2).

---

[5]The statement that there is no uncertainty about the return if the term to maturity equals the holding period is literally true only for a discount bond. For a coupon bond with a long holding period, there is some risk because coupon payments must be reinvested before the bond matures. Our analysis here is thus being conducted for discount bonds. However, the gist of the analysis remains the same for coupon bonds because the amount of this risk from reinvestment is small when coupon bonds have the same term to maturity as the holding period.

Because each of our two theories explains empirical facts that the other cannot, a logical step is to combine the theories, which leads us to the preferred habitat theory and closely related liquidity premium theory.

Preferred Habitat and Liquidity Premium Theories

The **preferred habitat theory** of term structure states that the interest rate on a long-term bond will equal an average of short-term interest rates expected to occur over the life of the long-term bond plus a term (liquidity) premium that responds to supply and demand conditions for that bond.

The preferred habitat theory's key assumption is that bonds of different maturities are substitutes, which means that the expected return on one bond *does* influence the expected return on a bond of a different maturity, but it allows investors to prefer one bond maturity over another. In other words, bonds of different maturities are assumed to be substitutes but not perfect substitutes. We might think of investors as having a preference for bonds of one maturity over another, a particular bond market where they are most comfortable to stay; we might then say that they have a preferred habitat. Investors still care about the expected returns on bonds with a maturity other than their preferred maturity, and so they will not allow expected returns on one bond to get too far out of line with that on another bond with a different maturity. Because they prefer bonds of one maturity over another, they will be willing to buy bonds that do not have the preferred maturity only if they earn a somewhat higher expected return.

If investors prefer the habitat of short-term bonds over longer-term bonds, for example, they might be willing to hold short-term bonds even though they have a lower expected return. This means that investors would have to be paid a positive term premium to be willing to hold a long-term bond. Such an outcome would modify the expectations hypothesis by adding a positive term premium to the equation that describes the relationship between long- and short-term interest rates. The preferred habitat theory is thus written as

$$i_{nt} = \frac{i_t + i_{t+1}^e + i_{t+2}^e + \cdots + i_{t+(n-1)}^e}{n} + k_{nt} \tag{3}$$

where k_{nt} = the term premium for the n-period bond at time t.

Closely related to the preferred habitat theory is the **liquidity premium theory,** which takes a somewhat more direct approach to modifying the expectations hypothesis. It reasons that a positive term (liquidity) premium must be offered to buyers of longer-term bonds to compensate them for their increased risk. This reasoning leads to the same Equation 3 implied by the preferred habitat theory, with the proviso that the term premium k_{nt} is always positive and rises with the term to maturity of the bond.

A simple numerical example similar to the one we used for the expectations hypothesis further clarifies what the preferred habitat and liquidity premium theories in Equation 3 are saying. Again suppose that the one-year interest rate over the next five years is expected to be 5%, 6%, 7%, 8%, and 9%, while investors' preferences for holding short-term bonds means that the term premiums for one-to five-year bonds are 0%, 0.25%, 0.5%, 0.75%, and 1.0%, respectively. Equation 3 then indicates that the interest rate on the two-year bond would be

$$\frac{5\% + 6\%}{2} + 0.25\% = 5.75\%$$

while for the five-year bond it would be

$$\frac{5\% + 6\% + 7\% + 8\% + 9\%}{5} + 1\% = 8\%$$

Doing a similar calculation for the one-, three-, and four-year interest rates, you should be able to verify that the one- to five-year interest rates are 5.0%, 5.75%, 6.5%, 7.25%, and 8.0%, respectively. Comparing these findings with those for the expectations hypothesis, we see that the preferred habitat and liquidity premium theories produce yield curves that slope more steeply upward because of investors' preferences for short-term bonds.

Let's see if the preferred habitat and liquidity premium theories are consistent with all three empirical facts we have discussed. They explain fact 1 that interest rates on different-maturity bonds move together over time: A rise in short-term interest rates indicates that short-term interest rates will, on average, be higher in the future, and the first term in Equation 3 then implies that long-term interest rates will rise along with them.

They also explain why yield curves tend to have an especially steep upward slope when short-term interest rates are low and to be inverted when short-term rates are high (fact 2). Because investors generally expect short-term interest rates to rise to some normal level when they are low, the average of future expected short-term rates will be high relative to the current short-term rate. With the additional boost of a positive term premium, long-term interest rates will be substantially above current short-term rates, and the yield curve would then have a steep upward slope. Conversely, if short-term rates are high, people usually expect them to come back down. Long-term rates would then drop below short-term rates because the average of expected future short-term rates would be so far below current short-term rates that despite positive term premiums, the yield curve would slope downward.

The preferred habitat and liquidity premium theories explain fact 3 that yield curves typically slope upward by recognizing that the term premium rises with a bond's maturity because of investors' preferences for short-term bonds. Even if short-term interest rates are expected to stay the same on average in the future, long-term interest rates will be above short-term interest rates, and yield curves will typically slope upward.

How can the preferred habitat and liquidity premium theories explain the occasional appearance of inverted yield curves if the term premium is positive? It must be that at times short-term interest rates are expected to fall so much in the future that the average of the expected short-term rates is well below the current short-term rate. Even when the positive term premium is added to this average, the resulting long-term rate will still be below the current short-term interest rate.

As our discussion indicates, a particularly attractive feature of the preferred habitat and liquidity premium theories is that they tell you what the market is pre-

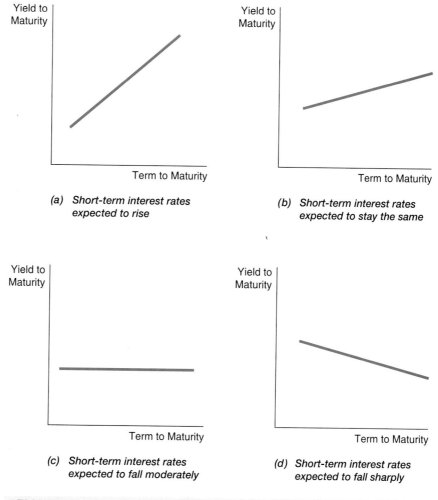

■FIGURE 5 Yield Curves and the Market's Expectations of Future Short-Term
Interest Rates

dicting about future short-term interest rates just by looking at the slope of the
yield curve. A steeply rising yield curve, as in panel (a) of Figure 5, indicates that
short-term interest rates are expected to rise in the future. A moderately steep
yield curve, as in panel (b), indicates that short-term interest rates are not
expected to rise or fall much in the future. A flat yield curve, as in panel (c), indicates that short-term rates are expected to fall moderately in the future. Finally,
an inverted yield curve, as in panel (d), indicates that short-term interest rates are
expected to fall sharply in the future.

Recent Evidence on the Term Structure

In the 1980s, researchers examining the term structure of interest rates ques-
tioned whether the slope of the yield curve provides information about move-

ments of future short-term interest rates.[6] They found that the spread between long- and short-term interest rates does not always help predict future short-term interest rates, a finding that may stem from substantial fluctuations in the term premium for long-term bonds. More recent research using more discriminating tests now favors a different view. It shows that the term structure contains quite a bit of information for the very short run, over the next several months, and the long run, over several years, but is unreliable at predicting movements in interest rates over the intermediate term, the time in between.[7]

Summary

The preferred habitat and liquidity premium theories are the most widely accepted theories of the term structure of interest rates because they explain the major empirical facts about the term structure so well. They combine the features of both the expectations hypothesis and the segmented markets theory by asserting that a long-term interest rate will be the sum of a term premium (liquidity) and the average of the short-term interest rates that are expected to occur over the life of the bond.

The preferred habitat and liquidity premium theories explain the following facts: (1) Interest rates on bonds of different maturities tend to move together over time, (2) yield curves usually slope upward, and (3) when short-term interest rates are low, yield curves are more likely to have a steep upward slope, whereas when short-term interest rates are high, yield curves are more likely to be inverted.

The theories also help us predict the movement of short-term interest rates in the future. A steep upward slope of the yield curve means that short-term rates are expected to rise, a mild upward slope means that short-term rates are expected to remain the same, a flat slope means that short-term rates are expected to fall moderately, and an inverted yield curve means that short-term rates are expected to fall sharply.

APPLICATION | INTERPRETING YIELD CURVES, 1980–1997

Figure 6 illustrates several yield curves that have appeared for U.S. government bonds in recent years. What do these yield curves tell us about the public's expectations of future movements of short-term interest rates?

---

[6]Robert J. Shiller, John Y. Campbell, and Kermit L. Schoenholtz, "Forward Rates and Future Policy: Interpreting the Term Structure of Interest Rates," *Brookings Papers on Economic Activity* 1 (1983): 173–217; N. Gregory Mankiw and Lawrence H. Summers, "Do Long-Term Interest Rates Overreact to Short-Term Interest Rates?" *Brookings Papers on Economic Activity* 1 (1984): 243–247.

[7]Eugene Fama, "The Information in the Term Structure," *Journal of Financial Economics* 13 (1984): 509–528; Eugene Fama and Robert Bliss, "The Information in Long-Maturity Forward Rates," *American Economic Review* 77 (1987): 680–692; John Y. Campbell and Robert J. Shiller, "Cointegration and Tests of the Present Value Models," *Journal of Political Economy* 95 (1987): 1062–1088; John Y. Campbell and Robert J. Shiller, "Yield Spreads and Interest Rate Movements: A Bird's Eye View," *Review of Economic Studies* 58 (1991): 495–514.

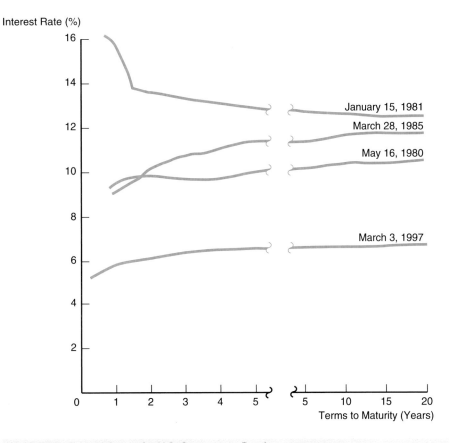

■FIGURE 6 Yield Curves for U.S. Government Bonds

Sources: Federal Reserve Bank of St. Louis; *U.S. Financial Data*, various issues; *Wall Street Journal*, various dates.

■ **S T U D Y   G U I D E**   Try to answer the question before reading further in the text. If you have trouble answering it with the preferred habitat and liquidity premium theories, first try answering it with the expectations hypothesis (which is simpler because you don't have to worry about the term premium). When you understand what the expectations of future interest rates are in this case, modify your analysis by taking the term premium into account.

The steep inverted yield curve that occurred on January 15, 1981, indicated that short-term interest rates were expected to decline sharply in the future. In order for longer-term interest rates with their positive term premium to be well below the short-term interest rate, short-term interest rates must be expected to decline so sharply that their average is far below the current short-term rate. Indeed, the public's expectations of sharply lower short-term interest rates evident in the yield curve were realized soon after January 15; by March, three-month Treasury bill rates had declined from the 16% level to 13%.

The steep upward-sloping yield curves on March 28, 1985, indicated that short-term interest rates would climb in the future. The long-term interest rate is above the short-term interest rate when short-term interest rates are expected to rise because their average plus the term premium will be above the current short-term rate. The moderately upward-sloping yield curves on May 16, 1980, and March 3, 1997, indicated that short-term interest rates were expected neither to rise nor to fall in the near future. In this case, their average remains the same as the current short-term rate, and the positive term premium for longer-term bonds explains the moderate upward slope of the yield curve.

■ THE PRACTICING FINANCIAL INSTITUTION MANAGER
Using the Term Structure to Forecast Interest Rates

As was discussed in Chapter 5, interest-rate forecasts are extremely important to managers of financial institutions because future changes in interest rates have a significant impact on the profitability of their institutions. Furthermore, interest-rate forecasts are needed when managers of financial institutions have to set interest rates on loans that are promised to customers in the future. Our discussion of the term structure of interest rates has indicated that the slope of the yield curve provides general information about the market's prediction of the future path of interest rates. For example, a steeply upward-sloping yield curve indicates that short-term interest rates are predicted to rise in the future, and a downward-sloping yield curve indicates that short-term interest rates are predicted to fall. However, a financial institution manager needs much more specific information on interest-rate forecasts than this. Here we show how the manager of a financial institution can generate specific forecasts of interest rates using the term structure.

To see how this is done, let's start the analysis using the approach we took in developing the expectations hypothesis. Recall that because bonds of different maturities are perfect substitutes, we assumed that the expected return over two periods from investing $1 in a two-period bond, which is $(1 + i_{2t})$ $(1 + i_{2t}) - 1$, must equal the expected return from investing $1 in one-period bonds, which is $(1 + i_t)(1 + i^e_{t+1}) - 1$. In other words,

$$(1 + i_t)(1 + i^e_{t+1}) - 1 = (1 + i_{2t})(1 + i_{2t}) - 1$$

Through some tedious algebra we can solve for i^e_{t+1}:

$$i^e_{t+1} = \frac{(1 + i_{2t})^2}{1 + i_t} - 1 \tag{4}$$

This measure of i^e_{t+1} is called the **forward rate** because it is the one-period interest rate that the expectations hypothesis of the term structure indicates is expected to prevail one period in the future. To differentiate forward rates derived from the term structure from actual interest rates that are observed at time t, we call these observed interest rates **spot rates.**

Going back to the numerical example we used to discuss the expectations hypothesis earlier in this chapter, at time t the one-year interest rate is 5% and the two-year rate is 5.5%. Plugging these numbers into Equation 4 yields the following estimate of the forward rate one period in the future:

$$i^e_{t+1} = \frac{(1 + 0.055)^2}{1 + 0.05} - 1 = 0.06 = 6\%$$

Not surprisingly, this 6% forward rate is identical to the expected one-year interest rate one year in the future that we used in the earlier numerical example. This is exactly what we should find, as our calculation here is just another way of looking at the expectations hypothesis.

We can also compare holding the three-year bond against holding a sequence of one-year bonds, which reveals the following relationship:

$$(1 + i_t)(1 + i^e_{t+1})(1 + i^e_{t+2}) - 1 = (1 + i_{3t})(1 + i_{3t})(1 + i_{3t}) - 1$$

and plugging in the estimate for i^e_{t+1} derived in Equation 4, we can solve for i^e_{t+2}

$$i^e_{t+2} = \frac{(1 + i_{3t})^3}{(1 + i_{2t})^2} - 1$$

Continuing with these calculations, we obtain the general solution for the forward rate n periods into the future:

$$i^e_{t+n} = \frac{(1 + i_{n+1t})^{n+1}}{(1 + i_{nt})^n} - 1 \tag{5}$$

Our discussion in the chapter indicated that the expectations hypothesis is not entirely satisfactory because investors must be compensated with term premiums to induce them to hold longer-term bonds. Hence we need to modify our analysis, as we did when discussing the preferred habitat and liquidity premium theories, by allowing for these term premiums in estimating predictions of future interest rates.

Recall from the discussion of those theories that because investors prefer to hold short-term rather than long-term bonds, the n-period interest rate differs from that indicated by the expectations hypothesis by a term premium of k_{nt}. So to allow for term premiums, we need merely subtract k_{nt} from i_{nt} in our formula to derive i^e_{t+n}:

$$i^e_{t+n} = \frac{(1 + i_{n+1t} - k_{n+1t})^{n+1}}{(1 + i_{nt} - k_{nt})^n} - 1 \tag{6}$$

This measure of i^e_{t+n} is referred to, naturally enough, as the *adjusted forward-rate forecast*.

In the case of i^e_{t+1}, Equation 6 produces the following estimate:

$$i^e_{t+1} = \frac{(1 + i_{2t} - k_{2t})^2}{1 + i_t} - 1$$

Using the numerical example in the discussion of the preferred habitat and liquidity premium theories, at time t the k_{2t} term premium is 0.25%, $k_{1t} = 0$, the one-year interest rate is 5%, and the two-year interest rate is 5.75%. Plugging these numbers into our equation yields the following adjusted forward-rate forecast for one period in the future:

$$i^e_{t+1} = \frac{(1 + 0.0575 - 0.0025)^2}{1 + 0.05} - 1 = 0.06 = 6\%$$

which is the same as the expected interest rate found in the numerical example, as it should be.

Our analysis of the term structure thus provides managers of financial institutions with a fairly straightforward procedure for producing interest-rate forecasts. First they need to estimate k_{nt}, the values of the term premiums for various n. Then they need merely apply the formula in Equation 6 to derive the market's forecasts of future interest rates.

To see how this might work in practice, suppose that a customer asks a bank if the bank would be willing to commit to making the customer a one-year loan at an interest rate of 8% one year from now. To compensate for the costs of making a loan, the bank needs to charge one percentage point more than the expected interest rate on a Treasury bond with the same maturity if it is to make a profit. If the bank manager estimates the term premium k_{2t} to be 0.4%, and the one-year Treasury bond rate is 6% and the two-year bond rate is 7%, should the manager be willing to make the commitment?

Using the formula in Equation 6, the bank manager calculates the forward rate to be

$$i^e_{t+1} = \frac{(1 + 0.07 - 0.004)^2}{1 + 0.06} - 1 = 0.072 = 7.2\%$$

The market's forecast of the one-year Treasury bond rate one year in the future is therefore 7.2%. Adding the 1% necessary to make a profit on the one-year loan to the 7.2% interest-rate forecast means that the one-year loan is expected to be profitable only if it has an interest rate of 8.2% or higher. Thus the bank manager regretfully tells the customer that the bank cannot make the commitment because at an interest rate of 8%, it is likely that the loan will be unprofitable.

As we will see in Chapter 7, the bond market's forecasts of interest rates may be the most accurate ones possible. If this is the case, the estimates of the market's forecasts of future interest rates using the simple procedure outlined here may be the best interest-rate forecasts that a financial institution manager can obtain.

■ **STUDY GUIDE**　To make sure you understand how to generate interest-rate forecasts from the term structure, calculate the forecasts of the one-year interest rates using Equation 6 for two, three, and four years in the future using the term premiums and one- through five-year interest rates in the numerical example in the discussion of the preferred habitat and liquidity premium theories. The resulting forecasts should equal the expected future interest rates found in the numerical example. Problems 14 and 15 at the end of the chapter will give you more practice in generating interest-rate forecasts from the term structure.

SUMMARY

1. Bonds with the same maturity will have different interest rates because of three factors: default risk, liquidity, and tax considerations. The greater a bond's default risk, the higher its interest rate relative to other bonds; the greater a bond's liquidity, the lower its interest rate; and bonds with tax-exempt status will have lower interest rates than they otherwise would. The relationship among interest rates on bonds with the same maturity that arise because of these three factors is known as the risk structure of interest rates.

2. Four theories of the term structure provide explanations of how interest rates on bonds with different terms to maturity are related. The expectations hypothesis views long-term interest rates as equaling the average of future short-term interest rates expected to occur over the life of the bond; by contrast, the segmented markets theory treats the determination of interest rates for each bond's maturity as the outcome of supply and demand in that market only. Neither of these theories by itself can explain both the fact that interest rates on bonds of different maturities move together over time and that yield curves usually slope upward.

3. The preferred habitat and liquidity premium theories combine the features of the other two theories and by so doing are able to explain the facts just mentioned. They view long-term interest rates as equaling the average of future short-term interest rates expected to occur over the life of the bond plus a term premium that reflects the supply of and demand for bonds of different maturities. These theories allow us to infer the market's expectations about the movement of future short-term interest rates from the yield curve. A steeply upward-sloping curve indicates that future short-term rates are expected to rise, a mildly upward-sloping curve indicates that short-term rates are expected to stay the same, a flat curve indicates that short-term rates are expected to decline slightly, and an inverted yield curve indicates that a substantial decline in short-term rates is expected in the future.

KEY TERMS

default-free bonds, p. 139
default risk, p. 139
expectations hypothesis, p. 148
forward rate, p. 158
inverted yield curve, p. 146
junk bonds, p. 141

liquidity premium theory, p. 153
preferred habitat theory, p. 153
risk premium, p. 139
risk structure of interest rates, p. 138

segmented markets theory, p. 151
spot rate, p. 158
term structure of interest rates, p. 138
yield curve, p. 146

QUESTIONS AND PROBLEMS

1. Which should have the higher risk premium on its interest rates, a corporate bond with a Moody's Baa rating or a corporate bond with a C rating? Why?

*2. Why do U.S. Treasury bills have lower interest rates than large-denomination negotiable bank CDs?

3. Risk premiums on corporate bonds are usually anticyclical; that is, they decrease during business cycle expansions and increase during recessions. Why is this so?

*4. "If bonds of different maturities are close substitutes, their interest rates are more likely to move together." Is this statement true, false, or uncertain? Explain your answer.

5. If yield curves, on average, were flat, what would this say about the term premiums in the term structure? Would you be more or less willing to accept the expectations hypothesis?

*6. Assuming that the expectations hypothesis is the correct theory of the term structure, calculate the interest rates in the term structure for maturities of one to five years, and plot the resulting yield curves for the following series of one-year interest rates over the next five years:
   a. 5%, 7%, 7%, 7%, 7%
   b. 5%, 4%, 4%, 4%, 4%

   How would your yield curves change if people preferred shorter-term bonds over longer-term bonds?

7. Assuming that the expectations hypothesis is the correct theory of the term structure, calculate the interest rates in the term structure for maturities of one to five years, and plot the resulting yield curves for the following path of one-year interest rates over the next five years:

a. 5%, 6%, 7%, 6%, 5%
b. 5%, 4%, 3%, 4%, 5%

How would your yield curves change if people preferred shorter-term bonds over longer-term bonds?

*8. If a yield curve looks like the one shown here, what is the market predicting about the movement of future short-term interest rates? What might the yield curve indicate about the market's predictions about the inflation rate in the future?

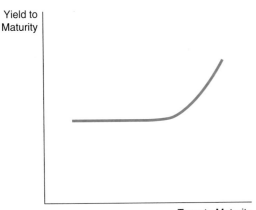

9. If a yield curve looks like the one shown here, what is the market predicting about the movement of future short-term interest rates? What might the yield curve indicate about the market's predictions about the inflation rate in the future?

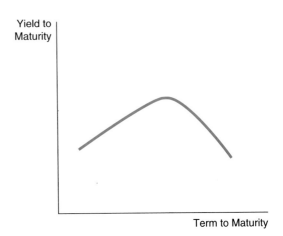

*10. What effect would reducing income tax rates have on the interest rates of municipal bonds? Would interest rates of Treasury securities be affected and, if so, how?

Predicting the Future

11. Predict what will happen to interest rates on a corporation's bonds if the federal government guarantees today that it will pay creditors if the corporation goes bankrupt in the future. What will happen to the interest rates on Treasury securities?

*12. Predict what would happen to the risk premiums on corporate bonds if brokerage commissions were lowered in the corporate bond market.

13. If the income tax exemption on municipal bonds were abolished, what would happen to the interest rates on these bonds? What effect would it have on interest rates on U.S. Treasury securities?

*14. If the interest rates on one- to five-year bonds are currently 4%, 5%, 6%, 7%, and 8% and the term premiums for one- to five-year bonds are 0%, 0.25%, 0.35%, 0.40%, and 0.50%, predict what the one-year interest rate will be two years from now.

15. If the interest rates on one- to five-year bonds are currently 7%, 6%, 5%, 6%, and 7% and the term premiums for one- to five-year bonds are 0%, 0.15%, 0.25%, 0.30%, and 0.60%, predict what the one-year interest rate will be four years from now.

CASE STUDY

Yield Curve Hypotheses and the Effects of Economic Events

CONCEPTS IN THIS CASE

term structure of interest rates
default risk
risk premium
yield curve
expectations hypotheses
segmented markets theory
preferred habitat theory
liquidity premium theory

Your employer (a bank) has decided to offer five-year loans to its small business customers. You have been presented the task of determining what the appropriate minimum interest rate should be for the most creditworthy customer. The decision to select a particular fixed rate for the loans depends on our forecast of the interest rates and our internal efficiency in managing the loan. This requires compensation for the costs of making the loan plus profit. You are to use the most recent five-year treasury bond as the basis for determining the minimum interest rate on the small business fixed-rate loans.

Your supervisor indicates that the bank needs to charge two percentage points more than the expected interest rate on treasury bonds for these loans. In addition, the bank has estimated the term premium to be 0.9%. Given this information, and the fact that you know you will need to defend your recommendation, you start to analyze current interest rates as follows:

1. Access local or internet articles that describe theories about the form of a yield curve.

2. Obtain current information on the U.S. Treasury Yield Curve.

3. Plot the current U.S. Treasury Yield Curve and interpret its shape using

a. The Expectations Hypothesis
b. The Segmented Markets Theory
c. The Preferred Habitat & Liquidity Preference Theories.
d. Which theory (a, b, or c) do you think best describes the curve?

4. Given the information in responses 1, 2, 3 above— use the expectations hypothesis to calculate and predict interest rates as follows:
a. If the one-year interest rate is expected to be the same as the yield curve over the next three years, what interest rate is expected on a two-year bond one year from now?
b. What interest rate is expected on a three-year bond one year from now?
c. What relationship do you find between interest rates and maturity?
d. If investors attach term premiums of 0.0025, 0.0075 and 0.0085 to the one-, two- and three-year bonds:
   i. What would be the interest rate on a two-year security?
   ii. What would be the interest rate on a three-year security?
   iii. What is the forward rate for one-year treasury bonds one year from now?
   iv. What is the adjusted forward rate for one-year treasury bonds one year out?

5. After describing the current yield curve and forecasting interest rates using both the expectations and preferred habitat and liquidity premium methods above,
a. What is your recommended minimum interest rate for the five-year fixed rate loans ?
b. How would this rate be adjusted for customers that have some credit risk?

CHAPTER 7

THE THEORY OF EFFICIENT CAPITAL MARKETS

◼ PREVIEW Throughout our discussion so far of how financial markets work, you may have noticed that the subject of expectations keeps cropping up again and again. Expectations of returns, risk, and liquidity are central elements in the theory of portfolio choice; expectations of inflation have a major impact on bond prices and interest rates; expectations about the likelihood of default are the most important factor that determines the risk structure of interest rates; expectations of future short-term interest rates play a central role in determining the term structure of interest rates; and expected returns on foreign deposits relative to domestic deposits are the key element in the determination of foreign exchange rates. Not only are expectations critical in understanding behavior in financial markets, but as we will see later in this book, they are also central to our understanding of how financial institutions and monetary policy operate.

To understand how expectations are formed so that we can understand how securities prices move over time, we look at the *theory of rational expectations*, which, when applied to financial markets, is called the *theory of efficient capital markets* (or simply *efficient markets theory*). In this chapter we examine the basic reasoning behind efficient markets theory in order to explain some puzzling features of the operation and behavior of financial markets. You will see, for example, why changes in stock prices are unpredictable and why listening to a stock broker's hot tips may not be a good idea.

Theoretically, efficient markets theory should be a powerful tool for analyzing behavior in financial markets. But to establish that it is *in reality* a useful tool, we must compare the theory with the data. Does the empirical evidence support the theory? Though mixed, the available evidence indicates that for many purposes, this theory is a good starting point for analyzing expectations.

■ THEORY OF RATIONAL EXPECTATIONS

In the 1950s and 1960s, economists regularly viewed expectations as formed from past experience only. Expectations of inflation, for example, were typically viewed as being an average of past inflation rates. This view of expectation formation, called **adaptive expectations,** suggests that changes in expectations will occur slowly over time as past data change.[1] So if inflation had formerly been steady at a 5% rate, expectations of future inflation would be 5% too. If inflation rose to a steady rate of 10%, expectations of future inflation would rise toward 10%, but slowly: In the first year, expected inflation might rise only to 6%; in the second year, to 7%; and so on.

Adaptive expectations have been faulted on the grounds that people use more information than just past data on a single variable to form their expectations of that variable. Their expectations of inflation will almost surely be affected by their predictions of future monetary policy as well as by current and past monetary policy. In addition, people often change their expectations quickly in the light of new information. To meet these objections to adaptive expectations, John Muth developed an alternative theory of expectations, called **rational expectations,** which can be stated as follows: ***Expectations will be identical to optimal forecasts (the best guess of the future) using all available information.***[2]

What exactly does this mean? To explain it more clearly, let's use the theory of rational expectations to examine how expectations are formed in a situation that most of us encounter at some point in our lifetime: our drive to work. Suppose that when Joe Commuter travels when it is not rush hour, it takes an average of 30 minutes for his trip. Sometimes it takes him 35 minutes, other times 25 minutes, but the average non-rush-hour driving time is 30 minutes. If, however, Joe leaves for work during the rush hour, it takes him, on average, an additional 10 minutes to get to work. Given that he leaves for work during the rush hour, the best guess of the driving time—the **optimal forecast**—is 40 minutes.

If the only information available to Joe before he leaves for work that would have a potential effect on his driving time is that he is leaving during the rush hour, what does rational expectations theory allow you to predict about Joe's expectations of his driving time? Since the best guess of his driving time using all available information is 40 minutes, Joe's expectation should also be the same. Clearly, an expectation of 35 minutes would not be rational because it is not equal to the optimal forecast, the best guess of the driving time.

Suppose that the next day, given the same conditions and the same expectations, it takes Joe 45 minutes to drive because he hits an abnormally large number

---

[1]More specifically, adaptive expectations, say, of inflation, are written as a weighted average of past inflation rates:

$$\pi_t^e = (1 - \lambda)\sum_{j=0}^{\infty} \lambda^j \pi_{t-j}$$

where
π_t^e = adaptive expectation of inflation at time t
π_{t-j} = inflation at time $t - j$
λ = a constant between the values of 0 and 1

[2]John Muth, "Rational Expectations and the Theory of Price Movements," *Econometrica* 29 (1961): 315–335.

of red lights, and the day after that he hits all the lights right and it takes him only 35 minutes. Do these variations mean that Joe's 40-minute expectation is irrational? No, an expectation of 40 minutes' driving time is still a rational expectation. In both cases, the forecast is off by 5 minutes, so the expectation has not been perfectly accurate. However, the forecast does not have to be perfectly accurate to be rational—it need only be the *best possible* given the available information; that is, it has to be correct *on average,* and the 40-minute expectation meets this requirement. Since there is bound to be some randomness in Joe's driving time regardless of driving conditions, an optimal forecast will never be completely accurate.

The example makes the following important point about rational expectations: ***Even though a rational expectation equals the optimal forecast using all available information, a prediction based on it may not always be perfectly accurate.***

What if an item of information relevant to predicting driving time is unavailable or ignored? Suppose that on Joe's usual route to work there is an accident that causes a two-hour traffic jam. If Joe has no way of ascertaining this information, his rush-hour expectation of 40 minutes' driving time is still rational because the accident information is not available to him for incorporation into his optimal forecast. However, if there was a radio or TV traffic report about the accident that Joe did not bother to listen to or heard but ignored, his 40-minute expectation is no longer rational. In light of the availability of this information, Joe's optimal forecast should have been two hours and 40 minutes.

Accordingly, there are two reasons why an expectation may fail to be rational:

1. People might be aware of all available information but find it takes too much effort to make their expectation the best guess possible.
2. People might be unaware of some available relevant information, so their best guess of the future will not be accurate.

Nonetheless, it is important to recognize that if an additional factor is important but information about it is not available, an expectation that does not take account of it can still be rational.

Formal Statement of the Theory

We can state the theory of rational expectations somewhat more formally. If X stands for the variable that is being forecast (in our example, Joe Commuter's driving time), X^e for the expectation of this variable (Joe's expectation of his driving time), and X^{of} for the optimal forecast of X using all available information (the best guess possible of his driving time), the theory of rational expectations then simply says

$$X^e = X^{of} \tag{1}$$

That is, the expectation of X equals the optimal forecast using all available information.

Rationale Behind the Theory

Why do people try to make their expectations match their best possible guess of the future using all available information? The simplest explanation is that it is costly for people not to do so. Joe Commuter has a strong incentive to make his expectation of the time it takes him to drive to work as accurate as possible. If he underpredicts his driving time, he will often be late to work and risk being fired. If he overpredicts, he will, on average, get to work too early and will have given up sleep or leisure time unnecessarily. Accurate expectations are desirable, and there are strong incentives for people to try to make them equal to optimal forecasts by using all available information.

The same principle applies to businesses. Suppose that an appliance manufacturer, say, General Electric, knows that interest-rate movements are important to the sales of appliances. If GE makes poor forecasts of interest rates, it will earn less profit because it might either produce too many appliances or too few. There are strong incentives for GE to acquire all available information to help it forecast interest rates and use the information to make the best possible guess of future interest-rate movements.

The incentives for equating expectations with optimal forecasts are especially strong in financial markets. In these markets, people with better forecasts of the future get rich. The application of the theory of rational expectations to financial markets (where it is called **efficient markets theory**) is thus particularly useful.

Implications of the Theory

Rational expectations theory leads to two commonsense implications for the forming of expectations that are important in the analysis of the aggregate economy.

1. If there is a change in the way a variable moves, the way in which expectations of this variable are formed will change as well. This tenet of rational expectations theory can be most easily understood through a concrete example. Suppose that interest rates move in such a way that they tend to return to a "normal" level in the future. If today's interest rate is high relative to the normal level, an optimal forecast of the interest rate in the future is that it will decline to the normal level. Rational expectations theory would imply that when today's interest rate is high, the expectation is that it will fall in the future.

Suppose now that the way in which the interest rate moves changes so that when the interest rate is high, it stays high. In this case, when today's interest rate is high, the optimal forecast of the future interest rate, and hence the rational expectation, is that it will stay high. Expectations of the future interest rate will no longer indicate that the interest rate will fall. The change in the way the interest-rate variable moves has therefore led to a change in the way that expectations of future interest rates are formed. The rational expectations analysis here is generalizable to expectations of any variable.

Hence when there is a change in the way any variable moves, the way in which expectations of this variable are formed will change too.

2. The forecast errors of expectations will on average be zero and cannot be predicted ahead of time. The forecast error of an expectation is $X - X^e$, the difference between the realization of a variable X and the expectation of the variable; that is, if Joe Commuter's driving time on a particular day is 45 minutes and his expectation of the driving time is 40 minutes, the forecast error is 5 minutes.

Suppose that in violation of the rational expectations tenet, Joe's forecast error is not, on average, equal to zero; instead, it equals 5 minutes. The forecast error is now predictable ahead of time because Joe will soon notice that he is, on average, 5 minutes late for work and can improve his forecast by increasing it by 5 minutes. Rational expectations theory implies that this is exactly what Joe will do because he will want his forecast to be the best guess possible. When Joe has revised his forecast upward by 5 minutes, on average, the forecast error will equal zero so that it cannot be predicted ahead of time. Rational expectations theory implies that forecast errors of expectations cannot be predicted.

■ EFFICIENT MARKETS THEORY: RATIONAL EXPECTATIONS IN FINANCIAL MARKETS

While the theory of rational expectations was being developed by monetary economists, financial economists were developing a parallel theory of expectation formation in financial markets. It led them to the same conclusion as the rational expectations theorists: Expectations in financial markets are equal to optimal forecasts using all available information.[3] Although financial economists gave their theory another name, calling it the *theory of efficient capital markets* or *efficient markets theory,* in fact their theory is just an application of rational expectations to the pricing of securities.

Efficient markets theory is based on the assumption that prices of securities in financial markets fully reflect all available information. You may recall from Chapter 3 that the rate of return from holding a security equals the sum of the capital gain on the security (the change in the price) plus any cash payments, divided by the initial purchase price of the security:

$$RET = \frac{P_{t+1} - P_t + C}{P_t} \tag{2}$$

where RET = rate of return on the security held from time t to time $t + 1$ (say, the end of 1997 to the end of 1998)

P_{t+1} = price of the security at time $t + 1$, the end of the holding period

P_t = the price of the security at time t, the beginning of the holding period

C = cash payment (coupon or dividend payments) made in the period t to $t + 1$

---

[3]The development of efficient markets theory was not wholly independent of the development of rational expectations theory in that finance scholars were aware of Muth's work.

Let's look at the expectation of this return at time t, the beginning of the holding period. Because the current price and the cash payment C are known at the beginning, the only variable in the definition of the return that is uncertain is the price next period P_{t+1}.[4] Denoting the expectation of the security's price at the end of the holding period as P^e_{t+1}, the expected return RET^e is

$$RET^e = \frac{P^e_{t+1} - P_t + C}{P_t}$$

Efficient markets theory also views expectations of future prices as equal to optimal forecasts using all currently available information. In other words, the market's expectations of future securities prices are rational, so that

$$P^e_{t+1} = P^{of}_{t+1}$$

which in turn implies that the expected return on the security will equal the optimal forecast of the return:

$$RET^e = RET^{of} \tag{3}$$

Unfortunately, we cannot observe either RET^e or P^e_{t+1}, so the rational expectations equations by themselves do not tell us much about how the financial market behaves. However, if we can devise some way to measure the value of RET^e, these equations will have important implications for how prices of securities change in financial markets.

The supply and demand analysis of the bond market developed in Chapter 5 shows us that the expected return on a security (the interest rate in the case of the bond examined) will have a tendency to head toward the equilibrium return that equates the quantity demanded to the quantity supplied. Supply and demand analysis enables us to determine the expected return on a security with the following equilibrium condition: The expected return on a security RET^e equals the equilibrium return RET^*, which equates the quantity of the security demanded to the quantity supplied; that is,

$$RET^e = RET^* \tag{4}$$

The academic field of finance explores the factors (risk and liquidity, for example) that influence the equilibrium returns on securities. For our purposes, it is sufficient to know that we can determine the equilibrium return and thus determine the expected return with the equilibrium condition.

We can derive an equation to describe pricing behavior in an efficient market by using the equilibrium condition to replace RET^e with RET^* in the rational expectations equation (Equation 3). In this way we obtain

$$RET^{of} = RET^* \tag{5}$$

This equation tells us that ***current prices in a financial market will be set so that the optimal forecast of a security's return using all available***

---

[4]There are cases where C might not be known at the beginning of the period, but that does not make a substantial difference to the analysis. We would in that case assume that not only price expectations but also the expectations of C are optimal forecasts using all available information.

information equals the security's equilibrium return. Financial economists state it more simply: A security's price fully reflects all available information in an efficient market.

Rationale Behind the Theory

Let's see what the efficient markets condition means in practice and why it is a sensible characterization of pricing behavior. Suppose that the equilibrium return on a security, say, Exxon common stock, is 10% at an annual rate, and its current price P_t is lower than the optimal forecast of tomorrow's price P^{of}_{t+1} so that the optimal forecast of the return at an annual rate is 50%, which is greater than the equilibrium return of 10%. We are now able to predict that, on average, Exxon's return would be abnormally high. This situation is called an **unexploited profit opportunity** because, on average, people would be earning more than they should, given the characteristics of that security. Knowing that, on average, you can earn such an abnormally high rate of return on Exxon because $RET^{of} > RET^*$, you would buy more, which would in turn drive up its current price relative to the expected future price P^{of}_{t+1}, thereby lowering RET^{of}. When the current price had risen sufficiently so that RET^{of} equals RET^* and the efficient markets condition (Equation 5) is satisfied, the buying of Exxon will stop, and the unexploited profit opportunity will have disappeared.

Similarly, a security for which the optimal forecast of the return is -5% while the equilibrium return is 10% ($RET^{of} < RET^*$) would be a poor investment because, on average, it earns less than the equilibrium return. In such a case, you would sell the security and drive down its current price relative to the expected future price until RET^{of} rose to the level of RET^* and the efficient markets condition is again satisfied. What we have shown can be summarized as follows:

$$\left.\begin{array}{l} RET^{of} > RET^* \to P_t\uparrow \to RET^{of}\downarrow \\ RET^{of} < RET^* \to P_t\downarrow \to RET^{of}\uparrow \end{array}\right\} \quad \text{until} \quad RET^{of} = RET^*$$

Another way to state the efficient markets condition is this: ***In an efficient market, all unexploited profit opportunities will be eliminated.***

An extremely important factor in this reasoning is that ***not everyone in a financial market must be well informed about a security or have rational expectations for its price to be driven to the point at which the efficient markets condition holds.*** Financial markets are structured so that many participants can play. As long as a few keep their eyes open for unexploited profit opportunities, they will eliminate the profit opportunities that appear because in so doing, they make a profit. The theory of efficient markets makes sense because it does not require everyone in a market to be cognizant of what is happening to every security.

Stronger Version of Efficient Markets Theory

Many financial economists take efficient markets theory one step further in their analysis of financial markets. Not only do they define efficient markets as those in which expectations are rational, that is, equal to optimal forecasts using all available information, but they also add the condition that an efficient market is one in which prices reflect the true fundamental (intrinsic) value of the securities. Thus in an efficient market, all prices are always correct and reflect **market fundamentals** (items that have a direct impact on future income streams of the securities). This stronger view of market efficiency has several important implications in the academic field of finance. First, it implies that in an efficient capital market, one investment is as good as any other because the securities' prices are correct. Second, it implies that a security's price reflects all available information about the intrinsic value of the security. Third, it implies that security prices can be used by managers of both financial and nonfinancial firms to assess their cost of capital (cost of financing their investments) accurately and hence that security prices can be used to help them make the correct decisions about whether a specific investment is worth making or not. The stronger version of market efficiency is a basic tenet of much analysis in the finance field.

■ EVIDENCE ON EFFICIENT MARKETS THEORY

Early evidence on efficient markets theory was quite favorable to it, but in recent years, deeper analysis of the evidence suggests that the theory may not always be entirely correct. Let's first look at the earlier evidence in favor of the theory and then examine some of the more recent evidence that casts some doubt on it.

Evidence in Favor of Market Efficiency

Evidence in favor of market efficiency has examined the performance of investment analysts and mutual funds, whether stock prices reflect publicly available information, the random-walk behavior of stock prices, and the success of so-called technical analysis.

Performance of Investment Analysts and Mutual Funds. We have seen that one implication of efficient markets theory is that when purchasing a security, you cannot expect to earn an abnormally high return, a return greater than the equilibrium return. This implies that it is impossible to beat the market. Many studies shed light on whether investment advisers and mutual funds (some of which charge steep sales commissions to people who purchase them) beat the market. One common test that has been performed is to take buy and sell recommendations from a group of advisers or mutual funds and compare the performance of the resulting selection of stocks with the market as a whole. Sometimes the advisers' choices have even been compared to a group of stocks chosen by putting a copy of the financial page of the newspaper on a dartboard and throwing darts. The *Wall Street Journal,* for example, has a regular feature called "Investment Dartboard" that compares how well stocks picked by investment advisers do relative to stocks picked by throwing darts. Do the advisers win? To their embarrassment, the dartboard beats them as often as they beat the dartboard.

BOX 1

An Exception That Proves the Rule Ivan Boesky

Efficient markets theory indicates that investment advisers should not have the ability to beat the market. Yet that is exactly what Ivan Boesky was able to do until 1986, when he was charged by the Securities and Exchange Commission with making unfair profits (rumored to be in the hundreds of millions of dollars) by trading on inside information. In an out-of-court settlement, Boesky was banned from the securities business, fined $100 million, and sentenced to three years in jail. (After serving his sentence, Boesky was released from jail in 1990.) If the stock market is efficient, can the SEC legitimately claim that Boesky was able to beat the market? The answer is yes.

Ivan Boesky was the most successful of the so-called *arbs* (short for *arbitrageurs*) who made hundreds of millions in profits for himself and his clients by investing in the stocks of firms that were about to be taken over by other firms at an above-market price. Boesky's con-

tinuing success was assured by an arrangement whereby he paid cash (sometimes in a suitcase) to Dennis Levine, an investment banker who had inside information about when a takeover was to take place because his firm was arranging the financing of the deal. When Levine found out that a firm was planning a takeover, he would inform Boesky, who would then buy the stock of the company being taken over and sell it after the stock had risen.

Boesky's ability to make millions year after year in the 1980s is an exception that proves the rule that financial analysts cannot continually outperform the market; yet it supports the efficient markets claim that only information *unavailable to the market* enables an investor to do so. Boesky profited from knowing about takeovers before the rest of the market; this information was known to him but unavailable to the market.

Furthermore, even when the comparison includes only advisers who have been successful in the past in predicting the stock market, the advisers still don't regularly beat the dartboard.

In studies of mutual fund performance, mutual funds are separated into groups according to whether they had the highest or lowest profits in a chosen period. When their performance is compared to a subsequent period, the mutual funds that did well in the first period do not beat the market in the second.[5]

The conclusion from the study of investment advisers and mutual fund performance is this: ***Having performed well in the past does not indicate that an investment adviser or a mutual fund will perform well in the future.*** This is not pleasing news to investment advisers, but it is exactly what the theory of efficient markets predicts. It says that some advisers will be lucky and some will be unlucky. Being lucky does not mean that a forecaster actually has the ability to beat the market. (An exception that proves the rule is discussed in Box 1.)

Do Stock Prices Reflect Publicly Available Information? Efficient markets theory predicts that stock prices will reflect all publicly available information. Thus if information is already publicly available, a positive announcement about a com-

---

[5]An early study that found that mutual funds do not outperform the market is Michael C. Jensen, "The Performance of Mutual Funds in the Period 1945–64," *Journal of Finance* 23 (1968): 389–416. More recent studies on mutual fund performance are Mark Grimblatt and Sheridan Titman, "Mutual Fund Performance: An Analysis of Quarterly Portfolio Holdings," *Journal of Business* 62 (1989): 393–416, and R. A. Ippolito, "Efficiency with Costly Information: A Study of Mutual Fund Performance, 1965–84," *Quarterly Journal of Economics* 104 (1989): 1–23.

pany will not, on average, raise the price of its stock because this information is already reflected in the stock price. Early empirical evidence also confirmed this conjecture from efficient markets theory: Favorable earnings announcements or announcements of stock splits (a division of a share of stock into multiple shares, which is usually followed by higher earnings) do not, on average, cause stock prices to rise.[6]

Random-Walk Behavior of Stock Prices. The term **random walk** describes the movements of a variable whose future changes cannot be predicted (are random) because, given today's value, the variable is just as likely to fall as to rise. An important implication of efficient markets theory is that stock prices should approximately follow a random walk; that is, *future changes in stock prices should, for all practical purposes, be unpredictable.* The random-walk implication of efficient markets theory is the one most commonly mentioned in the press because it is the most readily comprehensible to the public. In fact, when people mention the "random-walk theory of stock prices," they are in reality referring to efficient markets theory.

The case for random-walk stock prices can be demonstrated. Suppose that people could predict that the price of Happy Feet Corporation (HFC) stock would rise 1% in the coming week. The predicted rate of capital gains and rate of return on HFC stock would then be over 50% at an annual rate. Since this is very likely to be far higher than the equilibrium rate of return on HFC stock $(RET^{of} > RET^*)$, the theory of efficient markets indicates that people would immediately buy this stock and bid up its current price. The action would stop only when the predictable change in the price dropped to near zero so that $RET^{of} = RET^*$.

Similarly, if people could predict that the price of HFC stock would fall by 1%, the predicted rate of return would be negative $(RET^{of} < RET^*)$, and people would immediately sell. The current price would fall until the predictable change in the price rose back to near zero, where the efficient markets condition again holds. Efficient markets theory suggests that the predictable change in stock prices will be near zero, leading to the conclusion that stock prices will generally follow a random walk.[7]

Financial economists have used two types of tests to explore the hypothesis that stock prices follow a random walk. In the first, they examine stock market records to see if changes in stock prices are systematically related to past changes and hence could have been predicted on that basis. The second type of test examines the data to see if publicly available information other than past stock prices could have been used to predict changes. These tests are somewhat more stringent because additional information (money supply growth, government

---

[6]Ray Ball and Philip Brown, "An Empirical Evaluation of Accounting Income Numbers," *Journal of Accounting Research* 6 (1968): 159–178; Eugene F. Fama, Lawrence Fisher, Michael C. Jensen, and Richard Roll, "The Adjustment of Stock Prices to New Information," *International Economic Review* 10 (1969): 1–21.

[7]Note that the random-walk behavior of stock prices is only an *approximation* derived from efficient markets theory. It would hold exactly only for a stock for which an unchanged price leads to its having the equilibrium return. Then, when the predictable change in the stock price is exactly zero, $RET^{of} = RET^*$.

spending, interest rates, corporate profits) might be used to help forecast stock returns. Early results from both types of tests generally confirmed the efficient markets view that stock prices are not predictable and follow a random walk.[8]

Technical Analysis A popular technique used to predict stock prices, called *technical analysis*, is to study past stock price data and search for patterns such as trends and regular cycles. Rules for when to buy and sell stocks are then established on the basis of the patterns that emerge. The theory of efficient markets suggests that technical analysis is a waste of time. The simplest way to understand why is to use the random-walk result derived from efficient markets theory that holds that past stock price data cannot help predict changes. Therefore, technical analysis, which relies on such data to produce its forecasts, cannot successfully predict changes in stock prices.

Two types of tests bear directly on the value of technical analysis. The first performs the empirical analysis described earlier to evaluate the performance of any financial analyst, technical or otherwise. The results are exactly what efficient markets theory predicts: Technical analysts fare no better than other financial analysts; on average, they do not outperform the market, and successful past forecasting does not imply that their forecasts will outperform the market in the future. The second type of test (first performed by Sidney Alexander) takes the rules developed in technical analysis for when to buy and sell stocks and applies them to new data.[9] The performance of these rules is then evaluated by the profits that would have been made using them. These tests also discredit technical analysis: It does not outperform the overall market.

APPLICATION | **SHOULD FOREIGN EXCHANGE RATES FOLLOW A RANDOM WALK?**

Efficient markets theory can be used to show that foreign exchange rates, like stock prices, should generally follow a random walk. To see why this is the case, consider what would happen if people could predict that a currency would appreciate by 1% in the coming week. By buying this currency, they could earn a greater than 50% return at an annual rate, which is likely to be far above the equilibrium return for holding a currency. As a result, people would immediately buy the cur-

---

[8]The first type of test, using only stock market data, is referred to as a test of *weak-form efficiency* because the information that can be used to predict stock prices is restricted solely to past price data. The second type of test is referred to as a test of *semistrong-form efficiency* because the information set is expanded to include all publicly available information, not just past stock prices. A third type of test is called a test of *strong-form efficiency* because the information set includes insider information, known only to the owners of the corporation, as when they plan to declare a high dividend. Strong-form tests do sometimes indicate that insider information can be used to predict changes in stock prices. This finding does not contradict efficient markets theory because the information is not available to the market and hence cannot be reflected in market prices. In fact, there are strict laws against using insider information to trade in financial markets. For an early survey on the three forms of tests, see Eugene F. Fama, "Efficient Capital Markets: A Review of Theory and Empirical Work," *Journal of Finance* 25 (1970): 383–416.

[9]Sidney Alexander, "Price Movements in Speculative Markets: Trends or Random Walks?" *Industrial Management Review,* May 1961, pp. 7–26; and Sidney Alexander, "Price Movements in Speculative Markets: Trends or Random Walks? No. 2," in *The Random Character of Stock Prices,* ed. Paul Cootner (Cambridge, Mass.: MIT Press, 1964), pp. 338–372.

rency and bid up its current price, thereby reducing the expected return. The process would stop only when the predictable change in the exchange rate dropped to near zero so that the optimal forecast of the return no longer differed from the equilibrium return. Likewise, if people could predict that the currency would depreciate by 1% in the coming week, they would sell it until the predictable change in the exchange rate was again near zero. Efficient markets theory therefore implies that future changes in exchange rates should, for all practical purposes, be unpredictable; in other words, exchange rates should follow random walks. This is exactly what empirical evidence finds.[10]

Evidence Against Market Efficiency

All the early evidence supporting efficient markets theory appeared to be overwhelming, causing Eugene Fama, a prominent financial economist, to state in his famous 1970 survey of the empirical evidence on efficient markets theory, "The evidence in support of the efficient markets model is extensive, and (somewhat uniquely in economics) contradictory evidence is sparse."[11] However, in recent years, the theory has begun to show a few cracks, referred to as *anomalies*, and empirical evidence indicates that efficient markets theory may not always be generally applicable.

Small-Firm Effect   One of the earliest reported anomalies in which the stock market did not appear to be efficient is called the *small-firm effect*. Many empirical studies have shown that small firms have earned abnormally high returns over long periods of time, even when the greater risk for these firms has been taken into account.[12] The small-firm effect seems to have diminished in recent years but is still a challenge to the theory of efficient markets. Various theories have been developed to explain the small-firm effect, suggesting that it may be due to rebalancing of portfolios by institutional investors, tax issues, low liquidity of small-firm stocks, large information costs in evaluating small firms, or an inappropriate measurement of risk for small-firm stocks.

January Effect   Over long periods of time, stock prices have tended to experience an abnormal price rise from December to January that is predictable and hence inconsistent with random-walk behavior. This so-called **January effect** seems to have diminished in recent years for shares of large companies but still occurs for

---

[10]See Richard A. Meese and Kenneth Rogoff, "Empirical Exchange Rate Models of the Seventies: Do They Fit out of Sample?" *Journal of International Economics* 14 (1983): 3–24.

[11]Eugene F. Fama, "Efficient Capital Markets: A Review of Theory and Empirical Work," *Journal of Finance* 25 (1970): 383–416.

[12]For example, see Marc R. Reinganum, "The Anomalous Stock Market Behavior of Small Firms in January: Empirical Tests of Tax Loss Selling Effects," *Journal of Financial Economics* 12 (1983): 89–104; Jay R. Ritter, "The Buying and Selling Behavior of Individual Investors at the Turn of the Year," *Journal of Finance* 43 (1988): 701–717; and Richard Roll, "Vas Ist Das? The Turn-of-the-Year Effect: Anomaly or Risk Mismeasurement?" *Journal of Portfolio Management* 9 (1988): 18–28.

shares of small companies.[13] Some financial economists argue that the January effect is due to tax issues. Investors have an incentive to sell stocks before the end of the year in December because they can then take capital losses on their tax return and reduce their tax liability. Then when the new year starts in January, they can repurchase the stocks, driving up their prices and producing abnormally high returns. Although this explanation seems sensible, it does not explain why institutional investors such as private pension funds, which are not subject to income taxes, do not take advantage of the abnormal returns in January and buy stocks in December, thus bidding up their price and eliminating the abnormal returns.[14]

Market Overreaction Recent research suggests that stock prices may overreact to news announcements and that the pricing errors are corrected only slowly.[15] When corporations announce a major change in earnings, say, a large decline, the stock price may overshoot, and after an initial large decline, it may rise back to more normal levels over a period of several weeks. This violates efficient markets theory because an investor could earn abnormally high returns, on average, by buying a stock immediately after a poor earnings announcement and then selling it after a couple of weeks when it has risen back to normal levels.

Excessive Volatility A closely related phenomenon to market overreaction is that the stock market appears to display excessive volatility; that is, fluctuations in stock prices may be much greater than is warranted by fluctuations in their fundamental value. In an important paper, Robert Shiller of Yale University found that fluctuations in the S&P 500 stock index could not be justified by the subsequent fluctuations in the dividends of the stocks making up this index. There has been much subsequent technical work criticizing these results, but Shiller's work, along with research that finds that there are smaller fluctuations in stock prices when stock markets are closed, has produced a consensus that stock market prices appear to be driven by factors other than fundamentals.[16]

Mean Reversion Some researchers have also found that stock returns display **mean reversion:** Stocks with low returns today tend to have high returns in the future, and vice versa. Hence stocks that have done poorly in the past are more

---

[13]For example, see Donald B. Keim, "The CAPM and Equity Return Regularities," *Financial Analysts Journal* 42 (May-June 1986): 19–34.

[14]Another anomaly that makes the stock market seem less than efficient is the fact that the *Value Line Survey*, one of the most prominent investment advice newsletters, has produced stock recommendations that have yielded abnormally high returns on average. See Fischer Black, "Yes, Virginia, There Is Hope: Tests of the Value Line Ranking System," *Financial Analysts Journal* 29 (September-October 1973): 10–14, and Gur Huberman and Shmuel Kandel, "Market Efficiency and Value Line's Record," *Journal of Business* 63 (1990): 187–216. Whether the excellent performance of the *Value Line Survey* will continue in the future is, of course, a question mark.

[15]Werner F. M. De Bondt and Richard Thaler, "Further Evidence on Investor Overreaction and Stock Market Seasonality," *Journal of Finance* 62 (1987): 557–580.

[16]Robert Shiller, "Do Stock Prices Move Too Much to Be Justified by Subsequent Changes in Dividends?" *American Economic Review* 71 (1981): 421–436, and Kenneth R. French and Richard Roll, "Stock Return Variances: The Arrival of Information and the Reaction of Traders," *Journal of Financial Economics* 17 (1986): 5–26.

likely to do well in the future because mean reversion indicates that there will be a predictable positive change in the future price, suggesting that stock prices are not a random walk. Other researchers have found that mean reversion is not nearly as strong in data after World War II and so have raised doubts about whether it is currently an important phenomenon. The evidence on mean reversion remains controversial.[17]

Overview of the Evidence on Efficient Markets Theory

As you can see, the debate on efficient markets theory is far from over. The evidence seems to suggest that efficient markets theory may be a reasonable starting point for evaluating behavior in financial markets. However, there do seem to be important violations of market efficiency that suggest that efficient markets theory may not be the whole story and so may not be generalizable to all behavior in financial markets.

■ THE PRACTICING FINANCIAL INSTITUTION MANAGER
Practical Guide to Investing in the Stock Market

Efficient markets theory has numerous applications to the real world. It is especially valuable because it can be applied directly to an issue that concerns managers of financial institutions (and the general public as well): how to make profits in the stock market. A practical guide to investing in the stock market, which we develop here, provides a better understanding of the use and implications of efficient markets theory.

How Valuable Are Published Reports by Investment Advisers?

Suppose that you have just read in the "Heard on the Street" column of the *Wall Street Journal* that investment advisers are predicting a boom in oil stocks because an oil shortage is developing. Should you proceed to withdraw all your hard-earned savings from the bank and invest it in oil stocks?

Efficient markets theory tells us that when purchasing a security, we cannot expect to earn an abnormally high return, a return greater than the equilibrium return. Information in newspapers and in the published reports of

---

[17]Evidence for mean reversion has been reported by James M. Poterba and Lawrence H. Summers, "Mean Reversion in Stock Prices: Evidence and Implications," *Journal of Financial Economics* 22 (1988): 27–59; Eugene F. Fama and Kenneth R. French, "Permanent and Temporary Components of Stock Prices," *Journal of Political Economy* 96 (1988): 246–273; and Andrew W. Lo and A. Craig MacKinlay, "Stock Market Prices Do Not Follow Random Walks: Evidence from a Simple Specification Test," *Review of Financial Studies* 1 (1988): 41–66. However, Myung Jig Kim, Charles R. Nelson, and Richard Startz, "Mean Reversion in Stock Prices? A Reappraisal of the Evidence," *Review of Economic Studies* 58 (1991): 515–528, question whether some of these findings are valid. For an excellent summary of this evidence, see Charles Engel and Charles S. Morris, "Challenges to Stock Market Efficiency: Evidence from Mean Reversion Studies," Federal Reserve Bank of Kansas City *Economic Review,* September-October 1991, pp. 21–35. See also N. Jegadeesh and Sheridan Titman, "Returns to Buying Winners and Selling Losers: Implications for Stock Market Efficiency," *Journal of Finance* 48 (1993): 65–92, which shows that mean reversion also occurs for individual stocks.

investment advisers is readily available to many market participants and is already reflected in market prices. So acting on this information will not yield abnormally high returns, on average. As we have seen, the empirical evidence for the most part confirms that recommendations from investment advisers cannot help us outperform the general market. Indeed, as Box 2 suggests, human investment advisers in San Francisco do not on average even outperform an orangutan!

Probably no other conclusion is met with more skepticism by students than this one when they first hear it. We all know or have heard of somebody who has been successful in the stock market for a period of many years. We wonder, how could someone be so consistently successful if he or she did not really know how to predict when returns would be abnormally high? The following story, reported in the press, illustrates why such anecdotal evidence is not reliable.

A get-rich-quick artist invented a clever scam. Every week, he wrote two letters. In letter A, he would pick team A to win a particular football game, and in letter B, he would pick the opponent, team B. A mailing list would then be separated into two groups, and he would send letter A to the people in one group and letter B to the people in the other. The following week he would do the same thing but would send these letters only to the group who had received the first letter with the correct prediction. After doing this for ten games, he had a small cluster of people who had received letters predicting the correct winning team for every game. He then mailed a final letter to them, declaring that since he was obviously an expert predictor of the outcome of football games (he had picked winners ten weeks in a row) and since his predictions were profitable for the recipients who bet on the games, he would continue to send his predictions only if he were paid a substantial amount of money. When one of his clients figured out what he was up to, the con man was prosecuted and thrown in jail!

What is the lesson of the story? Even if no forecaster is an accurate predictor of the market, there will always be a group of consistent winners. A person who has done well regularly in the past cannot guarantee that he or she will do well in the future. Note that there will also be a group of persistent losers, but you rarely hear about them because no one brags about a poor forecasting record.

■ BOX 2

Should You Hire an Ape as Your Investment Adviser?

The *San Francisco Chronicle* has come up with an amusing way of evaluating how successful investment advisers are at picking stocks. They ask eight analysts to pick five stocks at the beginning of the year and then compare the performance of their stock picks to those chosen by Jolyn, an orangutan living at Marine World/Africa USA in Vallejo, California. Consistent with the results found in the "Investment Dartboard" feature of the *Wall Street Journal*, Jolyn beats the investment advisers as often as they beat her. Given this result, you might be just as well off hiring an orangutan as your investment adviser as you would hiring a human being!

Should You Be Skeptical of Hot Tips?

Suppose that your broker phones you with a hot tip to buy stock in the Happy Feet Corporation (HFC) because it has just developed a product that is completely effective in curing athlete's foot. The stock price is sure to go up. Should you follow this advice and buy HFC stock?

Efficient markets theory indicates that you should be skeptical of such news. If the stock market is efficient, it has already priced HFC stock so that its expected return will equal the equilibrium return. The hot tip is not particularly valuable and will not enable you to earn an abnormally high return.

You might wonder, though, if the hot tip is based on new information and would give you an edge on the rest of the market. If other market participants have gotten this information before you, the answer is no. As soon as the information hits the street, the unexploited profit opportunity it creates will be quickly eliminated. The stock's price will already reflect the information, and you should expect to realize only the equilibrium return. But if you are one of the first to know the new information (as Ivan Boesky was—see Box 1), it can do you some good. Only then can you be one of the lucky ones who, on average, will earn an abnormally high return by helping eliminate the profit opportunity by buying HFC stock.

Do Stock Prices Always Rise When There Is Good News?

If you follow the stock market, you might have noticed a puzzling phenomenon: When good news about a stock, such as a particularly favorable earnings report, is announced, the price of the stock frequently does not rise. Efficient markets theory and the random-walk behavior of stock prices explain this phenomenon.

Because changes in stock prices are unpredictable, when information is announced that has already been expected by the market, the stock price will remain unchanged. The announcement does not contain any new information that should lead to a change in stock prices. If this were not the case and the announcement led to a change in stock prices, it would mean that the change was predictable. Because that is ruled out in an efficient market, **stock prices will respond to announcements only when the information being announced is new and unexpected.** If the news is expected, there will be no stock price response. This is exactly what the evidence we described earlier, which shows that stock prices reflect publicly available information suggests will occur.

Sometimes a stock price declines when good news is announced. Although this seems somewhat peculiar, it is completely consistent with the workings of an efficient market. Suppose that although the announced news is good, it is not as good as expected. HFC's earnings may have risen 15%, but if the market expected earnings to rise by 20%, the new information is actually unfavorable, and the stock price declines.

Efficient Markets Prescription for the Investor

What does the theory of efficient markets recommend for investing in the stock market? It tells us that hot tips, investment advisers' published recommendations, and technical analysis—all of which make use of publicly available information—cannot help an investor outperform the market. Indeed, it indicates that anyone without better information than other market participants cannot expect to beat the market. So what is an investor to do?

Efficient markets theory leads to the conclusion that such an investor (and almost all of us fit into this category) should not try to outguess the market by constantly buying and selling securities. This process does nothing but boost the income of brokers, who earn commissions on each trade.[18] Instead, the investor should pursue a "buy and hold" strategy—purchase stocks and hold them for long periods of time. This will lead to the same returns, on average, but the investor's net profits will be higher because fewer brokerage commissions will have to be paid.[19]

It is frequently a sensible strategy for a small investor, whose costs of managing a portfolio may be high relative to its size, to buy into a mutual fund rather than individual stocks. Because efficient markets theory indicates that no mutual fund can consistently outperform the market, an investor should not buy into one that has high management fees or that pays sales commissions to brokers but rather should purchase a no-load (commission-free) mutual fund that has low management fees.

As we have seen, the evidence indicates that it will not be easy to beat the prescription suggested here, although some of the anomalies to efficient markets theory suggest that an extremely clever investor (which rules out most of us) may be able to outperform a buy-and-hold strategy.

APPLICATION **WHAT DOES THE STOCK MARKET CRASH OF 1987 TELL US ABOUT RATIONAL EXPECTATIONS AND EFFICIENT MARKETS?**

Some observers have suggested that the October 19, 1987, stock market crash should make us question the validity of efficient markets and rational expectations. They do not believe that a rational marketplace could have produced such a massive swing in share prices. To what degree should the stock market crash make us doubt the validity of rational expectations and efficient markets theory?

Nothing in rational expectations theory rules out large one-day changes in stock prices. A large change in stock prices can result from new information that produces a dramatic change in optimal forecasts of the future valuation of firms. Some financial economists have pointed out that there are many possible explanations for why rational expectations of the future value of firms dropped dra-

---

[18]The investor may also have to pay Uncle Sam capital gains taxes on any profits that are realized when a security is sold—an additional reason why continual buying and selling does not make sense.

[19]As we saw in Chapter 4, the investor can also minimize risk by holding a diversified portfolio. The investor will be better off by pursuing a buy-and-hold strategy with a diversified portfolio or with a mutual fund that has a diversified portfolio.

matically on October 19, 1987: moves in Congress to restrict corporate takeovers, the disappointing performance of the trade deficit, congressional failure to reduce the budget deficit substantially, increased fears of inflation, the decline of the dollar, and increased fears of financial distress in the banking industry. Other financial economists doubt whether these explanations are enough to explain the stock market drop because none of these market fundamentals seems important enough.

One lesson from the Black Monday stock market crash appears to be that factors other than market fundamentals may have had an effect on stock prices. The crash of 1987 has therefore convinced many financial economists that the stronger version of efficient markets theory, which states that asset prices reflect the true fundamental (intrinsic) value of securities, is incorrect. They attribute a large role in the determination of stock prices to market psychology and to the institutional structure of the marketplace. However, nothing in this view contradicts the basic reasoning behind rational expectations or efficient markets theory—that market participants eliminate unexploited profit opportunities. Even though stock market prices may not always solely reflect market fundamentals, this does not mean that rational expectations do not hold. As long as the stock market crash was unpredictable, the basic lessons of the theory of rational expectations hold.

Some financial economists have come up with theories of what they call *rational bubbles* to explain events such as the stock market crash. A **bubble** is a situation in which the price of an asset differs from its fundamental market value. In a rational bubble, investors can have rational expectations that a bubble is occurring because the asset price is above its fundamental value but continue to hold the asset anyway. They might do this because they believe that someone else will buy the asset for a higher price in the future. In a rational bubble, asset prices can therefore deviate from their fundamental value for a long time because the bursting of the bubble cannot be predicted and so there are no unexploited profit opportunities.

However, other financial economists believe that the stock market crash of 1987 suggests that there may be unexploited profit opportunities and that the theory of rational expectations and efficient markets theory may be fundamentally flawed. The controversy over whether capital markets are efficient or expectations are rational continues.

SUMMARY

1. The theory of rational expectations states that expectations will not differ from optimal forecasts (the best guesses of the future) using all available information. Rational expectations theory makes sense because it is costly for people not to have the best forecast of the future. The theory has two important implications: (a) If there is a change in the way a variable moves, there will be a change in the way expectations of this variable are formed, too, and (b) the forecast errors of expectations are unpredictable.

2. Efficient markets theory is the application of rational expectations to the pricing of securities in financial markets. Current security prices will fully reflect all available information because in an efficient market, all unexploited profit opportunities are eliminated. The elimination of unexploited profit opportunities necessary for a financial market to be efficient does not require that all market participants be well informed and have rational expectations.

3. The evidence on efficient markets theory is quite mixed. Early evidence on the performance of investment analysts and mutual funds, whether stock prices reflect publicly available information, the random-walk behavior of stock prices, and the success of so-called technical analysis was quite favorable to efficient markets theory. However, in recent years, evidence on the small-firm effect, the January effect, the *Value Line Survey*, market overreaction, excessive volatility, and mean reversion suggests that the theory may not always be entirely correct. The evidence seems to suggest that efficient markets theory may be a reasonable starting point for evaluating behavior in financial markets but may not be generalizable to all behavior in financial markets.

4. Efficient markets theory indicates that hot tips, investment advisers' published recommendations, and technical analysis cannot help an investor outperform the market. The prescription for investors is to pursue a buy-and-hold strategy—purchase stocks and hold them for long periods of time. Empirical evidence generally supports these implications of efficient markets theory in the stock market.

5. The stock market crash of 1987 has convinced many financial economists that the stronger version of efficient markets theory, which states that asset prices reflect the true fundamental (intrinsic) value of securities, is not correct. It is less clear that the stock market crash shows that rational expectations theory is wrong. Even if the stock market was driven by factors other than fundamentals, the crash does not clearly demonstrate that expectations were not rational as long as the crash could not have been predicted.

KEY TERMS

adaptive expectations, p. 165
bubble, p. 181
efficient markets theory, p. 167
January effect, p. 175

market fundamentals, p. 171
mean reversion, p. 176
optimal forecast, p. 165
random walk, p. 173

rational expectations, p. 165
unexploited profit opportunity, p. 170

QUESTIONS AND PROBLEMS

*1. "Forecasters' predictions of inflation are notoriously inaccurate, so their expectations of inflation cannot be rational." Is this statement true, false, or uncertain? Explain your answer.

2. "Whenever it is snowing when Joe Commuter gets up in the morning, he misjudges how long it will take him to drive to work. Otherwise, his expectations of the driving time are perfectly accurate. Considering that it snows only once every ten years where Joe lives, Joe's expectations are almost always perfectly accurate." Are Joe's expectations rational? Why or why not?

*3. If a forecaster spends hours every day studying data to forecast interest rates but his expectations are not as accurate as predicting that tomorrow's interest rates will be identical to today's interest rate, are his expectations rational?

4. "If stock prices did not follow a random walk, there would be unexploited profit opportunities in the market." Is this statement true, false, or uncertain? Explain your answer.

*5. Suppose that increases in the money supply lead to a rise in stock prices. Does this mean that when you see that the money supply has had a sharp rise in the past week, you should go out and buy stocks? Why or why not?

6. If the public expects a corporation to lose $5 a share this quarter and it actually loses $4, which is still the largest loss in the history of the company, what does efficient markets theory say will happen to the price of the stock when the $4 loss is announced?

*7. If I read in the *Wall Street Journal* that the "smart money" on Wall Street expects stock prices to fall, should I follow that lead and sell all my stocks?

8. If my broker has been right in her five previous buy and sell recommendations, should I continue listening to her advice?

*9. Can a person with rational expectations expect the price of IBM to rise by 10% in the next month?

10. "If most participants in the stock market do not follow what is happening to the monetary aggregates, prices of common stocks will not fully reflect information about them." Is this statement true, false, or uncertain? Explain your answer.

*11. "An efficient market is one in which no one ever profits from having better information than the rest." Is this statement true, false, or uncertain? Explain your answer.

12. If higher money growth is associated with higher future inflation and if announced money growth turns out to be extremely high but is still less than the market expected, what do you think would happen to long-term bond prices?

*13. "Foreign exchange rates, like stock prices, should follow a random walk." Is this statement true, false, or uncertain? Explain your answer.

14. Can we expect the value of the dollar to rise by 2% next week if our expectations are rational?

*15. "Human fear is the source of stock market crashes, so these crashes indicate that expectations in the stock market cannot be rational." Is this statement true, false, or uncertain? Explain your answer.

■ **CASE STUDY**
■
■ # Adaptive Expectations, Rational Expectations, Optimal Forecast, January Effect

CONCEPTS IN THIS CASE

adaptive expectations
rational expectations
optimal forecast
unexploited profit opportunity
random walk
January effect
mean reversion

You have been identified as someone in your firm who can make impressive presentations. This ability has grown over time. Although you were not pleased with this requirement in school, you are now convinced that this classroom experience will lead you quickly to higher positions in your company.

The presentation you have been asked to produce is about the general theory of how capital markets work. To explain how capital markets work, you have decided to provide definitions and practical examples of the concepts of adaptive expectations, rational expectations, optimal forecast, random walk, and mean reversion.

After gathering the information you need, you decide to use an example to make your points, assuming that the historical inflation rate has ranged between 4% and 6%, the average inflation rate has been 5%, and the inflation rate is 1% higher than the average when the unemployment rate is 4.5% or below.

1. Given that the unemployment rate dropped recently to 4.0%,
   a. What is the adaptive expectation of inflation?
   b. What is the rational expectation of inflation?

2. What does rational expectations theory state about forecast errors of expectations?

3. How does rational expectations theory relate to efficient markets theory?

4. If the current price of an asset is $100, the cash payment to be received is $5, and you expect the price to increase to $103 in one year,
   a. What is the expectation of return at the beginning of this investment?
   b. How does the forecast of the future price relate to the optimal forecast in the theory of rational expectations?

5. What is the "equilibrium" return of a security?

6. What is the relationship between the current prices in a financial market and the security's equilibrium return?

7. How does the market react to unexploited profits in an efficient market?

8. If an investment adviser has performed well in the past, what does this indicate about the future?

9. If stock prices follow a "random walk," what does this indicate about the predictability of future stock prices?

10. What is the performance record of "technical analysts" relative to the overall market?

11. What evidence exists against the theory of market efficiency, with respect to
    a. The small-firm effect?
    b. The January effect?
    c. Market overreaction?
    d. Excessive volatility?
    e. Mean reversion?

12. Explain why foreign exchange rates should or should not follow a random walk.

PART III

Financial Markets

CHAPTER 8

THE FOREIGN EXCHANGE MARKET

■ **PREVIEW** In the 1980s, American businesses became less competitive with their foreign counterparts; in the 1990s, their competitiveness has increased. Was this swing in competitiveness primarily the result of American management falling down on the job in the 1980s, then getting its act together in the 1990s? Not really. American businesses became less competitive in the 1980s because American dollars became worth more in terms of foreign currencies, making American goods more expensive relative to foreign goods. By the 1990s, the value of the U.S. dollar had fallen appreciably from its highs in the mid-1980s, making American goods cheaper and enabling American businesses to be more competitive.

The price of one currency in terms of another is called the **exchange rate.** It affects the economy because when the U.S. dollar becomes more valuable relative to foreign currencies, American goods become more expensive and foreign goods become cheaper. When the U.S. dollar falls in value, American goods become cheaper and foreign goods become more expensive. In addition, changes in the exchange rate have a major impact on financial institutions because many of their assets are denominated in foreign currencies; when the value of foreign currencies changes, the market value of financial institutions changes as well. To understand why exchange rates change, we need to examine the market in which they are determined, the **foreign exchange market.**

In the 1980s, exchange rates were highly volatile. As shown in Figure 1, from the beginning of 1980 to early 1985, the dollar strengthened, and its value relative to many other currencies climbed sharply—100% against the pound sterling, 90% against the German mark, and 75% against the Swiss franc. From early 1985 to the end of 1996, the dollar weakened and fell in value relative to other currencies— over 50% against the Japanese yen, 50% against the German mark, 50% against

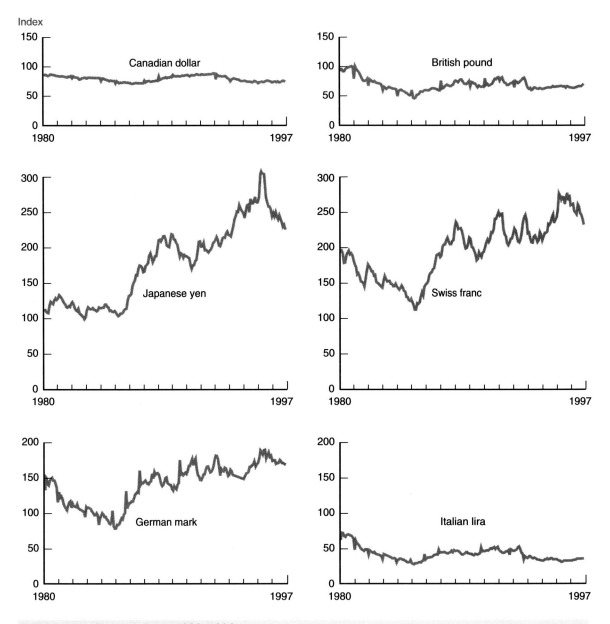

■FIGURE 1 Exchange Rates, 1980–1996

Dollar prices of selected foreign currencies (monthly averages; index: March 1973 = 100). Note that a decline in these plots means a strengthening of the dollar, and an increase indicates a weakening of the dollar. *Sources: International Financial Statistics*; Citibase databank.

the Swiss franc, and 15% against the pound sterling. What factors explain the former strength and later weakness of the dollar that has caused major swings in the competitiveness of American businesses? Why are exchange rates so volatile from day to day?

To answer these questions, we develop a modern view of exchange rate determination that explains recent behavior in the foreign exchange market.

■ FOREIGN EXCHANGE MARKET

Most countries of the world have their own currencies: The United States has its dollar; France, its franc; Brazil, its cruzeiro real; and India, its rupee. Trade between countries involves the mutual exchange of different currencies (or, more usually, bank deposits denominated in different currencies). When an American firm buys foreign goods, services, or financial assets, for example, U.S. dollars (typically, bank deposits denominated in U.S. dollars) must be exchanged for foreign currency (bank deposits denominated in the foreign currency).

The trading of currency and bank deposits denominated in particular currencies takes place in the foreign exchange market. The volume of these transactions worldwide averages over $1 trillion daily. Transactions conducted in the foreign exchange market determine the rates at which currencies are exchanged, which in turn determine the cost of purchasing foreign goods and financial assets.

What Are Foreign Exchange Rates?

There are two kinds of exchange rate transactions. The predominant ones, called **spot transactions,** involve the immediate (two-day) exchange of bank deposits. **Forward transactions** involve the exchange of bank deposits at some specified future date. The **spot exchange rate** is the exchange rate for the spot transaction, and the **forward exchange rate** is the exchange rate for the forward transaction.

When a currency increases in value, it experiences **appreciation;** when it falls in value and is worth fewer U.S. dollars, it undergoes **depreciation.** At the beginning of 1980, for example, the French franc was valued at 24 cents, and as indicated in the "Following the Financial News" box, on October 8, 1996, it was valued at 19.36 cents. The franc *depreciated* by 19%: $(19.36 - 24)/24 = -0.19 = -19\%$. Conversely, we could say that the U.S. dollar, which went from a value of 4.23 francs per dollar in 1980 to a value of 5.17 francs per dollar in October 1996, *appreciated* by 22%: $(5.17 - 4.23)/4.23 = 0.22 = 22\%$.

Why Are Exchange Rates Important?

Exchange rates are important because they affect the relative price of domestic and foreign goods. The dollar price of French goods to an American is determined by the interaction of two factors: the price of French goods in francs and the franc/dollar exchange rate.

Suppose that Wanda the Winetaster, an American, decides to buy a bottle of 1961 (a very good year) Château Lafite Rothschild to complete her wine cellar. If the price of the wine in France is 2000 francs and the exchange rate is $0.1936 to the franc, the wine will cost Wanda $387 (= 2000 francs × $0.1936/franc). Now suppose that Wanda delays her purchase by two months, at which time the French

Foreign Exchange Rates

Foreign exchange rates are published daily and appear in the "Currency Trading" column of the *Wall Street Journal*. The entries from one such column, shown here, are explained in the text.

The first entry for the French franc lists the exchange rate for the spot transaction (the spot exchange rate) on October 8, 1996, and is quoted in two ways: $0.1936 per franc and 5.1655 francs per dollar. Americans generally regard the exchange rate with France as $0.1936 per franc, while the French think of it as 5.1655 francs per dollar. The three entries immediately below the spot exchange rates give the rates for forward transactions (the forward exchange rates) that will take place 30, 90, and 180 days in the future. For example, Tuesday's 180-day forward rate for the French franc is $0.1956 per franc or, equivalently, 5.1131 francs per dollar.

CURRENCY TRADING

EXCHANGE RATES

Tuesday, October 8, 1996

The New York foreign exchange selling rates below apply to trading among banks in amounts of $1 million and more, as quoted at 3 p.m. Eastern time by Dow Jones Telerate Inc. and other sources. Retail transactions provide fewer units of foreign currency per dollar.

Country	U.S. $ equiv. Tue	U.S. $ equiv. Mon	Currency Per U.S. $ Tue	Currency Per U.S. $ Mon
Argentina (Peso)	1.0012	1.0012	.9988	.9988
Australia (Dollar)	.7911	.7878	1.2641	1.2694
Austria (Schilling)	.09319	.09289	10.731	10.766
Bahrain (Dinar)	2.6490	2.6490	.3775	.3775
Belgium (Franc)	.03176	.03173	31.485	31.520
Brazil (Real)	.9737	.9737	1.0270	1.0270
Britain (Pound)	1.5625	1.5630	.6400	.6398
30-Day Forward ...	1.5618	1.5623	.6403	.6401
90-Day Forward ...	1.5611	1.5615	.6406	.6404
180-Day Forward ...	1.5601	1.5604	.6410	.6409
Canada (Dollar)	.7386	.7390	1.3539	1.3532
30-Day Forward ...	.7398	.7401	1.3518	1.3512
90-Day Forward ...	.7420	.7424	1.3477	1.3470
180-Day Forward ...	.7453	.7457	1.3418	1.3410
Chile (Peso)	.002491	.002419	413.35	413.45
China (Renminbi)	.1200	.1200	8.3315	8.3307
Colombia (Peso)	.0009847	.0009847	1015.50	1015.50
Czech. Rep. (Koruna) ..	....	....		
Commercial rate	.03679	.03655	27.180	27.360
Denmark (Krone)	.1708	.1706	5.8545	5.8625
Ecuador (Sucre)	....	....		
Floating rate	.0003051	.0003047	3278.00	3282.00
Finland (Markka)	.2192	.2187	4.5619	4.5723
France (Franc)	.1936	.1933	5.1655	5.1730
30-Day Forward ...	.1939	.1937	5.1566	5.1638
90-Day Forward ...	.1946	.1943	5.1390	5.1467
180-Day Forward ...	.1956	.1952	5.1131	5.1217
Germany (Mark)	.6537	.6531	1.5297	1.5311
30-Day Forward ...	.6550	.6545	1.5267	1.5279
90-Day Forward ...	.6577	.6570	1.5205	1.5220
180-Day Forward ...	.6617	.6609	1.5113	1.5130
Greece (Drachma)	.004167	.004154	239.98	240.71
Hong Kong (Dollar) ..	.1293	.1293	7.7320	7.7323
Hungary (Forint)	.006310	.006296	158.47	158.84
India (Rupee)	.02801	.02807	35.705	35.630
Indonesia (Rupiah)	.0004309	.0004306	2320.75	2322.25
Ireland (Punt)	1.6026	1.6018	.6240	.6243
Israel (Shekel)	.3135	.3135	3.1903	3.1903
Italy (Lira)	.0006585	.0006588	1518.50	1518.00
Japan (Yen)	.008953	.008993	111.69	111.20
30-Day Forward ...	.008992	.009034	111.21	110.69
90-Day Forward ...	.009071	.009110	110.25	109.78
180-Day Forward ...	.009183	.009225	108.90	108.40
Jordan (Dinar)	1.4065	1.4065	.7110	.7110
Kuwait (Dinar)	3.3344	3.3434	.2999	.2991
Lebanon (Pound)	.0006420	.0006420	1557.75	1557.75
Malaysia (Ringgit)	.3996	.3998	2.5027	2.5010
Malta (Lira)	2.7739	2.7701	.3605	.3610
Mexico (Peso)	....	....		
Floating rate	.1326	.1329	7.5440	7.5260
Netherland (Guilder) ..	.5826	.5822	1.7163	1.7177
New Zealand (Dollar) .	.6916	.6912	1.4459	1.4468
Norway (Krone)	.1539	.1537	6.4970	6.5065
Pakistan (Rupee)	.02744	.02735	36.440	36.560
Peru (new Sol)	.3988	.3979	2.5074	2.5134
Philippines (Peso)	.03807	.03807	26.267	26.269
Poland (Zloty)	.3563	.3554	2.8070	2.8135
Portugal (Escudo)	.006461	.006470	154.78	154.56
Russia (Ruble) (a)	.0001846	.0001846	5417.00	5418.00
Saudia Arabia (Riyal) ..	.2666	.2666	3.7505	3.7505
Singapore (Dollar)	.7087	.7084	1.4111	1.4116
Slovak Rep. (Koruna) ..	.03263	.03263	30.650	30.650
South Africa (Rand) ..	.2205	.2205	4.5360	4.5355
South Korea (Won) ...	.001206	.001208	828.85	827.65
Spain (Peseta)	.007772	.007764	128.67	128.80
Sweden (Krona)	.1520	.1512	6.5808	6.6133
Switzerland (Franc) ...	.7974	.7971	1.2540	1.2545
30-Day Forward ...	.8002	.8000	1.2497	1.2500
90-Day Forward ...	.8054	.8051	1.2416	1.2421
180-Day Forward ...	.8134	.8131	1.2294	1.2298
Taiwan (Dollar)	.03637	.03638	27.495	27.485
Thailand (Baht)	.03932	.03929	25.434	25.453
Turkey (Lira)	.00001079	.00001079	92650.00	92646.00
United Arab (Dirham) ..	.2723	.2723	3.6720	3.6720
Uruguay (New Peso) .	....	....		
Financial	.1190	.1198	8.4000	8.3500
Venezuela (Bolivar) b .	.002151	.002148	465.00	465.62
Brady Rate	.002148	.002148	465.50	465.50
SDR	1.4409	1.4385	.6940	.6952
ECU	1.2531	1.2494		

Special Drawing Rights (SDR) are based on exchange rates for the U.S., German, British, French, and Japanese currencies.
Source: International Monetary Fund.

European Currency Unit (ECU) is based on a basket of community currencies.

a-fixing, Moscow Interbank Currency Exchange.

b-Changed to market rate effective Apr. 22.

Source: Wall Street Journal, October 9, 1996, p. C15.

franc has appreciated to $0.20 per franc. If the domestic price of the bottle of Lafite Rothschild remains 2000 francs, its dollar cost will have risen from $387 to $400.

The same currency appreciation, however, makes the price of foreign goods in that country less expensive. At an exchange rate of $0.1936 per franc, a Compaq computer priced at $2000 costs Claude the Programmer 10,331 francs; if the exchange rate increases to $0.20 per franc, the computer will cost only 10,000 francs.

A depreciation of the franc lowers the cost of French goods in America but raises the cost of American goods in France. If the franc drops in value to $0.10, Wanda's bottle of Lafite Rothschild will cost her only $200 instead of $387, and the Compaq computer will cost Claude 20,000 francs rather than 10,331.

Such reasoning leads to the following conclusion: ***When a country's currency appreciates (rises in value relative to other currencies), the country's goods abroad become more expensive and foreign goods in that country become cheaper (holding domestic prices constant in the two countries). Conversely, when a country's currency depreciates, its goods abroad become cheaper and foreign goods in that country become more expensive.***

Appreciation of a currency can make it harder for domestic manufacturers to sell their goods abroad and can increase competition at home from foreign goods because they cost less. From 1980 to early 1985, the appreciating dollar hurt U.S. industries. For instance, the U.S. steel industry was hurt not just because sales abroad of the more expensive American steel declined but also because sales of relatively cheap foreign steel in the United States increased. Although appreciation of the U.S. dollar hurt some domestic businesses, American consumers benefited because foreign goods were less expensive. Japanese videocassette recorders and cameras and the cost of vacationing in Europe fell in price as a result of the strong dollar.

How Is Foreign Exchange Traded?

You cannot go to a centralized location to watch exchange rates being determined; currencies are not traded on exchanges such as the New York Stock Exchange. Instead, the foreign exchange market is organized as an over-the-counter market in which several hundred dealers (mostly banks) stand ready to buy and sell deposits denominated in foreign currencies. Because these dealers are in constant telephone and computer contact, the market is very competitive; in effect, it functions no differently from a centralized market.

An important point to note is that while banks, companies, and governments talk about buying and selling currencies in foreign exchange markets, they do not take a fistful of dollar bills and sell them for British pound notes. Rather, most trades involve the buying and selling of bank deposits denominated in different currencies. So when we say that a bank is buying dollars in the foreign exchange market, what we actually mean is that the bank is buying deposits *denominated in dollars*.

Trades in the foreign exchange market consist of transactions in excess of $1 million. The market that determines the exchange rates in the "Following the Financial News" box is not where one would buy foreign currency for a trip abroad. Instead, we buy foreign currency in the retail market from dealers such as American Express or from banks. Because retail prices are higher than wholesale, when we buy foreign exchange, we obtain fewer units of foreign currency per dollar than exchange rates in the box indicate.

■ EXCHANGE RATES IN THE LONG RUN

Like the price of any good or asset in a free market, exchange rates are determined by the interaction of supply and demand. To simplify our analysis of exchange rates in a free market, we divide it into two parts. First, we examine how exchange rates are determined in the long run; then we use our knowledge of the long-run determinants of the exchange rate to help us understand how they are determined in the short run.

Law of One Price

The starting point for understanding how exchange rates are determined is a simple idea called the **law of one price:** If two countries produce an identical good, the price of the good should be the same throughout the world no matter which country produces it. Suppose that American steel costs $100 per ton and identical Japanese steel costs 10,000 yen per ton. The law of one price suggests that the exchange rate between the yen and the dollar must be 100 yen per dollar ($0.01 per yen) in order for one ton of American steel to sell for 10,000 yen in Japan (the price of Japanese steel) and one ton of Japanese steel to sell for $100 in the United States (the price of U.S. steel). If the exchange rate were 200 yen to the dollar, Japanese steel would sell for $50 per ton in the United States, or half the price of American steel, and American steel would sell for 20,000 yen per ton in Japan, twice the price of the Japanese steel. Because American steel would be more expensive than Japanese steel in both countries and is identical to Japanese steel, the demand for American steel would go to zero. Given a fixed dollar price for American steel, the resulting excess supply of American steel will be eliminated only if the exchange rate falls to 100 yen per dollar, making the price of American steel and Japanese steel the same in both countries.

Theory of Purchasing Power Parity

One of the most prominent theories of how exchange rates are determined is the **theory of purchasing power parity (PPP).** It states that exchange rates between any two currencies will adjust to reflect changes in the price levels of the two countries. The theory of PPP is simply an application of the law of one price to national price levels rather than to individual prices. Suppose that the yen price of Japanese steel rises 10% (to 11,000 yen) relative to the dollar price of American steel (unchanged at $100). For the law of one price to hold, the exchange rate must rise to 110 yen to the dollar, a 10% appreciation of the dollar. Applying the law of one price to the price levels in the two countries produces the theory of purchasing power parity, which maintains that if the Japanese price level rises 10% relative to the U.S. price level, the dollar will appreciate by 10%.

As our U.S./Japanese example demonstrates, the theory of PPP suggests that if one country's price level rises relative to another's, its currency should depreciate (the other country's currency should appreciate). As you can see in Figure 2, this prediction is borne out in the long run. From 1973 to 1996, the British price level rose 82% relative to the U.S. price level, and as the theory of PPP predicts, the dollar appreciated against sterling, though by 65%, an amount smaller than the 82% increase predicted by PPP.

Yet, as the same figure indicates, PPP theory often has little predictive power in the short run. From early 1985 to the end of 1987, for example, the British price level rose relative to that of the United States. Instead of appreciating, as PPP theory predicts, the U.S. dollar actually depreciated by 40%. So even though PPP theory provides some guidance to the long-run movement of exchange rates, it is not perfect and in the short run is a particularly poor predictor. What explains PPP theory's failure to predict well?

Why the Theory of Purchasing Power Parity Cannot Fully Explain Exchange Rates

The PPP conclusion that exchange rates are determined solely by changes in relative price levels rests on the assumption that all goods are identical in both countries. When this assumption is true, the law of one price states that the relative prices of all these goods (that is, the relative price level between the two

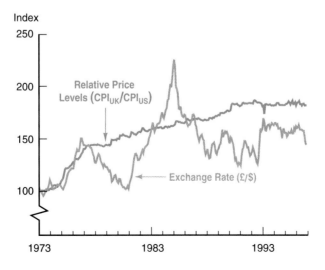

■FIGURE 2 Purchasing Power Parity, United States/United Kingdom, 1973–1996
(Index: March 1973 = 100)

Source: International Financial Statistics.

countries) will determine the exchange rate. The assumption that goods are identical may not be too unreasonable for American and Japanese steel, but is it a reasonable assumption for American and Japanese cars? Is a Toyota the equivalent of a Chevrolet?

Because Toyotas and Chevys are obviously not identical, their prices do not have to be equal. Toyotas can be more expensive relative to Chevys and both Americans and Japanese will still purchase Toyotas. Because the law of one price does not hold for all goods, a rise in the price of Toyotas relative to Chevys will not necessarily mean that the yen must depreciate by the amount of the relative price increase of Toyotas over Chevys.

PPP theory furthermore does not take into account that many goods and services (whose prices are included in a measure of a country's price level) are not traded across borders. Housing, land, and services such as restaurant meals, haircuts, and golf lessons are not traded goods. So even though the prices of these items might rise and lead to a higher price level relative to another country's, there would be little direct effect on the exchange rate.

Factors That Affect Exchange Rates in the Long Run

Our analysis indicates that relative price levels and additional factors affect the exchange rate. In the long run, there are four major ones: relative price levels, tariffs and quotas, preferences for domestic versus foreign goods, and productivity. We examine how each of these factors affects the exchange rate while holding the others constant.

The basic reasoning proceeds along the following lines: Anything that increases the demand for domestic goods relative to foreign goods tends to appreciate the domestic currency because domestic goods will continue to sell well even when the value of the domestic currency is higher. Similarly, anything that increases the demand for foreign goods relative to domestic goods tends to depreciate the domestic currency because domestic goods will continue to sell well only if the value of the domestic currency is lower.

Relative Price Levels In line with PPP theory, when prices of American goods rise (holding prices of foreign goods constant), the demand for American goods falls and the dollar tends to depreciate so that American goods can still sell well. By contrast, if prices of Japanese goods rise so that the relative prices of American goods fall, the demand for American goods increases, and the dollar tends to appreciate because American goods will continue to sell well even with a higher value of the domestic currency. ***In the long run, a rise in a country's price level (relative to the foreign price level) causes its currency to depreciate, and a fall in the country's relative price level causes its currency to appreciate.***

Tariffs and Quotas Barriers to free trade such as **tariffs** (taxes on imported goods) and **quotas** (restrictions on the quantity of foreign goods that can be imported) can affect the exchange rate. Suppose that the United States imposes a tariff or a quota on Japanese steel. These trade barriers increase the demand for

American steel, and the dollar tends to appreciate because American steel will still sell well even with a higher value of the dollar. ***Tariffs and quotas cause a country's currency to appreciate in the long run.***

Preferences for Domestic Versus Foreign Goods If the Japanese develop an appetite for American goods—say, for Florida oranges and American movies—the increased demand for American goods (exports) tends to appreciate the dollar because the American goods will continue to sell well even at a higher value for the dollar. Likewise, if Americans decide that they prefer Japanese cars to American cars, the increased demand for Japanese goods (imports) tends to depreciate the dollar. ***Increased demand for a country's exports causes its currency to appreciate in the long run; conversely, increased demand for imports causes the domestic currency to depreciate.***

Productivity If one country becomes more productive than other countries, businesses in that country can lower the prices of domestic goods relative to foreign goods and still earn a profit. As a result, the demand for domestic goods rises, and the domestic currency tends to appreciate because domestic goods will continue to sell well at a higher value for the currency. If, however, its productivity lags behind that of other countries, its goods become relatively more expensive, and the currency tends to depreciate. ***In the long run, as a country becomes more productive relative to other countries, its currency appreciates.***[1]

> ■ **STUDY GUIDE** The trick to figuring out what long-run effect a factor has on the exchange rate is to remember the following: ***If a factor increases the demand for domestic goods relative to foreign goods, the domestic currency will appreciate, and if a factor decreases the relative demand for domestic goods, the domestic currency will depreciate.*** See how this works by explaining what happens to the exchange rate when any of the factors in Table 1 declines rather than increases.

Our long-run theory of exchange rate behavior is summarized in Table 1. We use the convention that the exchange rate E is quoted so that an appreciation of the currency corresponds to a rise in the exchange rate. In the case of the United States, this means that we are quoting the exchange rate as units of foreign currency per dollar (say, yen per dollar).[2]

---

[1]A country might be so small that a change in productivity or the preferences for domestic or foreign goods would have no effect on prices of these goods relative to foreign goods. In this case, changes in productivity or changes in preferences for domestic or foreign goods affect the country's income but will not necessarily affect the value of the currency. In our analysis, we are assuming that these factors can affect relative prices and consequently the exchange rate.

[2]In professional writing, many economists quote exchange rates as units of domestic currency per foreign currency so that an appreciation of the domestic currency is portrayed as a fall in the exchange rate. The opposite convention is used in the text here because it is more intuitive to think of an appreciation of the domestic currency as a rise in the exchange rate.

SUMMARY TABLE 1	Factors That Affect Exchange Rates in the Long Run	

Factor	Change in Factor	Response of the Exchange Rate, E^*
Domestic price level†	↑	↓
Tariffs and quotas†	↑	↑
Import demand	↑	↓
Export demand	↑	↑
Productivity†	↑	↑

*Units of foreign currency per dollar: ↑ indicates currency appreciation; ↓, depreciation.

†Relative to other countries.

NOTE: Only increase (↑) in the factors are shown; the effects of decreases in the variables on the exchange rate are the opposite of those indicated in the "Response" column.

EXCHANGE RATES IN THE SHORT RUN

We have developed a theory of the long-run behavior of exchange rates. However, if we are to understand why exchange rates exhibit such large changes (sometimes several percent) from day to day, we must develop a theory of how current exchange rates (spot exchange rates) are determined in the short run.

The key to understanding the short-run behavior of exchange rates is to recognize that an exchange rate is the price of domestic bank deposits (those denominated in the domestic currency) in terms of foreign bank deposits (those denominated in the foreign currency). Because the exchange rate is the price of one asset in terms of another, the natural way to investigate the short-run determination of exchange rates is through an asset market approach that relies heavily on the theory of portfolio choice developed in Chapter 4. As you will see, however, the long-run determinants of the exchange rate we have just outlined also play an important role in the short-run asset market approach.[3]

Earlier approaches to exchange rate determination emphasized the role of import and export demand. The more modern asset market approach used here does not emphasize the flows of purchases of exports and imports over short periods because these transactions are quite small relative to the amount of domestic and foreign bank deposits at any given time. For example, foreign exchange transactions in the United States each year are well over 25 times greater than the amount of U.S. exports and imports. Thus over short periods such as a year, decisions to hold domestic or foreign assets play a much greater role in exchange rate determination than the demand for exports and imports does.

Comparing Expected Returns on Domestic and Foreign Deposits

In this analysis, we treat the United States as the home country, so domestic bank deposits are denominated in dollars. For simplicity, we use francs to stand for any foreign country's currency, so foreign bank deposits are denominated in francs.

---

[3]For a further description of the modern asset market approach to exchange rate determination that we use here, see Paul Krugman and Maurice Obstfeld, *International Economics,* 4th ed. (Reading, Mass.: Addison Wesley Longman, 1997).

The theory of portfolio choice suggests that the most important factor affecting the demand for domestic (dollar) deposits and foreign (franc) deposits is the expected return on these assets relative to each other. When Americans or foreigners expect the return on dollar deposits to be high relative to the return on foreign deposits, there is a higher demand for dollar deposits and a correspondingly lower demand for franc deposits. To understand how the demands for dollar and foreign deposits change, we need to compare the expected returns on dollar deposits and foreign deposits.

To illustrate further, suppose that dollar deposits have an interest rate (expected return payable in dollars) of i^D, and foreign bank deposits have an interest rate (expected return payable in the foreign currency, francs) of i^F. To compare the expected returns on dollar deposits and foreign deposits, investors must convert the returns into the currency unit they use.

First let us examine how François the Foreigner compares the returns on dollar deposits and foreign deposits denominated in his currency, the franc. When he considers the expected return on dollar deposits in terms of francs, he recognizes that it does not equal i^D; instead, the expected return must be adjusted for any expected appreciation or depreciation of the dollar. If the dollar were expected to appreciate by 7%, for example, the expected return on dollar deposits in terms of francs would be 7% higher because the dollar has become worth 7% more in terms of francs. Thus if the interest rate on dollar deposits is 10%, with an expected appreciation of the dollar of 7%, the expected return on dollar deposits in terms of francs is 17%: the 10% interest rate plus the 7% expected appreciation of the dollar. Conversely, if the dollar were expected to depreciate by 7% over the year, the expected return on dollar deposits in terms of francs would be only 3%: the 10% interest rate minus the 7% expected depreciation of the dollar.

Writing the currency exchange rate (the spot exchange rate) as E_t and the expected exchange rate for the next period as E^e_{t+1}, we can write the expected rate of appreciation of the dollar as $(E^e_{t+1} - E_t)/E_t$. Our reasoning indicates that the expected return on dollar deposits RET^D in terms of foreign currency can be written as the sum of the interest rate on dollar deposits plus the expected appreciation of the dollar[4]:

$$RET^D \text{ in terms of francs} = i^D + \frac{E^e_{t+1} - E_t}{E_t}$$

---

[4]This expression is actually an approximation of the expected return in terms of francs, which can be more precisely calculated by thinking how a foreigner invests in the dollar deposit. Suppose that François decides to put one franc into dollar deposits. First he buys $1/E_t$ of U.S. dollar deposits (recall that E_t, the exchange rate between dollar and franc deposits, is quoted in francs per dollar), and at the end of the period he is paid $(1 + i^D)(1/E_t)$ in dollars. To convert this amount into the number of francs he expects to receive at the end of the period, he multiplies this quantity by E^e_{t+1}. François's expected return on his initial investment of one franc can thus be written as $(1 + i^D)E^e_{t+1}/E_t)$ minus his initial investment of one franc:

$$(1 + i^D)\left(\frac{E^e_{t+1}}{E_t}\right) - 1$$

which can be rewritten as

$$i^D\left(\frac{E^e_{t+1}}{E_t}\right) + \frac{E^e_{t+1} - E_t}{E_t}$$

which is approximately equal to the expression in the text because E^e_{t+1}/E_t is typically close to 1.

However, François's expected return on foreign deposits RET^F in terms of francs is just i^F. Thus in terms of francs, the relative expected return on dollar deposits (that is, the difference between the expected return on dollar deposits and franc deposits) is calculated by subtracting i^F from the expression just given to yield

$$\text{Relative } RET^D = i^D - i^F + \frac{E^e_{t+1} - E_t}{E_t} \tag{1}$$

As the relative expected return on dollar deposits increases, foreigners will want to hold more dollar deposits and fewer foreign deposits.

Next let us look at the decision to hold dollar deposits versus franc deposits from Al the American's point of view. Following the same reasoning we used to evaluate the decision for François, we know that the expected return on foreign deposits RET^F in terms of dollars is the interest rate on foreign deposits i^F plus the expected appreciation of the foreign currency, equal to minus the expected appreciation of the dollar, $-(E^e_{t+1} - E_t)/E_t$, that is,

$$RET^F \text{ in terms of dollars} = i^F - \frac{E^e_{t+1} - E_t}{E_t}$$

If the interest rate on franc deposits is 5%, for example, and the dollar is expected to appreciate by 4%, then the expected return on franc deposits in terms of dollars is 1%. Al earns the 5% interest rate, but he expects to lose 4% because he expects the franc to be worth 4% less in terms of dollars as a result of the dollar's appreciation.

Al's expected return on the dollar deposits RET^D in terms of dollars is just i^D. Hence in terms of dollars, the relative expected return on dollar deposits is calculated by subtracting the expression just given from i^D to obtain

$$\text{Relative } RET^D = i^D - \left(i^F - \frac{E^e_{t+1} - E_t}{E_t} \right) = i^D - i^F + \frac{E^e_{t+1} - E_t}{E_t}$$

This equation is the same as the one describing François's relative expected return on dollar deposits (calculated in terms of francs). The key point here is that the relative expected return on dollar deposits is the same whether it is calculated by François in terms of francs or by Al in terms of dollars. Thus as the relative expected return on dollar deposits increases, both foreigners and domestic residents respond in exactly the same way—both will want to hold more dollar deposits and fewer foreign deposits.

Interest Parity Condition

We currently live in a world in which there is **capital mobility:** Foreigners can easily purchase American assets such as dollar deposits, and Americans can easily purchase foreign assets such as franc deposits. Because foreign bank deposits and American bank deposits have similar risk and liquidity and because there are few impediments to capital mobility, it is reasonable to assume that the deposits are perfect substitutes (that is, equally desirable). When capital is mobile and when bank deposits are perfect substitutes, if the expected return on dollar deposits is above that on foreign deposits, both foreigners and Americans will want to hold only dollar deposits and will be unwilling to hold foreign deposits. Conversely, if the expected return on foreign deposits is higher than on dollar deposits, both foreigners and Americans will not want to hold any dollar deposits and will want to hold only foreign deposits. For existing supplies of both dollar deposits and foreign deposits to be held, it must therefore be true that there is no difference in their expected returns; that is, the relative expected return in Equation 1 must equal zero. This condition can be rewritten as

$$i^D = i^F - \frac{E^e_{t+1} - E_t}{E_t} \tag{2}$$

This equation is called the **interest parity condition,** and it states that the domestic interest rate equals the foreign interest rate minus the expected appreciation of the domestic currency. Equivalently, this condition can be stated in a more intuitive way: The domestic interest rate equals the foreign interest rate plus the expected appreciation of the foreign currency. If the domestic interest rate is above the foreign interest rate, this means that there is a positive expected appreciation of the foreign currency, which compensates for the lower foreign interest rate. A domestic interest rate of 15% versus a foreign interest rate of 10% means that the expected appreciation of the foreign currency must be 5% (or, equivalently, that the expected depreciation of the dollar must be 5%).

There are several ways to look at the interest parity condition. First, we should recognize that interest parity means simply that the expected returns are the same on both dollar deposits and foreign deposits. To see this, note that the left side of the interest parity condition (Equation 2) is the expected return on dollar deposits, while the right side is the expected return on foreign deposits, both calculated in terms of a single currency, the U.S. dollar. Given our assumption that domestic and foreign bank deposits are perfect substitutes (equally desirable), the interest parity condition is an equilibrium condition for the foreign exchange market. Only when the exchange rate is such that expected returns on domestic and foreign deposits are equal—that is, when interest parity holds—will the outstanding domestic and foreign deposits be willingly held.

Equilibrium in the Foreign Exchange Market

To see how the interest parity equilibrium condition works in determining the exchange rate, our first step is to examine how the expected returns on franc and dollar deposits change as the current exchange rate changes.

Expected Return on Franc Deposits As we demonstrated earlier, the expected return in terms of dollars on foreign deposits RET^F is the foreign interest rate minus the expected appreciation of the domestic currency: $i^F - (E^e_{t+1} - E_t)/E_t$. Suppose that the foreign interest rate i^F is 10% and that the expected exchange rate next period E^e_{t+1} is 10 francs per dollar. When the current exchange rate E_t is 9.5 francs per dollar, the expected appreciation of the dollar is $(10.0 - 9.5)/9.5 = 0.052 = 5.2\%$, so the expected return on franc deposits RET^F in terms of dollars is 4.8% (equal to the 10% foreign interest rate minus the 5.2% dollar appreciation). This expected return when $E_t = 9.5$ francs per dollar is plotted as point A in Figure 3. At a higher current exchange rate of $E_t = 10$ francs per dollar, the expected appreciation of the dollar is zero because E^e_{t+1} also equals 10 francs per dollar. Hence RET^F, the expected dollar return on franc deposits, is now just $i^F = 10\%$. This expected return on franc deposits when $E_t = 10$ francs per dollar is plotted as point B. At an even higher exchange rate of $E_t = 10.5$ francs per dollar, the expected change in the value of the dollar is now -4.8% $[= (10.0 - 10.5)/10.5 = -0.048]$, so the expected dollar return on foreign deposits RET^F has now risen to 14.8% $[= 10\% - (-4.8\%)]$. This combination of exchange rate and expected return on franc deposits is plotted as point C.

The curve connecting these points is the schedule for the expected return on franc deposits in Figure 3, labeled RET^F, and as you can see, it slopes upward; that is, as the exchange rate E_t rises, the expected return on franc deposits rises. The intuition for this upward slope is that because the expected next-period exchange rate is held constant as the current exchange rate rises, there is less expected appreciation of the dollar. Hence a higher current exchange rate means a greater expected appreciation of the foreign currency in the future, which increases the expected return on foreign deposits in terms of dollars.

Expected Return on Dollar Deposits   The expected return on dollar deposits in terms of dollars RET^D is always the interest rate on dollar deposits i^D no matter

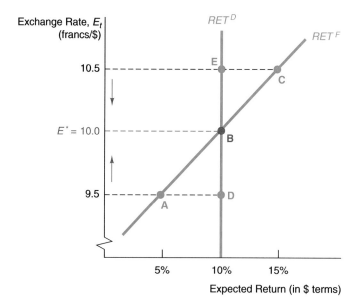

■FIGURE 3 Equilibrium in the Foreign Exchange Market

Equilibrium in the foreign exchange market occurs at the intersection of the schedules for the expected return on franc deposits RET^F and the expected return on dollar deposits RET^D at point B. The equilibrium exchange rate is $E^* = 10$ francs per dollar.

what the exchange rate is. Suppose that the interest rate on dollar deposits is 10%. The expected return on dollar deposits whether at an exchange rate of 9.5, 10.0, or 10.5 francs per dollar, is always 10% (points D, B, and E). The line connecting these points is the schedule for the expected return on dollar deposits, labeled RET^D in Figure 3.

Equilibrium   The intersection of the schedules for the expected return on dollar deposits RET^D and the expected return on franc deposits RET^F is where equilibrium occurs in the foreign exchange market; in other words,

$$RET^D = RET^F$$

At the equilibrium point B where the exchange rate E^* is 10 francs per dollar, the interest parity condition is satisfied because the expected returns on dollar deposits and on franc deposits are equal.

To see that the exchange rate actually heads toward the equilibrium exchange rate E^*, let's see what happens if the exchange rate is 10.5 francs per dollar, a value above the equilibrium exchange rate. As we can see in Figure 3, the expected return on franc deposits at point C is greater than the expected return on dollar deposits at point E. Since dollar and franc deposits are perfect substitutes, people will not want to hold any dollar deposits, and holders of dollar deposits will try to sell them for franc deposits in the foreign exchange market (which is referred to as "selling dollars" and "buying francs"). However, because the expected return on these dollar deposits is below that on franc deposits, no one holding francs will be willing to exchange them for dollar deposits. The resulting excess supply of dollar deposits means that the price of the dollar deposits relative to franc deposits must fall; that is, the exchange rate (amount of francs per dollar) falls as is illustrated by the downward arrow drawn in the figure at the exchange rate of 10.5 francs per dollar. The decline in the exchange rate will continue until point B is reached at the equilibrium exchange rate of 10 francs per dollar, where the expected return on dollar and franc deposits is now equalized.

Now let us look at what happens when the exchange rate is 9.5 francs per dollar, a value below the equilibrium level. Here the expected return on dollar deposits is greater than that on franc deposits. No one will want to hold franc deposits, and everyone will try to sell them to buy dollar deposits ("sell francs" and "buy dollars"), thus driving up the exchange rate as illustrated by the upward arrow. As the exchange rate rises, there is a smaller expected appreciation of the dollar and so a higher expected appreciation of the franc, thereby increasing the expected return on franc deposits. Finally, when the exchange rate has risen to $E^* = 10$ francs per dollar, the expected return on franc deposits has risen enough so that it again equals the expected return on dollar deposits.

■ EXPLAINING CHANGES IN EXCHANGE RATES

To explain how an exchange rate changes over time, we have to understand the factors that shift the expected-return schedules for domestic (dollar) deposits and foreign (franc) deposits.

Shifts in the Expected-Return Schedule for Foreign Deposits

As we have seen, the expected return on foreign (franc) deposits depends on the foreign interest rate i^F minus the expected appreciation of the dollar $(E_{t+1}^e - E_t)/E_t$. Because a change in the current exchange rate E_t results in a movement along the expected-return schedule for franc deposits, factors that shift this schedule must work through the foreign interest rate i^F and the expected future exchange rate E_{t+1}^e. We examine the effect of changes in these factors on the expected-return schedule for franc deposits RET^F, holding everything else constant.

■ **STUDY GUIDE** To grasp how the expected-return schedule for franc deposits shifts, just think of yourself as an investor who is considering putting funds into foreign deposits. When a variable changes (i^F for example), decide whether at a given level of the current exchange rate, holding all other variables constant, you would earn a higher or lower expected return on franc deposits.

Changes in the Foreign Interest Rate If the interest rate on foreign deposits i^F increases, holding everything else constant, the expected return on these deposits must also increase. Hence at a given exchange rate, the increase in i^F leads to a rightward shift in the expected-return schedule for franc deposits from RET_1^F to RET_2^F in Figure 4. As you can see in the figure, the outcome is a depreciation of the dollar from E_1 to E_2. An alternative way to see this is to recognize that the increase in the expected return on franc deposits at the original equilibrium exchange rate resulting from the rise in i^F means that people will want to buy francs and sell dollars, so the value of the dollar must fall. Our analysis thus generates the following conclusion: ***An increase in the foreign interest rate i^F shifts the RET^F schedule to the right and causes the domestic currency to depreciate ($E\downarrow$).***

Conversely, if i^F falls, the expected return on franc deposits falls, the RET^F schedule shifts to the left, and the exchange rate rises. This yields the following conclusion: ***A decrease in i^F shifts the RET^F schedule to the left and causes the domestic currency to appreciate ($E\uparrow$).***

Changes in the Expected Future Exchange Rate Any factor that causes the expected future exchange rate E_{t+1}^e to fall decreases the expected appreciation of the dollar and hence raises the expected appreciation of the franc. The result is a higher expected return on franc deposits, which shifts the schedule for the expected return on franc deposits to the right and leads to a decline in the exchange rate as in Figure 4. Conversely, a rise in E_{t+1}^e raises the expected appreciation of the dollar, lowers the expected return on foreign deposits, shifts the RET^F schedule to the left, and raises the exchange rate. To summarize, ***a rise in the expected future exchange rate shifts the RET^F schedule to the left and causes an appreciation of the domestic currency; a fall in the***

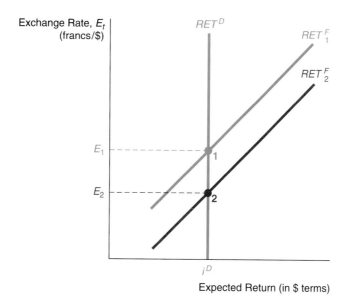

■FIGURE 4 Shifts in the Schedule for the Expected Return on Foreign Deposits RET^F

An increase in the expected return on foreign deposits, which occurs when either the foreign interest rate rises or the expected future exchange rate falls, shifts the schedule for the expected return on foreign deposits from RET^F_1 to RET^F_2, and the exchange rate falls from E_1 to E_2.

expected future exchange rate shifts the RET^F schedule to the right and causes a depreciation of the domestic currency.

Summary Our analysis of the long-run determinants of the exchange rate indicates the factors that influence the expected future exchange rate: the relative price level, relative tariffs and quotas, import demand, export demand, and relative productivity (refer to Table 1). The theory of purchasing power parity suggests that if a higher American price level relative to the foreign price level is expected to persist, the dollar will depreciate in the long run. A higher expected relative American price level should thus have a tendency to raise the expected return on franc deposits, shift the RET^F schedule to the right, and lower the current exchange rate.

Similarly, the other long-run determinants of the exchange rate we discussed earlier can also influence the expected return on franc deposits and the current exchange rate. Briefly, the following changes will increase the expected return on franc deposits, shift the RET^F schedule to the right, and cause a depreciation of the domestic currency, the dollar: (1) expectations of a rise in the American price level relative to the foreign price level, (2) expectations of lower American tariffs and quotas relative to foreign tariffs and quotas, (3) expectations of higher American import demand, (4) expectations of lower foreign demand for American exports, and (5) expectations of lower American productivity relative to foreign productivity.

Shifts in the Expected-Return Schedule for Domestic Deposits

Since the expected return on domestic (dollar) deposits is just the interest rate on these deposits i^D, this interest rate is the only factor that shifts the schedule for the expected return on dollar deposits.

Changes in the Domestic Interest Rate A rise in i^D raises the expected return on dollar deposits, shifts the RET^D schedule to the right, and leads to a rise in the exchange rate, as is shown in Figure 5. Another way of seeing this is to recognize that a rise in i^D, which raises the expected return on dollar deposits, creates an excess demand for dollar deposits at the original equilibrium exchange rate, and the resulting purchases of dollar deposits cause an appreciation of the dollar. *A rise in the domestic interest rate i^D shifts the RET^D schedule to the right and causes an appreciation of the domestic currency; a fall in i^D shifts the RET^D schedule to the left and causes a depreciation of the domestic currency.*

■ **STUDY GUIDE** As a study aid, the factors that shift the RET^F and RET^D schedules and lead to changes in the current exchange rate E_t are listed in Table 2. The table shows what happens to the exchange rate when there is an increase in each of these variables, holding everything else constant. To give yourself practice, see if you can work out what happens to the RET^F and RET^D schedules and to the exchange rate if each of these factors falls rather than rises. Check your answers by seeing if you get the opposite change in the exchange rate to those indicated in Table 2.

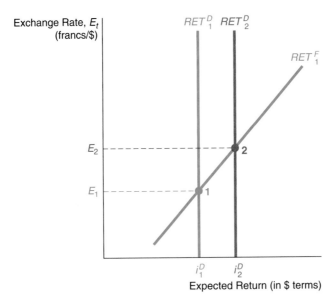

■ **FIGURE 5** Shifts in the Schedule for the Expected Return on Domestic Deposits RET^D

An increase in the expected return on dollar deposits i^D shifts the expected return on domestic (dollar) deposits from RET_1^D to RET_2^D and the exchange rate rises from E_1 to E_2.

SUMMARY TABLE 2	Factors That Shift the RET^F and RET^D Schedules and Affect the Exchange Rate		

Factor	Change in Factor	Response of the Exchange Rate, E_t	
Domestic interest rate, i^D	↑	↑	
Foreign interest rate, i^F	↑	↓	
Expected domestic price level*	↑	↓	
Expected tariffs and quotas*	↑	↑	
Expected import demand	↑	↓	
Expected export demand	↑	↑	
Productivity*	↑	↑	

*Relative to other countries.

NOTE: Only increases (↑) in the factors are shown; the effects of decreases in the variables on the exchange rate are the opposite of those indicated in the "Response" column.

APPLICATION | **CHANGES IN THE EQUILIBRIUM EXCHANGE RATE: TWO EXAMPLES**

Our analysis has revealed the factors that affect the value of the equilibrium exchange rate. Now we use this analysis to take a close look at the response of the exchange rate to changes in interest rates and money growth.

Changes in Interest Rates

Changes in domestic interest rates i^D are often cited as a major factor affecting exchange rates. For example, we see headlines in the financial press like this one: "Dollar Recovers As Interest Rates Edge Upward." But is the view presented in this headline always correct?

Not necessarily, because to analyze the effects of interest rate changes, we must carefully distinguish the sources of the changes. The Fisher equation (Chapter 3) states that a (nominal) interest rate equals the *real* interest rate plus expected inflation: $i = i_r + \pi^e$. The Fisher equation indicates that an interest rate i can change for two reasons: Either the real interest rate i_r changes or the expected inflation rate π^e changes. The effect on the exchange rate is quite different, depending on which of these two factors is the source of the change in the nominal interest rate.

Suppose that the domestic real interest rate increases so that the nominal interest rate i^D rises while expected inflation remains unchanged. In this case, it is reasonable to assume that the expected appreciation of the dollar will be unchanged because expected inflation is unchanged, and so the expected return on foreign deposits will remain unchanged for any given exchange rate. The result is that the RET^F schedule stays put and the RET^D schedule shifts to the right, and we end up with the situation depicted in Figure 5, which analyzes an increase in i^D, holding everything else constant. Our model of the foreign exchange market produces the following result: **When domestic real interest rates rise, the domestic currency appreciates.**

When the nominal interest rate rises because of an increase in expected inflation, we get a different result from the one shown in Figure 5. The rise in expected domestic inflation leads to a decline in the expected appreciation of the dollar (a higher appreciation of the franc), which is typically thought to be larger than the increase in the domestic interest rate i^D.[5] As a result, at any given exchange rate, the expected return on foreign deposits rises more than the expected return on dollar deposits. Thus, as we see in Figure 6, the RET^F schedule shifts to the right more than the RET^D schedule, and the exchange rate falls. Our analysis leads to

---

[5]This conclusion is standard in asset market models of exchange rate determination; see Rudiger Dornbusch, "Expectations and Exchange Rate Dynamics," *Journal of Political Economy* 84 (1976): 1061–1076. It is also consistent with empirical evidence that suggests that nominal interest rates do not rise one-for-one with increases in expected inflation. See Frederic S. Mishkin, "The Real Interest Rate: An Empirical Investigation," *Carnegie-Rochester Conference Series on Public Policy* 15 (1981): 151–200; and Lawrence Summers, "The Nonadjustment of Nominal Interest Rates: A Study of the Fisher Effect," in *Macroeconomics, Prices and Quantities*, ed. James Tobin (Washington, D.C.: Brookings Institution, 1983), pp. 201–240.

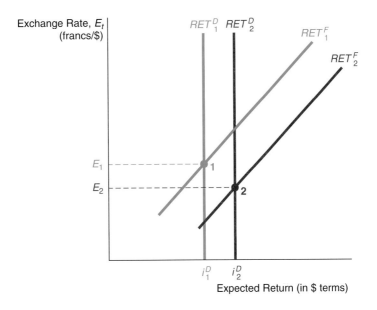

■FIGURE 6 Effect of a Rise in the Domestic Nominal Interest Rate as a Result of an Increase in Expected Inflation

Because a rise in domestic expected inflation leads to a decline in expected dollar appreciation that is larger than the resulting increase in the domestic interest rate, the expected return on foreign deposits rises by more than the expected return on domestic (dollar) deposits. RET^F shifts to the right more than RET^D, and the equilibrium exchange rate falls from E_1 to E_2.

this conclusion: ***When domestic interest rates rise due to an expected increase in inflation, the domestic currency depreciates.***

Because this conclusion is completely different from the one reached when the rise in the domestic interest rate is associated with a higher real interest rate, we must always distinguish between *real* and *nominal* measures when analyzing the effects of interest rates on exchange rates.

Changes in the Money Supply

Suppose that the Federal Reserve decides to increase the level of the money supply in order to reduce unemployment, which it believes to be excessive. The higher money supply will lead to a higher American price level in the long run and hence to a lower expected future exchange rate. The resulting decline in the expected appreciation of the dollar increases the expected return on foreign deposits at any given current exchange rate and so shifts the RET^F schedule rightward from RET^F_1 to RET^F_2 in Figure 7. In addition, the higher money supply will lead to a higher real money supply M/P because the price level does not immediately increase in the short run. As suggested in Chapter 5, the resulting rise in the real money supply causes the domestic interest rate to fall from i^D_1 to i^D_2, which lowers the expected return on domestic (dollar) deposits, shifting the RET^D schedule in from RET^D_1 to RET^D_2. As we can see in Figure 7, the result is a decline

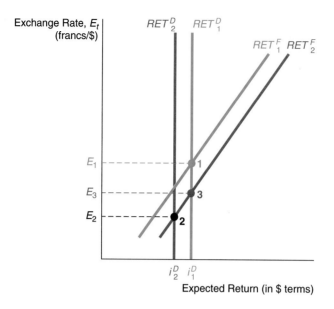

■FIGURE 7 Effect of a Rise in the Money Supply

A rise in the money supply leads to a higher domestic price level in the long run, which in turn leads to a lower expected future exchange rate. The resulting decline in the expected appreciation of the dollar raises the expected return on foreign deposits, shifting the RET^F schedule rightward from RET^F_1 to RET^F_2. In the short run, the domestic interest rate i^D falls, shifting RET^D from RET^D_1 to RET^D_2. The short-run outcome is that the exchange rate falls from E_1 to E_2. In the long run, however, the interest rate returns to i^D_1 and RET^D returns to RET^D_1. The exchange rate thus rises from E_2 to E_3 in the long run.

in the exchange rate from E_1 to E_2. The conclusion is this: ***A higher domestic money supply causes the domestic currency to depreciate.***

Exchange Rate Overshooting

Our analysis of the effect of a money supply increase on the exchange rate is not yet over—we still need to look at what happens to the exchange rate in the long run. A basic proposition in monetary theory, called **monetary neutrality,** states that in the long run, a onetime percentage rise in the money supply is matched by the same onetime percentage rise in the price level, leaving unchanged the real money supply and all other economic variables such as interest rates. An intuitive way to understand this proposition is to think of what would happen if our government announced overnight that an old dollar would now be worth 100 new dollars. The money supply in new dollars would be 100 times its old value and the price level would also be 100 times higher, but nothing in the economy would really have changed; interest rates and the real money supply would remain the same. Monetary neutrality tells us that in the long run, the rise in the money supply would not lead to a change in the domestic interest rate and so it would return to i^D_1 in the long run, and the schedule for the expected return on domestic deposits would return to RET_1^D. As we can see in Figure 7, this means that the exchange rate would rise from E_2 to E_3 in the long run.

The phenomenon we have described here in which the exchange rate falls by more in the short run than it does in the long run when the money supply increases is called **exchange rate overshooting.** It is important because, as we will see in the following application, it can help explain why exchange rates exhibit so much volatility.

Another way of thinking about why exchange rate overshooting occurs is to recognize that when the domestic interest rate falls in the short run, equilibrium in the foreign exchange market means that the expected return on foreign deposits must be lower. With the foreign interest rate given, this lower expected return on foreign deposits means that there must be an expected appreciation of the dollar (depreciation of the franc) in order for the expected return on foreign deposits to decline when the domestic interest rate falls. This can occur only if the current exchange rate falls below its long-run value.

| APPLICATION | WHY ARE EXCHANGE RATES SO VOLATILE? |

The high volatility of foreign exchange rates surprises many people. Thirty or so years ago, economists generally believed that allowing exchange rates to be determined in the free market would not lead to large fluctuations in their values. Recent experience has proved them wrong. If we return to Figure 1, we see that exchange rates over the 1980–1996 period have been very volatile.

The asset market approach to exchange rate determination that we have outlined in this chapter gives a straightforward explanation of volatile exchange rates. Because expected appreciation of the domestic currency affects the expected return on foreign deposits, expectations about the price level, inflation, tariffs and quotas, productivity, import demand, export demand, and the money supply play important roles in determining the exchange rate. When expectations about any of these variables change, our model indicates that there will be an immediate effect on the expected return on foreign deposits and therefore on the exchange rate. Since expectations on all these variables change with just about every bit of news that appears, it is not surprising that the exchange rate is volatile. In addition, we have seen that our exchange rate analysis produces exchange rate overshooting when the money supply increases. Exchange rate overshooting is an additional reason for the high volatility of exchange rates.

Because earlier models of exchange rate behavior focused on goods markets rather than asset markets, they did not emphasize changing expectations as a source of exchange rate movements, and so these earlier models could not predict substantial fluctuations in exchange rates. The failure of earlier models to explain volatility is one reason why they are no longer so popular. The more modern approach developed here emphasizes that the foreign exchange market is like any other asset market in which expectations of the future matter. The foreign exchange market, like other asset markets such as the stock market, displays substantial price volatility, and foreign exchange rates are notoriously hard to forecast.

APPLICATION **THE DOLLAR AND INTEREST RATES, 1973–1996**

In the chapter preview we mentioned that the dollar was weak in the late 1970s, rose substantially from 1980 to 1985, and declined thereafter. We can use our analysis of the foreign exchange market to understand exchange rate movements and help explain the dollar's rise and fall in the 1980s.

Some important information for tracing the dollar's changing value is presented in Figure 8, which plots measures of real and nominal interest rates and the value of the dollar in terms of a basket of foreign currencies (called an **effective exchange rate index**). We can see that the value of the dollar and the measure of real interest rates rise and fall together. In the late 1970s, real interest rates were at low levels, and so was the value of the dollar. Beginning in 1980, however, real interest rates in the United States began to climb sharply, and at the same time so did the dollar. After 1984, the real interest rate declined substantially, as did the dollar.

Our model of exchange rate determination helps explain the rise and fall in the dollar in the 1980s. As Figure 5 indicates, a rise in the U.S. real interest rate raises the expected return on dollar deposits while leaving the expected return on foreign deposits unchanged. The resulting increased demand for dollar deposits

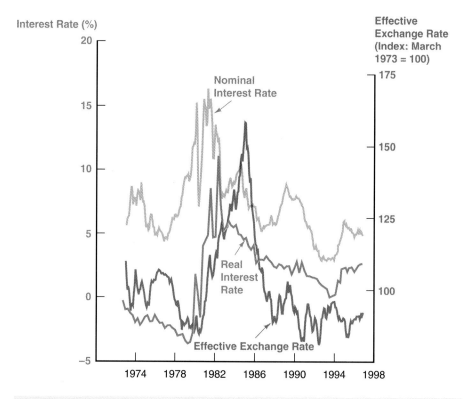

■FIGURE 8 Value of the Dollar and Interest Rates, 1973–1996

Sources: International Financial Statistics; real interest rate from Figure 3 in Chapter 3.

then leads to purchases of dollar deposits (and sales of foreign deposits), which raise the exchange rate. This is exactly what occurred in the 1980–1984 period. The subsequent fall in U.S. real interest rates then lowered the expected return on dollar deposits relative to foreign deposits, and the resulting sales of dollar deposits (and purchases of foreign deposits) lowered the exchange rate.

The plot of *nominal* interest rates in Figure 8 also demonstrates that the correspondence between nominal interest rates and exchange rate movements is not nearly as close as that between *real* interest rates and exchange rate movements. This is also exactly what our analysis predicts. The rise in nominal interest rates in the late 1970s was not reflected in a corresponding rise in the value of the dollar; indeed, the dollar actually fell in the late 1970s. Figure 8 explains why the rise in nominal rates in the late 1970s did not produce a rise in the dollar. As a comparison of the real and nominal interest rates in the late 1970s indicates, the rise in nominal interest rates reflected an increase in expected inflation and not an increase in real interest rates. As our analysis in Figure 6 demonstrates, the rise in nominal interest rates stemming from a rise in expected inflation should lead to a decline in the dollar, and that is exactly what transpired.

If there is a moral to the story, it is that a failure to distinguish between real and nominal interest rates can lead to poor predictions of exchange rate movements: The weakness of the dollar in the late 1970s and the strength of the dollar in the early 1980s can be explained by movements in *real* interest rates but not by movements in *nominal* interest rates.

<table>
<tr><td>**APPLICATION**</td><td>**THE "FOREIGN EXCHANGE" COLUMN**</td></tr>
</table>

READING THE *"WALL STREET JOURNAL"*

Now that we have an understanding of how exchange rates are determined, we can use our analysis to understand discussions about developments in the foreign exchange market reported in the financial press.

Every day, the *Wall Street Journal* reports on developments in the foreign exchange market on the previous business day in its "Foreign Exchange" column, an example of which is presented in the "Following the Financial News" box.

The column focuses on strong U.S. data and the prospect of higher U.S. and lower German interest rates as the source of the rise in the dollar relative to the mark. Our analysis of the foreign exchange market explains why these developments lead to an appreciation of the dollar against the mark.

The strong U.S. economy is seen as making it likely that U.S. interest rates will rise in the near future (a view that is consistent with the analysis in Chapter 5). The higher U.S. interest rates will shift the RET^D schedule to the right as in Figure 5 and will thereby cause the exchange rate to rise in the future. The comment from the Bundesbank official implying that German interest rates are likely to fall in the future decreases the expected return on mark deposits, thus shifting the RET^F curve to the left, providing an additional reason why the value of the dollar should rise against the mark in the future. The resulting expectation of a future rise in the dollar against the mark produces a rise in the dollar today because the expected appreciation of the dollar implies a depreciation of the mark, which decreases the expected return on mark deposits and shifts the RET^F schedule to the left.

The "Foreign Exchange" Column

The "Foreign Exchange" column appears daily in the *Wall Street Journal*; an example is presented here. It is found in the third section, "Money and Investing."

FOREIGN EXCHANGE

Dollar Continues Its Advance on Mark On Strong U.S. Data, Slips Against Yen

BY BETTY W. LIU
AP-Dow Jones News Service

NEW YORK–The dollar continued its climb against the mark yesterday, boosted by the robust U.S. economic outlook and a report indicating Germany could cut interest rates again.

However, the U.S. currency ended off slightly against the yen, though still above the psychologically important 110 yen level as traders took profits from Wednesday's two-month high.

"All the news continues to support the dollar with [U.S.] interest rates moving up, Bundesbank officials commenting that interest rates could move lower . . . and the Iraqi situation," said Roger Chapin, foreign-exchange manager at Bank One Columbus in Columbus, Ohio.

Early in the New York afternoon, Baghdad's official news agency confirmed that Iraq fired missiles at U.S. warplanes over the "no-fly zone" in southern Iraq.

Subdued U.S. producer prices for August showed inflation remains moderate, though the economy is expanding. Bonds and stocks rallied on the numbers, which in turn helped the dollar, traders said.

"We've got the best of all possible worlds here," said Kevin Raphael, foreign-exchange manager at Rabobank Nederland in New York. "We've got high levels of employment and few signs of inflation."

Late in New York, the dollar was quoted at 1.5126 marks, up from 1.5108 marks late Wednesday in New York. The U.S. currency also was quoted at 110.10 yen, down from 110.31 yen. Sterling was trading at $1.5557, up from $1.5551. About noon Friday in Tokyo, the dollar was trading at 1.5127 marks and at 110.16 yen; sterling was quoted at $1.5554.

Klaus Dieter Kuebacher, member of the Bundesbank's policymaking council, said in an interview yesterday that Germany's repurchase, or repo, rate "has leeway to fall some 20 basis points," from its current 3%.

A basis point is one-hundredth of a percentage point. The repo rate is the rate at which the Bundesbank does most of its lending to banks.

U.S. producer prices in August rose a seasonally adjusted 0.3% after remaining unchanged in July.

The Dow Jones Industrial Average ended just shy of its closing high—5778 points, set May 22—at 5771.94, up 17.02 points. The 30-year benchmark Treasury was at 95 30/32, up about $^{1}/_{2}$ point to yield 7.07%.

Market players interviewed were convinced the evidence of the economy's strength was overwhelming. Even if today's consumer price data is subdued, they say, it won't keep the Federal Reserve from raising interest rates by its next policy meeting in late September. This, in turn, will keep pushing the dollar up.

The discount and Federal-funds target rates are at 5% and 5.25%, respectively. The discount rate, at which the Fed lends to banks, is considered their fund source of last resort. Banks lend each other excess reserves overnight at the Fed-funds rate.

And a call for a stronger dollar by French central bank Governor Jean-Claude Trichet was an added element of support for the U.S. currency.

Regarding recent comments by Bundesbank officials about interest rates and the dollar, Wayne Grigull, managing director of foreign exchange at Merrill Lynch & Co. in New York, said: "It's vital for an economic union that the countries of Europe start to experience economic growth and that unemployment rates decline. They're not going to decline unless monetary conditions ease" and the mark weakens.

Source: Wall Street Journal, September 13, 1996, p. C17.

The comment about being in the best of all possible worlds provides an additional reason for the strong dollar because it suggests that although the economy is strong, there are few signs of inflation. The prospect of low inflation in the United States implies that it is more likely that the U.S. price level will be lower relative to the German price level in the future. The lower relative U.S. price level provides an additional reason for an expected appreciation of the dollar, which drives down the expected return on mark deposits because it implies an expected depreciation of the mark, thereby shifting the RET^F schedule to the left. As explained earlier, this leads to a rise in the value of the dollar today.

■ THE PRACTICING FINANCIAL INSTITUTION MANAGER
Profiting from Foreign Exchange Forecasts

Managers of financial institutions care a great deal about what foreign exchange rates will be in the future because these rates affect the value of assets on their balance sheet that are denominated in foreign currencies. In addition, financial institutions often engage in trading foreign exchange, both for their own account and for their customers. Forecasts of future foreign exchange rates can thus have a big impact on the profits that financial institutions make on their foreign exchange trading operations.

Managers of financial institutions obtain foreign exchange forecasts either by hiring their own staff economists to generate them or by purchasing forecasts from other financial institutions or economic forecasting firms. In predicting exchange rate movements, forecasters look at the factors mentioned in this chapter. For example, if they expect domestic real interest rates to rise, they will predict, in line with our analysis, that the domestic currency will appreciate; conversely, if they expect domestic inflation to increase, they will predict that the domestic currency will depreciate.

Managers of financial institutions, particularly those engaged in international banking, rely on foreign exchange forecasts to make decisions about which assets denominated in foreign currencies they should hold. For example, if a financial institution manager has a reliable forecast that the German mark will appreciate in the future but the French franc will depreciate, the manager will want to sell off assets denominated in francs and instead purchase assets denominated in marks. Alternatively, the manager might instruct loan officers to make more loans denominated in marks and fewer loans denominated in francs. Likewise, if the franc is forecast to appreciate and the mark to depreciate, the manager would want to switch out of mark-denominated assets into franc-denominated assets and would want to make more loans in francs and fewer in marks.

If the financial institution has a foreign exchange trading operation, a forecast of an appreciation of the franc means that the financial institution manager should tell foreign exchange traders to buy francs. If the forecast turns out to be correct, the higher value of the franc means that the trader can sell the francs in the future and pocket a tidy profit. If the mark is forecast to depreciate, the trader can sell marks and buy them back in the future at a lower price if the forecast turns out to be correct, and again the financial institution will make a profit.

Accurate foreign exchange rate forecasts can thus help a financial institution manager generate substantial profits for the institution. Unfortunately, exchange rate forecasters are no more or less accurate than other economic forecasters, and they often make large errors. Reports on foreign exchange rate forecasts and how well forecasters are doing appear from time to time in the *Wall Street Journal* and in the trade magazine *Euromoney.*

SUMMARY

1. Foreign exchange rates (the price of one country's currency in terms of another's) are important because they affect the price of domestically produced goods sold abroad and the cost of foreign goods bought domestically.

2. The theory of purchasing power parity suggests that long-run changes in the exchange rate between two countries are determined by changes in the relative price levels of the two countries. Other factors that affect exchange rates in the long run are tariffs and quotas, import demand, export demand, and productivity.

3. Exchange rates are determined in the short run by the interest parity condition, which states that the expected return on domestic deposits is equal to the expected return on foreign deposits.

4. Any factor that changes the expected returns on domestic or foreign deposits will lead to changes in the exchange rate. Such factors include changes in the interest rates on domestic and foreign deposits as well as changes in any of the factors that affect the long-run exchange rate and hence the expected future exchange rate. Changes in the money supply lead to exchange rate overshooting, causing the exchange rate to change by more in the short run than in the long run.

5. The asset market approach to exchange rate determination can explain both the volatility of exchange rates and the rise of the dollar in the 1980–1984 period and its subsequent fall.

6. Forecasts of foreign exchange rates are very valuable to managers of financial institutions because these rates influence decisions about which assets denominated in foreign currencies the institutions should hold and what kinds of trades should be made by their traders in the foreign exchange market.

KEY TERMS

appreciation, p. 189

capital mobility, p. 198

depreciation, p. 189

effective exchange rate index, p. 210

exchange rate, p. 187

exchange rate overshooting, p. 209

foreign exchange market, p. 187

forward exchange rate, p. 189

forward transaction, p. 189

interest parity condition, p. 199

law of one price, p. 192

monetary neutrality, p. 208

quotas, p. 194

spot exchange rate, p. 189

spot transaction, p. 189

tariffs, p. 194

theory of purchasing power parity (PPP), p. 192

QUESTIONS AND PROBLEMS

1. When the French franc appreciates, are you more likely to drink California or French wine?

*2. "A country is always worse off when its currency is weak (falls in value)." Is this statement true, false, or uncertain? Explain your answer.

3. Check in a newspaper the exchange rates for the foreign currencies listed in the "Following the Financial News" box on page 190. Which of these currencies have appreciated and which have depreciated since October 8, 1996?

*4. If the French price level rises by 5% relative to the price level in the United States, what does the the-

ory of purchasing power parity predict will happen to the value of the French franc in terms of dollars?

5. If the demand for a country's exports falls at the same time that tariffs on imports are raised, will the country's currency tend to appreciate or depreciate in the long run?

*6. In the mid- to late 1970s, the yen appreciated relative to the dollar even though Japan's inflation rate was higher than America's. How can this be explained by an improvement in the productivity of Japanese industry relative to American industry?

Predicting the Future

Answer the remaining problems by drawing the appropriate exchange market diagrams.

7. The president of the United States announces that he will reduce inflation with a new anti-inflation program. If the public believes him, predict what will happen to the U.S. exchange rate.

*8. If the British central bank prints money to reduce unemployment, what will happen to the value of the pound in the short run and the long run?

9. If the French government unexpectedly announces that it will be imposing higher tariffs and quotas on foreign goods one year from now, what will happen to the value of the franc today?

*10. If nominal interest rates in America rise but real interest rates fall, predict what will happen to the U.S. exchange rate.

11. If American auto companies make a breakthrough in automobile technology and are able to produce a car that gets 60 miles to the gallon, what will happen to the U.S. exchange rate?

*12. If Americans go on a spending spree and buy twice as much French perfume, Japanese TVs, English sweaters, Swiss watches, and Italian wine, what will happen to the value of the U.S. dollar?

13. If expected inflation drops in Europe so that interest rates fall there, predict what will happen to the U.S. exchange rate.

*14. If the German central bank decides to contract the money supply in order to fight inflation, what will happen to the value of the U.S. dollar?

15. If there is a strike in France, making it harder to buy French goods, what will happen to the value of the franc?

■ CASE STUDY

■ Determining the Effects of Changes in Exchange Rates, Purchasing Power Parity

CONCEPTS IN THIS CASE

exchange rate
foreign exchange market
spot versus forward transactions
law of one price
interest parity condition
tariffs versus quotas
purchasing power parity
capital mobility

As a new member of the international department at your company, you have been asked to conduct a review class on the foreign exchange market. You remember something about this from your undergraduate classes, but you are not quite sure how to proceed. The company library has older texts and other information, but you want to present more recent views on how to manage this important aspect of the company. International sales produce almost 35% of all revenues and are expected to increase considerably in the future. In fact, the only prospects for substantial growth will depend on the correct management of international markets and finances.

In setting up the review for others in your department, you decide to begin with fundamental definitions. These definitions will be a part of the handout you will provide at the time of your presentation.

1. What are the definitions of the following foreign exchange terms?
   a. Exchange rate
   b. Foreign exchange market
   c. Spot transactions
   d. Forward transactions
   e. Forward exchange rate
   f. Appreciating currency
   g. Depreciating currency
   h. Law of one price
   i. Interest parity condition
   j. Monetary neutrality
   k. Exchange rate overshooting
   l. Effective exchange rate index
   m. Tariffs
   n. Quotas
   o. Purchasing power parity
   p. Capital mobility

2. Explain why foreign exchange rates are important to your firm; how would changes in the exchange rate affect your firm's sales and net profits?

3. Explain how a 20% increase in the price of Turkish pistachios would affect the cost of the same product in U.S. dollars under the theory of purchasing power parity (PPP). What factors does this theory leave out?

4. In the long run, which four major factors affect the exchange rate?

5. State whether each of the following changes causes the U.S. dollar to appreciate or to depreciate relative to foreign currencies.
   a. The price level in the United States rises.
   b. The price level in the United States falls.
   c. The United States imposes or increases a tariff.
   d. The United States imposes or reduces a quota.
   e. Demand for U.S. exports increases.
   f. Demand for U.S. exports decreases.
   g. Productivity in the United States increases.
   h. Productivity in the United States decreases.

6. Use the dollar and interest rates figure in your text to explain the need to distinguish between real and nominal interest rates when predicting exchange rate movements.

7. Assume that today is January 1, U.S. $1.00 = 5.80 francs, and the interest rate on dollar deposits is 8%.
   a. If the dollar appreciates relative to the franc by 20%, what will be the return on dollar deposits in terms of francs?
   b. If the dollar depreciates relative to the franc by 10%, what will be the return on dollar deposits in terms of francs?
   c. If the expected exchange rate is U.S. $1.00 = 6.96 francs what is the expected rate of appreciation for the dollar?
   d. If the dollar is expected to appreciate 5%, what interest rate on franc deposits is required if the concepts of interest-rate parity and capital mobility hold?

CHAPTER 9

THE MONEY MARKETS

PREVIEW In November 1996, an interest-bearing checking account at Wachovia Bank paid 1% per year. This same money invested in a three-month Treasury bill would have paid 5.05%. It is no wonder that individuals, as well as businesses, have aggressively pursued alternatives to low-interest-rate bank accounts. One such alternative is provided by the money markets, which we first introduced in Chapter 2. Recall that money market securities are short-term, low-risk, and very liquid. Because of the high degree of safety and liquidity these securities exhibit, they are close to being money, hence their name.

The money markets have been active since the early 1800s but have become much more important in recent years as interest rates have risen above historic levels. In fact, the rise in short-term rates, coupled with a regulated ceiling on the rate that banks could pay for deposits, resulted in a rapid outflow of funds from financial institutions in the late 1970s and early 1980s. This outflow in turn caused many banks and savings and loans to fail. The industry regained its health only after massive changes were made to bank regulations with regard to money market interest rates.

This chapter carefully reviews the money markets and the securities that are traded there. In addition, we discuss why the money markets are important to our financial system.

THE MONEY MARKETS DEFINED

The term *money market* is actually a misnomer. Money—currency—is not traded in the money markets. Because the securities that do trade there are short-term and highly liquid, however, they are close to being money. Money market securities, which are discussed in detail later in this chapter, have three basic characteristics in common:

- They are usually sold in large denominations.
- They have low default risk.
- They mature in one year or less *from their original issue date.* Most money market instruments mature in less than 120 days.

Money market transactions do not take place in any one particular location or building. Instead, traders usually arrange purchases and sales between participants over the phone and complete them electronically. Because of this characteristic, money market securities usually have an active *secondary market.* Recall from Chapter 2 that this means that after the security has been sold initially, it is relatively easy to find buyers who will purchase it in the future. An active secondary market makes money market securities very flexible instruments to use to fill short-term financial needs.

Another characteristic of the money markets is that they are **wholesale markets.** This means that most transactions are very large, usually in excess of $1 million. The size of these transactions prevents most individual investors from participating directly in the money markets. Instead, dealers and brokers, operating in the trading rooms of large banks and brokerage houses, bring customers together. These traders will buy or sell $50 or $100 million in mere seconds—certainly not a job for the faint of heart!

As you may recall from Chapter 2, flexibility and innovation are two important characteristics of any financial market, and the money markets are no exception. Despite the wholesale nature of the money market, innovative securities and trading methods have been developed to give small investors access to money market securities. We will discuss these securities and their characteristics later in the chapter.

Why Do We Need the Money Markets?

In theory, the money markets should not be needed. The banking industry exists primarily to provide short-term loans and to accept short-term deposits. Banks should have an efficiency advantage in gathering information, an advantage that should eliminate the need for the money markets. Thanks to continuing relationships with customers, banks should be able to offer loans more cheaply than diversified markets, which must evaluate each borrower every time a new security is offered. Furthermore, short-term securities offered for sale in the money markets are neither as liquid nor as safe as deposits placed in banks and thrifts. Given the advantages that banks have, why do the money markets exist at all?

The banking industry exists primarily to mediate the asymmetric information problem between saver-lenders and borrower-spenders, and banks can earn profits by capturing economies of scale while providing this service. However, the banking industry is subject to more regulations and governmental costs than the money markets are. In situations where the asymmetric information problem is not severe, the money markets have a distinct cost advantage over banks in providing short-term funds.

Cost Advantages

Banks must put aside a portion of their deposits in the form of reserves that are held without interest at the Federal Reserve. Thus for every dollar deposited, the bank can invest only between 90 to 97 cents.[1] This means that it must pay a lower interest rate to the depositor than if the full deposit could be reinvested.

Interest-rate regulations were a second competitive obstacle for banks. One of the principal purposes of the banking regulations of the 1930s was to reduce competition among banks. Without competition, regulators felt, banks were less likely to fail. The cost to consumers of the greater profits banks earned because of the lack of free market competition was justified by the greater economic stability that a healthy banking system would provide.

One way that banking profits were assured was by regulations that set a ceiling on the rate of interest that banks could pay for funds. The Glass-Steagall Act of 1933 prohibited payment of interest on checking accounts and limited the interest that could be paid on time deposits. The limits on interest rates were not particularly relevant until the late 1950s. The limits became especially troublesome to banks in the late 1970s and early 1980s when inflation pushed short-term interest rates above the level that banks could pay. Investors pulled their money out of banks and put it into money market security accounts offered by many brokerage firms. These new investors caused the money markets to grow rapidly.

Banks continue to provide valuable intermediation, as we will see in several later chapters. In some situations, however, the cost structure of the banking industry makes it unable to compete effectively in the market for short-term funds against the less restricted money markets.

■ THE PURPOSE OF THE MONEY MARKETS

The well-developed secondary market for money market instruments makes the money market an ideal place for a firm or financial institution to "warehouse" surplus funds for short periods of time until they are needed. Similarly, the money markets provide a low-cost source of funds to firms, the government, and intermediaries that need a short-term infusion of funds.

Most investors in the money market who are temporarily warehousing funds are ordinarily not trying to earn unusually high returns on their money market funds. Rather, they use the money market as an interim investment that provides a higher return than holding cash or money in banks. They may feel that market conditions are not right to warrant the purchase of additional stock, or they may expect interest rates to rise and hence not want to purchase bonds. It is important to keep in mind that holding idle surplus cash is expensive for an investor because cash balances earn no income for the owner. Idle cash represents an *opportunity cost* in terms of lost interest income. Recall from Chapter 5 that an asset's opportunity cost is the amount of interest sacrificed by not holding an alternative asset.

---

[1]The reserve requirement on nonpersonal time deposits with an original maturity of less than $1\frac{1}{2}$ years was reduced from 3% to 0% in December 1990.

The money markets provide a means to invest idle funds and to reduce this opportunity cost.

Investment advisers often hold some funds in the money market so that they will be able to act quickly to take advantage of investment opportunities they identify. Most investment funds and financial intermediaries also hold money market securities to meet investment or deposit outflows.

The sellers of money market securities find that the money market provides a low-cost source of temporary funds. Table 1 shows the interest rates available on a variety of money market instruments sold by a variety of firms and institutions. For example, banks may issue federal funds (we will define the money market securities later in this chapter) to obtain funds in the money market to meet short-term reserve requirement shortages. The government funds a large portion of the U.S. debt with Treasury bills. Finance companies like GMAC (General Motors Acceptance Company, the financing division of General Motors) may raise in the money market the funds that it uses to make car loans.

Why do corporations and the U.S. government sometimes need to get their hands on funds quickly? The primary reason is that cash inflows and outflows are rarely synchronized. Government tax revenues, for example, usually come only at certain times of the year, but expenses are incurred all year long. The government can borrow short-term funds that it will pay back when it receives tax revenues. Businesses also face problems caused by revenues and expenses occurring at different times. The money markets provide an efficient, low-cost way of solving these problems.

■ WHO PARTICIPATES IN THE MONEY MARKETS?

An obvious way to discuss the players in the money market would be to list those who borrow and those who lend. The problem with this approach is that most money market participants operate on both sides of the market. For example, any large bank will borrow aggressively in the money market by selling large commercial CDs. At the same time, it will lend short-term funds to businesses through its

■ **TABLE 1** Sample Money Market Rates, February 26, 1997

Instrument	Interest Rate (%)
Prime rate	8.25
Federal funds	5.00
Commercial paper	5.35
Certificate of deposit	4.97
Banker's acceptance	5.22
London interbank offer rate	5.33
Foreign prime rates	
Canada	4.75
Germany	3.22
Japan	1.625
Treasury bills	5.01
Merrill Lynch Ready Assets Trust	4.88

Source: Wall Street Journal, February 26, 1997, p. C20.

commercial lending departments. Nevertheless, we can identify the primary money market players—the U.S. Treasury, the Federal Reserve System, commercial banks, businesses, investments and securities firms, and individuals—and discuss their roles (summarized in Table 2).

U.S. Treasury Department

The U.S. Treasury Department is unique because it is always a demander of money market funds and never a supplier. The U.S. Treasury is the largest of all money market borrowers worldwide. It issues Treasury bills (often called T-bills) and other securities that are popular with other money market participants. Short-term issues enable the government to raise funds until tax revenues are received. The Treasury also issues T-bills to replace maturing issues.

Federal Reserve System

The Federal Reserve is the Treasury's agent for the distribution of all government securities. The Fed holds vast quantities of Treasury securities that it sells if it believes that the money supply should be reduced. Similarly, the Fed will purchase Treasury securities if it believes that the money supply should be expanded. The Fed's responsibility for the money supply makes it the single most influential participant in the U.S. money market. The Federal Reserve's role in controlling the economy through money market transactions is discussed further in Chapter 23.

Commercial Banks

Commercial banks hold a larger percentage of U.S. government securities than any other group of financial institutions, approximately 12%. This is partly because of regulations that limit the investment opportunities available to banks. Specifically, banks are prohibited from owning risky securities, such as stocks or corporate bonds. There are no restrictions against holding Treasury securities because of their low risk and liquidity.

Banks are also the major issuer of negotiable certificates of deposit (CDs), banker's acceptances, federal funds, and repurchase agreements (we will discuss these securities in the next section). In addition to using money market securities to help manage their own liquidity, many banks trade on behalf of their customers.

Not all commercial banks deal for their customers in the secondary money market. The ones that do are among the largest in the country and are often referred to as *money center banks.* The biggest money center banks include Citibank, Bank of America, Chemical Bank, Morgan Guaranty, and Chase Manhattan.

Businesses

Many businesses buy and sell securities in the money markets. Such activity is usually limited to major corporations because of the large dollar amounts involved. As discussed earlier, the money markets are used extensively by businesses both to warehouse surplus funds and to raise short-term funds. We will discuss the specific money market securities that businesses issue later in this chapter.

Investment and Securities Firms

The other financial institutions that participate in the money markets are listed in Table 2.

Investment Companies Large diversified brokerage firms are active in the money markets. The largest of these include Bear Stearns, Smith Barney, Merrill Lynch, Paine Webber, and Morgan Stanley. The primary function of these dealers is to "make a market" for money market securities by maintaining an inventory from which to buy or sell. These firms are very important to the liquidity of the money market because they ensure that both buyers and sellers can readily market their securities. We discuss investment companies in Chapter 19.

Finance Companies Finance companies raise funds in the money markets primarily by selling commercial paper. They then lend the funds to consumers for the purchase of durable goods such as cars, boats, or home improvements. Finance companies and related firms are discussed in Chapter 18.

■ TABLE 2 Money Market Participants

Participant	Role
U.S. Treasury Department	Sells U.S. Treasury securities to fund the national debt
Federal Reserve System	Buys and sells U.S. Treasury securities as its primary method of controlling the money supply
Businesses	Buy and sell various short-term securities as a regular part of their cash management
Commercial banks	Buy U.S. Treasury Securities; sell certificates of deposit and make short-term loans; offer individual investors accounts that invest in money market securities
Investment companies (brokerage firms)	Trade on behalf of commercial accounts
Finance companies (commercial leasing companies)	Lend funds to individuals
Insurance companies (property and casualty insurance companies)	Maintain liquidity needed to meet unexpected demands
Pension funds	Maintain funds in money market instruments in readiness for investment in stocks and bonds
Individuals	Occasionally buy money market mutual funds
Money market mutual funds	Allow small investors to participate in the money market by aggregating their funds to invest in large-denomination money market securities

Insurance Companies Property and casualty insurance companies must maintain liquidity because of their unpredictable need for funds. When hurricane Fran hit North Carolina in 1996, for example, insurance companies paid out billions of dollars in benefits to policyholders. To meet this demand for funds, the insurance companies sold some of their money market securities to raise cash. Insurance companies are discussed in Chapter 17.

Pension Funds Pension funds invest a portion of their cash in the money markets so that they can take advantage of investment opportunities that they may identify in the stock or bond markets. Like insurance companies, pension funds must have sufficient liquidity to meet their obligations. However, because their obligations are reasonably predictable, large money market security holdings are unnecessary. Pension funds are discussed in Chapter 17.

Individuals

When inflation rose in the late 1970s, the interest rates that banks were offering on deposits became unattractive to individual investors. At this same time, brokerage houses began promoting money market mutual funds, which paid much higher rates.

Banks could not stop large amounts of cash from moving out to mutual funds because regulations capped the rate they could pay on deposits. To combat this flight of money from banks, the authorities revised the regulations. Banks quickly raised rates in an attempt to recapture individual investors' dollars. This halted the rapid movement of funds, but money market mutual funds remain a popular individual investment option. The advantage of mutual funds is that they give investors with relatively small amounts of cash to invest access to large-denomination securities. We will discuss money market mutual funds in more depth later in this chapter.

■ MONEY MARKET INSTRUMENTS

A variety of money market instruments are available to meet the diverse needs of market participants. One security will be perfect for one investor; a different security may be best for another. These securities—Treasury bills, federal funds, repurchase agreements, negotiable certificates of deposit, commercial paper, banker's acceptances, and Eurodollars—were briefly introduced in Chapter 2. Here we gain a greater understanding of their characteristics and how money market participants use them to manage their cash.

Treasury Bills

To finance the national debt, the U.S. Treasury Department issues a variety of debt securities. The most widely held liquid security is the Treasury bill. Treasury bills have 91-day, 182-day, or 12-month maturities. Treasury bills are issued in denominations of $10,000, $15,000, $50,000 $100,000, $500,000, and $1 million. The usual minimum purchase is a round lot of $5 million. Investors who wish to buy amounts smaller than $5 million contact one of the major dealers who will then purchase Treasury bills from the government and resell them to the investor.

As we noted in Chapter 2, the government does not actually pay interest on Treasury bills. Instead they are issued at a discount from par (their value at maturity). The investor's yield comes from the increase in the value of the security between the time it was purchased and the time it matures.

APPLICATION	DISCOUNTING THE PRICE OF TREASURY SECURITIES TO PAY THE INTEREST

Most money market securities do not pay interest. Instead, the investor pays less for the security than it will be worth when it matures, and the increase in price provides a return. This is called **discounting** and is common to short term securities because they often mature before the issuer could mail out interest checks. (We discussed discounting in Chapter 3.)

The yield on an investment is found by computing the increase in value in the security during its holding period and dividing by the amount paid for the security. This yield is converted into an annual yield by multiplying by 365 divided by the number of days until maturity. This gives the following equation:

$$Y_t = \frac{M - P}{P} \times \frac{365}{n} \tag{1}$$

where
$$Y_t = \text{annualized yield on the investment}$$
$$M = \text{price paid to the investor at maturity}$$
$$P = \text{purchase price}$$
$$n = \text{number of days until maturity}$$

Suppose that you purchased a 91-day Treasury bill for $9,850. If this bill will be worth $10,000 when it matures, what is the bond's annualized yield? Applying Equation 1, we find

$$Y_t = \frac{\$10,000 - \$9,850}{\$9,850} \times \frac{365}{91} = 6.11$$

So you would earn 6.11% on this 91-day investment in the Treasury bill.

Now suppose that you decided to sell the Treasury bill 31 days before it matured. If you received $9,948, what was your yield?

Use Equation 1, but M will now be the price you received when you sold the bill and n will be the number of days you held the bill, not the number of days until maturity.

$$Y_t = \frac{\$9,948 - \$9,850}{\$9,850} \times \frac{365}{60} = 6.05$$

You would have earned 6.05% on your 60-day investment.

Risk Treasury bills have virtually zero default risk because even if the government ran out of money, it could simply print more to pay them off when they mature. The risk of unexpected changes in inflation is also low because of the short term to maturity. The market for Treasury bills is extremely deep and liquid. A **deep market** is one with many different buyers and sellers. A **liquid market** is one in which securities can be bought and sold quickly and with low transaction costs. Investors in markets that are deep and liquid have little risk that they will not be able to sell their securities when they want to. The Treasury bill is so riskless that it is often used as the risk-free security in the capital asset pricing model (see Chapter 4).

The budget debates in early 1996 almost caused the government to default on its debt, despite the long-held belief that such a thing could not happen. Congress attempted to force President Clinton to sign a budget bill by refusing to approve a temporary spending package. If the stalemate had lasted much longer, we would have witnessed the first-ever U.S. government security default. We can only speculate what the long-term effect on interest rates might have been if the market decided to add a default risk premium to all government securities.

Treasury Bill Auctions Every Thursday, the Treasury announces how many 91-day (13-week) and 182-day (26-week) Treasury bills it will offer for sale. Buyers must submit bids by the following Monday, and awards are made the following morning. The 52-week Treasury bills are offered similarly but only once a month. The Treasury accepts the bids offering the highest price. The highest bidder is satisfied first. Subsequent bidders are satisfied in the order of their bid amount until the total amount of securities is distributed. Note that this implies that not everyone at the auction pays the same price for the securities.

As an alternative to the **competitive bidding** procedure just outlined, the Treasury also permits **noncompetitive bidding.** When competitive bids are offered, investors state both the amount of securities desired and the price they are willing to pay. By contrast, noncompetitive bids include only the amount of securities the investor wants. The price is set as the weighted average of the competitive bids accepted. For example, if 30% of the issue was sold for $98 per $100 of par value, 50% for $97, and the remaining 20% for $96, the weighted average would be

$$\text{Weighted average price} = 0.30(98) + 0.50(97) + 0.20(96) = \$97.10$$

Bidders submitting noncompetitive bids would pay $97.10 per $100 of Treasury bills purchased.

Table 3 presents the results of a typical Treasury auction as reported in the *Wall Street Journal.* About 38% of the bids submitted to the Fed were accepted

■ TABLE 3 Treasury Bill Auction Results, April 22, 1997

	13-Week	26-Week
Applications	$40,047,804,000	$36,176,808,000
Accepted bids	$6,094,918,000	$6,004,311,000
Accepted at low price	38%	33%
Accepted noncompetitively	$1,333,029,000	1,031,530,000
Average price (rate)	98.683 (5.21%)	97.280 (5.38%)
High price (rate)	98.691 (5.18%)	97.290 (5.36%)
Low price (rate)	98.683 (5.21%)	97.280 (5.38%)

Source: Wall Street Journal, April 22, 1997, p. C19.

for 13-week securities were accepted at the low price. A relatively small number of bids were submitted noncompetitively. It is interesting to note that the spread between the high and low bids was very small (98.683 versus 98.691 for the 13-week Treasury bill). That is due to the highly competitive nature of the auction.

In 1976, the Treasury switched the entire marketable portion of the federal debt over to **book entry** securities, replacing engraved pieces of paper. In a book entry system, ownership of Treasury securities is documented only in the Fed's computer: Essentially, a ledger entry replaces the actual security. This procedure reduces the cost of issuing Treasury securities as well as the cost of transferring them as they are bought and sold in the secondary market.

The Treasury auction of securities is supposed to be highly competitive and fair. To ensure proper levels of competition, no one dealer is allowed to purchase more than 35% of any one issue. About 40 primary dealers regularly participate in the auction. Solomon Brothers was caught violating the limits on the percentage of one issue a dealer may purchase. (See the Box on the Solomon Brothers Scandal.)

Treasury Bill Interest Rates Treasury bills are very close to being risk-free. As expected for a risk-free security, the interest rate earned on Treasury bill securities is among the lowest in the economy. Investors in Treasury bills have found that in some years, their earnings did not even compensate them for changes in purchasing power due to inflation. Figure 1 shows the interest rate on Treasury bills and the inflation rate over the period 1973–1995. As discussed in Chapter 3, the *real rate* of interest has occasionally been less than zero. For example, in 1973–1977 and again in 1990–1991, the inflation rate matched or exceeded the earnings on T-bills. Clearly, the T-bill is not an investment to be used for anything but temporary storage of excess funds because it barely keeps up with inflation.

BOX 1

Treasury Bill Auctions Go Haywire

Every Thursday the Treasury announces how many 91-day and 182-day Treasury bills it will offer for sale. Buyers must submit bids by the following Monday, and awards are made the following morning. Fifty two-week Treasury bills are offered similarly once per month. The Treasury accepts those bids offering the highest price.

The Treasury auction of securities is supposed to be highly competitive and fair. To ensure proper levels of competition, no one dealer is allowed to purchase more than 35% of any one issue. About 40 primary dealers regularly participate in the auction.

In 1991, the disclosure that Solomon Brothers had broken the rules to corner the market cast the fairness of the auction in doubt. Solomon Brothers purchased 35% of the Treasury securities in its own name by submitting a relatively high bid. It then bought additional securities in the names of its customers, often without their knowledge or consent. Solomon then bought the securities from the customers. As a result of these transactions Solomon cornered the market and was able to charge a monopoly-like premium. The investigation of Solomon Brothers revealed that during one auction in May 1991, Solomon managed to gain control of 94% of an $11 billion issue. During the scandal that followed this disclosure, John Gutfreund, the firm's chairman, and several other top executives with Solomon retired. The Treasury has instituted new rules since then to ensure that the market remains competitive.

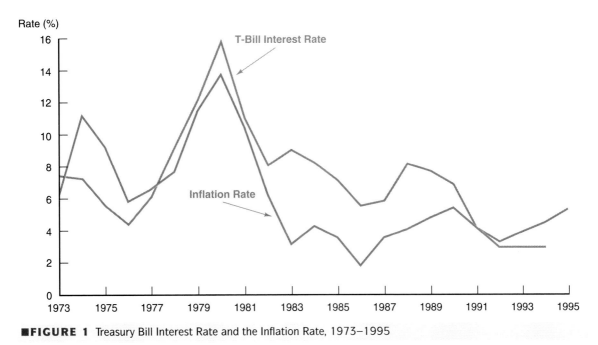

■FIGURE 1 Treasury Bill Interest Rate and the Inflation Rate, 1973–1995

Source: Wall Street Journal, February 26, 1997, p. C20.

Federal Funds

In Chapter 2 we defined *federal funds* as short-term funds transferred (loaned or borrowed) between financial institutions, usually for a period of one day. The term *federal funds* (or *fed funds*) is misleading. Fed funds really have nothing to do with the federal government. When the fed funds market began in the 1920s, banks with excess reserves loaned them to banks that needed them. The interest rate for borrowing these funds was close to the rate that was available from the Federal Reserve.

Purpose of Fed Funds The Federal Reserve has set minimum reserve requirements that all banks must maintain to ensure that they have adequate liquidity. To meet these reserve requirements, banks must maintain a certain percentage of their total deposits with the Federal Reserve. The main purpose for fed funds is to provide banks with an immediate infusion of reserves should they be short. Banks can borrow directly from the Federal Reserve, but many prefer to borrow from other banks so that they do not alert the Fed to any liquidity problems. The reason that banks like to lend in the fed funds market is that money held at the Federal Reserve in excess of what is required does not earn any interest. So even though the interest rate on fed funds is low, it beats the alternative. One indication of the popularity of fed funds is that on a typical day in June 1993, $257 billion in Fed funds were purchased. The calculation of reserve requirements is discussed in "The Practicing Financial Institutional Manager" in Chapter 16.

Terms for Fed Funds Fed funds are usually overnight investments. Banks analyze their reserve position on a daily basis and either borrow or invest in fed funds, depending on whether they have excess or deficit reserves. Suppose that a bank finds that it has $50 million in excess reserves. It will call its correspondent banks (banks that have reciprocal accounts) to see if they need reserves that day. The bank will sell its excess funds to the bank that offers the highest rate. Once an agreement has been reached, the bank with excess funds will wire the funds to the borrowing bank. This involves telecommunicating to the Federal Reserve bank instructions to take funds out of the seller's account at the Fed and deposit the funds in the borrower's account. The next day, the funds are transferred back, and the process begins again.

Most fed funds borrowings are unsecured. Typically, the entire agreement is supported only by oral communication between buyer and seller.

Federal Funds Interest Rates The forces of supply and demand set the fed funds interest rate. This is a competitive market that analysts watch closely for indications of what is happening to short-term rates.

The Federal Reserve cannot directly control fed funds rates. It can and does indirectly influence them by adjusting the level of reserves available to banks in the system. The Fed can increase the amount of money in the financial system by buying securities. When investors sell securities to the Fed, the proceeds are deposited in their banks' accounts at the Federal Reserve. These deposits increase the supply of reserves in the financial system and lower interest rates. If the Fed removes reserves by selling securities, fed funds rates will increase. The Fed will often announce its intention to raise or lower the fed funds rate in advance. Though these rates directly affect few businesses or consumers, analysts consider them an important indicator of the direction in which the Federal Reserve wants the economy to move. Figure 2 compares the fed funds rate with the T-bill rate. Clearly, the two track together.

Repurchase Agreements

As we learned in Chapter 2, repurchase agreements (repos) work much the same as fed funds except that nonbanks can participate. A firm can sell Treasury securities in a repurchase agreement whereby the firm agrees to buy back the securities at a specified future date. Most repos have a very short term, the most common being for 3 to 14 days. There is a market, however, for one- to three-month repos.

The Use of Repurchase Agreements Government securities dealers frequently engage in repos. The dealer may sell the securities to a bank with the promise to buy the securities back the next day. This makes the repo essentially a short-term collateralized loan. Securities dealers use the repo to manage their liquidity and to take advantage of anticipated changes in interest rates.

The Federal Reserve also uses repos in conducting monetary policy. We present the details of monetary policy in Chapter 24; for now, however, we need to

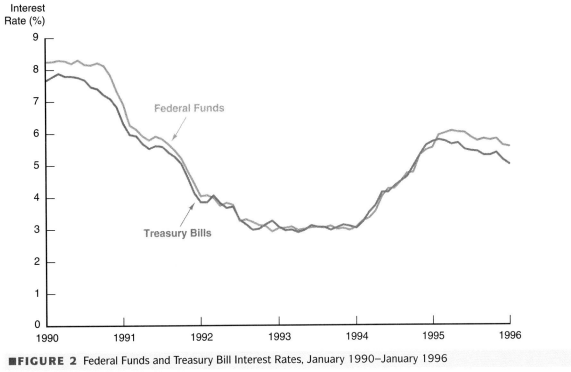

■FIGURE 2 Federal Funds and Treasury Bill Interest Rates, January 1990–January 1996

Source: Federal Reserve Bulletin, Various issues.

understand only that the conduct of monetary policy requires that the Fed adjust bank reserves on a temporary basis. To accomplish this adjustment, the Fed will buy or sell Treasury securities in the repo market. The maturities of Federal Reserve repos never exceed 15 days.

Interest Rate on Repos   Because repos are collateralized with Treasury securities, they are usually low-risk investments and therefore have low interest rates. Losses have occurred in these markets, however. In 1985, ESM Government Securities and Bevill, Bresler, and Schulman declared bankruptcy. These firms had used the same securities as collateral for more than one loan. The resulting losses to municipalities that had purchased the repos exceeded $500 million. Such losses also caused the failure of the state-insured thrift insurance system in Ohio.

Negotiable Certificates of Deposit

A negotiable certificate of deposit is a bank-issued security that documents a deposit and specifies the interest rate and the maturity date. Because a maturity date is specified, a CD is a **term security** as opposed to a **demand deposit:** Term securities have a specified maturity date; demand deposits can be withdrawn at any time. A CD is also called a **bearer instrument.** This means that whoever holds the instrument at maturity receives the principal and interest. The CD can be bought and sold until maturity.

Terms of Negotiable Certificates of Deposit The denominations of negotiable certificates of deposit range from $100,000 to $10 million. Few negotiable CDs are denominated less than $1 million. The reason that these instruments are so large is that dealers have established the round lot size to be $1 million. A round lot is the minimum quantity that can be traded without incurring higher than normal brokerage fees.

Negotiable CDs typically have a maturity of one to four months. Some have six-month maturities, but there is little demand for ones with longer maturities.

History of the CD Citibank issued the first large certificates of deposit in 1961. The bank offered the CD to counter the long-term trend of declining demand deposits at large banks. Corporate treasurers were minimizing their cash balances and investing their excess funds in safe, income-generating money market instruments such as T-bills. The attraction of the CD was that it paid a market interest rate. There was a problem, however. The rate of interest that banks could pay on CDs was restricted by Regulation Q. As long as interest rates on most securities were low, this regulation did not affect demand. But when interest rates rose above the level permitted by Regulation Q, the market for these certificates of deposit evaporated. In response, banks began offering the certificates overseas, where they were exempt from Regulation Q limits. In 1970, Congress amended Regulation Q to exempt certificates of deposit over $100,000. By 1972, the CD represented approximately 40 percent of all bank deposits. The certificate of deposit is now the second most popular money market instrument, behind only the T-bill.

Interest Rate on CDs Figure 3 plots the interest rate on negotiable CDs along with that on T-bills. The rates paid on negotiable CDs are negotiated between the bank and the customer. They are similar to the rate paid on other money market instruments because the level of risk is relatively low. Large money center banks can offer rates a little lower than other banks because many investors in the market believe that the government would never allow one of the nation's largest banks to fail. This belief makes these banks' obligations less risky. CD rates tend to be slightly above the T-bill rate because of the slightly greater chance of default.

Commercial Paper

In Chapter 2 we defined *commercial paper securities* as unsecured promissory notes, issued by corporations, that mature in no more than 270 days. Because these securities are unsecured, only the largest and most creditworthy corporations issue commercial paper. The interest rate the corporation is charged reflects the firm's level of risk.

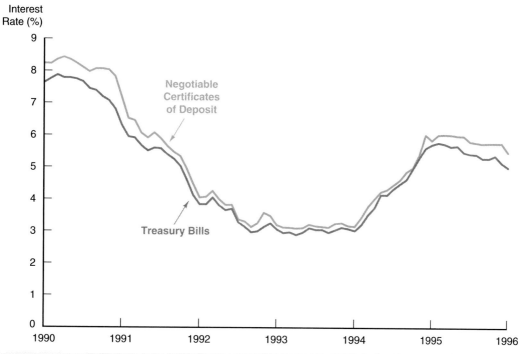

FIGURE 3 Interest Rates on Negotiable Certificates of Deposit and on Treasury Bills, January 1990–January 1996

Source: Federal Reserve Bulletin, Various issues.

Terms and Issuance Commercial paper always has an original maturity of less than 270 days. This is to avoid the need to register the security issue with the Securities and Exchange Commission. (To be exempt from SEC registration, the issue must have an original maturity of less than 270 days and be intended for current transactions.) Most commercial paper actually matures in 20 to 45 days. Like T-bills, most commercial paper is issued on a discounted basis.

About 60% of commercial paper is sold directly by the issuer to the buyer. The balance is sold by dealers in the commercial paper market. A strong secondary market for commercial paper does not exist. A dealer will redeem commercial paper if a purchaser has a dire need for cash, though this is generally not necessary.

History of Commercial Paper Commercial paper has been used in various forms since the 1920s. In 1969, a tight-money environment caused bank holding companies to issue commercial paper to finance new loans. In response, to keep control over the money supply, the Federal Reserve imposed reserve requirements on bank-issued commercial paper in 1970. These reserve requirements removed the major advantage to banks of using commercial paper. Bank holding companies still use commercial paper to fund leasing and consumer finance.

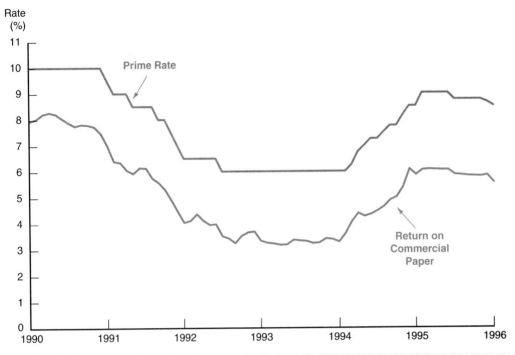

■**FIGURE 4** Return on Commercial Paper and the Prime Rate, January 1990–January 1996

Source: Federal Reserve Bulletin, Various issues.

The use of commercial paper increased substantially in the early 1980s because of the rising cost of bank loans. Figure 4 graphs the interest rate on commercial paper against the bank prime rate for the period January 1990–January 1996.

Commercial paper has become an important alternative to bank loans primarily because of its lower cost.

Market for Commercial Paper Nonbank corporations use commercial paper extensively to finance the loans that they extend to their customers. For example, General Motors Acceptance Corporation (GMAC) borrows money by issuing commercial paper and uses the money to make loans to consumers buying General Motors cars. Similarly, Household Finance and Chrysler Credit use commercial paper to fund loans made to consumers. The total number of firms issuing commercial paper varies between 600 to 800, depending on the level of interest rates. Most of these firms use one of about 30 commercial paper dealers who match up buyers and sellers. The large New York City money center banks are very active in this market. Some of the larger issuers of commercial paper choose to distribute their securities with **direct placements.** In a direct placement, the issuer bypasses the dealer and sells directly to the end investor. The advantage of this method is that the issuer saves the 0.125% commission that the dealer charges.

Most issuers of commercial paper back up their paper with a line of credit at a bank. This means that in the event that the issuer cannot pay off or roll over the maturing paper, the bank will lend the firm funds for this purpose. The line of credit reduces the risk to the purchasers of the paper and so lowers the interest rate. The bank that provides the backup line of credit agrees in advance to make a loan to the issuer if needed to pay off the outstanding paper. The bank charges a fee of 0.5% to 1% for this commitment. Issuers pay this fee because they are able to save more than this in lowered interest costs by having the line.

Commercial banks were the original purchasers of commercial paper. Today the market has greatly expanded to include large insurance companies, nonfinancial businesses, bank trust departments, and government pension funds. These firms are attracted by the relatively low default risk, short maturity, and high yields these securities offer.

Banker's Acceptances

A banker's acceptance is an order to pay a specified amount of money to the bearer on a given date. As noted in Chapter 2, banker's acceptances have been in use since the twelfth century. However, they were not major money market securities until the volume of international trade ballooned in the 1960s. They are used to finance goods that have not yet been transferred from the seller to the buyer. For example, suppose that Builtwell Construction Company wants to buy a bulldozer from Komatsu in Japan. Komatsu does not want to ship the bulldozer without being paid because Komatsu has never heard of Builtwell and realizes that it would be difficult to collect if payment were not forthcoming. Similarly, Builtwell is reluctant to send money to Japan before receiving the equipment. A bank can intervene in this standoff by issuing a banker's acceptance.

Using a Banker's Acceptance The transaction would begin with Builtwell's obtaining a letter of credit from its bank. A letter of credit simply says that if Builtwell has not paid its obligation by a certain time, the bank will make payment. This particular letter of credit will also authorize the exporter (Komatsu or its bank) to draw a time draft for the amount of the sale. A time draft is like a postdated check: It can be cashed only after a certain date. Builtwell sends the order for the bulldozer, along with the letter of credit, to Komatsu.

When Komatsu receives these documents, it is willing to ship the equipment because the bank's credit standing has been substituted for that of the actual buyer. Once the equipment has been shipped, Komatsu will present the letter of credit and the shipping documents to its own bank in Japan. This bank will create the time draft authorized by the letter of credit and send it to Builtwell's bank. When Builtwell's bank receives the time draft and the shipping documents, it will stamp the time draft "accepted" and return it to Komatsu's bank.

This accepted time draft is now a banker's acceptance. Because it is backed by the credit of a bank, it can be traded on the secondary market. Typically, the exporter's bank will sell it so that the exporter can receive funds before the maturity date. It will be sold at a discount so that the buyer can earn a fair return for holding it until its maturity date.

The transaction is completed when Builtwell deposits the funds in its bank to cover the amount of the time draft (now a banker's acceptance). When the banker's acceptance finally matures and is presented for payment, the issuing bank withdraws funds from Builtwell's account to make payment. Of course, if for some reason Builtwell was unable to make the required deposit, its bank would pay the acceptance anyway and attempt to collect from Builtwell later.

Let us summarize the steps for using banker's acceptances.

1. The importer requests its bank to send an irrevocable letter of credit to the exporter.
2. The exporter receives the letter, ships the goods, and is paid by presenting to its bank the letter along with proof that the merchandise was shipped.
3. The exporter's bank creates a time draft based on the letter of credit and sends it along with proof of shipment to the importer's bank.
4. The importer's bank stamps the time draft "accepted" and sends the banker's acceptance back to the exporter's bank so that the exporter's bank can sell it on the secondary market to collect payment.
5. The importer deposits funds at its bank sufficient to cover the banker's acceptance when it matures.

Advantages of Banker's Acceptances As the bulldozer example demonstrates, banker's acceptances are crucial to international trade. Without them, many transactions simply would not occur because the parties would not feel properly protected from losses. There are other advantages as well:

- The exporter is paid immediately. This is important when delivery times are long after shipment.
- The exporter is shielded from foreign exchange risk because the local bank pays in domestic funds.
- The exporter does not have to assess the creditworthiness of the importer because the importer's bank guarantees payment.

Secondary Market for Banker's Acceptances Because banker's acceptances are payable to the bearer, they can be bought and sold until they mature. They are sold on a discounted basis like commercial paper and T-bills. Dealers in this market match up firms that want to discount a banker's acceptance (sell it for immediate payment) with these companies wishing to invest in banker's acceptances.

Interest rates on banker's acceptances are low because the risk of default is very low. For example, no investor in banker's acceptances in the United States has suffered a loss of principal in more than 60 years. The reason is that only large money center banks are involved in this market.

 **Eurodollars**

Many contracts around the world call for payment in U.S. dollars due to the dollar's stability. For this reason, many companies and governments choose to hold dollars. Prior to World War II, most of these deposits were held in New York money center banks. However, as a result of the Cold War that followed, some governments (the Soviet government in particular) felt that there was a risk that deposits held on U.S. soil could be expropriated. Some large London banks responded to this opportunity by offering to hold dollar-denominated deposits in British banks. These deposits are called Eurodollars. Even as the Cold War threat lessened, these deposits remained popular. One reason was that Eurodollar banks were not subject to the regulatory costs imposed on U.S. banks. The Eurodollar market expanded during the 1970s and 1980s along with the money markets as a whole. Currently, the Eurodollar market has more than $4 trillion outstanding. To put this into perspective, the entire U.S. national debt could be paid off with the funds loaned in this market.

Why has the Eurodollar market grown so large so fast? The primary reason is that depositors receive a higher rate of return on a dollar deposit in the Eurodollar market than in the domestic market. At the same time, the borrower is able to receive a more favorable rate in the Eurodollar market than in the domestic market. This is because multinational banks are not subject to the same regulations restricting U.S. banks and because they are willing and able to accept narrower spreads between the interest paid on deposits and the interest earned on loans.

London Interbank Market Some large London banks act as brokers in the interbank Eurodollar market. Recall that fed funds are used by banks to make up temporary shortfalls in their reserves. Eurodollars are an alternative to fed funds. Banks from around the world buy and sell overnight funds in this market. The rate paid by banks buying funds is the **London interbank bid rate (LIBID).** Funds are offered for sale in this market at the **London interbank offer rate (LIBOR).** Because many banks participate in this market, it is extremely competitive. The spread between the bid and the offer rate seldom exceeds 0.125%. Eurodollar deposits are time deposits, which means that they cannot be withdrawn for a specified period of time. Although the most common time period is overnight, different maturities are available. Each maturity has a different rate.

The overnight LIBOR and the fed funds rate tend to be very close to each other. This is because they are near-perfect substitutes. Suppose that the fed funds rate exceeded the overnight LIBOR. Banks that need to borrow funds will borrow overnight Eurodollars, and banks with funds to sell will sell fed funds. The demand and supply pressure will cause a rapid adjustment that will drive the two rates together.

At one time, most short-term loans with adjustable interest rates were tied to the Treasury bill rate. However, the market for Eurodollars is so broad and deep that it has recently become the standard rate against which others are compared. For example, the U.S. commercial paper market now quotes rates as a spread over LIBOR, rather than over the T-bill rate.

The Eurodollar market is not limited to London banks anymore. The primary brokers in this market maintain offices in all of the major financial centers worldwide.

Eurodollar Certificates of Deposit Because Eurodollars are time deposits with fixed maturities, they are to a certain extent illiquid. As usual, the financial markets created new types of securities to combat this problem. These new securities were transferable negotiable certificates of deposit (negotiable CDs). Because most Eurodollar deposits have a relatively short term to begin with, the market for Eurodollar negotiable CDs is relatively limited, comprising less than 10% of the amount of regular Eurodollar deposits. The market for the negotiable CDs is still thin.

Other Eurocurrencies The Eurodollar market is by far the largest short term security in the world. This is due to the international popularity of the U.S. dollar for trade. However, the market is not limited to dollars. It is possible to have an account denominated in Japanese yen held in a London or New York bank. Such an account would be termed a Euroyen account. Similarly, you may also have Euromark or Europeso accounts denominated in marks and pesos, respectively, and held in various banks around the world. Keep in mind that if market participants have a need for a particular security and are willing to pay for it, the financial markets stand ready and willing to create it.

■ COMPARING MONEY MARKET SECURITIES

Although money market securities share many characteristics, such as liquidity, safety, and short maturities, they all differ in some aspects.

Interest Rates

Figure 5 compares the interest rates on each of the money market instruments we have discussed. The most notable feature of this graph is that all of the money market instruments appear to move very closely together over time. This is because all have a very low risk and a short term. They all have deep markets and so are priced competitively. In addition, because these instruments have so many of the same risk and term characteristics, they are close substitutes. Consequently, if one rate should temporarily depart from the others, market supply and demand forces would soon cause a correction.

The *Wall Street Journal* reports money market rates in a table called "Money Rates," which appears daily in the third section. This table contains a brief description of each security and the most recent available interest rate. The "Following the Financial News" box on p. 238 shows a "Money Rates" table from the *Wall Street Journal.*

Liquidity

As we discussed in Chapter 3, the *liquidity* of a security refers to how quickly, easily, and cheaply it can be converted into cash. Typically, the depth of the secondary market where the security can be resold determines its liquidity. For example, the secondary market for Treasury bills is extensive and well developed. As a result, Treasury bills can be converted into cash quickly and with little cost. By contrast, there is no well-developed secondary market for commercial paper.

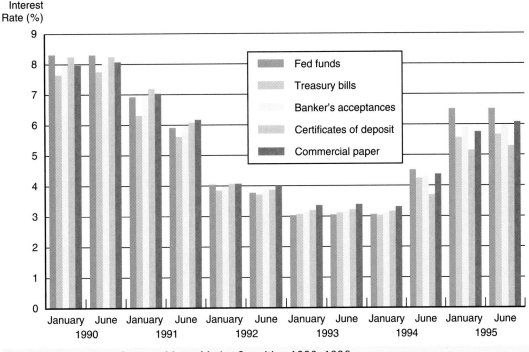

■FIGURE 5 Interest Rates on Money Market Securities, 1990–1996

Source: Federal Reserve Bulletin, Various issues.

Most holders of commercial paper hold the securities until maturity. In the event that a commercial paper investor needed to sell the securities to raise cash, it is likely that brokers would charge relatively high fees.

In some ways, the depth of the secondary market is not as critical for money market securities as it is for long-term securities such as stocks and bonds. This is because money market securities are short-term to start with. Nevertheless, many investors desire *liquidity intervention:* They seek an intermediary to provide liquidity where it did not previously exist. This is one function of money market mutual funds (discussed in the next section).

Table 4 summarizes the money market securities and the depth of the secondary market.

■ MONEY MARKET MUTUAL FUNDS

Earlier in this chapter we pointed out that the money markets are wholesale markets where most securities trade in large denominations. This characteristic effectively blocks most individuals from investing directly in these securities. However, the markets usually find a way to correct for such deficiencies, especially when potential customers are available. Money market mutual funds represent one such correction.

Money Market Rates

The *Wall Street Journal* publishes daily a listing of interest rates on many different financial instruments in its "Money Rates" column. (See "Today's Contents" on page 1 of the *Journal* for the location.)

The four interest rates in the "Money Rates" column that are discussed most frequently in the media are these:

Prime rate: The base interest rate on corporate bank loans, as indicator of the cost of business borrowing from banks.

Federal funds rate: The interest rate charged on overnight loans in the federal funds market, a sensitive indicator of the cost to banks of borrowing funds from other banks and the stance of monetary policy

Treasury bill rate: The interest rate on U.S. Treasury bills, an indicator of general interest-rate movements

Federal Home Loan Mortgage Corporation rates: Interest rates on "Freddie Mac"–guaranteed mortgages, an indicator of the cost of financing residential housing purchases

Source: Wall Street Journal, January 31, 1997, p. C17.

MONEY RATES

Thursday, January 30, 1997

The key U.S. and foreign annual interest rates below are a guide to general levels but don't always represent actual transactions.

PRIME RATE: 8.25% (effective 2/01/96). The base rate on corporate loans posted by at least 75% of the nation's 30 largest banks.

DISCOUNT RATE: 5%. The charge on loans to depository institutions by the Federal Reserve Banks.

FEDERAL FUNDS: 5 1/2% high, 4 3/4% low, 5% near closing bid, 5 1/4% offered. Reserves traded among commercial banks for overnight use in amounts of $1 million or more. Source: Prebon Yamane (U.S.A.) Inc.

CALL MONEY: 7%. The charge on loans to brokers on stock exchange collateral. Source: Dow Jones Telerate Inc.

COMMERCIAL PAPER placed directly by General Electric Capital Corp.: 5.30% 30 to 44 days; 5.31% 45 to 89 days; 5.33% 90 to 179 days; 5.35% 180 to 239 days; 5.36% 240 to 270 days.

COMMERCIAL PAPER: High-grade unsecured notes sold through dealers by major corporations: 5.45% 30 days; 5.45% 60 days; 5.46% 90 days.

CERTIFICATES OF DEPOSIT: 4.84% one month; 4.90% two months; 4.96% three months; 5.19% six months; 5.42% one year. Average of top rates paid by major New York banks on primary new issues of negotiable C.D.s, usually on amounts of $1 million and more. The minimum unit is $100,000. Typical rates in the secondary market: 5.32% one month; 5.40% three months; 5.50% six months.

BANKERS ACCEPTANCES: 5.25% 30 days; 5.25% 60 days; 5.28% 90 days; 5.29% 120 days; 5.30% 150 days; 5.30% 180 days. Offered rates of negotiable, bank-backed business credit instruments typically financing an import order.

LONDON LATE EURODOLLARS: 5 7/16%-5 5/16% one month; 5 1/2%-5 3/8% two months; 5 9/16%-5 7/16% three months; 5 19/32%-5 15/32 four months; 5 5/8%-5 1/2% five months; 5 11/16%-5 9/16% six months.

LONDON INTERBANK OFFERED RATES (LIBOR): 5 15/32% one month; 5 9/16% three months; 5 11/16% six months; 5 15/16% one year. The average of interbank offered rates for dollar deposits in the London market based on quotations at five major banks. Effective rate for contracts entered into two days from date appearing at top of this column.

FOREIGN PRIME RATES: Canada 4.75%; Germany 3.15%; Japan 1.625%; Switzerland 3.875%; Britain 6.00%. These rate indications aren't directly comparable; lending practices vary widely by location.

TREASURY BILLS: Results of the Monday, January 27, 1997, auction of short-term U.S. government bills, sold at a discount from face value in units of $10,000 to $1 million: 5.06% 13 weeks; 5.12% 26 weeks.

OVERNIGHT REPURCHASE RATE: 5.33%. Dealer financing rate for overnight sale and repurchase of Treasury securities. Source: Dow Jones Telerate Inc.

FEDERAL HOME LOAN MORTGAGE CORP. (Freddie Mac): Posted yields on 30-year mortgage commitments. Delivery within 30 days 7.97%, 60 days 8.03%, standard conventional fixed-rate mortgages; 5.625%, 2% rate capped one-year adjustable rate mortgages. Source: Dow Jones Telerate Inc.

FEDERAL NATIONAL MORTGAGE ASSOCIATION (Fannie Mae): Posted yields on 30 year mortgage commitments (priced at par) for delivery within 30 days 7.93%, 60 days 8.00%, standard conventional fixed rate-mortgages; 6.70%, 6/2 rate capped one-year adjustable rate mortgages. Source: Dow Jones Telerate Inc.

MERRILL LYNCH READY ASSETS TRUST: 4.91%. Annualized average rate of return after expenses for the past 30 days; not a forecast of future returns.

■ **TABLE 4** Money Market Securities and Their Markets

Money Market Security	Issuer	Buyer	Usual Maturity	Secondary Market
Treasury bills	U.S. government	Consumers and companies	13 weeks, 26 weeks, 1 year	Excellent
Federal funds	Banks	Banks	1 to 7 days	None
Repurchase agreements	Businesses and banks	Businesses and banks	1 to 15 days	Good
Negotiable certificates of deposit	Large money center banks	Businesses	14 to 120 days	Good
Commercial Paper	Finance companies and businesses	Businesses	1 to 270 days	Poor
Banker's Acceptance	Banks	Businesses	30 to 180 days	Good
Eurodollar deposits	Non-U.S. banks	Businesses, governments, and banks	1 day to 1 year	Poor

Money market mutual funds (MMMFs) are funds that aggregate money from a group of small investors and invest it in money market instruments. They have grown enormously popular since their inception in the early 1970s because they provide a means for small investors to take advantage of the returns offered on money market securities. These securities would be out of reach to most small investors because of their large minimum denominations.

History of Money Market Mutual Funds

Money market mutual funds have existed since the 1960s; however, the low market interest rates before 1977 (which were either below or just slightly above Regulation Q ceilings of 5.25% to 5.5%) kept them from being particularly advantageous relative to bank deposits. In 1978, Merrill Lynch recognized that it could provide better service to its customers if it offered an account that customers could use to warehouse money. Prior to the introduction of MMMFs as a small-investor account, customers had to bring checks to the brokerage house when they wanted to invest and had to pick up checks when they sold securities. Customers who had MMMF accounts, however, could simply direct the broker to take funds out of this account to buy stocks or to deposit funds in this account when they sold securities. Initially, Merrill Lynch did not look on the MMMF as a major source of income.

In the early 1980s, inflation and interest rates skyrocketed. Regulation Q restricted banks from paying more than 5.25% in interest on savings accounts. With interest rates in the money market exceeding 15%, investors flocked to MMMFs. Figure 6 shows the growth in money market mutual funds between 1975 and 1995.

The loss of deposits from banks and thrifts to these MMMFs caused serious liquidity and profitability problems in both the banking and thrift industries. These problems are discussed further in Chapter 13.

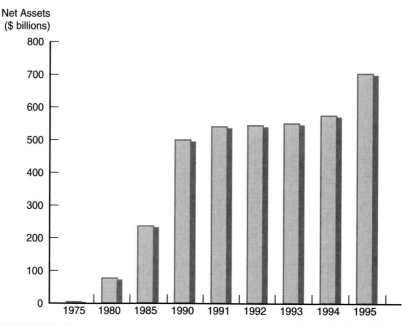

■FIGURE 6 Net Assets of Money Market Mutual Funds, 1975–1995

Source: 1996 Mutual Fund Fact Book, 36th edition, Investment Company Institute.

Description of Money Market Mutual Funds

MMFs are open-end investment funds that invest only in money market securities. An *open-ended fund* is one that invests in securities and sells direct claims on the securities to investors. Most funds do not charge investors any fee for purchasing or redeeming shares. The funds usually have a minimum initial investment of $500 to $20,000. The fund's yield depends entirely on the performance of the securities purchased.

An important feature of MMMFs is that many have check-writing privileges. They often do not charge a fee for writing checks or have any minimum check amount as long as the balance in the account is above a stated level. This convenience, along with market interest rates, makes the accounts very popular with small investors.

Brokerage houses do not have the computer facilities needed to handle the volume of transactions generated by MMMF accounts. Instead of incurring the cost of developing these facilities, most brokerage firms contract with banks to provide the processing. For example, Merrill Lynch set up a joint venture with BancOne Corporation of Columbus, Ohio, to service its tremendously popular Cash Management Account. Customers using MMMFs had to learn to bank by mail and over the telephone because brokerage houses did not have extensive branch systems. Once the customers became accustomed to this way of banking, many found it convenient and well worth the trouble for the extra income earned on these accounts.

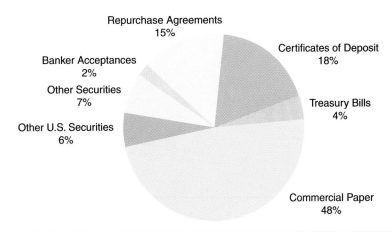

■FIGURE 7 Average Distribution of Money Market Fund Assets, 1995

Source: 1996 Mutual Fund Fact Book, 36th edition, Investment Company Institute.

MMMF Risk

Investors took their money out of federally *insured* banks and thrifts and put it into *uninsured* MMMFs. An important question is why they were willing to take this extra level of risk. The reason is that the extra risk was really very small. The money invested in MMMFs was in turn invested in money market instruments. Commercial paper is by far the largest component of these funds, followed by certificates of deposit and repurchase agreements and then by banker's acceptances. Figure 7 shows the average distribution of money market fund assets. Because the risk of default on these securities is very low, the risk of MMMFs is very low. Investors recognized this and so were willing to abandon the safety of their banks and thrifts.

Current Trends in MMMFs

Legislation in 1980 and 1982 removed most of the restrictions on bank interest-rate ceilings. These changes were aimed at reducing the flow of funds out of banks into brokerage houses. And by the mid-1980s, interest rates had begun to fall. The combined effect was to reduce the growth rate of MMMFs. Currently, investors can still earn a 0.5% to 1% higher return by investing in MMMFs rather than placing their money in a bank. For this reason, MMMFs remain popular.

SUMMARY

1. Money market securities are short-term instruments with an original maturity of less than one year. These securities trade in the money markets. They include Treasury bills, commercial paper, federal funds, repurchase agreements, negotiable certificates of deposit, banker's acceptances, and Eurodollars.

2. Money market securities are used to "warehouse" funds until needed. The returns earned on these investments are low due to their low risk and high liquidity.

3. Many participants in the money markets both buy and sell money market securities. The U.S. Treasury, commercial banks, businesses, and individuals all benefit by having access to low-risk short-term investments.

4. Interest rates on all money market securities tend to follow one another closely over time. Treasury bill returns are the lowest because they are virtually devoid of default risk. Banker's acceptances and negotiable certificates of deposit are next lowest because they are backed by the creditworthiness of large money center banks.

5. Money market mutual funds aggregate the funds of many small investors and purchase money market instruments. The returns on these instruments are passed on to the investors. Money market mutual funds have grown rapidly since 1978. Higher market interest rates occurred at a time when banks were limited as to the maximum rate they could pay to retain deposits. This made the returns to money market mutual funds very attractive.

KEY TERMS

bearer instrument, p. 230
book entry, p. 226
competitive bidding, p. 225
deep market, p. 225
demand deposit, p. 229

direct placement, p. 232
discounting, p. 224
liquid market, p. 225
London interbank bid rate, (LIBID), p. 235

London interbank offer rate, (LIBOR), p. 235
noncompetitive bidding, p. 225
term security, p. 229
wholesale market, p. 218

QUESTIONS AND PROBLEMS

*1. What characteristics define the money markets?

2. Is a Treasury bond issued 29 years ago with six months remaining before it matures a money market instrument?

*3. Why do banks not eliminate the need for money markets?

4. Distinguish between a term security and a demand security.

*5. What was the purpose motivating regulators to impose interest ceilings on bank savings accounts? What impact did this eventually have on the money markets?

6. Why does the U.S. government use the money markets?

*7. Why do businesses use the money markets?

8. What purpose initially motivated Merrill Lynch to offer money market mutual funds to its customers?

*9. Why are more funds from property and casualty insurance companies than funds from life insurance companies invested in the money markets?

10. Which of the money market securities is the most liquid and considered the most risk-free? Why?

*11. Distinguish between competitive bidding and noncompetitive bidding for Treasury securities.

12. Who issues federal funds, and what is the usual purpose of these funds?

*13. Does the Federal Reserve *directly* set the federal funds interest rate?

14. Who issues commercial paper and for what purpose?

*15. Why are banker's acceptances so popular for international transactions?

CASE STUDY

Participants in the Money Markets, Weighted Average Returns, Foreign Alternatives

CONCEPTS IN THIS CASE

money market securities
treasury bills
federal funds
repurchase agreements
negotiable CDs
Eurodollars
London interbank bid and offer rate
money market mutual funds

You have just been named as a beneficiary in a will. The initial amount is $2 million dollars. Due to poor estate planning, the executor must pay federal, state and local income taxes, estate (death) taxes, probate costs and other fees. This costs you $900 thousand dollars. You are not ready to commit your funds for the long run, since you do not know where you will be or what you will be doing in the future. You want to invest the funds in the money market as a "warehouse" until you are ready to make long-term decisions on your future. With this in mind, you begin to study the market for short-term securities that mature in one year or less from their original issue date. Your goal is to maximize your return for one-year while minimizing risk and maintaining trading flexibility.

1. To achieve your goal, you begin by answering the following questions.
   a. Who are the major players in the money market?
   b. What are the primary money market instruments?

2. All investments are based on one-year maturities or actual returns, beginning on the first day of business for the calendar year and ending on the last day of business for the same calendar year. You obtain the rates and share prices for the first and last business days for the previous calendar year (using library resources, the Internet, or other databases).
   a. What is the weighted average expected rate of return for all investments made in January?
   b. What is the weighted average actual rate of return for all investments ending in December?
   c. What is the weighted average expected rate of return for all investments between January and July 1?
   d. What is the weighted average actual rate of return for all investments between January and July 1?
   e. Which holding period would you prefer, 6 months or 12 months?

CHAPTER 10

THE CAPITAL MARKETS

■ **PREVIEW** In 1996, Netscape emerged as the leading software used for browsing the Internet. The firm needed additional cash to fund its explosive growth and to fight off efforts by Microsoft to capture the market. The managers of Netscape did not want to use short-term funds like those available in the money markets. Instead, they required long-term capital that could be used to fund long-term growth. Netscape's managers could have raised the funds using any of a number of long-term securities, but they decided to do it by offering stock for sale to the public in one of the decade's most closely watched stock offerings. The founders of Netscape became instant billionaires as a result.

This chapter discusses securities that have an original maturity that is *greater* than one year, such as the stock issued by Netscape. These securities trade in the capital markets. The best-known capital market securities are stocks and bonds. Mortgages, which also trade in the capital markets, are discussed in Chapter 11.

■ PURPOSE OF THE CAPITAL MARKET

Firms that issue capital market securities and the investors who buy them have very different motivations than they have when they operate in the money markets. Firms and individuals use the money markets primarily to warehouse funds for short periods of time until a more important need or a more productive use for the funds arises. By contrast, firms and individuals use the capital markets for long-term investments. The capital markets provide an alternative to investment in assets such as real estate or gold.

Suppose that after a careful financial analysis, your firm determines that it needs a new plant to meet the increased demand for its products. This analysis will be made using interest rates that reflect the *current* long-term cost of funds to the firm. Now suppose that your firm chooses to finance this plant by issuing money market securities, such as commercial paper. As long as interest rates do not rise, all is well: When these short-term securities mature, they can be reissued at the same interest rate. However, if interest rates rise, as they did in 1980, the firm may find that it does not have the cash flows or income to support the plant because when the short-term securities mature, the firm will have to reissue them at a higher interest rate. If long-term securities, such as bonds or stock, had been used, the increased interest rates would not have been as critical. The primary reason that individuals and firms choose to borrow long-term is to reduce the risk that interest rates will rise before they pay off their debt. This reduction in risk comes at a cost, however. As you may recall from Chapter 5, most long-term interest rates are higher than short-term rates due to risk premiums. Despite the need to pay higher interest rates to borrow in the capital markets, these markets remain very active.

CAPITAL MARKET PARTICIPANTS

The primary issuers of capital market securities are federal and local governments and corporations. The federal government issues long-term notes and bonds to fund the national debt. State and municipal governments also issue long-term notes and bonds to finance capital projects, such as school and prison construction. Governments never issue stock because they cannot sell ownership claims.

Corporations issue both bonds and stock. One of the most difficult decisions a firm faces can be whether it should finance its growth with debt or equity. The distribution of a firm's capital between debt and equity is its capital structure. (The factors that influence the capital structure decision are discussed in Chapter 12.) Corporations may enter the capital markets because they do not have sufficient capital to fund their investment opportunities. Alternatively, firms may choose to enter the capital markets because they want to preserve their capital to protect against unexpected needs. In either case, the availability of efficiently functioning capital markets is crucial to the continued health of the business sector.

The largest purchasers of capital market securities are households. Frequently, individuals and households deposit funds in financial institutions, such as mutual funds and pension funds, that use the funds to purchase capital market instruments such as bonds or stock.

CAPITAL MARKET TRADING

Capital market trading occurs in either the *primary market* or the *secondary market*. As you may recall from Chapter 2, the primary market is where new issues of stocks and bonds are introduced. Investment funds, corporations, and individual investors can all purchase securities offered in the primary market. You can think of a primary market transaction as one where the issuer of the security actually receives the proceeds of the sale. When firms sell securities for the very first time, the issue is an **initial public offering (IPO).** Subsequent sales of a firm's new stocks or bonds to the public are simply primary market transactions (as opposed to an initial one).

The capital markets have well-developed secondary markets. A secondary market is where the sale of previously issued securities takes place, and it is important because most investors plan to sell long-term bonds before they reach maturity and eventually to sell their holdings of stock as well. There are two types of exchanges in the secondary market for capital securities: *organized exchanges* and *over-the-counter exchanges*. Whereas most money market transactions originate over the phone, most capital market transactions, measured by volume, occur in organized exchanges.

Organized Securities Exchanges

An organized exchange has a building where securities (including stocks, bonds, options, and futures) trade. Exchange rules govern trading to ensure the efficient and legal operation of the exchange, and the exchange's board constantly reviews these rules to ensure that they result in competitive trading.

Organized exchanges account for over 72% of the total dollar volume of domestic stock shares traded. Organized exchanges also support trading in bonds. The largest of the organized stock exchanges in the United States is the New York Stock Exchange (NYSE). The NYSE occupies a building in downtown New York City, and only traders who are members of the exchange may engage in trading. To become a member, an individual or firm must buy a "seat." There are 1366 seats on the NYSE, most of them owned by brokerage houses. Today seats on the New York Stock Exchange sell for around $650,000, depending on the market's perception of the profit potential in being a trader. Average daily volume on the NYSE in 1995 was 346.1 million shares of stocks with a total of 87.2 billion shares traded during the year. By contrast, a total of about 7 million bonds were traded on organized exchanges during 1995.

There are also major organized stock exchanges around the world. The most active exchange in the world is the Nikkei in Tokyo. Other major exchanges include the London Stock Exchange in England, the DAX in Germany, and the Toronto Stock Exchange in Canada.

To have a stock listed for trading on one of the organized exchanges, a firm must file an application and meet certain criteria set by the exchange designed to enhance trading. For example, the NYSE encourages only the largest firms to list so that transaction volume will be high. To list on the NYSE, a firm must meet the following minimum requirements:

- At least 2000 stockholders, each owning 100 shares or more
- A minimum of 1.1 million shares traded publicly
- Pretax earnings of $2.5 million at the time of listing plus at least $2 million in pretax earnings in each of the prior two years
- Net assets of $18 million
- A total of $18 million in market value of publicly traded shares

More than 2675 companies around the world list their shares on the New York Stock Exchange. More than two-thirds of NYSE-listed companies have joined the exchange since 1986. The average new firm on the exchange had a market value of $305.6 million, revenues of $263.1 million, pretax income of $24 million, net income of $14.9 million, and 12.9 million shares outstanding.

The second-largest organized stock exchange in the United States is the American Stock Exchange. About 2500 firms trade on it. The American Stock Exchange has less restrictive listing requirements. Regional exchanges, such as the Philadelphia and Pacific Stock Exchanges, are even easier to list on. Some firms choose to list on more than one exchange, believing that more exposure will increase the demand for their stock and hence its price. Many firms also believe that there is a certain amount of prestige in being listed on one of the major exchanges. They may even include this fact in their advertising. There is little conclusive research to support this belief, however. Microsoft, for example, is not listed on any organized exchange, yet its stock had a total market value over $73 billion in early 1997.

Over-the-Counter Markets

If Microsoft's stock is not traded on any of the organized stock exchanges, where does it sell its stock? Securities not listed on one of the exchanges trade in the over-the-counter market. This market is not organized in the sense of having a building where trading takes place. Instead, trading occurs over a sophisticated telecommunications network, called the **National Association of Securities Dealers Automated Quotation System (NASDAQ).** This system, introduced in 1971, provides current bid and ask prices on about 4500 actively traded securities. Dealers "make a market" in these stocks by buying for inventory when investors want to sell and selling from inventory when investors want to buy. These dealers provide small stocks with the liquidity that is essential to their acceptance in the market. Total volume on the NASDAQ is usually slightly lower than on the NYSE; however, NASDAQ volume has been growing and occasionally exceeds NYSE volume.

Not all publicly traded stocks list on one of the organized exchanges or on NASDAQ. Securities that trade very infrequently or trade primarily in one region of the country are usually handled by the regional offices of various brokerage houses. These offices often maintain small inventories of regionally popular securities. Dealers that make a market for stocks that trade in low volume are very important to the success of the over-the-counter market. Without these dealers' standing ready to buy or sell shares, investors would be reluctant to buy shares of stock in regional or unknown firms, and it would be very difficult for start-up firms to raise needed capital.

■ CAPITAL MARKET SECURITIES: BONDS

The capital markets are where securities with original maturities of greater than one year trade. Capital market securities fall into three categories: bonds, stocks, and mortgages. In this section, we look at bonds.

As noted in Chapter 2, *bonds* are securities that represent a debt owed by the issuer to the investor. Bonds obligate the issuer to pay a specified amount at a given date, generally with periodic interest payments. The par, face, or maturity value of the bond is the amount that the issuer must pay at maturity. The coupon rate is the rate of interest that the issuer must pay. This rate is usually fixed for the duration of the bond and does not fluctuate with market interest rates. If the repayment terms of a bond are not met, the holder of a bond has a claim on the assets of the issuer.

Long-term bonds traded in the capital market include long-term government notes and bonds, municipal bonds, and corporate bonds.

■ TREASURY BONDS

The U.S. Treasury issues notes and bonds to finance the national debt. The difference between a note and a bond is that notes have an original maturity of 1 to 10 years while bonds have an original maturity of 10 to 30 years. (Recall from Chapter 9 that Treasury *bills* mature in less than one year.) Table 1 summarizes, the maturity differences among Treasury securities. The prices of Treasury notes, bonds, and bills are quoted as a percentage of $100 face value. Chapter 3 explains how newspaper bond quotes can be converted into market prices.

Federal government notes and bonds are free of default risk because the government can always print money to pay off the debt if necessary.[1] This does *not* mean that these securities are risk free. There is still the possibility that market interest rates will rise, making the bonds fall in value.

| APPLICATION | INTEREST-RATE RISK IN BOND INVESTMENT |

The risk that the value of a bond will fall when market interest rates rise is called *interest-rate risk* (discussed in Chapter 3). Suppose that you wanted to sell a bond that pays 4.5% for $1,000 when new ones are available that pay 5.5%. To sell an old bond when rates have risen, the holder will have to discount the bond until the yield to the buyer is the same as the market rate. In this example, if there were 20 years until the bond matured, the seller would have to drop the asking price to $879.61 to give the buyer a 5.5% yield. We did not discuss interest-rate risk in Chapter 9 because securities in the money market have short maturities and inter-

■ **TABLE 1** Treasury Securities

Type	Maturity
Treasury bill	Less than 1 year
Treasury note	1 to 10 years
Treasury bond	10 to 30 years

---

[1]In Chapter 9 we noted that Treasury bills were also considered default-risk-free except that a budget stalemate in 1996 almost caused default. The same small chance of default applies to Treasury bonds.

est rates do not usually change greatly in the short run. When they do, the change does not influence the price of the security as much as when the security has a long time until maturity.

Treasury Bond Interest Rates

Treasury bonds have very low interest rates because they have no default risk. Although investors in Treasury bonds have found themselves earning less than the rate of inflation in some years (see Figure 1), most of the time, the interest rate on Treasury notes and bonds is above that on money market securities because of interest-rate risk.

Figure 2 plots the yield on 20-year Treasury bonds against the yield on 91-day Treasury bills. Two things are noteworthy in this graph. First, in most years, the rate of return on the short-term bill is below that on the 20-year bond. Second, short-term rates are more volatile than long-term rates. Short-term rates are more influenced by the current rate of inflation. Investors in long-term securities expect extremely high or low inflation rates to return to more normal levels, so long-term rates do not typically change as much as short-term rates.

Treasury STRIPS

In addition to bonds, notes, and bills, in 1985 the Treasury began issuing to depository institutions bonds in book entry form called **Separate Trading of**

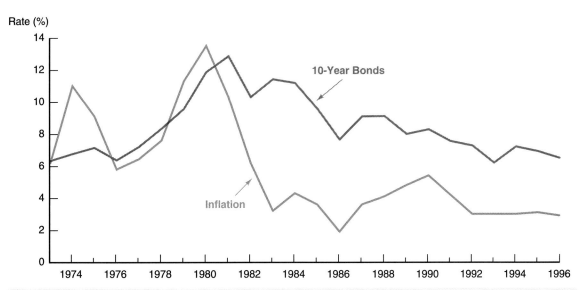

■FIGURE 1 Interest Rate on Treasury Notes and the Inflation Rate, 1973–1996

Source: Federal Reserve Bulletin, Various issues.

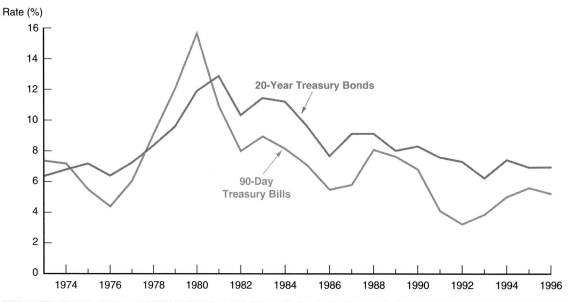

■FIGURE 2 Interest Rate on Treasury Bills and Treasury Bonds, 1973–1996 (December of each year)

Source: Federal Reserve Bulletin, Various issues.

Registered Interest and Principal Securities, more commonly called **STRIPS.** Recall from Chapter 9 that to be sold in book entry form means that no physical document exists; instead, the security is issued and accounted for electronically. A STRIP separates the periodic interest payments from the final principal repayment. In essence, this means that two securities are created from one. The first is a zero-coupon bond, which is the final principal repayment, and the second is an annuity consisting of the annual coupon interest payments.

Before the government introduced these securities, the private sector had created them indirectly. In the early 1980s, Merrill Lynch created the Treasury Investment Growth Fund (TIGRs, pronounced "tigers"), in which it purchased Treasury securities and then stripped them to create principal-only securities and interest-only securities. Currently, more than $50 billion in stripped Treasury securities are outstanding.

Agency Bonds

Congress has authorized a number of U.S. agencies to issue bonds. The government does not explicitly guarantee agency bonds, though most investors feel that the government would not allow the agencies to default. Issuers of agency bonds include the Government National Mortgage Association, the Farmers Home Administration, the Federal Housing Administration, the Veterans Administrations, the Federal National Mortgage Association, the Federal Land Banks, the

Federal Home Loan Mortgage Corporation, and the Student Loan Marketing Association. These agencies issue bonds to raise funds that are used for purposes that Congress has deemed to be in the national interest. For example, the Government National Mortgage Association (Ginnie Mae) issues bonds to raise funds that are used to finance home loans. Similarly, the Student Loan Marketing Association (Sallie Mae) issues bonds to fund student loans.

The risk on agency bonds is actually very low. They are usually secured by the loans that are made with the funds raised by the bond sales. In addition, the federal agencies may use their lines of credit with the Treasury Department should they have trouble meeting their obligations. Finally, it is unlikely that the federal government would permit its agencies to default on their obligations.

Despite this low level of risk, these securities offer interest rates that are significantly higher than those available on Treasury securities. For example, on March 4, 1997, Federal National Mortgage Association 30-year bonds yielded 7.95% while 30-year Treasury bonds yielded 6.80%. A portion of the higher yield available on agencies may be due to their lower liquidity: Though a secondary market in agency securities exists, it is not as well developed or as deep as the market for government securities. (Chapter 6 discusses the effect liquidity has on interest rates.) Many investors feel that agency bonds represent an attractive alternative to low-interest-rate Treasuries.

■ MUNICIPAL BONDS

Municipal bonds are securities issued by local, county, and state governments. The proceeds from these bonds are used to finance public interest projects such as schools, utilities, and transportation systems. Municipal bonds that are issued to pay for essential public projects are exempt from federal taxation. This allows the municipality to borrow at a lower cost because investors will be satisfied with lower interest rates on tax-exempt bonds. You can use the following equation to determine what tax-free rate of interest is equivalent to a taxable rate:

Tax-free municipal interest rate = taxable interest rate × (1 − marginal tax rate)

For example, suppose that the taxable corporate bond interest rate is 9%. The equivalent tax-free rate for an investor with a 28% marginal tax rate is:

$$9\% \times (1 - 0.28) = 6.48\%$$

There are two types of municipal bonds: general obligation bonds and revenue bonds. **General obligation bonds** do not have specific assets pledged as security or a specific source of revenue allocated for their repayment. Instead, they are backed by the "full faith and credit" of the issuer. This phrase means that the issuer promises to use every resource available to repay the bond as promised. Most general obligation bond issues must be approved by the taxpayers because the taxing authority of the government is pledged for their repayment.

Revenue bonds, by contrast, are backed by the cash flow of a particular revenue-generating project. For example, revenue bonds may be issued to build a toll bridge, with the tolls being pledged as repayment. If the revenues are not sufficient to repay the bonds, they may go into default, and investors may suffer losses. This occurred on a large scale in 1983 when the Washington Public Power Supply System (since called "WHOOPS") used revenue bonds to finance the construction of two nuclear power plants. As a result of falling energy costs and tremendous cost overruns, the plants never became operational, and buyers of these bonds lost their investments. Revenue bonds tend to be issued more frequently than general obligation bonds (see Figure 3).

Risk in the Municipal Bond Market

Municipal bonds are not default-free. For example, defaults on municipal bonds amounted to $1.4 billion in 1990. This was primarily attributed to the weaker economy in 1990; however, it points out that governments are not exempt from financial distress. Unlike the federal government, local governments cannot print money, and there are real limits on how high they can raise taxes without driving the population away.[2]

■ CORPORATE BONDS

When large corporations need to borrow funds for long periods of time, they may issue bonds. Most corporate bonds have a face value of $1000, pay interest semiannually (twice per year), and can be redeemed anytime the issuer wishes.

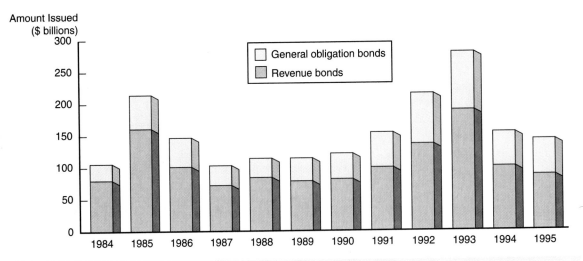

■FIGURE 3 Issuance of Revenue and General Obligation Bonds, 1984–1995

Source: Federal Reserve Bulletin, Various issues.

---

[2]Review Chapter 6 for a complete discussion on the determinants of interest rates for securities.

The **bond indenture** is a contract that states the lender's rights and privileges and the borrower's obligations. Any collateral offered as security to the bondholders will also be described in the indenture.

The degree of risk varies widely among issues because the risk of default depends on the company's health, which can be affected by a number of variables. The interest rate on corporate bonds varies with the level of risk, as we discussed in Chapter 6. As Figure 4 shows, bonds with lower risk and a higher rating (AAA being the highest) have lower interest rates than more risky bonds (BBB). A bond's interest rate will depend on its features and characteristics, which are described in the following sections.

Characteristics of Corporate Bonds

Early bonds, called *bearer bonds* because payments were made to whoever had physical possession of the bonds, were sold with coupons attached that the owner of the bond clipped and mailed to the firm to receive interest payments. The Internal Revenue Service did not care for this method of payment, however, because it made tracking interest income difficult. Bearer bonds have now been largely replaced by **registered bonds,** which do not have coupons. Instead, the owner must register with the firm to receive interest payments. The firms are required to report to the IRS who receives interest income. Despite the fact that

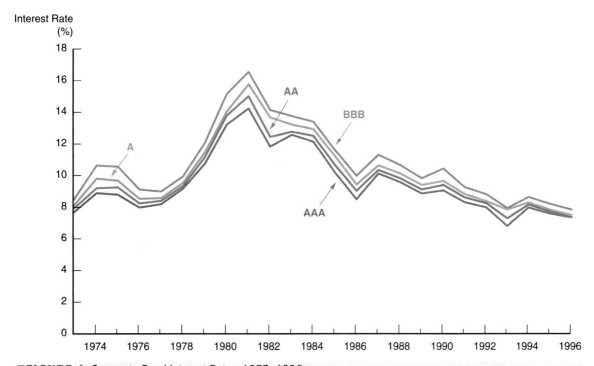

■FIGURE 4 Corporate Bond Interest Rates, 1973–1996

Source: Federal Reserve Bulletin, Various issues.

bearer bonds with attached coupons have been phased out, the interest paid on bonds is still called the "coupon interest payment" and the interest rate on bonds is the coupon interest rate.

Restrictive Covenants A corporation's financial managers are hired, fired, and compensated at the direction of the board of directors, which represents the corporation's *stockholders*. This arrangement implies that the managers will be more interested in protecting stockholders than they are in protecting bondholders. Since bondholders cannot look to managers for protection when the firm gets into trouble, they must include rules and restrictions on managers designed to protect the bondholders' interests. These are known as **restrictive covenants.** They usually limit the amount of dividends the firm can pay and the ability of the firm to issue additional debt. Other financial policies, such as the firm's involvement in mergers, may also be restricted. Restrictive covenants are included in the bond indenture. Typically, the interest rate will be lower the more restrictions are placed on management through restrictive covenants because the bonds will be considered safer by buyers.

Call Provisions Most corporate indentures include a **call provision,** which states that the issuer has the right to force the holder to sell the bond back. The call provision usually requires a waiting period between the time the bond is initially issued and the time when it can be called. The price bondholders are paid for the bond is set at the bond's par price or slightly higher (usually by one year's interest cost). For example, a 10%-coupon-rate $1000 bond may have a call price of $1100.

If interest rates fall, the price of the bond will rise. If rates fall enough, the price will rise above the call price, and the firm will call the bond. Because call provisions put a limit on the amount that bondholders can earn from the appreciation of a bond's price, investors do not like call provisions.

A second reason that issuers of bonds include call provisions is to make it possible for them to buy back their bonds according to the terms of the **sinking fund.** A sinking fund is a requirement in the bond indenture that the firm pay off a portion of the bond issue each year. This provision is attractive to bondholders because it reduces the probability of default when the issue matures. Because a sinking fund provision makes the issue more attractive, the firm can reduce the bond's interest rate.

A third reason firms usually issue only callable bonds is that firms may have to retire a bond issue if the covenants of the issue restrict the firm from some activity that it feels is in the best interest of stockholders. Suppose that a firm needed to borrow additional funds to expand its storage facilities. If the firm's bonds carried a restriction against adding debt, the firm would have to retire its existing bonds before issuing new bonds or taking out a loan to build the new warehouse.

Finally, a firm may choose to call bonds if it wishes to alter its capital structure. A maturing firm with excess cash flow may wish to reduce its debt load if few attractive investment opportunities are available.

Because bondholders do not generally like call provisions, callable bonds must have a higher yield than comparable noncallable bonds. Despite the higher cost, firms still typically issue callable bonds because of the flexibility this feature provides the firm.

Conversion Some bonds can be converted into shares of common stock. This feature permits bondholders to share in the firm's good fortunes if the stock price rises. Most convertible bonds will state that the bond can be converted into a certain number of common shares at the discretion of the bondholder. The conversion ratio will be such that the price of the stock must rise substantially before conversion is likely to occur.

Issuing convertible bonds is one way firms avoid sending a negative signal to the market. If a firm chooses to issue stock, the market usually interprets this action as indicating that the stock price is relatively high or that it is going to fall in the future. The market makes this interpretation because it believes that managers are most concerned with looking out for the interests of existing stockholders and will not issue stock when it is undervalued. If managers believe that the firm will perform well in the future, they can, instead, issue convertible bonds. If the managers are correct and the stock price rises, the bondholders will convert to stock at a relatively high price that managers believe is fair. Alternatively, bondholders have the option not to convert if managers turn out to be wrong about the company's future.

Bondholders like a conversion feature. It is very similar to buying just a bond but receiving both a bond and a stock option. The price of the bond will reflect the value of this option and so will be higher than the price of comparable non-convertible bonds. The higher price received for the bond by the firm implies a lower interest rate.

Types of Corporate Bonds

A variety of corporate bonds are available. They are usually distinguished by the type of collateral that secures the bond and by the order in which the bond is paid off if the firm defaults.

Secured Bonds *Mortgage bonds* are used to finance a specific project. For example, a building may be the collateral for bonds issued for its construction. In the event that the firm fails to make payments as promised, mortgage bondholders have the right to liquidate the property in order to be paid. Because these bonds have specific property pledged as collateral, they are less risky than comparable unsecured bonds. As a result, they will have a lower interest rate.

Equipment trust certificates are bonds secured by tangible non–real estate property, such as heavy equipment or airplanes. Typically, the collateral backing these bonds is more easily marketed than the real property backing mortgage bonds. As with mortgage bonds, the presence of collateral reduces the risk of the bonds and so lowers their interest rates.

Unsecured Bonds *Debentures* are long-term unsecured bonds that are backed only by the general creditworthiness of the issuer. No specific collateral is pledged to repay the debt. In the event of default, the bondholders must go to court to seize assets. Collateral that has been pledged to other debtors is not available to the holders of debentures. *Debentures* usually have a contract attached to them that spells out the terms of the bond and the responsibilities of management. The contract attached to the debenture is called an *indenture*. (Be careful not to confuse the terms *debenture* and *indenture*.) Debentures have lower priority than secured bonds if the firm defaults. As a result, they will have a higher interest rate than otherwise comparable secured bonds.

Subordinated debentures are similar to debentures except that they have a lower priority claim. This means that in the event of a default, subordinated debenture holders are paid only after nonsubordinated bondholders have been paid in full. As a result, subordinated debenture holders are at greater risk of loss.

Variable-rate bonds (which may be secured or unsecured) are a financial innovation spurred by increased interest-rate variability in the 1980s and 1990s. The interest rate on these securities is tied to another market interest rate, such as the rate on Treasury bonds, and is adjusted periodically. The interest rate on the bonds will change over time as market rates change.

Junk Bonds Recall from Chapter 6 that all bonds are rated by various companies according to their default risk. These companies study the issuer's financial characteristics and make a judgment about the issuer's possibility of default. A bond with a rating of AAA has the highest grade possible. Bonds *above* Moody's Baa or Standard and Poor's BBB rating are considered of investment grade. Those rated *below* this level are usually considered speculative. Speculative-grade bonds are often called **junk bonds.** Before the late 1970s, primary issues of speculative-grade securities were very rare; almost all new bond issues consisted of investment-grade bonds. However, when companies ran into financial difficulties, their bond ratings would fall. Holders of these downgraded bonds found that they were difficult to sell because no well-developed secondary market existed. It is easy to understand why investors would be leery of these securities, as they were usually unsecured.

In 1977, Michael Milken, at the investment banking firm of Drexel Burnham Lambert, recognized that there were many investors who would be willing to take on greater risk if they were compensated with greater returns. First, however, Milken had to address two problems that hindered the market for low-grade bonds. The first was that they suffered from poor liquidity. Whereas underwriters of investment-grade bonds continued to make a market after the bonds were issued, no such market maker existed for junk bonds. Drexel agreed to assume this role as market maker for junk bonds. That assured that a secondary market existed, an important consideration for investors, who seldom want to hold the bonds to maturity.

The second problem with the junk bond market was that there was a very real chance that the issuing firms would default on their bond payments. By comparison, the default risk on investment-grade securities was negligible. To reduce the probability of losses, Milken acted much as a commercial bank for junk bond issuers. He would renegotiate the firm's debt or advance additional funds if needed to prevent the firm from defaulting. Milken's efforts substantially reduced the default risk, and the demand for junk bonds soared.

During the early and mid-1980s, many firms took advantage of junk bonds to finance the takeover of other firms. These acquisitions were called **leveraged buyouts (LBOs).** In an LBO, a firm greatly increases its debt level (by issuing junk bonds) to finance the purchase of another firm's stock. It was this increase in leverage that made the bonds high-risk. Frequently, part of the acquired firm was eventually sold to pay down the debt incurred by issuing the junk bonds. Some 1800 firms accessed the junk bond market during the 1980s.

Milken and his brokerage firm were very well compensated for their efforts. Milken earned a fee of 2% to 3% of each junk bond issue, which made Drexel the most profitable firm on Wall Street in 1987. Milken's personal income between 1983 and 1987 was in excess of $1 billion.

Unfortunately for holders of junk bonds, both Milken and Drexel were caught and convicted of insider trading. With Drexel unable to support the junk bond market, 250 companies defaulted between 1989 and 1991. Drexel itself filed bankruptcy in 1990 due to losses on its own holdings of junk bonds. Milken was sentenced to three years in prison for his part in the scandal. *Fortune* magazine reported that Milken's personal fortune still exceeded $400 million.[3]

The junk bond market has recovered since its low in 1990 and now continues to permit medium-size firms to obtain financing that might otherwise be unavailable to them because of the relatively high risk.

◼ FINANCIAL GUARANTEES FOR BONDS

Financially weaker security issuers frequently purchase **financial guarantees** to lower the risk of their bonds. A financial guarantee ensures that the lender (bond purchaser) will be paid both principal and interest in the event the issuer defaults. Large, well-known insurance companies write what are actually insurance policies to back bond issues. With such a financial guarantee, bond buyers no longer have to be concerned with the financial health of the bond issuer. Instead, they are only interested in the strength of the insurer. Essentially, the credit rating of the insurer is substituted for the credit rating of the issuer. The resulting reduction in risk lowers the interest rate demanded by bond buyers. Of course, issuers must pay a fee to the insurance company for the guarantee. Financial guarantees make sense only when the cost of the insurance is less than the interest savings that result.

Financial guarantees were developed in the early 1970s to insure municipal bonds. More recently, their use has been expanded to cover a variety of corporate bonds as well.

---

[3]A complete history of Milken and details of his current dealings were reported in *Fortune,* September 30, 1996, pp. 80–105.

■ TRENDS IN THE BOND MARKET

During the first half of the 1980s, interest rates were very high, and firms were reluctant to borrow in the long-term market. In the second half of the 1980s, declining interest rates and a healthy economy combined to encourage bond issuance. Issuance again fell in 1990 when the economy entered a recession, and interest rates rose. Falling interest rates and a rebounding economy have again contributed toward record-breaking volumes in the bond markets. Figure 5 shows the volume of new bonds issued by all entities between 1983 and 1994 in comparison with the volume of new stocks issued in the same period.

■ CAPITAL MARKET SECURITIES: STOCK

A share of stock in a firm represents ownership. A stockholder owns a percentage interest in a firm consistent with the percentage of outstanding stock held. This ownership is in contrast to a bondholder, who holds no ownership interest but is rather a creditor of the firm.

Investors can earn a return from stock in one of two ways. Either the price of the stock rises over time, or the firm pays the stockholder dividends. Frequently, investors earn a return from both sources. Stock is more risky than bonds because stockholders have a lower priority than bondholders when the firm is in trouble, the returns to investors are less assured because dividends can be easily changed, and stock price increases are not guaranteed. Despite these risks, it is possible to make a great deal of money by investing in stock, whereas that is very unlikely by

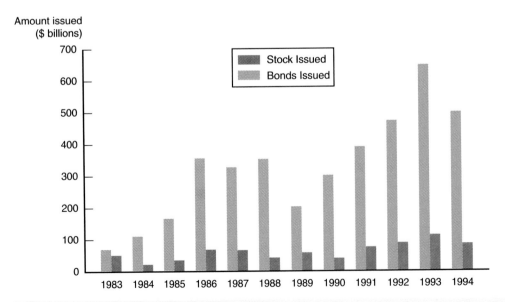

■FIGURE 5 Bonds and Stocks Issued, 1983–1994

Source: NYSE Fact Book, 1995 data, May 1996.

investing in bonds. Another distinction between stock and bonds is that stock does not mature.

Ownership of stock gives the stockholder certain rights regarding the firm. One is the right of a *residual claimant:* Stockholders have a claim on all assets and income left over after all other claimants have been satisfied. If nothing is left over, they get nothing. As noted, however, it is possible to get rich as a stockholder if the firm does well.

Most stockholders have the *right to vote* for directors and on certain issues, such as amendments to the corporate charter and whether new shares should be issued.

Common Stock Versus Preferred Stock

There are two types of stock, common and preferred. A share of **common stock** in a firm represents an ownership interest in that firm. Common stockholders vote, receive dividends, and hope that the price of their stock will rise. There are various classes of common stock, usually denoted as type A, type B, and so on. Unfortunately, the type does not have any meaning that is standard across all companies. The differences among the types usually involve either the distribution of dividends or voting rights. It is important for an investor in stocks to know exactly what rights go along with the shares of stock being contemplated.

Preferred stock is a form of equity from a legal and tax standpoint. However, it differs from common stock in several important ways. First, because preferred stockholders receive a fixed dividend that never changes, a share of preferred stock is as much like a bond as it is like common stock. Second, because the dividend does not change, the price of preferred stock is relatively stable. Third, preferred stockholders do not usually vote unless the firm has failed to pay the promised dividend. Finally, preferred stockholders hold a claim on assets that has priority over the claims of common shareholders but after that of creditors such as bondholders.

Figure 6 shows the proportion of preferred versus common stock issued each year between 1984 and 1995. The figure reveals two general characteristics of stocks: First, firms issue common stock in far greater amounts than preferred. This may be because preferred dividends are not tax-deductible to the firm but bond interest payments are. Consequently, issuing preferred stock usually costs the firm more than issuing debt, even though it shares many of the characteristics of a bond.

The second thing to note is that the total volume of stock issued is much less than the volume of bonds issued. Over $500 million in new bonds was offered to the public in 1995 but Figure 6 shows that just over $100 million in stock was issued. One reason for this may be that because the interest payments on debt are tax-deductible, the cost of borrowing is lower than the cost of equity. This issue is addressed in greater detail in Chapter 12.

Valuing Stock

The price of a share of stock is the present value of expected future cash flows, which consist of dividends plus a final selling price. (The "Following the Financial

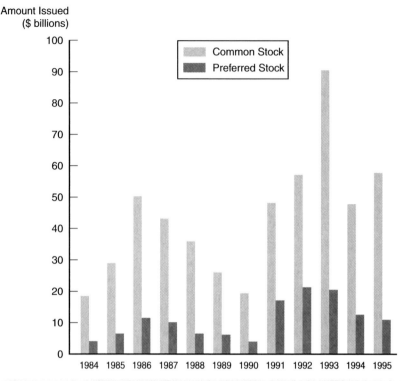

■FIGURE 6 New Issues of Preferred and Common Stock, 1984–1995

Source: NYSE Fact Book, 1995 data, May 1996.

News" box on p. 261 shows how stock market prices are reported each day.) Investors are willing to pay a price for stock that reflects the sum of all of the future cash flows the security will generate, after adjusting for the time value of money. The problem, of course, is predicting the future cash flows of the firm. If a firm does well, the residual cash flows available for dividends can be large, and a high share price is justified. If a firm does poorly, there may not be any cash flows available to pay any dividend at all.

The theory of efficient markets, discussed in Chapter 7, suggests that stocks will always be correctly priced. If a stock were incorrectly priced, traders who specialize in that stock would quickly recognize the profit potential, and buy or sell the stock until the profit opportunity has disappeared. As a result of competition in the market, the opportunity to earn extraordinary returns should not exist. Of course, as we discussed in Chapter 7, there are strong arguments against the concept of market efficiency as well.

APPLICATION | THE VALUATION OF COMMON STOCK

The value of any asset is simply the present value of the cash flows the holder will receive. The possible cash flows the holder of stock may receive are future divi-

Stock Prices

Stock prices are published daily, and in the *Wall Street Journal* they are reported in the sections "NYSE—Composite Transactions," "Amex—Composite Transactions," and "Over-the-Counter Markets." The New York Stock Exchange (NYSE) and American Stock Exchange (Amex) stocks' prices are quoted in the following format:

52 Weeks		Stock	Sym	Div	Yld %	PE	Vol 100s	Hi	Lo	Close	Net Chg
Hi	Lo										
31	24	IntAlum	IAL	1.00	3.7	17	52	$27^1/_8$	27	$27^1/_8$	$-^1/_8$
$170^1/_8$	$89^1/_8$	IBM	IBM	1.40	.9	15	45740	$158^1/_4$	$155^3/_4$	$157^1/_4$	$+^7/_8$
$27^1/_2$	$25^1/_2$	IBM dep pf		1.88	7.1	...	372	$26^5/_8$	$26^3/_8$	$26^5/_8$	$+^1/_4$
$19^1/_8$	$12^7/_8$	IntFamEntn B	FAM		...	42	328	18	$17^5/_8$	18	$+^1/_8$
$4^1/_4$	$3^3/_8$	IntFinBear wt			...	...	83	$3^1/_2$	$3^1/_4$	$3^1/_2$	...

Source: Wall Street Journal, January 30, 1997, p. C5.

The following information is included in each column. International Business Machines (IBM) common stock is used as an example.

52 Weeks Hi: Highest price of a share in the past 52 weeks: $170\frac{1}{8}$ for IBM stock

52 Weeks Lo: Lowest price of a share in the past 52 weeks: $89\frac{1}{8}$ for IBM stock

Stock: Company name: IBM for International Business Machines

Sym: Symbol that identifies company: IBM

Div: Annual dividends per share: $1.40 for IBM

Yld %: Yield for stock expressed as annual dividends divided by today's closing price: 0.9% (= 1.40 ÷ $157\frac{1}{4}$) for IBM stock

PE: Price-earnings ratio; the stock price divided by the annual earnings per share: 15.

Vol 100s: Number of shares (in hundreds) traded that day: 4,574,000 shares for IBM

Hi: Highest price of a share that day: $158\frac{1}{4}$

Lo: Lowest price of a share that day: $155\frac{3}{4}$

Close: Closing price (last price) that day: $157\frac{1}{4}$

Net Chg: Change in the closing price from the previous day: $+\frac{7}{8}$

Prices quoted for shares traded over-the-counter (through dealers rather than on an organized exchange) are sometimes quoted with the same information, but in many cases only the bid price (the price the dealer is willing to pay for the stock) and the asked price (the price the dealer is willing to sell the stock for) are quoted.

dends and the price the stock will sell for in the future. The future stock price, however, is itself the present value of the dividends that follow and an even more distant sales price. Taken to an extreme, the current price of stock is simply the present value of the dividends that follow because the present value of a future price, if very far in the future, is too small to be of consequence. Hence

$$P_0 = \frac{D_1}{1 + i} + \frac{D_2}{(1 + i)^2} + \frac{D_3}{(1 + i)^3} + \cdots + \frac{D_\infty}{(1 + i)^\infty} \tag{1}$$

where P_0 = price of stock at time 0 (the present)

D_n = dividend paid at time n

i = discount rate applied to computing the present value of the dividends

Unfortunately, although Equation 1 accurately reflects the cash flows that determine the stock's value, it is not very useful for actually computing the price of a share of stock. By assuming that dividends increase at a constant rate, however, Equation 1 converts to this one:

$$P_0 = \frac{D_1}{i - g} \tag{2}$$

where P_0, D_1, and i are as defined before and g is the constant dividend growth rate expected. This equation is known as the *Gordon growth model* and is appropriate to use when dividends are expected to follow a constant growth pattern in the future.

For example, suppose that you want to compute the price of a share of stock when the next dividend is expected to be $2, the discount rate is estimated to be 12% and the dividends are projected to increase at a constant rate of 5% per year indefinitely. Applying Equation 2, we find

$$P_0 = \frac{\$2}{0.12 - 0.05} = \frac{\$2}{0.07} = \$28.57$$

Thus the stock should sell for $28.57.

Stock Market Indexes

A stock market index is used to monitor the behavior of a group of stocks. By reviewing the average behavior of a group of stocks, investors are able to gain some insight as to how a broad group of stocks may have performed. Various stock market indexes are reported to give investors an indication of the performance of different groups of stocks. The most commonly quoted index is the Dow Jones Industrial Average, an index based on the performance of the stocks of 30 large companies. The 30 stocks that make up the DJIA are listed in Table 2. Box 1 provides more background on this index.

■ **TABLE 2** The Thirty Stocks in the Dow Jones Industrial Average

AT&T	Hewlett-Packard
Allied-Signal	IBM
Aluminum Company of America	International Paper
American Express	Johnson & Johnson
Boeing	McDonald's
Caterpillar	Merck
Chevron	Minnesota Mining & Manufacturing
Coca-Cola	J. P. Morgan
Walt Disney	Philip Morris
DuPont	Procter & Gamble
Eastman Kodak	Sears, Roebuck
Exxon	Travelers Group
General Electric	Union Carbide
General Motors	UnitedTechnologies
Goodyear Tire & Rubber	Wal-Mart

BOX 1

The History of the Dow Jones Industrial Average

The Dow Jones Industrial Average (DJIA) is an index composed of 30 "blue chip" industrial firms. On May 26, 1896, Charles H. Dow added up the prices of 12 of the best-known stocks and created an average by dividing by the number of stocks. In 1916, eight more stocks were added, and in 1928, the 30-stock average made its debut.

Today the editors of the *Wall Street Journal* select the firms that make up the DJIA. They take a broad view of the type of firm that is considered "industrial": In essence, it is almost any company that is not in the transportation or utility business (because there are also Dow Jones averages for those kinds of stocks). In choosing a new company for the DJIA, they look among substantial industrial companies with a history of successful growth and wide interest among investors. The

components of the DJIA are not changed often, but they were altered in 1997, when Bethlehem Steel, Texaco, Westinghouse and Woolworth were replaced with Hewlett-Packard, Johnson and Johnson, Travelers Group and Wal-Mart.

Most market watchers agree that the DJIA is not the best indicator of the market's overall day-to-day performance. Indeed, it varies substantially from broader-based stock indexes in the short run. It continues to be followed so closely primarily because it is the oldest index and was the first to be quoted by other publications. But it tracks the performance of the market reasonably well over the long run.

Table 3 shows the greatest one-day gains and losses since the initiation of the DJIA.

Other indexes, such as Standard and Poor's 500 Index, the NASDAQ composite, and the NYSE composite, may be more useful for following the performance of different groups of stocks. The *Wall Street Journal* reports on 23 different indexes in its "Stock Market Daily Data Bank."

 Buying Foreign Stocks

In Chapter 4 we learned that diversification of a portfolio reduces nonsystematic risk, the risk unique to an asset that can be diversified away. In a properly diversified portfolio, only systematic risk, the risk of the market as whole, remains. In recent years, investors have come to realize that in fact some systematic risk can

■ TABLE 3 Greatest One-Day Changes in the Dow Jones Industrial Average

Rank	Date	Percent Gain	Date	Percent Loss
1	October 6, 1931	14.87	October 19, 1987	−22.61
2	October 30, 1929	12.34	October 28, 1929	−12.82
3	September 21, 1932	11.36	October 29, 1929	−11.73
4	October 21, 1987	10.15	November 6, 1929	−9.92
5	August 3, 1932	9.52	December 18, 1899	−8.72
6	February 11, 1932	9.47	August 12, 1932	−8.40
7	November 14, 1929	9.36	March 14, 1907	−8.29
8	December 18, 1931	9.35	October 26, 1987	−8.04
9	February 13, 1932	9.19	July 21, 1933	−7.84
10	May 6, 1932	9.08	October 18, 1937	−7.75

Source: Dow Jones Corp.

be eliminated by holding the securities of different countries. When one country is suffering from a recession, the other may be booming. If inflationary concerns in the United States cause stock prices to drop, falling inflation in Japan may cause Japanese stocks to rise.

The problem with buying foreign stocks is that most foreign companies are not listed on any of the U.S. stock exchanges, so the purchase of shares is difficult. Intermediaries have found a way to solve this problem by selling **American depository receipts (ADRs).** A U.S. bank buys the shares of a foreign company and places them in its vault. The bank then issues receipts against these shares, and these receipts can be traded domestically, usually on the NASDAQ. Trade in ADRs is conducted entirely in U.S. dollars, and the bank converts stock dividends into U.S. currency. One advantage of the ADR is that it allows foreign firms to trade in the United States without the firm's having to meet the disclosure rules required by the SEC.

Foreign stock trading has been growing rapidly. Since 1979, cross-border trade in equities has grown at a rate of 28% a year and now exceeds $2 trillion annually. Interest is particularly keen in the stocks of firms in emerging economies such as Mexico, Brazil, and South Korea.

■ PUBLIC ISSUES OF STOCKS AND BONDS

Once a firm determines that it should issue stocks or bonds, it must somehow get them into the public's hands at the highest price possible. The more the public pays for either the stocks or the bonds of a firm, the lower the cost of capital to that firm, all other things being equal.

There are two principal ways for a firm to sell securities to the public: through a public sale organized by investment bankers who are underwriting the issue or through a private placement. **Underwriting** means that the investment bankers handle the details of placing the securities in the public's hands.

Using Investment Bankers In the first method, **investment bankers** perform a number of tasks required to sell securities to the public, among them pricing the security, preparing the filings required by the Securities and Exchange Commission, arranging for the security to be rated, and marketing the security through their contacts with brokerage houses. Investment bankers were mentioned in Chapter 2 and will be discussed in greater detail in Chapter 19 when we investigate securities markets and firms.

Firms decide to use investment bankers to facilitate a public issue for a number of reasons, one of which is that the market trusts the investment banker to exercise due diligence in the process of evaluating the risk of the firm and pricing the issue. If the investment banker fails to use reasonable care when investigating an issue, buyers can sue for losses. Investment bankers exercise care for another reason as well. The top ten investment bankers are responsible for approximately 90% of all securities issued to the public. The competition among these firms for new business is extremely intense. The primary distinguishing feature among the investment bankers is their reputation. If an investment banker mispriced an offering or sells an issue that subsequently performs poorly, its reputation will fall, and issuers will avoid it in the future.

In addition to the credibility investment bankers add to a security issue, for many firms it is wise to issue securities using an investment banker because the firm's managers may be unfamiliar with the process. Remember that even for relatively large firms, issuing stock is an unusual event that requires stockholder approval. Most managers may be involved in the process only a few times in their careers. They will need the advice, expertise, and marketing ability provided by investment bankers.

One of the tasks required of investment bankers is establishing a price for the security. This is not difficult if the firm already has similar securities trading in the market. However, about half of all security issues are initial public offerings (IPOs), securities being offered to the public for the very first time. It can be difficult to determine the fair market value of securities that have had no public exposure. Frequently, the firm's founder is attempting to raise money for expansion and to pull some personal wealth out of the firm. The founder will want the stock sold high. But if the investment bankers set the price too high, the security may not sell.

It is crucial that the price of the security be set correctly because when an investment banker underwrites a security, the bank may promise to pay the issuing firm the specified price for the *whole issue*. The investment bank then attempts to resell the issue through its network of brokerage houses to the public. This is called **firm-commitment underwriting** and is the most common method. If the price set by the investment banker is too high, the brokerage houses may not be able to sell the securities without incurring a loss.

An alternative to firm-commitment underwriting is **best-efforts underwriting,** whereby the underwriter sells the security on a commission basis with no guarantee regarding the price. Investors tend to discount the prices of best-efforts issues because the underwriters seem unwilling to put their own money or reputation behind such securities.

Often an investment banker may not want to incur the entire risk of underwriting a large security issue. In such situations, risk may be spread among different brokerage houses by forming a **syndicate,** a group of investment bankers, each of which agrees to sell a portion of an issue. The advantages of syndication are that the risks are spread among several investment bankers and a larger number of brokers participate in the marketing effort. Securities markets and firms are also discussed in Chapter 19.

Once the firm and the investment bankers have agreed on a price and a method of underwriting, the investment bankers can begin getting SEC approval. The typical security issue will be registered with the SEC. Registration is a lengthy, costly process that is required before securities may be offered to the public. The Securities and Exchange Act of 1934 requires issuers to register securities intended for public sale. The intent of this act was to protect the public by requiring issuers to disclose certain information about the firm and the security. The SEC passed a rule in 1982 offering an alternative. Instead of registering each issue separately, firms that will be offering multiple issues may avail themselves of

shelf registration, submitting one registration statement detailing the firms' financing plans for the next two years. Shelf registration allows a firm to rush securities to market when it feels conditions are right, and it lowers the cost of issuing securities if securities are issued frequently.

While a security is in the process of receiving SEC approval, the investment banker may arrange for the issue to be rated by a rating agency such as Moody's or Standard and Poor's. The rating given by these firms helps investors decide whether the security meets their investment needs.

The last step in the process is for the investment bankers to market the issue to the public. In most cases, brokers across the country will have been soliciting commitments from investors to buy part of the issue. Once the issue becomes available, these orders are filled.

Private Placement A second way of issuing securities is through a private placement. In a private placement, the seller contacts a large investor and negotiates a price for the issue. Often the buyer will be a large institutional investor that already holds a block of the firm's stock or a large number of its bonds. The SEC waives the registration requirement for private placements under certain conditions. The buyer must agree to hold the securities for about two years or until the company registers the issue, and there can be no more than 35 investors involved. The rationale behind the exemption is that large institutional and corporate buyers should be capable of looking out for themselves without the need for government intervention.

Thus one advantage of the private placement is that registration costs, which can run into hundreds of thousands of dollars, are saved. A second advantage is that a private placement can be conducted much more quickly than a public sale.

The private placement market has grown in recent years as institutional investors have become more influential. This growth led the SEC to adopt new rules in 1990 that permitted secondary market trading of private placement issues by large institutional investors. Some institutions historically avoided private placements because they restricted liquidity. With the rule change, however, liquidity is increased and private placements are more attractive.

SUMMARY

1. The capital markets exist to provide financing for long-term capital assets. Households, often through investments in pension and mutual funds, are net investors in the capital markets. Corporations and the federal and state governments are net users of these funds.

2. The three main capital market instruments are bonds, stocks, and mortgages. Bonds represent borrowing by the issuing firm. Stock represents ownership in the issuing firm. Mortgages are long-term loans secured by real property. Only corporations can issue stock. Corporations and governments can issue bonds. In any given year, far more funds are raised with bonds than with stock.

3. There are both organized and over-the-counter exchanges. Organized exchanges are distinguished by a physical building where trading takes place. The over-the-counter market operates primarily over phone lines and computer links. Typically, larger firms trade on organized exchanges and smaller firms in the over-the-counter market, though there are exceptions to this rule.

4. Firm managers are hired by stockholders to protect and increase their wealth. Bondholders must rely on a contract called an indenture to protect their interests. Bond indentures contain covenants that restrict the firm from activities that increase risk and hence the chance of default on the bonds. Bond indentures also contain many provisions that make them more or less attractive to investors, such as a call option, convertibility, or a sinking fund.

5. The primary market for stocks and bonds is aided by investment bankers who will issue securities on either a firm-commitment or best-efforts basis. An alternative method of selling new securities is the private placement. This method is gaining popularity.

KEY TERMS

American depository receipts
   (ADRs), p. 264
best-efforts underwriting,
   p. 265
bond indenture, p. 253
call provision, p. 254
common stock, p. 259
financial guarantee, p. 257
firm-commitment underwriting,
   p. 265
general obligation bonds, p. 251

initial public offering (IPO),
   p. 246
investment banker, p. 264
junk bond, p. 256
leveraged buyout (LBO), p. 257
National Association of
   Securities Dealers
   Automated Quotation System
   (NASDAQ), p. 247
preferred stock, p. 259
registered bonds, p. 253

restrictive covenants, p. 254
revenue bonds, p. 251
Separate Trading of Registered
   Interest and Principal
   Securities (STRIPS),
   p. 249-250
shelf registration, p. 266
sinking fund, p. 254
syndicate, p. 265
underwriting, p. 264

QUESTIONS AND PROBLEMS

*1. Contrast investors' use of capital markets with their use of money markets.

2. What are the primary capital market securities, and who are the primary purchasers of these securities?

*3. Distinguish between the primary market and the secondary market for securities.

4. Discuss the features that differentiate organized exchanges from the over-the-counter market.

*5. What is the National Association of Securities Dealers Automated Quotation System (NASDAQ)?

6. A bond provides information about its par value, coupon interest rate, and maturity date. Define each of these.

*7. The U.S. Treasury issues bills, notes, and bonds. How do these three securities differ?

8. As interest rates in the market change over time, the market price of bonds rises and falls. The change in the value of bonds due to changes in interest rates is a risk incurred by bond investors. What is this risk called?

*9. In addition to Treasury securities, some agencies of the government issue bonds. List three such agencies, and state what the funds raised by the bond issues are used for.

10. A call provision on a bond allows the issuer to redeem the bond at will. Investors do not like call provisions and so require higher interest on callable bonds. Why do issuers continue to issue callable bonds anyway?

*11. What is a sinking fund? Do investors like bonds that contain this feature?

12. What is the document called that lists the terms of a bond?

*13. What distinguishes stocks from bonds?

14. Describe the two ways whereby capital market securities pass from the issuer to the public.

*15. Why do investment bankers often form syndicates to issue securities?

CASE STUDY

Capital Markets, Comparing Weighted Average Returns Versus Money Markets

CONCEPTS IN THIS CASE

Capital markets
capital structure
primary market
secondary market
initial public offering (IPO)
NASDAQ

Having invested your inheritance in the money market for one year in Chapter 9, you are now prepared to make a commitment to longer-term instruments. To make the best-informed decision, you have started to study the capital markets alternatives in the United States.

1. You begin your analysis by defining the following terms (include risk and return factors where appropriate)
   a. Capital markets
   b. NYSE
   c. AMEX
   d. OTC
   e. NASDAQ
   f. Bonds
   g. Stocks
   h. Mortgages
   i. Strips
   j. Agency bonds
   k. Municipal bonds
   l. Corporate bonds
   m. Call and sinking fund provisions
   n. Junk bonds
   o. Common stock

   p. Preferred stock
   q. Investment bankers and underwriting
   r. General obligation municipal bonds
   s. Revenue bonds

2. Your inheritance has grown to $1.2 million, and you are prepared to make long-term investment decisions. After considering the alternatives in the capital markets, you decide to divide the funds equally among the following financial instruments: U.S. Treasury notes (2-year maturity), U.S. Treasury bonds (20-year maturity), Ginnie Mae (10-year maturity), municipal bonds from your state (10-year maturity), corporate bonds from your company (nonconvertible 20-year maturity), junk bonds (10-year maturity), common stock, and preferred stock. (All returns are one-year returns with beginning prices and rates from the first business day of the calendar year, and all ending prices and rates are from the last business day of the calendar year.)
   a. What is the return on the U.S. Treasury notes?
   b. What is the return on the U.S. Treasury bonds?
   c. What is the return on the Ginnie Mae bonds?
   d. What is the return on the municipal bonds?
   e. What is the return on the corporate bonds?
   f. What is the return on the junk bonds?
   g. What is the return on the common stock?
   h. What is the return on the preferred stock?
   i. What is the weighted-average return for the capital market portfolio?
   j. How does this weighted average return compare to the money market portfolio in Chapter 9?

CHAPTER 11

THE MORTGAGE MARKETS

■ **PREVIEW** Part of the classic American dream is to own your own home. With the price of the average house now over $120,000, few of us could hope to do this until late in life if we were not able to borrow the bulk of the purchase price. Similarly, businesses rely on borrowed capital far more than on equity investment to finance their growth. Many small firms do not have access to the bond market and must find alternative sources of funds. Consider the state of the mortgage loan markets 100 years ago. They were organized mostly to accommodate the needs of businesses and the very wealthy. Much has changed since then. The purpose of this chapter is to discuss these changes.

Chapter 9 discussed the *money markets,* the markets for short term-funds. Chapter 10 discussed the *capital markets,* the markets for long-term funds. This chapter discusses the *mortgage markets,* where borrowers—individuals, businesses, and governments—can obtain long-term collateralized loans. From one perspective, the mortgage markets form a subcategory of the capital markets because mortgages involve long-term funds. But the mortgage markets differ from the stock and bond markets in several important ways. First, the usual borrowers in the capital markets are government entities and businesses, whereas the usual borrowers in the mortgage markets are individuals. Second, the majority of capital market borrowing is unsecured; by contrast, real estate secures most mortgages. Third, mortgage loans are made for varying amounts and maturities, depending on the borrowers' needs, features that cause problems for developing a secondary market.

In this chapter we will identify the characteristics of typical residential mortgages, discuss the usual term and types of mortgages available, and review who provides and services these loans. We will also discuss the growth of the mortgage-backed security market.

■ WHAT ARE MORTGAGES?

As we have noted, a **mortgage** is a long-term loan secured by real estate. A developer may obtain a mortgage loan to finance the construction of an office building, or a family may obtain a mortgage loan to finance the purchase of a home. In either case, the loan is **amortized:** The borrower pays it off over time in some combination of principal and interest payments that result in full payment of the debt by maturity. Table 1 shows the distribution of mortgage loan borrowers. Because over 83% of mortgage loans finance residential home purchases, that will be the primary focus of this chapter.

One way to understand the modern mortgage is to review its history. Originally, many states had laws that prevented banks from funding mortgages so that banks would not tie up their funds in long-term loans. The National Banking Act of 1863 further restricted mortgage lending. As a result, most mortgage contracts in the past were arranged between individuals, usually with the help of a lawyer who brought the parties together and drew up the papers. Such loans were generally available only to the wealthy and socially connected. As the demand for long-term funds increased, however, more mortgage brokers surfaced. They often originated loans in the rapidly developing western part of the country and sold them to savings banks and insurance companies in the East.

By 1880, mortgage bankers had learned to streamline their operations by selling bonds to raise the long-term funds they lent. They would gather a portfolio of mortgage contracts and use them as security for an issue of bonds that were sold publicly. Many of these loans were used to finance agricultural expansion in the Midwest. Unfortunately, an agricultural recession in the 1890s resulted in many defaults. Land prices fell, and a large number of the mortgage bankers went bankrupt.

Thereafter, it was very difficult to obtain long-term loans until after World War I, when national banks were authorized to make mortgage loans. This regulatory change caused a tremendous real estate boom, and mortgage lending expanded rapidly.

The mortgage market was again devastated by the Great Depression in the 1930s. Millions of borrowers were without work and were unable to make their loan payments. This led to foreclosures and land sales that caused property values to collapse. Mortgage-lending institutions were again hit hard, and many failed.

One reason that so many borrowers defaulted on their loans was the type of mortgage loan they had. Most mortgages in this period were **balloon loans:** The

■ TABLE 1 Mortgage Loan Borrowing, 1995

Type of Property	Mortgage Loans Issued ($ billions)	Proportion of Total (%)
One- to four-family dwelling	3640.1	77.05
Multifamily dwelling	289.2	6.12
Commercial building	710.5	15.04
Farm	84.3	1.79

Source: Federal Reserve Bulletin, 1996.

borrower paid only interest for three to five years, at which time the entire loan amount became due. The lender was usually willing to renew the debt with some reduction in principal. However, if the borrower were unemployed, the lender would not renew, and the borrower would default.

As part of the recovery program from the depression, the federal government stepped in and restructured the mortgage market. The government took over delinquent balloon loans and allowed borrowers to repay them over long periods of time. It is no surprise that these new types of loans were very popular. The surviving savings and loans began offering home buyers similar loans, and the high demand contributed to restoring the health of the mortgage industry.

■ CHARACTERISTICS OF THE RESIDENTIAL MORTGAGE

The modern mortgage lender has continued to refine the long-term loan to make it more desirable to borrowers. Even in the past 20 years, both the nature of the lenders and the instruments have undergone substantial changes. One of the biggest changes is the development of an active secondary market for mortgage contracts. We will examine the nature of mortgage loan contracts and then look at their secondary market.

The mortgage market has become very competitive in recent years. Twenty years ago, savings and loan institutions and the mortgage departments of large banks originated most mortgage loans. Currently, there are many loan production offices that compete in real estate financing. Some of these offices are subsidiaries of banks, and others are independently owned. As a result of the competition for mortgage loans, borrowers can choose from a variety of terms and options.

Mortgage Interest Rates

The interest rate borrowers pay on their mortgages is probably the most important factor in their decision of how much and from whom to borrow. The interest rate on the loan is determined by three factors: current long-term market rates, the life (term) of the mortgage, and the number of discount points paid.

1. *Market rates.* Long-term market rates are determined by the supply of and demand for long-term funds, which are in turn influenced by a number of global, national, and regional factors. As Figure 1 shows, mortgage rates tend to stay above the less risky Treasury bonds most of the time but tend to track along with them.

2. *Term.* Longer-term mortgages have higher interest rates than shorter-term mortgages. The usual mortgage lifetime is either 15 or 30 years. Lenders also offer 20-year loans, though they are not as popular. Because interest-rate risk falls as the term to maturity decreases, the interest rate on the 15-year loan will be substantially less than on the 30-year loan.

3. *Discount points.* **Discount points** (or simply *points*) are interest payments made at the beginning of a loan. A loan with one discount point means that the borrower pays 1% of the loan at *closing,* the moment when the borrower signs the loan paper and receives the proceeds of the loan. In

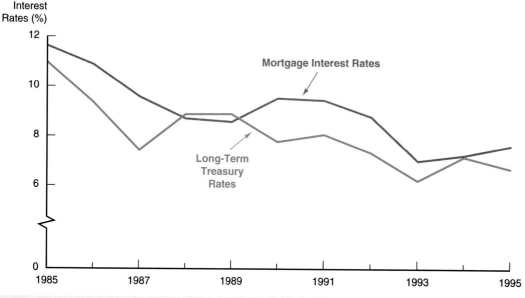

■FIGURE 1 Mortgage Rates and Long-Term Treasury Interest Rates, 1985–1995

Source: Federal Reserve Bulletin, Various issues.

exchange for the points, the lender reduces the interest rate on the loan. In considering whether to pay points, borrowers must determine whether the reduced interest rate over the life of the loan fully compensates for the increased up-front expense. To make this determination, borrowers must take into account how long they will hold on to the loan.

APPLICATION | THE DISCOUNT POINT DECISION

Suppose that you are offered two loan alternatives. In the first, you pay no discount points and the interest rate is 12%. In the second, you pay 2 discount points but receive a lower interest rate of 11.5%. Which alternative do you choose?

To answer this question you must first compute the effective annual rate without discount points. Since the loan is compounded monthly, you pay 1% per month. Because of the compounding, the effective annual rate is greater than the simple annual rate. To compute the effective rate, raise 1 plus the monthly rate to the twelfth power and subtract 1. The effective annual rate on the no-point loan is thus

$$\text{Effective annual rate} = (1.01)^{12} - 1 = 0.1268 = 12.68\%$$

Because of monthly compounding, a 12% annual percentage rate has an effective annual rate of 12.68%. On a 30-year, $100,000 house loan, your payment will be $1028.61 as found on a financial calculator.

Now compute the effective annual rate if you pay 2 discount points. Let's assume that the amount of the loan is still $100,000. If you pay 2 points, instead of receiving $100,000, you will receive only $98,000 ($100,000 − $2000). Your payment is computed on the $100,000, but at the lower interest rate. Using a financial calculator, we find that the monthly payment is $990.29 and your monthly rate is 0.9804%.[1] The effective annual rate after compounding is

$$\text{Effective annual rate} = (1.009804)^{12} - 1 = 0.1242 = 12.42\%$$

As a result of paying the 2 discount points, the effective annual rate has dropped from 12.68% to 12.42%. On the surface, it would seem like a good idea to pay the points. The problem is that these calculations were made assuming the loan would be held for 30 years. What happens if you sell the house before the loan matures?

If the loan is paid off early, the borrower will benefit from the lower interest rate for a shorter length of time, and the discount points are spread over a shorter period of time. The result of these two factors is that the effective interest rate rises the shorter the time the loan is held before being paid. This relationship is demonstrated in Table 2. If the 2-point loan is held for 15 years, the effective rate is 12.45%. At 10 years, the effective rate is up to 12.52%. Even at six years, when the effective rate is 12.65%, paying the discount points has saved the borrower money. However, if the loan is paid off at 5 years, the effective rate is 12.73%, which is higher than the 12.68% effective rate if no points were paid.[2]

Loan Terms

Mortgage loan contracts contain many legal and financial terms, most of which protect the lender from financial loss.

Collateral One characteristic common to mortgage loans is the requirement that collateral, usually the real estate being financed, be pledged as security. The lending institution will place a **lien** against the property, and this remains in effect until the loan is paid off. A lien is a public record that attaches to the title of the

■ **TABLE 2** Effective Rate of Interest on a 2-Point Loan at 12%

Year of Prepayment	Effective Rate of Interest (%)	Year of Prepayment	Effective Rate of Interest (%)
1	14.54	6	12.65
2	13.40	7	12.60
3	13.02	10	12.52
4	12.84	15	12.45
5	12.73	30	12.42

---

[1]The application box on page 276 discusses how mortgage loan payments are computed.

[2]For example, to compute the effective rate if the loan is prepaid after 2 years, find the FV if I = 11.5%, PV = 100,000, N = 24, and PMT = 990.29. Now set PV equal to 98,000 and compute I. Divide this I by 12, add 1, and raise result to the twelfth power.

property, advising that the property is security for a loan, and it gives the lender the right to sell the property if the underlying loan defaults.

No one can buy the property and obtain clear title to it without paying off this lien. For example, if you purchased a piece of property with a loan secured by a lien, the lender would file notice of this lien at the public recorder's office. The lien gives notice to the world that if there is a default on the loan, the lender has the right to seize the property. If you try to sell the property without paying off the loan, the lien would remain attached to the title or deed to the property. Since the lender can take the property away from whoever owns it, no one would buy it unless you paid off the loan. The existence of liens against real estate explains why a title search is an important part of any mortgage loan transaction. During the title search, a lawyer or title company searches the public record for any liens. Title insurance is then sold that guarantees the buyer that the property is free of *encumbrances,* any questions about the state of the title to the property, including the existence of liens.

Down Payments To obtain a mortgage loan, the lender also requires the borrower to make a **down payment** on the property, that is, to pay a portion of the purchase price. The balance of the purchase price is paid by the *loan proceeds.* Down payments (like liens) are intended to make the borrower less likely to default on the loan. A borrower who does not make a down payment could walk away from the house and the loan and lose nothing. Furthermore, if real estate prices drop even a small amount, the balance due on the loan will exceed the value of the collateral. As we discussed in Chapter 2, the down payment reduces *moral hazard* in the borrower. The amount of the down payment depends on the type of mortgage loan. Many lenders require that the borrower pay 5% of the purchase price; in other situations, up to 20% may be required.

Private Mortgage Insurance Another way that lenders protect themselves against default is by requiring the borrower to purchase **private mortgage insurance (PMI)**. PMI is an insurance policy that guarantees to make up any discrepancy between the value of the property and the loan amount, should a default occur. For example, if the balance on your loan was $120,000 at the time of default and the property was worth only $100,000, PMI would pay the lending institution $20,000. The default still appears on the credit record of the borrower, but the lender avoids sustaining the loss. PMI is usually required on loans that have less than a 20% down payment. If the loan-to-value ratio falls because of payments being made or because the value of the property increases, the borrower can request that the PMI requirement be dropped. PMI usually costs between $20 and $30 per month for a $100,000 loan.

Borrower Qualification Before granting a mortgage loan, the lender will determine whether the borrower qualifies for it. Qualifying for a mortgage loan is different from qualifying for a bank loan because most lenders sell their mortgage loans to one of a few federal agencies in the secondary mortgage market. These agencies establish very precise guidelines that must be followed before they will accept the loan. If the lender gives a mortgage loan to a borrower who does not fit these guidelines, the lender may not be able to resell the loan. That ties up the lender's funds. Banks can be more flexible with loans that will be kept on the bank's own books.

The rules for qualifying a borrower are complex and constantly changing, but a rule of thumb is that the loan payment, including taxes and insurance, should not exceed 25% of gross monthly income. Furthermore, the sum of the monthly payments on all loans to the borrower, including car loans and credit cards, cannot exceed 33% of gross monthly income. A borrower who fails this income test can pay off some of the outstanding debt, increase the down payment, or find a less expensive house to buy.

Mortgage Loan Amortization

Mortgage loan borrowers agree to pay a monthly amount of principal and interest that will fully amortize the loan by its maturity. "Fully amortize" means that the payments will pay off the outstanding indebtedness by the time the loan matures. During the early years of the loan, the lender applies most of the payment to the interest on the loan and a small amount to the outstanding principal balance. Many borrowers are surprised to find that after years of making payments, their loan balance has not dropped appreciably.

Table 3 shows the distribution of principal and interest for a 30-year, $130,000 loan at 8.5% interest. Only $78.75 of the first payment is applied to reduce the loan balance. At the end of two years, the balance due is $127,947, and at the end of five years, the balance due is $124,137. Put another way, of $59,975.40 in loan payments made during the first five years, only $5862.69 is applied to the principal. Over the life of the $130,000 loan, a total of $229,850 in interest will be paid.

If the loan in Table 3 had been financed for 15 years instead of for 30, the payment would have increased by about $280 per month to $1279.59, but the interest savings over the life of the loan would be nearly $130,000. It is no wonder why so many borrowers prefer the shorter-term loans.

■ TABLE 3 Amortization of a 30-Year, $130,000 Loan at 8.5%

Payment Number	Beginning Balance of Loan	Monthly Payment	Amount Applied to Interest	Amount Applied to Principal	Ending Balance of Loan
1	130,000	999.59	920.83	78.75	129,921.24
24	128,040.25	999.59	906.95	92.66	127,947.62
60	124,256.74	999.59	880.15	119.43	124,137.31
120	115,365.63	999.59	817.17	182.41	115,183.22
180	101,786.23	999.59	720.99	278.60	101,507.63
240	81,046.41	999.59	574.08	425.51	80,620.90
360	991.77	999.59	7.82	991.77	0

APPLICATION | **COMPUTING THE PAYMENT ON MORTGAGE LOANS**

We can apply the techniques for computing loan payments introduced in Chapter 3 to computing the payment on mortgage loans. Suppose that you have graduated and want to buy a condominium instead of renting an apartment. The condo costs $100,000, and a 5% down payment is required by your mortgage lender. How much will your monthly loan payment be?

To compute fixed-amount loan payments, we recognize that the lender must equate the present value of the stream of payments you will pay to the amount of the loan. In equation form,

$$\text{Loan amount} = \frac{FP}{1+i} + \frac{FP}{(1+i)^2} + \frac{FP}{(1+i)^3} + \cdots + \frac{FP}{(1+i)^n} \qquad (1)$$

where

FP = fixed payment
i = interest rate on the loan
n = term of the loan

An alternative form for Equation 1, which takes advantage of present value tables included at the end of most introductory finance texts, is

$$\text{Loan amount} = FP \, (PVIFA_{i,n}) \qquad (2)$$

where $PVIFA$ is the present value interest factor with an interest rate of i for n periods. FP can then be found by looking up the factor for the term and interest rate on the loan you are interested in and dividing this factor into the loan amount. Most factor tables include only 50 or 60 periods, so we cannot use this method to compute the payment on 30-year loans with monthly payments ($30 \times 12 = 360$ periods). Instead, a close approximation of the monthly payment can be found by computing the annual payment and dividing by 12.

Let us assume that you can obtain a 30-year loan at 8% on the $95,000 you need to finance your condo ($100,000 minus the $5000 down payment). Using the portion of the present value interest factor table provided in Table 4 and Equation 2, we obtain

$$\$95,000 = FP_{ann}(PVIFA_{8\%, 30})$$
$$\$95,000 = FP_{ann}(11.2578)$$
$$FP_{ann} = \frac{\$95,000}{11.2578}$$
$$FP_{ann} = \$8439$$

$$FP_{mo} = \frac{FP_{ann}}{12} = \frac{\$8439}{12} = \$703 \text{ per month}$$

When this problem is solved using a financial calculator, the monthly payment is found to be $697. Although using the present value table is not perfectly accurate, it has the advantage of allowing you to compute loan payments at any whole interest rate using commonly available tables.

Your actual payment will be increased to include amounts that are used to pay taxes and insurance on the property.

■ **TABLE 4** Present Value Interest Factor at Various Rates of Interest

Payment Periods	Interest Rate					
	5%	6%	7%	8%	9%	10%
15	10.3797	9.7122	9.1079	8.5595	8.0607	7.6061
20	12.4622	11.4699	10.5940	9.8181	9.1285	8.5136
25	14.0939	12.7834	11.6536	10.6748	9.8226	9.0770
30	15.3725	13.7648	12.4090	11.2578	9.8226	9.0770

■ TYPES OF MORTGAGE LOANS

A number of types of mortgage loans are available in the market. Different borrowers may qualify for different ones. A skilled mortgage banker can help find the best type of mortgage loan for each particular situation.

Insured and Conventional Mortgages

Mortgages are classified as either *insured* or *conventional.* **Insured mortgages** are originated by banks or other mortgage lenders but are guaranteed by either the Federal Housing Administration (FHA) or the Veterans Administration (VA). Applicants for FHA and VA loans must meet certain qualifications, such as having served in the military or having income below a given level, and can borrow only up to a certain amount. The FHA or VA then guarantees the bank making the loans against any losses—that is, the agency guarantees that it will pay off the mortgage loan if the borrower defaults. One important advantage to a borrower who qualifies for an FHA or VA loan is that only a very low or zero down payment is required.

Conventional mortgages are originated by the same sources as insured loans but are not guaranteed. Private mortgage companies now insure many conventional loans against default. As we noted, most lenders require the borrower to obtain private mortgage insurance on all loans with a loan-to-value ratio exceeding 80%.

Fixed- and Adjustable-Rate Mortgages

In standard mortgage contracts, borrowers agree to make regular payments on the principal and interest they owe to lenders. As we saw earlier, the interest rate significantly affects the size of this monthly payment. In *fixed-rate mortgages,* the interest rate and the monthly payment do not vary over the life of the mortgage.

The interest rate on *adjustable-rate mortgages (ARMs)* is tied to some market interest rate and therefore changes over time. ARMs usually have limits, called *caps,* on how high (or low) the interest rate can move in one year and during the term of the loan. A typical ARM might tie the interest rate to the average Treasury bill rate plus 2%, with caps of 2% per year and 6% over the lifetime of the mortgage. Caps make ARMs more palatable to borrowers.

Borrowers tend to prefer fixed-rate loans to ARMs because ARMs may cause financial hardship if interest rates rise. However, fixed-rate borrowers do not benefit if rates fall unless they are willing to refinance their mortgage (pay it off by obtaining a new mortgage at a lower interest rate). The fact that individuals are risk-averse means that fear of hardship most often overwhelms anticipation of savings.

Lenders, by contrast, prefer ARMs because ARMs lessen interest-rate risk. Recall from Chapter 3 that interest-rate risk is the risk that rising interest rates will cause the value of debt instruments to fall. The effect on the value of the debt is greatest when the debt has a long term to maturity. Since mortgages are usually long-term, their value is very sensitive to interest-rate movements. Lending institutions can reduce the sensitivity of their portfolios by making ARMs instead of standard fixed-rate loans.

Seeing that lenders prefer ARMs and borrowers prefer fixed-rate mortgages, lenders must entice borrowers by offering lower initial interest rates on ARMs than on fixed-rate loans. For example, in early 1997, the reported interest rate for 30-year fixed-rate mortgage loans was 7.75%. The rate at that time for adjustable-rate mortgages was 5.50%. The rate on the ARM would have to rise over 2 percentage points before the borrower of the ARM would be in a worse position than the fixed-rate borrower.

Other Types of Mortgages

As the market for mortgage loans becomes more competitive, lenders are offering more innovative mortgage contracts in an effort to attract borrowers. We discuss some of these mortgages here.

Graduated-Payment Mortgages (GPMs) Graduated-payment mortgages are useful for home buyers who expect their incomes to rise. The GPM has lower payments in the first few years; then the payments rise. The early payments may not even be sufficient to cover the interest due, in which case the principal balance increases. As time passes, the borrower expects income to increase so that the higher payment will not be a burden.

The advantage of the GPM is that borrowers will qualify for a larger loan than if they requested a conventional mortgage. This may help buyers purchase adequate housing now and avoid the need to move to more expensive homes as their family size increases. The disadvantage is that the payments escalate whether the borrower's income does or not.

Growing-Equity Mortgages (GEMs) Lenders designed the growing-equity mortgage loan to help the borrower pay off the loan in a shorter period of time. With a GEM, the payments will initially be the same as on a conventional mortgage. However, over time, the payment will increase. This increase will reduce the principal more quickly than the conventional payment stream would. For example, a typical contract may call for level payments for the first two years. The payments may increase by 5% per year for the next five years, then remain the same until maturity. The result is to reduce the life of the loan from 30 years to about 17.

GEMs are popular among borrowers who expect their incomes to rise in the future. It gives them the benefit of a small payment at the beginning while still retiring the debt early. Although the increase in payments is *required* in GEMs, most mortgage loans have no prepayment penalty. This means that a borrower with a 30-year loan could create a GEM by simply increasing the monthly payments beyond what is required and designating that the excess be applied entirely to the principal.

The GEM is similar to the graduated-payment mortgage; the difference is that the goal of the GPM is to help the borrower qualify by reducing the first few years' payments. The loan still pays off in 30 years. The goal of the GEM is to let the borrower pay off early.

Shared-Appreciation Mortgages (SAMs) When interest rates are high, the monthly payments on mortgage loans are also high. That prevents many borrowers from qualifying for loans. To help borrowers qualify and to keep loan volume high, lenders created the shared-appreciation mortgage. In a SAM, the lender lowers the interest rate on the mortgage in exchange for a share of any appreciation in the real estate (if the property sells for more than a stated amount, the lender is entitled to a portion of the gain). As interest rates and inflation fell in the late 1980s and into the 1990s, the popularity of these loans also diminished.

Equity Participation Mortgages In a shared-appreciation mortgage, the lender shares in the appreciation of the property. In an equity participation mortgage, an outside investor shares in the appreciation rather than the lender. This investor will either provide a portion of the purchase price of the property or supplement the monthly payments. In return, the investor receives a portion of any appreciation in the property. As with the SAM, the borrower benefits by being able to qualify for a larger loan than without such help.

Second Mortgages Second mortgages are loans that are secured by the same real estate that is used to secure the first mortgage. The second mortgage is junior to the original loan. This means that should a default occur, the second mortgage holder will be paid only after the original loan has been paid off, if sufficient funds remain.

Second mortgages have two purposes. The first is to give borrowers a way to use the equity they have in their homes as security for another loan. An alternative to the second mortgage would be to refinance the home at a higher loan amount than is currently owed. The cost of obtaining a second mortgage is often much lower than refinancing.

The second purpose of the second mortgage is to take advantage of one of the few remaining tax deductions available to the middle class. The interest on loans secured by residential real estate is tax-deductible (the tax laws allow borrowers to deduct the interest on the primary residence and one vacation home). No other kind of consumer loan has this tax deduction. Many banks now offer lines of credit secured by second mortgages. In most cases, the value of the security is not of great interest to the bank. Consumers prefer that the line of credit be secured so that they can deduct the interest on the loan from their taxes.

Reverse Annuity Mortgages (RAMs) The reverse annuity mortgage is an innovative method for retired people to live on the equity they have in their homes. The contract for an RAM has the bank advancing funds on a monthly schedule. This increasing-balance loan is secured by the real estate. The borrower does not make any payments against the loan. When the borrower dies, the borrower's estate sells the property to retire the debt.

The advantage of the RAM is that it allows retired people to use the equity in their homes without the necessity of selling it. For retirees in need of supplemental funds to meet living expenses, the RAM can be a desirable option.

■ MORTGAGE-LENDING INSTITUTIONS

Originally, the thrift industry was established with the mandate from Congress to provide mortgage loans to families. Congress gave these institutions the ability to attract depositors by allowing S&Ls to pay slightly higher interest rates on deposits. For many years, the thrift industry did its job well. Thrifts raised short-term funds by attracting deposits and used these funds to make long-term mortgage loans. The growth of the housing industry owes much of its success to these institutions. (The thrift industry is discussed further in Chapter 15.)

Until the 1970s, interest rates remained relatively stable, and when fluctuations occurred, they tended to be small and short-lived. But in the 1970s, interest rates rose rapidly, along with inflation, and thrifts became the victims of interest-rate risk. As market interest rates rose, the value of their fixed-rate mortgage loan portfolios fell. Because of the losses the thrifts suffered, they stopped being the primary source of mortgage loans.

Another serious problem with the early mortgage market was that thrift institutions were restricted from nationwide branching by federal and state laws and were forbidden to lend outside of their normal lending territory, about 100 miles from their offices. So even if an institution appeared very diversified, with thousands of different loans, all of the loans were from the same region. When that region had economic problems, many of the loans would default at the same time. For example, Texas and Oklahoma experienced a recession in the mid-1980s due to falling oil prices. Many mortgage loans defaulted because real estate values fell at the same time as the region's unemployment rate rose. That other areas of the country remained healthy was of no help to local lenders.

Figure 2 shows the share of the total mortgage market held by the major mortgage-lending institutions in the United States. (Mortgage pools and trusts are discussed later in this chapter.)

■ LOAN SERVICING

Many of the institutions making mortgage loans do not want to hold large portfolios of long-term securities. Commercial banks, for example, obtain their funds from short-term sources. Investing in long-term loans would subject them to unacceptably high interest-rate risk. Commercial banks, thrifts, and most other loan

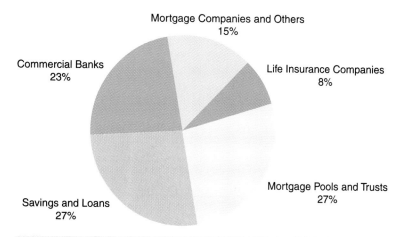

■FIGURE 2 Share of the Mortgage Market Held by Major Mortgage-Lending Institutions

Source: Federal Reserve Bulletin, 1996.

originators do, however, make money through the fees that they earn for packaging loans for other investors to hold. Loan origination fees are typically 1% of the loan amount, though this varies with the market.

Once a loan has been made, many lenders immediately sell the loan to another investor. The borrower may not even be aware that the original lender transferred the loan. By selling the loan, the originator frees up funds that can be lent to another borrower, thereby generating additional fee income.

Some of the originators also provide servicing of the loan. The loan-servicing agent collects payments from the borrower, passes the principal and interest on to the investor, keeps required records of the transaction, and maintains **reserve accounts.** Reserve accounts are established for most mortgage loans to permit the lender to make tax and insurance payments for the borrower. Lenders prefer to make these payments because they protect the security of the loan. Loan-servicing agents usually earn 0.5% per year of the total loan amount for their efforts.

In summary, there are three distinct elements to most mortgage loans.

1. The originator packages the loan for an investor.
2. The investor holds the loan.
3. The servicing agent handles the paperwork.

One, two, or three different intermediaries may provide these functions.

■ SECONDARY MORTGAGE MARKET

The federal government founded the secondary market for mortgages. As we noted earlier, the mortgage market had all but collapsed during the Great Depression. To help spur the nation's economic activity, the government established several agencies to buy mortgages. The Federal National Mortgage Association (Fannie Mae) was set up to buy mortgages from thrifts so that these institutions could make more mortgage loans. This agency would fund these purchases by selling bonds to the public.

At about the same time, the Federal Housing Administration was established to insure certain mortgage contracts. This made it easier to sell the mortgages because the buyer did not have to be concerned with the borrower's credit history or the value of the collateral. A similar insurance program was set up through the Veterans Administration to insure loans to veterans after World War II.

One advantage of the insured loans was that they were required to be written on a standard loan contract. This standardization was an important factor in the growth of the secondary market for mortgages.

As the secondary market for mortgage contracts took shape, a new intermediary, the mortgage bank, emerged. Because this firm did not accept deposits, it was able to open offices across the country. The mortgage bank originated the loans, funding them initially with its own capital. After a group of similar loans were made, they would be bundled and sold, either to one of the federal agencies or to an insurance or pension fund. There were several advantages to the mortgage banks. Because of their size, they were able to capture economies of scale in loan origination and servicing. They were also able to bundle loans from different regions together, which helped reduce their risk. The increased competition for loans among these intermediaries led to lower rates for borrowers.

■ MORTGAGE-BACKED SECURITIES

Intermediaries still faced several problems when trying to sell mortgages. The first was that mortgages are usually too small to be wholesale instruments. The average mortgage loan is now about $130,000. This is far below the $5 million round lot established for commercial paper, for example. Many institutional investors do not want to deal in such small denominations.

The second problem with selling mortgages in the secondary market was that they were not standardized. They have different times to maturity, interest rates, and contract terms. That makes it difficult to bundle a large number of mortgages together.

Third, mortgage loans are relatively costly to service. Compare the servicing a mortgage loan requires to that of a corporate bond. The lender must collect monthly payments, often pay property taxes and insurance premiums, and service reserve accounts. None of this is required if a bond is purchased.

Finally, mortgages have unknown default risk. Investors in mortgages do not want to spend a lot of time evaluating the credit of borrowers. These problems inspired the creation of the **mortgage-backed security.**

What Is a Mortgage-Backed Security?

By the late 1960s, the secondary market for mortgages was declining, mostly because fewer veterans were obtaining guaranteed loans. The government reorganized Fannie Mae and created two new agencies, the Government National

Mortgage Association (GNMA, or Ginnie Mae) and the Federal Home Loan Mortgage Corporation (FHLMC, or Freddie Mac). These three agencies were now able to offer new securities backed by both insured and, for the first time, uninsured mortgages.

An alternative to selling mortgages directly to investors is to create a new security backed by (secured by) a large number of mortgages assembled into what is called a *mortgage pool.* A trustee, such as a bank or a government agency, holds the mortgage pool, which serves as collateral for the new security. The most common type of mortgage-backed security is the **mortgage pass-through,** a security that has the borrower's mortgage payments pass through the trustee before being disbursed to the investors in the mortgage pass-through. If borrowers prepay their loans, investors receive more principal than expected. For example, investors may buy mortgage-backed securities on which the average interest rate is 9%. If interest rates fall and borrowers refinance at lower rates, the securities will pay off early. The possibility that mortgages will prepay and force investors to seek alternative investments, usually with lower returns, is called *prepayment risk.* As is evident in Figure 3, the dollar volume of outstanding mortgage pools increased steadily between 1984 and 1995. The reason that mortgage pools have become so popular is that they permit the creation of new securities (like mortgage pass-throughs) that make investing in mortgage loans much more efficient. For example, an institutional investor can invest in one large mortgage pass-through secured by a mortgage pool rather than investing in many small and dissimilar mortgage contracts.

Types of Pass-Through Securities

There are several types of mortgage pass-through securities: GNMA pass-throughs, FHLMC pass-throughs, and private pass-throughs.

GNMA Pass-Through Securities Ginnie Mae began guaranteeing pass-through securities in 1968. Since then, the popularity of these instruments has increased dramatically.

A variety of financial intermediaries, including commercial banks and mortgage companies, originate Ginnie Mae mortgages. Ginnie Mae aggregates these mortgages into a pool and issues pass-through securities that are collateralized by the interest and principal payments from the mortgages. Ginnie Mae also guarantees the pass-through securities against default. The usual minimum denomination for pass-throughs is $25,000. The minimum pool size is $1 million. One pool may back up many pass-through securities.

FHLMC Pass-Throughs Freddie Mac was created to assist savings and loan associations, which are not eligible to originate Ginnie Mae–guaranteed loans. Freddie Mac purchases mortgages for its own account and also issues pass-through securities similar to those issued by Ginnie Mae. Pass-through securities issued by Freddie Mac are called *participation certificates (PCs).* Freddie Mac pools are distinct from Ginnie Mae pools in that they contain conventional (nonguaranteed)

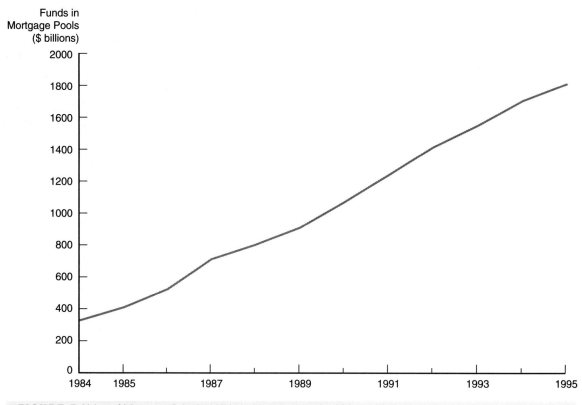

Funds in
Mortgage Pools
($ billions)

FIGURE 3 Value of Mortgage Principal Held in Mortgage Pools, 1984–1995

Source: Federal Reserve Bulletin, Various issues.

mortgages, are not federally insured, contain mortgages with different rates, are larger (ranging up to several hundred million dollars), and have a minimum denomination of $100,000.

A relatively recent innovation in the FHLMC pass-through market has been the **collateralized mortgage obligation (CMO).** CMOs are securities classified by when prepayment is likely to occur and are issued by Freddie Mac. These differ from traditional mortgage-backed securities in that they are offered in different maturity groups. These securities help reduce prepayment risk, which is a problem with other types of pass-through securities.

CMOs backed by a particular mortgage pool are divided into classes. When principal is repaid, the investors in the first class are paid first, then those in the second class, and so on. Investors choose a class that matches their maturity requirements. For example, if they will need cash from their investment in a few years, they purchase class 1 or 2 CMOs. If they want the investment to be long-term, they can purchase CMOs from the last class.

Even when an investor purchases a CMO, there are no guarantees about how long the investment will last. If interest rates fall significantly, many borrowers will pay off their mortages early by refinancing at lower rates.

Private Pass-Through Securities (PIPs) In addition to the agency pass-throughs, intermediaries in the private sector have offered privately issued pass-through securities. The first of these PIPs was offered by BankAmerica in 1977.

One mortgage market opportunity available to private institutions is for mortgages larger than the maximum size set by the government. These so-called *jumbo mortgages* are often bundled into pools to back private pass-throughs.

Mortgage Backed Securities Clearing Corporation

The Mortgage Backed Securities Clearing Corporation (MBSCC) was formed by the Midwest Stock Exchange in 1979 to automate the trading of mortgage-backed securities. Both parties to an exchange of mortgage-backed securities submit information to the MBSCC. The computer system checks that the information is in agreement and then confirms the trade.

■ THE IMPACT OF SECURITIZED MORTGAGES ON THE MORTGAGE MARKET

Mortgage-backed securities (also called **securitized mortgages**) have been a very important development in the financial markets in recent years. These new debt instruments compete for funds with government bonds, corporate bonds, and stocks. Securitized mortgages are low-risk securities that have higher yields than comparable government bonds and attract funds from around the world.

One benefit of the securitized mortgage is that it reduces the problems caused by regional lending institutions' sensitivity to local economic fluctuations. Because the loans are packaged and sold nationwide and worldwide, regional variations are no longer as great a source of risk to lenders.

A second benefit of the securitized mortgage is that borrowers now have access to a national capital market. In the early twentieth century, borrowers could choose among mortgages offered by only a few local lenders. The new securitized mortgages function much more like the rest of the capital markets. As a result, rates in the mortgage market follow other capital market rates much more closely.

Another benefit of the securitized mortgages is that an investor can enjoy the low-risk and long-term nature of investing in mortgages without having to service the loan.

A side effect of the development of securitized mortgages has been that mortgage rates are now more open to national and international influences. As a result, mortgage rates are more volatile than they were in the past.

SUMMARY

1. Mortgages are long-term loans secured by real estate. Both individuals and businesses obtain mortgage loans to finance real estate purchases.

2. Mortgage interest rates are relatively low due to competition among various institutions that want to make mortgage loans. In addition to keeping interest rates low, the competition has resulted in a variety of terms and options for mortgage loans. For example, borrowers may choose to obtain a 30-year fixed-rate loan or an adjustable-rate loan that has its interest rate tied to the Treasury bill rate.

3. Several features of mortgage loans are designed to reduce the likelihood that the borrower will default. For example, a down payment is usually required so that the borrower will suffer a loss if the lender repossesses the property. Most lenders also require that the borrower purchase private mortgage insurance unless the loan-to-value ratio drops below 80%.

4. A variety of mortgages are available to meet the needs of most borrowers. The graduated-payment mortgage has low initial payments that increase over time. The growing-equity mortgage has increasing payments that cause the loan to be paid off in a

shorter period than a level-payment loan. Shared-appreciation loans were used when interest rates and inflation were high. The lender shared in the increase in the real estate's value in exchange for lower interest rates.

5. Mortgage-backed securities have been growing in popularity in recent years as institutional investors look for attractive investment opportunities. Mortgage-backed securities are securities collateralized by a pool of mortgages. The payments on the pool are passed through to the investors. Ginnie Mae, Freddie Mac, and private banks issue pass-through securities.

KEY TERMS

amortized, p. 270
balloon loan, p. 270
collateralized mortgage
    obligation (CMO), p. 284
conventional mortgage, p. 277
discount points, p. 271
down payment, p. 274

insured mortgage, p. 277
lien, p. 273
mortgage, p. 270
mortgage-backed security
    (securitized mortgage),
    p. 282, 285
mortgage pass-through, p. 283

private mortgage insurance
    (PMI), p. 274
reserve account, p. 281

QUESTIONS AND PROBLEMS

*1. What distinguishes the mortgage markets from other capital markets?

2. Most mortgage loans once had balloon payments; now most current mortgage loans fully amortize. What is the difference between a balloon loan and an amortizing loan?

*3. What features contribute to keeping long-term mortgage interest rates low?

4. What are discount points, and why do some mortgage borrowers choose to pay them?

*5. What is a lien, and when is it used in mortgage lending?

6. What is the purpose of requiring that a borrower make a down payment before receiving a loan?

*7. What kind of insurance do lenders usually require of borrowers who have less than an 80% loan-to-value ratio?

8. Lenders tend not to be as flexible about the qualifications required of mortgage customers as they can be for other types of bank loans. Why is this so?

*9. Distinguish between conventional mortgage loans and insured mortgage loans.

10. Interpret what is meant when a lender quotes the terms on a loan as "floating with the T-bill plus 2 with caps of 2 and 6"?

*11. The monthly payments on both graduated-payment loans and growing-equity loans increase over time. Despite this similarity, the two types of loans have different purposes. What is the motivation behind each type of loan?

12. Many banks offer lines of credit that are secured by a second mortgage (or lien) on real property. These loans have been very popular among bank customers. Why are homeowners so willing to pledge their homes as security for these lines of credit?

*13. The reverse annuity mortgage (RAM) allows retired people to live off the equity they have in their homes without having to sell the home. Explain how a RAM works.

14. What is a mortgage-backed security?

*15. Describe how a mortgage pass-through works.

CASE STUDY

Mortgage Loans, Qualifying for a Mortgage, Finding the Lowest Interest Rate, Effective Cost of the Loan, Prepayment Options

CONCEPTS IN THIS CASE

mortgage loans

fixed-rate v variable rate loans

calculating loan amounts

the effect of loan timing

internet alternatives to local mortgages

adjustments needed to remain competitive

alternatives to basic mortgages

the effect of discount points

Your bank has a mortgage loan department/subsidiary. It has been suggested that this area of the bank is not competitive in terms of interest rates and options available to homeowners. You have been given the opportunity to evaluate the products offered by your bank and how it compares to alternatives that homeowners are considering when selecting a mortgage company.

You decide that the best way of learning how your bank's mortgage department works is to experience the mortgage application process using internet resources first, then compare your findings with what would occur if you obtained the mortgage from your own employer.

The following information applies to your mortgage qualification process:

Monthly Gross Income	$3,000
Money you have in savings for a down payment	$25,000
You have monthly payments for all existing debts of	$400
The property tax rate in your area is	1%
The hazard/home insurance rate in your area is	0.5%

You are an acceptable credit risk, with a respectable credit history.

1. Assume your bank offers the following mortgage terms and rates:

Term of loan:	15 or 30 years
Down payment required:	10% to 20%
Closing costs of:	Discount Points of 1%
	Origination Fees of 2%
	Lender Fees of $300
	Credit Report Cost of $20
	Escrow Fee of $300

Lender's Title Insurance fee of $400

Recording Fee of $25

Appraisal Report of $300

Survey Fee of $200

Termite Infestation Report of $50

A 15-year fixed mortgage has an interest rate of 6.5%

A 30-year fixed mortgage has an interest rate of 7.0%

A 15-year adjustable-rate mortgage (ARM) has an interest rate of 5.0%, adjusted every 12 months

The bank uses a payment-to-income (PTI) ratio range of 28% to 33%

Using internet mortgage calculators answer the following:

a. How much do you qualify to borrow (assume 28% PTI)

   i. for a 15-year fixed-rate mortgage (10% down)?

   ii. for a 30-year fixed-rate mortgage (10% down)?

   iii. for a 15-year fixed-rate mortgage (20% down)?

   iv. for a 30-year fixed-rate mortgage (20% down)?

b. How much do you qualify to borrow (assume 33% PTI)

   i. for a 15-year fixed-rate mortgage (10% down)?

   ii. for a 30-year fixed-rate mortgage (10% down)?

   iii. for a 15-year fixed-rate mortgage (20% down)?

   iv. for a 30-year fixed-rate mortgage (20% down)?

c. Assuming closing costs are paid from savings:

   i. What is the monthly payment on a 30-year, fixed-rate loan of $100,000?

   ii. What is the monthly payment on a 15-year, fixed-rate loan of $100,000?

   iii. What is the monthly payment on an adjustable-rate loan of $100,000 for the first year?

   iv. How much is the total interest paid on the 30-year loan in year 5?

v. How much is the total interest paid on the 15-year loan in year 5?

d. Given the following information on the adjustable-rate loan:

Maximum Rate is 12%
Months Before First Adjustment is 36
Months Between Adjustments is 12
Rate Change Per Adjustment is 2%
Years before Sell/Pay Off Loan is 7
Your Savings Rate is 4%
Your State + Federal Tax Rate is 40%

i. What is the cost difference between the adjustable-rate loan and the 30-year fixed rate loan if interest rates decrease?

ii. What is the cost difference between the adjustable rate loan and the 30-year fixed-rate loan if interest rates increase?

iii. Which loan would you prefer, and why?

2. Use local mortgage lenders and/or libraries/ Internet resources to find terms and rates for competing mortgage lenders. Re-calculate your responses to questions 1(a), 1(b), and 1(c). Indicate the strengths and weaknesses of your bank's mortgage loan area relative to what you find locally or on the Internet. What changes should your company consider in order to improve its position as a mortgage lender? What recommendations would you make to your supervisor?

3. What is the effective annual interest rate of the 15-year mortgage in question 1 if the discount rate is zero?

4. What is the effective annual interest rate of the 15-year mortgage in question 1 if the discount rate is 2%?

PART IV

The Financial Institutions Industry

CHAPTER 12

THEORY OF FINANCIAL STRUCTURE

■ PREVIEW A healthy and vibrant economy requires a financial system that moves funds from people who save to people who have productive investment opportunities. But how does the financial system make sure that your hard-earned savings get channeled to those with productive investment opportunities?

This chapter answers that question by providing a theory for understanding how our financial structure is designed to promote economic efficiency. The theoretical analysis focuses on a few simple but powerful economic concepts that enable us to explain features of our financial markets such as why financial contracts are written as they are, why financial intermediaries are more important than securities markets for getting funds to borrowers, and why financial crises occur and have such severe consequences for the health of the economy.

 ## BASIC PUZZLES ABOUT FINANCIAL STRUCTURE THROUGHOUT THE WORLD

The financial system is complex in structure and function throughout the world. There are many different types of institutions: banks, insurance companies, mutual funds, stock and bond markets, and so on—all of which are regulated by government. The financial system channels billions of dollars per year from savers to people with productive investment opportunities. If we take a close look at financial structure all over the world, we find eight basic puzzles that we need to solve in order to understand how the financial system works.

The pie chart in Figure 1 indicates how American businesses financed their activities using external funds (those obtained from outside the business itself) in

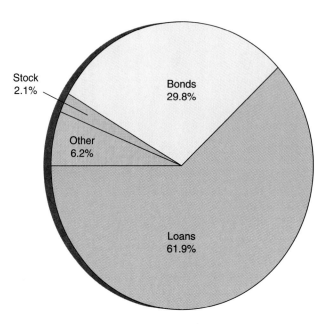

■FIGURE 1 Sources of External Funds for Nonfinancial Businesses in the United States

The categories of external funds are as follows: *Loans* is made up primarily of bank loans, but it also includes loans made by other financial intermediaries. *Bonds* includes marketable debt securities such as corporate bonds and commercial paper. *Stock* consists of stock market shares. *Other* includes other loans such as government loans, loans by foreigners, and trade debt (loans made by businesses to other businesses when they purchase goods). *Source:* Colin Mayer, "Financial Systems, Corporate Finance, and Economic Development," in *Asymmetric Information, Corporate Finance, and Investment,* ed. R. Glenn Hubbard (Chicago: University of Chicago Press, 1990), p. 312.

the period 1970–1985. The *loans* category is made up primarily of bank loans, but it also includes loans made by other financial intermediaries; the *bonds* category includes marketable debt securities such as corporate bonds and commercial paper; *stock* consists of stock market shares; and *other* includes other loans such as government loans, loans by foreigners, and trade debt (loans made by businesses to other businesses when they purchase goods). Figure 2 uses the same classifications as Figure 1 and compares the U.S. data to those of five other industrialized countries.

Now let us explore the eight financial puzzles.

1. *Stocks are not the most important source of external financing for businesses.* Because so much attention in the media is focused on the stock market, many people have the impression that stocks are the most important sources of financing for American corporations. However, as we can see from the pie chart in Figure 1, the stock market accounted for only a small fraction of the external financing of American businesses in the

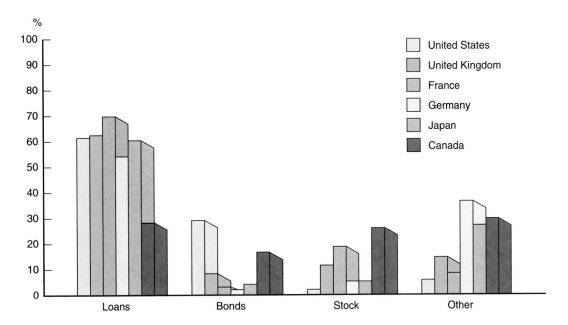

■FIGURE 2 Sources of External Funds for Nonfinancial Businesses: A Comparison of the United States and Five
Other Industrialized Countries

The categories of external funds are the same as in Figure 1. *Source:* Colin Mayer, "Financial Systems, Corporate Finance, and Economic Development,"
in *Asymmetric Information, Corporate Finance, and Investment,* ed. R. Glenn Hubbard (Chicago: University of Chicago Press, 1990), p. 312.

1970–1985 period, 2.1%.[1] (In fact, in the mid- to late 1980s, American corporations generally stopped issuing shares to finance their activities; instead they purchased large numbers of shares, meaning that the stock market was actually a *negative* source of corporate finance in those years.) Similarly small figures apply in the other countries presented in Figure 2 as well. Why is the stock market less important than other sources of financing in the United States and other countries?

2. *Issuing marketable debt and equity securities is not the primary way in which businesses finance their operations.* Figure 1 shows that bonds are a far more important source of financing than stocks in the United States (29.8% versus 2.1%). However, stocks and bonds combined (31.9%), which make up the total share of marketable securities, still supply

----

[1]The 2.1% figure for the percentage of external financing provided by stocks is based on the flows of external funds to corporations. However, this flow figure is somewhat misleading because when a share of stock is issued, it raises funds permanently, whereas when a bond is issued, it raises funds only temporarily until they are paid back at maturity. To see this, suppose that a firm raises $1000 by selling a share of stock and another $1000 by selling a $1000 one-year bond. In the case of the stock issue, the firm can hold on to the $1000 it raised this way, but to hold on to the $1000 it raised through debt, it has to issue a new $1000 bond every year. If we look at the flow of funds to corporations over a 15-year period, as in Figure 1, the firm will have raised $1000 with a stock issue only once in the 15-year period, while it will have raised $1000 with debt 15 times, once in each of the 15 years. Thus it will look like debt is 15 times more important than stocks in raising funds, even though our example indicates that they are actually equally important for the firm.

less than one-third of the external funds corporations need to finance their activities. The fact that issuing marketable securities is not the most important source of financing is true elsewhere in the world as well. Indeed, as we see in Figure 2, most countries, with the exception of Canada, have a much smaller share of external financing supplied by marketable securities than the United States. Why don't businesses use marketable securities more extensively to finance their activities?

3. *Indirect finance, which involves the activities of financial intermediaries, is many times more important than direct finance, in which businesses raise funds directly from lenders in financial markets.* Direct finance involves the sale to households of marketable securities such as stocks and bonds. The 31.9% share of stocks and bonds as a source of external financing for American businesses actually greatly overstates the importance of direct finance in our financial system. Since 1970, less than 5% of newly issued corporate bonds and commercial paper and around 50% of stocks have been sold directly to American households. The rest of these securities have been bought primarily by financial intermediaries such as insurance companies, pension funds, and mutual funds. These figures indicate that direct finance is used in less than 5% of the external funding of American business. Because in most countries marketable securities are an even less important source of finance than in the United States, direct finance is also far less important than indirect finance in the rest of the world. Why are financial intermediaries and indirect finance so important in financial markets?

4. *Banks are the most important source of external funds used to finance businesses.* As we can see in Figures 1 and 2, the primary sources of external funds for businesses throughout the world are loans (61.9% in the United States). Most of these loans are bank loans, so the data suggest that banks have the most important role in financing business activities. An extraordinary fact that surprises most people is that in an average year in the United States, 25 times more funds are raised with bank loans than with stocks. Banks are even more important in countries such as France than they are in the United States, and in developing countries banks play an even more important role in the financial system than they do in the industrialized countries. What makes banks so important to the workings of the financial system?

5. *The financial system is among the most heavily regulated sectors of the economy.* You learned in Chapter 2 that the financial system is heavily regulated, not only in the United States but in all other developed countries as well. Governments regulate financial markets primarily to promote the provision of information and to ensure the soundness of the financial system. Why are financial markets so extensively regulated throughout the world?

6. *Only large, well-established corporations have access to securities markets to finance their activities.* Individuals and smaller businesses that are not well established almost never raise funds by issuing marketable securities. Instead, they obtain their financing from banks. Why do only large, well-known corporations have the ability to raise funds in securities markets?

7. *Collateral is a prevalent feature of debt contracts for both households and businesses.* **Collateral** is property that is pledged to the lender to guarantee payment in the event that the borrower should be unable to make debt payments. Collateralized debt (which is also known as **secured debt** to contrast it with **unsecured debt,** such as credit card debt, which is not collateralized) is the predominant form of household debt and is widely used in business borrowing as well. The majority of household debt in the United States consists of collateralized loans: Your automobile is collateral for your auto loan, and your house is collateral for your mortgage. Commercial and farm mortgages, for which property is pledged as collateral, make up one-quarter of borrowing by nonfinancial businesses; corporate bonds and other bank loans also often involve pledges of collateral. Why is collateral such an important feature of debt contracts?

8. *Debt contracts are typically extremely complicated legal documents that place substantial restrictions on the behavior of the borrower.* Many students think about a debt contract as a simple IOU that can be written on a single piece of paper. The reality of debt contracts is far different, however. In all countries, bond or loan contracts are typically long legal documents with provisions (called **restrictive covenants**) that restrict and specify certain activities that the borrower can engage in. Restrictive covenants are not just a feature of debt contracts for businesses; for example, personal automobile loan and home mortgage contracts have restrictive covenants that require the borrower to maintain sufficient insurance on the automobile or house purchased with the loan. Why are debt contracts so complex and restrictive?

As you might recall from Chapter 2, an important feature of financial markets is that they have substantial transaction and information costs. A theoretical analysis of how these costs affect financial markets provides us with solutions to the eight puzzles, which in turn provide us with a much deeper understanding of how our financial system works. In the next section we examine the impact of transaction costs on the structure of our financial system. Then we turn to how information costs affect financial structure.

■ TRANSACTION COSTS

Transaction costs are a major problem in financial markets. An example will make this clear.

How Transaction Costs Influence Financial Structure

Say you have $5000 you would like to invest, and you think about investing in the stock market. Because you have only $5000, you can buy only a small number of shares. The stockbroker tells you that your purchase is so small that the brokerage commission for buying the stock you picked will be a large percentage of the purchase price of the shares. If instead you decide to buy a bond, the problem is even worse because the smallest denomination for some bonds you might want to buy is as much as $10,000 and you do not have that much to invest. Indeed, the broker may not even be interested in your business at all because the small size of your account doesn't make spending time on it worthwhile. You are disappointed and realize that you will not be able to use financial markets to earn a return on your hard-earned savings. You can take some consolation, however, in the fact that you are not alone in being stymied by high transaction costs. This is a fact of life for most of us: Most American households never own any securities.

You also face another problem because of transaction costs. Because you have only a small amount of funds available, you can make only a restricted number of investments. That is, you have to put all your eggs in one basket, and your inability to diversify will subject you to a lot of risk.

How Financial Intermediaries Reduce Transaction Costs

This example of the problems posed by transaction costs and the example outlined in Chapter 2 when legal costs kept you from making a loan to Carl the Carpenter illustrate that small savers like you are frozen out of financial markets and are unable to benefit from them. Fortunately, financial intermediaries, an important part of the financial structure, have evolved to reduce transaction costs and allow small savers and borrowers to benefit from the existence of financial markets.

Economies of Scale One solution to the problem of high transaction costs is to bundle the funds of many investors together so that they can take advantage of *economies of scale,* the reduction in transaction costs per dollar of investment as the size (scale) of transactions increases. By bundling investors' funds together, transaction costs for each individual investor are far smaller. Economies of scale exist because the total cost of carrying out a transaction in financial markets increases only a little as the size of the transaction grows. For example, the cost of arranging a purchase of 10,000 shares of stock is not much greater than the cost of arranging a purchase of 50 shares of stock.

The presence of economies of scale in financial markets helps explain why financial intermediaries developed and are such an important part of our financial structure. The clearest example of a financial intermediary that arose because of economies of scale is a mutual fund. A *mutual fund* is a financial intermediary that sells shares to individuals and then invests the proceeds in bonds or stocks. Because it buys large blocks of stocks or bonds, a mutual fund can take advantage of lower transaction costs. These cost savings are then passed on to individual investors after the mutual fund has taken its cut in the form of management fees for administering their accounts. An additional benefit for individual investors is that a mutual fund is large enough to purchase a widely diversified portfolio of securities. The increased diversification for individual investors reduces their risk, thus making them better off.

Economies of scale are also important in lowering the costs of things such as computer technology that financial institutions need to accomplish their tasks. Once a large mutual fund has invested a lot of money in setting up a telecommunications system, for example, it can be used for a huge number of transactions at a low cost per transaction.

Expertise Financial intermediaries also arise because they are better able to develop expertise to lower transaction costs. Mutual funds, banks, and other financial intermediaries develop expertise in computer technology so that they can cheaply provide convenient services such as toll-free numbers that allow you to check on how well your investments are doing or the ability to write checks on your account.

An important outcome of a financial intermediary's low transaction costs is that they allow a financial intermediary to provide its customers with *liquidity services,* services that make it easier for customers to conduct transactions. Money market mutual funds, for example, allow shareholders to write checks that enable them to pay their bills easily while at the same time paying them high interest rates.

■ ASYMMETRIC INFORMATION: ADVERSE SELECTION AND MORAL HAZARD

The presence of transaction costs in financial markets explains in part why financial intermediaries and indirect finance play such an important role in financial markets (puzzle 3). To understand financial structure more fully, however, we turn to the role of information in financial markets.[2]

Asymmetric information—one party's having insufficient knowledge about the other party involved in a transaction to make accurate decisions—is an important aspect of financial markets. For example, managers of a corporation know whether they are honest or have better information about how well their business is doing than the stockholders do. The presence of asymmetric information leads to adverse selection and moral hazard problems, which were introduced in Chapter 2.

Adverse selection is an asymmetric information problem that occurs *before* the transaction occurs: Potential bad credit risks are the ones who most actively seek out loans. Thus the parties who are the most likely to produce an undesirable outcome are most likely to want to engage in the transaction. For example, big risk takers or outright crooks might be the most eager to take out a loan because they know that they are unlikely to pay it back. Because adverse selection increases the chances that a loan might be made to a bad credit risk, lenders may decide not to make any loans even though there are good credit risks in the marketplace.

Moral hazard arises *after* the transaction occurs: The lender runs the risk that the borrower will engage in activities that are undesirable from the lender's point of view because they make it less likely that the loan will be paid back. For example, once borrowers have obtained a loan, they may take on big risks (which have possible high returns but also run a greater risk of default) because they are playing with someone else's money. Because moral hazard lowers the probability that the loan will be repaid, lenders may decide that they would rather not make a loan.

---

[2]An excellent survey of the literature on information and financial structure that expands on the topics discussed in the rest of this chapter is contained in Mark Gertler, "Financial Structure and Aggregate Economic Activity: An Overview," *Journal of Money, Credit and Banking* 20 (1988): 559–588.

■ THE LEMONS PROBLEM: HOW ADVERSE SELECTION INFLUENCES FINANCIAL STRUCTURE

A particular characterization of the adverse selection problem and how it interferes with the efficient functioning of a market was outlined in a famous article by George Akerlof. It is referred to as the "lemons problem" because it resembles the problem created by lemons in the used-car market.[3] Potential buyers of used cars are frequently unable to assess the quality of the car; that is, they can't tell whether a particular used car is a good car that will run well or a lemon that will continually give them grief. The price that a buyer pays must therefore reflect the *average* quality of the cars in the market, somewhere between the low value of a lemon and the high value of a good car.

The owner of a used car, by contrast, is more likely to know whether the car is a peach or a lemon. If the car is a lemon, the owner is more than happy to sell it at the price the buyer is willing to pay, which, being somewhere between the value of a lemon and a good car, is greater than the lemon's value. However, if the car is a peach, the owner knows that the car is undervalued by the price the buyer is willing to pay, and so the owner may not want to sell it. As a result of this adverse selection, very few good used cars will come to the market. Because the average quality of a used car available in the market will be low and because very few people want to buy a lemon, there will be few sales. The used-car market will then function poorly, if at all.

Lemons in the Stock and Bond Markets

A similar lemons problem arises in securities markets, that is, the debt (bond) and equity (stock) markets. Suppose that our friend Irving the Investor, a potential buyer of securities such as common stock, can't distinguish between good firms with high expected profits and low risk and bad firms with low expected profits and high risk. In this situation, Irving will be willing to pay only a price that reflects the *average* quality of firms issuing securities—a price that lies between the value of securities from bad firms and the value of those from good firms. If the owners or managers of a good firm have better information than Irving and *know* that they are a good firm, they know that their securities are undervalued and will not want to sell them to Irving at the price he is willing to pay. The only firms willing to sell Irving securities will be bad firms (because the price is higher than the securities are worth). Our friend Irving is not stupid; he does not want to hold securities in bad firms, and hence he will decide not to purchase securities in the market. In an outcome similar to that in the used-car market, this securities market will not work very well because few firms will sell securities in it to raise capital.

---

[3]George Akerlof, "The Market for 'Lemons': Quality, Uncertainty and the Market Mechanism," *Quarterly Journal of Economics* 84 (1970): 488–500. Two important papers that have applied the lemons problem analysis to financial markets are Stewart Myers and N. S. Majluf, "Corporate Financing and Investment Decisions When Firms Have Information That Investors Do Not Have," *Journal of Financial Economics* 13 (1984): 187–221, and Bruce Greenwald, Joseph E. Stiglitz, and Andrew Weiss, "Information Imperfections in the Capital Market and Macroeconomic Fluctuations," *American Economic Review* 74 (1984): 194–199.

The analysis is similar if Irving considers purchasing a corporate debt instrument in the bond market rather than an equity share. Irving will buy a bond only if its interest rate is high enough to compensate him for the average default risk of the good and bad firms trying to sell the debt. The knowledgeable owners of a good firm realize that they will be paying a higher interest rate than they should, and so they are unlikely to want to borrow in this market. Only the bad firms will be willing to borrow, and because investors like Irving are not eager to buy bonds issued by bad firms, they will probably not buy any bonds at all. Few bonds are likely to sell in this market, and so it will not be a good source of financing.

The analysis we have just conducted explains puzzle 2—why marketable securities are not the primary source of financing for businesses in any country in the world. It also partly explains puzzle 1—why stocks are not the most important source of financing for American businesses. The presence of the lemons problem keeps securities markets such as the stock and bond markets from being effective in channeling funds from savers to borrowers.

Tools to Help Solve Adverse Selection Problems

In the absence of asymmetric information, the lemons problem goes away. If buyers know as much about the quality of used cars as sellers so that all involved can tell a good car from a bad one, buyers will be willing to pay full value for good used cars. Because the owners of good used cars can now get a fair price, they will be willing to sell them in the market. The market will have many transactions and will do its intended job of channeling good cars to people who want them.

Similarly, if purchasers of securities can distinguish good firms from bad, they will pay the full value of securities issued by good firms, and good firms will sell their securities in the market. The securities market will then be able to move funds to the good firms that have the most productive investment opportunities.

Private Production and Sale of Information The solution to the adverse selection problem in financial markets is to eliminate asymmetric information by furnishing people supplying funds with full details about the individuals or firms seeking to finance their investment activities. One way to get this material to saver-lenders is to have private companies collect and produce information that distinguishes good from bad firms and then sell it to purchasers of securities. In the United States, companies such as Standard and Poor's, Moody's, and Value Line gather information on firms' balance sheet positions and investment activities, publish these data, and sell them to subscribers (individuals, libraries, and financial intermediaries involved in purchasing securities).

The system of private production and sale of information does not completely solve the adverse selection problem in securities markets, however, because of the so-called **free-rider problem.** The free-rider problem occurs when people who do not pay for information take advantage of the information that other people have paid for. The free-rider problem suggests that the private sale of information will be only a partial solution to the lemons problem. To see why, suppose that you have just purchased information that tells you which firms are good and which are bad. You believe that this purchase is worthwhile because you can make up the cost of acquiring this information, and then some, by purchasing the securities of good firms that are undervalued. However, when our savvy (free-riding) investor Irving sees you buying certain securities, he buys right along with you, even though he has not paid for any information. If many other investors act as Irving does, the increased demand for the undervalued good securities will cause their low price to be bid up immediately to reflect the securities' true value. As a result of all these free riders, you can no longer buy the securities for less than their true value. Now because you will not gain any extra profits from purchasing the information, you realize that you never should have paid for this information in the first place. If other investors come to the same realization, private firms and individuals may not be able to sell enough of this information to make it worth their while to gather and produce it. The weakened ability of private firms to profit from selling information will mean that less information is produced in the marketplace, and so adverse selection (the lemons problem) will still interfere with the efficient functioning of securities markets.

Government Regulation The free-rider problem prevents the private market from producing enough information to eliminate all the asymmetric information that leads to adverse selection. Could financial markets benefit from government intervention? The government could, for instance, produce information to help investors distinguish good from bad firms and provide it to the public free of charge. This solution, however, would involve the government in releasing negative information about firms, a practice that might be politically difficult. A second possibility (and one followed by the United States and most governments throughout the world) is for the government to regulate securities markets in a way that encourages firms to reveal honest information about themselves so that investors can determine how good or bad the firms are. In the United States, the Securities and Exchange Commission (SEC) is the government agency that requires firms selling their securities in public markets to adhere to standard accounting principles and to disclose information about their sales, assets, and earnings. Similar regulations are found in other countries.

The asymmetric information problem of adverse selection in financial markets helps explain why financial markets are among the most heavily regulated sectors in the economy (puzzle 5). Government regulation to increase information for investors is needed to reduce the adverse selection problem, which interferes with the efficient functioning of securities (stock and bond) markets.

Although government regulation lessens the adverse selection problem, it does not eliminate it. Even when firms provide information to the public about their sales, assets, or earnings, they still have more information than investors: There is a lot more to knowing the quality of a firm than statistics can provide. Furthermore, bad firms have an incentive to make themselves look like good firms because this would enable them to fetch a higher price for their securities. Bad firms will slant the information they are required to transmit to the public, thus making it harder for investors to sort out the good firms from the bad.

Financial Intermediation So far we have seen that private production of information and government regulation to encourage provision of information lessen but do not eliminate the adverse selection problem in financial markets. How, then, can the financial structure help promote the flow of funds to people with productive investment opportunities when there is asymmetric information? A clue is provided by the structure of the used-car market.

An important feature of the used-car market is that most used cars are not sold directly by one individual to another. An individual considering buying a used car might pay for privately produced information by subscribing to a magazine like *Consumer Reports* to find out if a particular make of car has a good repair record. Nevertheless, reading *Consumer Reports* does not solve the adverse selection problem because even if a particular make of car has a good reputation, the specific car someone is trying to sell could be a lemon. The prospective buyer might also bring the used car to a mechanic for a once-over. But what if the prospective buyer doesn't know a mechanic who can be trusted or if the mechanic would charge a high fee to evaluate the car?

Because these roadblocks make it hard for individuals to acquire enough information about used cars, most used cars are not sold directly by one individual to another. Instead, they are sold by an intermediary, a used-car dealer who purchases used cars from individuals and resells them to other individuals. Used-car dealers produce information in the market by becoming experts in determining whether a car is a peach or a lemon. Once they know that a car is good, they can sell it with some form of a guarantee: either a guarantee that is explicit, such as a warranty, or an implicit guarantee in which they stand by their reputation for honesty. People are more likely to purchase a used car because of a dealer's guarantee, and the dealer is able to make a profit on the production of information about automobile quality by being able to sell the used car at a higher price than the dealer paid for it. If dealers purchase and then resell cars on which they have produced information, they avoid the problem of other people free-riding on the information they produced.

Just as used-car dealers help solve adverse selection problems in the automobile market, financial intermediaries play a similar role in financial markets. A financial intermediary such as a bank becomes an expert in the production of information about firms so that it can sort out good credit risks from bad ones. Then it can acquire funds from depositors and lend them to the good firms. Because the bank is able to lend mostly to good firms, it is able to earn a higher return on its loans than the interest it has to pay to its depositors. As a result, the bank earns a profit, which allows it to engage in this information production activity.

An important element in the ability of the bank to profit from the information it produces is that it avoids the free-rider problem by primarily making private loans rather than by purchasing securities that are traded in the open market. Because a private loan is not traded, other investors cannot watch what the bank is doing and bid up the loan's price to the point that the bank receives no compensation for the information it has produced. The bank's role as an intermediary that holds mostly nontraded loans is the key to its success in reducing asymmetric information in financial markets.

Our theoretical analysis of adverse selection indicates that financial intermediaries in general, and banks in particular because they hold a large fraction of nontraded loans, should play a greater role in moving funds to corporations than securities markets do. Our analysis thus explains puzzles 3 and 4: why indirect finance is so much more important than direct finance and why banks are the most important source of external funds for financing businesses.

Another important fact that is explained by the analysis here is the greater importance of banks in the financial systems of developing countries. As we have seen, when the quality of information about firms is better, asymmetric information problems will be less severe, and it will be easier for firms to issue securities. Information about private firms is even harder to collect in developing countries than in industrialized countries; therefore, the smaller role played by securities markets leaves a greater role for financial intermediaries such as banks. A corollary of this analysis is that as information about firms becomes easier to acquire, the role of banks should decline. A major development in the past 20 years in the United States has been huge improvements in information technology. Thus the analysis here suggests that the lending role of financial institutions such as banks in the United States should have declined, and this is exactly what has occurred (see Chapter 14).

Our analysis of adverse selection also explains which firms are more likely to obtain funds from banks and financial intermediaries, an indirect route, rather than directly from the securities markets. The better known a corporation is, the more information about its activities is available in the marketplace. Thus it is easier for investors to evaluate the quality of the corporation and determine whether it is a good firm or a bad one. Because investors have fewer worries about adverse selection with well-known corporations, they will be willing to invest directly in their securities. Hence we have an explanation for puzzle 6: The larger and more mature a corporation is, the more information investors have about it, and the more likely it is that the corporation can raise funds in securities markets.

Collateral and Net Worth Adverse selection interferes with the functioning of financial markets only if a lender suffers a loss when a borrower is unable to make loan payments and thereby defaults. Collateral, property promised to the lender if the borrower defaults, reduces the consequences of adverse selection because it reduces the lender's losses in the event of a default. If a borrower defaults on a loan, the lender can sell the collateral and use the proceeds to make up for the losses on the loan. For example, if you fail to make your mortgage payments, the lender can take title to your house, auction it off, and use the receipts to pay off the loan. Lenders are thus more willing to make loans secured by collateral, and borrowers are willing to supply collateral because the reduced risk for the lender makes it more likely they will get the loan in the first place and perhaps at a better loan rate. The presence of adverse selection in credit markets thus provides an explanation for why collateral is an important feature of debt contracts (puzzle 7).

Net worth (also called **equity capital**), the difference between a firm's assets (what it owns or is owed) and its liabilities (what it owes), can perform a similar role to collateral. If a firm has a high net worth, then even if it engages in investments that cause it to have negative profits and so defaults on its debt payments, the lender can take title to the firm's net worth, sell it off, and use the proceeds to recoup some of the losses from the loan. In addition, the more net worth a firm has in the first place, the less likely it is to default because the firm has a cushion of assets that it can use to pay off its loans. Hence when firms seeking credit have high net worth, the consequences of adverse selection are less important and lenders are more willing to make loans. This analysis lies behind the often-heard lament, "Only the people who don't need money can borrow it!"

Summary So far we have used the concept of adverse selection to explain seven of the eight puzzles about financial structure introduced earlier: The first four emphasize the importance of financial intermediaries and the relative unimportance of securities markets for the financing of corporations; the fifth, that financial markets are among the most heavily regulated sectors of the economy; the sixth, that only large, well-established corporations have access to securities markets; and the seventh, that collateral is an important feature of debt contracts. In the next section we will see that the other asymmetric information concept of moral hazard provides additional reasons for the importance of financial intermediaries and the relative unimportance of securities markets for the financing of corporations, the prevalence of government regulation, and the importance of collateral in debt contracts. In addition, the concept of moral hazard can be used to explain our final puzzle (puzzle 8) of why debt contracts are complicated legal documents that place substantial restrictions on the behavior of the borrower.

■ HOW MORAL HAZARD AFFECTS THE CHOICE BETWEEN DEBT AND EQUITY CONTRACTS

Moral hazard is the asymmetric information problem that occurs after the financial transaction takes place, when the seller of a security may have incentives to hide information and engage in activities that are undesirable for the purchaser of the security. Moral hazard has important consequences for whether a firm finds it easier to raise funds with debt rather than with equity contracts.

Moral Hazard in Equity Contracts: The Principal-Agent Problem

Equity contracts, such as common stock, are claims to a share in the profits and assets of a business. Equity contracts are subject to a particular type of moral hazard called the **principal-agent problem.** When managers own only a small fraction of the firm they work for, the stockholders who own most of the firm's equity (called the *principals*) are not the same people as the managers of the firm, who are the *agents* of the owners. This separation of ownership and control involves moral hazard in that the managers in control (the agents) may act in their own interest rather than in the interest of the stockholder-owners (the principals) because the managers have less incentive to maximize profits than the stockholder-owners do.

To understand the principal-agent problem more fully, suppose that your friend Steve asks you to become a silent partner in his ice-cream store. The store requires an investment of $10,000 to set up, but Steve has only $1000. So you purchase an equity stake (stock shares) for $9000, which entitles you to 90% of the ownership of the firm, while Steve owns only 10%. If Steve works hard to make tasty ice cream, keeps the store clean, smiles at all the customers, and hustles to wait on tables quickly, after all expenses (including Steve's salary), the store will have $50,000 in profits per year, of which Steve receives 10% ($5000) and you receive 90% ($45,000).

But if Steve doesn't provide quick and friendly service to his customers, uses the $50,000 in income to buy artwork for his office, and even sneaks off to the beach while he should be at the store, the store will not earn any profit. Steve can only earn the additional $5000 (his 10% share of the profits) over his salary if he works hard and forgoes unproductive investments (such as art for his office). Steve might decide that the extra $5000 just isn't enough to make him want to expend the effort to be a good manager; he might decide that it would be worth his while only if he earned an extra $10,000. If Steve feels this way, he does not have enough incentive to be a good manager and will end up with a beautiful office, a good tan, and a store that doesn't show any profits. Because the store won't show any profits, Steve's decision not to act in your interest will cost you $45,000 (your 90% of the profits if he had chosen to be a good manager instead).

The moral hazard arising from the principal-agent problem might be even worse if Steve were not totally honest. Because his ice-cream store is a cash business, Steve has the incentive to pocket $50,000 in cash and tell you that the profits were zero. He now gets a return of $50,000, but you get nothing. The moral hazard incentive to underreport profits is illustrated by the experience with accounting practices in the movie industry described in Box 1.

BOX 1

"Hollywood Accounting"

Has *Forrest Gump* Been a Money Loser?

Accounting practices in the movie industry are notorious, giving the phrase "Hollywood accounting" a dubious reputation. A standard practice at movie studios is to keep two sets of books, a practice that might not be tolerated in other businesses but is in the movie business, where standards of morality are not always the highest. One set is maintained according to the generally accepted accounting principles in other industries; that set is used to report profits to management and to shareholders. The second set of books, referred to as "contractual accounting," is used when a studio commits to paying out percentages of a movie's "net profits" among actors, directors, writers, and other parties as part of contractual arrangements. Given that the movie studios have a moral hazard incentive to minimize these "net profits," not surprisingly they are rarely

positive. For example, *Forrest Gump*, which has taken in over $600 million at the box office, is yet to show any profits according to Paramount, the filmmaker. The same has also been the case for other blockbusters such as the first *Batman* movie, *J.F.K.*, and *Coming to America*. Can we really believe that *Forrest Gump*, one of the most successful movies of all time, is a money loser, or is this just an example of the principal-agent problem at work?

The dubious accounting practices of the movie industry have been coming under attack as a result of numerous lawsuits. In addition, the squeaky-clean Walt Disney Company is trying to change industry practices by going on record that it will not use contractual accounting and a second set of books when it compensates movie actors, directors, and writers.

Further indications that the principal-agent problem created by equity contracts can be severe are provided by examples of managers who build luxurious offices for themselves or drive high-priced corporate automobiles. Besides pursuing personal benefits, managers might also pursue corporate strategies (such as the acquisition of other firms) that enhance their personal power but do not increase the corporation's profitability.

The principal-agent problem would not arise if the owners of a firm had complete information about what the managers were up to and could prevent wasteful expenditures or fraud. The principal-agent problem, which is an example of moral hazard, arises only because a manager, like Steve, has more information about his activities than the stockholder does—that is, there is asymmetric information. The principal-agent problem would also not arise if Steve alone owned the store and there were no separation of ownership and control. If this were the case, Steve's hard work and avoidance of unproductive investments would yield him a profit (and extra income) of $50,000, an amount that would make it worth his while to be a good manager.

Tools to Help Solve the Principal-Agent Problem

Production of Information: Monitoring You have seen that the principal-agent problem arises because managers have more information about their activities and actual profits than stockholders do. One way for stockholders to reduce this moral hazard problem is for them to engage in a particular type of information production, the monitoring of the firm's activities: auditing the firm frequently and checking on what the management is doing. The problem is that the monitoring process can be expensive in terms of time and money, as reflected in the name financial economists give it, **costly state verification.** Costly state verification makes the equity contract less desirable, and it explains, in part, why equity is not a more important element in our financial structure.

As with adverse selection, the free-rider problem decreases the amount of information production that would reduce the moral hazard (principal-agent) problem. In this example, the free-rider problem decreases monitoring. If you know that other stockholders are paying to monitor the activities of the company you hold shares in, you can take a free ride on their activities. Then you can use the money you save by not engaging in monitoring to vacation on a Caribbean island. If you can do this, though, so can other stockholders. Perhaps all the stockholders will go to the islands, and no one will spend any resources on monitoring the firm. The moral hazard problem for shares of common stock will then be severe, making it hard for firms to issue them to raise capital.

Government Regulation to Increase Information As with adverse selection, the government has an incentive to try to reduce the moral hazard problem created by asymmetric information. Governments everywhere have laws to force firms to adhere to standard accounting principles that make profit verification easier. They also pass laws to impose stiff criminal penalties on people who commit the fraud of hiding and stealing profits. However, these measures can only be partly effective. Catching this kind of fraud is not easy; fraudulent managers have the incentive to make it very hard for government agencies to find or prove fraud.

Financial Intermediation Financial intermediaries have the ability to avoid the free-rider problem in the face of moral hazard. One financial intermediary that helps reduce the moral hazard arising from the principal-agent problem is the **venture capital firm.** Venture capital firms pool the resources of their partners and use the funds to help budding entrepreneurs start new businesses. In exchange for the use of the venture capital, the firm receives an equity share in the new business. Because verification of earnings and profits is so important in eliminating moral hazard, venture capital firms usually insist on having several of their own people participate as members of the managing body of the firm, the board of directors, so that they can keep a close watch on the firm's activities. When a venture capital firm supplies start-up funds, the equity in the firm is not marketable to anyone *but* the venture capital firm. Thus other investors are unable to take a free ride on the venture capital firm's verification activities. As a result of this arrangement, the venture capital firm is able to garner the full benefits of its verification activities and is given the appropriate incentives to reduce the moral hazard problem.

Debt Contracts Moral hazard arises with an equity contract, which is a claim on profits in all situations, whether the firm is making or losing money. If a contract could be structured so that moral hazard would exist only in certain situations, there would be a reduced need to monitor managers, and the contract would be more attractive than the equity contract. The debt contract has exactly these attributes because it is a contractual agreement by the borrower to pay the lender *fixed* dollar amounts at periodic intervals. When the firm has high profits, the lender receives the contractual payments and does not need to know the exact profits of the firm. If the managers are hiding profits or are pursuing activities that are personally beneficial but don't increase profitability, the lender doesn't care as long as these activities do not interfere with the ability of the firm to make its debt payments on time. Only when the firm cannot meet its debt payments, thereby being in a state of default, is there a need for the lender to verify the state of the firm's profits. Only in this situation do lenders involved in debt contracts need to act more like equity holders; now they need to know how much income the firm has in order to get their fair share.

The advantage of a less frequent need to monitor the firm, and thus a lower cost of state verification, helps explain why debt contracts are used more frequently than equity contracts to raise capital. The concept of moral hazard thus helps explain puzzle 1, why stocks are not the most important source of financing for businesses.[4]

---

[4]Another factor that encourages the use of debt contracts rather than equity contracts in the United States is our tax code. Debt interest payments are a deductible expense for American firms, whereas dividend payments to equity shareholders are not.

■ HOW MORAL HAZARD INFLUENCES FINANCIAL STRUCTURE IN DEBT MARKETS

Even with the advantages just described, debt contracts are still subject to moral hazard. Because a debt contract requires the borrowers to pay out a fixed amount and lets them keep any profits above this amount, the borrowers have an incentive to take on investment projects that are riskier than the lenders would like.

For example, suppose that because you are concerned about the problem of verifying the profits of Steve's ice-cream store, you decide not to become an equity partner. Instead, you lend Steve the $9000 he needs to set up his business and have a debt contract that pays you an interest rate of 10%. As far as you are concerned, this is a surefire investment because there is a strong and steady demand for ice cream in your neighborhood. However, once you give Steve the funds, he might use them for purposes other than you intended. Instead of opening up the ice-cream store, Steve might use your $9000 loan to invest in chemical research equipment because he thinks he has a 1-in-10 chance of inventing a diet ice cream that tastes every bit as good as the premium brands but has no fat or calories.

Obviously, this is a very risky investment, but if Steve is successful, he will become a multimillionaire. He has a strong incentive to undertake the riskier investment with your money because the gains to him would be so large if he succeeded. You would clearly be very unhappy if Steve used your loan for the riskier investment because if he were unsuccessful, which is highly likely, you would lose most, if not all, of the money you gave him. And if he were successful, you wouldn't share in his success—you would still get only a 10% return on the loan because the principal and interest payments are fixed. Because of the potential moral hazard (Steve might use your money to finance a very risky venture), you would probably not make the loan to Steve, even though an ice-cream store in the neighborhood is a good investment that would provide benefits for everyone.

Tools to Help Solve Moral Hazard in Debt Contracts

Net Worth   When borrowers have more at stake because their *net worth* (the difference between their assets and their liabilities) is high, the risk of moral hazard—the temptation to act in a manner that lenders find objectionable—will be greatly reduced because the borrowers themselves have a lot to lose. Let's return to Steve and his ice-cream business. Suppose that the cost of setting up either the ice-cream store or the research equipment is $100,000 instead of $10,000. So Steve needs to put $91,000 of his own money into the business (instead of $1000) in addition to the $9000 supplied by your loan. Now if Steve is unsuccessful in inventing the no-calorie nonfat ice cream, he has a lot to lose, the $91,000 of net worth ($100,000 in assets minus the $9000 loan from you). He will think twice about undertaking the riskier investment and is more likely to invest in the ice-cream store, which is more of a sure thing. Hence when Steve has more of his own money (net worth) in the business, you are more likely to make him the loan.

One way of describing the solution that high net worth provides to the moral hazard problem is to say that it makes the debt contract **incentive-compatible;** that is, it aligns the incentives of the borrower with those of the lender. The greater the borrower's net worth, the greater the borrower's incentive to behave in the way that the lender expects and desires, the smaller the moral hazard problem in the debt contract is, and the easier it is for the firm to borrow. Conversely, when the borrower's net worth is lower, the moral hazard problem is greater, and it is harder for the firm to borrow.

Monitoring and Enforcement of Restrictive Covenants As the example of Steve and his ice-cream store shows, if you could make sure that Steve doesn't invest in anything riskier than the ice-cream store, it would be worth your while to make him the loan. You can ensure that Steve uses your money for the purpose *you* want it to be used for by writing provisions (restrictive covenants) into the debt contract that restrict his firm's activities. By monitoring Steve's activities to see whether he is complying with the restrictive covenants and enforcing the covenants if he is not, you can make sure that he will not take on risks at your expense.

Restrictive covenants are directed at reducing moral hazard either by ruling out undesirable behavior or by encouraging desirable behavior. There are four types of restrictive covenants that achieve this objective:

1. Covenants can be designed to lower moral hazard by keeping the borrower from engaging in the undesirable behavior of undertaking risky investment projects. Some such covenants mandate that a loan can be used only to finance specific activities, such as the purchase of particular equipment or inventories. Others restrict the borrowing firm from engaging in certain risky business activities, such as purchasing other businesses.

2. Restrictive covenants can encourage the borrower to engage in desirable activities that make it more likely that the loan will be paid off. One restrictive covenant of this type requires the breadwinner in a household to carry life insurance that pays off the mortgage upon that person's death. Restrictive covenants of this type for businesses focus on encouraging the borrowing firm to keep its net worth high because higher borrower net worth reduces moral hazard and makes it less likely that the lender will suffer losses. These restrictive covenants typically specify that the firm must maintain minimum holdings of certain assets relative to the firm's size.

3. Because collateral is an important protection for the lender, restrictive covenants can encourage the borrower to keep the collateral in good condition and make sure that it stays in the possession of the borrower. This is the type of covenant ordinary people encounter most often. Automobile loan contracts, for example, require the car owner to maintain a minimum amount of collision and theft insurance and prevent the sale of the car unless the loan is paid off. Similarly, the recipient of a home mortgage must have adequate insurance on the home and must pay off the mortgage when the property is sold.

4. Restrictive covenants also require a borrowing firm to provide information about its activities periodically in the form of quarterly accounting and income reports, thereby making it easier for the lender to monitor the firm and reduce moral hazard. This type of covenant may also stipulate that the lender has the right to audit and inspect the firm's books at any time.

We now see why debt contracts are often complicated legal documents with numerous restrictions on the borrower's behavior (puzzle 8): Debt contracts require complicated restrictive covenants to lower moral hazard.

Financial Intermediation Although restrictive covenants help reduce the moral hazard problem, they do not eliminate it completely. It is almost impossible to write covenants that rule out *every* risky activity. Furthermore, borrowers may be clever enough to find loopholes in restrictive covenants that make them ineffective.

Another problem with restrictive covenants is that they must be monitored and enforced. A restrictive covenant is meaningless if the borrower can violate it knowing that the lender won't check up or is unwilling to pay for legal recourse. Because monitoring and enforcement of restrictive covenants are costly, the free-rider problem arises in the debt securities (bond) market just as it does in the stock market. If you know that other bondholders are monitoring and enforcing the restrictive covenants, you can free-ride on their monitoring and enforcement. But other bondholders can do the same thing, so the likely outcome is that not enough resources are devoted to monitoring and enforcing the restrictive covenants. Moral hazard therefore continues to be a severe problem for marketable debt.

As we have seen before, financial intermediaries, particularly banks, have the ability to avoid the free-rider problem as long as they primarily make private loans. Private loans are not traded, so no one else can free-ride on the intermediary's monitoring and enforcement of the restrictive covenants. The intermediary making private loans thus receives the benefits of monitoring and enforcement and will work to shrink the moral hazard problem inherent in debt contracts. The concept of moral hazard has provided us with additional reasons why financial intermediaries play a more important role in channeling funds from savers to borrowers than marketable securities do, as described in puzzles 1 through 4.

Summary

The presence of asymmetric information in financial markets leads to adverse selection and moral hazard problems that interfere with the efficient functioning of those markets. Tools to help solve these problems involve the private production and sale of information, government regulation to increase information in financial markets, the importance of collateral and net worth to debt contracts, and the use of monitoring and restrictive covenants. A key finding from our theoretical analysis is that the existence of the free-rider problem for traded securities such as stocks and bonds indicates that financial intermediaries, particularly banks, should play a greater role than securities markets in financing the activities of businesses. Theoretical analysis of the consequences of adverse selection and moral hazard has helped explain the basic features of our financial system and has provided solutions to the eight puzzles about our financial structure outlined at the beginning of this chapter.

APPLICATION	FINANCIAL DEVELOPMENT AND ECONOMIC GROWTH

Recent research has found that an important reason why many developing countries experience very low rates of growth is that their financial systems are underdeveloped (a situation referred to as *financial repression*).[5] The theoretical analysis of financial structure helps explain how an underdeveloped financial system leads to a low state of economic development and economic growth.

The financial systems in developing countries face several difficulties that keep them from operating efficiently. As we have seen, two important tools used to help solve adverse selection and moral hazard problems in credit markets are collateral and restrictive covenants. In many developing countries, the legal system functions poorly, making it hard to make effective use of these two tools. In these countries, bankruptcy procedures are often extremely slow and cumbersome. For example, in many countries, **creditors** (holders of debt) must first sue the defaulting debtor for payment, which can take several years, and then once a favorable judgment has been obtained, the creditor has to sue again to obtain title to the collateral. The process can take in excess of five years, and by the time the lender acquires the collateral, it well may have been neglected and thus have little value. In addition, governments often block lenders from foreclosing on borrowers in politically powerful sectors such as agriculture. Where the market is unable to use collateral effectively, the adverse selection problem will be worse because the lender will need even more information about the quality of the borrower in order to screen out a good loan from a bad one. The result is that it will be harder for lenders to channel funds to borrowers with the most productive investment opportunities, thereby leading to less productive investment and hence a slower-growing economy. Similarly, a poorly developed legal system may make it extremely difficult for borrowers to enforce restrictive covenants. Thus they may have a much more limited ability to reduce moral hazard on the part of borrowers and so will be less willing to lend. Again the outcome will be less productive investment and a lower growth rate for the economy.

Governments in developing countries have also often decided to use their financial systems to direct credit to themselves or to favored sectors of the economy by setting interest rates at artificially low levels for certain types of loans, by creating so-called development finance institutions to make specific types of loans, or by directing existing institutions to lend to certain entities. As we have seen, private institutions have an incentive to solve adverse selection and moral hazard problems and lend to borrowers with the most productive investment opportunities. Governments have less incentive to do so because they are not driven by the profit motive and so their directed credit programs may not channel

[5]See Nouriel Roubini and Xavier Sala-i-Martin, "A Growth Model of Inflation, Tax Evasion and Financial Repression," *Journal of Monetary Economics* 35 (1995): 275–301, for a survey of this literature and a list of further references.

funds to sectors that will produce high growth for the economy. The outcome is again likely to result in less efficient investment and slower growth.

In addition, banks in many developing countries have been nationalized by their governments. Again because of the absence of the profit motive, these nationalized banks have little incentive to allocate their capital to the most productive uses. Indeed, the primary loan customer of these nationalized banks is often the government, which does not always use the funds wisely.

We have seen that government regulation can increase the amount of information in financial markets to make them work more efficiently. Many developing countries have an underdeveloped regulatory apparatus that retards the provision of adequate information to the marketplace. For example, developing countries often have weak accounting standards, making it very hard to ascertain the quality of a borrower's balance sheet. As a result, asymmetric information problems are more severe, and the financial system is severely hampered in channeling funds to the most productive uses.

The institutional environment of a poor legal system, weak accounting standards, inadequate government regulation, and government intervention through directed credit programs and nationalization of banks all help explain why many countries stay poor while others grow richer.

FINANCIAL CRISES AND AGGREGATE ECONOMIC ACTIVITY

Our theoretical analysis of the effects of adverse selection and moral hazard can help us understand **financial crises,** major disruptions in financial markets that are characterized by sharp declines in asset prices and the failures of many financial and nonfinancial firms. Financial crises have been common in most countries throughout modern history. The United States experienced major financial crises in 1819, 1837, 1857, 1873, 1884, 1893, 1907, and 1930–1933 but has had none since then.[6] Studying financial crises is worthwhile because they have led to severe economic downturns in the past and have the potential for doing so in the future.

Financial crises occur when there is a disruption in the financial system that causes such a sharp increase in adverse selection and moral hazard problems in financial markets that the markets are unable to channel funds efficiently from savers to people with productive investment opportunities. As a result of this inability of financial markets to function efficiently, economic activity contracts sharply.

Factors Causing Financial Crises

To understand why banking and financial crises occur and more specifically how they lead to contractions in economic activity, we need to examine the factors that

---

[6]Although we in the United States have not experienced any financial crises since the Great Depression, we have had several close calls—the October 1987 stock market crash, for example. An important reason why we have escaped financial crises is the timely action of the Federal Reserve to prevent them during episodes like that of October 1987. We look at the issue of the Fed's role in preventing financial crises in Chapter 24.

cause them. Four categories of factors can trigger financial crises: increases in interest rates, increases in uncertainty, asset market effects on balance sheets, and bank panics.

Increases in Interest Rates As we saw earlier, individuals and firms with the riskiest investment projects are exactly those who are willing to pay the highest interest rates. If market interest rates are driven up sufficiently because of increased demand for credit or because of a decline in the money supply, good credit risks are less likely to want to borrow while bad credit risks are still willing to borrow. Because of the resulting increase in adverse selection, lenders will no longer want to make loans. The substantial decline in lending will lead to a substantial decline in investment and aggregate economic activity.

Increases in Uncertainty A dramatic increase in uncertainty in financial markets, due perhaps to the failure of a prominent financial or nonfinancial institution, a recession, or a stock market crash, makes it harder for lenders to screen good from bad credit risks. The resulting inability of lenders to solve the adverse selection problem makes them less willing to lend, which leads to a decline in lending, investment, and aggregate activity.

Asset Market Effects on Balance Sheets The state of firms' balance sheets has important implications for the severity of asymmetric information problems in the financial system. A sharp decline in the stock market is one factor that can cause a serious deterioration in firms' balance sheets that can increase adverse selection and moral hazard problems in financial markets and provoke a financial crisis. A decline in the stock market means that the net worth of corporations has fallen because share prices are the valuation of a corporation's net worth. The decline in net worth as a result of a stock market decline makes lenders less willing to lend because, as we have seen, the net worth of a firm plays a role similar to that of collateral. When the value of collateral declines, it provides less protection to lenders, meaning that losses on loans are likely to be more severe. Because lenders are now less protected against the consequences of adverse selection, they decrease their lending, which in turn causes investment and aggregate output to decline. In addition, the decline in corporate net worth as a result of a stock market decline increases moral hazard by providing incentives for borrowing firms to make risky investments, as they now have less to lose if their investments go sour. The resulting increase in moral hazard makes lending less attractive—another reason why a stock market decline and hence a decline in net worth leads to decreased lending and economic activity.

In economies in which inflation has been moderate, which characterizes most industrialized countries, many debt contracts are typically of fairly long maturity with fixed interest rates. In this institutional environment, unanticipated declines in the aggregate price level also decrease the net worth of firms. Because debt payments are contractually fixed in nominal terms, an unanticipated decline in the price level raises the value of firms' liabilities in *real* terms (increases the burden of the debt) but does not raise the real value of firms' assets. The result is that net worth in *real* terms (the difference between assets and liabilities in *real* terms) declines. A sharp drop in the price level therefore causes a substantial decline in real net worth and an increase in adverse selection and moral hazard problems facing lenders. An unanticipated decline in the aggregate price level thus leads to a drop in lending and economic activity.

Because of uncertainty about the future value of the domestic currency in developing countries (and in some industrialized countries), many nonfinancial firms, banks, and governments in these countries find it easier to issue debt denominated in foreign currencies. This can lead to a financial crisis in a fashion similar to an unanticipated decline in inflation. With debt contracts denominated in foreign currency, when there is an unanticipated depreciation or devaluation of the domestic currency, the debt burden of domestic firms increases. Since assets are typically denominated in domestic currency, there is a resulting deterioration in firms' balance sheets and a decline in net worth, which then increases adverse selection and moral hazard problems along the lines just described. The increase in asymmetric information problems leads to a decline in investment and economic activity.

Although we have seen that increases in interest rates have a direct effect on increasing adverse selection problems, increases in interest rates also play a role in promoting a financial crisis through their effect on both firms' and households' balance sheets. A rise in interest rates and therefore in households' and firms' interest payments decreases firms' **cash flow,** the difference between cash receipts and cash expenditures. The decline in cash flow causes a deterioration in the balance sheet because it decreases the liquidity of the household or firm and thus makes it harder for lenders to know whether the firm or household will be able to pay its bills. As a result, adverse selection and moral hazard problems become more severe for potential lenders to these firms and households, leading to a decline in lending and economic activity. There is thus an additional reason why sharp increases in interest rates can be an important factor leading to financial crises.

Bank Panics Banks perform an important financial intermediation role by engaging in information-producing activities that facilitate productive investment for the economy. Consequently, a financial crisis in which many banks go out of business (called a **bank panic**) reduces the amount of financial intermediation undertaken by banks and so leads to a decline in investment and aggregate economic activity. Indeed, even if the banks do not fail but instead just suffer a substantial contraction in their net worth because of bad loans, the banks will have fewer resources to lend and so bank lending will decline, thereby leading to a contraction in economic activity. A decrease in bank lending during a financial crisis also decreases the supply of funds to borrowers, which in turn leads to higher interest rates. Since a rise in interest rates also increases adverse selection in credit markets, bank panics further intensify the decrease in economic activity through this channel as well.

APPLICATION | FINANCIAL CRISES IN THE UNITED STATES

As mentioned, the United States has a long history of banking and financial crises, such crises having occurred every 20 years or so in the nineteenth and early twentieth centuries—in 1819, 1837, 1857, 1873, 1884, 1893, 1907, and 1930–33. Our analysis of the factors that lead to a financial crisis can explain why these crises took place and why they were so damaging to the U.S. economy.

> ■ **STUDY GUIDE** To understand fully what took place in a U.S. financial crisis, make sure that you can state the reasons why each of the factors—increases in interest rates, increases in uncertainty, asset market effects on balance sheets, and bank panics—increases adverse selection and moral hazard problems, which in turn lead to a decline in economic activity. To help you understand these crises, you might want to refer to Figure 3, a diagram that traces the sequence of events in a U.S. financial crisis.

As shown in Figure 3, most financial crises in the United States have begun with a sharp rise in interest rates (frequently stemming from increases in interest rates abroad), a steep stock market decline, and an increase in uncertainty resulting from a failure of major financial or nonfinancial firms (the Ohio Life Insurance & Trust Company in 1857, the Northern Pacific Railroad and Jay Cooke & Company in 1873, Grant & Ward in 1884, the National Cordage Company in 1893, the Knickerbocker Trust Company in 1907, and the Bank of the United States in 1930). During these crises, the increase in uncertainty, the rise in interest rates, and the stock market decline increased the severity of adverse selection problems in credit markets; the stock market decline also increased moral hazard problems. The rise in adverse selection and moral hazard problems then made it less attractive for lenders to lend and led to a decline in investment and aggregate economic activity.

Because of the worsening business conditions and uncertainty about their bank's health (perhaps banks would go broke), depositors began to withdraw their funds from banks, and the massive withdrawal of deposits led to bank failures, which, if they snowballed, led to a full-scale bank panic. The resulting decline in the number of banks raised interest rates even further and decreased the amount of financial intermediation by banks. Worsening of the problems created by adverse selection and moral hazard led to further economic contraction.

Finally, there was a sorting out of firms that were **insolvent** (that had a negative net worth and hence were bankrupt) from healthy firms by bankruptcy proceedings. The same process occurred for banks, often with the help of public and private authorities. Once this sorting out was complete, uncertainty in financial markets declined, the stock market underwent a recovery, and interest rates fell. The overall result was that adverse selection and moral hazard problems diminished and the financial crisis subsided. With the financial markets able to operate well again, the stage was set for the recovery of the economy.

If, however, the economic downturn led to a sharp decline in prices, the recovery process was short-circuited. In this situation, shown in Figure 3, a

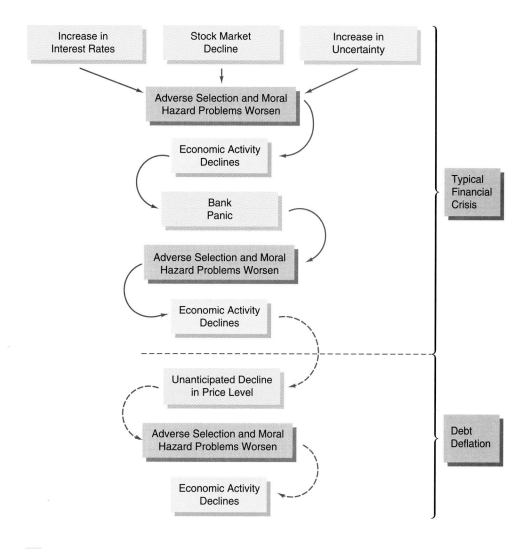

Factors Causing Financial Crises

Consequences of Changes in Factors

■FIGURE 3 Sequence of Events in U.S. Financial Crises

The solid arrows trace the sequence of events in a typical financial crisis; the dotted arrows show the additional set of events that occur if the crisis develops into a debt deflation.

process called **debt deflation** occurred, in which a substantial decline in the price level set in, leading to a further deterioration in firms' net worth because of the increased burden of indebtedness. When debt deflation set in, the adverse selection and moral hazard problems continued to increase so that lending, investment spending, and aggregate economic activity remained depressed for a long time. The most significant financial crisis that included debt deflation was the Great Depression, the worst economic contraction in U.S. history (see Box 2).

| APPLICATION | FINANCIAL CRISES IN DEVELOPING COUNTRIES: MEXICO, 1994–1995 |

In recent years, many developing countries have experienced financial crises, the most dramatic of which was the Mexican crisis of 1994–1995. An important puzzle is how a developing country can shift dramatically from a path of reasonable growth before a financial crisis, as was the case in Mexico in 1994, to a sharp decline in economic activity after a crisis occurs that is very damaging to both the economy and the social fabric of the country. We can again apply our asymmetric information analysis of financial crises to explain this puzzle and to understand the Mexican financial crisis of 1994–95.

BOX 2

Case Study of a Financial Crisis

The Great Depression

Federal Reserve officials viewed the stock market boom of 1928 and 1929, during which stock prices doubled, as excessive speculation. To curb it, they pursued a tight monetary policy to raise interest rates. The Fed got more than it bargained for when the stock market crashed in October 1929.

Although the 1929 crash had a great impact on the minds of a whole generation, most people forget that by the middle of 1930, more than half of the stock market decline had been reversed. What might have been a normal recession turned into something far different, however, with adverse shocks to the agricultural sector, a continuing decline in the stock market after the middle of 1930, and a sequence of bank collapses from October 1930 until March 1933 in which over one-third of the banks in the United States went out of business.

The continuing decline in stock prices after mid-1930 (by mid-1932 stocks had declined to 10% of their value at the 1929 peak) and the increase in uncertainty from the unsettled business conditions created by the economic contraction made adverse selection and moral hazard problems worse in the credit markets. The loss of one-third of the banks reduced the amount of financial intermediation. This intensified adverse selection and moral hazard problems, thereby decreas-

ing the ability of financial markets to channel funds to firms with productive investment opportunities. As our analysis predicts, the amount of outstanding commercial loans fell by half from 1929 to 1933, and investment spending collapsed, declining by 90% from its 1929 level.

The short-circuiting of the process that kept the economy from recovering quickly, which it does in most recessions, occurred because of a fall in the price level by 25% in the 1930–1933 period. This huge decline in prices triggered a debt deflation in which net worth fell because of the increased burden of indebtedness borne by firms. The decline in net worth and the resulting increase in adverse selection and moral hazard problems in the credit markets led to a prolonged economic contraction in which unemployment rose to 25% of the labor force. The financial crisis in the Great Depression was the worst ever experienced in the United States, and it explains why this economic contraction was also the most severe one ever experienced by the nation.*

---

*See Ben Bernanke, "Nonmonetary Effects of the Financial Crisis in the Propagation of the Great Depression," *American Economic Review* 73 (1983): 257–276, for a discussion of the role of asymmetric information problems in the Great Depression period.

Because of the different institutional features of Mexico's debt markets, the sequence of events in the 1994–1995 Mexican banking and financial crisis, which began in December 1994, is different from that which occurred in the United States in the nineteenth and twentieth centuries. Figure 4 provides a diagrammatic exposition of the sequence of events that occurred in the Mexican case.

An important factor leading up to the Mexican financial crisis was the deterioration in banks' balance sheets because of increasing loan losses. When the Mexican banks were privatized in the early 1990s and financial markets were

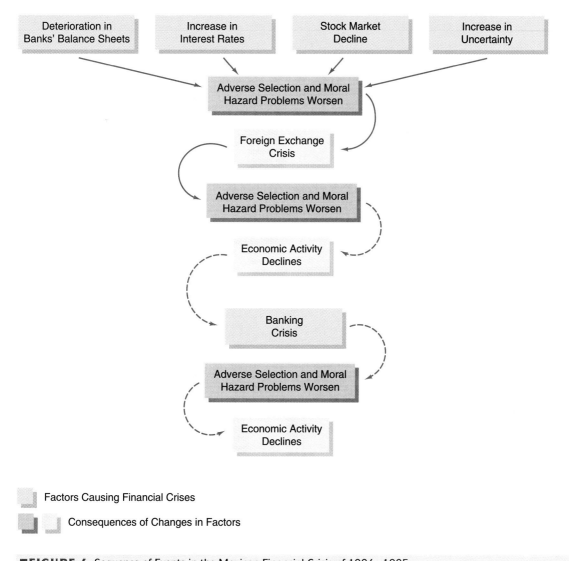

■FIGURE 4 Sequence of Events in the Mexican Financial Crisis of 1994–1995
The arrows trace the sequence of events during the Mexican financial crisis.

deregulated, a lending boom ensued in which bank credit to the private nonfinancial business sector as a fraction of GDP accelerated dramatically, going from 10% of GDP in 1988 to over 40% of GDP in 1994. Because of weak supervision by bank regulators and a lack of expertise in screening and monitoring borrowers at the commercial banks, losses on their loans began to mount, thereby causing an erosion of banks' net worth (capital). As we have seen, this decline in bank capital would mean that the banks would have fewer resources to lend, and this lack of lending would eventually lead to a contraction in economic activity.

Consistent with the U.S. experience in the nineteenth and early twentieth centuries, another precipitating factor to the Mexican financial crisis was a rise in interest rates abroad. Beginning in February 1994, the Federal Reserve began to raise the federal funds rate to head off inflationary pressures. Although the policy was quite successful in keeping inflation in check in the United States, it put upward pressure on Mexican interest rates, increasing asymmetric information problems in the Mexican financial system. Furthermore, the Mexican central bank, the Banco de Mexico, raised interest rates to protect the value of the peso in the foreign exchange market when the peso came under attack beginning in early 1994. The rise in interest rates directly added to increased adverse selection in Mexican financial markets because, as discussed earlier, it made it more likely that the parties willing to take on the most risk would seek loans.

Even more important, increased interest payments caused reductions in households' and firms' cash flow, which led to a deterioration in their balance sheets. A feature of Mexican debt markets is that debt contracts have very short durations, typically less than one month. Thus the rise in Mexican short-term interest rates, which occurred partly as a result of rising short-term rates in the United States, meant that the effect on cash flow and hence on balance sheets would be substantial. As our asymmetric information analysis suggests, this deterioration in households' and firms' balance sheets increased adverse selection and moral hazard problems in Mexican financial markets, making lenders less willing to lend.

Also consistent with the U.S. experience in the nineteenth and early twentieth centuries, increases in uncertainty in Mexican financial markets and a stock market decline precipitated the full-blown financial crisis. The Mexican economy was hit by political shocks in 1994, specifically the assassination of Luis Donaldo Colosio, the ruling party's presidential candidate, and an uprising in the southern state of Chiapas. These events increased general uncertainty in Mexican financial markets. In addition, by the middle of December 1994, stock prices on the Bolsa (stock exchange) had fallen nearly 20% from their September 1994 peak. As we have seen, an increase in uncertainty and the decrease in net worth as a result of the stock market decline increase asymmetric information problems because it becomes harder to screen out good from bad borrowers and the decline in net worth decreases the value of firms' collateral and increases their incentives to make risky investments because there is less equity to lose if the investments are unsuccessful. The increase in uncertainty and the stock market decline, along with increases in interest rates and the deterioration in banks' balance sheets, were the initial conditions that worsened adverse selection and moral hazard problems (shown in the top of the diagram in Figure 4) and made the Mexican economy ripe for a serious financial crisis when a full-blown speculative attack developed in the foreign exchange market.

With the Colosio assassination, the Chiapas uprising, and other political developments, the Mexican peso began to come under attack. Even though the Mexican central bank raised interest rates sharply, it was unable to stem the attack and was forced to devalue the peso on December 20, 1994. (We will return to this in Chapter 25.)

The institutional structure of debt markets in Mexico now interacted with the peso devaluation to propel the economy into a full-fledged financial crisis. When the peso had lost half its value by March 1995, actual and expected inflation rose dramatically, and interest rates on debt denominated in pesos went to sky-high levels, exceeding 100% a year. The Mexican stock market crashed, falling another 30% in peso terms and over 60% in dollar terms. Given the resulting huge increase in interest payments because of the short duration of the Mexican debt, households' and firms' cash flow dropped dramatically, leading to a deterioration in their balance sheets. In addition, because many firms had debts denominated in dollars, the depreciation of the peso resulted in an immediate sharp increase in their indebtedness in pesos, even though the value of their assets remained unchanged. The depreciation of the peso starting in December 1994 led to an especially sharp negative shock to the net worth of private firms, causing a dramatic increase in adverse selection and moral hazard problems. These asymmetric information problems were severe for domestic lenders and foreign lenders as well because they had difficulty obtaining information about what was going on in the Mexican economy. Foreign lenders were thus eager to pull their funds out of Mexico, and this is exactly what they did. Foreign portfolio investment inflows to Mexico, which had been on the order of $20 billion (a year) in 1993 and early 1994, reversed course, and the outflows exceeded $10 billion a year by the fourth quarter of 1994. Consistent with the theory of financial crises outlined in this chapter, the sharp decline in lending helped lead to a collapse of economic activity, with real GDP growth falling from around 4% to 4.5% annually in the last half of 1994 to very negative growth rates in the vicinity of −10% in 1995. Only in 1996, with financial assistance from the United States and the IMF, did the Mexican economy finally start to recover, having suffered serious damage.

As shown in Figure 4, further deterioration to the economy occurred because the collapse in economic activity and the deterioration in the cash flow and balance sheets of both firms and households led to a worsening banking crisis. The problems of firms and households meant that many were no longer able to pay off their debts, resulting in substantial loan losses for the banks. Even more problematic for the Mexican banks was that they had many short-term liabilities denominated in foreign currency, and the sharp increase in the value of these liabilities after the devaluation led to a further deterioration in the banks' balance sheets. Under these circumstances, the banking system would have collapsed in the absence of a government safety net, but the Mexican government came forth with funds to protect depositors, thereby avoiding a bank panic. However, given the banks' loss of capital and the need for the government to intervene to prop up the banks, the banks' ability and willingness to lend were sharply curtailed. As we have seen, a banking crisis of this type hinders the ability of banks to lend and also makes adverse selection and moral hazard problems worse in financial markets because banks are no longer as capable of playing their traditional financial intermediation role. The banking crisis, along with the other factors that increased adverse selection and moral hazard problems in Mexican credit markets, explains the collapse of lending and hence in economic activity in the aftermath of the financial crisis.

SUMMARY

1. There are eight basic puzzles about our financial structure. The first four emphasize the importance of financial intermediaries and the relative unimportance of securities markets for the financing of corporations; the fifth recognizes that financial markets are among the most heavily regulated sectors of the economy; the sixth states that only large, well-established corporations have access to securities markets; the seventh indicates that collateral is an important feature of debt contracts; and the eighth presents debt contracts as complicated legal documents that place substantial restrictions on the behavior of the borrower.

2. Transaction costs freeze many small savers and borrowers out of direct involvement with financial markets. Financial intermediaries can take advantage of economies of scale and are better able to develop expertise to lower transaction costs, thus enabling their savers and borrowers to benefit from the existence of financial markets.

3. Asymmetric information results in two problems: adverse selection, which occurs before the transaction, and moral hazard, which occurs after the transaction. Adverse selection refers to the fact that bad credit risks are the ones most likely to seek loans, and moral hazard refers to the risk of the borrower's engaging in activities that are undesirable from the lender's point of view.

4. Adverse selection interferes with the efficient functioning of financial markets. Tools to help reduce the adverse selection problem include private production and sale of information, government regulation to increase information, financial intermediation, and collateral and net worth. The free-rider problem occurs when people who do not pay for information take advantage of information that other people have paid for. This problem explains why financial intermediaries, particularly banks, play a more important role in financing the activities of businesses than securities markets do.

5. Moral hazard in equity contracts is known as the principal-agent problem because managers (the agents) have less incentive to maximize profits than stockholders (the principals). The principal-agent problem explains why debt contracts are so much more prevalent in financial markets than equity contracts. Tools to help reduce the principal-agent problem include monitoring, government regulation to increase information, and financial intermediation.

6. Tools to reduce the moral hazard problem in debt contracts include net worth, monitoring and enforcement of restrictive covenants, and financial intermediaries.

7. Financial crises are major disruptions in financial markets. They are caused by increases in adverse selection and moral hazard problems that prevent financial markets from channeling funds to people with productive investment opportunities, leading to a sharp contraction in economic activity. The four types of factors that lead to financial crises are increases in interest rates, increases in uncertainty, asset market effects on balance sheets, and bank panics.

KEY TERMS

bank panic, p. 313
cash flow, p. 313
collateral, p. 295
costly state verification, p. 305
creditor, p. 310
debt deflation, p. 315

financial crisis, p. 311
free-rider problem, p. 299
incentive-compatible, p. 308
insolvent, p. 314
net worth (equity capital),
    p. 302

principal-agent problem, p. 303
restrictive covenants, p. 295
secured debt, p. 295
unsecured debt, p. 295
venture capital firm, p. 306

QUESTIONS AND PROBLEMS

1. How can economies of scale help explain the existence of financial intermediaries?

*2. Describe two ways in which financial intermediaries help lower transaction costs in the economy.

3. Would moral hazard and adverse selection still arise in financial markets if information were not asymmetric? Explain your answer.

*4. How do standard accounting principles required by the government help financial markets work more efficiently?

5. Do you think the lemons problem would be more severe for stocks traded on the New York Stock Exchange or those traded over-the-counter? Explain your answer.

*6. Which firms are most likely to use bank financing rather than to issue bonds or stocks to finance their activities? Why?

7. How can the existence of asymmetric information provide a rationale for government regulation of financial markets?

*8. Would you be more willing to lend to a friend if she put all of her life savings into her business than you would if she had not done so? Why?

9. Rich individuals often worry that people will seek to marry them only for their money. Is this a problem of adverse selection?

*10. "The more collateral there is backing a loan, the less the lender has to worry about adverse selection." Is this statement true, false, or uncertain? Explain your answer.

11. How does the free-rider problem aggravate adverse selection and moral hazard problems in financial markets?

*12. Explain how the separation of ownership and control in American corporations might lead to poor management.

13. Is a financial crisis more likely to occur when the economy is experiencing deflation or inflation? Explain your answer.

*14. How can a stock market crash provoke a financial crisis?

15. How can a sharp rise in interest rates provoke a financial crisis?

CHAPTER 13

THE BANKING FIRM AND BANK MANAGEMENT

PREVIEW Because banks (depository institutions) play such a major role in channeling funds to borrowers with productive investment opportunities, they are important in ensuring that the financial system and the economy run smoothly and efficiently. In the United States, banks supply over $5 trillion of credit annually. They provide loans to businesses, help us finance our college educations or the purchase of a new car or home, and provide us with services such as checking and savings accounts.

In this chapter we examine how banks, the most important of all the financial intermediaries, operate to earn the highest profits possible: how and why they make loans, how they acquire funds and manage their assets and liabilities (debts), and how they earn income. Although we focus on commercial banks because they hold over two-thirds of the assets in the banking system, the principles are equally applicable to other types of banking institutions, such as savings and loans, mutual savings banks, and credit unions. Furthermore, many of the principles of bank management discussed here also apply to many other financial institutions.

THE BANK BALANCE SHEET

To understand how a bank operates, first we need to examine its **balance sheet,** a list of the bank's assets and liabilities. As the name implies, this list balances; that is, it has the characteristic that

$$\text{Total assets} = \text{total liabilities} + \text{capital}$$

Furthermore, a bank's balance sheet lists *sources* of bank funds (liabilities) and *uses* to which they are put (assets). Banks obtain funds by borrowing and by issuing other liabilities such as deposits. They then use these funds to acquire assets such as securities and loans. Banks make profits by charging an interest rate on their holdings of securities and loans that is higher than the expenses on their liabilities. The balance sheet of all commercial banks at the end of 1996 appears in Table 1.

Liabilities

A bank acquires funds by issuing (selling) liabilities, which are consequently also referred to as *sources of funds*. The funds obtained from issuing liabilities are used to purchase income-earning assets.

Checkable Deposits Checkable deposits are bank accounts that allow the owner of the account to write checks to third parties. Checkable deposits include all accounts on which checks can be drawn: non-interest-bearing checking accounts (demand deposits), interest-bearing NOW (negotiable order of withdrawal) accounts, and money market deposit accounts (MMDAs). Introduced with the Depository Institutions Act in 1982, MMDAs have similar features to money market mutual funds and are included in the checkable deposits category. However, MMDAs differ from checkable deposits in that they are not subject to reserve requirements (discussed later in the chapter) like checkable deposits. Table 1 shows that the category of checkable deposits is an important source of bank funds, making up 17% of bank liabilities. Once checkable deposits were the most important source of bank funds (over 60% of bank liabilities in 1960), but with the appearance of new, more attractive financial instruments such as money market mutual funds, the share of checkable deposits in total bank liabilities has shrunk over time.

■ TABLE 1   Balance Sheet of All Commercial Banks (items as a percentage of the total, end of 1996)

Assets (Uses of Funds)*		Liabilities (Sources of Funds)	
Reserves	1	Checkable deposits	17
Cash items in process of collection +		Nontransaction deposits	
deposits at other banks	4	Small-denomination time deposits	
Securities		(< $100,000) + savings deposits	37
U.S. government and agency	15	Large-denomination time deposits	12
State and local government and		Borrowings	26
other securities	6	Bank capital	8
Loans			
Commercial and industrial	18		
Real estate	25		
Consumer	12		
Interbank	5		
Other	8		
Other assets (for example,	6		
physical capital)			
Total	100	Total	100

*In order of decreasing liquidity.
Source: Federal Reserve *Bulletin.*

Checkable deposits and money market deposit accounts are payable on demand; that is, if a depositor shows up at the bank and requests payment by making a withdrawal, the bank must pay the depositor immediately. Similarly, if a person who receives a check written on an account from a bank presents that check at the bank, it must pay the funds out immediately (or credit them to that person's account).

A checkable deposit is an asset for the depositor because it is part of his or her wealth. Conversely, because the depositor can withdraw funds from an account that the bank is obligated to pay, checkable deposits are a liability for the bank. They are usually the lowest-cost source of bank funds because depositors are willing to forgo some interest in order to have access to a liquid asset that can be used to make purchases. The bank's costs of maintaining checkable deposits include interest payments and the costs incurred in servicing these accounts—processing and storing canceled checks, preparing and sending out monthly statements, providing efficient tellers (human or otherwise), maintaining an impressive building and conveniently located branches, and advertising and marketing to entice customers to deposit their funds with a given bank. In recent years, interest paid on deposits (checkable and time) has accounted for around 45% of total bank operating expenses, while the costs involved in servicing accounts (employee salaries, building rent, and so on) have been approximately 50% of operating expenses.

Nontransaction Deposits Nontransaction deposits are the primary source of bank funds (49% of bank liabilities in Table 1). Owners cannot write checks on nontransaction deposits, but the interest rates are usually higher than those on checkable deposits. There are two basic types of nontransaction deposits: savings accounts and time deposits (also called certificates of deposit, or CDs).

Savings accounts were once the most common type of nontransaction deposit. In these accounts, to which funds can be added or from which funds can be withdrawn at any time, transactions and interest payments are recorded in a monthly statement or in a small book (the passbook) held by the owner of the account.

Time deposits have a fixed maturity length, ranging from several months to over five years, and have substantial penalties for early withdrawal (the forfeiture of several months' interest). Small-denomination time deposits (deposits of less than $100,000) are less liquid for the depositor than passbook savings, earn higher interest rates, and are a more costly source of funds for the banks.

Large-denomination time deposits (CDs) are available in denominations of $100,000 or over and are typically bought by corporations or other banks. Large-denomination CDs are negotiable; like bonds, they can be resold in a secondary market before they mature. For this reason, negotiable CDs are held by corporations, money market mutual funds, and other financial institutions as alternative assets to Treasury bills and other short-term bonds. Since 1961, when they first appeared, negotiable CDs have become an important source of bank funds (12%).

Borrowings Banks obtain funds by borrowing from the Federal Reserve System, other banks, and corporations. Borrowings from the Fed are called **discount loans** (also known as *advances*). Banks also borrow reserves overnight in the federal (fed) funds market from other U.S. banks and financial institutions. Banks borrow funds overnight in order to have enough deposits at the Federal Reserve to meet the amount required by the Fed. Other sources of borrowed funds are loans made to banks by their parent companies (bank holding companies), loan arrangements with corporations (such as repurchase agreements), and borrowings of Eurodollars (deposits denominated in U.S. dollars residing in foreign banks or foreign branches of U.S. banks). Borrowings have become a more important source of bank funds over time: In 1960, they made up only 2% of bank liabilities; currently, they exceed 25% of bank liabilities.

Bank Capital The final category on the liabilities side of the balance sheet is bank capital, the bank's net worth, which equals the difference between total assets and liabilities (8% of total bank assets in Table 1). The funds are raised by selling new equity (stock) or from retained earnings. Bank capital is a cushion against a drop in the value of its assets, which could force the bank into insolvency (when the value of bank assets falls below its liabilities, meaning that the bank is bankrupt). One important component of bank capital is *loan loss reserves,* which are described in Box 1.

Assets

A bank uses the funds that it has acquired by issuing liabilities to purchase income-earning assets. Bank assets are thus naturally referred to as *uses of funds,* and the interest payments earned on them are what enable banks to make profits.

Reserves All banks hold some of the funds they acquire as deposits in an account at the Fed. **Reserves** are these deposits plus currency that is physically held by banks (called **vault cash** because it is stored in bank vaults overnight). Although reserves currently do not pay any interest, banks hold them for two reasons. First, some reserves, called **required reserves,** are held because, by law, the Fed requires that for every dollar of checkable deposits at a bank, a certain fraction (10 cents, for example) must be kept as reserves. This fraction (10% in the example) is called the **required reserve ratio.** Banks hold additional reserves, called **excess reserves,** because they are the most liquid of all bank assets and can be used by a bank to meet its obligations when funds are withdrawn, either directly by a depositor or indirectly when a check is written on an account.

Cash Items in Process of Collection Suppose that a check written on an account at another bank is deposited in your bank and the funds for this check have not yet been received (collected) from the other bank. The check is classified as a cash item in process of collection, and it is an asset for your bank because it is a claim on another bank for funds that will be paid within a few days.

Deposits at Other Banks Many small banks hold deposits in larger banks in exchange for a variety of services, including check collection, foreign exchange transactions, and help with securities purchases. This is an aspect of a system called *correspondent banking.*

■ **BOX 1**

Understanding Loan Loss Reserves

Perhaps you have seen headlines in the press about a bank's large increase in loan loss (bad debt) reserves. Often there is confusion about loan loss reserves, perhaps because they have a similar-sounding name to the "reserves" item on a bank's balance sheet. Actually, loan loss reserves have nothing to do with the reserves shown on the assets side of the balance sheet; rather, they are a component of the liabilities item known as bank capital.

To see how loan loss reserves work, suppose that a bank suspects that some of its loans, say, $1 million worth, might prove to be bad debts that will have to be written off (valued at zero) in the future. The bank can set aside $1 million of its earnings and put it into its loan loss reserves account. Because the $1 million is now retained earnings, it adds to the difference between the bank's assets and liabilities and so increases bank capital. The fact that adding to loan loss reserves increases bank capital explains why loan loss reserves are counted as a component of capital. As a result of adding to loan loss reserves, the bank reduces its reported earnings by $1 million, even though it has

not yet actually lost the $1 million—in effect, taking its lumps even before the bad debt is written off.

If the bank eventually determines that the $1 million loan will never be paid back and formally writes it off, it reduces the value of its assets by $1 million. The resulting $1 million decline in bank capital is reflected as a decrease in the loan loss reserves account by $1 million. At this time, however, reported earnings are unaffected by the loan write-off because they were reduced earlier when the bank set aside $1 million of earnings as loan loss reserves.

Banks add to loan loss reserves before a bad loan has to be written off because it is better for them to allow for the loss when they have plenty of earnings rather than to wait and find that they must take the loss when they have little in earnings to write the loan off against. In addition, adding to loan loss reserves, which reduces reported earnings, can reduce the amount of taxes a bank has to pay and is also a way of informing the bank's stockholders, depositors, and regulators of potential future losses on loans.

Collectively, reserves, cash items in process of collection, and deposits at other banks are often referred to as *cash items*. In Table 1 they constitute only 5% of total assets, and their importance has been shrinking over time: In 1960, for example, they accounted for 20% of total assets.

Securities A bank's holdings of securities are an important income-earning asset: Securities (made up entirely of debt instruments for commercial banks because banks are not allowed to hold stock) account for 21% of bank assets in Table 1, and they provide commercial banks with about 15% of their revenue. These securities can be classified into three categories: U.S. government and agency securities, state and local government securities, and other securities. U.S. government and agency securities are the most liquid because they can be easily traded and converted into cash with low transaction costs. Because of their high liquidity, short-term U.S. government securities are called **secondary reserves.**

State and local government securities are desirable for banks to hold primarily because state and local governments are more likely to do business with banks that hold their securities. In addition, state and local government securities purchased before August 1986 have substantial tax advantages for banks because their interest payments are deductible from income taxes, and 80% of the interest costs associated with the funding of their purchase is deductible. State and local government and other securities are less marketable (hence less liquid) and are also riskier than U.S. government securities, primarily because of default risk: There is some possibility that the issuer of the securities may not be able to make its interest payments or pay back the face value of the securities when they mature.

Loans Banks make their profits primarily by issuing loans. In Table 1, some 68% of bank assets are in the form of loans, and in recent years they have generally produced more than half of bank revenues. A loan is a liability for the individual or corporation receiving it but an asset for a bank because it provides income to the bank. Loans are typically less liquid than other assets because they cannot be turned into cash until the loan matures. If the bank makes a one-year loan, for example, it cannot get its funds back until the loan comes due in one year. Loans also have a higher probability of default than other assets. Because of the lack of liquidity and higher default risk, the bank earns its highest return on loans.

As you can see in Table 1, the largest categories of loans for commercial banks are commercial and industrial loans made to businesses and real estate loans. Commercial banks also make consumer loans and lend to each other. The bulk of these interbank loans are overnight loans lent in the federal funds market. The major difference in the balance sheets of the various depository institutions is primarily in the type of loan in which they specialize. Savings and loans and mutual savings banks, for example, specialize in residential mortgages, while credit unions tend to make consumer loans.

Other Assets The physical capital (bank buildings, computers, and other equipment) owned by the banks is included in this category.

■ BASIC OPERATION OF A BANK

Before proceeding to more detailed study of how a bank manages its assets and liabilities in order to make the highest profit, you should understand the basic operation of a bank.

In general terms, banks make profits by selling liabilities with one set of characteristics (a particular combination of liquidity, risk, and return) and using the proceeds to buy assets with a different set of characteristics. This process is often referred to as *asset transformation.* Instead of making a mortgage loan directly to a neighbor, a person can hold a savings deposit that enables a bank to use the funds provided by the deposit to make the loan to the neighbor. The bank has, in effect, transformed the savings deposit (an asset held by the depositor) into a mortgage loan (an asset held by the bank). Another way this process of asset transformation is described is to say that the bank "borrows short and lends long" because it makes long-term loans and funds them by issuing short-dated deposits.

The process of transforming assets and providing a set of services (check clearing, record keeping, credit analysis, and so forth) is like any other production process in a firm. If the bank produces desirable services at low cost and earns substantial income on its assets, it earns profits; if not, the bank suffers losses.

To make our analysis of the operation of a bank more concrete, we use a tool called a **T-account.** A T-account is a simplified balance sheet, with lines in the form of a T, that lists only the changes that occur in balance sheet items starting from some initial balance sheet position. Let's say that Jane Brown has heard that the First National Bank provides excellent service, so she opens a checking account with a $100 bill. She now has a $100 checkable deposit at the bank, which shows up as a $100 liability on the bank's balance sheet. The bank now puts her $100 bill into its vault so that the bank's assets rise by the $100 increase in vault cash. The T-account for the bank looks like this:

First National Bank

Assets		Liabilities	
Vault cash	+$100	Checkable deposits	+$100

Since vault cash is also part of the bank's reserves, we can rewrite the T-account as follows:

Assets		Liabilities	
Reserves	+$100	Checkable deposits	+$100

Note that Jane Brown's opening of a checking account leads to *an increase in the bank's reserves equal to the increase in checkable deposits.*

If Jane had opened her account with a $100 check written on an account at another bank, say, the Second National Bank, we would get the same result. The initial effect on the T-account of the First National Bank is as follows:

Assets		Liabilities	
Cash items in process of collection	+$100	Checkable deposits	+$100

Checkable deposits increase by $100 as before, but now the First National Bank is owed $100 by the Second National Bank. This asset for the First National Bank is entered in the T-account as $100 of cash items in process of collection because the First National Bank will now try to collect the funds that it is owed. It could go directly to the Second National Bank and ask for payment of the funds, but if the two banks are in separate states, that would be a time-consuming and costly process. Instead, the First National Bank deposits the check in its account at the Fed, and the Fed collects the funds from the Second National Bank. The result is that the Fed transfers $100 of reserves from the Second National Bank to the First National Bank, and the final balance sheet positions of the two banks are as follows:

First National Bank			**Second National Bank**		
Assets		Liabilities	Assets		Liabilities
Reserves +$100		Checkable deposits +$100	Reserves −$100		Checkable deposits −$100

The process initiated by Jane Brown can be summarized as follows: When a check written on an account at one bank is deposited in another, the bank receiving the deposit gains reserves equal to the amount of the check, while the bank on which the check is written sees its reserves fall by the same amount. Therefore, ***when a bank receives additional deposits, it gains an equal amount of reserves; when it loses deposits, it loses an equal amount of reserves.***

> **■ STUDY GUIDE** T-accounts are used to study various topics throughout this text. Whenever you see a T-account, try to analyze what would happen if the opposite action were taken; for example, what would happen if Jane Brown decided to close her $100 account at the First National Bank by writing a $100 check and depositing it in a new checking account at the Second National Bank?

Now that you understand how banks gain and lose reserves, we can examine how a bank rearranges its balance sheet to make a profit when it experiences a change in its deposits. Let's return to the situation when the First National Bank has just received the extra $100 of checkable deposits. As you know, the bank is obliged to keep a certain fraction of its checkable deposits as required reserves. If the fraction (the required reserve ratio) is 10%, the First National Bank's required reserves have increased by $10, and we can rewrite its T-account as follows:

	First National Bank		
Assets		Liabilities	
Required reserves	+$10	Checkable deposits	+$100
Excess reserves	+$90		

Let's see how well the bank is doing as a result of the additional checkable deposits. Because reserves pay no interest, it has no income from the additional $100 of assets. But servicing the extra $100 of checkable deposits is costly because the bank must keep records, pay tellers, return canceled checks, pay for check clearing, and so forth. The bank is making a loss! The situation is even worse if the bank makes interest payments on the deposits, as with NOW accounts. If it is to make a profit, the bank must put to productive use all or part of the $90 of excess reserves it has available.

Let us assume that the bank chooses not to hold any excess reserves but to make loans instead. The T-account then looks like this:

Assets		Liabilities	
Required reserves	+$10	Checkable deposits	+$100
Loans	+$90		

The bank is now making a profit because it holds short-term liabilities such as checkable deposits and uses the proceeds to buy longer-term assets such as loans with higher interest rates. As mentioned earlier, this process of asset transformation is frequently described by saying that banks are in the business of "borrowing short and lending long." For example, if the loans have an interest rate of 10% per year, the bank earns $9 in income from its loans over the year. If the $100 of checkable deposits is in a NOW account with a 5% interest rate and it costs another $3 per year to service the account, the cost per year of these deposits is $8. The bank's profit on the new deposits is then $1 per year (a 1% return on assets).

■ GENERAL PRINCIPLES OF BANK MANAGEMENT

Now that you have some idea of how a bank operates, let's look at how a bank manages its assets and liabilities in order to earn the highest possible profit. The bank manager has four primary concerns. The first is to make sure that the bank has enough ready cash to pay its depositors when there are **deposit outflows,** that is, when deposits are lost because depositors make withdrawals and demand payment. To keep enough cash on hand, the bank must engage in **liquidity management,** the acquisition of sufficiently liquid assets to meet the bank's obligations to depositors. Second, the bank manager must pursue an acceptably low level of risk by acquiring assets that have a low rate of default and by diversifying asset holdings **(asset management).** The third concern is to acquire funds at low cost **(liability management).** Finally, the manager must decide the amount of capital the bank should maintain and then acquire the needed capital **(capital adequacy management).**

To understand bank management fully, we must go beyond the general principles of bank asset and liability management described next and look in more detail at how a bank manages its assets. In Chapter 20 we look at how managers of financial institutions such as banks manage risk, specifically, **credit risk,** the risk arising because borrowers may default, and **interest-rate risk,** the riskiness of earnings and returns on bank assets that results from fluctuations in interest rates.

Liquidity Management and the Role of Reserves

Let us see how a typical bank, the First National Bank, can deal with deposit outflows that occur when its depositors withdraw cash from checking or savings accounts or write checks that are deposited in other banks. In the example that follows, we assume that the bank has ample excess reserves and that all deposits have the same required reserve ratio of 10% (the bank is required to keep 10% of its time and checkable deposits as reserves). Suppose that the First National Bank's initial balance sheet is as follows:

Assets		Liabilities	
Reserves	$20 million	Deposits	$100 million
Loans	$80 million	Bank capital	$ 10 million
Securities	$10 million		

The bank's required reserves are 10% of $100 million, or $10 million. Since it holds $20 million of reserves, the First National Bank has excess reserves of $10 million. If a deposit outflow of $10 million occurs, the bank's balance sheet becomes

Assets		Liabilities	
Reserves	$10 million	Deposits	$90 million
Loans	$80 million	Bank capital	$10 million
Securities	$10 million		

The bank loses $10 million of deposits *and* $10 million of reserves, but since its required reserves are now 10% of only $90 million ($9 million), its reserves still exceed this amount by $1 million. In short, ***if a bank has ample reserves, a deposit outflow does not necessitate changes in other parts of its balance sheet.***

The situation is quite different when a bank holds insufficient excess reserves. Let's assume that instead of initially holding $10 million in excess reserves, the First National Bank makes loans of $10 million, so that it holds no excess reserves. Its initial balance sheet would be

Assets		Liabilities	
Reserves	$10 million	Deposits	$100 million
Loans	$90 million	Bank capital	$ 10 million
Securities	$10 million		

When it suffers the $10 million deposit outflow, its balance sheet becomes

Assets		Liabilities	
Reserves	$ 0	Deposits	$90 million
Loans	$90 million	Bank capital	$10 million
Securities	$10 million		

After $10 million has been withdrawn from deposits and hence reserves, the bank has a problem: It has a reserve requirement of 10% of $90 million, or $9 million, but it has no reserves! To eliminate this shortfall, the bank has four basic options. One is to acquire reserves to meet a deposit outflow by borrowing them from other banks in the federal funds market or by borrowing from corporations.[1] If the First National Bank acquires the $9 million shortfall in reserves by borrowing it from other banks or corporations, its balance sheet becomes

Assets		Liabilities	
Reserves	$ 9 million	Deposits	$90 million
Loans	$90 million	Borrowings from other	
Securities	$10 million	banks or corporations	$ 9 million
		Bank capital	$10 million

---

[1]One way that the First National Bank can borrow from other banks and corporations is by selling negotiable certificates of deposit. This method for obtaining funds is discussed in the section on liability management.

The cost of this activity is the interest rate on these loans, such as the federal funds rate.

A second alternative is for the bank to sell some of its securities to help cover the deposit outflow. For example, it might sell $9 million of its securities and deposit the proceeds with the Fed, resulting in the following balance sheet:

Assets		Liabilities	
Reserves	$ 9 million	Deposits	$90 million
Loans	$90 million	Bank capital	$10 million
Securities	$ 1 million		

The bank incurs some brokerage and other transaction costs when it sells these securities. The U.S. government securities that are classified as secondary reserves are very liquid, so the transaction costs of selling them are quite modest. However, the other securities the bank holds are less liquid and the transaction costs can be appreciably higher.

A third way that the bank can meet a deposit outflow is to acquire reserves by borrowing from the Fed. In our example, the First National Bank could leave its security and loan holdings the same and borrow $9 million in discount loans from the Fed. Its balance sheet would be

Assets		Liabilities	
Reserves	$ 9 million	Deposits	$90 million
Loans	$90 million	Discount loans from	
Securities	$10 million	the Fed	$ 9 million
		Bank capital	$10 million

There are two costs associated with discount loans. First is the interest rate that must be paid to the Fed (called the **discount rate**). The second is a nonexplicit cost resulting from the Fed's discouragement of too much borrowing from it. If a bank takes out too many discount loans, the Fed may refuse to let it borrow further. In popular parlance, the Fed can "close down the discount window" for that bank.

Finally, a bank can acquire the $9 million of reserves to meet the deposit outflow by reducing its loans by this amount and depositing the $9 million it then receives with the Fed, thereby increasing its reserves by $9 million. This transaction changes the balance sheet as follows:

Assets		Liabilities	
Reserves	$ 9 million	Deposits	$90 million
Loans	$81 million	Bank capital	$10 million
Securities	$10 million		

The First National Bank is once again in good shape because its $9 million of reserves satisfies the reserve requirement.

However, this process of reducing its loans is the bank's costliest way of acquiring reserves when there is a deposit outflow. If the First National Bank has numerous short-term loans renewed at fairly short intervals, it can reduce its total amount of loans outstanding fairly quickly by *calling in* loans—that is, by not renewing some loans when they come due. Unfortunately for the bank, this is likely to antagonize the customers whose loans are not being renewed because they have not done anything to deserve such treatment. Indeed, they are likely to take their business elsewhere in the future, a very costly consequence for the bank.

A second method for reducing its loans is for the bank to sell them off to other banks. Again, this is very costly because other banks do not personally know the customers who have taken out the loans and so may not be willing to buy the loans at their full value.

The foregoing discussion explains why banks hold excess reserves even though loans or securities earn a higher return. When a deposit outflow occurs, holding excess reserves allows the bank to escape the costs of (1) borrowing from other banks or corporations, (2) selling securities, (3) borrowing from the Fed, or (4) calling in or selling off loans. ***Excess reserves are insurance against the costs associated with deposit outflows. The higher the costs associated with deposit outflows, the more excess reserves banks will want to hold.***

Just as you and I would be willing to pay an insurance company to insure us against a casualty loss such as the theft of a car, a bank is willing to pay the cost of holding excess reserves (the opportunity cost, which is the earnings forgone by not holding income-earning assets such as loans or securities) in order to insure against losses due to deposit outflows. Because excess reserves, like insurance, have a cost, banks also take other steps to protect themselves; for example, they might shift their holdings of assets to more liquid securities (secondary reserves).

■ **STUDY GUIDE**   Bank management is easier to grasp if you put yourself in the banker's shoes and imagine what you would do in the situations described. To understand a bank's possible responses to deposit outflows, imagine how you as a banker might respond to two successive deposit outflows of $10 million.

Asset Management

Now that you understand why a bank has a need for liquidity, we can examine the basic strategy a bank pursues in managing its assets. To maximize its profits, a bank must simultaneously seek the highest returns possible on loans and securities, reduce risk, and make adequate provisions for liquidity by holding liquid assets. Banks try to accomplish these three goals in four basic ways.

First, banks try to find borrowers who will pay high interest rates and are unlikely to default on their loans. They seek out loan business by advertising their borrowing rates and by approaching corporations directly to solicit loans. It is up to the bank's loan officer to decide if potential borrowers are good credit risks who will make interest and principal payments on time. Typically, banks are conservative in their loan policies; the default rate is usually less than 1%. It is important, however, that banks not be so conservative that they miss out on attractive lending opportunities that earn high interest rates.

Second, banks try to purchase securities with high returns and low risk. Third, in managing their assets, banks must attempt to lower risk by diversifying. They accomplish this by purchasing many different types of assets (short- and long-term, U.S. Treasury, and municipal bonds) and approving many types of loans to a number of customers. Banks that have not sufficiently sought the benefits of diversification often come to regret it later. For example, banks that had overspecialized in making loans to energy companies, real estate developers, or farmers suffered huge losses in the 1980s with the slump in energy, property, and farm prices. Indeed, many of these banks went broke because they had "put too many eggs in one basket."

Finally, the bank must manage the liquidity of its assets so that it can satisfy its reserve requirements without bearing huge costs. This means that it will hold liquid securities even if they earn a somewhat lower return than other assets. The bank must decide, for example, how much excess reserves must be held to avoid costs from a deposit outflow. In addition, it will want to hold short-term U.S. government securities as secondary reserves so that even if a deposit outflow forces some costs on the bank, these will not be terribly high. Again, it is not wise for a bank to be too conservative. If it avoids all costs associated with deposit outflows by holding only excess reserves, losses are suffered because reserves earn no interest, while the bank's liabilities are costly to maintain. The bank must balance its desire for liquidity against the increased earnings that can be obtained from less liquid assets such as loans.

Liability Management

Before the 1960s, liability management was a staid affair: For the most part, banks took their liabilities as fixed and spent their time trying to achieve an optimal mix of assets. There were two main reasons for the emphasis on asset management. First, over 60% of the sources of bank funds were obtained through checkable (demand) deposits that by law could not pay any interest. Thus banks could not actively compete with one another for these deposits, and so their amount was effectively a given for an individual bank. Second, because the markets for making overnight loans between banks were not well developed, banks rarely borrowed from other banks to meet their reserve needs.

Starting in the 1960s, however, large banks (called **money center banks**) in key financial centers, such as New York, Chicago, and San Francisco, began to explore ways in which the liabilities on their balance sheets could provide them with reserves and liquidity. This led to an expansion of overnight loans markets, such as the federal funds market, and the development of new financial instruments such as negotiable CDs (first developed in 1961), which enabled money center banks to acquire funds quickly.[2]

---

[2]Because small banks are not as well known as money center banks and so might be a higher credit risk, they find it harder to raise funds in the negotiable CD market. Hence they do not engage nearly as actively in liability management.

This new flexibility in liability management meant that banks could take a different approach to bank management. They no longer needed to depend on checkable deposits as the primary source of bank funds and as a result no longer treated their sources of funds (liabilities) as given. Instead, they aggressively set target goals for their asset growth and tried to acquire funds (by issuing liabilities) as they were needed.

For example, today, when a money center bank finds an attractive loan opportunity, it can acquire funds by selling a negotiable CD. Or if it has a reserve shortfall, funds can be borrowed from another bank in the federal funds market without incurring high transaction costs. The federal funds market can also be used to finance loans.

The emphasis on liability management explains some of the important changes over the past three decades in the composition of banks' balance sheets. While negotiable CDs and bank borrowings have greatly increased in importance as a source of bank funds in recent years (rising from 2% of bank liabilities in 1960 to 38% by the end of 1996), checkable deposits have decreased in importance (from 61% of bank liabilities in 1960 to 17% by the end of 1996). Newfound flexibility in liability management and the search for higher profits have also stimulated banks to increase the proportion of their assets held in loans, which earn higher income (from 46% of bank assets in 1960 to 68% by the end of 1996).

Capital Adequacy Management

Banks have to make decisions about the amount of capital they need to hold for three reasons. First, bank capital helps prevent *bank failure,* a situation in which the bank cannot satisfy its obligations to pay its depositors and other creditors and so goes out of business. Second, the amount of capital affects returns for the owners (equity holders) of the bank. And third, a minimum amount of bank capital (bank capital requirements) is required by regulatory authorities.

How Bank Capital Helps Prevent Bank Failure Let's consider two banks with identical balance sheets, except that the High Capital Bank has a ratio of capital to assets of 10% while the Low Capital Bank has a ratio of 4%.

High Capital Bank				Low Capital Bank			
Assets		Liabilities		Assets		Liabilities	
Reserves	$10 million	Deposits	$90 million	Reserves	$10 million	Deposits	$96 million
Loans	$90 million	Bank		Loans	$90 million	Bank	
		capital	$10 million			capital	$ 4 million

Suppose that both banks got caught up in the euphoria of the real estate market in the 1980s, only to find that $5 million of their real estate loans became worthless in the 1990s. When these bad loans are written off (valued at zero), the total value of assets declines by $5 million, and so bank capital, which equals total assets minus liabilities, also declines by $5 million. The balance sheets of the two banks now look like this:

High Capital Bank				Low Capital Bank			
Assets		Liabilities		Assets		Liabilities	
Reserves	$10 million	Deposits	$90 million	Reserves	$10 million	Deposits	$96 million
Loans	$85 million	Bank		Loans	$85 million	Bank	
		capital	$ 5 million			capital	−$1 million

The High Capital Bank takes the $5 million loss in stride because its initial cushion of $10 million in capital means that it still has a positive net worth (bank capital) of $5 million after the loss. The Low Capital Bank, however, is in big trouble. Now the value of its assets has fallen below its liabilities, and its net worth is now −$1 million. Because the bank has a negative net worth, it is insolvent (bankrupt): It does not have sufficient assets to pay off all holders of its liabilities (creditors). When a bank becomes insolvent, government regulators close the bank, its assets are sold off, and its managers are fired. Since the owners of the Low Capital Bank will find their investment wiped out, they would clearly have preferred the bank to have had a larger cushion of bank capital to absorb the losses, as was the case for the High Capital Bank. We therefore see an important rationale for a bank to maintain a high level of capital: ***A bank maintains bank capital to lessen the chance that it will become insolvent.***

How the Amount of Bank Capital Affects Returns to Equity Holders Because owners of a bank must know whether their bank is being managed well, they need good measures of bank profitability. A basic measure of bank profitability is the **return on assets *(ROA),*** the net profit after taxes per dollar of assets:

$$ROA = \frac{\text{net profit after taxes}}{\text{assets}}$$

The return on assets provides information on how efficiently a bank is being run because it indicates how much profits are generated on average by each dollar of assets.

However, what the bank's owners (equity holders) care about most is how much the bank is earning on their equity investment. This information is provided by the other basic measure of bank profitability, the **return on equity *(ROE),*** the net profit after taxes per dollar of equity capital:

$$ROE = \frac{\text{net profit after taxes}}{\text{equity capital}}$$

There is a direct relationship between the return on assets (which measures how efficiently the bank is run) and the return on equity (which measures how well the owners are doing on their investment). This relationship is determined by the so-called **equity multiplier *(EM),*** which is the amount of assets per dollar of equity capital:

$$EM = \frac{\text{assets}}{\text{equity capital}}$$

To see this, we note that

$$\frac{\text{Net profit after taxes}}{\text{Equity capital}} = \frac{\text{net profit after taxes}}{\text{assets}} \times \frac{\text{assets}}{\text{equity capital}}$$

which, using our definitions, yields

$$ROE = ROA \times EM \tag{1}$$

The formula in Equation 1 tells us what happens to the return on equity when a bank holds a smaller amount of capital (equity) for a given amount of assets. As we have seen, the High Capital Bank initially has $100 million of assets and $10 million of equity, which gives it an equity multiplier of 10 (= $100 million/$10 million). The Low Capital Bank, by contrast, has only $4 million of equity, so its equity multiplier is higher, equaling 25 (= $100 million/$4 million). Suppose that these banks have been equally well run so that they both have the same returns on assets of 1%. The return on equity for the High Capital Bank equals 1% × 10 = 10%, while the return on equity for the Low Capital Bank equals 1% × 25 = 25%. The equity holders in the Low Capital Bank are clearly a lot happier than the equity holders in the High Capital Bank because they are earning more than twice as high a return. We now see why owners of a bank may not want it to hold a lot of capital. ***Given the return on assets, the lower the bank capital, the higher the return for the owners of the bank.***

Trade-Off Between Safety and Returns to Equity Holders We now see that bank capital has benefits and costs. Bank capital benefits the owners of a bank in that it makes their investment safer by reducing the likelihood of bankruptcy. But bank capital is costly because the higher it is, the lower will be the return on equity for a given return on assets. In determining the amount of bank capital, managers must decide how much of the increased safety that comes with higher capital (the benefit) they are willing to trade off against the lower return on equity that comes with higher capital (the cost).

In more uncertain times, when the possibility of large losses on loans increases, bank managers might want to hold more capital to protect the equity holders. Conversely, if they have confidence that loan losses won't occur, they might want to reduce the amount of bank capital, have a high equity multiplier, and thereby increase the return on equity.

Bank Capital Requirements Banks also hold capital because they are required to do so by regulatory authorities. Because of the high costs of holding capital for the reasons just described, bank managers often want to hold less bank capital than is required by the regulatory authorities. In this case, the amount of bank capital is determined by the bank capital requirements. We discuss the details of bank capital requirements and why they are such an important part of bank regulation in Chapter 16.

■ THE PRACTICING FINANCIAL INSTITUTION MANAGER
Strategies for Managing Bank Capital

Mona, the manager of the First National Bank, has to make decisions about the appropriate amount of bank capital. Looking at the balance sheet of the bank, which has a ratio of bank capital to assets of 10% ($10 million of capital and $100 million of assets), Mona is concerned that the large amount of bank capital is causing the return on equity to be too low. She concludes that the bank has a capital surplus and should increase the equity multiplier to increase the return on equity. To lower the amount of capital relative to assets and raise the equity multiplier, she can do any of three things: (1) She can reduce the amount of bank capital by buying back some of the bank's stock. (2) She can reduce the bank's capital by paying out higher dividends to its stockholders, thereby reducing the bank's retained earnings. (3) She can keep bank capital constant but increase the bank's assets by acquiring new funds, say, by issuing CDs, and then seeking out loan business or purchasing more securities with these new funds. Because the bank manager feels that she will enhance her position with the stockholders, she decides to pursue the second alternative and raises the dividends on First National Bank stock.

Now suppose that the First National Bank is in a similar situation to the Low Capital Bank and has a ratio of bank capital to assets of 3%. The bank manager now might worry that the bank is short on capital relative to assets because it does not have a sufficient cushion to prevent bank failure. To raise the amount of capital relative to assets, she now has the following three choices: (1) She can raise capital for the bank by having it issue equity (common stock). (2) She can raise capital by reducing the bank's dividends to shareholders, thereby increasing retained earnings that it can put into its capital account. (3) She can keep capital at the same level but reduce the bank's assets by making fewer loans or by selling off securities and then using the proceeds to reduce its liabilities. Suppose that raising bank capital is not easy to do at the current time because capital markets are tight or because shareholders will protest if their dividends are cut. Then Mona might have to choose the third alternative and decide to shrink the size of the bank.

In recent years, many banks have experienced capital shortfalls and have had to restrict asset growth, as Mona did, when the bank is short of capital. The important consequences of this for the credit markets are discussed in the application that follows.

APPLICATION | **DID THE CAPITAL CRUNCH CAUSE A CREDIT CRUNCH IN THE EARLY 1990s?**

During the 1990–1991 recession and the year following, there occurred a slowdown in the growth of credit that was unprecedented in the post–World War II era. Many economists and politicians have claimed that there was a "credit crunch" during this period in which credit was hard to get, and as a result the performance of the economy in 1990–1992 was very weak. Was the slowdown in credit growth a manifestation of a credit crunch, and if so, what caused it?

Our analysis of how a bank manages bank capital suggests that a credit crunch was likely to have occurred in 1990–1992 and that it was caused at least in part by the so-called capital crunch in which shortfalls of bank capital led to slower credit growth.

The period of the late 1980s saw a boom and then a major bust in the real estate market that led to huge losses for banks on their real estate loans. As our example on how bank capital helps prevent bank failures demonstrates, the loan losses caused a substantial fall in the amount of bank capital. At the same time, regulators were raising capital requirements (a subject we will discuss in Chapter 16). The resulting capital shortfalls meant that banks had either to raise new capital or to restrict their asset growth by cutting back on lending. Because of the weak economy at the time, raising new capital was extremely difficult for banks, so they chose the latter course. Banks did restrict their lending, and borrowers found it harder to obtain loans, leading to complaints from banks' customers.[3] Only with the stronger recovery of the economy in 1993, helped by a low-interest-rate policy at the Federal Reserve, did these complaints subside.

■ OFF-BALANCE-SHEET ACTIVITIES

Although asset and liability management has traditionally been the major concern of banks, in the more competitive environment of recent years banks have been aggressively seeking out profits by engaging in off-balance-sheet activities. **Off-balance-sheet activities** involve trading financial instruments and generating income from fees and loan sales, activities that affect bank profits but do not appear on bank balance sheets. Indeed, off-balance-sheet activities have been growing in importance for banks: The income from these activities as a percentage of assets has nearly doubled since 1979.

Loan Sales

One type of off-balance-sheet activity that has grown in importance in recent years involves income generated by loan sales. A **loan sale,** also called a *secondary loan participation,* involves a contract that sells all or part of the cash stream from a specific loan and thereby removes the loan from the bank's balance sheet. Banks earn profits by selling loans for an amount slightly greater than the amount of the original loan. Because the high interest rate on these loans makes them attractive, institutions are willing to buy them even though the higher price means that they earn a slightly lower interest rate than the original interest rate on the loan, usually on the order of 0.15 percentage point.

---

[3]As we will see in Chapter 16, not only were capital requirements raised, but also risk-based capital requirements were imposed that required even more capital if loans were made but not if banks bought government securities. The risk-based capital requirements thus encouraged banks to switch out of loans and into government securities, and this was an additional factor that led to a decline in bank lending. For a discussion of the evidence on how the capital crunch caused the credit crunch of 1990–1992, see "The Role of the Credit Slowdown in the Recent Recession," *Federal Reserve Bank of New York Quarterly Review,* Spring 1993.

Generation of Fee Income

Another type of off-balance-sheet activity involves the generation of income from fees that banks receive for providing specialized services to their customers, such as making foreign exchange trades on a customer's behalf, servicing a mortgage-backed security by collecting interest and principal payments and then paying them out, guaranteeing debt securities such as banker's acceptances (the bank promises to make interest and principal payments if the party issuing the security cannot), and providing backup lines of credit. There are several types of backup lines of credit. The most important is the **loan commitment,** under which for a fee the bank agrees to provide a loan at the customer's request, up to a given dollar amount, over a specified period of time. Credit lines are also now available to bank depositors with "overdraft privileges"—these bank customers can write checks in excess of their deposit balances and, in effect, write themselves a loan. Other lines of credit for which banks get fees include standby letters of credit to back up issues of commercial paper and other securities, and credit lines (called **note issuance facilities,** NIFs, and **revolving underwriting facilities,** RUFs) for underwriting Euronotes, which are medium-term Eurobonds.

Off-balance-sheet activities involving guarantees of securities and backup credit lines increase the risk a bank faces. Even though a guaranteed security does not appear on a bank balance sheet, it still exposes the bank to default risk: If the issuer of the security defaults, the bank is left holding the bag and must pay off the security's owner. Backup credit lines also expose the bank to risk because the bank may be forced to provide loans when it does not have sufficient liquidity or when the borrower is a very poor credit risk.

Trading Activities and Risk Management Techniques

We have already mentioned that banks' attempts to manage interest-rate risk led them to trading in financial futures, options for debt instruments, and interest-rate swaps. Banks engaged in international banking also conduct transactions in the foreign exchange market. All transactions in these markets are off-balance-sheet activities because they do not have a direct effect on the bank's balance sheet. Although bank trading in these markets is often directed toward reducing risk or facilitating other bank business, banks also try to outguess the markets and engage in speculation. This speculation can be a very risky business and indeed has led to bank insolvencies, the most dramatic being the failure of Barings, a British bank, in 1995.

Trading activities, although often highly profitable, are dangerous because they make it easy for financial institutions and their employees to make huge bets both easily and quickly. A particular problem for management of trading activities is that the principal-agent problem, discussed in Chapter 12, is especially severe. Given the ability to place large bets, a trader (the agent), whether she trades in bond markets, in foreign exchange markets, or in financial derivatives, has an incentive to take on excessive risks: If her trading strategy leads to large profits, she is likely to receive a high salary and bonuses, but if she takes large losses, the financial institution (the principal) will have to cover them. As the Barings Bank failure in 1995 so forcefully demonstrated, a trader subject to the principal-agent problem can take a bank that is quite healthy and drive it into insolvency very fast (see Box 2).

To reduce the principal-agent problem, bank management must set up internal controls to prevent debacles like the one at Barings. Such controls include the complete separation of the people in charge of trading activities and those in

BOX 2   A GLOBL PERSPECTIVE

Barings, Daiwa, and Sumitomo

Rogue Traders and the Principal-Agent Problem

 The demise of Barings, a venerable British bank over a century old, is a sad morality tale of how the principal-agent problem operating through a rogue trader can take a financial institution that has a healthy balance sheet one month and turn it into an insolvent tragedy the next.

In July 1992, Nick Leeson, Barings's new head clerk at its Singapore branch, began to speculate on the Nikkei, the Japanese version of the Dow Jones index. By late 1992, Leeson had suffered losses of $3 million, which he hid from his superiors by stashing the losses in a secret account. He even fooled his superiors into thinking he was generating large profits thanks to a failure of internal controls at his firm, which allowed him to execute trades on the Singapore exchange *and* oversee the bookkeeping of those trades. (As anyone who runs a cash business, such as a bar, knows, there is always a lower likelihood of fraud if more than one person handles the cash. Similarly for trading operations, you never mix management of the back room with management of the front room; this principle was grossly violated by Barings management.) Things didn't get better for Leeson, who by late 1994 had losses exceeding $250 million. In January and February 1995, he bet the bank. On January 17, 1995, the day of the Kobe earthquake, he lost $75 million, and by the end of the week had lost more than $150 million. When the stock market declined on February 23, leaving him with a further loss of $250 million, he called it quits and fled Singapore. Three days later, he turned himself in at the Frankfurt airport. By the end of his wild ride, Leeson's losses, $1.3 billion in all, ate up Barings's capital and caused the bank to fail.

Our asymmetric information analysis of the principal-agent problem explains Leeson's behavior and the danger of Barings's management lapse. By letting Leeson control both his own trades and the back room,

it increased asymmetric information because it reduced the principal's (Barings's) knowledge about Leeson's trading activities. This lapse increased the moral hazard incentive for him to take risks at the bank's expense, as he was now less likely to be caught. Furthermore, once he had experienced large losses, he had even greater incentives to take on even higher risk because if his bets worked out, he could reverse his losses and keep in good standing with the company, whereas if his bets soured, he had little to lose since he was out of a job anyway. Indeed, the bigger his losses, the more he had to gain by bigger bets, which explains the escalation of the amount of his trades as his losses mounted. If Barings's managers had understood the principal-agent problem, they would have been more vigilant in learning what Leeson was up to, and the bank might still be here today.

Unfortunately, Nick Leeson is no longer a rarity in the rogue traders' billionaire club, those who have lost more than $1 billion. Over 11 years, Toshihide Iguchi, an officer in the New York branch of Daiwa Bank, also had control of both the bond trading operation and the back room, and he racked up $1.1 billion in losses over the period. In July 1995, Iguchi disclosed his losses to his superiors, but the management of the bank did not disclose them to its regulators. The result was that Daiwa was slapped with a $340 million fine and the bank was thrown out of the country by U.S. bank regulators. Yasuo Hamanaka is the latest member of the billionaire club. In July 1996, he topped Leeson's and Iguchi's record, losing $2.6 billion for his employer, the Sumitomo Corporation, one of Japan's top trading companies. The moral of these stories is that management of firms engaged in trading activities must reduce the principal-agent problem by closely monitoring their traders' activities.

charge of the bookkeeping for trades. In addition, bank management must set limits on the total amount of traders' transactions and on the bank's risk exposure. Bank management must also scrutinize risk assessment procedures using the latest computer technology. One such method involves the so-called value-at-risk approach. In this approach, the bank develops a statistical model with which it can calculate the maximum loss that its portfolio is likely to sustain over a given time interval, dubbed the value at risk, or VAR. For example, a bank might estimate that the maximum loss that it would be likely to sustain over one day with a probability of 1 in 100 is $1 million; the $1 million figure is the bank's calculated value at risk. Another approach is called "stress testing." In this approach, the bank asks models what would happen if a doomsday scenario occurs; that is, it looks at the losses it would sustain if an unusual combination of bad events occurred. With the value-at-risk approach and stress testing, a bank can assess its risk exposure and take steps to reduce it.

Because of the increased risk that banks are facing from their off-balance-sheet activities, U.S. bank regulators have become concerned about increased risk from banks' off-balance-sheet activities and, as we will see in Chapter 16, are encouraging banks to pay increased attention to risk management. In addition, the Bank for International Settlements is developing additional bank capital requirements based on value-at-risk calculations for a bank's trading activities.

■ MEASURING BANK PERFORMANCE

To understand how well a bank is doing, we need to start by looking at a bank's income statement, the description of the sources of income and expenses that affect the bank's profitability.

Bank's Income Statement

The 1995 income statement for all federally insured commercial banks appears in Table 2.

Operating Income **Operating income** is the income that comes from a bank's ongoing operations. Most of a bank's operating income is generated by interest on its assets, particularly loans. As we see in Table 2, in 1995 interest income represented 78.6% of commercial banks' operating income. Interest income fluctuates with the level of interest rates, and so its percentage of operating income is highest when interest rates are at peak levels. That is exactly what happened in 1981, when interest rates rose above 15% and interest income rose to 93% of total bank operating income.

Noninterest income, which made up 21.4% of operating income in 1995, is generated partly by service charges on deposit accounts, but the bulk of it comes from the off-balance-sheet activities mentioned earlier, which generate fees or trading profits for the bank. The importance of these off-balance-sheet activities to bank profits has been growing in recent years. Whereas in 1980 other noninterest income from off-balance-sheet activities represented only 5% of operating income, it reached 17.2% in 1995.

■ **TABLE 2** Income Statement for All Federally Insured Commercial Banks, 1995

	Amount ($ billions)	Share of Operating Income or Expenses (%)
Operating Income		
Interest income	302.6	78.6
Interest on loans	223.5	58.1
Interest on securities	51.2	13.3
Other interest	27.9	7.2
Noninterest income	82.4	21.4
Service charges on deposit accounts	16.0	4.2
Other noninterest income	66.4	17.2
Total operating income	385.0	100.0
Operating Expenses		
Interest expenses	148.4	47.8
Interest on deposits	105.4	33.9
Interest on fed funds and repos	18.5	6.0
Other	24.5	7.9
Noninterest expenses	149.6	48.2
Salaries and employee benefits	63.4	20.4
Premises and equipment	19.6	6.3
Other	66.6	21.5
Provisions for loan losses	12.6	4.0
Total operating income	310.6	100.0
Net Operating Income	74.4	
Income taxes	26.2	
Gains (losses) on securities	0.5	
Extraordinary items, net	0.2	
Net Income	48.8	

Source: Federal Deposit Insurance Corporation, *Statistics on Banking, 1995.*

Operating Expenses Operating expenses are the expenses incurred in conducting the bank's ongoing operations. An important component of a bank's operating expenses is the interest payments that it must make on its liabilities, particularly on its deposits. Just as interest income varies with the level of interest rates, so do interest expenses. Interest expenses as a percentage of total operating expenses reached a peak of 74% in 1981, when interest rates were at their highest, and fell to 47.8% in 1995 as interest rates moved lower. Noninterest expenses include the costs of running a banking business: salaries for tellers and officers, rent on bank buildings, purchases of equipment such as desks and vaults, and servicing costs of equipment such as computers.

The final item listed under operating expenses is provisions for loan losses. When a bank has a bad debt or anticipates that a loan might become a bad debt in the future, it can write up the loss as a current expense in its income statement under the "provision for loan losses" heading. Provisions for loan losses are directly related to loan loss reserves (discussed in Box 1 earlier in the chapter). When a bank wants to increase its loan loss reserves account by, say, $1 million, it does this by adding $1 million to its provisions for loan losses. Loan loss reserves rise when this is done because by increasing expenses when losses have not yet occurred, earnings are being set aside to deal with the losses in the future.

Provisions for loan losses have been a major element in fluctuating bank profits in recent years. The 1980s brought the third-world debt crisis mentioned in Chapter 16; a sharp decline in energy prices in 1986, which caused substantial losses on loans to energy producers; and a collapse in the real estate market. As a result, provisions for loan losses were particularly high in the late 1980s, reaching a peak of 13% of operating expenses in 1987. Since then, losses on loans have begun to subside, and in 1995 provisions for loan losses dropped to only 4% of operating expenses.

Income Subtracting the $310.6 billion in operating expenses from the $385.0 billion of operating income in 1995 yields net operating income of $74.4 billion. Net operating income is closely watched by bank managers, bank shareholders, and bank regulators because it indicates how well the bank is doing on an ongoing basis.

Two items, gains (or losses) on securities sold by banks ($0.5 billion) and net extraordinary items, which are events or transactions that are both unusual and infrequent ($0.2 billion), are added to the $74.4 billion net operating income figure to get the $75.1 billion figure for net income before taxes. Net income before taxes is more commonly referred to as profits before taxes. Subtracting the $26.2 billion of income taxes then results in $48.8 billion of net income. Net income, more commonly referred to as profits after taxes, is the figure that tells us most directly how well the bank is doing because it is the amount that the bank has available to keep as retained earnings or to pay out to stockholders as dividends.

Measures of Bank Performance

Although net income gives us an idea of how well a bank is doing, it suffers from one major drawback: It does not adjust for the bank's size, thus making it hard to compare how well one bank is doing relative to another. A basic measure of bank profitability that corrects for the size of the bank is the return on assets (*ROA*), mentioned earlier in the chapter, which divides the net income of the bank by the amount of its assets. *ROA* is a useful measure of how well a bank manager is doing on the job because it indicates how well a bank's assets are being used to generate profits. At the beginning of 1995, the assets of all federally insured commercial banks amounted to $4,010.2 billion, so using the $48.8 billion net income figure from Table 2 gives us a return on assets of

$$ROA = \frac{\text{net income}}{\text{assets}} = \frac{48.8}{4010.7} = 0.0122 = 1.22\%$$

Although *ROA* provides useful information about bank profitability, we have already seen that it is not what the bank's owners (equity holders) care about most. They are more concerned about how much the bank is earning on their equity investment, an amount that is measured by the return on equity (*ROE*), the net income per dollar of equity capital. At the beginning of 1995, equity capital for all federally insured commercial banks was $312.2 billion, so the ROE was therefore

$$ROE = \frac{\text{net income}}{\text{capital}} = \frac{48.8}{312.2} = 0.156 = 15.6\%$$

Another commonly watched measure of bank performance is called the **net interest margin** (*NIM*), the difference between interest income and interest expenses as a percentage of total assets:

$$NIM = \frac{\text{interest income} - \text{interest expenses}}{\text{assets}}$$

As we have seen earlier in the chapter, one of a bank's primary intermediation functions is to issue liabilities and use the proceeds to purchase income-earning assets. If a bank manager has done a good job of asset and liability management such that the bank earns substantial income on its assets and has low costs on its liabilities, profits will be high. How well a bank manages its assets and liabilities is affected by the spread between the interest earned on the bank's assets and the interest costs on its liabilities. This spread is exactly what the net interest margin measures. If the bank is able to raise funds with liabilities that have low interest costs and is able to acquire assets with high interest income, the net interest margin will be high, and the bank is likely to be highly profitable. If the interest cost of its liabilities rises relative to the interest earned on its assets, the net interest margin will fall, and bank profitability will suffer.

Recent Trends in Bank Performance Measures

Table 3 provides measures of return on assets (*ROA*), return on equity (*ROE*), and the net interest margin (*NIM*) for all federally insured commercial banks from 1980 to 1995. Because the relationship between bank equity capital and total assets for all commercial banks remained fairly stable in the 1980s, both the *ROA* and *ROE* measures of bank performance move closely together and indicate that from the early to the late 1980s, there was a sharp decline in bank profitability. The rightmost column, net interest margin, indicates that the spread between interest income and interest expenses remained fairly stable throughout the 1980s and even improved in the late 1980s and early 1990s, which should have helped bank profits. The *NIM* measure thus tells us that the poor bank performance in the late 1980s was not the result of interest-rate movements.

The explanation of the weak performance of commercial banks in the late 1980s is that they had made many risky loans in the early 1980s that turned sour. The resulting huge increase in loan loss provisions in that period directly decreased net income and hence caused the fall in *ROA* and *ROE*. (Why bank profitability deteriorated and the consequences for the economy are discussed in Chapters 14 and 16.)

Beginning in 1992, bank performance improved substantially. The return on equity rose to nearly 14% in 1992 and remained at 15% or above in the 1993–1995

■ TABLE 3 Measures of Bank Performance, 1980–1995

Year	Return on Assets (ROA) (%)	Return on Equity (ROE) (%)	Net Interest Margin (NIM)(%)
1980	0.77	13.38	3.33
1981	0.79	13.68	3.31
1982	0.73	12.55	3.39
1983	0.68	11.60	3.34
1984	0.66	11.04	3.47
1985	0.72	11.67	3.62
1986	0.64	10.30	3.48
1987	0.09	1.54	3.40
1988	0.82	13.74	3.57
1989	0.50	7.92	3.58
1990	0.49	7.81	3.50
1991	0.53	8.25	3.60
1992	0.94	13.86	3.89
1993	1.23	16.3	3.97
1994	1.20	15.0	3.95
1995	1.22	15.6	3.85

Sources: Federal Deposit Insurance Corporation, *Historical Statistics on Banking, 1934–1991; Statistics on Banking, 1992, 1993, 1994, 1995.*

period. Similarly, the return on assets rose from the 0.5% level in the 1990–1991 period to around the 1.2% level in 1993–1995. The performance measures in Table 3 suggest that the banking industry has returned to health in the mid-1990s with slightly less than half of the 0.7-percentage-point increase in the return on assets from 1991 to 1995 attributable to the unusually large (0.3%) increase in the net interest margin.

■ FINANCIAL INNOVATION

Like other industries, the financial industry is in business to earn profits by selling its products. If a soap company perceives that there is a need in the marketplace for a laundry detergent with fabric softener, it develops a product to fit the need. Similarly, in order to maximize their profits, financial institutions develop new products to satisfy their own needs as well as those of their customers; in other words, innovation—which can be extremely beneficial to the economy—is driven by the desire to get (or stay) rich. This view of the innovation process leads to the following simple analysis: ***A change in the financial environment will stimulate a search by financial institutions for innovations that are likely to be profitable.***

Starting in the 1960s, individuals and financial institutions operating in financial markets were confronted with drastic changes in the economic environment: Inflation and interest rates climbed sharply and became harder to predict, a situation that changed demand conditions in financial markets. Computer technology advanced rapidly, which changed supply conditions. In addition, financial regulations became more burdensome. Financial institutions found that many of the old ways of doing business were no longer profitable; the financial services and products they had been offering to the public were not selling. Many financial intermediaries found that they were no longer able to acquire funds with their traditional financial instruments, and without these funds they would soon be out of business. To survive in the new economic environment, financial institutions had to research and develop new products and services that would meet customer needs and prove profitable, a process referred to as **financial engineering.** In their case, necessity was the mother of innovation.

Our discussion of why financial innovation occurs suggests that there are three basic types of financial innovations: responses to changes in demand conditions, responses to changes in supply conditions, and avoidance of regulations. Now that we have a framework for understanding why financial institutions such as banks produce innovations, let's look at examples of how financial institutions in their search for profits have produced financial innovations of the three basic types.

Responses to Changes in Demand Conditions

The most significant change in the economic environment that altered the demand for financial products in recent years has been the dramatic increase in the volatility of interest rates. In the 1950s, the interest rate on three-month Treasury bills fluctuated between 1.0% and 3.5%; in the 1970s, it fluctuated between 4.0% and 11.5%. This volatility became even more pronounced in the 1980s, during which the three-month T-bill rate ranged from 5% to over 15%. We have seen in Chapter 3 (Table 2) that a rise in the interest rate from 10% to 20% would result in a capital loss of nearly 50% on a 30-year bond and a negative return of almost 40%. Large fluctuations in interest rates lead to substantial capital gains or losses and greater uncertainty about returns on investments. Recall that the risk that is related to the uncertainty about interest-rate movements and returns is called *interest-rate risk,* and high volatility of interest rates, such as we saw in the 1970s and 1980s, leads to a higher level of interest-rate risk.

We would expect the increase in interest-rate risk to increase the demand for financial products and services that could reduce that risk. This change in the economic environment would thus stimulate a search for profitable innovations by financial institutions that meet this new demand and would spur the creation of new financial instruments that help lower interest-rate risk. One financial innovation in the banking industry that appeared in the 1970s confirms this prediction: the development of adjustable-rate mortgages.

Adjustable-Rate Mortgages Like other investors, financial institutions find that lending is more attractive if interest-rate risk is lower. They would not want to make a mortgage loan at a 10% interest rate and two months later find that they could obtain a 12% interest rate on the same mortgage. To reduce interest-rate risk, in 1975 savings and loans in California began to issue adjustable-rate mortgages, mortgage loans on which the interest rate changes when a market interest rate (usually the Treasury bill rate) changes. Initially, an adjustable-rate mortgage might have a 5% interest rate. In six months, this interest rate might increase or decrease by the amount of the increase or decrease in, say, the six-month Treasury bill rate, and the mortgage payment would change. Because adjustable-rate mortgages allow mortgage-issuing institutions to earn higher interest rates on mortgages when rates rise, profits are kept higher during these periods.

This attractive feature of adjustable-rate mortgages has encouraged mortgage-issuing institutions to issue adjustable-rate mortgages with lower initial interest rates than on conventional fixed-rate mortgages, making them popular with many households. However, because the mortgage payment on a variable-rate mortgage can increase, many households continue to prefer fixed-rate mortgages. Hence both types of mortgages are widespread.

Responses to Changes in Supply Conditions

The most important source of the changes in supply conditions that stimulate financial innovation has been the improvement in computer and telecommunications technology. These changes have made it profitable to supply for financial institutions to create new financial products and services to the public. When computer technology that substantially lowered the cost of processing financial transactions became available, financial institutions conceived new financial products and instruments dependent on this technology that might appeal to the public, including the bank credit card and electronic banking facilities.

Bank Credit and Debit Cards Credit cards have been around since well before World War II. Many individual stores (Sears, Macy's, Goldwater's) institutionalized charge accounts by providing customers with credit cards that allowed them to make purchases at these stores without cash. Nationwide credit cards were not established until after World War II, when Diners Club developed one to be used in restaurants all over the country (and abroad). Similar credit card programs were started by American Express and Carte Blanche, but because of the high cost of operating these programs, cards were issued only to selected persons and businesses who could afford expensive purchases.

A firm issuing credit cards earns income from loans it makes to credit card holders and from payments made by stores on credit card purchases (a percentage of the purchase price, say, 5%). A credit card program's costs arise from loan defaults, stolen cards, and the expense involved in processing credit card transactions.

Bankers saw the success of Diners Club, American Express, and Carte Blanche and wanted to share in the profitable credit card business. Several commercial banks attempted to expand the credit card business to a wider market in the 1950s, but the cost per transaction when running these programs was so high that their early attempts failed.

In the late 1960s, improved computer technology, which lowered the transaction costs for providing credit card services, made it more likely that bank credit card programs would be profitable. The banks tried to enter this business again, and this time their efforts led to the creation of two successful bank credit card programs: BankAmericard (originally started by the Bank of America but now an independent organization called Visa) and MasterCharge (now MasterCard, run by the Interbank Card Association). These programs have become phenomenally successful; more than 200 million of their cards are in use. Indeed, bank credit cards have been so profitable that nonfinancial institutions such as Sears (which launched the Discover card), General Motors, and AT&T have also entered the credit card business. Consumers have benefited because credit cards are more widely accepted than checks when paying for purchases (particularly abroad), and they allow consumers to take out loans more easily.

The success of bank credit cards has led these institutions to come up with a new financial innovation, *debit cards.* Debit cards often look just like credit cards and can be used to make purchases in an identical fashion. However, in contrast to credit cards, which extend the purchaser a loan that does not have to be paid off immediately, a debit card purchase is immediately deducted from the card holder's bank account. Debit cards depend even more on low costs of processing transactions, since their profits are generated entirely from the fees paid by merchants on debit card purchases at their stores. Debit cards have been growing increasingly popular in recent years.

Electronic Banking Facilities The wonders of modern computer technology have also enabled banks to lower the cost of bank transactions by having the customer interact with an electronic banking facility rather than with a human being. One important form of electronic banking facility is the automated teller machine (ATM), which has the advantage that it does not have to be paid overtime and never sleeps, thus being available for use 24 hours a day. Not only does this result in cheaper transactions for the bank, but it also provides more convenience for the customer. Furthermore, because of its low cost, ATMs can be put at locations other than a bank or its branches, further increasing customer convenience. The low cost of ATMs has meant that they have sprung up everywhere and now number over 100,000 in the United States alone. Furthermore, it is now as easy to get foreign currency from an ATM when you are traveling in Europe as it is to get cash from your local bank. In addition, transactions with ATMs are so much cheaper for the bank than ones conducted with human tellers that some banks charge customers less if they use the ATM than if they use a human teller.

With the drop in the cost of telecommunications, banks have developed another financial innovation, home banking. It is now cost-effective for banks to set up an electronic banking facility in which the bank's customer is linked up with the bank's computer to carry out transactions either by using a telephone or a personal computer. Now a bank's customers can conduct many of their bank transactions without ever leaving the comfort of home. The advantage for the customer is the convenience of home banking, while banks find that the cost of transactions is substantially less than having the customer come to the bank.

With the decline in the price of personal computers and their increasing presence in the home, we have seen a further innovation in the home banking area, the appearance of a new type of banking institution, the **virtual bank,** a bank that has no physical location but rather exists only in cyberspace. In 1995, Security First Network Bank became the first virtual bank, planning to offer an array of banking services on the Internet—accepting checking account and savings deposits, selling certificates of deposits, issuing ATM cards, providing bill-paying facilities, and so on. In 1996, Bank of America and Wells Fargo, two of the largest banks in the United States, entered the virtual banking market, providing home banking services via the Internet. The virtual bank thus takes home banking one step further, enabling a customer to have a full set of banking services at home, 24 hours a day.

Avoidance of Existing Regulations

The process of financial innovation we have discussed so far is much like innovation in other areas of the economy: It occurs in response to changes in demand and supply conditions. However, because the financial industry is more heavily regulated than other industries, government regulation is a much greater spur to innovation in this industry. Government regulation leads to financial innovation by creating incentives for firms to skirt regulations that restrict their ability to earn profits. Edward Kane describes this process of avoiding regulations as "loophole mining."[4] The economic analysis of innovation suggests that when the economic environment changes such that regulatory constraints are so burdensome that large profits can be made by avoiding them, loophole mining and innovation are more likely to occur.

Because banking is one of the most heavily regulated industries in America, loophole mining is especially likely to occur. The rise in inflation and interest rates from the late 1960s to 1980 made the regulatory constraints imposed on this industry even more burdensome. Under these circumstances, we would expect the pace of financial innovation in banking to be rapid, and, indeed, it has been.

Two sets of regulations have seriously restricted the ability of banks to make profits: reserve requirements that force banks to keep a certain fraction of their deposits as reserves (deposits in the Federal Reserve System) and restrictions on the interest rates that can be paid on deposits. For the following reasons, these regulations have been among the major forces behind financial innovation in recent years.

Reserve Requirements The key to understanding why reserve requirements affect financial innovation is to recognize that they act, in effect, as a tax on deposits. Because the Fed does not pay interest on reserves, the opportunity cost of holding them is the interest that a bank could otherwise earn by lending the reserves out. For each dollar of deposits, reserve requirements therefore impose a cost on the bank equal to the interest rate that could be earned if the reserves could be lent out i times the fraction of deposits required as reserves r_D. The cost of $i \times r_D$ imposed on the bank is just like a tax on bank deposits of $i \times r_D$.

It is a great tradition to avoid taxes if possible, and banks also play this game. Just as taxpayers look for loopholes to lower their tax bills, banks seek to increase their profits by mining loopholes and by producing new financial innovations that allow them to escape the tax on deposits imposed by reserve requirements.

Restrictions on Interest Paid on Deposits Until 1980, legislation prohibited banks in most states from paying interest on checking account deposits, and through Regulation Q, the Fed set maximum limits on the interest rate that could be paid on time deposits. The desire to avoid these **deposit rate ceilings** also led to financial innovations.

---

[4]"Banking Takes a Beating," *Time*, December 3, 1984, p. 49.

If market interest rates rose above the maximum rates that banks paid on time deposits under Regulation Q, depositors withdrew funds from banks to put them into higher-yielding securities. This loss of deposits from the banking system restricted the amount of funds that banks could lend (called **disintermediation**) and thus limited bank profits. Banks had an incentive to get around deposit rate ceilings because by so doing, they could acquire more funds to make loans and earn higher profits.

We can now look at how the desire to avoid restrictions on interest payments and the tax effect of reserve requirements led to several important financial innovations.

Eurodollars and Bank Commercial Paper In the late 1960s, inflation was accelerating, and (as we would expect from our analysis of the Fisher effect in Chapter 5) interest rates began to rise. The tax on deposits from reserve requirements $i \times r_D$ also began to rise, and the incentives to avoid this tax increased. In addition, higher interest rates meant that market interest rates exceeded the maximum rate payable on time deposits under Regulation Q, and as market interest rates climbed to then record highs in 1969, investors reduced their time deposits to invest in higher-yielding securities. By the late 1960s, commercial banks had a strong incentive to search for new funds that would not be subject to reserve requirements and so escape the tax of $i \times r_D$ and not be subject to the interest rate ceiling set by Regulation Q.

As the economic analysis of innovation predicts, the banks began to mine loopholes and discovered two sources of funds that avoided both reserve requirements and deposit rate ceilings: Eurodollars and bank commercial paper. Because Eurodollars (deposits abroad denominated in dollars) were borrowed from banks outside the United States, they were not subject to reserve requirements or to Regulation Q. Similarly, commercial paper issued by a bank's parent holding company was not treated as deposits and so was also exempt from these regulations. Not surprisingly, the markets for Eurodollars and bank commercial paper began to expand rapidly in the late 1960s.

NOW Accounts, ATS Accounts, and Overnight Repos The rise in interest rates in the late 1960s, which made the avoidance of restrictions on deposit rates profitable, stimulated the development of new types of checking accounts. Because of Regulation Q ceilings, savings and loans and mutual savings banks were hit especially hard by the rise in interest rates in the late 1960s. They lost large amounts of funds to financial instruments that paid higher interest rates, and they needed to find new sources of funds to continue to make profitable loans.

In 1970, as a result of diligent loophole mining, a mutual savings bank in Massachusetts struck gold by discovering a loophole in the prohibition of interest payments on checking accounts. In effect, by calling a check a "negotiable order of withdrawal" (NOW), accounts on which these NOWs could be written were not legally checking accounts. Hence NOW accounts were not subject to regulations on checking accounts and could pay interest. In May 1972, after two years of litigation, mutual savings banks in Massachusetts were allowed to issue NOW accounts that paid interest. Subsequently, in September 1972, the courts approved NOW accounts in New Hampshire.

NOW accounts were immediately successful in Massachusetts and New Hampshire, and they enabled savings and loans and mutual savings banks in those states to earn higher profits because they were able to attract more funds that could be loaned out. Since commercial banks did not want competition from other financial intermediaries for checking account deposits (at the time only commercial banks were legally allowed to issue checking accounts), they mounted a campaign to prevent the spread of these accounts to other states. The result was congressional legislation enacted in January 1974 that limited NOW accounts to New England. Legislation in 1980 finally authorized NOW accounts nationwide for savings and loans, mutual savings banks, and commercial banks, and similar accounts **(share draft accounts)** were authorized for credit unions.

Another innovation that enables banks to pay interest on checking accounts is the ATS (automatic transfer from savings) account. Balances above a certain amount in a checking account are automatically transferred into a savings account that pays interest. When a check is written on the ATS account, the necessary funds to cover the check are automatically transferred from the savings account into the checking account. Thus balances earning interest in a savings account are effectively part of the depositor's checking account because they are available for writing checks. Legally, however, it is the savings account and not the checking account that pays interest to the depositor.

Commercial banks provide a variant of the ATS account to their corporate depositors, which involves the use of a so-called *sweep account* to engage in overnight repurchase agreements (repos). In this type of arrangement, any balances above a certain amount in a corporation's checking account at the end of a business day are "swept out" of the account and invested in overnight repos that pay the corporation interest. (As you may recall from Chapter 2, the repo is an agreement whereby a corporation purchases Treasury bills that the bank agrees to repurchase the next day at a slightly higher price.) Again, although the checking account does not legally pay interest, in effect the corporation is receiving interest on balances that are available for writing checks.

The financial innovations of ATS accounts and overnight repo arrangements were stimulated not only by deposit rate ceilings but also by new technology. Without low-cost computers to process inexpensively the additional transactions required by these accounts, neither of these innovations would be profitable and therefore would not have been developed. Technological factors often combine with other incentives, such as the desire to get around restrictions on deposit rates, to produce financial innovation.

Conclusion Our discussion of financial innovation and the challenges that are facing managers of banks indicate that banking is no longer the staid profession it once was, prompting one banker to state, "Despite all the dark suits worn by its leaders, banking is a very dynamic industry."[5]

---

[5]Ibid.

■ **THE PRACTICING FINANCIAL INSTITUTION MANAGER**

Profiting from a New Financial Product: A Case Study of Treasury Strips

We have seen that the advent of high-speed computers, which lowered the cost of processing financial transactions, led to such financial innovations as bank credit and debit cards. Because there is money to be made from financial innovation, it is important for managers of financial institutions to understand the thinking that goes into producing new, highly profitable financial products that take advantage of computer technology. To illustrate how financial institution managers can figure out ways to increase profits through financial innovation, we look at Treasury strips, a financial instrument first developed in 1982 by Salomon Brothers and Merrill Lynch.

One problem for investors in long-term coupon bonds, even when investors have a long holding period, is that there is some uncertainty in their returns arising from what is called *reinvestment risk*. Even if an investor holding a long-term coupon bond has a holding period of ten years, the return on the bond is not certain. The problem is that coupon payments are made before the bond matures in ten years, and these coupon payments must be reinvested. Because the interest rates at which the coupon payments will be reinvested fluctuate, the eventual return on the bond fluctuates as well. In contrast, long-term zero-coupon bonds have no reinvestment risk because they make no cash payments before the bond matures. The return on a zero-coupon bond if it is held to maturity is known at the time of purchase. The absence of reinvestment risk is an attractive feature of zero-coupon bonds, and as a result, investors are willing to accept a slightly lower interest rate on them than on coupon bonds, which do bear some reinvestment risk.

The fact that zero-coupon bonds have lower interest rates, along with the ability to use computers to create so-called hybrid securities, which are securities derived from other underlying securities, gave employees of Salomon Brothers and Merrill Lynch a brilliant idea for making profits. They could use computers to separate ("strip") a long-term Treasury coupon bond into a set of zero-coupon bonds. For example, a $1 million ten-year Treasury bond might be stripped into ten $100,000 zero-coupon bonds, which, naturally enough, are called *Treasury strips*. The lower interest rates on the more desirable Treasury strip zero-coupon bonds would mean that the value of these bonds would exceed the price of the underlying long-term Treasury bond, allowing Salomon Brothers and Merrill Lynch to make a profit by purchasing the long-term Treasury bond, separating it into Treasury strips, and selling them off as zero-coupon bonds.

To see in more detail how their thinking worked, let's look more closely at a $1 million ten-year Treasury bond with a coupon rate of 10% whose yield to maturity is also 10%, so it is selling at par. The cash payments for this bond are listed in the second column of Table 4. To make things simple, let's assume that the yield curve is absolutely flat so that the interest rate used to discount all the future cash payments is the same. Because zero-coupon bonds, which have no

■ TABLE 4 Market Value of Treasury Strip Zero-Coupon Bonds Derived from a $1
Million Ten-Year Treasury Bond with a 10% Coupon Rate and Selling at Par

(1) Year	(2) Cash Payment $	(3) Interest Rate on Zero-Coupon Bond (%)	(4) Present Discounted Value of Zero-Coupon Bond ($)
1	100,000	9.75	91,116
2	100,000	9.75	83,022
3	100,000	9.75	75,646
4	100,000	9.75	68,926
5	100,000	9.75	62,802
6	100,000	9.75	57,223
7	100,000	9.75	52,140
8	100,000	9.75	47,508
9	100,000	9.75	43,287
10	100,000	9.75	39,442
10	1,000,000	9.75	394,416
Total			$1,015,528

reinvestment risk, are more desirable than the ten-year Treasury coupon bond, the interest rate on the zero-coupon bonds is 9.75%, a little lower than the 10% interest rate on the coupon bond.

How would Fran, a smart and sophisticated financial institution manager, figure out if she could make a profit from creating and selling the Treasury strips? Her first step is to figure out what the zero-coupon Treasury strips would sell for. She would find this easy to do if she had read Chapter 3 of this book: Using Equation 1 in that chapter, she would figure out that each of the Treasury strip zero-coupon bonds would sell for its present discounted value:

$$\frac{\text{Cash payment in year } n}{(1 + 0.0975)^n}$$

The results of this calculation for each year are listed in column (4) of Table 4. When Fran adds up the values of the collection of the Treasury strip zero-coupon bonds, she gets a figure of $1,015,528, which is greater than the $1 million purchase price of the Treasury bond. As long as it costs less than $15,528 to collect the payments from the Treasury and then pass them through to the owners of the zero-coupon strips, which is likely to be the case since computer technology makes the cost of conducting these financial transactions low, the zero-coupon strips will be profitable for her financial institution. Fran would thus recommend that her firm go ahead and market the new financial product. Because the financial institution can now generate much higher profits by selling substantial numbers of Treasury strips, it would amply reward Fran with a spanking new red BMW and a $100,000 bonus!

SUMMARY

1. The balance sheet of commercial banks can be thought of as a list of the sources and uses of bank funds. The bank's liabilities are its sources of funds, which include checkable deposits, time deposits, discount loans from the Fed, borrowings from other banks and corporations, and bank capital. The bank's assets are its uses of funds, which include reserves, cash items in process of collection, deposits at other banks, securities, loans, and other assets (mostly physical capital).

2. Banks make profits through the process of asset transformation: They borrow short (accept deposits) and lend long (make loans). When a bank takes in additional deposits, it gains an equal amount of reserves; when it pays out deposits, it loses an equal amount of reserves.

3. Although more liquid assets tend to earn lower returns, banks still desire to hold them. Specifically, banks hold excess and secondary reserves because they provide insurance against the costs of a deposit outflow. Banks manage their assets to maximize profits by seeking the highest returns possible on loans and securities while at the same time trying to lower risk and making adequate provisions for liquidity. Although liability management was once a staid affair, large (money center) banks now actively seek out sources of funds by issuing liabilities such as negotiable CDs or by actively borrowing from other banks and corporations. Banks manage the amount of capital they hold to prevent bank failure and to meet bank capital requirements set by the regulatory authorities. However, they do not want to hold too much capital because by so doing they will lower the returns to equity holders.

4. Off-balance-sheet activities consist of trading financial instruments and generating income from fees and loan sales, all of which affect bank profits but are not visible on bank balance sheets. Because these off-balance-sheet activities expose banks to increased risk, bank management must pay particular attention to risk assessment procedures and internal controls to restrict employees from taking on too much risk.

5. A bank's net operating income equals operating income minus operating expenses. Adding gains (or losses) on securities and net extraordinary items to net operating income and then subtracting taxes yields net income (profits after taxes). Additional measures of bank performance include the return on assets *(ROA)*, the return on equity *(ROE)*, and the net interest margin *(NIM)*.

6. A change in the economic environment will stimulate financial institutions to search for financial innovations that are likely to be profitable. Changes in demand conditions, especially the rise in interest-rate risk, have stimulated a search for profits that has resulted in financial innovations such as adjustable-rate mortgages, while changes in supply conditions because of advances in computer technology have led to financial innovations such as bank credit cards and electronic banking facilities. Regulation leads to financial innovation at banks by encouraging loophole mining. Starting in the late 1960s, for example, higher interest rates (resulting from higher inflation) combined with deposit rate ceilings and the "tax" on deposits to limit bank profits. The desire to avoid these regulations encouraged financial innovations, including NOW accounts, ATS accounts, and overnight repos.

KEY TERMS

QUESTIONS AND PROBLEMS

1. Why might a bank be willing to borrow funds from other banks at a higher rate than it can borrow from the Fed?

*2. Rank the following bank assets from most to least liquid:
   a. Commercial loans
   b. Securities
   c. Reserves
   d. Physical capital

3. Using the T-accounts of the First National Bank and the Second National Bank, describe what happens when Jane Brown writes a $50 check on her account at the First National Bank to pay her friend Joe Green, who in turn deposits the check in his account at the Second National Bank.

*4. What happens to reserves at the First National Bank if one person withdraws $1000 of cash and another person deposits $500 of cash? Use T-accounts to explain your answer.

5. The bank you own has the following balance sheet:

Assets		Liabilities	
Reserves	$75 million	Deposits	$500 million
Loans	$525 million	Bank	
		capital	$100 million

If the bank suffers a deposit outflow of $50 million with a required reserve ratio on deposits of 10%, what actions must you take to make sure that your bank meets its reserve requirements?

*6. If a deposit outflow of $50 million occurs, which balance sheet would a bank rather have initially, the balance sheet in Problem 5 or the following balance sheet? Why?

Assets		Liabilities	
Reserves	$100 million	Deposits	$500 million
Securities	$500 million	Bank	
		capital	$100 million

7. If the president of a bank told you that the bank was so well run that it has never had to call in loans, sell securities, or borrow as a result of a deposit outflow, would you be willing to buy stock in that bank? Why or why not?

*8. If the bank you own has no excess reserves and a sound customer comes in asking for a loan, should you automatically turn the customer down, explaining that you don't have any excess reserves to loan out? Why or why not? What options are available for you to provide the funds your customer needs?

9. Why has the development of overnight loan markets made it more likely that banks will hold fewer excess reserves?

*10. If you are a banker and expect interest rates to rise in the future, would you want to make short-term or long-term loans?

11. "Bank managers should always seek the highest return possible on their assets." Is this statement true, false, or uncertain? Explain your answer.

*12. "Banking has become a more dynamic industry because of more active liability management." Is this statement true, false, or uncertain? Explain your answer.

13. Why has noninterest income been growing as a source of bank operating income?

*14. Which components of operating expenses experience the greatest fluctuations? Why?

15. Why do equity holders care more about *ROE* than about *ROA*?

*16. What does the net interest margin measure, and why is it important to bank managers?

17. If a bank doubles the amount of its capital and *ROA* stays constant, what will happen to *ROE*?

*18. If a bank finds that its *ROE* is too low because it has too much bank capital, what can it do to raise its *ROE*?

19. What are the benefits and costs for a bank when it decides to increase the amount of its bank capital?

*20. If a bank is falling short of meeting its capital requirements by $1 million, what three things can it do to rectify the situation?

CASE STUDY

Bank Performance Analysis

CONCEPTS IN THIS CASE

balance sheet
liquidity management
asset management
liability management
return on assets (ROA)
return on equity (ROE)
operating income
operating expenses
net interest margin (NIM)

Your supervisor has recently promoted you to a financial analysis position in the bank. The chief financial officer (your supervisor's boss) is concerned about the bank's financial position in comparison with past trends and recent positions of similar banks in the region. To analyze the firm, you have been assigned the task of producing a bank performance analysis. You have done this type of report in your money and banking classes, and you know that the first step is to collect financial data on your bank and similar banks in order to make the necessary comparisons and suggestions for performance improvements. You collect the data in Tables 1 and 2 from internal annual reports and government publications.*

Using balance sheet and income statement data, create a bank analysis and performance report for your supervisor that addresses the following issues:

1. Using the balance sheet for each year,
   a. Create a balance sheet showing all items as a percentage of total assets. Which items on your bank's balance sheet increased over the last three years? Which items on your bank's balance sheet declined over the last three years?
   b. Examine the liquidity management practices of your bank over the last three years. How has the liquidity position of the bank changed over time? How does the liquidity position of your bank compare to the regional banks in year 3? Would your bank have sufficient reserves if deposits declined 20% in year 4? (Assume that

the reserve requirement is 8% on all deposits.)
   c. Calculate the equity multiplier ratio for each year. How has the equity multiplier of your bank changed over time? How does the equity multiplier of your bank compare to the regional banks in year 3?

2. Using the income statement for each year,
   a. Create an income statement with operating income items expressed as a percentage of total operating income. Which items improved over the last three years? Which trends need to be reversed? How does your bank compare to the regional banks?
   b. Create an income statement with operating expenses expressed as a percentage of total operating expenses. Which items improved over the last three years? Which trends need to be reversed? How does your bank compare to the regional banks?

3. Analyze the performance of the bank for each year.
   a. Calculate the net interest margin (NIM) for each year. How has the NIM trend changed over the last three years? How does your bank compare to the regional banks?
   b. Calculate the return on assets (ROA) for each year. How has the ROA trend changed over the last three years? How does your bank compare to the regional banks?
   c. Calculate the return on equity (ROE) for each year. How has the ROE trend changed over the last three years? How does your bank compare to the regional banks?
   d. Compare years 2 and 3 for your bank in terms of the relationship between changes in capital balances and ROE = ROA × EM.

4. Identify the strengths and weaknesses of your bank relative to trends over time and in year 3 for all regional banks. What is the relationship between your bank trends and the year 3 comparison with the region?

---

*The Internet site http://www.fdic.gov/research provides financial data for all insured banks, states, regions, and other areas; the site http://www.sec.gov allows a search of the EDGAR database.

■ **TABLE 1** Balance Sheet Data ($ millions)

	Your Bank, Year 3	Your Bank, Year 2	Your Bank, Year 1	Banks in Your Region, Year 3
Assets (Uses of Funds)				
Reserves	892	648	558	12,184
Cash items in process of collection	369	236	169	6,513
Deposits at other banks	246	124	179	4,242
Securities				
U.S. government and agency	2,062	2,243	1,694	40,020
State and local government and other securities	739	673	538	13,026
Loans				
Commercial and industrial	1,970	1,795	1,436	34,736
Real estate	2,708	2,467	1,974	47,762
Consumer	1,846	1,682	1,346	32,565
Interbank	348	318	254	6,143
Other	267	243	194	4,712
Other assets (e.g., physical capital)	862	785	628	15,197
Total	12,309	11,214	8,970	217,100
Liabilities (Sources of Funds)				
Checkable deposits	2,954	2,691	2,152	52,104
Nontransaction deposits				
Savings deposits	2,585	1,855	1,884	45,591
Small-denomination time deposits	1,723	1,570	1,256	30,394
Large-denomination time deposits	1,354	1,234	987	23,881
Borrowings	2,954	2,691	2,153	41,104
Bank capital	739	1,173	538	24,026
Total	12,309	11,214	8,970	217,100

■ **TABLE 2** Income Statement Data ($ millions)

	Your Bank, Year 3	Your Bank, Year 2	Your Bank, Year 1	Banks in Your Region, Year 3
Operating Income				
Interest on loans	605	601	441	12,671
Interest on securities	133	151	97	2,347
Other interest	52	47	38	913
Interest income	790	799	576	15,931
Service charges on deposit accounts	399	374	291	7,041
Other noninterest income	244	169	119	3,885
Noninterest income	643	543	410	10,926
Total operating income	1,433	1,342	986	26,857
Operating Expenses				
Interest expenses				
Interest on deposits	304	402	286	9,264
Interest on fed funds and repos	104	31	25	504
Other	61	56	45	872
Noninterest expenses				
Salaries and employee benefits	307	272	306	4,998
Premises and equipment	178	162	30	3,139
Other	173	158	96	3,047
Provisions for loan losses	134	122	87	2,355
Total operating expenses	1,261	1,203	875	24,179
Net Operating Income	172	139	111	2,678
Income taxes	28	26	21	498
Gains (losses) on securities	7	7	16	128
Extraordinary items, net	0	3	2	67
Net income	137	103	72	1,985

CHAPTER 14

COMMERCIAL BANKING INDUSTRY: STRUCTURE AND COMPETITION

■ **PREVIEW** The operations of individual banks (how they acquire, use, and manage funds to make a profit) are roughly similar throughout the world. In all countries, banks are financial intermediaries in the business of earning profits. When you consider the structure and operation of the banking industry as a whole, however, the United States is in a class by itself. In most countries, four or five large banks typically dominate the banking industry, but in the United States there are on the order of 10,000 commercial banks.

Is more better? Does this diversity mean that the American banking system is more competitive and therefore more economically efficient and sound than banking systems in other countries? What in the American economic and political system explains this large number of banking institutions? In this chapter we try to answer these questions by examining the historical trends in the commercial banking industry and its overall structure.

We start by examining the industry in detail. In addition to looking at our domestic banking system, we also examine the forces behind the growth in international banking to see how it has affected us in the United States. Finally, we examine how financial innovation has increased the competitive environment for the banking industry and is causing fundamental changes in it.

■ HISTORICAL DEVELOPMENT OF THE BANKING SYSTEM

The modern commercial banking industry began when the Bank of North America was chartered in Philadelphia in 1782. With the success of this bank, other banks opened for business, and the American banking industry was off and running. (As

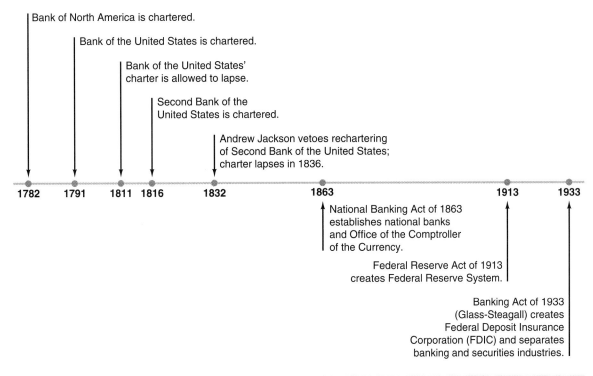

Bank of North America is chartered.

Bank of the United States is chartered.

Bank of the United States' charter is allowed to lapse.

Second Bank of the United States is chartered.

Andrew Jackson vetoes rechartering of Second Bank of the United States; charter lapses in 1836.

1782   1791   1811   1816   1832   1863   1913   1933

National Banking Act of 1863 establishes national banks and Office of the Comptroller of the Currency.

Federal Reserve Act of 1913 creates Federal Reserve System.

Banking Act of 1933 (Glass-Steagall) creates Federal Deposit Insurance Corporation (FDIC) and separates banking and securities industries.

■FIGURE 1 Time Line of the Early History of Commercial Banking in the United States

a study aid, Figure 1 provides a time line of the most important dates in the history of American banking before World War II.)

A major controversy involving the industry in its early years was whether the federal government or the states should charter banks. The Federalists, particularly Alexander Hamilton, advocated greater centralized control of banking and federal chartering of banks. Their efforts led to the creation in 1791 of the Bank of the United States, which had elements of both a private and a **central bank,** a government institution that has responsibility for the amount of money and credit supplied in the economy as a whole. Agricultural and other interests, however, were quite suspicious of centralized power and hence advocated chartering by the states. Furthermore, their distrust of moneyed interests in the big cities led to political pressures to eliminate the Bank of the United States, and in 1811 their efforts met with success when its charter was not renewed. Because of abuses by state banks and the clear need for a central bank to help the federal government raise funds during the War of 1812, Congress was stimulated to create the Second Bank of the United States in 1816. The tensions between advocates and opponents of centralized banking power were a recurrent theme during the operation of this second attempt at central banking in the United States, and with the election of Andrew Jackson, a strong advocate of states' rights, the fate of the Second Bank was sealed. After the election in 1832, Jackson vetoed the rechartering of the Second Bank of the United States as a national bank, and its charter lapsed in 1836.

Until 1863, all commercial banks in the United States were chartered by the banking commission of the state in which each operated. No national currency existed, and banks obtained funds primarily by issuing *banknotes* (currency circulated by the banks that could be redeemed for gold). Because banking regulations were extremely lax in many states, banks regularly failed due to fraud or lack of sufficient bank capital; their banknotes became worthless.

To eliminate the abuses of the state-chartered banks (called **state banks**), the National Banking Act of 1863 (and subsequent amendments to it) created a new banking system of federally chartered banks (called **national banks**), supervised by the Office of the Comptroller of the Currency, a department of the U.S. Treasury. This legislation was originally intended to dry up sources of funds to state banks by imposing a prohibitive tax on their banknotes while leaving the banknotes of the federally chartered banks untaxed. The state banks cleverly escaped extinction by acquiring funds by accepting deposits. As a result, today the United States has a **dual banking system** in which banks supervised by the federal government and banks supervised by the states operate side by side.

Central banking did not reappear in this country until the Federal Reserve System (the Fed) was created in 1913 to promote an even safer banking system. All national banks were required to become members of the Federal Reserve System and became subject to a new set of regulations issued by the Fed. State banks could choose (but were not required) to become members of the system, and most did not because of the high costs of membership stemming from the Fed's regulations.

During the Great Depression years 1930–1933, some 9000 bank failures wiped out the savings of many depositors at commercial banks. To prevent future depositor losses from such failures, banking legislation in 1933 established the Federal Deposit Insurance Corporation (FDIC), which provided federal insurance on bank deposits. Member banks of the Federal Reserve System were required to purchase FDIC insurance for their depositors, and non–Federal Reserve commercial banks could choose to buy this insurance (almost all of them did). The purchase of FDIC insurance made banks subject to another set of regulations imposed by the FDIC.

Because investment banking activities of the commercial banks were blamed for many bank failures, provisions in the banking legislation of 1933 (also known as the Glass-Steagall Act) prohibited commercial banks from underwriting or dealing in corporate securities (commercial banks were allowed to sell new issues of government securities, however) and limited banks to the purchase of debt securities approved by the bank regulatory agencies. Likewise it prohibited investment banks from engaging in commercial banking activities. In effect, the Glass-Steagall Act separated the activities of commercial banks from those of the securities industry.

Under the conditions of the Glass-Steagall Act, commercial banks had to sell off their investment banking operations. The First National Bank of Boston, for example, spun off its investment banking operations into the First Boston

Corporation, now one of the most important investment banking firms in America. Investment banking firms typically discontinued their deposit business, although J. P. Morgan discontinued its investment banking business and reorganized as a commercial bank; however, some senior officers of J. P. Morgan went on to organize Morgan Stanley, another one of the largest investment banking firms today.

Multiple Regulatory Agencies

Commercial bank regulation in the United States has developed into a crazy-quilt system of multiple regulatory agencies with overlapping jurisdictions. The Office of the Comptroller of the Currency has the primary supervisory responsibility for the 3000 national banks that own more than half of the assets in the commercial banking system. The Federal Reserve and the state banking authorities have joint primary responsibility for the 1000 state banks that are members of the Federal Reserve System. The Fed also has sole regulatory responsibility over companies that own one or more banks (called **bank holding companies**) and secondary responsibility for the national banks. The FDIC and the state banking authorities jointly supervise the 6000 state banks that have FDIC insurance but are not members of the Federal Reserve System. The state banking authorities have sole jurisdiction over the fewer than 500 state banks without FDIC insurance. (Such banks hold less than 0.2% of the deposits in the commercial banking system.)

If you find the U.S. bank regulatory system confusing, imagine how confusing it is for the banks, which have to deal with multiple regulatory agencies. Several proposals have been raised by the U.S. Treasury to rectify this situation by centralizing the regulation of all depository institutions under one independent agency. However, none of these has been successful in Congress, and whether there will be regulatory consolidation in the future is highly uncertain.

■ STRUCTURE OF THE U.S. COMMERCIAL BANKING INDUSTRY

There are around 10,000 commercial banks in the United States, far more than in any other country in the world. As Table 1 indicates, we have an extraordinary number of small banks. Eighteen percent of the banks have less than $25 million

■ TABLE 1 Size Distribution of Insured Commercial Banks, End of 1995

Assets	Number of Banks	Share of Banks (%)	Share of Assets Held (%)
Less than $25 million	1,756	17.7	0.7
$25–$50 million	2,369	23.8	2.0
$50–$100 million	2,534	25.5	4.2
$100–$500 million	2,593	26.1	11.9
$500 million–$1 billion	268	2.7	4.3
$1–$10 billion	346	3.5	24.4
More than $10 billion	75	0.8	52.5
Total	9,941	100.0	100.0

Source: Federal Deposit Insurance Corporation, *1995 Statistics on Banking.*

in assets. Far more typical is the size distribution in Canada or the United Kingdom, where five or fewer banks dominate the industry. In contrast, the ten largest commercial banks in the United States (listed in Table 2) together hold just 37% of the assets in their industry.

Most industries in the United States have far fewer firms than the commercial banking industry; typically, large firms tend to dominate these industries to a greater extent than in the commercial banking industry. (Consider the computer software industry, which is dominated by Microsoft, or the automobile industry, which is dominated by General Motors, Ford, Chrysler, Toyota, and Honda.) Does the large number of banks in the commercial banking industry and the absence of a few dominant firms suggest that commercial banking is more competitive than other industries?

Restrictions on Branching

The presence of so many commercial banks in the United States actually reflects past regulations that restricted the ability of these financial institutions to open **branches** (additional offices for the conduct of banking operations). Each state had its own regulations on the type and number of branches that a bank could open. Regulations on both coasts, for example, tended to allow banks to open branches throughout a state; in the middle part of the country, regulations on branching were more restrictive. The McFadden Act of 1927, which was designed to put national banks and state banks on an equal footing (and the Douglas Amendment of 1970, which closed a loophole in the McFadden Act) effectively prohibited banks from branching across state lines and forced all national banks to conform to the branching regulations in the state of their location.

The result of the McFadden Act and the state branching regulations was that many small banks stayed in existence because a large bank capable of driving them out of business was often restricted from opening a branch nearby. Indeed, it was often easier for a U.S. bank to open a branch in a foreign country than to open one in another state!

■ **TABLE 2** Ten Largest U.S. Banks, 1996

Bank	Assets ($ billions)	Share of All Commercial Bank Assets (%)
1. Citicorp, New York	256.9	6.0
2. BankAmerica Corp., San Francisco	232.4	5.4
3. NationsBank, Charlotte, N.C.	187.3	4.3
4. J. P. Morgan & Co., New York	184.9	4.3
5. Chemical Banking Corp., New York	182.9	4.2
6. First Chicago NBD Corp., Chicago	122.0	2.8
7. Chase Manhattan Corp., New York	121.7	2.8
8. Bankers Trust Corp., New York	104.0	2.4
9. First Union Corp., Charlotte, N.C.	96.7	2.2
10. Banc One Corp., Columbus, Ohio	90.2	2.1
Total	1579.0	36.6

Source: American Banker, July 1996.

Advocates of restrictive state branching regulations argue that these regulations foster competition by keeping so many banks in business. But the existence of large numbers of banks in the United States must be seen as an indication of a *lack* of competition, *not* the presence of vigorous competition. Inefficient banks have been able to remain in business because their customers could not find a conveniently located branch of another bank in which to conduct their business.

The McFadden Act and state branching regulations constituted strong anticompetitive forces in the commercial banking industry. If competition is beneficial to society, why have regulations restricting branching arisen in America? The simplest explanation is that the American public has historically been hostile to large banks. States with the most restrictive branching regulations were typically ones in which populist antibank sentiment was strongest in the nineteenth century. (These states usually had large farming populations whose relations with banks periodically became tempestuous when banks would foreclose on farmers who couldn't pay their debts.) The legacy of nineteenth-century politics was a banking system with restrictive branching regulations and hence an inordinate number of small banks. However, as we will see later in this chapter, branching restrictions are being eliminated, and we are heading toward nationwide banking.

Response to Branching Restrictions

An important feature of the U.S. banking industry is that competition can be repressed by regulation but not completely quashed. As we saw in Chapter 13, the existence of restrictive regulation will stimulate banking institutions to go "loophole mining," coming up with financial innovations that get around these regulations in the banks' search for profits. Regulations restricting branching have stimulated similar economic forces and have promoted the development of three financial innovations: bank holding companies, nonbank banks, and automated teller machines.

Bank Holding Companies A holding company is a corporation that owns several different companies. This form of corporate ownership has important advantages for banks in that (1) it has allowed them to circumvent restrictive branching regulations, because the holding company can own a controlling interest in several banks even if branching is not permitted; (2) a bank holding company can engage in other activities related to banking, such as the provision of investment advice, data processing and transmission services, leasing, credit card services, and servicing of loans in other states; and (3) the holding company can issue commercial paper, allowing the bank to tap into nondeposit sources of funds.

At the current time, bank holding companies are restricted to owning businesses that are "closely related to banking." Permissible activities, which are specified by the Federal Reserve's Regulation Y, include the activities mentioned here as well as others, ranging from providing courier services to real estate appraisal. In the past, the Fed and congressional legislation have prohibited bank holding companies from engaging in activities such as brokering real estate, underwriting securities, operating travel agencies, and offering general management consulting. However, in their continuing search for profits, bank holding companies have been seeking ways to get around these regulations and have been entering previously prohibited areas.

Bank holding companies also have the advantage that many states would allow bank holding companies headquartered in other states to purchase banks in their state. In addition, starting in 1982, banks were permitted to purchase out-of-state banks that were failing. For example, bank holding companies headquartered in New York, Ohio, North Carolina, Michigan, and California gained entry into the Texas market by purchasing failing institutions in that state. The result was that the McFadden Act's restrictions on branching no longer prevented these companies from providing banking services in other states.

The growth of the bank holding companies has been dramatic over the past three decades. Today bank holding companies (including Citicorp, BankAmerica, Chase Manhattan, NationsBank, and Wells Fargo) own almost all large banks, and over 90% of all commercial bank deposits are held in banks owned by holding companies.

Nonbank Banks Another way banks could avoid branching restrictions was through a loophole in the Bank Holding Act of 1956, which defined a bank as a financial institution that accepts deposits *and* makes loans. Once bank holding companies recognized this loophole, they realized that if they opened limited-service banks that either took deposits but did not make commercial loans or did not take deposits but made commercial loans, these so-called **nonbank banks** would not be subject to branching regulations. Thus the bank holding companies discovered a way of branching across state lines. However, the Competitive Equality Bank Act passed in 1987 placed a moratorium on new nonbank banks, thus closing this loophole.

Automated Teller Machines Another financial innovation that avoided the restrictions on branching is the electronic banking facility known as the automated teller machine (ATM). Banks realized that if they did not own or rent the ATM, but instead let it be owned by someone else and paid for each transaction with a fee, the ATM would probably not be considered a branch of the bank and thus would not be subject to branching regulations. This is exactly what the regulatory agencies and courts in most states concluded. Because they enable banks to widen their markets, a number of these shared facilities (such as Cirrus and NYCE) have been established nationwide. Furthermore, even when an ATM is owned by a bank, states typically have special provisions that allow wider establishment of ATMs than is permissible for traditional "brick and mortar" branches.

As we saw in Chapter 13, avoiding regulation was not the only reason for the development of the ATM. The advent of cheaper computer and telecommunications technology enabled banks to provide ATMs at low cost, making them a profitable innovation. This further illustrates that technological factors often combine with incentives such as the desire to avoid restrictive regulations like branching restrictions to produce financial innovation.

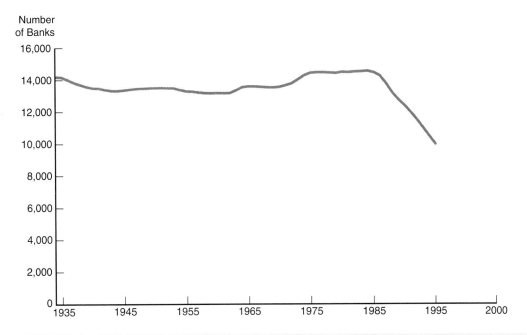

■FIGURE 2 Number of Insured Commercial Banks in the United States, 1934–1995

Sources: Federal Deposit Insurance Corporation, *1995 Statistics on Banking; Historical Statistics on Banking.*

■ NATIONWIDE BANKING AND BANK CONSOLIDATION

As we can see in Figure 2, after a remarkable period of stability from 1934 to the mid-1980s, the number of commercial banks has begun to fall dramatically. Why is this sudden decline taking place?

The banking industry hit some hard times in the 1980s and early 1990s, with bank failures running at a rate of over 100 per year from 1985 to 1992 (more on this in Chapter 16). But bank failures are only part of the story. In the years 1985–1992, the number of banks declined by 3000—more than double the number of failures. And in the period 1992–1996, when the banking industry returned to health, the number of commercial banks declined by a little over 1500, less than 15 percent of which were bank failures, and most of those were of small banks. Thus we see that bank failures played an important, though not predominant, role in the decline in the number of banks in the 1985–1992 period and an almost negligible role in the decline in the number of banks since then.

So what explains the rest of the story? The answer is bank consolidation. Banks have been merging to create larger entities or have been buying up other banks. This gives rise to a new question: Why has bank consolidation been taking place in recent years?

As we have seen, loophole mining by banks has reduced the effectiveness of branching restrictions, with the result that many states have recognized that it would be in their best interest if they allowed ownership of banks across state lines. The result has been the formation of regional compacts in which banks in the region are allowed to own banks in other states in the region. In 1975, Maine enacted the first interstate banking legislation that allowed out-of-state bank holding companies to purchase banks in that state. In 1982, Massachusetts enacted a regional compact with other New England states to allow interstate banking, and many other regional compacts were adopted thereafter until by the early 1990s, almost all states allowed some form of interstate banking.

With the barriers to interstate banking breaking down in the early 1980s, banks recognized that they could gain the benefits of diversification because they would now be able to make loans in many states rather than just one. This gave them the advantage that if one state's economy was weak, another in which they operated might be strong, thus decreasing the likelihood that loans in different states would default at the same time. In addition, allowing banks to own banks in other states meant that they could take advantage of economies of scale by increasing their size through out-of-state acquisition of banks or by merging with banks in other states. Mergers and acquisitions explain the first phase of banking consolidation which has played such an important role in the decline in the number of banks since 1985. Another result of the loosening of restrictions on interstate branching is the development of a new class of bank, the so-called **superregional banks,** bank holding companies that have begun to rival the money center banks in size but whose headquarters are not based in one of the money center cities (New York, Chicago, and San Francisco). Examples of these superregional banks are NationsBank of Charlotte, North Carolina, and Banc One of Columbus, Ohio.

Riegle-Neal Interstate Banking and Branching Efficiency Act of 1994

Banking consolidation has been given further stimulus by the passage in 1994 of the Riegle-Neal Interstate Banking and Branching Efficiency Act. This legislation expands the regional compacts to the entire nation and overturns the McFadden Act and Douglas Amendment's prohibition of interstate banking. Not only does this act allow bank holding companies to acquire banks in any other state, notwithstanding any state laws to the contrary, but it allows interstate branching by allowing bank holding companies to merge the banks they own into one bank with branches in different states beginning June 1, 1997. States do have the option of allowing interstate branching to occur earlier than this date, and several have done so; they also have the option of opting out of interstate branching, a choice only Texas has made.

The Riegle-Neal Act finally establishes the basis for a true nationwide banking system. Although interstate banking was accomplished previously by out-of-state purchase of banks by bank holding companies, up until 1994 interstate branching was virtually nonexistent because very few states had enacted interstate branching legislation. Allowing banks to conduct interstate banking through branching is especially important because many bankers feel that economies of scale cannot be fully exploited through the bank holding company structure; they can only be fully exploited through branching networks in which all of the bank's operations are fully coordinated.

What Will the Structure of the U.S. Banking Industry Look like in the Future?

With true nationwide banking becoming a reality, the benefits of bank consolidation for the banking industry have increased substantially, thus driving the next phase of mergers and acquisitions and accelerating the decline in the number of commercial banks. Great changes are occurring in the structure of this industry, and the natural question arises: What will the industry look like in, say, ten years?

One view is that the industry will become more like that in many other countries (see Box 1) and we will end up with only a couple of hundred banks. A more extreme view is that it will look like that of Canada or the United Kingdom with a few large banks dominating the industry. Research on this question, however, comes up with a different answer. The structure of the U.S. banking industry will still be unique, but not as unique as it once was. Most experts predict that the consolidation surge will settle down as the U.S. banking industry approaches several thousand, rather than several hundred, banks. One simple way of seeing why the number of banks will continue to be substantial is to recognize that California, which has unrestricted branching throughout the state, has close to 400 commercial banks. Blowing up the number of banks by the share of banking assets in California relative to the whole country produces an estimate of the number of banks with unrestricted nationwide branching on the order of 4000. More sophisticated research suggests that the number of banks in the United States will ultimately be somewhat fewer than this, but not much.[1]

Banking consolidation will not only result in a smaller number of banks, but as the recent merger between Chase Manhattan Bank and Chemical Bank and the purchase of Boatsmen's Bank by NationsBank suggest, a shift in assets from smaller banks to larger banks as well. Within ten years, the share of bank assets in banks with less than $100 million in assets is expected to halve, while the amount

---

BOX 1   A GLOBAL PERSPECTIVE

Comparison of Banking Structure in the United States and Abroad

 The structure of the commercial banking industry in the United States is radically different from that in other industrialized nations. The United States is the only country that is just now developing a true national banking system in which banks have branches throughout the country. One result is that there are many more banks in the United States than in other industrialized countries. In contrast to the United States, which has on the order of 10,000 commercial banks, every other industrialized country has well under 1000. Japan, for example, has fewer than 100 commercial banks—just 1% of the number in the United States, even though its economy and population are half the size of the United States. Another result of the past restrictions on branching in the United States is that our banks tend to be much smaller than those in other countries.

---

[1]For example, see Allen N. Berger, Anil K. Kashyap, and Joseph Scalise, "The Transformation of the U.S. Banking Industry: What a Long, Strange Trip It's Been," *Brookings Papers on Economic Activity* 2 (1995): 55–201, and Timothy Hannan and Stephen Rhoades, "Future U.S. Banking Structure, 1990–2010," in *Antitrust Bulletin* 37 (1992): 737–798. For a more detailed treatment of the bank consolidation process taking place in the United States, see Frederic S. Mishkin, "Bank Consolidation: A Central Banker's Perspective," National Bureau Working Paper No. 5849, December 1996.

at the so-called megabanks, those with over $100 billion in assets, is expected to more than double.

Are Bank Consolidation and Nationwide Banking Good Things?

Advocates of nationwide banking believe that it will produce more efficient banks and a healthier banking system less prone to bank failures. However, critics of bank consolidation fear that it will eliminate small banks, referred to as *community banks,* and that this will result in less lending to small businesses. In addition, they worry that a few banks will come to dominate the industry, making the banking business less competitive.

Most economists are skeptical of these criticisms of bank consolidation. As we have seen, research indicates that even after bank consolidation is completed, the United States will still have plenty of banks. Furthermore, megabanks will not dominate the banking industry. This research suggests that there will be more than ten banks with assets over $100 billion, and their collective share of bank assets will be less than 50%. The banking industry will thus remain highly competitive, probably even more so than now considering that banks that have been protected from competition from out-of-state banks will now have to compete with them vigorously to stay in business.

It also does not look as though community banks will disappear. When New York State liberalized branching laws in 1962, there were fears that community banks upstate would be driven from the market by the big New York City banks. Not only did this not happen, but some of the big boys found that the small banks were able to run rings around them in the local markets. Similarly, California, which has had unrestricted statewide branching for a long time, continues to have a thriving collection of community banks.

Economists see some important benefits of bank consolidation and nationwide banking. The elimination of geographic restrictions on banking will increase competition and drive inefficient banks out of business, thus raising the efficiency of the banking sector. The move to larger banking organizations also means that there will be some increase in efficiency because of economies of scale. The increased diversification of banks' loan portfolios may lower the probability of a banking crisis in the future. In the 1980s and early 1990s, bank failures were often concentrated in states with weak economies. For example, after the decline in oil prices in 1986, all the major commercial banks in Texas, which had been very profitable, now found themselves in trouble. At that time, banks in New England were doing fine. However, when the 1990–1991 recession hit New England hard, New England banks started failing. With nationwide banking, a bank could make loans in both New England and Texas and would thus be less likely to fail because when the loans were going sour in one location, they would likely be doing well in the other. Thus nationwide banking is seen as a major step toward creating a healthy banking system that is less prone to banking crises.

The two potential negatives to bank consolidation are that it might lead to a reduction in lending to small businesses because of the reduction in assets at small banks who specialize in small business lending and that the rush of banks to expand into new geographic markets might lead them into increased risk taking, which might lead to bank failures. The jury is still out on these concerns, but most economists see the benefits of bank consolidation and nationwide banking as outweighing the costs.

■ SEPARATION OF THE BANKING AND SECURITIES INDUSTRIES

Another important feature of the structure of the banking industry in the United States is the separation of the banking and securities industry. The Glass-Steagall Act of 1933 forced a separation between these industries. Glass-Steagall allowed commercial banks to sell new offerings of government securities but prohibited them from underwriting corporate securities or from engaging in brokerage activities. It also prohibited investment banks from engaging in commercial banking activities and thus has protected banks from competition.

Repeal of the Glass-Steagall Act

An issue that has received much attention in Congress is repeal of the Glass-Steagall Act. In 1995 and 1996, Representative Jim Leach, chair of the House Banking Committee, proposed a bill to repeal the Glass-Steagall Act and allow banks to enter the securities business. Leach was unsuccessful in getting the bill passed, but it is clear that Glass-Steagall reform will be on the agenda of future Congresses.

The Case for Allowing Banks to Enter the Securities Business As we have seen, the Glass-Steagall Act of 1933 prohibited banks from engaging in securities market activities such as securities underwriting or the sale of mutual funds. Advocates of allowing banks to participate in securities market activities argue that it is unfair to keep commercial banks from pursuing these activities in competition with investment banking and brokerage firms. Brokerage firms have been able to pursue traditional banking activities with the development of money market mutual funds and cash management accounts. Why shouldn't banks be allowed to compete with brokerage firms in those firms' traditional areas of business, the selling of corporate securities and the management of mutual funds?

Another argument in favor of allowing banks to enter the securities business is increased competition. Bank entry will mean that in the case of a new issue of securities, there will be more bidders to underwrite the issue. As a result, the spread between the price guaranteed to the issuer of the security and the price paid for the security by the general public will fall. This reduction in the spread will mean that both borrowers and lenders in financial markets will be better off: Issuers of securities (borrowers) will receive a higher price for their securities and will thus bear a lower interest cost, while the purchasers of securities (lenders) will be able to buy the securities at a lower price, thereby giving them a higher interest rate. The fact that underwriting spreads for investment-grade bonds have dropped substantially since commercial banks have been allowed to underwrite these securities is powerful evidence in support of this view. Banks' entry into the brokerage business (which has been occurring through bank holding companies) might also increase competition in this industry which could lead to lower brokerage commissions—another advantage to investors.

The Case Against Allowing Banks to Enter the Securities Business   Opponents of bank entry into the securities business argue that banks have an unfair advantage in competing against brokerage firms. Deposits provide banks with an artificially low cost of funds because they are insured by the FDIC.[2] Brokerage firms have higher costs on the funds they acquire, which are usually obtained through loans from banks.

The securities business, particularly investment banking, may involve more risk than traditional banking activities. An investment bank can suffer substantial losses if it is unable to sell securities it has underwritten for the price that it has agreed to pay the issuer. So allowing commercial banks to engage in investment banking might produce more bank failures and a less stable financial system. This problem would be even more acute because of the existence of federal deposit insurance. Allowing commercial banks to take advantage of additional risky activities increases the potential for moral hazard and adverse selection problems to arise. However, there is no compelling evidence that engaging in investment banking activities increased risk taking by banks before Glass-Steagall was passed.

Another argument against allowing banks to enter the securities business is that commercial banks face a potential conflict of interest if they engage in underwriting of securities. Congressional hearings prior to enactment of the Glass-Steagall Act in 1933 turned up some abuses that were tied to commercial banking's activities in the investment banking area. Banks that were underwriting new issues of securities sold them to trust funds that they managed when they could not sell them to anyone else, and these trust funds often took substantial losses when the securities were sold later. Cases surfaced in which the bank itself would buy securities that it was underwriting when the securities could not be sold elsewhere. The resulting lower quality of the bank's assets could have contributed to a failure later on.

Proponents of allowing banks to enter the securities business counter this argument by saying that the securities markets and commercial banking are very different industries today from what they were before 1933. Bank regulation and the SEC could probably prevent many of the abuses that occurred before the Glass-Steagall Act and the extent of the abuses that occurred before the passage of the act was probably exaggerated. Regulatory authorities now have much greater power than before 1933 to find and punish people who would abuse commercial banking's securities activities, and erection of "fire walls" to separate various bank operations can help prevent conflicts of interest. Although proponents do not guarantee that no abuses would occur, they suggest that abuses would be

---

[2]Note that the cost of funds will be artificially low only if the FDIC subsidizes the insurance by charging premiums that are too low. The past losses to the FDIC suggest that this was the case until 1991. However, with the development of risk-based deposit insurance premiums, it is no longer clear that the FDIC is subsidizing deposit insurance. So the argument that banks have an unfair advantage because they have an artificially low cost of funds is no longer as persuasive.

infrequent enough that any costs associated with them would be far smaller than the benefits of increased competition in the securities industry.

Future Prospects The debate about whether banks should be involved in securities activities has not been resolved. However, the pursuit of profits and financial innovation has stimulated both banks and other financial institutions to bypass the intent of the Glass-Steagall Act and encroach on each other's traditional territory. In addition, even primarily nonfinancial corporations have entered the banking and securities business. Companies like General Motors, Ford, and General Electric provide installment loans to their customers through their finance company subsidiaries, and retailers like J. C. Penney, Montgomery Ward, and Sears have experimented with selling insurance, securities, money market mutual funds, and real estate in their stores. (However, in 1992, Sears decided that this business was not sufficiently profitable and sold off some of its financial services businesses.)

Because commercial banks' market share in financial services had been falling, in 1987 the Federal Reserve used a loophole in Section 20 of the Glass-Steagall Act to begin to allow bank holding companies to underwrite several previously prohibited classes of securities. The loophole allows affiliates of approved commercial banks to engage in underwriting activities as long as the revenue doesn't exceed a specified amount, currently 25%, of the affiliates' total revenue. The remainder of the affiliates' revenue can be obtained by underwriting municipal bonds and selling Treasury securities, activities that were never precluded under Glass-Steagall. After the U.S. Supreme Court validated the Fed's action in July 1988, the Federal Reserve took the historic steps of allowing a commercial bank holding company, J. P. Morgan, to underwrite corporate debt securities (in January 1989) and to underwrite stocks (September 1990), with the privilege subsequently extended to other bank holding companies. The regulatory agencies have also allowed banks to invest in real estate and to engage in some insurance activities.

The regulatory trend seems to be accepting what has already been occurring in the marketplace. An important factor is that foreign commercial banks are often allowed to engage in the securities business, giving them a competitive edge over American banks. Regulators may thus be reluctant to restrict commercial banks' securities activities if it puts American banks at a competitive disadvantage relative to foreign banks. The trend away from the separation of banking and the securities industry is therefore likely to continue, and the demise of the Glass-Steagall Act may not be far off.

 ## Separation of the Banking and Securities Industries in Other Countries

Not many other countries have followed the lead of the United States in separating the banking and securities industries. In fact, this separation is the most prominent difference between banking regulation in the United States and in other countries. Around the world, there are three basic frameworks for the banking and securities industries.

The first framework is *universal banking,* which exists in Germany, the Netherlands, and Switzerland. It provides no separation at all between the banking and securities industries. In a universal banking system, commercial banks provide a full range of banking, securities, and insurance services, all within a single legal entity. Banks are allowed to own sizable equity shares in commercial firms, and often they do.

The British-style universal banking system, the second framework, is found in the United Kingdom and countries with close ties to it, such as Canada and Australia. The British-style universal bank engages in securities underwriting, but it differs from the German-style universal bank in three ways: Separate legal subsidiaries are more common, bank equity holdings of commercial firms are less common, and combinations of banking and insurance firms are less common.

The third framework features legal separation of the banking and securities industries, as in the United States and Japan. A major difference between the U.S. and Japanese banking systems is that Japanese banks are allowed to hold substantial equity stakes in commercial firms, whereas American banks cannot. In addition, most American banks use a bank-holding-company structure, but bank holding companies are illegal in Japan. Although the banking and securities industries are legally separated under the Glass-Steagall Act in the United States and Section 65 of the Japanese Securities Act, in both countries commercial banks are increasingly being allowed to engage in securities activities and are thus becoming more like British-style universal banks.

 ## INTERNATIONAL BANKING

In 1960, only eight U.S. banks operated branches in foreign countries, and their total assets were less than $4 billion. Currently, over 100 American banks have branches abroad, with assets totaling over $500 billion. The spectacular growth in international banking can be explained by three factors.

First is the rapid growth in international trade and multinational (worldwide) corporations that has occurred since 1960. When American firms operate abroad, they need banking services in foreign countries to help finance international trade. For example, they might need a loan in a foreign currency to operate a factory abroad. And when they sell goods abroad, they need to have a bank exchange the foreign currency they have received for their goods into dollars. Although these firms could use foreign banks to provide them with these international banking services, many of them prefer to do business with the U.S. banks with which they have established long-term relationships and which understand American business customs and practices. As international trade has grown, international banking has grown with it.

Second, when American banks go abroad, they are allowed to pursue activities that are prohibited in the United States under the Glass-Steagall Act. American banks are very active in global investment banking, in which they underwrite foreign securities. They also sell insurance abroad, and they derive substantial profits from these investment banking and insurance activities. The desire to escape burdensome regulations, an important factor that has stimulated financial innovations, has therefore also been a major spur to international banking.

Third, American banks have wanted to tap into the large pool of dollar-denominated deposits in foreign countries known as Eurodollars. To understand the structure of U.S. banking overseas, let us first look at the Eurodollar market, an important source of growth for international banking.

Eurodollar Market

Eurodollars are created when deposits in accounts in the United States are transferred to a bank outside the country and are kept in the form of dollars. For example, if Rolls-Royce PLC deposits a $1 million check, written on an account at an American bank, in its bank in London—specifying that the deposit is payable in dollars—$1 million in Eurodollars is created.[3] Over 90% of Eurodollar deposits are time deposits, more than half of them certificates of deposit with maturities of 30 days or more. The total amount of Eurodollars outstanding exceeds $2 trillion, making the Eurodollar market (which was born in an ironic way—see Box 2) one of the most important financial markets in the world economy.

Why would companies like Rolls-Royce want to hold dollar deposits outside the United States? First, the dollar is the most widely used currency in international trade, so Rolls-Royce might want to hold deposits in dollars to conduct its international transactions. Second, Eurodollars are "offshore" deposits—they are held in countries that will not subject them to regulations such as reserve requirements or restrictions (called *capital controls*) on taking the deposits outside the country.[4]

The main center of the Eurodollar market is London, a major international financial center for hundreds of years. Eurodollars are also held outside of Europe

---

BOX 2   A GLOBAL PERSPECTIVE

Ironic Birth of the Eurodollar Market

 One of capitalism's great ironies is that the Eurodollar market, one of the most important financial markets used by capitalists, was fathered by the Soviet Union. In the early 1950s, during the height of the Cold War, the Soviets had accumulated a substantial amount of dollar balances held by banks in the United States. Because the Russians feared that the U.S. government might freeze these assets in the United States, they wanted to move the deposits to Europe, where they would be safe from expropriation. (This fear was not unjustified—consider the U.S. freeze on Iranian assets in 1979 and Iraqi assets in 1990.) However, they also wanted to keep the deposits in dollars so that they could be used in their international transactions. The solution to the problem was to transfer the deposits to European banks but to keep the deposits denominated in dollars. When the Soviets did this, the Eurodollar was born.

---

[3]Note that the London bank has acquired the deposit at the American bank formerly owned by Rolls-Royce, so the creation of Eurodollars has not caused a reduction in the amount of bank deposits in the United States.

[4]Although most offshore deposits are denominated in dollars, some are also denominated in other currencies. Collectively, these offshore deposits are referred to as Eurocurrencies. A German mark–denominated deposit held in London, for example, is called a Euromark, and a French franc–denominated deposit held in London is called a Eurofranc.

in locations that provide offshore status to these deposits—for example, Hong Kong, Singapore, and the Caribbean (Bahamas, Cayman Islands).

The minimum-sized transaction in the Eurodollar market is typically $1 million, and approximately 75% of Eurodollar deposits are held by banks. Plainly, you and I are unlikely to come into direct contact with Eurodollars. The Eurodollar market is, however, an important source of funds to U.S. banks, whose borrowing of these deposits is over $100 billion. Rather than using an intermediary and borrowing all the deposits from foreign banks, American banks decided that they could earn higher profits by opening their own branches abroad to attract these deposits. Consequently, the Eurodollar market has been an important stimulus to U.S. banking overseas.

Structure of U.S. Banking Overseas

U.S. banks have most of their foreign branches in Latin America, the Far East, the Caribbean, and London. The largest volume of assets is held by branches in London because it is a major international financial center and the central location for the Eurodollar market. Latin America and the Far East have many branches because of the importance of U.S. trade with these regions. Parts of the Caribbean (especially the Bahamas and the Cayman Islands) have become important as tax havens, with minimal taxation and few restrictive regulations. In actuality, the bank branches in the Bahamas and the Cayman Islands are "shell operations" because they function primarily as bookkeeping centers and do not provide normal banking services.

An alternative corporate structure for U.S. banks that operate overseas is the **Edge Act corporation,** which is a special subsidiary engaged primarily in international banking. This corporate structure, created by the Edge Act of 1919, allows American banks to compete more effectively against foreign banks by exempting Edge Act corporations from certain U.S. banking regulations. For example, Edge Act corporations are exempt from the prohibition on branching across state lines; they can have branches in different states to facilitate the financing of trade with different parts of the world—an office on the West Coast to handle the financing of trade with Japan, an office in Miami to handle the financing of trade with Latin America, and so forth.

U.S. banks (through their holding companies) can also own a controlling interest in foreign banks and in foreign companies that provide financial services, such as finance companies. The international activities of member banks of the Federal Reserve System, bank holding companies, and Edge Act corporations (which account for almost all international banking conducted by U.S. banks) are governed by the Federal Reserve's Regulation K. As in the case of bank holding companies, these international activities must be "closely related to banking."

In late 1981, the Federal Reserve approved the creation of **international banking facilities (IBFs)** within the United States that can accept time deposits from foreigners but are not subject to either reserve requirements or restrictions on interest payments. IBFs are also allowed to make loans to foreigners, but they are not allowed to make loans to domestic residents. States have encouraged the establishment of IBFs by exempting them from state and local taxes. In essence, IBFs are treated like foreign branches of U.S. banks and are not subject to domestic regulations and taxes. The purpose of establishing IBFs is to encourage American and foreign banks to do more banking business in the United States rather than abroad. From this point of view, IBFs have been a success: Their assets climbed to nearly $200 billion in the first two years and currently exceed that amount.

Foreign Banks in the United States

The growth in international trade has not only encouraged U.S. banks to open offices overseas but also encouraged foreign banks to establish offices in the United States. Foreign banks have been extremely successful in the United States. Over the past 20 years, foreign banks have more than doubled their market share in the United States. Currently, they hold more than 20% of total U.S. bank assets and do almost as much commercial lending as U.S.-owned banks, with nearly a 50% share of the market lending to U.S. corporations.

Foreign banks engage in banking activities in the United States by operating an agency office of the foreign bank, a subsidiary U.S. bank, or a branch of the foreign bank. An agency office can lend and transfer funds in the United States, but it cannot accept deposits from domestic residents. Agency offices have the advantage of not being subject to regulations that apply to full-service banking offices (such as requirements for FDIC insurance and restrictions on branching). A subsidiary U.S. bank is just like any other U.S. bank (it may even have an American-sounding name) and is subject to the same regulations, but it is owned by the foreign bank. A branch of a foreign bank bears the foreign bank's name and is usually a full-service office. Foreign banks may also form Edge Act corporations and IBFs.

Before 1978, foreign banks were not subject to many regulations that applied to domestic banks: They could open branches across state lines and were not expected to meet reserve requirements, for example. The passage of the International Banking Act of 1978, however, put foreign and domestic banks on a more equal footing. Now foreign banks may open new full-service branches only in the state they designate as their home state or in states that allow the entry of out-of-state banks. Limited-service branches and agency offices in any other state are permitted, however, and foreign banks are allowed to retain any full-service branches opened before ratification of the International Banking Act of 1978.

The internationalization of banking, both by U.S. banks going abroad and by foreign banks entering the United States, has meant that financial markets throughout the world have become more integrated. As a result, there is a growing trend toward international coordination of bank regulation, one example of which is the 1988 Basel agreement to standardize minimum capital requirements in industrialized countries, discussed in Chapter 16. Another development has been the increased importance of foreign banks in international banking. As is shown in Table 3, in 1996, all of the ten largest banks in the world were foreign. The implications of this financial market integration for the operation of our econ-

■ TABLE 3 Ten Largest Banks in the World, 1996

Bank	Assets (U.S. $ billions)
1. Deutsche Bank, Germany	503.4
2. Sanwa Bank, Japan	501.0
3. Sumitomo Bank, Japan	499.9
4. Dai-Ichi Kangyo Bank, Japan	498.6
5. Fuji Bank, Japan	487.3
6. Industrial Bank of Japan, Japan	361.4
7. Credit Suisse, Switzerland	358.7
8. HSBC Holdings, United Kingdom	351.6
9. ABN-Amro, Netherlands	340.6
10. Credit Lyonnais, France	339.4

Source: American Banker, July 1996.

omy is examined further in Chapter 20 when we discuss the international financial system in more detail.

■ FINANCIAL INNOVATION AND THE DECLINE OF TRADITIONAL BANKING

The traditional financial intermediation role of banking has been to make long-term loans and fund them by issuing short-dated deposits, a process of asset transformation commonly referred to as "borrowing short and lending long." Earlier in the chapter, we saw that changes in regulations restricting bank branching have been increasing the competitive environment in the banking industry in the United States. Another source of increasing competition for this industry is coming from financial innovations. Here we examine how the same economic forces we examined in Chapter 13 have generated financial innovations that present the banking industry with competitive challenges that are causing traditional banking business to decline. The decline in traditional banking has important implications for the future of the banking industry and creates new challenges for regulators.

Behind the Decline: Four Financial Innovations

Four financial innovations have played an important role in the decline of traditional banking: money market mutual funds, junk bonds, the rise of the commercial paper market, and securitization.

Money Market Mutual Funds As we saw in Chapter 13, the desire to avoid regulations such as deposit rate ceilings and the restrictions on interest paid on deposits resulted in innovations developed by banks such as NOW and ATS accounts. These same forces produced a new financial institution, the money market mutual fund, that now competes with banks for deposits.

Money market mutual funds issue shares that are redeemable at a fixed price (usually $1) by writing checks. For example, if you buy 5000 shares for $5000, the money market fund uses these funds to invest in short-term money market securities (Treasury bills, certificates of deposit, commercial paper) that provide you with interest payments. In addition, you are able to write checks up to the $5000 held as shares in the money market fund. Although money market fund shares effectively function as checking account deposits that earn interest, they are not legally deposits and so are not subject to reserve requirements or prohibitions on interest payments. For this reason, they can pay higher interest rates than deposits at banks.

The first money market mutual fund was created by two Wall Street mavericks, Bruce Bent and Henry Brown, in 1971. However, the low market interest rates from 1971 to 1977 (which were just slightly above Regulation Q ceilings of 5.25% to 5.5%) kept them from being particularly advantageous relative to bank deposits. In early 1978, the situation changed rapidly as market interest rates began to climb over 10%, well above the 5.5% maximum interest rates payable on savings accounts and time deposits under Regulation Q. In 1977, money market mutual funds had assets under $4 billion; in 1978, their assets climbed to close to $10 billion; in 1979, to over $40 billion; and in 1982, to $230 billion. Currently, their assets are around $900 billion. To say the least, money market mutual funds have been a successful financial innovation, which is exactly what we would have predicted to occur in the late 1970s and early 1980s when interest rates soared beyond Regulation Q ceilings.

Junk Bonds Before the advent of computers and advanced telecommunications, it was difficult to acquire information about the financial situation of firms that might want to sell securities. Because of the difficulty in screening out bad from good credit risks, the only firms that were able to sell bonds were very well established corporations that had high credit ratings.[5] Before the 1980s, then, only corporations that could issue bonds with ratings of Baa or above could raise funds by selling newly issued bonds. Some firms that had fallen on bad times, so-called *fallen angels,* had previously issued long-term corporate bonds that now had ratings that had fallen below Baa, bonds that were pejoratively dubbed "junk bonds."

With the improvement in information technology in the 1970s, it became easier for investors to screen out bad from good credit risks, thus making it more likely that they would buy long-term debt securities from less well-known corporations with lower credit ratings. With this change in supply conditions, we would expect that some smart individual would pioneer the concept of selling new public issues of junk bonds, not for fallen angels but for companies that had not yet achieved investment-grade status. This is exactly what Michael Milken of Drexel Burnham, an investment banking firm, started to do in 1977. Junk bonds became an important factor in the corporate bond market, with the amount outstanding exceeding $200 billion by the late 1980s. Although there was a sharp slowdown in activity in the junk bond market after Milken was indicted for securities law violations in 1989, it has heated up again in the 1990s.

---

[5]The discussion of adverse selection problems in Chapter 12 provides a more detailed analysis of why only well-established firms with high credit ratings were able to sell securities.

Commercial Paper Market Recall that *commercial paper* is a short-term debt security issued by large banks and corporations. As we saw in Chapter 2, the commercial paper market has undergone tremendous growth since 1970, when there was $33 billion outstanding, to over $750 billion outstanding at the end of 1996. Indeed, commercial paper has been one of the fastest-growing money market instruments.

Improvements in information technology also help provide an explanation for the rapid rise of the commercial paper market. We have seen that the improvement in information technology made it easier for investors to screen out bad from good credit risks, thus making it easier for corporations to issue debt securities. Not only did this make it easier for corporations to issue long-term debt securities as in the junk bond market, but it also meant that they could raise funds by issuing short-term debt securities like commercial paper more easily. Many corporations that used to do their short-term borrowing from banks now frequently raise short-term funds in the commercial paper market instead.

The development of money market mutual funds has been another factor in the rapid growth in the commercial paper market. Because money market mutual funds need to hold liquid, high-quality, short-term assets such as commercial paper, the growth of assets in these funds to around $900 billion has created a ready market in commercial paper. The growth of pension and other large funds that invest in commercial paper has also stimulated the growth of this market.

Securitization An important example of a financial innovation arising from improvements in both transaction and information technology is securitization, one of the most important financial innovations in the past two decades. **Securitization** is the process of transforming otherwise illiquid financial assets (such as residential mortgages), which have typically been the bread and butter of banking institutions, into marketable capital market securities. As we have seen, improvements in the ability to acquire information have made it easier to sell marketable capital market securities. In addition, with low transaction costs because of improvements in computer technology, financial institutions find that they can cheaply bundle together a portfolio of loans (such as mortgages) with varying small denominations (often less than $100,000), collect the interest and principal payments on the mortgages in the bundle, and then "pass them through" (pay them out) to third parties. By dividing the portfolio of loans into standardized amounts, the financial institution can then sell the claims to these interest and principal payments to third parties as securities. The standardized amounts of these securitized loans make them liquid securities, and the fact that they are made up of a bundle of loans helps diversify risk, making them desirable. The financial institution selling the securitized loans makes a profit by servicing the loans (collecting the interest and principal payments and paying them out) and charging a fee to the third party for this service.

Securitization first started in 1970 when the GNMA (now known as Ginnie Mae) began a program in which it guaranteed interest and principal payments on bundles of standardized mortgages, thereby encouraging the creation of a new financial instrument, the mortgage-backed security. The guarantee of the interest and principal payments made it easy for private financial institutions such as savings and loans and commercial banks to sell a bundle of GNMA-guaranteed mortgages as a security and to pass through these payments to the owner of the security.

In the usual Ginnie Mae pass-through security, the buyer has direct ownership of a pro rata share of the portfolio of mortgage loans. Other types of mortgage-backed securities do not provide ownership of the mortgage portfolio to the buyer but are instead debt obligations of the mortgage-lending institution for which the mortgage loans are the collateral. Mortgage-backed securities continue to be the most common form of securitization. Securitization of mortgages has expanded enormously; two-thirds of all residential mortgages are now securitized, and over $1 trillion of securitized mortgages are currently outstanding.

Securitization has not stopped with mortgages, however: Securitization of automobile loans, credit card receivables, and commercial and computer leases began in the mid-1980s. Securitized credit card receivables have been particularly successful: By 1989, the amount outstanding of these so-called plastic bonds had surpassed $30 billion and is currently over $100 billion.

Computer technology has also enabled financial institutions to tailor securitization to produce securities that have payment streams considered especially desirable by the market. Collateralized mortgage obligations (CMOs), which are bonds that pass through the payments from a portfolio of mortgages, are a good example of such tailoring; they first appeared in 1983. Computerization enables a CMO to be split into several classes known as *tranches*. The first tranches receive interest payments according to the coupon rate on the CMO, with class 1 first receiving all principal payments and prepayments from the collateralized pool of mortgages. After the class 1 bonds have been paid off, the principal payments and prepayments are used to retire the remaining classes sequentially. The last class, called *accrual* or *Z bonds,* receives interest and principal payments only after the other classes have been paid off. The basic CMO described here has the advantage of containing bonds of both short maturity (class 1) and long maturity (the later classes or the accrual bond), thus increasing its potential market. Indeed, the financial innovation process has led to even more complicated CMOs that fit additional niches in the marketplace.

Although securitization could not take place without modern computer technology (think of the cost of collecting payments and paying them out by hand), technology is not the only factor encouraging it; the government has played an important role too. Securitization first started with GNMA guarantees of mortgage payments and even today involves mostly assets directly or indirectly guaranteed by the government. Tax rules have also stimulated new securitized instruments. A change in IRS regulations made possible real estate mortgage investment conduits (REMICs), which are essentially CMOs with a more favorable tax treatment.

Decline of Traditional Banking

In the United States, the importance of commercial banks as a source of funds to nonfinancial borrowers has shrunk dramatically. As we can see in Figure 3, in 1974 commercial banks provided 35% of these funds; yet by 1996, their market share was down to near 20%. The decline in market share for thrift institutions has been

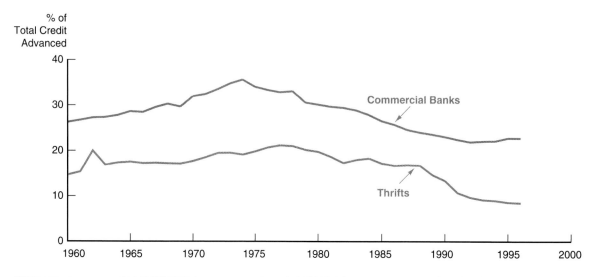

■FIGURE 3 Bank Share of Total Nonfinancial Borrowing, 1960–1996

Source: Federal Reserve Flow of Funds Accounts.

even more precipitous: from over 20% in the late 1970s to below 10% today. Another way of viewing the declining role of banking in traditional financial intermediation is to look at the size of banks' balance sheet assets relative to those of other financial intermediaries. Commercial banks' share of total financial intermediary assets has fallen from around 40% in the 1960–1980 period to below 30% by the end of 1996. Similarly, the share of total financial intermediary assets held by thrift institutions has declined even more from the 20% level of the 1960–1980 period to below 10% by 1995.

Clearly, the traditional financial intermediation role of banking, whereby banks make loans that are funded with deposits, is no longer as important in our financial system. However, the decline in the market share of banks in total lending and total financial intermediary assets does not necessarily indicate that the banking industry is in decline. If we look at bank profitability relative to GDP, there is no evidence of a declining trend. As we can see in Figure 4, after a dismal performance in the late 1980s and early 1990s, bank profits have rebounded sharply, with strong profits posted every year since 1992. It seems as though the worst is over for the American banking industry and that predictions of its demise may have been exaggerated.[6]

---

[6]For a further discussion of whether the banking industry is in decline, see John H. Boyd and Mark Gertler, "Are Banks Dead? Or Are the Reports Greatly Exaggerated?" in *The Declining(?) Role of Banking*, (Chicago: Federal Reserve Bank of Chicago, 1994), pp. 85–117; Gary Gorton and Richard Rosen, "Corporate Control, Portfolio Choice, and the Decline in Banking," *Journal of Finance* (1995) and Franklin Edwards and Frederic S. Mishkin, "The Decline of Traditional Banking: Implications for Financial Stability and Regulatory Policy," Federal Reserve Bank of New York *Economic Policy Review*, July 1995, pp. 27–45.

■FIGURE 4 Commercial Bank Profitability, 1970–1995

Sources: Federal Deposit Insurance Corporation, *Historical Statistics on Banking; Economic Report of the President.*

However, overall bank profitability is not a good indicator of the profitability of traditional banking because it includes an increasing amount of income from nontraditional off-balance-sheet activities discussed in Chapter 13. As you can see in Figure 5, noninterest income derived from off-balance-sheet activities, as a share of total bank income, increased from around 19% in the 1960–1980 period to 35% of total bank income by 1995. Given that the overall profitability of banks has not risen, the increase in income from off-balance-sheet activities implies that the profitability of traditional banking business has declined. This decline in profitability then explains why banks have been reducing their traditional business.

Reasons for the Decline

To understand why traditional banking business has declined in both size and profitability, we need to look at how the financial innovations described earlier have caused banks to suffer declines in their cost advantages in acquiring funds, that is, on the liabilities side of their balance sheet, while at the same time they have lost income advantages on the assets side of their balance sheet. The simultaneous decline of cost and income advantages has resulted in reduced profitability of traditional banking and an effort by banks to leave this business and engage in new and more profitable activities.

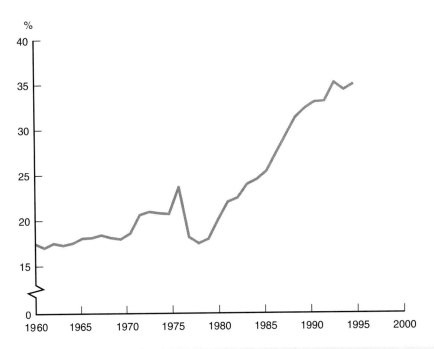

■FIGURE 5 Share of Noninterest Income in Total Bank Income, 1960–1995

Sources: Federal Deposit Insurance Corporation, *Historical Statistics on Banking; Quarterly Banking Profile.*

Decline in Cost Advantages in Acquiring Funds (Liabilities) Until 1980, banks were subject to deposit rate ceilings that restricted them from paying any interest on checkable deposits and (under Regulation Q) limited them to paying a maximum interest rate of a little over 5% on time deposits. Until the 1960s, these restrictions worked to the banks' advantage because their major source of funds (over 60%) was checkable deposits, and the zero interest cost on these deposits meant that the banks had a very low cost of funds. Unfortunately, this cost advantage for banks did not last. The rise in inflation from the late 1960s on led to higher interest rates, which made investors more sensitive to yield differentials on different assets. The result was the so-called disintermediation process in which people began to take their money out of banks, with their low interest rates on both checkable and time deposits, and began to seek out higher-yielding investments. Also, as we have seen, at the same time, attempts to get around deposit rate ceilings and reserve requirements led to the financial innovation of money market mutual funds, which put the banks at an even further disadvantage because depositors could now obtain checking account–like services while earning high interest on their money market mutual fund accounts. One manifestation of these changes in the financial system was that the low-cost source of funds, checkable deposits, declined dramatically in importance for banks, falling from over 60% of bank liabilities to below 20% today.

The growing difficulty for banks in raising funds led to their supporting legislation in the 1980s that eliminated Regulation Q ceilings on time deposit interest rates and allowed checkable deposits like NOW accounts that paid interest. Although these changes in regulation helped make banks more competitive in their quest for funds, it also meant that their cost of acquiring funds had risen substantially, thereby reducing their earlier cost advantage over other financial institutions.

Our discussion of international banking earlier in the chapter documented the encroachment of foreign (particularly Japanese) banks in U.S. financial markets. The loss of cost advantages of American banks helps explain this trend. With the high savings by the Japanese public, Japanese banks were able to tap a large savings pool and thus had access to a cheaper source of funds than American banks. This cost advantage for Japanese banks meant that they could more aggressively seek out loan business in the United States, which is exactly what they did. As a result, they grew at the expense of American banks. Before 1980, two U.S. banks, Citicorp and BankAmerica, were at the top of the heap, whereas in the 1990s, neither even ranks in the top ten of the world's largest banks.

Decline in Income Advantages on Uses of Funds (Assets) The loss of cost advantages on the liabilities side of the balance sheet for American banks is one reason that they have become less competitive, but they have also been hit by a decline in income advantages on the assets side from the financial innovations we discussed earlier, junk bonds, securitization, and the rise of the commercial paper market.

We have seen that improvements in information technology have made it easier for firms to issue securities directly to the public. This has meant that instead of going to banks to finance short-term credit needs, many of the banks' best business customers now find it cheaper to go to the commercial paper market for funds instead. The loss of this competitive advantage for banks is evident in the fact that before 1970, nonfinancial commercial paper equaled less than 5% of commercial and industrial bank loans, whereas the figure has risen to over 20% today. In addition, this growth in the commercial paper market has allowed finance companies, which depend primarily on commercial paper to acquire funds, to expand their operations at the expense of banks. Finance companies, which lend to many of the same businesses that borrow from banks, have increased their market share relative to banks: Before 1980, finance company loans to business equaled around 30% of commercial and industrial bank loans; currently, they are 60%.

The rise of the junk bond market has also eaten into banks' loan business, as the following headline from the *Wall Street Journal* indicated: "Wall Street Is Using Junk Bonds to Take Another Slice of Banks' Lending Pie."[7] Improvements in information technology have made it easier for corporations to sell their bonds to the public directly, thereby bypassing banks. Although *Fortune* 500 companies started taking this route in the 1970s, now lower-quality corporate borrowers are using banks less often because they have access to the junk bond market.

We have also seen that improvements in computer technology have led to securitization, whereby illiquid financial assets such as bank loans or mortgages

---

[7]May 18, 1993, p. C1.

are transformed into marketable securities. Computers enable other financial institutions to originate loans because they can now accurately evaluate credit risk with statistical methods, while computers have lowered transaction costs, making it possible to bundle these loans and sell them as securities. As a result, banks no longer have an advantage in making loans when default risk can be easily evaluated with computers. Without their former advantages, banks have lost loan business to other financial institutions even though the banks themselves are involved in the process of securitization. Securitization has been a particular problem for mortgage-issuing institutions such as S&Ls because most residential mortgages are now securitized.

Banks' Responses

In any industry, a decline in profitability usually results in exit from the industry (often due to widespread bankruptcies) and a shrinkage of market share. This occurred in the banking industry in the United States during the 1980s via consolidations and bank failures. As we see in Figure 6, in the 1960–1980 period, bank failures in the United States averaged fewer than ten per year, but during the 1980s bank failures soared, exceeding 200 a year by the end of the decade.

In the attempt to survive and maintain adequate profit levels, many U.S. banks face two alternatives. First, they can attempt to maintain their traditional lending activity by expanding into new and riskier areas of lending. For example, U.S. banks have increased their risk taking by placing a greater percentage of their

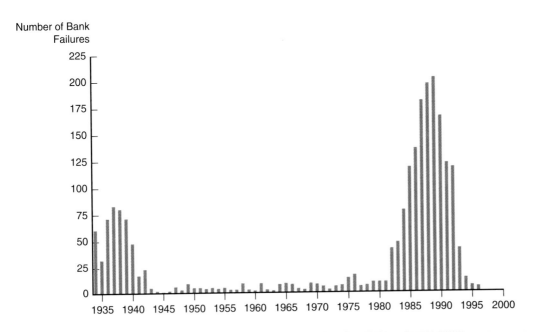

Number of Bank Failures

■FIGURE 6 Bank Failures in the United States, 1934–1996

Source: Federal Deposit Insurance Corporation.

total funds in commercial real estate loans, traditionally a riskier type of loan. In addition, they have increased lending for corporate takeovers and leveraged buyouts, which are highly leveraged transaction loans. The decline in the profitability of banks' traditional business may thus have helped lead to the crisis in banking that we discuss in Chapter 16.

The second way banks have sought to maintain former profit levels is to pursue new off-balance-sheet activities that are more profitable. As we saw in Figure 5, U.S. commercial banks did this during the early 1980s, nearly doubling the share of their income coming from off-balance-sheet, noninterest-income activities.[8] This strategy, however, has generated concerns about what are proper activities for banks and about whether nontraditional activities might be riskier and result in banks' taking excessive risks.

The decline of banks' traditional business has thus meant that the banking industry has been driven to seek out new lines of business. This could be beneficial because by so doing, banks can keep vibrant and healthy. Indeed, bank profitability has been high in recent years, and nontraditional, off-balance-sheet activities have been playing an important role in the resurgence of bank profits. However, there is a danger that the new directions in banking could lead to increased risk taking, and thus the decline in traditional banking requires regulators to be more vigilant. It also poses new challenges for bank regulators, who, as we will see in Chapter 16, must now be far more concerned about banks' off-balance-sheet activities.

 ## Decline of Traditional Banking in Other Industrialized Countries

Similar forces to those in the United States have been leading to the decline of traditional banking in other industrialized countries. The loss of banks' monopoly power over depositors has occurred outside the United States as well. Financial innovation and deregulation are occurring worldwide and have created attractive alternatives for both depositors and borrowers. In Japan, for example, deregulation has opened a wide array of new financial instruments to the public, causing a disintermediation process similar to that in the United States. In European countries, innovations have steadily eroded the barriers that have traditionally protected banks from competition.

In other countries, banks have also faced increased competition from the expansion of securities markets. Both financial deregulation and fundamental economic forces in other countries have improved the availability of information in securities markets, making it easier and less costly for firms to finance their activities by issuing securities rather than going to banks. Further, even in countries where securities markets have not grown, banks have still lost loan business because their best corporate customers have had increasing access to foreign and offshore capital markets, such as the Eurobond market. In smaller economies, like Australia, which still do not have well-developed corporate bond or commercial

---

[8]Note that some off-balance-sheet activities, such as loan commitments and letters of credit, which produce fee income, can be classified as being in the category of traditional banking business. The data in Figure 5 overstate somewhat the importance of nontraditional banking business.

paper markets, banks have lost loan business to international securities markets. In addition, the same forces that drove the securitization process in the United States are at work in other countries and will undercut the profitability of traditional banking in these countries as well. Thus although the decline of traditional banking has occurred earlier in the United States than in other countries, the same forces are resulting in competitive problems for banks in these countries as well.

The increase in the competitive environment for foreign banks has meant that some of them have found themselves in financial difficulties. Return on assets and return on equity have fallen in Japan and many European countries, and banks in these countries have sometimes been finding themselves in financial difficulties. France's largest bank, Crédit Lyonnais, required a $10 billion bailout in 1995, and the following year, the Italian government injected over $1 billion to help keep the Banco di Napoli afloat. Even in countries like Switzerland and Germany, banks have been running into trouble. For example, in January 1993, BfG Bank, a German bank, needed a capital infusion from its parent company, Crédit Lyonnais, because it suffered huge losses in 1992. In Chapter 16, we will discuss the extensive problems in the Japanese banking industry. The United States is not unique in seeing its banks face a more difficult competitive environment.

SUMMARY

1. The history of banking in the United States has left us with a dual banking system, with commercial banks chartered by the states and the federal government. Multiple agencies regulate commercial banks: the Office of the Comptroller, the Federal Reserve, the FDIC, and the state banking authorities.

2. Restrictive state branching regulations and the McFadden Act, which prohibits branching across state lines, have led to a large number of small commercial banks. The large number of commercial banks in the United States reflects the past *lack* of competition, not the presence of vigorous competition. Bank holding companies, nonbank banks, and ATMs were important responses to branching restrictions that have weakened the restrictions' anticompetitive effect.

3. Since the mid-1980s, bank consolidation has been occurring at a rapid pace. The first phase of bank consolidation was the result of bank failures and the reduced effectiveness of branching restrictions. The second phase has been stimulated by the Riegle-Neal Interstate Banking and Branching Efficiency Act of 1994, which establishes the basis for a nationwide banking system. Once banking consolidation has settled down, we are likely to be left with a banking system with several thousand banks. Most economists believe that the benefits of bank consolidation and nationwide banking will outweigh the costs.

4. The Glass-Steagall Act separated commercial banking from the securities industry. Competitive forces have been bypassing the intent of the act, causing a breakdown in the separation of the banking and the securities industries, and the Glass-Steagall Act's days may be numbered.

5. With the rapid growth of world trade since 1960, international banking has grown dramatically. U.S. banks engage in international banking activities by opening branches abroad, owning controlling interests in foreign banks, forming Edge Act corporations, and operating international banking facilities (IBFs) located in the United States. Foreign banks operate in the United States by owning a subsidiary American bank or by operating branches or agency offices in the United States.

6. Financial innovation has caused banks to suffer declines in cost advantages in acquiring funds and in income advantages on their assets. The resulting squeeze has hurt profitability in banks' traditional lines of business and has led to a decline in traditional banking.

KEY TERMS

bank holding companies, p. 363
branches, p. 364
central bank, p. 361
dual banking system, p. 362

Edge Act corporation, p. 376
international banking facilities
   (IBFs), p. 376
national banks, p. 362

nonbank banks, p. 366
securitization, p. 380
state banks, p. 362
superregional banks, p. 368

QUESTIONS AND PROBLEMS

1. Why was the United States one of the last of the major industrialized countries to have a central bank?

*****2.** Which regulatory agency has the primary responsibility for supervising the following categories of commercial banks?
 a. National banks
 b. Bank holding companies
 c. Non–Federal Reserve member state banks
 d. Federal Reserve member state banks

3. "The commercial banking industry in Canada is less competitive than the commercial banking industry in the United States because in Canada only a few large banks dominate the industry, while in the United States there are around 10,000 commercial banks." Is this statement true, false, or uncertain? Explain your answer.

*****4.** Why has new technology made it harder to enforce limitations on bank branching?

5. Why has there been such a dramatic increase in bank holding companies?

*****6.** What incentives have regulatory agencies created to encourage international banking? Why have they done this?

7. How could the approval of international banking facilities (IBFs) by the Fed in 1981 have reduced employment in the banking industry in Europe?

*****8.** If the bank at which you keep your checking account is owned by Saudi Arabians, should you worry that your deposits are less safe than if the bank were owned by Americans?

9. If reserve requirements were eliminated in the future, as some economists advocate, what effects would this have on the size of money market mutual funds?

*****10.** Why have banks been losing cost advantages in acquiring funds in recent years?

11. "If inflation had not risen in the 1960s and 1970s, the banking industry might be healthier today." Is this statement true, false, or uncertain? Explain your answer.

*****12.** Why have banks been losing income advantages on their assets in recent years?

13. "The invention of the computer is the major factor behind the decline of the banking industry." Is this statement true, false, or uncertain? Explain your answer.

CHAPTER 15

THRIFTS: SAVINGS AND LOANS AND CREDIT UNIONS

■ PREVIEW Suppose that you are a typical middle-class worker in New York in 1820. You work hard and earn fair wages as a craftsman. You are married and about to have a child, so you decide that you would like to own your own home. There are many commercial banks in the city, but as their name implies, these institutions exist to serve commerce, not the working class, because that is where the profits are. Where could you go to borrow the money to buy a home? Your options at that time are very limited. Later in the century, however, a new institution will emerge that will open the possibility of home ownership to more than the very wealthy. That institution was the savings and loan association.

The middle class also had problems finding financial institutions willing to offer small consumer-type loans. Again, banks had determined that loans to these customers were not profitable. Another type of institution, the credit union, emerged at about the same time as savings and loans to service the borrowing needs of this segment of the economy.

In Chapter 14 we discussed commercial banks, the largest of the depository institutions. Though smaller, savings and loan associations, mutual savings banks, and credit unions, collectively called thrift institutions or thrifts, are important to the servicing of consumer borrowing needs. Thrifts are primarily concerned with lending to individuals and households, as opposed to banks, which still tend to be more concerned with lending to businesses. We begin our discussion by reviewing the history of the thrift industry. We then describe the nature of the industry today and project where it might be in the future.

■ MUTUAL SAVINGS BANKS

The first pure savings banks were established by philanthropists in Scotland and England to encourage saving by the poor. The founders of the institutions would often provide subsidies that allowed the institution to pay interest rates above the current market level. Because of the nature of the savings banks' customers, the institutions were very conservative with their funds and placed most of them in commercial banks. The first savings banks in the United States were chartered by Congress and founded in the Northeast in 1816. These institutions quickly lost their distinction of being strictly for the poor and instead became a popular place for members of the middle class to store their excess money.

Savings banks were originally organized as **mutual banks,** meaning that the depositors were the owners of the firm. This form of ownership led to a more conservative investment posture, which prevented many of the mutual savings banks from failing during the recession at the end of the nineteenth century or during the Great Depression in the 1930s. In fact, between 1930 and 1937, deposits in mutual savings banks grew while those in commercial banks actually shrank. Following World War II, savings banks made mortgage lending their primary business. This focus made them similar to savings and loans.

Mutual ownership means that no stock in the bank is issued or sold; the depositors own a share of the bank in proportion to their deposits. There are currently about 500 mutual savings banks operating in 17 states, primarily concentrated on the eastern seaboard. Most are state-chartered (federal chartering of savings banks did not begin until 1978.) Because they are state-chartered, they are regulated and supervised by the state as well as the federal government.

The mutual form of ownership has both advantages and disadvantages. On the one hand, since the capital of the institution is contributed by the depositors, more capital is available because all deposits represent equity. This leads to greater safety in that mutual savings banks have far fewer liabilities than other banking organizations. On the other hand, the mutual form of ownership accentuates the principal-agent problem that exists in corporations. In corporations, managers are hired by the board of directors, who are in turn elected by the shareholders. Because most shareholders do not own a very large percentage of the firm, when there is a disagreement with management, it makes more sense to sell shares than to try to change policy. This problem also exists for the mutual form of ownership. Most depositors do not have a large enough stake in the firm to make it cost-effective for them to monitor the firm's managers closely.

The corporation, however, has alternative methods of aligning managers' goals with those of shareholders. For example, managers can be offered a stake in the firm, or stock options can be part of their compensation package. Similarly, managers of corporations are always under the threat of takeover by another firm if they fail to manage effectively. These alternatives are not available in the mutual form of ownership. As a result, there may be less control over management.

Another advantage to the mutual form of ownership is that managers are more risk-averse than in the corporate form. This is because mutual managers gain nothing if the firm does very well, since they do not own a stake in the firm, but they lose everything if the firm fails. This incentive arrangement appeals to the very risk-averse investor, but its importance has diminished now that the government provides deposit insurance.

SAVINGS AND LOAN ASSOCIATIONS

In the early part of the nineteenth century, commercial banks focused on short-term loans to businesses, so it was very difficult for families to obtain loans for the purchase of a house. In 1816, Congress decided that home ownership was part of the American dream, and to make that possible, Congress passed regulations creating savings and loans and mutual savings institutions. Congress chartered the first savings and loans 15 years after the first mutual savings banks received their charters. The original mandate to the industry was to provide a source of funds for families wanting to buy a home.

These institutions were to aggregate depositors' funds and use the money to make long-term mortgage loans. The institutions were not to take in demand deposits but instead were authorized to offer savings accounts that paid slightly higher interest than that offered by commercial banks.

There were about 12,000 savings and loans in operation by the 1920s. Mortgages accounted for about 85% of their total assets. The rest of their assets were usually deposited in commercial banks. One of every four mortgages in the country was held by a savings and loan institution, making S&Ls the single largest provider of mortgage loans in the country.

Despite the large number of separate savings and loan institutions, they were not an integrated industry. Each state regulated its own S&Ls, and regulations differed substantially from state to state. In 1913, Congress created the Federal Reserve System to regulate and help commercial banks. No such system existed for savings and loans.

Before any significant legislation could be passed, the Great Depression caused the failure of thousands of thrift institutions. In response to the problems facing the industry and to the loss of $200 million in savings, Congress passed the **Federal Home Loan Bank Act of 1932.** This act created the **Federal Home Loan Bank Board (FHLBB)** and a network of regional home loan banks, similar to the organization of the Federal Reserve System. The act gave thrifts the choice of being state or federally chartered. In 1934, Congress continued its efforts to support savings and loans by establishing the **Federal Savings and Loan Insurance Corporation (FSLIC),** which insured deposits in much the same way as the FDIC did for commercial banks.

Savings and loans were successful, low-risk businesses for many years following these regulatory changes (see Chapter 16). Their main source of funds was individual savings accounts, which tended to be stable and low-cost, and their primary assets (about 57% of their total assets) were mortgage loans (see Figure 1). Since real estate secured virtually all of these loans and since real estate values increased steadily through the mid-1970s, loan losses were very small. Thrifts provided the fuel for the home-building boom that for almost half a century, from 1934 to 1978, was the centerpiece of America's domestic economy.

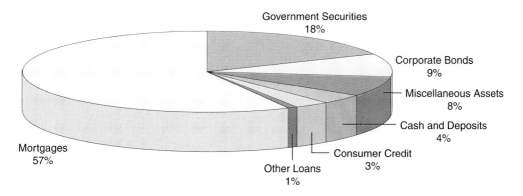

■FIGURE 1 Distribution of Savings and Loan Assets, 1995

Source: Federal Reserve *Bulletin,* 1996.

Mutual Savings Banks and Savings and Loans Compared

Mutual savings banks and savings and loan associations are similar in many ways; however, they do differ in ways other than ownership structure.

- Mutual savings banks are concentrated in the northeastern United States; savings and loans are located throughout the country.
- Mutual savings banks may insure their deposits with the state or with the Federal Deposit Insurance Corporation; S&Ls may not.
- Mutual savings banks are not as heavily concentrated in mortgages and have had more flexibility in their investing practices than savings and loans.

Because the similarities between mutual savings banks and savings and loans are more important than the differences, the focus of this chapter will be more on savings and loans.

■ SAVINGS AND LOANS IN TROUBLE: THE THRIFT CRISIS

As part of the regulatory changes following the Great Depression, Congress imposed a cap on the rate of interest that savings and loans could pay on savings accounts. The theory was that if S&Ls obtained funds at a low cost, they could make loans to home borrowers at a low cost. The interest-rate caps became a serious problem for savings and loans in the 1970s when inflation rose. Chapter 13 provides an in-depth discussion of the capital adequacy and interest-rate problems depository institutions faced at that time.

By 1979, inflation was running at 13.3%, but savings and loans were restricted to paying a maximum of 5.5% on deposits. These rates were far from even maintaining depositors' purchasing power with inflation running almost 8% higher than their interest return—in effect, the real interest rate they were earning was −7.8%. They were actually losing money leaving it in savings and loans.

At this same time, securities houses began offering a new product that circumvented interest-rate caps. *Money market accounts* paid market rates on short-term funds (see Chapter 19 for details). Though not insured, the bulk of the cash placed in money market funds was in turn invested in Treasury securities or commercial paper. Because the savings and loan customers were not satisfied with the low returns they were earning on their funds, they left S&Ls in droves for the high returns these accounts offered.

Financial innovation and deregulation in the permissive atmosphere of the Reagan years led to expanded powers for the S&L industry that led to several problems. First, many S&L managers did not have the required expertise to manage risk appropriately in these new lines of business. Second, the new expanded powers meant that there was a rapid growth in new lending, particularly to the real estate sector. Even if the required expertise was available initially, rapid credit growth might outstrip the available information resources of the banking institution, resulting in excessive risk taking. Third, these new powers of the S&Ls and lending boom meant that their activities were expanding in scope and were becoming more complicated, requiring an expansion of regulatory resources to monitor these activities appropriately. Unfortunately, regulators of the S&Ls at the Federal Savings and Loan Insurance Corporation (FSLIC) had neither the expertise nor the resources that would have enabled them to monitor these new activities sufficiently. Given the lack of expertise in both the S&L industry and the FSLIC, the weakening of the regulatory apparatus, and the moral hazard incentives provided by deposit insurance, it is no surprise that S&Ls took on excessive risks, which led to huge losses on bad loans.

In addition, the incentives of moral hazard were increased dramatically by an historical accident: the combination of the sharp increases in interest rates from late 1979 until 1981 and a severe recession in 1981–1982, both of which were engineered by the Federal Reserve to bring down inflation. The sharp rises in interest rates produced rapidly rising costs of funds for the savings and loans that were not matched by higher earnings on the S&Ls' principal asset, long-term residential mortgages (whose rates had been fixed at a time when interest rates were far lower). The 1981–1982 recession and a collapse in the prices of energy and farm products hit the economies of certain parts of the country such as Texas very hard. As a result, there were defaults on many S&Ls' loans. Losses for savings and loan institutions mounted to $10 billion in 1981–1982, and by some estimates over half of the S&Ls in the United States had a negative net worth and were thus insolvent by the end of 1982.

Later Stages of the Crisis: Regulatory Forbearance

At this point, a logical step might have been for the S&L regulators—the Federal Home Loan Bank Board and its deposit insurance subsidiary, the Federal Savings and Loan Insurance Fund (FSLIC), both now abolished—to close the insolvent S&Ls. Instead, these regulators adopted a stance of **regulatory forbearance:**

They refrained from exercising their regulatory right to put the insolvent S&Ls out of business. To sidestep their responsibility to close ailing S&Ls, they adopted irregular regulatory accounting principles that in effect substantially lowered capital requirements. For example, they allowed S&Ls to include in their capital calculations a high value for intangible capital, called *goodwill.*

There were three main reasons why the Federal Home Loan Bank Board and FSLIC opted for regulatory forbearance. First, the FSLIC did not have sufficient funds in its insurance fund to close the insolvent S&Ls and pay off their deposits. Second, the Federal Home Loan Bank Board was established to encourage the growth of the savings and loan industry, so the regulators were probably too close to the people they were supposed to be regulating. Third, because bureaucrats do not like to admit that their own agency is in trouble, the Federal Home Loan Bank Board and the FSLIC preferred to sweep their problems under the rug in the hope that they would go away.

Regulatory forbearance increases moral hazard dramatically because an operating but insolvent S&L (nicknamed a "zombie S&L" by Edward Kane of Ohio State University because it is the "living dead") has almost nothing to lose by taking on great risk and "betting the bank": If it gets lucky and its risky investments pay off, it gets out of insolvency. Unfortunately, if, as is likely, the risky investments don't pay off, the zombie S&L's losses will mount, and the deposit insurance agency will be left holding the bag.

This strategy is similar to the "long bomb" strategy in football. When a football team is almost hopelessly behind and time is running out, it often resorts to a high-risk play: the throwing of a long pass to try to score a touchdown. Of course, the long bomb is unlikely to be successful, but there is always a small chance that it will work. If it doesn't, the team has lost nothing, since it would have lost the game anyway.

Given the sequence of events we have discussed here, it should be no surprise that savings and loans began to take huge risks: They built shopping centers in the desert, bought manufacturing plants to convert manure to methane, and purchased billions of dollars of high-risk, high-yield junk bonds. The S&L industry was no longer the staid industry that once operated on the so-called *3-6-3 rule:* You took in money at 3%, lent it at 6%, and played golf at 3 P.M. Although many savings and loans were making money, losses at other S&Ls were colossal.

Another outcome of regulatory forbearance was that with little to lose, zombie S&Ls attracted deposits away from healthy S&Ls by offering higher interest rates. Because there were so many zombie S&Ls in Texas pursuing this strategy, above-market interest rates on deposits at Texas S&Ls were said to have a "Texas premium." Potentially healthy S&Ls now found that to compete for deposits, they had to pay higher interest rates, which made their operations less profitable and frequently pushed them into the zombie category. Similarly, zombie S&Ls in pursuit of asset growth made loans at below-market interest rates, thereby lowering loan interest rates for healthy S&Ls, and again made them less profitable. The zombie S&Ls had actually taken on attributes of vampires—their willingness to pay above-market rates for deposits and take below-market interest rates on loans was sucking the lifeblood (profits) out of healthy S&Ls.

Competitive Equality in Banking Act of 1987

Toward the end of 1986, the growing losses in the savings and loan industry were bankrupting the insurance fund of the FSLIC. The Reagan administration sought $15 billion in funds for the FSLIC, a completely inadequate sum considering that many times this amount was needed to close down insolvent S&Ls. The legislation passed by Congress, the Competitive Equality in Banking Act (CEBA) of 1987, did not even meet the administration's requests. It allowed the FSLIC to borrow only $10.8 billion through a subsidiary corporation called Financing Corporation (FICO) and, what was worse, included provisions that directed the Federal Home Loan Bank Board to continue to pursue regulatory forbearance (allow insolvent institutions to keep operating), particularly in economically depressed areas such as Texas.

The failure of Congress to deal with the savings and loan crisis was not going to make the problem go away, and consistent with our analysis, the situation deteriorated rapidly. Losses in the savings and loan industry surpassed $10 billion in 1988 and approached $20 billion in 1989. The crisis was reaching epidemic proportions. The collapse of the real estate market in the late 1980s led to additional huge loan losses that greatly exacerbated the problem.

■ POLITICAL ECONOMY OF THE SAVINGS AND LOAN CRISIS

Although we now have a grasp of the regulatory and economic forces that created the S&L crisis, we still need to understand the political forces that produced the regulatory structure and activities that led to it. The key to understanding the political economy of the S&L crisis is to recognize that the relationship between voter-taxpayers and the regulators and politicians creates a particular type of moral hazard problem, discussed in Chapter 12: the *principal-agent problem*, which occurs when representatives (agents) such as managers have incentives that differ from those of their employer (the principal) and so act in their own interest rather than in the interest of the employer.

Principal-Agent Problem for Regulators and Politicians

Regulators and politicians are ultimately agents for voter-taxpayers (principals) because in the final analysis, taxpayers bear the cost of any losses by the deposit insurance agency. The principal-agent problem occurs because the agent (a politician or regulator) does not have the same incentives to minimize costs to the economy as the principal (the taxpayer).

To act in the taxpayer's interest and lower costs to the deposit insurance agency, regulators have several tasks, as we have seen. They must set tight restrictions on holding assets that are too risky, must impose high capital requirements, and must not adopt a stance of regulatory forbearance, which allows insolvent institutions to continue to operate. However, because of the principal-agent problem, regulators have incentives to do the opposite. Indeed, as our sad saga of the S&L debacle indicates, they have at times loosened capital requirements and restrictions on risky asset holdings and pursued regulatory forbearance. One important incentive for regulators that explains this phenomenon is their desire to escape blame for poor performance by their agency. By loosening capital requirements and pursuing regulatory forbearance, regulators can hide the problem of an insolvent bank and hope that the situation will improve. Edward Kane characterizes such behavior on the part of regulators as "bureaucratic gambling."

Another important incentive for regulators is that they want to protect their careers by acceding to pressures from the people who most influence their careers. These people are not the taxpayers but the politicians who try to keep regulators from imposing tough regulations on institutions that are major campaign contributors. Members of Congress have often lobbied regulators to ease up on a particular S&L that contributed large sums to their campaigns (as we see in the following application). Regulatory agencies that have little independence from the political process are more vulnerable to these pressures.

In addition, both Congress and the presidential administration promoted banking legislation in 1980 and 1982 that made it easier for savings and loans to engage in risk-taking activities. After the legislation passed, the need for monitoring the S&L industry increased because of the expansion of permissible activities. The S&L regulatory agencies needed more resources to carry out their monitoring activities properly, but Congress (successfully lobbied by the S&L industry) was unwilling to allocate the necessary funds. As a result, the S&L regulatory agencies became so shortstaffed that they actually had to cut back on their on-site examinations just when these were needed most. In the period from January 1984 to July 1986, for example, several hundred S&Ls were not examined once. Even worse, spurred on by the intense lobbying efforts of the S&L industry, Congress passed the Competitive Equality in Banking Act of 1987, which, as we have seen, provided inadequate funding to close down the insolvent S&Ls and also hampered the S&L regulators from doing their job properly by including provisions encouraging regulatory forbearance.

As these examples indicate, the structure of our political system has created a serious principal-agent problem; politicians have strong incentives to act in their own interests rather than in the interests of taxpayers. Because of the high cost of running campaigns, American politicians must raise substantial contributions. This situation may provide lobbyists and other campaign contributors with the opportunity to influence politicians to act against the public interest, as we see in the following application.

APPLICATION **PRINCIPAL-AGENT PROBLEM IN ACTION: CHARLES KEATING AND THE LINCOLN SAVINGS AND LOAN SCANDAL**

We see that the principal-agent problem for regulators and politicians creates incentives that may cause excessive risk taking on the part of banking institutions, which then cause substantial losses to the taxpayer. The scandal associated with Charles H. Keating Jr. and the Lincoln Savings and Loan Association provides a graphic example of the principal-agent problem at work. As Edwin Gray, a former chairman of the Federal Home Loan Bank Board, stated, "This is a story of incredible corruption. I can't call it anything else."[1]

Charles Keating was allowed to acquire Lincoln Savings and Loan of Irvine, California, in early 1984, even though he had been accused of fraud by the SEC less than five years earlier. For Keating, whose construction firm, American Continental, planned to build huge real estate developments in Arizona, the S&L was a gold mine: In the lax regulatory atmosphere at the time, controlling the S&L gave his firm easy access to funds without being scrutinized by outside bankers. Within days of acquiring control, Keating got rid of Lincoln's conservative lending officers and internal auditors, even though he had promised regulators he would keep them. Lincoln then plunged into high-risk investments such as currency futures, junk bonds, common stock, hotels, and vast tracts of desert land in Arizona.

Because of a shortage of savings and loan examiners at the time, Lincoln was able to escape a serious examination until 1986, whereupon examiners from the Federal Home Loan Bank of San Francisco discovered that Lincoln had exceeded the 10% limit on equity investments by $600 million. Because of these activities and some evidence that Lincoln was deliberately trying to mislead the examiners, the examiners recommended federal seizure of the bank and all its assets. Keating was not about to take this lying down; he engaged hordes of lawyers—eventually 77 law firms—and accused the bank examiners of bias. He also sued unsuccessfully to overturn the 10% equity limit. Keating is said to have bragged that he spent $50 million fighting regulators.

Lawyers were not Keating's only tactic for keeping regulators off his back. After receiving $1.3 million of contributions to their campaigns from Keating, five senators—Dennis De Concini and John McCain of Arizona, Alan Cranston of California, John Glenn of Ohio, and Donald Riegle of Michigan (subsequently nicknamed the "Keating Five")—met with Edwin Gray, the chairman of the Federal Home Loan Board, and later with four top regulators from San Francisco in April 1987. They complained that the regulators were being too tough on Lincoln and urged the regulators to quit dragging out the investigation. After Gray was replaced by M. Danny Wall, Wall took the unprecedented step of removing the San Francisco examiners from the case in September 1987 and transferred the investigation to the bank board's headquarters in Washington. No examiners called on Lincoln for the next ten months, and as one of the San Francisco examiners described it, Lincoln dropped into a "regulatory black hole."

Lincoln Savings and Loan finally failed in April 1989, with estimated costs to taxpayers of $2.6 billion, making it possibly the most costly S&L failure in history. Keating was convicted for abuses (such as having Lincoln pay him and his family $34 million), but after serving four and a half years in jail, his conviction was overturned in 1996. Wall was forced to resign as head of the Office of Thrift Supervision because of his involvement in the Keating scandal. As a result of their activities on behalf of Keating, the Keating Five senators were made the object of

---

[1]Quoted in Tom Morganthau, Rich Thomas, and Eleanor Clift, "The S&L Scandal's Biggest Blowout," *Newsweek*, November 6, 1989, p. 35.

a congressional ethics investigation, but given Congress's propensity to protect its own, they were subjected only to minor sanctions.

■ SAVINGS AND LOAN BAILOUT: FINANCIAL INSTITUTIONS REFORM, RECOVERY, AND ENFORCEMENT ACT OF 1989

Immediately after taking office, the Bush administration proposed new legislation to provide adequate funding to close down the insolvent S&Ls. The resulting legislation, the **Financial Institutions Reform, Recovery, and Enforcement Act** (FIRREA), was signed into law on August 9, 1989. It was the most significant legislation to affect the thrift industry since the 1930s. FIRREA's major provisions were as follows: The regulatory apparatus was significantly restructured without the Federal Home Loan Bank Board and the FSLIC, both of which had failed in their regulatory tasks. The regulatory role of the Federal Home Loan Bank Board was relegated to the Office of Thrift Supervision (OTS), a bureau within the U.S. Treasury Department, and its responsibilities are similar to those that the Office of the Comptroller of the Currency has over the national banks. The regulatory responsibilities of the FSLIC were given to the FDIC, and the FDIC became the sole administrator of the federal deposit insurance system with two separate insurance funds: the Bank Insurance Fund (BIF) and the Savings Association Insurance Fund (SAIF). Another new agency, the Resolution Trust Corporation (RTC), was established to manage and resolve insolvent thrifts placed in conservatorship or receivership. It was made responsible for selling more than $450 billion of real estate owned by failed institutions. After seizing the assets of about 750 insolvent S&Ls, over 25% of the industry, the RTC sold over 95% of them, with a recovery rate of over 85%. After this success, the RTC went out of business on December 31, 1995.

Initially, the total cost of the bailout was estimated to be $159 billion over the ten-year period through 1999, but more recent estimates indicated that the cost would be far higher. Indeed, the General Accounting Office placed a cost for the bailout at more than $500 billion over 40 years. However, as pointed out in Box 1 in Chapter 3, this estimate was misleading because, for example, the value of a payment 30 years from now is worth much less in today's dollars. The present value of the bailout cost actually ended up being on the order of $150 billion. The funding for the bailout came partly from capital in the Federal Home Loan Banks (owned by the S&L industry) but mostly from the sale of government debt by both the Treasury and the Resolution Funding Corporation (RefCorp).

To replenish the reserves of the Savings Association Insurance Fund, insurance premiums for S&Ls were increased from 20.8 cents per $100 of deposits to 23 cents and can rise as high as 32.5 cents. Premiums for banks immediately rose from 8.3 cents to 15 cents per $100 of deposits and were raised further to 23 cents in 1991.

FIRREA also imposed new restrictions on thrift activities that in essence reregulated the S&L industry to the asset choices it had before 1982. S&Ls can no longer purchase junk bonds and had to sell their holdings by 1994. Commercial real estate loans are restricted to four times capital rather than the previous limit of 40% of assets, and so this new restriction is a reduction for all institutions whose capital is less than 10% of assets. S&Ls must also hold at least 70%—up from 60%—of their assets in investments that are primarily housing-related. Among the most important provisions of FIRREA was the increase in the core capital leverage requirement from 3% to 8% and the eventual adherence to the same risk-based capital standards imposed on commercial banks.[2]

FIRREA also enhanced the enforcement powers of thrift regulators by making it easier for them to remove managers, issue cease and desist orders, and impose civil penalties. The Justice Department was also given $75 million per year for three years to uncover and prosecute fraud in the banking industry, and maximum fines rose substantially.

As a result of the failure of savings and loans and the passage of the FIRREA, the total assets of savings and loans has fallen since 1988. Figure 2 shows the total assets of savings and loans between 1979 and 1996; note the rapid decrease after 1988.

The Savings and Loan Industry Today

Despite the problems and turmoil surrounding the industry in the 1980s, the savings and loan industry managed to survive, although somewhat changed. In this section we review the current state of the industry.

Number of Institutions The savings and loan industry has witnessed a substantial reduction in the number of institutions. Many failed or were taken over by the RTC; others merged with stronger institutions to avoid failure. The number of S&Ls declined about 36% between the end of 1986, when there were 3600 savings and loans, and the end of 1996, when there were fewer than 2300. As mentioned earlier, only one savings and loan failed during the first nine months of 1994. This suggests that both the industry and the economy are now stronger.

Types of Loans The 1982 reforms allowed S&Ls to make consumer and commercial loans. The intent of this legislation was to give S&Ls a source for assets with short maturities. The problem was that commercial loans are far riskier and require lending expertise that many S&Ls did not possess. The FIRREA severely curtailed S&Ls from commercial lending. In the four years following the passage of the law, the number of loans made for commercial purposes dropped by about 50%.

S&L Size Figure 3 shows the average total assets for savings and loans between 1984 and 1995. From this graph we can see that there is no strong evidence that the savings and loan industry has consolidated, although the average size has increased in recent years and in 1995 surpassed the previous peak achieved in 1988. It may be that the reduction in asset size between 1988 and 1991 resulted from the FIRREA, passed in 1989, which called for increased capital-to-assets

---

[2]Thrifts are now restricted from accepting brokered deposits, short term large denomination deposits placed in thrifts by funds managers. Brokered deposits are discussed further in Chapter 16.

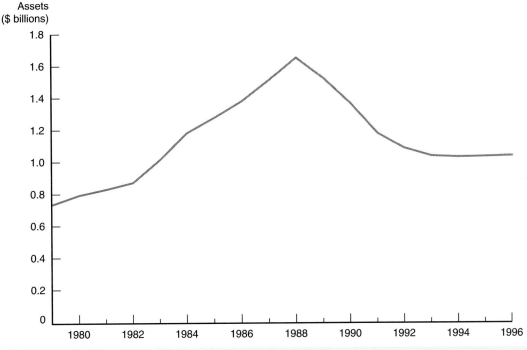

■**FIGURE 2** Total Assets of Savings and Loan Associations, 1979–1996

Source: Federal Reserve *Bulletin,* various issues.

ratios. One way to increase the capital-to-assets ratio is to reduce the institution's assets. The increase in the average size of the institutions since 1991 may be due to consolidation. It will be interesting to follow this trend for the next several years to determine whether this increase represents a permanent trend.

A second point to note about Figure 3 is that the average size of savings and loans is substantially greater than that of commercial banks. Recall from Chapter 14 that the growth of commercial banks was often constrained by restrictive banking regulations. As a result, the average size of commercial banks at the end of 1993 was $338.23 million in assets. Thus the average commercial bank is smaller than the average savings and loan by more than 30%. Now that Congress has removed most of the restrictions on interstate branching by commercial banks, many industry observers expect a period of rapid consolidation in that industry.

S&L Assets Figure 4 provides a consolidated balance sheet for the savings and loan industry. Let us first discuss the assets side.

As with banks, the primary asset of savings and loans is their loan portfolio. As of the end of 1995, loans and leases comprised over 63% of total assets. Not surprisingly, of these loans, 93% are secured by real estate. The balance of the loans are to businesses, consumers, and other financial institutions. Note that these figures do not show the number of loans that are made and then sold to various agencies.

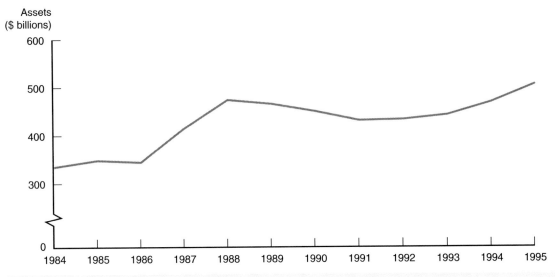

■FIGURE 3 Average Assets per Savings and Loan Association, 1984–1995

Source: Federal Reserve *Bulletin*, various issues.

Savings and loans are subject to reserve requirements, just like banks. Recall from Chapter 13 that reserve requirements are cash deposits that must be held in the vault or at the Federal Reserve in non-interest-bearing accounts. The purpose of reserve requirements is to limit the expansion of the money supply and to ensure adequate liquidity for the institutions. About 2.2% of total S&L assets are kept in cash.

In addition to cash, savings and loans hold securities, such as corporate, Treasury, and government agency bonds. Unlike reserve deposits, these assets earn interest. The 1982 legislation allowed savings and loans to hold up to 11% of their assets in junk bonds. S&Ls were a major source of funds during the mid-1980s for corporations looking for capital to use in acquiring other firms. In 1989, the FIRREA required that savings and loans divest themselves of these high-risk securities. Currently, only relatively safe securities can be purchased.

S&L Liabilities and Net Worth Now let's look at the right-hand side of the balance sheet in Figure 4. The primary liabilities of savings and loans are deposits and borrowed funds.

The largest liability of savings and loans are customer funds held on deposit. In the past, the bulk of the deposits were from **passbook savings accounts,** interest-bearing savings accounts. In the past, banks issued small books to savers to use for keeping track of their savings balances. The customer would present this book to the teller every time a deposit or withdrawal was made, and the teller

Savings and Loan Associations

Assets		Liabilities	
Cash	22,285	Deposits	730,143
Securities	272,296	Fed funds purchased	58,649
Fed funds sold	9,750	Other borrowed money	144,983
Loans	680,466	Notes and debentures	2,443
Banks premises and fixed		All other liabilities	13,932
assets	11,164	Total liabilities	950,150
Other real estate owned	3,238		
Intangible assets	8,121	Total equity	84,159
All other assets	26,989	Total of liabilities and	1,034,309
Total assets	1,034,309	equity	

■FIGURE 4 Consolidated Balance Sheet for Savings and Loan Associations ($ millions, September 30, 1996)

Source: Federal Reserve *Bulletin*, March 1997.

would validate the entry. The physical passbook has almost been phased out over the years with the advent of computerized record keeping.

The second major liability is *borrowings*, funds obtained in either the money or capital markets. Since savings and loan deposits are typically short-term, one way to lengthen their average maturity is to borrow long-term funds. Borrowed funds have become a major source of funds for savings and loans, now accounting for nearly 20% of total assets, up from 11% in 1990.

Capital The capital of financial institutions is often measured by the *net worth ratio*, total equity (also known as *net worth*) divided by total assets. This figure is closely watched by regulators for indications that a financial institution may be undercapitalized. The average net worth–to–assets ratio was about 3% in 1984. Many institutions had a negative net worth at this time. Since 1989, the average net worth ratio has improved. At the end of 1995, it stood at 8.3%. This is still below the 9.3% average net worth ratio for commercial banks, but not by much. One reason for the improvement in the capital of savings and loans is that the FIRREA mandated that it be increased. (We discuss the importance of capital in the functioning of a financial institution in Chapter 13.)

The accounting for savings and loans permitted extensive use of goodwill, an asset account on the balance sheet that supposedly reflects the value of a firm's good name and reputation. For example, in 1987, goodwill accounted for $29.6 billion of savings and loan assets. This represented more than half of the $53.8 billion in total capital. If we removed goodwill from capital before calculating the net worth–to–assets ratio in 1987, we find that the ratio is only 1.6%, not the 3.7% including goodwill. The value of goodwill fell steadily since its high that year and stood at just under $6.9 billion by early 1996. Listing large amounts of goodwill as an asset was another way that savings and loans were able to hide the fact that they were insolvent.

The Future of the Savings and Loan Industry

One indication that the health of savings and loans has improved in recent years is that their earnings have increased. From 1987 through 1990, the industry suffered net losses. But in 1991, net after-tax income for the industry was $859 million, and by 1995, it had reached $7.6 billion (see Figure 5). These net income figures, when coupled with the increase in capital, suggest that the industry has turned the corner to profitability. But is this trend likely to continue?

One issue that has received considerable attention in recent years is whether the savings and loan industry is still needed. Observers who favor eliminating S&L charters altogether point out that there are now a large number of alternative mortgage loan outlets available for home buyers. In Chapter 12 we introduced the securitized mortgage. This new instrument has provided the majority of the funds needed by the mortgage market. A reasonable question to ask is whether there is a need for an industry dedicated exclusively to providing a service efficiently provided elsewhere in the financial system.

Let us review the history of the savings and loan industry for a moment. S&Ls were established to provide mortgages to home buyers. The industry was healthy until interest rates increased and they were stuck holding low-interest fixed-rate

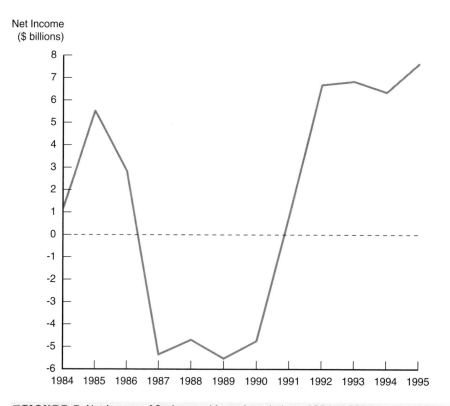

■FIGURE 5 Net Income of Savings and Loan Associations, 1984–1995

Source: Federal Reserve *Bulletin,* various issues.

mortgages financed with high-cost funds. Congress attempted to provide relief by giving S&Ls a great deal of flexibility in their capital structure and lending functions. Due to abuses, poor market conditions, inadequate supervision by FSLIC, and fraud, tremendous losses accrued. Finally, Congress reregulated the industry and again required that its primary business be mortgage lending. The only trouble now is that mortgage loans are available from many other sources.

Just as efficient markets develop new securities and services when the need for them arises, efficient markets should eliminate unneeded institutions when they are no longer required. Many industry analysts expect the savings and loan industry to disappear, perhaps by existing savings and loans being acquired by other institutions or by commercial banks. We can examine the evidence to see if this is beginning to happen.

We noted earlier that the number of savings and loans has decreased by 36% since its high in 1986. There were 122 fewer S&Ls in 1995 than in 1994. However, the drop in the number of institutions could be due to consolidation within the industry, much like what is happening in commercial banking. A better indication of the future of the industry may be provided by the trend in total assets. Figure 2 shows that the total assets of savings and loans have increased slightly since 1993. This suggests that there is at least not a rapid trend to eliminate these institutions. It may be that they will continue to be a provider of mortgage loans along with a number of other sources.

Congress will be pressured again to deregulate the industry to allow S&Ls to perform more of the functions allowed by commercial banks. Although this may happen, the losses sustained as a result of the last attempt at deregulation are still fresh in the minds of regulators. It is unlikely that we will again witness an attempt at rapid deregulation. Instead, we can expect to see gradual changes in the industry that will continue to blur the distinction between savings and loans and commercial banks.

■ CREDIT UNIONS

The third type of thrift institution is the **credit union,** a financial institution that focuses on servicing the banking and lending needs of its members. These institutions are also designed to service the needs of consumers, not businesses, and are distinguished by their ownership structure and their "common bond" membership requirement. Most credit unions are relatively small.

History and Organization

In the early 1900s, commercial banks focused most of their attention on the business borrower. This left the small consumer without a ready source of funds. Because Congress was concerned that commercial banks were not meeting the needs of consumers, it established savings banks and savings and loan associations to help consumers obtain mortgage loans. In the early 1900s, the credit union was established to help consumers with *other* types of loans. A secondary purpose was to provide a place for small investors to place their savings.

The concept behind credit unions originated in Germany in the nineteenth century. A group of consumers would pool their assets as collateral for a loan from a bank. The funds so raised were then loaned to the members of the group, and each member of the group was personally liable for repayment of the loan. Defaults were very rare because members knew one another well.

The first two credit unions in the United States were established in Massachusetts in 1910. The Massachusetts Credit Union (MCU) was organized in 1914 as a functioning credit union but with the additional purpose of encouraging the formation of additional credit unions. The MCU evolved into a kind of central credit union facility. In 1921, the MCU was reorganized as the **Credit Union National Extension Bureau (CUNEB),** which worked to have credit unions established in every state. In 1935, CUNEB was replaced by the **Credit Union National Association (CUNA).**

In 1934, Congress passed the **Federal Credit Union Act,** which allowed federal chartering of credit unions in all states. Prior to this, most credit unions were chartered by the state in which they operated. Currently, about 40% of credit unions have state charters and 60% have federal charters.

One reason for the growth of credit unions has been the support they received from employers. They realized that employee morale could be raised and time saved if banking-type facilities were readily available. In many cases, employers donated space on business property for the credit union to operate. The convenience of this institution soon attracted a large number of customers.

Mutual Ownership Credit unions are organized as *mutuals;* that is, they are owned by their depositors. A customer receives shares when a deposit is made. Rather than earning interest on deposited funds, the customer earns dividends. The amount of the dividend is not guaranteed, like the interest rate earned on accounts at banks. Instead, the amount of the dividend is estimated in advance and is paid if at all possible.

Each depositor has one vote, regardless how much money he or she may have with the institution. Depositors vote for directors, who in turn hire managers to run the credit union.

Because credit unions are cooperative businesses, they are managed somewhat differently from other businesses. For example, many credit unions make extensive use of volunteer help to reduce their costs. Since any cost reductions are passed on to the depositors, volunteers feel that they are working for the common good. Similarly, as noted, operating facilities may be donated.

Common Bond Membership The single most important feature of credit unions that distinguishes them from other depository institutions is the common bond member rule. The idea behind **common bond membership** is that only members of a particular association, occupation, or geographic region are permitted to join the credit union. A credit union's common bonds define its field of membership.

The most frequent type of common bond applies to employees of a single occupation or employer. For example, most state employees are eligible to join their state credit union. Similarly, the Navy Credit Union is open to all U.S. Navy personnel. Other credit unions accept members from the same religious or professional background.

One problem with the common bond membership rule is that it prevents credit unions from diversifying their risk. If most of a credit union's members are employed by one business and that business is forced to lay off workers, it is likely that the credit union will have high default rates on loans. A recent trend among credit unions has been for several to merge, a move that helps reduce the risk of having all members linked by a single bond. To make mergers easier, regulators have interpreted the common bond requirement less strictly. For example, most credit unions now let members of the immediate family of an eligible member join, and many credit unions have adopted a "once a member, always a member" policy. In 1982, the National Credit Union Administration ruled that credit unions could accept members from several employee groups instead of just one. In 1988, regulators determined that the bond between members of the American Association of Retired People was sufficient and authorized the organization to open its own credit union. The American Automobile Association, however, was rejected. (See Box 1, which discusses legal battles over the common bond membership rule.)

Nonprofit, Tax-Exempt Status The Federal Credit Union Act of 1934 contained the provision that credit unions were to be nonprofit and consequently exempt from federal taxation. All of the income earned by the institutions is to be spent on their members. Credit unions are currently the only financial institutions that are tax-exempt. This makes it easier for them to accumulate retained earnings than it is for other institutions. Banks and S&Ls are questioning this tax-exempt status as credit unions become larger and more significant competitors. Savings and loans lost their tax-exempt status in 1951. The American Bankers Association estimates that the subsidy reduces the cost of funds to credit unions by almost 2.5% and gives them a cost advantage of $1 billion per year. The credit unions themselves dispute this number and assign their cost advantage to their use of

<hr>

■ BOX 1   A GLOBAL PERSPECTIVE

The Common Bond Controversy

The commercial bank lobby violently disagrees with relaxed membership rules that in some instances have allowed credit unions to admit virtually everyone in a community. Commercial banks view credit unions as government-supported and hence unfair competitors due to their tax advantages (to be discussed shortly). For example, in Texas between 1991 and 1995, commercial bank deposits fell $3.4 billion while credit union deposits increased by $4.6 billion. Many bankers feel that the threat posed by credit unions could cause the more vulnerable banks to fail.

A group of Tennessee bankers sued to change the National Credit Unions Administration's opinion that federal law allows multiple occupational groups—each of which independently shares a common bond—to join a single credit union. In April of 1997 an appeals court ruled in favor of the bankers.

On February 24, 1997, the Supreme Court agreed to review a different lower court ruling that placed sharp limits on membership in federally chartered credit unions. This case affects almost 3,600 credit unions. Both banks and credit unions view the outcome of this suit as critical to their growth and prosperity.

volunteer help. It remains a question how long the favorable tax treatment for credit unions can be maintained.

Partly as a result of being nonprofit and partly due to the cost advantage of being tax-exempt, credit union fees tend to be lower than those of banks (see Table 1.)

Regulation and Insurance The **National Credit Union Act of 1970** established the **National Credit Union Administration (NCUA).** This independent federal agency is charged with the task of regulating and supervising federally chartered credit unions and state-chartered credit unions that receive federal deposit insurance. The remaining credit unions are regulated by state credit union or banking departments, which generally follow federal practices.

The National Credit Union Act of 1970 also established the **National Credit Union Share Insurance Fund (NCUSIF),** to be controlled by the NCUA. This fund insures the deposits of all nationally chartered credit unions and most state-chartered credit unions for up to $100,000 per account. The remaining state-chartered credit unions are insured by one of the state insurance systems. Since the savings and loan crisis, most states are eager to get out of the insurance business. It is likely that in the future, all credit union deposit insurance will be provided by the NCUSIF.

Central Credit Unions Because many credit unions are small and have very little diversification, they are often susceptible to seasonal cash flow problems. Most credit unions also lack the size needed to support large administrative staffs. One way they overcome these problems is with "state central" or "corporate" credit unions, which service the credit unions in their area by providing computer and financial assistance. There are currently 44 state central credit unions, which provide a number of valuable services, including these:

- They may help with member institutions' credit needs. The state central can invest excess funds and make loans to cover short-term shortages.
- They can invest excess funds with the **U.S. Central Credit Union,** which in turn can invest in the financial markets.
- They can hold clearing balances.
- They can provide educational services.

■ TABLE 1 Comparison of Average Credit Union and Bank Fees, 1995

	Fee ($)	
Service	Credit Union	Bank
Returned check	14.90	16.73
Annual credit card	11.54	15.83
Check overdraft	9.55	14.41
Stop payment	9.10	14.41
Regular checking account	3.59 per month	5.97 per month
Money order	0.89	1.94

Source: Consumer Federation of America.

The U.S. Central Credit Union was organized in 1974 to act as a central bank for credit unions. It is chartered as a commercial bank in Kansas, and its primary function is to provide banking services to the 44 state central credit unions. It allows these institutions access to the money markets and to long-term capital markets. Most individual credit unions and even most state central credit unions lack sufficient size and transaction volume to operate efficiently in these whole-sale markets.

In 1978, the **Financial Institutions Reform Act** created the **Central Liquidity Facility (CLF)** as the lender of last resort for credit unions. This agency provides many of the same functions for credit unions that the Federal Reserve provides for commercial banks. Although most day-to-day liquidity needs of credit unions are met by the state central organizations, in the event of a national liquidity crisis, a federal agency can raise far more funds. For example, in a crisis, the CLF can borrow directly from the Federal Reserve.

Membership in the CLF is voluntary, and any state or federally chartered credit union may join the CLF by pledging 0.5% of capital. Most of the funds in the CLF are borrowed from the federal government.

Credit Union Size Credit unions are small relative to other depository financial institutions. The industry only accounts for about 10% of all consumer deposits and about 15% of all consumer loans. One reason for credit unions' limited size is the common bond restraint. Because credit unions can enroll only members who satisfy the common bond, their growth potential is severely restricted. Nevertheless, some credit unions have grown quite large. The Navy Credit Union dwarfs the others, with well over $7 billion in total assets. However, most credit unions have less than $1 billion in assets, and many have less than $5 million.

As discussed earlier, mergers between credit unions help them capture economies of scale and diversify their risk. This trend has resulted in fewer but larger credit unions. Figure 6 reports the number of credit unions active from 1933 to 1996. The number has fallen steadily since 1970 as credit unions merged.

Trade Associations Because credit unions are so small, they often lack the economies of scale necessary to service their customers at competitive costs. For example, a credit union with only $5 million of deposits cannot afford the costs of maintaining a computer center for processing checks and sending out statements. Similarly, most credit unions cannot afford to maintain their own automated teller machine network. One solution to this problem is the use of **trade associations,** groups of credit unions that have organized together. These associations provide services to large numbers of credit unions.

The largest of the trade associations is the Credit Union National Association (CUNA). CUNA has a number of affiliations that provide specific services.

- CUNA Service Group provides new products for credit unions.
- CUNA Supply, Inc., provides for bulk purchases of supplies to lower supply costs.

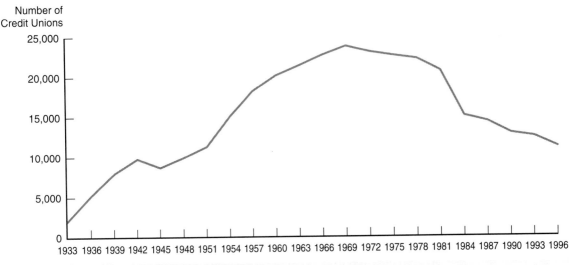

■FIGURE 6 Number of Credit Unions, 1933–1996

Source: Credit Union National, web page.

- ICU Services, Inc., provides various investment options, automated payment services, credit card programs, and IRA plans.
- CUNA Mortgage provides a liquidity facility for mortgage lending by credit unions.

In addition to using trade associations, many credit unions contract with commercial banks for data processing services. Checks written by credit union customers are automatically routed to the bank, which takes the funds out of a credit union account. The bank then provides a transaction history in electronic form that is given to the credit union. The tie-in with the servicing bank may be so close that the credit union's teller terminals are linked to the bank's computer system, just like the bank's own teller terminals. The credit union customer may never be aware that a bank is involved in the process.

Sources of Funds

Over 89.4% of credit union funds come from customer savings and share draft accounts. Unlike commercial banks, credit unions seldom purchase funds in the capital or money markets. Three types of accounts are offered by credit unions: regular share accounts, share certificates, and share draft accounts.

Regular Share Accounts Regular share accounts are savings accounts. Customers cannot write checks against these accounts, although they can withdraw funds without giving prior notice or incurring any penalties. These accounts make up the bulk of the credit unions' liabilities (over 70% in 1993). Customers do not receive interest on these accounts. Instead they receive dividends that are not guaranteed in advance but are estimated. The credit union tries to pay the estimated amount.

Share Certificates Share certificates are comparable to CDs offered by commercial banks. The customer agrees to leave the funds on deposit with the credit union for a specified length of time and in exchange receives a higher return.

Share Draft Accounts Share drafts were first developed in 1974 and made legal nationally in 1980. They are virtually identical to the checks written by customers of commercial banks. Share draft accounts usually pay interest and permit depositors to write share drafts against them. These accounts represent less than 10% of credit union liabilities.

Capital Credit union capital cannot be measured in the usual way because credit union share accounts are in fact equity accounts. A more meaningful approach is to measure capital as the difference between total assets and total liabilities where liabilities include all share accounts. Using this approach, we find that the average capital-to-asset ratio was 9.5% in June 1993. One reason for this strong capital position is that regulations require a capital-to-loan ratio of at least 10% for credit unions.

Uses of Funds

In June 1993, 53.5% of credit union assets were invested in loans. Most credit union loans are relatively small. For example, the average credit union loan in 1993 was $4386. This is in keeping with the mission of credit unions to provide loans to small borrowers. Credit union loan losses are usually quite small. The average ratio of delinquent loans to total loans is just over 1%. This compares favorably to the loan loss ratio for commercial banks.

The balance of credit union assets are in cash, government securities, deposits at other institutions, and fixed assets. Credit unions tend not to make risky investments and are limited by regulations to certain types of investment securities that assure low risk.

Advantages and Disadvantages of Credit Unions

Figure 7 traces the membership in credit unions from 1933 to 1996. The steady increase is expected to continue because credit unions enjoy several advantages over other depository institutions. These advantages have contributed toward their growth and popularity.

- *Employer support.* Many employers recognize that it is in their own best interest to help their employees manage their funds. This motivates the firm to support the employee credit union. Businesses will frequently provide free office space, utilities, and other help to the credit unions.

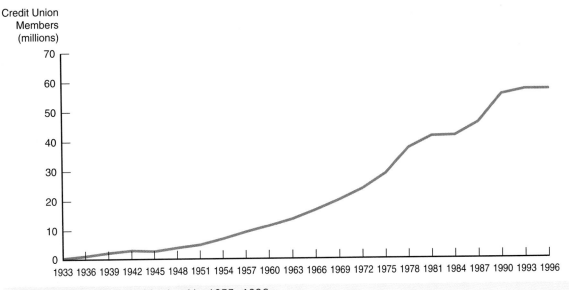

■FIGURE 7 Credit Union Membership, 1933–1996

Source: Credit Union National, web page.

- *Tax advantage.* Because credit unions are exempt from paying taxes by federal regulation, this savings can be passed on to the members in the form of higher dividends or lower account-servicing costs.
- *Strong trade associations.* Credit unions have formed many trade associations, which lower their costs and provide the means to offer services the institutions could not otherwise offer.

The main disadvantage of credit unions is that the common bond requirement keeps many of them very small. The cost disadvantage can prevent them from offering the range of services available from larger institutions. This disadvantage is not entirely equalized by the use of trade associations.

SUMMARY

1. Congress mandated that savings and loans and mutual savings banks provide mortgage loan opportunities for consumers. For most of the twentieth century, they profitably satisfied this need.

2. In the late 1970s and the 1980s, savings and loans lost money because interest rates on their deposits rose while the return on their mortgage portfolios was fixed. These losses initially led to deregulation. Savings and loans continued to lose money despite regulatory reform.

3. Due to mounting losses among savings and loans the industry was reregulated in 1987. It has since recovered in terms of both profitability and net worth. The industry continues to consolidate, though total assets are remaining about constant. It is too early to determine whether the industry will simply merge with commercial banks or remain independent.

4. Credit unions were established to serve the public's demand for consumer-type loans. They are unique because members must satisfy a common bond

requirement to join. This common bond requirement has restricted the growth of credit unions. Most are small compared to savings and loans and commercial banks.

5. Because of their small size, credit unions have benefited by forming cooperative organizations. These coops, such as CUNA, provide technical, liquidity, mortgage, and insurance services that would be impossible for the individual credit unions to have otherwise.

6. Credit unions enjoy several advantages that should keep them viable in the future. First, as nonprofit organizations, they are exempt from federal taxation. Second, many have strong support from a sponsoring company or business, which lowers the operating cost of the institution. The use of volunteers also helps keep costs low.

KEY TERMS

Central Liquidity Facility (CLF), p. 409
common bond membership, p. 406
credit union, p. 405
Credit Union National Association (CUNA), p. 406
Credit Union National Extension Bureau (CUNEB), p. 406
Federal Credit Union Act, p. 406
Federal Home Loan Bank Act of 1932, p. 392

Federal Home Loan Bank Board (FHLBB), p. 392
Federal Savings and Loan Insurance Corporation (FSLIC), p. 392
Financial Institutions Reform Act (FIRREA), p. 409
mutual bank, p. 391
National Credit Union Act of 1970, p. 408
National Credit Union Administration (NCUA), p. 408

National Credit Union Share Insurance Fund (NCUSIF), p. 408
passbook savings account, p. 402
regulatory forbearance, p. 394
Resolution Trust Corporation (RTC), p. 399
Savings Association Insurance Fund (SAIF), p. 399
trade association, p. 409
U.S. Central Credit Union, p. 408

QUESTIONS AND PROBLEMS

*1. How does the mutual form of ownership differ from the typical corporate form of ownership?

2. What is the primary disadvantage of the mutual form of ownership?

*3. What are the primary assets of savings and loan institutions?

4. Name three factors that led to the thrift crisis.

*5. Why did depositors not object to the risky loans and investments made by savings and loans in the early and mid-1980s?

6. How was the thrift crisis ended?

*7. What is the most common measure of the capital adequacy of a financial institution?

8. What has been the trend in S&L net income in the mid-1990s?

*9. What type of customers are credit unions focused on servicing?

10. What is the purpose of the Credit Union National Association (CUNA)?

*11. Describe the common bond membership rule.

12. Why does the commercial banking lobby object to the nonprofit, tax-exempt status enjoyed by credit unions?

*13. Are most credit unions larger or smaller than commercial banks? Why?

14. What are share accounts, share certificates, and share drafts?

*15. What are the primary advantages enjoyed by credit unions?

CHAPTER 16

BANKING REGULATION

PREVIEW As we have seen in earlier chapters, the financial system is among the most heavily regulated sectors of the economy, and banks are among the most heavily regulated of financial institutions. In this chapter we develop an economic analysis of why regulation of banking takes the form it does.

Unfortunately, the regulatory process may not always work very well, as evidenced by recent crises in the banking systems, not only in the United States but in many countries throughout the world. Here we also use our analysis of banking regulation to explain the worldwide crises in banking and how the regulatory system can be reformed to prevent future disasters.

ASYMMETRIC INFORMATION AND BANK REGULATION

In earlier chapters we have seen how asymmetric information, the fact that different parties in a financial contract do not have the same information, leads to adverse selection and moral hazard problems that have an important impact on our financial system. The concepts of asymmetric information, adverse selection, and moral hazard are especially useful in understanding why government has chosen the form of banking regulation we see in the United States and in other countries. There are seven basic categories of banking regulation: the government safety net, restrictions on bank asset holdings and capital requirements, chartering and bank examination, disclosure requirements, consumer protection, restrictions on competition, and separation of the banking and securities industries.

Government Safety Net: Deposit Insurance and the FDIC

As we saw in Chapter 12, banks are particularly well suited to solving adverse selection and moral hazard problems because they make private loans that help avoid the free-rider problem. However, this solution to the free-rider problem creates another asymmetric information problem because depositors lack information about the quality of these private loans. This asymmetric information problem leads to two reasons why the banking system might not function well.

First, before the FDIC started operations in 1934, a **bank failure** (in which a bank is unable to meet its obligations to pay its depositors and other creditors and so must go out of business) meant that depositors would have to wait to get their deposit funds until the bank was liquidated (until its assets had been turned into cash); at that time, they would be paid only a fraction of the value of their deposits. Unable to learn if bank managers were taking on too much risk or were outright crooks, depositors would be reluctant to put money in the bank, thus making banking institutions less viable. Second is that depositors' lack of information about the quality of bank assets can lead to bank panics, which, as we saw in Chapter 12, can have serious harmful consequences for the economy. To see this, consider the following situation. There is no deposit insurance, and an adverse shock hits the economy. As a result of the shock, 5% of the banks have such large losses on loans that they become insolvent (have a negative net worth and so are bankrupt). Because of asymmetric information, depositors are unable to tell whether their bank is a good bank or one of the 5% that are insolvent. Depositors at bad *and* good banks recognize that they may not get back 100 cents on the dollar for their deposits and will want to withdraw them. Indeed, because banks operate on a "sequential service constraint" (a first-come, first-served basis), depositors have a very strong incentive to show up at the bank first because if they are last in line, the bank may run out of funds and they will get nothing. Uncertainty about the health of the banking system in general can lead to runs on banks both good and bad, and the failure of one bank can hasten the failure of others (referred to as the *contagion effect*). If nothing is done to restore the public's confidence, a bank panic can ensue.

Indeed, bank panics were a fact of American life in the nineteenth and early twentieth centuries, with major ones occurring every 20 years or so in 1819, 1837, 1857, 1873, 1884, 1893, 1907, and 1930–1933. Bank failures were a serious problem even during the boom years of the 1920s, when the number of bank failures averaged around 600 per year.

A government safety net for depositors can short-circuit runs on banks and bank panics, and by providing protection for the depositor, it can overcome reluctance to put funds in the banking system. One form of the safety net is deposit insurance, a guarantee such as that provided by the Federal Deposit Insurance Corporation (FDIC) in the United States in which depositors are paid off in full on the first $100,000 they have deposited in the bank no matter what happens to the bank. With fully insured deposits, depositors don't need to run to the bank to make withdrawals—even if they are worried about the bank's health—because their deposits will be worth 100 cents on the dollar no matter what. From 1930 to 1933, the years immediately preceding the creation of the FDIC, the number of bank failures averaged over 2000 per year. After the establishment of the FDIC in 1934, bank failures averaged fewer than 15 per year until 1981.

The FDIC uses two primary methods to handle a failed bank. In the first, called the *payoff method,* the FDIC allows the bank to fail and pays off deposits up to the $100,000 insurance limit (with funds acquired from the insurance premiums paid by the banks who have bought FDIC insurance). After the bank has been liquidated, the FDIC lines up with other creditors of the bank and is paid its share of the proceeds from the liquidated assets. Typically, when the payoff method is used, account holders with deposits in excess of the $100,000 limit get back more than 90 cents on the dollar, although the process can take several years to complete.

In the second method, called the *purchase and assumption method,* the FDIC reorganizes the bank, typically by finding a willing merger partner who assumes (takes over) all of the failed bank's deposits so that no depositor loses a penny. The FDIC may help the merger partner by providing it with subsidized loans or by buying some of the failed bank's weaker loans. The net effect of the purchase and assumption method is that the FDIC has guaranteed *all* deposits, not just those under the $100,000 limit. The purchase and assumption method was the FDIC's most common procedure for dealing with a failed bank before new banking legislation in 1991.

Deposit insurance is not the only way in which governments provide a safety net for depositors. In other countries, governments have often stood ready to provide support to domestic banks when they face runs even in the absence of explicit deposit insurance. This support is sometimes provided by lending from the central bank to troubled institutions and is often referred to as the "lender of last resort" role of the central bank. In other cases, funds are provided directly by the government to troubled institutions, or these institutions are taken over by the government and the government then guarantees that depositors will receive their money in full.

Moral Hazard and the Government Safety Net Although a government safety net has been successful at protecting depositors and preventing bank panics, it is a mixed blessing. The most serious drawback of the government safety net stems from moral hazard, the incentives of one party to a transaction to engage in activities detrimental to the other party. Moral hazard is an important concern in insurance arrangements in general because the existence of insurance provides increased incentives for taking risks that might result in an insurance payoff. For example, some drivers with automobile collision insurance that has a low deductible might be more likely to drive recklessly because if they get into an accident, the insurance company pays most of the costs for damage and repairs.

Moral hazard is a prominent concern in government arrangements to provide a safety net. Because with a safety net depositors know that they will not suffer losses if a bank fails, they do not impose the discipline of the marketplace on banks by withdrawing deposits when they suspect that the bank is taking on too much risk. Consequently, banks with a government safety net have an incentive to take on greater risks than they otherwise would.

Adverse Selection and the Government Safety Net A further problem with a government safety net like deposit insurance arises because of adverse selection, the fact that the people who are most likely to produce the adverse outcome insured against (bank failure) are those who most want to take advantage of the insurance. For example, bad drivers are more likely than good drivers to take out automobile collision insurance with a low deductible. Because depositors protected by a government safety net have little reason to impose discipline on the bank, risk-loving entrepreneurs might find the banking industry a particularly attractive one to enter—they know that they will be able to engage in highly risky activities. Even worse, because protected depositors have so little reason to monitor the bank's activities, without government intervention outright crooks might also find banking an attractive industry for their activities because it is easy for them to get away with fraud and embezzlement.

"Too Big to Fail" The moral hazard created by a government safety net and the desire to prevent bank failures have presented bank regulators with a particular quandary. Because the failure of a very large bank makes it more likely that a major financial disruption will occur, bank regulators are naturally reluctant to allow a big bank to fail and cause losses to its depositors. Indeed, consider Continental Illinois, one of the ten largest banks in the United States when it became insolvent in May 1984. Not only did the FDIC guarantee depositors up to the $100,000 insurance limit, but it also guaranteed accounts exceeding $100,000 and even prevented losses for Continental Illinois bondholders. Shortly thereafter, the Comptroller of the Currency (the regulator of national banks) testified to Congress that the FDIC's policy was to regard the 11 largest banks as "too big to fail"—in other words, the FDIC would bail them out so that no depositor or creditor would suffer a loss. The FDIC would do this by using the purchase and assumption method, giving the insolvent bank a large infusion of capital and then finding a willing merger partner to take over the bank and its deposits. As Box 1 indicates, the too-big-to-fail policy has been extended to big banks that are not even among the 11 largest. (Note that "too big to fail" is somewhat misleading because when a bank is closed or merged into another bank, the managers are usually fired and the stockholders in the bank lose their investment.)

One problem with the too-big-to-fail policy is that it increases the moral hazard incentives for big banks. If the FDIC were willing to close a bank using the alternative payoff method, paying depositors only up to the $100,000 limit, large depositors with more than $100,000 would suffer losses if the bank failed. Thus they would have an incentive to monitor the bank by examining the bank's activities closely and pulling their money out if the bank was taking on too much risk. To prevent such a loss of deposits, the bank would be more likely to engage in less risky activities. However, once large depositors know that a bank is too big to fail, they have no incentive to monitor the bank and pull out their deposits when it takes on too much risk: No matter what the bank does, large depositors will not suffer any losses. The result of the too-big-to-fail policy is that big banks might take on even greater risks, thereby making bank failures more likely.[1]

Another serious problem with the too-big-to-fail policy is that it is basically unfair. Small banks are put at a competitive disadvantage because they will be

---

[1]Recent evidence reveals, as our analysis predicts, that large banks have taken on riskier loans than smaller banks and that this has led to higher loan losses for big banks; see John Boyd and Mark Gertler, "U.S. Commercial Banking: Trends, Cycles and Policy," *NBER Macroeconomics Annual, 1993,* pp. 319–368.

BOX 1

A Tale of Two Bank Collapses

Bank of New England and Freedom National Bank

The FDIC's procedures for handling two bank collapses, those of the Bank of New England and Freedom National Bank, illustrate how the too-big-to-fail policy works.

The Bank of New England, based in Boston, was the thirty-third-largest bank holding company in the United States, with over $20 billion of assets. In the 1980s, it was the region's most aggressive real estate lender; over 30% of its loan portfolio was in commercial real estate. With the collapse of real estate prices in New England beginning in the late 1980s (commercial real estate values dropped by more than 25%), many of the bank's loans went sour. On Friday, January 4, 1991, the bank announced a projected $450 million fourth-quarter loss that exceeded the bank's capital of $255 million. Expecting the failure of the bank, in the next 48 hours depositors lined up at the bank and withdrew over $1 billion in funds, much of it from automated teller machines.

The chairman of the FDIC, William Seidman, expressed his concern over the ramifications of the potential failure: "Given the condition of the financial system in New England, it would be unwise to send a signal that large depositors weren't going to be protected."* The FDIC invoked its too-big-to-fail policy. Sunday night, January 6, the FDIC moved in to stop the run on the bank and agreed to guarantee all Bank of New England deposits, including those in excess of the $100,000 insurance limit. To keep the bank in operation until a buyer could be found and the purchase and assumption method could be used to make sure that no depositors would suffer any loss, the FDIC created what is called a *bridge bank*. In this arrangement, the FDIC creates a new corporation to run the bank and immediately injects capital ($750 million in the case of the Bank of New England). The FDIC and the buyer of the bank then put additional capital into the bank over

time, and eventually the acquirer buys out the FDIC's share. The net result of these transactions was that the FDIC spent $2.3 billion bailing out the Bank of New England, the third-costliest bailout in the FDIC's history. However, when all was said and done and spent, none of the depositors lost a penny.

The very different FDIC treatment of a small insolvent bank in Harlem several months earlier raised serious questions of fairness. The Freedom National Bank was founded in 1964 by baseball great Jackie Robinson and other minority investors. Despite its small size (under $100 million of deposits), it was one of the most prominent black-owned banks.

As a result of numerous speculative loans that went bad, the bank became insolvent in November 1990. Because of the bank's small size, the FDIC was not concerned that the failure of the bank would have serious repercussions for the rest of the banking system, so it decided to close the bank on November 9 using the payoff method. The Freedom National Bank was liquidated, and large depositors were paid only 50 cents on the dollar for deposits in excess of $100,000. Not only fat cats suffered losses when this bank failed. Charitable organizations like the United Negro College Fund, the National Urban League, and several churches were among the large depositors at the bank. Seidman described the unfairness of the treatment of the Freedom National Bank to Congress: "My first testimony when I came to this job was that it's unfair to treat big banks in a way that covers all depositors but not small banks. I promised to do my best to change that. Five years later, I can report that my best wasn't good enough."†

*Quoted in John Meehan, "A Shock to the System: How Far Will Banking's Crisis of Confidence Spread?" *Business Week*, January 21, 1991, p. 26.
†Quoted in Kenneth H. Bacon, "Failures of a Big Bank and a Little Bank Bring Fairness of Deposit-Security Policy into Question," *Wall Street Journal*, December 5, 1990, p. A18.

allowed to fail, creating potential losses for their large depositors, while big banks' large depositors are immune from losses. The unfairness of the too-big-to-fail doctrine came to a head with the different FDIC treatment of two insolvent banks in late 1990 and early 1991 described in Box 1.

Restrictions on Asset Holdings and Bank Capital Requirements

As we have seen, the moral hazard associated with a government safety net encourages too much risk taking on the part of banks. Bank regulations that restrict asset holdings and bank capital requirements are directed at minimizing this moral hazard, which can cost the taxpayers dearly.

Even in the absence of a government safety net, banks still have the incentive to take on too much risk. Risky assets may provide the bank with higher earnings when they pay off; but if they do not pay off and the bank fails, depositors are left holding the bag. If depositors were able to monitor the bank easily by acquiring information on its risk-taking activities, they would immediately withdraw their deposits if the bank was taking on too much risk. To prevent such a loss of deposits, the bank would be more likely to reduce its risk-taking activities. Unfortunately, acquiring information on a bank's activities to learn how much risk the bank is taking can be a difficult task. Hence most depositors are incapable of imposing discipline that might prevent banks from engaging in risky activities. A strong rationale for government regulation to reduce risk taking on the part of banks therefore existed even before the establishment of federal deposit insurance.

Bank regulations that restrict banks from holding risky assets such as common stock are a direct means of making banks avoid too much risk. Bank regulations also promote diversification, which reduces risk by limiting the amount of loans in particular categories or to individual borrowers. Requirements that banks have sufficient bank capital are another way to change the bank's incentives to take on less risk. When a bank is forced to hold a large amount of equity capital, the bank has more to lose if it fails and is thus more likely to pursue less risky activities.

Bank capital requirements take three forms. The first type is based on the so-called **leverage ratio,** the amount of capital divided by the bank's total assets. To be classified as well capitalized, a bank's leverage ratio must exceed 5%; a lower leverage ratio, especially one below 3%, triggers increased regulatory restrictions on the bank. Through most of the 1980s, minimum bank capital in the United States was set solely by specifying a minimum leverage ratio.

In the wake of the Continental Illinois and savings and loans bailouts, regulators in the United States and the rest of the world have become increasingly worried about banks' holdings of risky assets and about the increase in banks' **off-balance-sheet activities**, activities that involve trading financial instruments and generating income from fees, which do not appear on bank balance sheets but nevertheless expose banks to risk. Under an agreement among banking officials from industrialized nations (who met under the auspices of the Bank for International Settlements in Basel, Switzerland), the Federal Reserve, the FDIC, and the Office of the Comptroller of the Currency have implemented an additional second type of bank-based capital requirement, which was fully phased in by December 1992. Under this risk-based capital requirement, which the banks must meet along with the leverage ratio capital requirement, minimum capital standards are linked to off-balance-sheet activities such as interest-rate swaps and trading positions in futures and options. Box 2 outlines the structure of these capital requirements in more detail.

■ BOX 2   A GLOBAL PERSPECTIVE

The Basel Accord on Risk-Based Capital Requirements

 The increased integration of financial markets across countries and the need to make the playing field level for banks from different countries led to the June 1988 Basel accord to standardize bank capital requirements internationally. The stated purposes of the agreement were (1) to promote world financial stability by coordinating supervisory definitions of capital, risk assessments, and standards for capital adequacy across countries and (2) to link a bank's capital requirements systematically to the riskiness of its activities, including various off-balance-sheet forms of risk exposure.

The Basel capital requirements work as follows. Assets and off-balance-sheet activities are allocated into four categories, each with a different weight to reflect the degree of credit risk. The lowest risk category carries a zero weight and includes items that have no default risk, such as reserves and government securities. The next lowest risk category has a weight of 20% and includes assets with a low default risk, such as interbank deposits, fully backed mortgage bonds, and securities issued by government agencies. The third category has a weight of 50% and includes municipal bonds and residential mortgages. The last risk category has the maximum weight of 100% and includes all remaining securities (such as commercial paper), loans (such as commercial and real estate construction loans), and fixed assets (bank building, computers, and other property). Off-balance-sheet activities are treated in a similar manner by assigning a credit equivalent percentage that converts them to on-balance-sheet items, and then the appropriate risk weight applies. For example, a standby letter of credit backing a customer's commercial paper is assigned a 100% credit-equivalent percentage and then has a risk weight of 100% because it exposes the bank to the same risk as a direct loan to this customer.

Once all the bank's assets and off-balance-sheet items have been assigned to a risk category, they are weighted by the corresponding risk factor and are added up to compute the total "risk-adjusted assets." The bank must then meet two capital requirements: It must have "core" or Tier 1 capital (stockholder equity capital) of at least 4% of total risk-adjusted assets, and total capital (Tier 1 capital plus Tier 2 capital, which is made up of loan loss reserves and subordinated debt) must come to 8% of total risk-adjusted assets. (Subordinated debt is debt that is paid off only after depositors and other creditors have been paid.) For regulators to classify a bank as well capitalized, it must meet an even more stringent total-capital requirement of 10% of risk-adjusted assets and Tier 1 capital of 6% of risk-adjusted assets.

In addition, in 1996, the Federal Reserve announced a third type of capital requirement to take effect by January 1998 to cover risk in trading activities at the largest banks. The Fed will require these banks to use their own internal models to calculate how much they could lose over a ten-day period and then set aside additional capital equal to three times that amount. Banks can meet this new capital requirement with more standard forms of capital or by issuing a new form of capital, called Tier 3, which consists of short-term securities that holders can't cash in at maturity if the bank is undercapitalized.

Bank Supervision: Chartering and Examination

Overseeing who operates banks and how they are operated, referred to as **bank supervision** or more generally as **prudential supervision,** is an important method for reducing adverse selection and moral hazard in the banking business. Because banks can be used by crooks or overambitious entrepreneurs to engage in highly speculative activities, such undesirable people would be eager to run a bank. (Charles Keating Jr., discussed in Chapter 15, was one such person.) Chartering banks is one method for preventing this adverse selection problem; through chartering, proposals for new banks are screened to prevent undesirable people from controlling them.

Regular on-site bank examinations, which allow regulators to monitor whether the bank is complying with capital requirements and restrictions on asset holdings, also function to limit moral hazard. Bank examiners give banks a so-called *CAMEL rating* (the acronym is based on the five areas assessed: capital adequacy, asset quality, management, earnings, and liquidity). With this information about a bank's activities, regulators can enforce regulations by taking such formal actions as *cease and desist orders* to alter the bank's behavior or even close a bank if its CAMEL rating is sufficiently low. Actions taken to reduce moral hazard by restricting banks from taking on too much risk help reduce the adverse selection problem further because with less opportunity for risk taking, risk-loving entrepreneurs will be less likely to be attracted to the banking industry.[2]

A commercial bank obtains a charter either from the Comptroller of the Currency (in the case of a national bank) or from a state banking authority (in the case of a state bank). To obtain a charter, the people planning to organize the bank must submit an application that shows how they plan to operate the bank. In evaluating the application, the regulatory authority looks at whether the bank is likely to be sound by examining the quality of the bank's intended management, the likely earnings of the bank, and the amount of the bank's initial capital. Before 1980, the chartering agency typically explored the issue of whether the community needed a new bank. Often a new bank charter would not be granted if existing banks in a community would be severely hurt by its presence. Today this anticompetitive stance (justified by the desire to prevent bank failures of existing banks) is no longer as strong in the chartering agencies.

Once a bank has been chartered, it is required to file periodic (usually quarterly) *call reports* that reveal the bank's assets and liabilities, income and dividends, ownership, foreign exchange operations, and other details. The bank is also subject to examination by the bank regulatory agencies to ascertain its financial condition at least once a year. To avoid duplication of effort, the three federal agencies work together and usually accept each other's examinations. This means that, typically, national banks are examined by the Office of the Comptroller of the Currency, the state banks that are members of the Federal Reserve System are examined by the Fed, and nonmember state banks are examined by the FDIC.

Bank examinations are conducted by bank examiners, who sometimes make unannounced visits to the bank (so that nothing can be "swept under the rug" in anticipation of their examination). The examiners study a bank's books to see whether it is complying with the rules and regulations that apply to its holdings of

---

[2]Note that the methods regulators use to cope with adverse selection and moral hazard have their counterparts in private financial markets (see Chapter 12). Chartering is similar to the screening of potential borrowers, regulations restricting risky asset holdings are similar to restrictive covenants that prevent borrowing firms from engaging in risky investment activities, bank capital requirements act like restrictive covenants that require minimum amounts of net worth for borrowing firms, and regular bank examinations are similar to the monitoring of borrowers by lending institutions.

assets. If a bank is holding securities or loans that are too risky, the bank examiner can force the bank to get rid of them. If a bank examiner decides that a loan is unlikely to be repaid, the examiner can force the bank to declare the loan worthless (to write off the loan). If, after examining the bank, the examiner feels that it does not have sufficient capital or has engaged in dishonest practices, the bank can be declared a "problem bank" and will be subject to more frequent examinations.

A New Trend in Bank Supervision: Assessment of Risk Management

Traditionally, on-site bank examinations have focused primarily on assessment of the quality of the bank's balance sheet at a point in time and whether it complies with capital requirements and restrictions on asset holdings. Although the traditional focus is important for reducing excessive risk taking by banks, it is no longer felt to be adequate in today's world in which financial innovation has produced new markets and instruments that make it easy for banks and their employees to make huge bets easily and quickly. In this new financial environment, a bank that is quite healthy at a particular point in time and can be driven into insolvency extremely rapidly from trading losses, as forcefully demonstrated by the failure of Barings in 1995 (discussed in Chapter 13). Thus an examination that focuses only on a bank's position at a point in time, may not be effective in indicating whether a bank will in fact be taking on excessive risk in the near future.

This change in the financial environment for banking institutions has resulted in a major shift in thinking about the bank supervisory process throughout the world. Bank examiners are now placing far greater emphasis on evaluating the soundness of a bank's management processes with regard to controlling risk. This shift in thinking was reflected in a new focus on risk management in the Federal Reserve System's 1993 guidelines to examiners on trading and derivatives activities. The focus was expanded and formalized in the Trading Activities Manual issued early in 1994, which provided bank examiners with tools to evaluate risk management systems. In late 1995, the Federal Reserve and the Comptroller of the Currency announced that they would be assessing risk management processes at the banks they supervise. Now bank examiners give a separate risk management rating from 1 to 5 that feeds into the overall management rating as part of the CAMEL system. Four elements of sound risk management are assessed to come up with the risk management rating: (1) The quality of oversight provided by the board of directors and senior management, (2) the adequacy of policies and limits for all activities that present significant risks, (3) the quality of the risk measurement and monitoring systems, and (4) the adequacy of internal controls to prevent fraud or unauthorized activities on the part of employees.

This shift toward focusing on management processes is also reflected in recent guidelines adopted by the U.S. bank regulatory authorities to deal with interest-rate risk. At one point, U.S. regulators were contemplating requiring banks to use a standard model to calculate the amount of capital a bank would need to have to allow for the interest-rate risk it bears. Because coming up with a one-size-fits-all model that would work for all banks has proved difficult, the regulatory agencies have instead decided to adopt guidelines for the management of interest-rate risk, although bank examiners will continue to consider interest-rate risk in deciding on the bank's capital requirements. These guidelines require the bank's board of directors to establish interest-rate risk limits, appoint officials of the bank to manage this risk, and monitor the bank's risk exposure. The guidelines also require that senior management of a bank develop formal risk management policies and procedures, to ensure that the board of director's risk limits are not violated and to implement internal controls to monitor interest-rate risk and compliance with the board's directives.

Disclosure Requirements

The free-rider problem described in Chapter 12 indicates that individual depositors and other bank creditors will not have enough incentive to produce private information about the quality of a bank's assets. To ensure that there is better information for depositors and the marketplace, regulators can require that banks adhere to certain standard accounting principles and disclose a wide range of information that helps the market assess the quality of a bank's portfolio and the amount of the bank's exposure to risk. More public information about the risks incurred by banks and the quality of their portfolio can better enable stockholders, creditors, and depositors to evaluate and monitor banks and so act as a deterrent to excessive risk taking. This view is consistent with a recent position paper issued by the Eurocurrency Standing Committee of the G-10 Central Banks, which recommends that estimates of financial risk generated by firms' own internal risk management systems be adapted for public disclosure purposes.[3] Such information would supplement disclosures based on traditional accounting conventions by providing information about risk exposure and risk management that is not normally included in conventional balance sheet and income statement reports. Disclosure requirements can also be the primary focus of a bank regulatory system, as with a new approach recently implemented in New Zealand (Box 3).

Consumer Protection

The existence of asymmetric information also suggests that consumers may not have enough information to protect themselves fully. Consumer protection regulation has taken several forms. First is "truth in lending," mandated under the Consumer Protection Act of 1969, which requires all lenders, not just banks, to provide information to consumers about the cost of borrowing including a standardized interest rate (called the annual percentage rate, or APR) and the total finance charges on the loan. The Fair Credit Billing Act of 1974 requires creditors, especially credit card issuers, to provide information on the method of assessing finance charges and requires that billing complaints be handled quickly. Both of these acts are administered by the Federal Reserve System under Regulation Z.

---

[3]See Eurocurrency Standing Committee of Central Banks of Group of Ten Countries (Fisher Group), "Discussion Paper on Public Disclosure of Markets and Credit Risks by Financial Intermediaries," September 1994, and a companion piece to this report, Federal Reserve Bank of New York, "A Discussion Paper on Public Disclosure of Risks Related to Market Activity," September 1994.

BOX 3   A GLOBAL PERSPECTIVE

New Zealand's Disclosure-Based Experiment in Bank Regulation

 Until 1995, New Zealand took a conventional approach to bank regulation that relied on regular examinations by the central bank to ensure that the banks complied with capital requirements and asset restrictions and followed good management practices. At the start of 1996, this system has been scrapped for one based on disclosure requirements that uses the market to police the behavior of the banks.

As part of this new system, every bank in New Zealand must supply a comprehensive, quarterly financial statement that provides information on the quality of its assets, its lending activities, and its ratings from private credit-rating agencies, among other things. These financial statements must be audited two times a year, and not only must they be provided to the central bank, which will monitor them, but they must also be made public, with a two-page summary posted in all bank branches. In addition, bank directors are required to validate these statements and state publicly that their bank's risk management systems are adequate and being properly implemented. A most unusual feature of this system is that a bank's directors now face unlimited liability—that is, they can lose all their assets, not just their holdings in the bank—if they are found to have made false or misleading statements. Directors are thus in the dangerous position that they can be sued by creditors for everything they are worth if the bank goes bust.

The rationale for this approach is that the market will now provide the necessary discipline to prevent bankers from taking excessive risks because it will have sufficient information about banks' activities—depositors have the incentive to monitor the banks because there is no deposit insurance in New Zealand. Furthermore, banks will now have the incentive to improve their financial health in order to acquire good credit ratings. The system also has the advantage that it reduces regulatory costs for the banks because it will eliminate examination fees and burdensome rules on management procedures.

Critics of New Zealand's new approach point out that even with the new disclosure requirements, the asymmetric information problem may still not be solved. Banks may be less willing to admit to problems if the information has to be made public. In addition, depositors may not have the sophistication to understand the information provided and thus may not impose the necessary discipline on the banks. Furthermore, unlimited liability for directors might discourage top people from taking these positions, thereby weakening the management of the banks.

Although advocates of the New Zealand system think that it may prove to be a model for the rest of the world, skeptics point out that it might work only because of the peculiar features of the New Zealand banking system. Almost all New Zealand banks are foreign-owned, and around 90% of deposits are at foreign-owned banks. Thus these skeptics contend that in effect, bank regulation has been outsourced to the regulators of the foreign banks that own the New Zealand banks—central banks such as the Bank of England and the Reserve Bank of Australia that supervise the banks with subsidiaries in New Zealand.

Congress has also passed legislation to reduce discrimination in credit markets. The Equal Credit Opportunity Act of 1974 and its extension in 1976 forbid discrimination by lenders based on race, gender, marital status, age, or national origin. It is administered by the Federal Reserve under Regulation B. The Community Reinvestment Act (CRA) of 1977 was enacted to prevent "redlining," a lender's refusal to lend in a particular area (marked off by a hypothetical red line on a map). The Community Reinvestment Act requires that banks show that they lend in all areas in which they take deposits, and if banks are found to be in noncompliance with the act, regulators can reject their applications for mergers, branching, or other new activities. The increased enforcement of CRA provisions in recent years has been controversial (see Box 4).

The Community Reinvestment Act

A Political Hot Button

The Community Reinvestment Act (CRA) has become more controversial recently because of the strengthening of its provisions in recent years and increased enforcement by bank regulators. Banks now have new reporting requirements on such items as small business lending and community involvement, and they complain that the increased paperwork is both burdensome and costly. The CRA has also received more attention recently because of increased merger activity in the banking industry, which raises its importance because meeting its provisions affects the merger approval process.

Many congressional Republicans regard the act as a heavy-handed affirmative action program that increases the burden of regulation unnecessarily and have strongly advocated its abolishment or at least the exemption of many banks and savings and loans from its provisions. Advocates of the act, who feel just as strongly, have pointed out that in the past minorities have been discriminated against by banks, and it has increased lending to minorities, which has recently begun to rise at a much faster rate than to whites. Considering that affirmative action has become a hot political topic, the Community Reinvestment Act is sure to remain controversial.

Restrictions on Competition

Increased competition can also increase moral hazard incentives for banks to take on more risk. Declining profitability as a result of increased competition could tip the incentives of bankers toward assuming greater risk in an effort to maintain former profit levels. Thus governments in many countries have instituted regulations to protect banks from competition. These regulations have taken two forms in the United States. First are restrictions on branching, such as those described in Chapter 14, which reduce competition between banks. The second form involves preventing nonbank institutions from competing with banks by engaging in banking business.

Although restricting competition may prop up the health of banks, restrictions on competition can also have serious disadvantages: They can lead to higher charges to consumers and can decrease the efficiency of banking institutions, which do not have to compete as hard. Thus although the existence of asymmetric information provides a rationale for anticompetitive regulations, it does not mean that they will be beneficial. Indeed, in recent years, the impulse of governments in industrialized countries to restrict competition has been waning.

Separation of the Banking and Securities Industries: The Glass-Steagall Act

Before 1933, commercial banks engaged in investment banking activities as well as traditional banking activities. Because investment banking is inherently risky, allowing banks to pursue these activities may have increased their moral hazard opportunities for risk taking. After sensational congressional hearings documenting abuses of commercial banks in their securities activities during the Great

Depression collapse—which were as widely followed by the public as the Watergate or Iran-*contra* hearings in recent decades—Congress passed the Glass-Steagall Act in 1933. Glass-Steagall allowed commercial banks to sell new offerings of government securities but prohibited them from underwriting corporate securities or from engaging in brokerage activities. It also prohibited investment banks from engaging in commercial banking activities and has thus protected banks from competition. Additional regulations prohibited banks from selling insurance and engaging in other nonbank activities that were considered risky.

> ■ **STUDY GUIDE** Because so many laws regulating banking have been passed in the United States, it is hard to keep track of it all. As a study aid, Table 1 lists the major banking legislation in the twentieth century and its key provisions.

INTERNATIONAL BANKING REGULATION

Because asymmetric information problems in the banking industry are a fact of life throughout the world, bank regulation in other countries is similar to that in the United States. Banks are chartered and supervised by government regulators, just as they are in the United States—for example, by the Ministry of Finance in Japan and by the Bank of England in the United Kingdom. Deposit insurance is also a feature of the regulatory systems in most other developed countries, although its coverage is often smaller than in the United States and is purposely not advertised. We have also seen that bank capital requirements are in the process of being standardized across countries with agreements like the Basel accord.

Problems in Regulating International Banking

Particular problems in bank regulation occur when banks are engaged in international banking and thus can readily shift their business from one country to another. Bank regulators closely examine the domestic operations of banks in their country, but they often do not have the knowledge or ability to keep a close watch on bank operations in other countries, either by domestic banks' foreign affiliates or by foreign banks with domestic branches. In addition, when a bank operates in many countries, it is not always clear which national regulatory authority should have primary responsibility for keeping the bank from engaging in overly risky activities. The difficulties inherent in regulating international banking were highlighted by the BCCI scandal discussed in Box 5. Cooperation among regulators in different countries and standardization of regulatory requirements provide potential solutions to the problems of regulating international banking. The world has been moving in this direction through agreements like the Basel accord on capital requirements in 1988 and the new regulatory oversight procedures announced by the Basel Committee in July 1992 (see Box 2). However, whether agreements of this type will solve the problem of regulating international banking in the future is an open question.

■ TABLE 1 Major Banking Legislation in the United States in the Twentieth Century

Federal Reserve Act (1913)
Created the Federal Reserve System

McFadden Act of 1927
Put national and state banks on equal footing regarding branching
Effectively prohibited banks from branching across state lines

Banking Acts of 1933 (Glass-Steagall) and 1935
Created the FDIC
Separated commercial banking from the securities industry
Prohibited interest on checkable deposits and restricted such deposits to commercial banks
Put interest-rate ceilings on other deposits

Bank Holding Company Act (1956) and Douglas Amendment (1970)
Clarified the status of bank holding companies (BHCs)
Gave the Federal Reserve regulatory responsibility for BHCs

Depository Institutions Deregulation and Monetary Control Act (DIDMCA) of 1980
Gave thrift institutions wider latitude in activities
Approved NOW and ATS accounts nationwide
Phased out interest rate ceilings on deposits
Imposed uniform reserve requirements on depository institutions
Eliminated usury ceilings on loans
Increased deposit insurance to $100,000 per account

Depository Institutions Act of 1982 (Garn–St Germain)
Gave the FDIC and the FSLIC emergency powers to merge banks and thrifts across state lines
Allowed depository institutions to offer money market deposit accounts (MMDAs)
Granted thrifts wider latitude in commercial and consumer lending

Competitive Equality in Banking Act (CEBA) of 1987
Provided $10.8 billion to the FSLIC
Made provisions for regulatory forbearance in depressed areas

Financial Institutions Reform, Recovery, and Enforcement Act (FIRREA) of 1989
Provided funds to resolve S&L failures
Eliminated the FSLIC and the Federal Home Loan Bank Board
Created the Office of Thrift Supervision to regulate thrifts
Created the Resolution Trust Corporation to resolve insolvent thrifts
Raised deposit insurance premiums
Reimposed restrictions on S&L activities

Federal Deposit Insurance Corporation Improvement Act (FDICIA) of 1991
Recapitalized the FDIC
Limited brokered deposits and the too-big-to-fail policy
Set provisions for prompt corrective action
Instructed the FDIC to establish risk-based premiums
Increased examinations, capital requirements, and reporting requirements
Included the Foreign Bank Supervision Enhancement Act (FBSEA), which strengthened the Fed's authority to supervise
    foreign banks

Riegle-Neal Interstate Banking and Branching Efficiency Act of 1994
Overturned prohibition of interstate banking
Allowed branching across state lines

BOX 5   A GLOBAL PERSPECTIVE

The BCCI Scandal

 The Bank of Credit and Commerce International (BCCI) was chartered in Luxembourg in 1972 by a Pakistani businessman, Agha Hasan Abedi. The bank grew rapidly to $20 billion in assets and by 1991 was operating in more than 70 countries. Unfortunately, the bank was siphoning off funds to secret accounts in the Cayman Islands, where much of this money was stolen. Indeed, estimates suggest that nearly half of the bank's assets may have "disappeared." Fraud was not the only shady activity BCCI engaged in. BCCI supposedly helped dictators such as Saddam Hussein of Iraq, Manuel Noriega of Panama, and Ferdinand Marcos of the Philippines steal huge sums from their countries, helped the CIA channel funds to the *contra* rebels in Nicaragua, and acted as a banker for the notorious Abu Nidal terrorist group. Not surprisingly, BCCI has been dubbed the "Bank of Crooks and Criminals, Inc."

How did BCCI get away with these fraudulent activities for so long? The answer illustrates the difficulties of regulating banks with operations in many countries. Although BCCI's headquarters were in London, regulatory oversight fell to the chartering country, Luxembourg, whose tiny bank regulator, the Institut Monétaire Luxembourgeois (IML), was not up to the task. As a result, BCCI effectively operated free of government regulatory oversight for 15 years. In 1987, the IML reached an agreement with seven other countries' regulators to oversee BCCI jointly, but even this larger group was unable to keep track of the bank's activities. Only in spring 1990 did these regulators uncover some evidence of fraud, and not until July 1991 did the Price Waterhouse accounting firm document the pervasiveness of the fraud to the Bank of England, which then closed BCCI down.

The losses to depositors and stockholders from the BCCI collapse were immense, and national regulators, particularly the Bank of England, have been severely criticized for their slowness in uncovering the scandal. A year after the BCCI collapse, in July 1992, the Basel Committee announced an agreement to standardize further the regulation of international banks. Now a bank's worldwide operations will be under the scrutiny of a single home-country regulator with enhanced powers to acquire information on the bank's activities. Furthermore, regulators in other countries will have the right to restrict operations of a foreign bank if they feel that it lacks effective oversight. Despite this improvement in the regulation of international banks, fears remain that a BCCI-like scandal could happen again.

Summary

Asymmetric information analysis explains what types of banking regulations are needed to reduce moral hazard and adverse selection problems in the banking system. However, understanding the theory behind regulation does not mean that regulation and supervision of the banking system are easy in practice. Getting bank regulators and supervisors to do their job properly is difficult for several reasons. First, as we learned in the discussion of financial innovation in Chapter 13, in their search for profits, financial institutions have strong incentives to avoid existing regulations by loophole mining. Thus regulation applies to a moving target: Regulators are continually playing cat and mouse with financial institutions—financial institutions think up clever ways to avoid regulations, which then causes regulators to modify their regulation activities. Regulators continually face new challenges in a dynamically changing financial system, and unless they can respond rapidly to change, they may not be able to keep financial institutions from taking on excessive risk. This problem can be exacerbated if regulators and supervisors do not have the resources or expertise to keep up with clever people in financial institutions who think up ways to hide what they are doing or ways to get around the existing regulations.

Bank regulation and supervision are difficult for two other reasons. In the regulation and supervision game, the devil is in the details. Subtle differences in the details may have unintended consequences; unless regulators get the regulation and supervision just right, they may be unable to prevent excessive risk taking. In addition, regulators and supervisors may be subject to political pressure not to do their jobs properly. For all these reasons, there is no guarantee that bank regulators and supervisors will be successful in promoting a healthy financial system. Indeed, as we will see, bank regulation and supervision have not always worked well, leading to banking crises in the United States and throughout the world.

■ THE 1980S U.S. BANKING CRISIS

Before the 1980s, federal deposit insurance seemed to work exceedingly well. In contrast to the pre-1934 period, when bank failures were common and depositors frequently suffered losses, the period from 1934 to 1980 was one in which bank failures were a rarity, averaging 15 a year for commercial banks. After 1981, this rosy picture changed dramatically. Failures of commercial banks climbed to levels more than ten times greater than in earlier years. Why did this happen? How did a deposit insurance system that seemed to be working well for half a century find itself in so much trouble?

Why?

The story starts with the burst of financial innovation in the 1960s, 1970s, and early 1980s: NOW accounts, money market mutual funds, junk bonds, securitization and the rise of the commercial paper market (discussed in Chapters 13 and 14). Financial innovation decreased the profitability of certain traditional business for commercial banks. Banks now faced increased competition for their sources of funds from new financial institutions such as money market mutual funds while they were losing commercial lending business to the commercial paper market and securitization.

With the decreasing profitability of their traditional business, by the mid 1980s commercial banks were forced to seek out new and potentially risky business to keep their profits up, by placing a greater percentage of their total loans in real estate and in credit extended to assist corporate takeovers and leveraged buyouts (called *highly leveraged transaction loans*).

The existence of deposit insurance increased moral hazard for banks because insured depositors had little incentive to keep the banks from taking on too much risk. Regardless of how much risk banks were taking, deposit insurance guaranteed that depositors would not suffer any losses.

Adding fuel to the fire, financial innovation produced new financial instruments that widened the scope for risk taking. New markets in financial futures, junk bonds, swaps, and other instruments made it easier for banks to take on extra risk—making the moral hazard problem more severe.

In addition, the Depository Institutions Deregulation and Monetary Control Act of 1980 increased the mandated amount of federal deposit insurance from

$40,000 per account to $100,000 and phased out Regulation Q deposit-rate ceilings. Banks that wanted to pursue rapid growth and take on risky projects could now attract the necessary funds by issuing larger-denomination insured certificates of deposit with interest rates much higher than those being offered by their competitors. Without deposit insurance, high interest rates would not have induced depositors to provide the high-rolling banks with funds because of the realistic expectation that they might not get the funds back. But with deposit insurance, the government was guaranteeing that the deposits were safe, so depositors were more than happy to make deposits in banks with the highest interest rates.

A financial innovation that made it even easier for high-rolling banks to raise funds is known as **brokered deposits,** which enable depositors to circumvent the $100,000 limit on deposit insurance. Brokered deposits work as follows: A large depositor with $10 million goes to a broker, who breaks the $10 million into 100 packages of $100,000 each and then buys $100,000 CDs at 100 different banks. Because the amount of each CD is within the $100,000 limit for deposits at each bank, the large depositor has in effect obtained deposit insurance on all $10 million. The federal deposit insurance agencies passed a regulation to ban brokered deposits in 1984, but a federal court judgment overturned the ban.

As a result of these forces, commercial banks did take on excessive risks and began to suffer substantial losses. The outcome was that bank failures rose to a level of 200 per year by the late 1980s. The resulting losses for the FDIC meant that it would have depleted its Bank Insurance Fund by 1992, requiring that this fund be recapitalized. Although the Financial Institutions Reform, Recovery, and Enforcement Act (FIRREA) of 1989 (described in Chapter 15) did not focus on the underlying adverse selection and moral hazard problems created by deposit insurance, it did, however, mandate that the U.S. Treasury produce a comprehensive study and plan for reform of the federal deposit insurance system. After this study appeared in 1991, Congress passed the Federal Deposit Insurance Corporation Improvement Act (FDICIA), which engendered major reforms in the bank regulatory system.

■ FEDERAL DEPOSIT INSURANCE CORPORATION IMPROVEMENT ACT OF 1991

FDICIA's provisions were designed to serve two purposes: to recapitalize the Bank Insurance Fund of the FDIC and to reform the deposit insurance and regulatory system so that taxpayer losses would be minimized.

FDICIA recapitalized the Bank Insurance Fund by increasing the FDIC's ability to borrow from the Treasury to $30 billion (up from $5 billion). FDICIA also allowed the FDIC to borrow $45 billion for working capital—money that would be repaid as the FDIC sold the assets of failed banks. FDICIA also mandated that the FDIC assess higher deposit insurance premiums until it could pay back its loans and achieve a level of reserves in its insurance funds that would equal 1.25% of insured deposits within 15 years, a goal that was reached for the Bank Insurance Fund (BIF) more than ten years early in 1995 because of the return to health of the commercial banking industry. However, despite a return to profitability of most S&Ls, the Savings Association Insurance Fund was still far from the mandated goal, leading to legislation in 1996 to return this fund to health (see Box 6).

The bill reduced the scope of deposit insurance in several ways. First, the FDIC is allowed to insure brokered deposits or accounts only if they are established under pension plans at well-capitalized banks. Second, and more important, the too-big-to-fail doctrine has been substantially limited: The FDIC must now close failed banks using the least-costly method, thus making it far more likely that uninsured depositors will suffer losses. An exception to this provision, whereby a bank would be declared too big to fail so that all depositors, both insured and uninsured, would be fully protected, would be allowed only if not doing so would "have serious adverse effects on economic conditions or financial stability." Furthermore, to invoke the too-big-to-fail policy, a two-thirds majority of both the Board of Governors of the Federal Reserve System and the directors of the FDIC, as well as the approval of the secretary of the Treasury, would be required. Furthermore, FDICIA requires that the Fed share in the FDIC's losses if long-term Fed lending to a bank that fails increases the FDIC's losses.

Probably the most important feature of FDICIA is its prompt corrective action provisions, which require the FDIC to intervene earlier and more vigorously when a bank gets into trouble. Banks are now classified into five groups based on bank

---

■ BOX 6

The SAIF Fix and the Future of the S&L Industry

Although the FDIC's Bank Insurance Fund (BIF) has returned to health and has reached its mandated level of 1.25% of insured deposits, this was not yet true for the FDIC's Savings Association Insurance Fund (SAIF) in 1996. The primary reason for the poor state of SAIF is the drain from the nearly $8 billion of outstanding Financing Corporation (FICO) bonds that were used to finance S&L bailouts under the Competitive Equality Banking Act of 1987. Insurance premiums from the S&Ls, which would otherwise be used to beef up SAIF, must first be used to pay off the interest on the FICO bonds instead. The result is that the funds in SAIF were well below the mandated level so that insurance premiums for even the best-capitalized S&Ls remained at 23 cents per $100 of deposits, a level more than five times the premium of 4 cents for well-capitalized commercial banks. The higher premiums for S&Ls put them at a serious competitive disadvantage, and this caused a substantial shrinkage of S&Ls' deposits relative to commercial banks. Indeed, the shrinkage of S&L deposits was so severe that there was fear that there would not be enough insurance premiums collected to cover the

FICO bond payments, with the result that these bonds could default.

The growing SAIF-FICO problem was resolved by legislation passed in late 1996 that tapped not only savings institutions but also commercial banks for the needed funds to make the FICO bond payments and to beef up SAIF. The law levied a onetime assessment of nearly $5 billion (an estimated 68 cents per $100 of deposits) on savings institutions to restore the funds in SAIF to the statutory 1.25% of insured deposits. Then through 1999, the savings institutions would pay 6.5 cents per $100 of deposits, compared to 1.3 cents for commercial banks, to make the payments on the FICO bonds. If the two industries remain separate, each would pay equal rates of 2.4 cents per $100 of deposits beginning in the year 2000. However, the law expects the merging of savings and loan charters into commercial bank charters and the merger of BIF-SAIF into one fund before the year 2000. Thus the final cleanup of the S&L mess may be the demise of the S&L industry.

capital. Group 1, classified as "well capitalized," are banks that significantly exceed minimum capital requirements and are allowed privileges such as insurance on brokered deposits and the ability to do some securities underwriting. Banks in group 2, classified as "adequately capitalized," meet minimum capital requirements and are not subject to corrective actions but are not allowed the privileges of the well-capitalized banks. Banks in group 3, "undercapitalized," fail to meet capital requirements. Banks in groups 4 and 5 are "significantly undercapitalized" and "critically undercapitalized," respectively, and are not allowed to pay interest on their deposits at rates that are higher than average. In addition, for group 3 banks, the FDIC is required to take prompt corrective actions such as requiring them to submit a capital restoration plan, restrict their asset growth, and seek regulatory approval to open new branches or develop new lines of business. Banks that are so undercapitalized as to have equity capital less than 2% of assets fall into group 5, and the FDIC must take steps to close them down.

FDICIA also instructed the FDIC to come up with risk-based insurance premiums. The system the FDIC has put in place uses the bank capital classifications just outlined and other supervisory criteria to assess these premiums. For example, after a reduction in insurance premiums in September 1995 when the Bank Insurance Fund reached its mandated level, well-capitalized banks with the best supervisory rating (over 90% of the banks) only had to pay an insurance premium of 4 cents per $100, while the most undercapitalized banks with a low supervisory rating had to pay 31 cents per $100. (The current premium ranges from 0 to 27 cents; over 90% of banks, with over 95% of total deposits, pay nothing.) However, because the Savings Association Insurance Fund had not yet reached its mandated level, S&Ls continued to pay higher premiums.

Other provisions of FDICIA require regulators to perform annual on-site examinations, restrict real estate lending, and mandate stricter and more burdensome reporting requirements. The act also requires that the existing risk-based capital standards, which focus solely on credit risk, be modified to take account of interest-rate risk as well. FDICIA also provides securities firms with access to Federal Reserve discount lending during a financial crisis.

FDICIA also includes the Foreign Bank Supervision Enhancement Act (FBSEA), which in the wake of the BCCI scandal gives supervisory responsibility for foreign banks to the Federal Reserve and gives the Fed increased powers to acquire information on the foreign banks' activities. In addition, the Fed now has the right to prevent the operation of a foreign bank in the United States if it feels that the home country's supervision is not adequate or if the foreign bank is engaging in unsound banking practices.

APPLICATION · **EVALUATING FDICIA AND OTHER PROPOSED REFORMS OF THE BANKING REGULATORY SYSTEM**

FDICIA is a major step in reforming the banking regulatory system. How well will it work to solve the adverse selection and moral hazard problems of the bank regulatory system? Let's use the analysis in the chapter to evaluate the most important provisions of this legislation to answer this question.

■ **S T U D Y G U I D E** Before looking at the evaluation for each set of provisions and proposals in this application, try to reason out how well they will solve the current problems with banking regulation. This exercise will help you develop a deeper understanding of the material in this chapter.

Limits on the Scope of Deposit Insurance

FDICIA's reduction of the scope of deposit insurance by limiting insurance on brokered deposits and restricting the use of the too-big-to-fail policy might have increased the incentives for uninsured depositors to monitor banks and to withdraw funds if the bank is taking on too much risk. Because banks might now fear the loss of deposits when they engage in risky activities, they might have less incentive to take on too much risk. Limitations on the use of the too-big-to-fail policy starting in 1992 have resulted in increased losses to uninsured depositors at failed banks as planned.

Although the cited elements of FDICIA strengthen the incentive of depositors to monitor banks, some critics of FDICIA would take these limitations on the scope of deposit insurance even further. Some suggest that deposit insurance should be eliminated entirely or should be reduced in amount from the current $100,000 limit to, say, $50,000 or $20,000. Another proposed reform would institute a system of **coinsurance** in which only a percentage of a deposit, say, 90%, would be covered by insurance. In this system, the insured depositor would suffer a percentage of the losses along with the deposit insurance agency. Because depositors facing a lower limit on deposit insurance or coinsurance would suffer losses if the bank goes broke, they will have an incentive to monitor the bank's activities. Other critics believe that FDICIA still contains too much scope for the too-big-to-fail policy. Because under FDICIA the Fed, the Treasury, and the FDIC can still agree to implement too-big-to-fail and thus bail out uninsured as well as insured depositors, big banks will not be subjected to enough discipline by uninsured depositors. These critics advocate eliminating the too-big-to-fail policy entirely, thereby decreasing the incentives of big banks to take on too much risk.

However, other experts do not believe that depositors are capable of monitoring banks and imposing discipline on them. The basic problem with reducing the scope of deposit insurance even further as proposed is that banks would be subject to runs, sudden withdrawals by nervous depositors. Such runs could by themselves lead to bank failures. In addition to protecting individual depositors, the purpose of deposit insurance is to prevent a large number of bank failures, which would lead to an unstable banking system and an unstable economy as occurred periodically before the establishment of federal deposit insurance in 1934. From this perspective, federal deposit insurance has been a resounding success. Bank panics, in which there are simultaneous failures of many banks and consequent disruption of the financial system, have not occurred since federal deposit insurance was established.

On the one hand, evidence that the largest banks benefiting from the de facto too-big-to-fail policy before 1991 were also the ones that took on the most risk suggests that limiting its application, as FDICIA does, may substantially reduce risk taking. On the other hand, eliminating the too-big-to-fail policy altogether would also cause some of the same problems that would occur if deposit insurance were eliminated or reduced: The probability of bank panics would increase. If a big bank were allowed to fail, the repercussions in the financial system might be immense. Other banks with a correspondent relationship with the failed bank (those that have deposits at the bank in exchange for a variety of services) would suffer large losses and might fail in turn, leading to a full-scale panic. In addition, the problem of liquidating the big bank's loan portfolio might create a major disruption in the financial market.

Prompt Corrective Action

The prompt corrective action provisions of FDICIA should also substantially reduce incentives for bank risk taking and reduce taxpayer losses. FDICIA uses a carrot-and-stick approach to get banks to hold more capital. If they are well capitalized, they receive valuable privileges; if their capital ratio falls, they are subject to more and more onerous regulation. Increased bank capital reduces moral hazard incentives for the bank because the bank now has more to lose if it fails and so is less likely to take on too much risk.

In addition, encouraging banks to hold more capital reduces potential losses for the FDIC because increased bank capital is a cushion that makes bank failure less likely. Furthermore, forcing the FDIC to close banks once their net worth is less than 2% (group 5) rather than waiting until net worth has fallen to zero makes it more likely that when a bank is closed, it will still have a positive net worth, thus limiting FDIC losses.

Prompt corrective action, which requires regulators to intervene early when bank capital begins to fall, is a serious attempt to reduce the principal-agent problem for politicians and regulators. With prompt corrective action provisions, regulators no longer have the option of regulatory forbearance, which, as we have seen, can greatly increase moral hazard incentives for banks.

Some critics of FDICIA feel that there are too many loopholes in the bill that still allow regulators too much discretion, thus leaving open the possibility of regulatory forbearance. However, an often overlooked part of the bill increases the accountability of regulators. FDICIA requires a mandatory review of any bank failure that imposes costs on the FDIC. The resulting report must be made available to any member of Congress and to the general public upon request, and the General Accounting Office must do an annual review of these reports. Opening up the actions of the regulators to public scrutiny will make regulatory forbearance less attractive to them, thereby reducing the principal-agent problem. It will also reduce the incentives of politicians to lean on regulators to relax their regulatory supervision of banks.

Risk-Based Insurance Premiums

Under FDICIA, banks deemed to be taking on greater risk, in the form of lower capital or riskier assets, will be subjected to higher insurance premiums. Risk-based insurance premiums will consequently reduce the moral hazard incentives for banks to take on higher risk because if they do so, they will have to pay higher premiums. In addition, the fact that risk-based premiums drop as the bank's capital increases encourages the bank to hold more capital, which has the benefits already mentioned.

One problem with risk-based premiums is that the scheme for determining the amount of risk the bank is taking may not be very accurate. For example, it might be hard for regulators to determine when a bank's loans are risky. Some critics have also pointed out that the classification of banks by such measures as the Basel risk-based capital standard solely reflects credit risk and does not take sufficient account of interest-rate risk. The regulatory authorities, however, are encouraged by FDICIA to modify existing risk-based standards to include interest-rate risk and, as we have seen earlier in this chapter, have proposed guidelines to encourage banks to manage interest-rate risk.

Other FDICIA Provisions

FDICIA's requirements that regulators perform bank examinations at least once a year are necessary for monitoring banks' compliance with bank capital requirements and asset restrictions. As the S&L debacle illustrates, frequent supervisory examinations of banks are necessary to keep them from taking on too much risk or committing fraud. Similarly, beefing up the ability of the Federal Reserve to monitor foreign banks might help dissuade international banks from engaging in these undesirable activities.

The stricter and more burdensome reporting requirements for banks have the advantage of providing more information to regulators to help them monitor bank activities. However, these reporting requirements have been criticized by banks, which claim that the requirements make it harder to lend to small businesses.

Other Proposed Changes in Banking Regulations

Regulatory Consolidation The current bank regulatory system in the United States has banking institutions supervised by four federal agencies: the FDIC, the Office of the Comptroller of the Currency, the Office of Thrift Supervision, and the Federal Reserve. Critics of this system of multiple regulatory agencies with overlapping jurisdictions believe that it creates a system that is too complex and too costly because it is rife with duplication. The Clinton administration proposed a consolidation in which the duties of the four regulatory agencies would be given to a new Federal Banking Commission governed by a five-member board with one member from the Treasury, one from the Federal Reserve, and three independent members appointed by the president and confirmed by the Senate. The Federal Reserve strongly opposed this proposal because it believed that it needed to have hands-on supervision of the largest banks through their bank holding companies (as is the case currently) in order to have the information that would enable the Fed to respond sufficiently quickly in a crisis. The Fed also pointed out that a monolithic regulator might be less effective than two or more regulators in providing checks and balances for regulatory supervision. The Clinton administration's proposal was not passed by Congress, but the issue of regulatory consolidation is sure to come up again.

Market-Value Accounting for Capital Requirements We have seen that the requirement that a bank have substantial equity capital makes the bank less likely to fail. The requirement is also advantageous because a bank with high equity capital has more to lose if it takes on risky investments and so will have less incentive to hold risky assets. Unfortunately, capital requirements, including new risk-based measures, are calculated on a historical-cost (book value) basis in which the value of an asset is set at its initial purchase price. The problem with historical-cost accounting is that changes in the value of assets and liabilities because of changes in interest rates or default risk are not reflected in the calculation of the firm's equity capital. Yet changes in the market value of assets and liabilities and hence changes in the market value of equity capital are what indicate if a firm is truly insolvent. Furthermore, it is the market value of capital that determines the incentives for a bank to hold risky assets.

Market-value accounting when calculating capital requirements is another reform that receives substantial support. All assets and liabilities could be updated to market value periodically, say, every three months, to determine if a bank's capital is sufficient to meet the minimum requirements. This market-value accounting information would let the deposit insurance agency know quickly when a bank was falling below its capital requirement. The bank could then be closed down before its net worth fell below zero, thus preventing a loss to the deposit insurance agency. The market-value-based capital requirement would also ensure that banks would not be operating with negative capital, thereby preventing the bet-the-bank strategy of taking on excessive risk.

Objections to market-value-based capital requirements center on the difficulty of making accurate and straightforward market-value estimates of capital. Historical-cost accounting has an important advantage in that accounting rules are easier to define and standardize when the value of an asset is simply set at its purchase price. Market-value accounting, by contrast, requires estimates and approximations that are harder to standardize. For example, it might be hard to assess the market value of your friend Joe's car loan, whereas it would be quite easy to value a government bond. In addition, conducting market-value accounting would prove costly to banks because estimation of market values requires the collection of more information about the characteristics of assets and liabilities. Nevertheless, proponents of market-value accounting for capital requirements point out that although market-value accounting involves some estimates and approximations, it would still provide regulators with more accurate assessment of bank equity capital than historical-cost accounting does.

Overall Evaluation

FDICIA appears to be an important step in the right direction because it increases the incentives for banks to hold capital and decreases their incentives to take on excessive risk. However, more could be done to improve the incentives for banks to limit their risk taking. Yet eliminating deposit insurance and the too-big-to-fail policy altogether may be going too far because these proposals might make the banking system too prone to a banking panic.

BANKING CRISES THROUGHOUT THE WORLD

Because misery likes company, it might make you feel better to know that the United States has by no means been alone in suffering a banking crisis. Indeed, as Figure 1 and Table 2 illustrate, banking crises have struck a large number of countries throughout the world, and many of them have been substantially worse than ours. We will examine what took place in several of these other countries and see that the same forces that produced a banking crisis in the United States have been at work elsewhere too.

Systemic
bank crisis

Borderline and
smaller banking crisis

No bank crisis
or insufficient
information

■FIGURE 1 Banking Crises Throughout the World Since 1970

Source: Gerard Caprio, Jr. and Daniela Klingbiel, "Bank Insolvency: Bad Luck, Bad Policy, or Bad Banking?" paper prepared for the World Bank's Annual Bank Conference on Development Economics, Washington, D.C., April 25–26, 1996.

■ TABLE 2 The Cost of Rescuing Banks in Several Countries

Date	Country	Cost as a % of GDP
1980–1982	Argentina	55
1981–1983	Chile	41
1994–1995	Venezuela	18
1995	Mexico	12–15
1994–1995	Brazil	5–10
1991–1993	Finland	8
1981–1984	Uruguay	7
1991	Sweden	6
1982–1987	Colombia	5
1987–1989	Norway	4
1984–1991	United States	3

Source: Gerard Caprio, Jr. and Daniela Klingbiel, "Bank Insolvency: Bad Luck, Bad Policy, or Bad Banking?" paper prepared for the World Bank's Annual Bank Conference on Development Economics, Washington, D.C., April 25–26, 1996.

Scandinavia

As in the United States, an important factor in the banking crises in Norway, Sweden, and Finland was the financial liberalization that occurred in the 1980s. Before the 1980s, banks in the Scandinavian countries were highly regulated and subject to restrictions on the interest rates they could pay to depositors and on the interest rates they could earn on loans. In this noncompetitive environment, and with artificially low rates on both deposits and loans, these banks lent only to the best credit risks, and both banks and their regulators had little need to develop expertise in screening and monitoring borrowers. With the deregulated environment, a lending boom ensued, particularly in the real estate sector. Given the lack of expertise in both the banking industry and its regulatory authorities in keeping risk taking in check, banks engaged in risky lending. When real estate prices collapsed in the late 1980s, massive loan losses resulted. The outcome of this process was similar to what happened in the savings and loan industry in the United States. The government was forced to bail out almost the entire banking industry in these countries in the late 1980s and early 1990s on a scale that was even larger relative to GDP than in the United States (see Table 2).

Latin America

The Latin American banking crises show a similar pattern to those in the United States and in Scandinavia. Before the 1980s, banks in many Latin American countries were owned by the government and were subject to interest-rate restrictions as in Scandinavia. Their lending was restricted to the government and other low-risk borrowers. With the deregulation trend that was occurring worldwide, many of these countries liberalized their credit markets and privatized their banks. We then see the same pattern we saw in the United States and Scandinavia, a lending boom in the face of inadequate expertise on the part of both bankers and regulators. The result was again massive loan losses and the inevitable government bailout. What is particularly striking about the Latin American experience is that the cost of the bailout relative to GDP dwarfs that in the United States. For example, in the recent banking crises in Mexico and Venezuela, the cost to the taxpayer of the government bailouts exceeded 10% of GDP.

Eastern Europe

Before the end of the Cold War, in the communist countries of Eastern Europe and the Soviet Union, banks were owned by the state. When the downfall of communism occurred, banks in these countries had little expertise in screening and monitoring loans. Furthermore, bank regulatory and supervisory apparatus that could rein in the banks and keep them from taking on excessive risk barely existed. Given the lack of expertise on the part of regulators and banks, not surprisingly, substantial loan losses ensued, resulting in the failure or government bailout of many banks. For example, in the second half of 1993, eight banks in Hungary with 25% of the financial system's assets were insolvent, and in Bulgaria, an estimated 75% of all loans in the banking system were estimated to be substandard in 1995. On August 24, 1995, a bank panic requiring government intervention occurred in Russia when the interbank loan market seized up and stopped functioning because of concern about the solvency of many new banks.

Japan

Japan was a latecomer to the banking crisis game. Before 1990, the vaunted Japanese economy looked unstoppable. Unfortunately, it has recently experienced many of the same pathologies that we have seen in other countries. Before the 1980s, Japan's financial markets were among the most heavily regulated in the world, with very strict restrictions on the issuing of securities and interest rates. Financial deregulation and innovation produced a more competitive environment that set off a lending boom, with banks lending aggressively in the real estate sector. As in the other countries we have examined here, financial disclosure and monitoring by regulators did not keep pace with the new financial environment. The result was that banks could and did take on excessive risks, and when property values collapsed in the early 1990s, the banks were left holding massive amounts of bad loans. For example, Japanese banks decided to get into the mortgage lending market by setting up the so-called *jusen*, home mortgage lending companies that raised funds by borrowing from banks and then loaned these funds out to households. Seven of these *jusen* are now insolvent, leaving banks with $60 billion or so of bad loans.

The result is that the Japanese have experienced their first bank failures since World War II. In July 1995, Tokyo-based Cosmo Credit Corporation, Japan's fifth-largest credit union, failed and on August 30, the Osaka authorities announced the imminent closing of Kizu Credit Cooperative, Japan's second-largest credit union. (Kizu's story is remarkably similar to that of many U.S. savings and loans. Kizu, like many American S&Ls, began offering high rates on large time deposits and grew at a blistering pace, with deposits rising from $2.2 billion in 1988 to $12 billion by 1995 and real estate loans growing by a similar amount. When the property market collapsed, so did Kizu.) On the same day, the Ministry of Finance announced that it was liquidating Hyogo Bank, a midsize Kobe bank that was the first commercial bank to fail. Other banks have followed the same path. The Ministry of Finance has estimated total loan losses for the banking sector to be on the order of $350 billion, although many private analysts think the number may be far higher.

The Japanese seem to be going through the same cycle of forbearance as occurred in the United States. It has proved very difficult to arrange bailout packages to close down insolvent banking institutions, and so, not surprisingly, regulators have been reluctant to close them down. Bank regulators have promised that none of Japan's 21 largest banks will be allowed to fail, an admission of a too-big-to-fail policy similar to that found in the United States.

"Déjà Vu All Over Again"

What we see in banking crises in these different countries is that history has kept on repeating itself. The parallels between the banking crisis episodes in all these countries are remarkably similar, leaving us with a feeling of déjà vu. Although financial liberalization is generally a good thing because it promotes competition and can make a financial system more efficient, as we have seen in the countries examined here, it can lead to an increase in moral hazard risk taking on the part of banks if there is lax regulation and supervision; the result can then be banking crises. However, these episodes do differ in that deposit insurance has not played an important role in many of the countries experiencing banking crises. For example, the size of the Japanese equivalent of the FDIC, the Deposit Insurance Corporation, was so tiny relative to the FDIC that it did not play a prominent role in the banking system and exhausted its resources almost immediately with the first bank failures. This means that deposit insurance is not to blame for some of these banking crises. However, what is common to all the countries discussed here is the existence of a government safety net, in which the government stands ready to bail out banks whether deposit insurance is an important feature of the regulatory environment or not. It is the existence of a government safety net, and not deposit insurance per se, that increases moral hazard incentives for excessive risk taking on the part of banks.

■ THE PRACTICING FINANCIAL INSTITUTION MANAGER
Calculating Capital Requirements

As we have seen in this chapter, capital requirements are one of the most important elements of regulation that concern bank managers. Because capital requirements are somewhat complicated, here we look at what a bank manager has to go through to make sure that the bank is meeting its capital requirements.

Suppose that the First National Bank has the following balance sheet: (a list of the bank's assets and liabilities):

First National Bank

Assets		Liabilities	
Reserves	$ 3 million	Checkable deposits	$20 million
Treasury securities	$10 million	Nontransaction	
Government agency		deposits	$60 million
securities	$ 7 million	Borrowings	$11 million
Municipal bonds	$10 million	Loan loss reserves	$ 2 million
Residential mortgages	$10 million	Bank capital	$ 7 million
Real estate loans	$20 million		
Commercial loans	$35 million		
Fixed assets	$ 5 million		

Recall that a bank must meet two types of capital requirements, one involving the leverage ratio and the other the Basel risk-based requirements. Because it is very easy to do, Mona, the manager of the First National Bank, first calculates the leverage ratio, the amount of bank capital divided by the total amount of assets. In this case, bank capital is $7 million and total assets are $100 million, so the leverage ratio is 7%, well above the 5% ratio required for the bank to be classified as well capitalized.

Mona next examines whether her bank meets the risk-based capital requirements. To do this, she proceeds in several steps. The first step is to allocate each of the assets on the balance sheet to one of the four risk categories in order to determine the appropriate risk-based weight. Reserves and Treasury securities are put in the lowest risk category and so have a zero weight, government agency securities are in the next lowest category and so have a weight of 20%, municipal bonds and residential mortgages are considered riskier and so are put in the category with a 50% risk-based weight, and real estate and commercial loans and fixed assets like the bank building are considered the riskiest assets of all and so are assigned a risk-based weight of 100%.

The next step in calculating the risk-based capital requirements is to determine the risk-based weight for the off-balance-sheet activities of the bank. Suppose that First National bank has $20 million of standby letters of credit outstanding. These standby letters of credit are assigned a 100% "credit equivalent" percentage because they are considered fully equivalent to commercial loans. Then they have the same risk-based weight of 100% that commercial loans have.

The final step for the bank manager is to add up all these weighted balance sheet and off-balance-sheet items to compute the total "risk-adjusted assets." Using the numbers given above, Mona is able to calculate the risk-adjusted assets as follows:

Assets	Amount	×	Weighting Factor	=	Total
Reserves	$ 3 million	×	0.00	=	$ 0
Treasury securities	$10 million	×	0.00	=	$ 0
Government agency securities	$ 7 million	×	0.20	=	$ 1.4 million
Municipal bonds	$10 million	×	0.50	=	$ 5.0 million
Residential mortgages	$10 million	×	0.50	=	$ 5.0 million
Real estate loans	$20 million	×	1.00	=	$20.0 million
Commercial loans	$35 million	×	1.00	=	$35.0 million
Fixed assets	$ 5 million	×	1.00	=	$ 5.0 million
Standby letters of credit	$20 million	×	1.00	=	$20.0 million
Total risk-adjusted assets					$91.4 million

The Basel risk-based capital requirements are of two types. The "core" capital requirement is 4% of total risk-adjusted assets, which in this case is $3.66 million (= 0.04 × $91.4 million). Because the First National Bank has $7 million of bank capital, it meets this requirement easily. The second requirement is that the bank have total capital (core capital plus loan loss reserves and subordinated debt) of 8% of total risk-adjusted assets, which in this case is $7.31 million (= 0.08 × $91.4 million). Because the First National Bank has $2 million of loan loss reserves as well as $7 million of core capital, its total capital of $9 million exceeds this second capital requirement.

After Mona has done all these calculations, she breathes a sigh of relief because she knows that her bank is meeting both the Basel risk-based capital requirements and the leverage ratio requirement. She can now go home and get a good night's sleep, for her bank does not need to raise any more capital to satisfy the regulators.

SUMMARY

1. The concepts of asymmetric information, adverse selection, and moral hazard help explain the seven types of banking regulation that we see in the United States and other countries: the government safety net, restrictions on bank asset holdings and capital requirements, bank supervision, disclosure requirements, consumer protection, restrictions on competition, and the separation of the banking and securities industries.

2. Because asymmetric information problems in the banking industry are a fact of life throughout the world, bank regulation in other countries is similar to that in the United States. It is particularly problematic to regulate banks engaged in international banking because they can readily shift their business from one country to another.

3. Because of financial innovation and deregulation, adverse selection and moral hazard problems increased in the 1980s and resulted in a banking crisis in the United States.

4. The Federal Deposit Insurance Corporation Improvement Act (FDICIA) of 1991 recapitalized the Bank Insurance Fund of the FDIC and included reforms for the deposit insurance and regulatory system so that taxpayer losses would be minimized. This legislation limited brokered deposits and the use of the too-big-to-fail policy, mandated prompt corrective action to deal with troubled banks, and instituted risk-based deposit insurance premiums. These provisions have helped reduce the incentives of banks to take on excessive risk and so should help reduce taxpayer exposure in the future.

5. Proposals for reforming the banking regulatory system include elimination of deposit insurance, lower limits on the amount of deposit insurance, outright elimination of the too-big-to-fail policy, coinsurance,

risk-based insurance premiums, regulatory consolidation, and market-value accounting for capital requirements.

6. The parallels between the banking crisis episodes that have occurred in other countries are striking, indicating that similar forces are at work.

KEY TERMS

bank failure, p. 415

bank supervision (prudential supervision), p. 420

brokered deposits, p. 430

coinsurance, p. 433

leverage ratio, p. 419

off-balance-sheet activities, p. 419

QUESTIONS AND PROBLEMS

1. Give one example each of moral hazard and adverse selection in private insurance arrangements.

*2. If casualty insurance companies provided fire insurance without any restrictions, what kind of adverse selection and moral hazard problems might result?

3. What bank regulation is designed to reduce adverse selection problems for deposit insurance? Will it always work?

*4. What bank regulations are designed to reduce moral hazard problems created by deposit insurance? Will they completely eliminate the moral hazard problem?

5. What are the costs and benefits of a too-big-to-fail policy?

*6. Why did the S&L crisis not occur until the 1980s?

7. Why is regulatory forbearance a dangerous strategy for a deposit insurance agency?

*8. The FIRREA legislation of 1989 is the most comprehensive banking legislation since the 1930s. Describe its major features.

9. What steps were taken in the FDICIA legislation of 1991 to improve the functioning of federal deposit insurance?

*10. Some advocates of campaign reform believe that government funding of political campaigns and restrictions on campaign spending might reduce the principal-agent problem in our political system. Do you agree? Explain your answer.

11. How can the S&L crisis be blamed on the principal-agent problem?

*12. Do you think that eliminating or limiting the amount of deposit insurance would be a good idea? Explain your answer.

13. Do you think that removing the impediments to a nationwide banking system will be beneficial to the economy? Explain.

*14. How could higher deposit insurance premiums for banks with riskier assets benefit the economy?

15. How could market-value accounting for bank capital requirements benefit the economy? How difficult would it be to implement?

CHAPTER 17

Insurance Companies and Pension Funds

■ PREVIEW In this chapter we continue our discussion of financial institutions by looking at two nonbank institutions: insurance companies and pension funds. Insurance is an important industry in the United States. Most people hold one or more types of insurance policies (health, life, homeowners, automobile, disability, and so on), and the annual revenues of insurance companies exceed $600 billion. Insurance companies are also a major employer, especially of business majors. Figure 1 shows the number of persons employed by the insurance industry between 1960 and 1995. The numbers rose rapidly during the 1960s, 1970s, and early 1980s. (Currently, well over 2 million Americans are employed in the insurance industry.) In recent years, the rate of growth has slowed however. There are a couple of possible explanations for this. First, technology has streamlined claims processing so that fewer back-office workers are needed. Second, competition by other financial institutions such as commercial banks and brokerage houses may be cutting into some of the business traditionally reserved for insurance companies.

One major competitor to insurance has been the private, company-sponsored pension plan. Better-educated and longer-lived workers are putting more money into pension funds than ever before. Over 65 million individuals are now invested in a private pension fund. These plans are also reviewed in this chapter.

Insurance companies and pension funds are considered financial intermediaries for several reasons. First, they receive investment funds from their customers. For example, when a person buys a whole life insurance policy, the person receives a life insurance benefit and accumulates a cash balance. Many people use insurance companies as their primary investment avenue. Similarly, private pension funds also take in investment dollars from their customers. Second, both of these institutions place their money in a variety of money-earning investments. Insurance companies and pension funds make large commercial mortgage loans, invest in stocks, and buy bonds. Thus these institutions are financial intermediaries in that they take in funds from one sector and invest it in another.

■ INSURANCE COMPANIES

Insurance companies are in the business of assuming risk on behalf of their customers in exchange for a fee, called a *premium.* Insurance companies make a profit by charging premiums that are sufficient to pay the expected claims on the company plus a profit. Why do people pay for insurance when they know that over the lifetime of their policy, they will probably pay more in premiums than the expected amount of any loss they will suffer? Because most people are risk averse: They would rather pay a **certainty equivalent** (the insurance premium) than accept the gamble that they will lose their house or their car. Thus it is because people are risk-averse that they prefer to buy insurance and know with certainty what their wealth will be (their current wealth minus the insurance premium) than to incur the risk and run the chance that their wealth may fall.

Consider how people's lives would change if insurance were not available. Instead of knowing that the insurance company would help if an emergency occurred, everyone would have to set aside reserves. These reserves could not be invested long-term but would have to be kept in an extremely liquid form. Furthermore, people would be constantly worried that their reserves would be inadequate to pay for catastrophic events such as the loss of their house to fire or

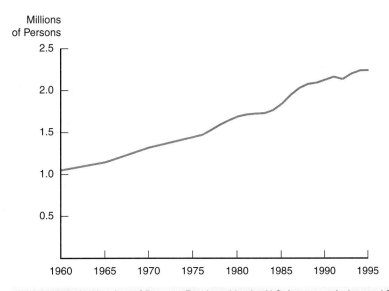

■FIGURE 1 Number of Persons Employed in the U.S. Insurance Industry, 1960–1995

Source: Insurance Company Fact Book.

their car to theft or the death or prolonged illness of the family breadwinner. Insurance allows us the peace of mind that a single event can have only a limited effect on our lives.

FUNDAMENTALS OF INSURANCE

Although there are many types of insurance and insurance companies, all insurance is subject to several basic principles.

1. There must be a relationship between the *insured* (the party covered by insurance) and the *beneficiary* (the party who receives the payment should a loss occur). In addition, the beneficiary must be someone who may suffer potential harm. For example, you could not take out a policy on your neighbor's teenage driver because you are unlikely to suffer harm if the teenager gets into an accident. The reason for this rule is that insurance companies do not want people to buy policies as a way of gambling.
2. The insured must provide full and accurate information to the insurance company.
3. The insured is not to profit as a result of insurance coverage.
4. If a third party compensates the insured for the loss, the insurance company's obligation is reduced by the amount of the compensation.
5. The insurance company must have a large number of insureds so that the risk can be spread out among many different policies.
6. The loss must be quantifiable. For example, an oil company could not buy a policy on an unexplored oil field.
7. The insurance company must be able to compute the probability of the loss's occurring.

The purpose of these principles is to maintain the integrity of the insurance process. Without them, people may be tempted to use insurance companies to gamble or speculate on future events. Taken to an extreme, this behavior could undermine the ability of insurance companies to protect persons in real need. In addition, these principles provide a way to spread the risk among many policies and to establish a price for each policy that will provide an expectation of a profitable return. Despite following these guidelines, insurance companies suffer greatly from the problems of asymmetric information that we first described in Chapter 2.

Adverse Selection and Moral Hazard in Insurance

Recall that adverse selection occurs when the individuals most likely to benefit from a transaction are the ones who most actively seek out the transaction and are thus most likely to be selected. In Chapter 2, we discussed adverse selection in the context of borrowers with the worst credit being the ones who most actively seek loans. The problem also occurs in the insurance market. Who is more likely to apply for health insurance, someone who is seldom sick or someone with chronic health problems? Who is more likely to buy flood insurance, someone who lives on a mountain or someone who lives in a river valley? In both cases, the party most likely to suffer a loss is the party likely to seek insurance. The implication of adverse selection is that loss probability statistics gathered for the entire population may not accurately reflect the loss potential for the persons who actually want to buy policies.

The adverse selection problem raises the issue of which policies an insurance company should accept. Because someone in poor health is more likely to buy a supplemental health insurance policy than someone in perfect health, we might predict that insurance companies should turn down anyone who applies. Since this does not happen, insurance companies must have found alternative solutions. For example, most insurance companies require physical exams and may examine previous medical records before issuing a health or life insurance policy. If some previous illness is found to be a factor in the person's health, the company may issue the policy but charge a higher premium. Insurance firms often offer better rates to insure groups of people, such as everyone working at a particular business, because the adverse selection problem is then avoided.

In addition to the adverse selection problem, moral hazard plagues the insurance industry. Moral hazard occurs when the insured fails to take proper precautions to avoid losses because losses are covered by insurance. For example, moral hazard may cause you not to lock your car doors if you will be reimbursed by insurance if the car is stolen. When Hurricane Fran approached the North Carolina coast in 1996, many yacht owners did not take down their old canvas covers because they hoped the covers would be destroyed by the hurricane, in which case the owners could file a claim with the insurance company and get money to buy new covers.

One way that insurance companies combat moral hazard is by requiring a **deductible.** A deductible is the amount of any loss that must be paid by the insured before the insurance company will pay anything. For example, if new canvas yacht covers cost $5000 and the yacht owner has $1000 deductible, the owner will pay the first $1000 of the loss and the insurance company will pay $4000. In addition to deductibles, there may be other terms in the insurance contract aimed at reducing risk. For example, a business insured against fire may be required to install and maintain a sprinkler system on its premises to reduce the loss should a fire occur.

Although contract terms and deductibles help with the moral hazard problem, these issues remain a constant difficulty for insurance companies. The insurance industry's reaction to moral hazard and adverse selection are discussed in greater detail in "The Practicing Financial Institutional Manager" later in this chapter.

Selling Insurance

Another problem common to insurance companies is that people often fail to seek as much insurance as they actually need. Human nature tends to cause people to ignore their mortality, for example. For this reason, insurance, unlike many banking services, does not sell itself. Instead, insurance companies must hire large sales forces to sell their products. The expense of marketing may account for up to 20% of the total cost of a policy. A good sales force can convince people to buy insurance coverage that they never would have pursued on their own yet may have a need for.

Insurance is unique in that agents sell a product that commits the company to a risk. The relationship between the agent and the company varies: *Independent agents* may sell insurance for a number of different companies. They do not have any particular loyalty to any one firm and simply try to find the best product for their customer. There are in excess of 60,000 independent agents in the United States. *Exclusive agents* sell the insurance products for only one insurance company.

Most agents, whether independent or exclusive, are compensated by being paid a commission. The agents themselves are usually not at all concerned with the level of risk of any one policy because they have little to lose if a loss occurs. (Rarely are commissions influenced by the claims submitted by an agent's customers.) To keep control of the risk that agents are incurring on behalf of the company, insurance companies employ **underwriters,** people who review and sign off on each policy an agent writes and have the authority to turn down a policy if they deem the risk unacceptable. If underwriters have questions about the quality of customers, they may order an independent inspector to review the property being insured or request additional medical information. A final decision to accept the policy may depend on the inspector's report (see Box 1).

■ GROWTH AND ORGANIZATION OF INSURANCE COMPANIES

Figure 2 shows the number of life insurance companies from 1950 to 1994. There was a steady increase in the number until 1988. After this the number has fallen steadily. Another interesting point to note about Figure 2 is that insurance companies can be organized as either *stock* or *mutual* firms. A **stock company** is owned by stockholders and has the objective of making a profit.

Mutual insurance companies are owned by the policyholders. The objective of mutual insurance firms is to provide insurance at the lowest possible cost

---

■ BOX 1

Insurance Agent:

Ally of the Customer

An underwriter working for Prudential Insurance was responsible for a number of agents selling property insurance in Southern California in 1985. One agent sold a large number of fire insurance policies and was always careful to document clearly when a fire hydrant was on the property by including it in a photograph attached to the policy application. The agent made a mistake on one policy, however, when he included his car in a picture of a different view of the property. The picture showed a plastic fire hydrant lying in the open trunk of his car. He had been putting this fire hydrant on property for years when he needed to give a low quote to get business.

The agent was neither fired nor sued. He was simply advised to halt the practice, and his policies continued to be accepted by the company.

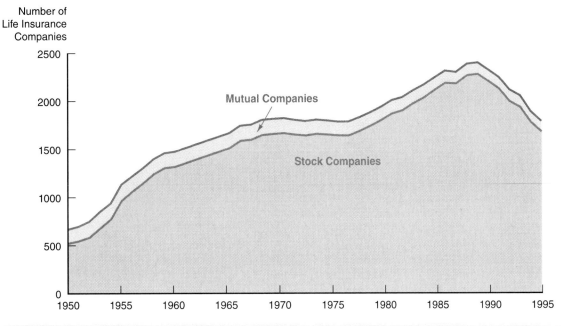

■FIGURE 2 Number of Life Insurance Companies in the United States, 1950–1994

Source: Life Insurance Fact Book.

to the insured. Policyholders are paid dividends that reflect the surplus of premiums over costs. Because the policyholders share in reducing the cost of insurance, there may be some reduction in the moral hazard that most insurance companies face. A unique feature of mutual insurance dividends is that they are not taxed like dividends received from other types of corporations. The Internal Revenue Service regards the dividends as refunds of overcharges on insurance premiums.

Most new insurance companies organize as stock corporations. As Figure 2 shows, at the end of 1994, only 106 of 1639 insurance companies were organized as mutuals. (See Box 2 for a description of a unique form of insurance ownership.)

■ TYPES OF INSURANCE

Insurance is classified by which type of undesirable event is insured. The most common types are life insurance and property and casualty insurance. In its simplest form, life insurance provides income for the heirs of the deceased. Many insurance companies offer policies that provide retirement benefits as well as life insurance. In this case, the premium combines the cost of the life insurance with a savings program. The cost of life insurance depends on such factors as the age of the insured, average life expectancies, the health and lifestyle of the insured (whether the insured smokes, engages in a dangerous hobby such as skydiving, and so on), and the insurance company's operating costs.

Property and casualty insurance protects property (houses, cars, boats, and so on) against losses due to accidents, fire, disasters, and other calamities. Marine

BOX 2   A GLOBAL PERSPECTIVE

The Woes of Lloyd's of London

In June 1993, Lloyd's of London announced the biggest loss in its history, $4.33 billion for the year 1990 (Lloyd's waits three years to allow all claims to be processed before reporting profits or losses). The chairman of Lloyd's stated that the 1990 deficit "represents in every way the low point of Lloyd's history in the last 305 years."* Things continued to get worse for Lloyd's, with losses continuing until 1992, for a cumulative amount of more than $12 billion over the five-year period 1988–1992.

Lloyd's began in 1688 in a London coffeehouse owned by Edward Lloyd, which was a meeting place for merchants, shipowners, and sea captains. Lloyd's became a marketplace in which members, known as "names," trade pieces of insurance policies in order to spread the risk, a process called *reinsurance*. An unusual feature of Lloyd's is that names are directly exposed to losses because they accept unlimited personal liability for any claims they have to pay. Many of those participating in Lloyd's have come to regret it in recent years, having lost their entire personal fortunes.

Indeed, the average loss per name was over $150,000 in 1990. The losses at Lloyd's have also resulted in a slew of lawsuits, with members suing each other right and left over who should be responsible for paying claims.

To survive, the basic structure of Lloyd's has had to change. Lloyd's has opened itself up to corporate capital with only limited liability, has taken measures to lower central spending by the organization, and has altered the way it is governed. In 1996, Lloyd's was able to announce record profits for the year 1993. However, to settle its lawsuits, Lloyd's offered a $4.8 billion rescue package to its 34,000 names, including the creation of a new corporation called Equitas that took over Lloyd's liabilities incurred before 1993. A victim of the worldwide woes of the property and casualty insurance industry, Lloyd's of London, after three centuries, will never be the same.

---

*"Lloyd's of London Posts Big Loss, Raising Fears on Market's Viability," *Wall Street Journal*, June 23, 1993, p. A10.

insurance, for example, which insures against the loss of the ship and its cargo, is the oldest form of insurance, predating even life insurance. Property and casualty policies tend to be short-term contracts subject to frequent renewal. Another significant distinction between life insurance policies and property and casualty policies is that the latter do not have a savings component. Property and casualty premiums are based simply on the probability of sustaining the loss. That is why car insurance premiums are higher if a driver has had speeding tickets, has caused accidents, or lives in a high-crime area. Each of these events increases the likelihood that the insurance company will have to pay a claim.

Life Insurance

Life is assumed to unfold in a predictable sequence: You work for a number of years while saving for retirement; then you retire, live off the fruits of your earlier labor, and die at a ripe old age. The problem is that you could die too young and not have time to provide for your loved ones, or you could live too long and run out of retirement assets. Either option is very unappealing to most people. The purpose of life insurance is to relieve some of the concern associated with either eventuality. Although insurance cannot make you comfortable with the idea of a premature death, it can at least allow you the peace of mind that comes with knowing that you have provided for your heirs. Life insurance companies also want to help people save for their retirement. In this way, the insurance company provides for the customer's whole life.

The basic products of life insurance companies are life insurance proper, disability insurance, annuities, and health insurance. Life insurance pays off if you die, protecting those who depend on your continued earnings. As mentioned, the person who receives the insurance payment after you die is called the *beneficiary* of the policy. Disability insurance replaces part of your income should you become unable to continue working due to illness or an accident. An **annuity** is an insurance product that will help if you live longer than you expect. For an initial fixed sum or stream of payments, the insurance company agrees to pay you a fixed amount for as long as you live. If you live a short life, the insurance company pays out less than expected. Conversely, if you live unusually long, the insurance company may pay out much more than expected.

Notice one curiosity among these various types of insurance: Although predicting any one individual's life expectancy or probability of being disabled is very difficult, when many people are insured, the actual amount to be paid out by the insurance company can be predicted very accurately. Insurance companies collect and analyze statistics on life expectancies, health claims, disability claims, and other relevant matters.

For example, a life insurance company can predict with a high degree of accuracy when death benefits must be paid by using *actuarial tables* that predict life expectancies. Table 1 lists the expected life of persons at various ages. A 25-year-old female can expect to live another 55.2 years; a 25-year-old male, however, can only expect to live another 49 years.

The **law of large numbers** says that when many people are insured, the probability distribution of the losses will assume a normal probability distribution, a distribution that allows accurate predictions. This distribution is important: Because insurance companies insure so many millions of people, the law of large numbers tends to make the company's predictions quite accurate and allows companies to price the policies so that they can earn a profit.

Life insurance policies protect against an interruption in the family's stream of income. The broad categories of life insurance products are *term, whole life,* and *universal life.*

■ TABLE 1 Life Expectancy at Various Ages in the United States, 1995

Age	Male	Female	Total Population
0	72.5	79.1	75.7
15	58.2	65.0	61.6
25	49.0	55.2	52.2
35	39.8	45.6	42.8
45	31.0	36.2	33.7
55	22.5	27.2	25.0
65	15.4	19.2	17.5
75	9.5	12.2	11.1
85	5.3	6.7	6.2

Source: Life Insurance Fact Book.

Term Life The simplest form of life insurance is the *term insurance policy,* which pays out if the insured dies while the policy is in force. This form of policy contains no savings element. Once the policy period expires, there are no residual benefits.

As the insured ages, the probability of death increases, so the cost of the policy rises. For example, Table 2 shows the estimated premiums for a 40-year-old male nonsmoker for $100,000 of term life insurance. The premium for the first year is $134. This rises to $147 when the insured is 41 years old, $153 when the insured is 42, and so on. By the time the insured is 60 years old, $100,000 of life insurance costs $810 per year. Of course, rates vary among insurance companies, but these sample rates demonstrate how the annual cost of a term policy rises with the age of the insured.

Some term policies fix the premiums for a set number of years, usually five or ten. Alternatively, *decreasing term policies* have a constant premium, but the amount of the insurance coverage declines each year.

Term policies have been historically hard to sell because once they expire, the policyholder has nothing to show for the premium paid. This problem is solved with whole life policies.

Whole Life A *whole life insurance* policy pays a death benefit if the policyholder dies. Whole life policies usually require the insured to pay a level premium for the duration of the policy. In the beginning, the insured pays more than if a term policy had been purchased. This overpayment accumulates as a cash value that can be borrowed by the insured at reasonable rates.

Survivorship benefits also contribute to the accumulated cash values. When members of the insured pool die, any remaining cash values are divided among the survivors. If the policyholder lives until the policy matures, it can be surrendered for its cash value. This cash value can be used to purchase an annuity. In this way, the whole life policy is advertised as covering the insured for the duration of his or her life.

Universal Life In the late 1970s, whole life policies fell into disfavor because the rates of return earned on the policy premiums were well below rates available on other investments. For example, say that an investor bought a term policy instead of a whole life policy and invested the difference in the premiums. If she did this each year for the term of the whole life policy, she would be able to pay for term

■**TABLE 2** Typical Annual Premiums on a $100,000 Term Policy for a 40-Year-Old Male Nonsmoker

Age of Insured	Cost ($)
40	134
41	147
42	153
45	192
50	286
55	461
60	810

insurance and still have a greater amount in her investment account than if she had initially purchased the whole life policy. Investment advisers and insurance agents began steering customers away from whole life policies. The sales pitch became "buy term and invest the difference." Because the agents were also selling other investments, they did not suffer from this change in insurance plans. To combat the flow of funds out of their companies, insurance firms introduced the *universal life policy.*

Universal life policies combine the benefits of the term policy with those of the whole life policy. The major benefit of the universal life policy is that the cash value accumulates at a much higher rate.

The universal life policy is structured to have two parts, one for the term life insurance and one for savings. One important advantage that universal life policies have over many alternative investment plans is that the interest earned on the savings portion of the account is tax-exempt until withdrawn. To keep this favorable tax treatment, the cash value of the policy cannot exceed the death benefit.

Universal life policies were introduced in the early 1980s when interest rates were at record high levels. They immediately became very popular and by 1984 accounted for 32% of the volume of life insurance sold. Later, as interest rates fell, their popularity ebbed.

Annuities If we think of term life insurance as insuring against death, the annuity can be viewed as insuring against life. As we noted earlier, one risk people have is outliving their retirement funds. If they live longer than they projected when they initially retired, they could spend all of their money and end up in poverty. One way to avoid this outcome is by purchasing annuities. Once an annuity has been purchased for a fixed amount, it makes payments as long as the beneficiary lives.

Annuities are particularly susceptible to the adverse selection problem. When people retire, they know more about their life expectancy than the insurance company knows. People who are in good health, have a family history of longevity, and have attended to their health all of their lives are more likely to live longer and hence to want to buy an annuity than people in poor or average health. To avoid this problem, insurance companies tend to price individual annuities expensively. Most annuities are sold to members of large groups where all employees covered by a particular pension plan automatically receive their benefit distribution by purchasing an annuity from the insurance company. Because the annuity is automatic, the adverse selection problem is eliminated.

Assets and Liabilities of Life Insurance Companies Life insurance companies derive funds from two sources. First, they receive premiums that represent future obligations that must be met when the insured dies. Second, they receive premiums paid into pension funds managed by the life insurance company. These funds are long-term in nature.

Since life insurance liabilities are predictable and long-term, life insurance companies can invest in long-term assets. Figure 3 shows the distribution of assets of the average life insurance company at the end of 1996. Most of the assets are in long-term investments such as corporate stocks and bonds.

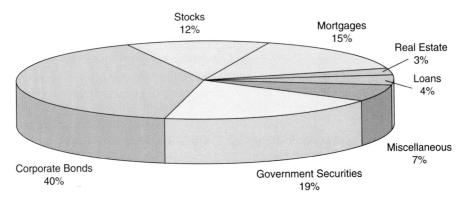

■FIGURE 3 Distribution of Life Insurance Company Assets (end of 1996)

Source: Insurance Company Fact Book.

Insurance companies have also invested heavily in mortgages and real estate over the years. In 1992, about 17.9% of life insurance assets were invested either in mortgage loans or directly in real estate. This percentage is down substantially from historic levels. Figure 4 displays the percentage of assets invested in mort-

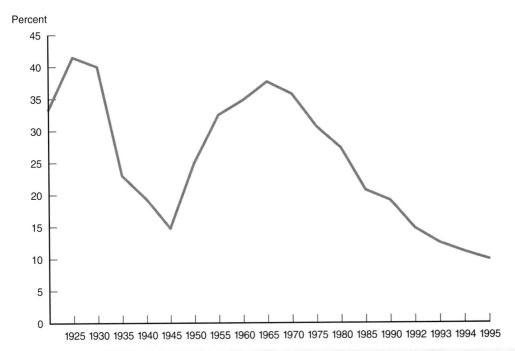

■FIGURE 4 Percentage of Life Insurance Company Assets Invested in Mortgages, 1920–1995

Source: Federal Reserve Bulletin, various issues.

gages from 1920 to 1995. The decline in mortgage investment, which represents a shift to lower-risk assets, has been offset by increased investment in corporate bonds and government securities.

The shift to less risky securities may be the result of losses suffered by some insurance companies in the late 1980s. As insurance companies competed against mutual funds and money market funds for retirement dollars, they found that they needed higher-return investments. This led some insurance companies to invest in real estate and junk bonds. Deteriorating real estate values brought on by over-building during the 1980s caused some firms to suffer large losses. The combination of large real estate losses and junk bond investment contributed to the failure of several large firms in 1991, including Executive Life, with assets of $15 billion, and Mutual Benefit Life, with $14 billion in assets.

Health Insurance

Individual health insurance coverage is very vulnerable to adverse selection problems. People who know that they are likely to get ill are the most likely to seek health insurance coverage. This causes individual health insurance to be very expensive. Most policies are offered through company-sponsored programs in which the company pays all or part of the employee's policy premium.

Most life insurance companies also offer health insurance. Health insurance premiums account for about 25% of total premium income. Life insurance companies compete with Blue Cross and Blue Shield organizations, nonprofit firms that are sponsored by hospitals. Blue Cross usually covers hospital care and Blue Shield, doctors' services. One national agency coordinates and monitors the 73 Blue Cross/Blue Shield organizations.

The government is also involved in health insurance through Medicare and Medicaid. Medicare provides medical coverage for the elderly, and Medicaid provides coverage for people on welfare.

Health insurance was a major political issue in the 1992 presidential election and continues to be the subject of regulation. In 1996, Congress passed legislation making it more difficult for insurance companies to refuse to insure a person with a preexisting medical problem.

One reason for the extensive debate over medical insurance has been the spiraling costs of health care. For most of the past decade, the cost of health care has risen much faster than the cost of living and real wages. Insurance companies have dealt with these rising costs in a number of ways. For example, today the risk of most company-sponsored plans is borne by the company, with the insurance company administering the plan and covering catastrophic expenses. This increases the sponsoring company's incentive to maintain a healthy workforce and to encourage responsible use of medical facilities by its employees. For example, many large firms have found it cost-effective to employ physician assistants on site to reduce medical fees and absenteeism.

Another way that insurance companies are attempting to deal with increased medical costs is by controlling them. This is done by negotiating contracts with physician groups to provide services at reduced cost and through *managed care,* where approval is required before services can be rendered. *Health maintenance organizations (HMOs)* shift the risk from the insurance company to the provider. The insurance company pays the HMO a fixed payment per person covered in exchange for medical services. One problem many people find with the HMO form of health care is that the provider has an incentive to limit medical services. Recent regulation was required, for example, to ensure mothers at least 48 hours in the hospital following a delivery.

Though it appears that a national health insurance overhaul is not going to come out of Congress, the attention focused on the problem has prompted many changes at the state and local levels. These changes are likely to continue in the future, due largely to pressure from insurance companies.

Property and Casualty Insurance

Property and casualty insurance was the earliest form of insurance. It began in the Middle Ages when merchants sent ships off to foreign ports to trade. A merchant, though willing to accept the risk that the trading might not turn a profit, was often unwilling to accept the risk that the ship might sink or be captured by pirates. To reduce such risks, merchants began to band together and insure each other's ships against loss. The process became more sophisticated as time went on, and insurance policies were written that were then traded in the major commercial centers of the time.

In 1666, the Great Fire of London did much to advance the case for fire insurance. The first fire insurance company was founded in London in 1680. In the United States, the first fire insurance company was formed by a group led by Benjamin Franklin in 1752. By the beginning of the nineteenth century, the assets of property and casualty insurance firms exceeded even those of commercial banks, making these firms the most important financial intermediary. The invention of the automobile did a great deal to spur the growth of property and casualty insurance companies during the twentieth century.

Property and Casualty Insurance Today Property and casualty insurance protects against losses from fire, theft, storm, explosion, and even neglect. **Property insurance** protects businesses and owners from the impact of risk associated with owning property. This includes replacement and loss of earnings from income-producing property as well as financial losses to owners of residential property. **Casualty insurance** (or **liability insurance**) protects against liability for harm the insured may cause to others as a result of product failure or accidents. For example, part of your car insurance is property insurance (which pays if your car is damaged), and part is casualty insurance (which pays if you cause an accident).

Property and casualty insurance is different from life insurance. First, policies tend to be short-term, usually for one year or less. Second, whereas life insurance is limited to insuring against one event, property and casualty companies insure against many different events. Finally, the amount of the potential loss is much more difficult to predict than for life insurance. These characteristics cause property and casualty companies to hold more liquid assets than those of life insurance companies.

Property insurance can be provided in either **named-peril policies** or **all-risk policies.** Named-peril policies insure against loss only from perils that are specifically named in the policy, whereas all-risk policies insure against all perils except those specifically excluded by the policy. For example, many homeowners in low-lying areas are required to buy flood insurance. This insurance covers only losses due to flooding so is a named-peril policy. A homeowner's insurance policy, which protects the house from fire, hurricane, tornado, and other damage, is an example of an all-risk policy.

Casualty or liability insurance protects against financial losses because of a claim of negligence. Liability insurance is bought not only by manufacturers who might be sued because of product defects but also by many types of professionals, including physicians, lawyers, and building contractors. Whereas the risk exposure in property insurance policies is relatively easy to predict, since it is usually limited to the value of the property, liability risk exposure is much more difficult to determine. And liability risk exposure can have long lag times (often referred to as "tails"). This means that a liability claim may be filed long after the policy expires.

Consider liability claims filed against the manufacturers of light airplanes. Cessna and Piper produced airplanes in the 1950s, 1960s, and 1970s that are still being used today. The companies often get sued when one of these old planes crashes. Insurance premiums grew so large in the 1980s due to the extensive lag time that both Cessna and Piper had to stop producing private airplanes. The cost of the liability insurance put the price of the planes out of reach of most private pilots.

There has been extensive publicity about high liability awards given by juries. These awards have often been well above what the insurance companies could have predicted. Liability insurance premiums continue to rise as a result. Some states have attempted to limit liability awards in an effort to contain these insurance costs.

Reinsurance   One way that insurance companies may reduce their risk exposure is to obtain **reinsurance**. Reinsurance allocates a portion of the risk to another company in exchange for a portion of the premium. Reinsurance allows insurance companies to write larger policies because a portion of the policy is actually held by another firm.

About 10% of all property and casualty insurance is reinsured. Smaller insurance firms obtain reinsurance more frequently than large firms. You can think of it as insurance for the insurance company.

Since the originator of the policy usually has more to lose than the reinsurer, the moral hazard and adverse selection problems are small. This means that little specific information about the risk being reinsured is required. As a result of the simplified information requirements, the reinsurance market consists of relatively standardized contracts. One problem with the market is the risk that the reinsurer can fail. For example, in 1990, insurance firms were owed about $20 billion in unrecovered reinsurance.

Insurance Regulation

Insurance companies are subject to less federal regulation than many other financial institutions. In fact, the McCarran-Ferguson Act of 1945 explicitly exempts insurance from federal regulation. The primary federal regulator is the Internal Revenue Service, which administers special taxation rules.

Most insurance regulation occurs at the state level. Not only must an insurance company follow the standards set by the state in which it is chartered, but it must also comply with the regulations set in any state in which it does business. New York requires that any insurance company doing business in the state comply with its investment standards. Because New York is such a big market, virtually every company complies. This makes the New York State regulations almost the same as national regulations.

The purpose of most regulations is to protect policyholders from losses due to the insolvency of the company. To accomplish this, insurance companies are restricted as to their asset composition and minimum capital ratio. All states also require that insurance agents and brokers obtain state licenses to sell each kind of insurance: life, property and casualty, and health. These licenses are to ensure that all agents have a minimum level of knowledge about the products they sell.

◼ THE PRACTICING FINANCIAL INSTITUTION MANAGER
Insurance Management

Insurance companies, like banks, are in the financial intermediation business of transforming one type of asset into another for the public. Insurance companies use the premiums paid on policies to invest in assets such as bonds, stocks, mortgages, and other loans; the earnings from these assets are then used to pay out claims on the policies. In effect, insurance companies transform assets such as bonds, stocks, and loans into insurance policies that provide a set of services (for example, claim adjustments, savings plans, friendly insurance agents). If the insurance company's production process of asset transformation efficiently provides its customers with adequate insurance services at low cost and if it can earn high returns on its investments, it will make profits; if not, it will suffer losses.

In Chapters 2 and 12 the concepts of adverse selection and moral hazard allowed us to understand why financial intermediaries like insurance companies are important in the economy. Here we use the adverse selection and moral hazard concepts to explain many management practices specific to the insurance industry.

In the case of an insurance policy, moral hazard arises when the existence of insurance encourages the insured party to take risks that increase the likelihood of an insurance payoff. For example, a person covered by burglary insurance might not take as many precautions to prevent a burglary because the insurance company will reimburse most of the losses if a theft occurs. Adverse selection holds that the people most likely to receive large insurance payoffs are the ones who will want to purchase insurance the most. For example, a person suffering from a terminal disease would want to take out the biggest life and medical insurance policies possible, thereby exposing the insurance company to potentially large losses. Both adverse selection and moral hazard can result in large losses to insurance companies because they lead to higher payouts on insurance claims. Minimizing adverse selection and moral hazard to reduce these payouts is therefore an extremely important goal for insurance companies, and this goal explains the insurance practices we discuss here.

Screening

To reduce adverse selection, insurance companies try to screen out poor insurance risks from good ones. Effective information collection procedures are therefore an important principle of insurance management.

When you apply for auto insurance, the first thing your insurance agent does is ask you questions about your driving record (number of speeding tickets and accidents), the type of car you are insuring, and certain personal matters (age, marital status). If you are applying for life insurance, you go through a similar grilling, but you are asked even more personal questions about such things as your health, smoking habits, and drug and alcohol use. The life insurance company even orders a medical evaluation (usually done by an independent company) that involves taking blood and urine samples. The insurance company uses the information you provide to allocate you to a risk class—a statistical estimate of how likely you are to have an insurance claim. Based on this information, the insurance company can decide whether to accept you for the insurance or to turn you down because you pose too high a risk and thus would be an unprofitable customer for the insurance company.

Risk-Based Premium

Charging insurance premiums on the basis of how much risk a policyholder poses for the insurance company is a time-honored principle of insurance management. Adverse selection explains why this principle is so important to insurance company profitability.

To understand why an insurance company finds it necessary to have risk-based premiums, let's examine an example of risk-based insurance premiums that at first glance seems unfair. Harry and Sally, both college students with no accidents or speeding tickets, apply for auto insurance. Normally, Harry will be charged a much higher premium than Sally. Insurance companies do this because young males have a much higher accident rate than young females. Suppose, though, that one insurance company did not base its premiums on a risk classification but rather just charged a premium based on the average combined risk for males and females. Then Sally would be charged too much and

Harry too little. Sally could go to another insurance company and get a lower rate, while Harry would sign up for the insurance. Because Harry's premium isn't high enough to cover the accidents he is likely to have, on average the company would lose money on Harry. Only with a premium based on a risk classification, so that Harry is charged more, can the insurance company make a profit.[1]

Restrictive Provisions

Restrictive provisions in policies are another insurance management tool for reducing moral hazard. Such provisions discourage policyholders from engaging in risky activities that make an insurance claim more likely. One type of restrictive provision keeps the policyholder from benefiting from behavior that makes a claim more likely. For example, life insurance companies have provisions in their policies that eliminate death benefits if the insured person commits suicide within the first two years the policy is in effect. Restrictive provisions may also require certain behavior on the part of the insured that makes a claim less likely. A company renting motor scooters may be required to provide helmets for renters in order to be covered for any liability associated with the rental. The role of restrictive provisions is not unlike that of restrictive covenants on debt contracts described in Chapter 12: Both serve to reduce moral hazard by ruling out undesirable behavior.

Prevention of Fraud

Insurance companies also face moral hazard because an insured person has an incentive to lie to the company and seek a claim even if the claim is not valid. For example, a person who has not complied with the restrictive provisions of an insurance contract may still submit a claim. Even worse, a person may file claims for events that did not actually occur. Thus an important management principle for insurance companies is conducting investigations to prevent fraud so that only policyholders with valid claims receive compensation.

Cancellation of Insurance

Being prepared to cancel policies is another insurance management tool. Insurance companies can discourage moral hazard by threatening to cancel a policy when the insured person engages in activities that make a claim more likely. If your auto insurance company makes it clear that if a driver gets too many speeding tickets, coverage will be canceled, you will be less likely to speed.

Deductibles

The deductible is the fixed amount by which the insured's loss is reduced when a claim is paid off. A $250 deductible on an auto policy, for example, means that

---

[1]You may recognize that the example here is in fact the lemons problem described in Chapter 12.

if you suffer a loss of $1000 because of an accident, the insurance company will pay you only $750. Deductibles are an additional management tool that helps insurance companies reduce moral hazard. With a deductible, you experience a loss along with the insurance company when you make a claim. Because you also stand to lose when you have an accident, you have an incentive to drive more carefully. A deductible thus makes a policyholder act more in line with what is profitable for the insurance company; moral hazard has been reduced. And because moral hazard has been reduced, the insurance company can lower the premium by more than enough to compensate the policyholder for the existence of the deductible.

Coinsurance

When a policyholder shares a percentage of the losses along with the insurance company, their arrangement is called **coinsurance.** For example, some medical insurance plans provide coverage for 80% of medical bills, and the insured person pays 20% after a certain deductible has been met. Coinsurance works to reduce moral hazard in exactly the same way that a deductible does. A policyholder who suffers a loss along with the insurance company has less incentive to take actions, such as going to the doctor unnecessarily, that involve higher claims. Coinsurance is thus another useful management tool for insurance companies.

Limits on the Amount of Insurance

Another important principle of insurance management is that there should be limits on the amount of insurance provided, even though a customer is willing to pay for more coverage. The higher the insurance coverage, the more the insured person can gain from risky activities that make an insurance payoff more likely and hence the greater the moral hazard. For example, if Zelda's car were insured for more than its true value, she might not take proper precautions to prevent its theft, such as making sure that the key is always removed or putting in an alarm system. If it were stolen, she comes out ahead because the excessive insurance payoff would allow her to buy an even better car. By contrast, when the insurance payment is lower than the value of her car, she will suffer a loss if it is stolen and will thus take the proper precautions to prevent this from happening. Insurance companies must always make sure that their coverage is not so high that moral hazard leads to large losses.

Summary

Effective insurance management requires several practices: information collection and screening of potential policyholders, risk-based premiums, restrictive provisions, prevention of fraud, cancellation of insurance, deductibles, coinsurance, and limits on the amount of insurance. All of these practices reduce moral hazard and adverse selection by making it harder for policyholders to benefit from engaging in activities that increase the amount and likelihood of claims. With smaller benefits available, the poor insurance risks (those who are more likely to engage in the activities in the first place) see less benefit from the insurance and are thus less likely to seek it out.

■ PENSIONS

A **pension plan** is an asset pool that accumulates over an individual's working years and is paid out during the nonworking years. Pension plans represent the fastest-growing financial intermediary. There are a number of reasons for this rapid growth.

As the United States became more urban, people realized that they could not rely on their children to care for them in their retirement. In a rural culture, families tend to stay together on the farm. The property passes from generation to generation with an implicit understanding that the younger generations will care for the older ones. When families became more dispersed and moved off farms, both the opportunity for and the expectation of extensive financial support of the older generations declined.

A second factor contributing to the growth of pension plans is that people are living longer and retiring younger. Again, in the rural setting, people often remained productive well into their retirement years. Many companies in urban America, however, encourage older workers to retire. They are often earning high wages as a result of seniority, yet may be less productive than younger workers. The result of this trend toward younger retirement and longer lives is that the average person can expect to spend more years in retirement. These years must be funded somehow, and the pension plan is often the vehicle of choice.

■ TYPES OF PENSIONS

Pension plans can be categorized in several ways. They may be defined-benefit or defined-contribution plans, and they may be public or private.

Defined-Benefit Pension Plans

Under a **defined-benefit plan,** the plan sponsor promises the employees a specific benefit when they retire. The payout is usually determined with a formula that uses the number of years worked and the employee's final salary. For example, a pension benefit may be calculated by the following formula:

Annual payment = 2% × average of final 3 years' income × years of service

In this case, if a worker had been employed for 35 years and the average wages during the last three years were $50,000, the annual pension benefit would be

$$0.02 \times \$50,000 \times 35 = \$35,000 \text{ per year}$$

The defined-benefit plan puts the burden on the employer to provide adequate funds to ensure that the agreed payments can be made. External audits of pension plans are required to determine whether sufficient funds have been contributed by the company. If sufficient funds are set aside by the firm for this purpose, the plan is **fully funded.** If more than enough funds are available, the plan is **overfunded.** More commonly, insufficient funds are available and the fund is **underfunded.** For example, if Jane Brown contributes $100 per year into her pension plan and the interest rate is 10%, after ten years, the contributions and their interest earnings would be worth $1753.[2] If the defined benefit on her pension plan is $1753 or less after ten years, the plan is fully funded because her contributions and earnings will cover this payment in full. But if the defined benefit is $2000, the plan is underfunded because her contributions and earnings do not cover this amount. Underfunding is most common when the employer fails to contribute adequately to the plan. Surprisingly, it is not illegal for a firm to sponsor an underfunded plan. The General Motors Corporation pension plan has been underfunded by billions of dollars for most of the past decade. The degree of funding does not affect the sponsor's responsibility to pay its obligations under the plan. Difficulties arise, however, when firms go bankrupt. If the pension fund is underfunded, retirees may not receive their benefits.

Defined-Contribution Pension Plans

As the name implies, instead of defining what the pension plan will pay, **defined-contribution plans** specify only what will be contributed into the fund. The retirement benefits are entirely dependent on the earnings of the fund. Corporate sponsors of defined-contribution plans usually put a fixed percentage of each employee's wages into the pension fund each pay period. In some instances, the employee also contributes to the plan. An insurance company or fund manager acts as trustee and invests the fund's assets. Frequently, employees are allowed to specify how the funds in their individual accounts will be invested. For example, an employee who is a conservative investor may prefer government securities, while one who is a more aggressive investor may prefer to have her retirement funds invested in corporate stock. When the employee retires, the balance in the pension account can be transferred into an annuity or some other form of distribution.

Defined-contribution pension plans are becoming increasingly popular. Many existing defined-benefit plans are converting to this form, and virtually all new plans are established as defined-contribution. One reason the defined-contribution plan is becoming so popular is that the onus is put on the employee rather than the employer to look out for the pension plan's performance. This reduces the liability of the employer.

One problem with defined-contribution plans is that many employees are not familiar enough with investments to make wise long-term choices. For example,

---

[2]The $100 contributed in year 1 would become worth $100 \times (1 + 0.10)^{10} = 259.37 at the end of ten years; the $100 contributed in year 2 would become worth $100 \times (1 + 0.10)^9 = 235.79$; and so on until the $100 contributed in year 10 would become worth $100 \times (1 + 0.10) = 110. Adding these together, we get the total value of these contributions and their earnings at the end of ten years as $1753.

only 3.7% of plan participants choose to put any more than half of their investment in stocks, even though long-term growth potential is greatest in the stock market.

Private and Public Pension Plans

Private pension plans, sponsored by employers, groups, and individuals, have grown rapidly as people have become more concerned about the viability of Social Security and more sophisticated about preparing for retirement (see Figure 5). In the past, private pension plans invested mostly in government securities and corporate bonds. Although these instruments are still important pension plan assets, corporate stocks, mortgages, open market paper, and time deposits now play a significant role. Figure 6 shows the distribution of private pension plan assets. They are now the largest institutional investor in the stock market. This makes pension plan managers a potentially powerful force if they choose to exercise control over firm management.

An alternative to privately sponsored pension plans are the public plans, though in many cases there is very little difference between the two. A **public pension plan** is one that is sponsored by a governmental body.

The largest of the public plans is the Federal Old Age and Disability Insurance Program (often called simply Social Security). This pension plan was established in 1935 to provide a safety net for aging Americans and is a "pay as you go" system—money that workers contribute today pays benefits to current recipients. Future generations will be called on to pay benefits to the individuals who are currently contributing. Many people fear that the fund will be unable to meet its

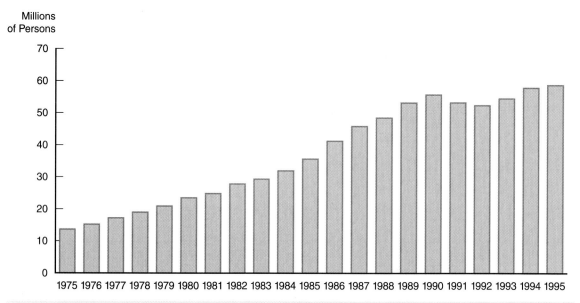

■**FIGURE 5** Number of Americans Covered by Private Pension Plans, 1975–1995

Source: 1996 Mutual Fund Fact Book, 36 edition, Investment Company Institute.

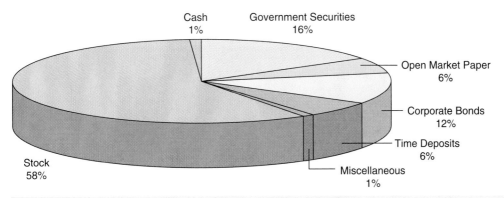

Cash
1%

Government Securities
16%

Open Market Paper
6%

Corporate Bonds
12%

Time Deposits
6%

Miscellaneous
1%

Stock
58%

■FIGURE 6 Distribution of Private Pension Plan Assets (end of 1996)

Source: 1996 Mutual Fund Fact Book, 3rd Edition, Investment Company Institute.

obligations by the time they retire. This fear is based on problems that the fund encountered in the 1970s and on the realization that a large number of people from the baby boom generation (born between 1946 and 1960) will swell the ranks of retirees in the rapidly approaching future.

The amount of the Social Security benefits a retiree receives is based on the person's earnings history. Workers contribute 7.5% of wages up to a current maximum wage of $53,400. Employers contribute the same amount. There is a certain amount of redistribution in the benefits, with low-income workers receiving a relatively larger return on their investment than high-income workers. One way to evaluate the amount of the benefits of a pension plan is to determine how the monthly benefits compare to preretirement income. This replacement ratio ranged from 49% for someone earning $15,000 a year to 24% for someone earning $53,400.

Figure 7 shows that the total assets in the Social Security fund decreased at the same time that the number of insured people was increasing. This situation led to a restructuring that included raising the program's contributions and reducing the program's benefits. To build public confidence, the Social Security system has started accumulating reserves to be used when the baby boom generation begins retiring. Currently, the plan is healthy. However, as the number of retirees increases relative to the number of workers paying retirement taxes, a problem will occur. By 2012, expenses are projected to exceed revenues. By 2029, unless the plan is modified, it will be bankrupt. Few analysts expect this actually to happen. More likely, retirement taxes will be increased and benefits reduced. For example, people may not be able to draw benefits as early as they now can, and the benefits may not be adjusted as fully for inflation as they are now. Already, Congress has scheduled over the next 20 years, two increases in the age of which social security benefits can be collected. As a result, you will have to wait until age 67 before collecting benefits.

Another solution, currently gaining support, is to privatize Social Security. Under a privatized plan, retirement dollars are invested in stocks and bonds rather than being paid out to current workers. Analysts estimate that the cost of making

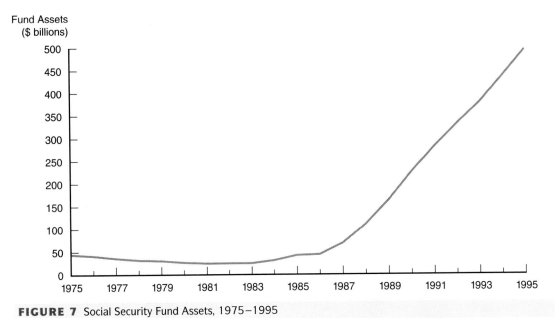

FIGURE 7 Social Security Fund Assets, 1975–1995

Source: Federal Reserve Board Statistical Releases Web Site.

a transition to a fully funded privatized plan would be enormous—about $100 billion—because payroll taxes would be diverted from current retirees into private accounts. To cover payments to current beneficiaries, the government would have to borrow the bulk of the money. Over time, analysts argue, privatization would gradually transform Social Security from an unfunded, pay-as-you-go system to a fully funded pension with real assets. Privatization is expected to gain public support because of the decreasing returns earned by contributors to the current system. Workers who retired 20 years ago received all that they paid in, plus interest and much more. But those who retire today get only about a 2.2% return, adjusted for inflation. A 30-year-old worker will lose money in absolute terms upon retirement. The debate over how to save Social Security will make headlines for many years to come.

The second-largest group of public plans is state and local employee pension plans. Currently, these plans cover more than 17 million government workers. The Federal Civilian Employees plan is next largest, covering over 5.5 million federal employees. The Railroad Retirement Plan covers 1.1 million workers.

■ REGULATION OF PENSION PLANS

For many years, pension plans were relatively free of government regulation. Many companies provided pension benefits as rewards for long years of good service and used the benefits as an incentive. Frequently, pension benefits were paid out of current income. When the firm failed or was acquired by another firm, the benefits ended. During the Great Depression, widespread pension plan failures led to increased regulation and to the establishment of the Social Security system.

A major U.S. Supreme Court decision in 1949 established that pension benefits were a legitimate part of collective bargaining, the negotiation of contracts by unions. This decision led to a great increase in the number of plans in existence as unions pressured employers to establish such plans for union members.

Employee Retirement Income Security Act

The most important and most comprehensive legislation affecting pension funds is the **(Employee Retirement Income Security Act) (ERISA),** passed in 1974. ERISA set certain standards that must be followed by all pension plans. Failure to follow the provisions of the act may cause a plan to lose its advantageous tax status. The motivation for the act was that many workers who had contributed to plans for many years were losing their benefits when plans failed. The principal features of the act are the following:

- ERISA established guidelines for funding.
- It provided that employees switching jobs may transfer their credits from one employer plan to the next.
- It said that plans must have minimum vesting requirements. *Vesting* refers to how long an employee must work for the company to be eligible for pension benefits. The maximum permissible vesting period is ten years, though most plans allow for vesting in less time.
- It increased the disclosure requirements for pension plans, providing employees with more ample information about the health and investments of their pension plans.
- It assigned the responsibility of regulatory oversight to the Department of Labor.

ERISA also established the **Pension Benefit Guarantee Corporation** (called **Penny Benny**), a government agency that performs a role similar to that of the FDIC. It insures pension benefits up to a limit (currently just over $30,000 per year per person) if a company with an underfunded pension plan goes bankrupt or is unable to meet its pension obligations for other reasons. Penny Benny charges pension plans a premium to pay for this insurance, but it can also borrow funds up to $100 million from the U.S. Treasury. Unfortunately, the problem of pension plan underfunding has been growing worse in recent years. In 1993, the secretary of labor indicated that underfunding had reached levels in excess of $45 billion, with one company's pension plan alone, that of General Motors, underfunded to the tune of $11.8 billion. As a result, Penny Benny, which insures the pensions of one of every three workers, is encountering severe financial difficulties that may necessitate a federal bailout (see Box 3).

▎**BOX 3**

The Perils of Penny Benny

A Repeat of the S&L Bailout?

The current woes of the Pension Benefit Guarantee Corporation, the U.S. government's pension insurance agency, commonly called "Penny Benny," display many of the characteristics of the savings and loan crisis we discussed in Chapter 15. When an insured company with an underfunded pension plan files for bankruptcy, Penny Benny must pay the company's workers their retirement benefits. Again, we see the moral hazard principle at work: A company is more likely to risk underfunding its pension plan if Penny Benny will foot the pension bill if it goes bankrupt. For example, the LTV Steel Company's bankruptcy in February 1987 resulted in Penny Benny's paying out $400 million per year to LTV pensioners alone, even though Penny Benny was taking in only $280 million in premiums in total.

As we have seen, to keep the costs of government insurance programs from getting out of hand, the insurance agency must reduce moral hazard by monitoring the firms it is insuring to make sure that they are not subjecting the agency to too much risk. In the case of Penny Benny, this means that Penny Benny must audit pension plans to make sure that they are not becoming too severely underfunded. A decrease in the amount of monitoring of S&Ls was one reason for the huge losses to their government insurance agency, the FSLIC; unfor-

tunately, we see a similar pattern for Penny Benny. Since the establishment of Penny Benny, the number of pension funds has more than doubled, yet the number of federal audits of pension plans has declined. As a result, fewer than 1% of private plans insured by Penny Benny are audited each year. Not surprisingly, given the agency's failure to control moral hazard, the liabilities arising from its responsibility for troubled pension plans have grown at an alarming rate and are now estimated to exceed its assets by more than $15 billion. Taxpayers are likely to be hit with another massive government bailout, the size of which will keep growing unless the government makes a concerted effort to reduce the underfunding of corporate pension plans.

The Clinton administration has proposed legislation to deal with some of these problems. It would require underfunded pension plans to make larger insurance contributions, thereby providing Penny Benny with more funding and making it less attractive for companies to underfund their pension plans. In addition, the legislation would tighten the rules for calculating the degree of underfunding and would also give Penny Benny greater powers to enforce compliance with its regulations, thus making it easier for it to discourage underfunding.

Individual Retirement Plans

The Pension Reform Act of 1978 updated the Self-Employed Individuals Tax Retirement Act of 1962 to authorize **individual retirement accounts (IRAs).** IRAs permitted people (such as those who are self-employed) who are not covered by other pension plans to contribute into a tax-deferred savings account. Legislation in 1981 and 1982 expanded the eligibility of these accounts to make them available to almost everyone. IRAs proved extremely popular, to the extent that their use resulted in significant losses of tax revenues to the government. That led Congress to include provisions in the Tax Reform Act of 1986 sharply curtailing eligibility.

Keogh plans are a retirement savings option for the self-employed. Funds can be deposited with a depository institution, life insurance company, or securities firm. The owner of the Keogh is often allowed some discretion as to how the funds will be invested.

SUMMARY

1. Insurance companies exist because people are risk-averse and prefer to transfer risk away from themselves. Insurance benefits people's lives by reducing the size of reserves they would have to maintain to cover possible loss of life or property.

2. Adverse selection and moral hazard are problems inherent to the insurance business. Many of the provisions of insurance policies—including deductibles, application screening, and risk-based premiums—are aimed at reducing their effects.

3. Insurance is usually divided into two primary types, life insurance and property and casualty insurance. Many life insurance products also serve as savings vehicles. Property and casualty insurance usually has a much shorter term than most life insurance.

4. Because life insurance liabilities are very predictable, these insurers are able to invest in long-term assets. Property and casualty insurance companies must keep their assets more liquid to pay out on unexpected losses.

5. Pension plans are rapidly growing as a longer-lived generation plan for early retirement.

6. There are two primary types of pension plans: defined-benefit and defined-contribution. Defined-benefit plans pay benefits according to a formula that is established in advance. Defined-contribution plans specify only how much is to be saved; benefits depend on the returns generated by the plans.

7. The largest public pension plan is Social Security, which is a pay-as-you-go system. Current retirees receive payments from current workers. Many people are concerned that as the number of retirees increases, the amount paid in to the Social Security system will not be sufficient to cover the sums being paid out.

8. Most private pension plans are insured by the Pension Benefit Guarantee Corporation, which pays benefits when a plan's sponsor goes bankrupt or is otherwise unable to make payments.

KEY TERMS

all-risk policy, p. 457
annuity, p. 451
casualty (liability) insurance,
    p. 456
certainty equivalent, p. 445
coinsurance, p. 461
deductible, p. 447
defined-benefit plan, p. 462
defined-contribution plan,
    p. 463
Employee Retirement Income
    Security Act (ERISA), p. 467

fully funded, p. 463
individual retirement account
    (IRA), p. 468
law of large numbers, p. 451
mutual insurance company,
    p. 448
named-peril policy, p. 457
overfunded, p. 463
Pension Benefit Guarantee
    Corporation (Penny Benny),
    p. 467
pension plan, p. 462

private pension plan, p. 464
property insurance, p. 456
public pension plan, p. 464
reinsurance, p. 457
stock company, p. 448
underfunded, p. 463
underwriter, p. 448

QUESTIONS AND PROBLEMS

*1. Why do people choose to buy insurance even if their expected loss is less than the payments they will make to the insurance company?

2. Why do insurance companies not allow people to buy insurance on personally unrelated risks?

*3. What is information asymmetry, and how does it affect insurance companies?

4. Distinguish between adverse selection and moral hazard as they relate to the insurance industry.

*5. How do insurance companies protect themselves against losses due to adverse selection and moral hazard?

6. Distinguish between independent agents and exclusive agents.

*7. Are most insurance companies organized as mutuals or stock companies?

8. How are insurance companies able to predict their losses from claims accurately enough to let them price their policies such that they will make a profit?

*9. What is the difference between term life insurance and whole life insurance?

10. What risk do property and casualty insurance policies protect against?

*11. What is the purpose behind reinsurance?

12. Distinguish between defined-benefit and defined-contribution pension plans.

*13. Why have private pension plans grown rapidly in recent years?

14. What is a pay-as-you-go pension plan?

*15. Why is Social Security in danger of eventually going bankrupt?

CHAPTER 18

FINANCE COMPANIES AND FINANCIAL CONGLOMERATES

■ PREVIEW Suppose that you are graduating from college and about to start work at that high-paying job you were offered. You may decide that your first purchase must be a car. If you are not mechanically inclined, you may opt to buy a new one. The problem, of course, is that you do not have the $20,000 needed for the purchase. A finance company may come to your rescue. Most automobile financing is provided by finance companies owned by the automobile companies.

Now suppose that you have gone to work and your first assignment is to acquire a new piece of equipment. After doing some math, you may decide that the company should lease the equipment. Again, you may find yourself dealing with another type of finance company.

Finally, you are asked to see what you can do to increase your company's liquidity. You may again find that finance companies can help by purchasing your accounts receivable in a transaction called *factoring*.

It is clear that finance companies are an important intermediary to many segments of the economy. In this chapter we discuss the different types of finance companies and describe what they do.

■ HISTORY OF FINANCE COMPANIES

The earliest examples of finance companies date back to the beginning of the 1800s when retailers offered **installment credit** to customers. With an installment credit agreement, a loan is made that requires the borrower to make a series of equal payments over some fixed length of time. Prior to installment credit agreements, loans were usually of the single-payment or balloon type. A **balloon loan** requires the borrower to make a single large payment at the loan's maturity to retire the debt. Installment loans appealed to consumers because they allowed them to make small payments on the loan out of current income.

Finance companies came into their own when automobile companies began mass marketing. In the early 1900s, banks did not offer car loans because cars were considered consumer purchases rather than productive assets. Many people wanted to buy cars but found it difficult to raise the purchase price. The automobile companies established subsidiaries, called *finance companies*, to provide installment loans to car buyers.

Soon many other retailers adopted the idea of providing financing for consumers who wanted to buy their goods. They found not only that sales increased but also the subsidiary finance company was profitable.

Eventually, banks recognized the value of consumer loans and began offering installment credit loans too. By offering lower interest rates, banks rapidly gained the larger part of the consumer credit market. By the end of 1996, banks held $500 billion in consumer loans, compared to $203 billion by finance companies.

As the proportion of credit offered by finance companies to consumers declined, the proportion offered to businesses in the form of sales and leasing increased. At the end of 1996, for example, finance companies held $411 billion of business loans.

■ PURPOSE OF FINANCE COMPANIES

Finance companies are money market intermediaries. Recall from Chapter 9 that the money markets are wholesale markets. This means that most securities that trade there have very large denominations. The minimum investment of $100,000 makes it impossible for individuals and most small companies to trade in this market. A second obstacle is that consumers and small companies lack the credit standing necessary to borrow in the money markets. These factors exclude consumers and small businesses from being able to take advantage of the low interest rates available on money market securities.

Finance companies allow smaller participants access to this market by selling commercial paper and using the proceeds to make loans. (In Chapter 9 we noted that finance companies were the largest sellers of commercial paper.)

The financial intermediation process of finance companies can be described by saying that they borrow in large amounts but often lend in small amounts—a process quite different from that of commercial banks, which collect deposits in small amounts and then often make large loans.

A key feature of finance companies is that although they lend to many of the same customers that borrow from banks, they are virtually unregulated compared to commercial banks and thrift institutions. States regulate the maximum amount they can loan to individual consumers and the terms of the debt contract, but there are no restrictions on branching, the assets they hold, or how they raise their funds. The lack of restrictions enables finance companies to tailor their loans to customer needs better than banking institutions can.

Finance companies exist to service both individuals and businesses. Consumer finance companies that focus on loans to individuals differ from banks in significant ways. First, consumer finance companies often accept loans with much higher risk than banks would. These high-risk customers may not have any source of loans other than the consumer finance company. Second, consumer finance companies are often wholly owned by a manufacturer who uses the company to make loans to consumers interested in purchasing the manufacturer's products. For example, all U.S. automobile companies own consumer finance companies that fund auto loans. Often these loans are made on very favorable terms to encourage product sales.

Business finance companies exist to fill financing needs not served by banks, such as lease financing. Manufacturers of business products often own finance companies for the same reasons as automobile companies: Sales can be increased if attractive financing terms are available.

■ RISK IN FINANCE COMPANIES

Like other financial institutions, finance companies face several types of risk. The greatest is **default risk,** the chance that customers will fail to repay their loans. As mentioned earlier, many consumer finance companies lend to borrowers who are unable to obtain credit from other sources. Naturally, these borrowers tend to default more frequently. Finance company delinquency rates are usually higher than those for banks or thrifts. Finance companies recoup the losses they suffer from bad loans by charging higher interest rates, often as much as twice that charged by banks. Despite high interest rates, when economic conditions deteriorate, their customers are often the first to be unemployed because they tend to be less educated, and defaults cause losses.

Another type of risk finance companies face is **liquidity risk.** Liquidity risk refers to problems that arise when a firm runs short of cash. For example, a bank may have a liquidity problem if many depositors withdraw their funds at once. Finance companies run the risk of liquidity problems because their assets, consumer and business loans, are not easily sold in the secondary financial markets. Thus if they are in need of cash, they must borrow. This is not difficult for larger finance companies because they have access to the money markets and can sell commercial paper, but borrowing may be more difficult for smaller firms.

Offsetting the lack of a secondary market for finance company assets is the fact that none of the firm's funds come from deposits, so unexpected withdrawals do not occur. The greater problem is that a change in the perceived risk of the finance company may make it difficult to **roll over** its short-term debt instruments. The term *roll over* means to renew the debt each time it matures.

Interest-rate risk is a major problem for banks and thrifts but not of great concern to finance companies. Recall that interest-rate risk refers to a decline in value of fixed-rate loans when market interest rates rise. Banks and thrifts hold more long-term loans than finance companies do and hence are subject to greater interest-rate risk. Finance companies can be affected by changing interest-rate levels because their assets (loans) are not as interest-rate-sensitive as their liabilities (borrowings). We discuss risk management in financial institutions and in finance companies in particular in greater detail in Chapter 20.

■ TYPES OF FINANCE COMPANIES

There are three types of finance companies: business, sales, and consumer. Figure 1 shows the distribution of loans for finance companies. Over half are made for business purposes. Note that loans secured by real estate can be made to both businesses and consumers but more often result when consumers obtain second mortgages on their homes. (Second mortgage loans are discussed in Chapter 11.)

Business (Commercial) Finance Companies

In the early 1900s, commercial banks were reluctant to lend money secured by a company's accounts receivable (funds owed to the company by other businesses and individuals) because the Federal Reserve discounted or bought only promissory notes that were related to productive purposes, such as financing for a factory. Not until after the Great Depression did commercial banks begin competing for loans secured by accounts receivable. By this time, finance companies were offering to make loans to businesses that were secured by equipment and inventory as well. Finance companies gained the reputation of being more innovative than banks at finding ways to finance small businesses. One reason they could be more flexible was their near-total absence of regulation. Because there are no depositors to protect, the government has never found the need to restrict the activities of these types of firms. Figure 2 reports the different types of business loans made by finance companies. Equipment financing is the most prevalent. Loans secured by motor vehicles, which include loans to buy autos for business use and for resale, are second most common.

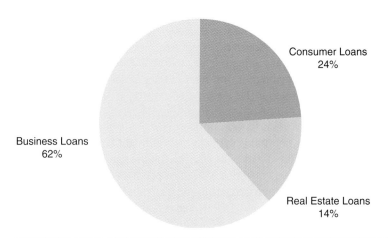

■FIGURE 1 Types of Loans Made by Finance Companies

Source: Federal Reserve *Bulletin,* 1996.

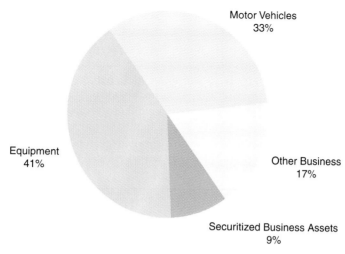

■FIGURE 2 Types of Business Loans Made by Finance Companies

Source: Federal Reserve Bulletin, 1996.

Factoring Business finance companies provide specialized forms of credit to businesses by making loans and purchasing accounts receivable at a discount; this provision of credit is called **factoring.** For example, a dressmaking firm might have outstanding bills (accounts receivable) of $100,000, owed by the retail stores that have bought its dresses. If this firm needs cash to buy 100 new sewing machines, it can sell its accounts receivable for, say, $90,000 to a finance company, which is now entitled to collect the $100,000 owed to the firm.

Factoring is a very common practice in the apparel industry. One advantage of factoring is that the finance company (called a *factor* in this situation) usually assumes responsibility for collecting the debt. If the debt becomes uncollectable, the factor suffers the loss. This removes the need for the apparel company to have a credit department or be involved in the collection effort.

Factors usually check the credit of the firm's receivables before accepting them. The factoring arrangement works well because the factor is able to specialize in bill processing and collections and to take advantage of economies of scale. Besides the cost savings from reduced salary expenses, many firms like to use factors because they do not want their relationship with their customers spoiled by having to collect money from them.

Finance companies also provide financing of accounts receivable without taking ownership of the accounts receivable. In this case, the finance company receives documents from the business giving it the right to collect and keep the accounts receivable should the business fail to pay its debt to the finance company. Many firms prefer this arrangement over factoring because it leaves them in control of their accounts receivable. They can work with their customers if special arrangements are required to assure payment.

Leasing Business finance companies also specialize in **leasing** equipment (such as railroad cars, jet planes, and computers), which they purchase and then lease to businesses for a set number of years. Indeed, much of the growth in finance companies in recent years has come from business leasing. Under a lease, the finance company buys the asset and then leases it back to the business. One advantage of leasing is that **repossession** of the asset is easier. Repossession occurs when the finance company takes the asset back when the lessee (the firm that is leasing the asset) fails to make the payments on time. Lenders can repossess an asset under loans and lease contracts, but it is easier under a lease because the finance company already owns the asset, so no transfer of title of ownership is required.

Finance companies that are subsidiaries of equipment manufacturers have an additional advantage over banks. When a piece of equipment must be repossessed, the manufacturer is in a better position to re-lease or resell the asset.

The owner of an asset is able to depreciate the asset over time and to capture a tax savings as a result. If the firm that plans to use the asset does not have income to offset with the depreciation, the tax saving may be more valuable to the finance company. Part of this tax benefit can be passed on to the lessee in the form of lower payments than on a straight loan. In effect, the government is supporting the equipment purchase in the amount of the tax savings. This support is lost unless a firm earning income actually owns the asset.

A final advantage to leasing is that the lessee is often not required to make as large an up-front payment as is usually required on a straight loan. This conserves valuable working capital and is often the critical factor in leasing decisions.

Floor Plan Loans Some auto manufacturers require that dealers accept auto deliveries throughout the year, even though sales tend to be seasonal. To help dealers pay for their inventories of cars, finance companies began offering **floor plans.** In a floor plan arrangement, the finance company pays for the car dealership's inventory of cars received from the manufacturer and puts a lien on each car on the showroom floor. When a car is sold, the dealer must pay off the debt owed on that car before the finance company will provide a clear title of ownership. The dealer must pay the finance company interest on the floor loans until the inventory has been sold off. Floor plan financing is most common in the auto industry because cars have titles that the finance company can hold to secure its loans. Floor plan financing exists in other industries where assets with titles are involved, such as construction equipment and boats.

A close relationship usually evolves between the finance company and the dealer. Consider that each sale requires correspondence between the firms. As a result of the close relationship, it is common to find that the same finance company also provides retail financing for the dealer's customers. The help that an aggressive finance company can provide by financing weak credit customers also helps the finance company's floor loans get paid.

Note that banks also provide floor plan financing; however, such loans tend to be high-maintenance. The unregulated, lower-cost structure of finance companies often makes them the preferred intermediaries.

Consumer Finance Companies

Consumer finance companies make loans to consumers to buy particular items such as furniture or home appliances, to make home improvements, or to help refinance small debts. Consumer finance companies are separate corporations (like Household Finance Corporation) or are owned by banks (Citicorp owns Person-to-Person Finance Company, which operates offices nationwide). Typically, these companies make loans to consumers who cannot obtain credit from other sources due to low income or poor credit history. Finance companies will often accept items for security, such as old cars or old mobile homes, that would be unacceptable to banks. Because these loans are often high in both risk and maintenance, they usually carry high interest rates.

There are two exceptions: Finance companies are becoming more active in making home equity loans, loans secured by a second mortgage on the borrower's home. The Tax Reform Act of 1986 ended the ability to deduct most consumer interest from income when computing taxes. Unchanged, however, was the right to deduct interest paid on loans against a principal residence.[1] This lowers the effective interest rate by 1 minus the tax rate in decimal form. For example, if the interest rate on a home equity loan is given as 12% and the marginal tax rate is 28%, the effective after-tax cost of the loan is $12\% \times (1 - 0.28) = 12\% \times 0.72 = 8.64\%$. The reduced effective interest rates have made home equity loans very popular. Most consumers continue to obtain home equity loans through banks. However, lower-income consumers and those with poor credit histories obtain them from finance companies.

The disadvantage to home equity lending is that the lender will usually be in second position on the title. This requires the lender to pay off the first mortgage before taking ownership of the property. We discussed second mortgages in detail in Chapter 11.

Another growth area for consumer finance companies is in retail credit cards. Many retailers like to offer their customers a "private label" credit card to increase sales. Many large retailers operate their own credit card programs either in-house or through finance subsidiaries, but smaller retailers may contract with a finance company. When the retailers accept applications for credit cards, they pass them on to the finance company for approval. The finance company then sends the retailer's card to the customers. The finance company provides billing and collection services for the account. The consumer may never be aware that a finance company is involved in these transactions. Finance companies allow smaller retailers to provide a service that only larger retailers could offer otherwise.

Sales Finance Companies

Sales finance companies make loans to consumers to purchase items from a particular retailer or manufacturer. Sears, Roebuck Acceptance Corporation, for example, finances consumer purchases of all goods and services at Sears stores,

---

[1]Interest on loans made against a second home is also deductible.

and General Motors Acceptance Corporation (GMAC) finances purchases of GM cars. Sales finance companies compete directly with banks for consumer loans and are used by consumers because loans can frequently be obtained faster and more conveniently at the location where an item is purchased.

A sales finance company, also called a **captive finance company,** is owned by the manufacturer to make loans to consumers to help finance the purchase of the manufacturer's products (GMAC is the largest of these). These captive finance companies often offer interest rates below those of banks and other finance companies to increase sales. Profits made on the sale offset any losses made on the loans. Other major manufacturers also own captive finance companies (Box 1 profiles Ford Motor Credit).

■ REGULATION OF FINANCE COMPANIES

As noted, because there are no depositors to protect and no government deposit insurance is involved, finance companies are far less regulated than banks and thrifts. The exception to this is when a finance company is acting as a bank holding company or is a subsidiary of a bank holding company. (Recall from Chapter 14 that bank holding companies are firms that own the stock of one or more banking institutions.) In these cases, federal regulations are imposed. Finance companies without a direct relationship to a bank are regulated by the state.

BOX 1

The Expansion of Ford Motor Credit

In December 1996, Ford Motor Credit announced its intention to expand its lending operations to include subprime loans, loans to individuals with poor credit records. The lure to make these types of loans is that $100 billion is lent to people with flawed credit each year to buy new and used cars. Most of this business now goes to a number of smaller finance companies, which specialize in high-risk lending, often charging very high rates to compensate for the risk. Ford Motor Credit thinks it can compete effectively for these loans.

Ford is very interested in the income generated by its finance operations. Its credit program began in 1923 when customers were permitted to pay $5 per week toward the purchase of a $265 Ford. Only when the full amount had been paid was the customer allowed to drive the car home. By 1995, credit operations had expanded to the point where Ford earned $671 million from financial services, compared to $15 million from its automotive operations. Ford's financial service operations consists of the Ford Motor Credit Company,

which is primarily an auto lender; the Associates, which is the second-biggest independent finance company in the United States; and International Businesses, which makes auto loans internationally.

Ford's entry into high-risk lending is a departure from the usual lending practices of the major automotive finance companies. Ford admits that it will be difficult to balance the need to protect its assets by repossessing cars while they can still be located against protecting Ford's reputation. The new subsidiary, to be named Fairlane Credit, hopes to identify customers who have once had problems but have recovered, such as college students who overextended on credit cards or people who unexpectedly lost their jobs but are now employed. Whereas a normal, high-credit loan is usually approved in less than an hour, Fairlane expects to spend several days evaluating its subprime customers. It hopes to be rewarded for its effort with loyal, long-term Ford customers and high profits due to the high interest rates these types of loans command.

What regulations do affect finance companies are aimed at protecting unsophisticated customers from being taken advantage of. **Regulation Z** (the "truth in lending" regulation) requires that banks and finance companies disclose the annual percentage rate charged on loans in a prominent and understandable fashion. The lender must also disclose what the total interest cost of the credit will be over the life of the loan.

Federal bankruptcy laws were revised in 1979 to increase the protection provided to consumers who declare bankruptcy. The homestead exemption in the revised law allows consumers to declare bankruptcy, thereby eliminating their debts, while still retaining ownership of many of their assets. Because many finance company customers have few assets to begin with, they lose little if they declare bankruptcy. This is a serious concern for finance companies and is one reason they usually demand adequate security before making a loan.

The level of interest rates that finance companies can charge customers is limited by **usury** statutes. Usury is charging an excessive or inordinate interest rate on a loan. The permissible interest-rate ceiling depends on the size and maturity of the loan, with small, short-term loans having the highest rates. The usury limits vary by state, but most are sufficiently high not to be a limiting factor to reputable finance companies.

State and federal government regulations impose restrictions on finance companies' ability to collect on delinquent and defaulted loans. For example, many states restrict how aggressive a finance company can be when calling customers and prohibit them from calling late at night or at work. Regulations also require that certain legal procedures be followed and that the lender bear the expense of collecting on the bad debt.

In contrast to consumer lending, few regulations limit finance companies in the business loan market. Regulators feel that businesses should be financially sophisticated enough to protect themselves without government intervention.

■ FINANCE COMPANY BALANCE SHEET

Figure 3 presents the aggregate balance sheet for finance companies.

Assets

The primary asset of finance companies is their loan portfolio, consisting of consumer, business, and real estate loans. The largest category of loans is to businesses, currently representing 50% of total assets and 61% of all loans made.

Because of the high risk of loans made to consumers, more loans default. To protect their income against these defaults, finance companies allocate a portion of income each period to an account to be used to offset losses, called the **reserve for loan losses.** The reason for having a reserve for loan losses is to smooth losses over time. By recognizing a set amount of loss each period, different losses in one period over another do not show up on the bottom line. Banks and thrifts also maintain a reserve for loan losses; however, it does not need to be as large as that for finance companies.

Assets	Billions of dollars	Percent of Total
Consumer loans	112.6	19%
Business loans	287.8	50%
Real estate loans	67.2	12%
Less reserve for loan losses	59.0	−10%
Other assets	169.7	29%
Total Assets	578.3	100%
Liabilities		
Bank loans	25.8	5%
Commercial paper	149.9	26%
Owned to parent	47.9	8%
Debt not elsewhere	198.1	34%
Other liabilities	87.6	15%
Equity	68.9	12%
Total Liabilites and Equity	578.3	100%

■**FIGURE 3** Consolidated Finance Company Balance Sheet ($ billions, end of year 1996)

Source: Federal Reserve *Bulletin,* March 1997.

Liabilities

Because finance companies do not accept deposits, they must raise funds from other sources to fund their loans. An important source of funds is commercial paper (discussed in detail in Chapter 9). Recall, however, that this commercial paper is unsecured, short-term debt issued by low-risk companies. Its advantage over bank loans and other sources of funds is that it carries a low interest rate. Finance companies also obtain funds by borrowing from other money market sources and occasionally from banks (about 5% of assets). Captive finance companies have the option of borrowing directly from their parent corporation.

On average, finance companies have a 12% capital-to-total-assets ratio. This is relatively strong when compared to the 9% to 10% usually observed for banks and savings and loans.

Income

Finance company income derives from several sources. The primary source, of course, is interest income from its loan portfolio. Finance companies also earn income from loan origination fees. These are fees they charge borrowers for making a loan. These fees cover the processing costs involved. Many finance companies also sell credit insurance, which pays off any balance due on a loan if the borrower should die or become disabled. Credit insurance tends to generate very high profits compared to other types of life insurance coverage. Some finance companies earn additional income from expanding their operations to include income tax preparation services.

Finance Company Growth

Finance companies grew rapidly during the 1980s. This growth was fueled by the expansive economy, which caused the demand for finance company business loans to increase. The percentage of assets in loans made to businesses increased from 35% in 1970 to over 46% in 1991. As the recession took hold in the early 1990s, the demand for business loans decreased, as did the growth in assets. Figure 4 traces the growth in finance company assets from 1979 to 1996.

■ FINANCIAL CONGLOMERATES

A financial conglomerate is a firm that owns and manages a large number of different types of financial intermediaries. For example, in 1981, Sears, in addition to its ownership of consumer finance subsidiaries, Allstate Insurance Company, and Allstate Life Insurance Company, acquired Coldwell Banker Real Estate and Dean Witter (a brokerage firm). It also introduced its Discover card and acquired a $6 billion California-based savings bank. By putting all of these businesses under one roof, the goal was to achieve economies of scale and of scope.

Economies of scale reflect the savings that can be achieved through increased size. For example, one computer system could provide service to several subsidiaries. Similarly, existing management could oversee operations for a number of similar firms.

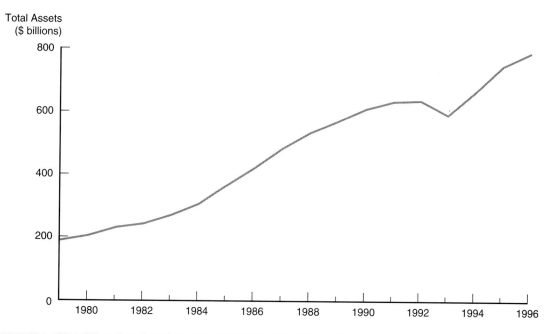

■FIGURE 4 Growth of Finance Company Assets, 1979–1996

Source: Federal Reserve *Bulletin,* various issues.

Economies of scope reflect increased business from offering many products in one easy-to-reach location. For example, a customer wanting auto insurance could also be sold a life insurance policy and shares in a mutual fund at the same time. Sears, as well as other large retailers, felt that customers would rather deal with one well-known and trusted business than with a variety of smaller firms. Xerox, for example, owned a securities business and an insurance company. Ford, Chrysler, Westinghouse, AT&T, and Kodak all established or expanded their finance company subsidiaries to compete for retail business.

Although the concept of a one-stop-shopping financial conglomerate seemed reasonable, it was often not successful. The types of businesses tackled by these conglomerates were highly competitive. Consumers did not perceive any great benefit to dealing with a single firm for all of their financial needs and instead shopped for the best deals available.

By 1989, Sears recognized that in-store offices of Coldwell Banker and Dean Witter were losing money. In response, it sold off the Coldwell Banker commercial group. In 1992, Sears announced its intent to dispose of its securities and remaining real estate businesses, the Discover card, and 20% of its interest in Allstate. Other financial conglomerates are doing the same. All of those listed here have either sold or announced plans to sell all or part of their financial intermediary holdings.

One exception is General Electric Capital Services. GE purchased Eastman Kodak's finance subsidiary for $1 billion. It also owns Kidder Peabody, a major investment bank, and Employers Reinsurance, one of the largest property and casualty reinsurers. GEFSCO, a subsidiary, is a leading supplier of private-label credit cards to retailers as well as a major servicer of home mortgages. Earnings from this conglomerate account for up to one-third of GE's total income.

Despite the success of General Electric Capital Services, the luster has apparently vanished from the conglomerate concept. It is more important to be flexible than big and to be an expert at one business than involved in many. While captive finance companies continue to grow and prosper, further growth of financial conglomerates seems unlikely.

SUMMARY

1. Finance companies were initially owned by manufacturers who wanted to provide easy financing to help the sales of their products. The concept rapidly expanded when automobile financing became more commonplace.

2. Finance companies sell short-term securities in the money markets and use the proceeds to make small consumer and business loans. In this way, they act as intermediaries in the money markets. They typically borrow in large amounts and lend in small.

3. Another purpose served by consumer finance companies is servicing higher-risk customers. As a result

of making these high-risk loans, default is the primary risk finance companies face. Finance companies compensate for default risk by charging higher interest rates. Finance companies also make business loans and offer leases.

4. The three types of finance companies are business, consumer, and sales. Business finance companies finance accounts receivable (often through an arrangement called factoring) and provide inventory loans and leases. Consumer finance companies make loans to high-risk customers for the purchase of autos and appliances and to refinance other debt. Sales

finance companies finance a firm's sales, often through in-house credit or credit cards.

5. Because there are no deposits at risk, finance companies are less regulated than banks and thrifts. They are subject, however, to consumer regulations that limit interest rates and require disclosure of the cost of loans.

6. Financial conglomerates are firms offering a variety of financial services under one umbrella. These services may include consumer loans, credit cards, insurance, real estate sales, and brokerage services. Most of the efforts to provide a one-stop financial superstore have not fared well. Many early efforts are being dismantled.

KEY TERMS

balloon loan, p. 471
captive finance company, p. 478
default risk, p. 473
economies of scale, p. 481
economies of scope, p. 482

factoring, p. 475
floor plan, p. 476
installment credit, p. 471
leasing, p. 476
liquidity risk, p. 473

Regulation Z, p. 479
repossession, p. 476
reserve for loan losses, p. 479
roll over, p. 473
usury, p. 479

QUESTIONS AND PROBLEMS

*1. What is the difference between an installment loan and a balloon loan?

2. What caused finance companies to grow rapidly in the early 1900s?

*3. Who are the typical customers of consumer finance companies, and why do they not go to commercial banks, where interest rates are lower?

4. How do consumer finance companies maintain their income in the face of high default rates on their loans?

*5. Do finance companies face liquidity risk? Why?

6. Do finance companies face interest-rate risk? Why?

*7. What is factoring?

8. What is the advantage of leasing assets to the lessor? To the lessee?

*9. Many auto dealers finance their inventory using floor plan loans advanced by finance companies. What is a floor plan loan?

10. Many manufacturers own finance companies that finance the purchase of the manufacturers' products. What are these finance companies called?

*11. Why are home equity loans popular?

12. Why are finance companies so concerned that their customers may file bankruptcy?

*13. What does Regulation Z require of finance companies?

14. What types of statutes limit the interest rates that finance companies can charge their customers?

*15. Have financial conglomerates been successful at providing one-stop shopping for financial services?

◼ CASE STUDY

◼ Purchase of a Finance Company, Analysis of Balance Sheet, Risk Difference Relative to a Bank, Leasing Function

CONCEPTS IN THIS CASE

balloon loan
liquidity risk
interest-rate risk
factoring
leasing

floor plan
Regulation Z
reserve for loan losses
economies of scale
economies of scope

Your bank is considering the purchase of a finance company. The financial information you have been given is as follows:

Assets ($ millions)	
Consumer loans	60.0
Business loans	140.0
Real estate loans	50.0
Less reserve for loan losses	–20.0
Other assets	50.0
Total assets	280.0
Liabilities ($ millions)	
Bank loans	35.0
Commercial paper	130.0
Owed to parent	22.0
Debt not elsewhere	44.0
Other liabilities	19.0
Total liabilities	250.0
Equity	30.0
Total liabilities and equity	280.0

Given the typical finance company balance sheet in Figure 3,

1. What would be the typical amount held as reserve for loan losses?

2. What would be the typical amount held as business loans?

3. How much commercial paper would be expected for this company?

4. How much in bank loans would be expected for this company?

5. How does the firm compare to the average capital-to-total-asset ratio of 12%?

6. After reviewing the firm's position relative to Figure 3, what recommendation would you make to your management regarding the purchase of this finance company?

7. What economies of scale would you expect if your larger bank purchased this finance company?

8. What economies of scope would you expect if your larger bank purchased this finance company?

9. What is the difference between the risk of the finance company and the bank in terms of government regulations?

10. What advantages (if any) could the bank gain by purchasing the finance company and using it to own and lease productive assets (such as computers) to the parent company (bank)?

CHAPTER 19

SECURITIES FIRMS

█ PREVIEW If you decide to take advantage of that hot stock tip you just heard from your roommate or if you want to earn more than 1.5% on funds you have on deposit at your bank, you will need to interact with one of many securities companies. Similarly, as the new CFO of WWCF, a candy manufacturer, you may need a securities company if you are asked to coordinate a bond sale or to issue additional stock. If your grandfather decides to sell his firm to the public, you may need to help him by working with investment bankers at that securities company. Finally, if you are looking for a high-paying job, your next stop may be a securities firm.

The smooth functioning of securities markets, in which bonds and stocks are traded, involves several financial institutions, including securities brokers and dealers, investment banks, and organized exchanges. None of these institutions were included in our list of financial intermediaries in Chapter 2 because they do not perform the intermediation function of acquiring funds by issuing liabilities and then using the funds to acquire financial assets. Nonetheless, they are important in the process of channeling funds from savers to spenders.

To begin our look at how securities markets work, we must recall the distinction between primary and secondary securities markets discussed in Chapter 2. In a primary market, new issues of a security are sold to buyers by the corporation or government agency borrowing the funds. A secondary market then trades the securities that have been sold in the primary market (and so are secondhand). Investment banks assist in the initial sale of securities in the primary market; securities brokers and dealers assist in the trading of securities in the secondary markets, some of which are organized into exchanges.

■ INVESTMENT BANKS

An investment bank is a financial institution that helps corporations raise funds. As discussed in Chapter 10, when a corporation wants to borrow or raise funds, it may decide to issue long-term debt or equity instruments. It then usually hires an investment bank to facilitate the issuance and subsequent sale of the securities. (Despite its name, an investment bank is not a bank in the ordinary sense; that is, it is not a financial intermediary that takes in deposits and then lends them out.) Some of the well-known investment banking firms are Morgan Stanley, Merrill Lynch, Salomon Brothers, First Boston Corporation, and Goldman, Sachs.

In the early 1800s, most American securities had to be sold in Europe. As a result, most securities firms developed from merchants who operated securities businesses as a sideline to their primary business. For example, the Morgans built their initial fortune with the railroads. To help raise the money to finance railroad expansion, J. P. Morgan's father resided in London and sold Morgan railroad securities to European investors. Over time, the profitability of the securities businesses became evident, and the securities industry expanded.

Prior to the Great Depression, many large money center banks in New York sold securities and simultaneously conducted conventional banking activities. During the depression, about 10,000 banks failed (about 40% of all commercial banks), and the Banking Act of 1933, popularly known as the **Glass-Steagall Act** after the bill's sponsors, was passed to separate commercial banking from investment banking.

The Glass-Steagall Act made it illegal for a commercial bank to buy or sell securities on behalf of its customers. The original reasoning behind this legislation was to insulate commercial banks from the greater risk inherent in the securities business. There were also concerns that conflicts of interest might arise that would subject commercial banks to increased risk. For example, suppose that an investment banker working at a commercial bank made a mistake pricing a new stock offering. After promising the customer that he could sell the stock for $20, no sales materialized. There might be a temptation for the investment banker to go down the hall to the commercial bank's investment department and talk a manager there into bailing him out. This would subject depositors to the risk that the bank could lose money on poor investments.

Regulators thought another problem existed. Suppose that the investment banker still cannot sell all of that $20 stock issue. He could call up bank customers and offer to lend them 100% of the funds needed to buy a portion of the stock issue. This would not cause a problem if the stock price rose in the future, but if it fell, the bank would be undercollateralized because the value of the securities would be less than the amount of the loan and the customer may not feel a great obligation to repay the loan. Many industry observers felt that this practice was partly to blame for some of the bank failures that occurred during the depression. However, bank lobbyists currently argue that because only large banks were involved in issuing securities and most banks that failed were small, there is no evidence that security abuses led directly to any bank failures.

When the Glass-Steagall Act separated commercial banking from investment banking, new securities firms were created, many of which currently offer both investment banking services (selling new securities to the public) and brokerage services (selling existing securities to the public). We discuss each type of business separately because they tend to be relatively specialized.

Underwriting Stocks and Bonds

In Chapter 10, we learned that the primary function of investment bankers is underwriting securities. The process of underwriting a stock or bond issue requires that the securities firm *purchase* the entire issue at a predetermined price and then resell it in the market. A number of services are provided in the process of underwriting.

Giving Advice Most firms do not issue capital market securities very frequently. Over 80% of all corporate expansion is financed using profits retained from prior-period earnings. As a result, the financial managers at most firms are not familiar with how to proceed with a new security offering. Investment bankers, who participate in this market daily, can provide advice to firms contemplating a sale. For instance, a firm may not know if it should raise capital by selling stocks or by selling bonds. The investment bankers may be able to help by pointing out, for example, that the market is currently paying high prices for stocks in the firm's industry, while bonds are currently carrying relatively high interest rates (and therefore low prices).

Firms may also need advice as to *when* securities should be offered. If, for example, competitors have recently released earnings reports that show poor profits, it may be better to wait before attempting a sale: Firms want to sell stock when it will obtain the highest possible price. Again, because of daily interaction with the securities markets, investment bankers should be able to advise firms on the timing of their offerings.

Possibly the most difficult advice an investment banker must give a customer concerns at what *price* the security should be sold. Here the investment banker and the issuing firm have somewhat differing motives. The firm wants to sell the stock for the highest price possible. Suppose that you started a firm and ran it well for 20 years. You now wish to sell it to the public and retire to Tahiti. If 500,000 shares are to be offered and sold at $10 each, you will receive $5 million for your company. If you can sell the stock for $12, you will receive $6 million.

The investment bankers, however, do not want to overprice the stock because in most underwriting agreements, the investment bankers will buy the entire issue at the agreed price and then resell it through their brokerage houses. They earn a profit by selling the stock at a slightly higher price than they paid the issuing firm. If the issue is priced too high, the investment bank will not be able to resell, and it will suffer a loss.

Pricing securities is not too hard if the firm has prior issues currently selling in the market, called **seasoned issues.** When a firm issues stock for the first time in an *initial public offering (IPO),* it is much more difficult to determine what the correct price should be. All of the skill and expertise of the investment banking firm will be used to determine the most appropriate price. If the issuing firm and the investment banking firm can come to agreement on a price, the investment banker can assist with the next stage, filing the required documents.

Filing Documents In addition to advising companies, investment bankers will assist with making the required Securities and Exchange Commission filings. The activities of investment banks and the operation of primary markets are heavily regulated by the SEC, which was created by the Securities and Exchange Acts of 1933 and 1934 to ensure that adequate information reaches prospective investors. Issuers of new securities to the general public (for amounts greater than $1.5 million in a year and with a maturity longer than 270 days) must file a **registration statement** with the SEC. This statement contains information about the firm's financial condition, management, competition, industry, and experience. The firm also discloses what the funds will be used for and management's assessment of the risk of the securities. The SEC will review the registration statement, and if it does not object during a 20-day waiting period, the securities can then be sold.

The SEC review in no way represents an endorsement of the offering by the SEC. Approval merely means that all of the required statements and disclosures have been made. Nor does SEC approval mean that the information is accurate. Inaccuracies in the registration statement open the issuing firm's management up to lawsuits if investors incur losses. In extreme cases, inaccuracies could result in criminal charges.

A portion of the registration statement is reproduced and made available to investors for review. This widely circulated document is called a **prospectus** (see Figure 1). By law, investors must be given a prospectus before they can invest in a new security.

While the registration document is in the process of obtaining approval, the investment banker has other chores to attend to. For issues of debt, the investment banker must do the following:

- Secure a credit rating from one or more of the credit review companies such as Standard and Poor's or Moody's
- Hire a bond counsel, who will issue a statement attesting to the legality of the issue
- Select a trustee who is responsible for seeing that the issuer fulfills its obligations as stated in the security's contract
- Have the securities printed and prepared for distribution

For equity issues, the investment banker may arrange for the securities to appear on one of the stock exchanges. Clearly, the investment banker can be of great assistance to an issuer well before any securities are actually offered for sale.

Underwriting Once all of the paper work has been completed, the investment banker can proceed with the actual underwriting of the issue. At a prespecified time and date, the issuer will sell all of the stock or bond issue to the investment banking firm at the agreed price. The investment banker must now distribute this issue to the public at a greater price to earn a profit. The ten largest underwriters in the United States are listed in Table 1.

Information contained herein is subject to completion or amendment. A registration statement relating to these securities has been filed with the Securities and Exchange Commission. These securities may not be sold nor may offers to buy be accepted prior to the time the registration statement becomes effective. This prospectus shall not constitute an offer to sell or the solicitation of an offer to buy nor shall there be any sale of these securities in any State in which such offer, solicitation or sale would be unlawful prior to registration or qualification under the securities laws of any such State.

SUBJECT TO COMPLETION, DATED JUNE 19, 1996

2,500,000 Shares

LaserVision®
CENTERS

Common Stock

The 2,500,000 shares of common stock, par value $0.01 per share (the "Common Stock"), offered hereby (this "Offering") are being offered by Laser Vision Centers, Inc. (the "Company"). The Common Stock has been approved for quotation on the Nasdaq National Market under the symbol "LVCI" upon consummation of this Offering. The Common Stock is currently traded on the over-the-counter market through Nasdaq under the symbol "LVCI" and on the Boston Stock Exchange under the symbol "LVS." On June 17, 1996, the last reported sale price of the Common Stock by Nasdaq was $13 per share. See "Price Range of Common Stock and Dividend Policy."

For a discussion of certain risks of an investment in the shares of Common Stock offered hereby, see "Risk Factors" on pages 6 to 12.

THESE SECURITIES HAVE NOT BEEN APPROVED OR DISAPPROVED BY THE SECURITIES AND EXCHANGE COMMISSION OR ANY STATE SECURITIES COMMISSION NOR HAS THE SECURITIES AND EXCHANGE COMMISSION OR ANY STATE SECURITIES COMMISSION PASSED UPON THE ACCURACY OR ADEQUACY OF THIS PROSPECTUS. ANY REPRESENTATION TO THE CONTRARY IS A CRIMINAL OFFENSE.

	Price to Public	Underwriting Discounts and Commissions*	Proceeds to Company†
Per Share	$	$	$
Total‡	$	$	$

* The Company and certain stockholders of the Company (the "Selling Stockholders") have agreed to indemnify the Underwriters against certain liabilities, including liabilities under the Securities Act of 1933, as amended. See "Underwriting."

† Before deducting expenses of this Offering payable by the Company estimated to be $320,000.

‡ The Company and the Selling Stockholders have granted the Underwriters a 30-day option to purchase up to 375,000 additional shares of Common Stock on the same terms per share solely to cover over-allotments, if any. If such option is exercised in full, the total price to public will be $, the total underwriting discounts and commission will be $, the total proceeds to the Company will be $ and the total proceeds to the Selling Stockholders will be $ See "Underwriting."

The Common Stock is being offered by the Underwriters as set forth under "Underwriting" herein. It is expected that the delivery of certificates therefor will be made at the offices of Dillon, Read & Co. Inc., New York, New York on or about , 1996. The Underwriters include:

Dillon, Read & Co. Inc. **A.G. Edwards & Sons, Inc.**

The date of this Prospectus is , 1996

FIGURE 1 Front Page of a Prospectus

■ TABLE 1 Top Ten Underwriters of U.S. Debt and Equity Issues, 1994

Underwriter	Market Share (%)
1. Merrill Lynch	16.5
2. Lehman Brothers	11.1
3. Crédit Suisse First Boston	10.4
4. Goldman, Sachs	9.1
5. Morgan Stanley	8.3
6. Salomon Brothers	8.1
7. Kidder Peabody	6.9
8. Bear, Stearns	4.8
9. J. P. Morgan	3.7
10. Donaldson, Lufkin & Jenrette	3.3
Total for top ten	82.2

Source: Wall Street Journal, January 3, 1995, p. C1.

The investment banking firm is clearly taking a huge risk at this point. One way that they can reduce the risk is by forming a **syndicate.** A syndicate is a group of investment banking firms each of which buys a portion of the security issue. Each firm in the syndicate is then responsible for reselling its share of the securities. Most securities issues are sold by syndicates because it is such an effective way to spread the risk among many firms.

Investment banks advertise upcoming securities offerings with block ads in the *Wall Street Journal.* These ads, called **tombstones** because of their shape and their stark text-only format, list all of the primary investment banking firms included in the syndicate. Review the tombstone reproduced in the "Following the Financial News" box. Notice the prominent statement "This announcement is not an offer of securities for sale or a solicitation of an offer to buy securities." The actual offer to sell can be made only in the prospectus. Also note the large number of investment banking firms involved in the syndicate.

The longer the investment banker holds the securities before reselling them to the public, the greater the risk that a drop in the price will cause losses. One way that the investment banking firm speeds the sale is to solicit offers to buy the securities from investors prior to the date the investment bankers actually take ownership. Then, when the securities are available, the orders are filled and the securities are quickly transferred to the final buyers.

Most investment bankers are attached to larger brokerage houses (multifunction securities firms) that have nationwide sales offices. Each of these offices will be contacted prior to the issue date, and the sales agents will contact their customers to see if they would like to review a prospectus on the new security. The goal is to subscribe (sell off) the entire issue. A **fully subscribed** issue is one for which all of the securities available for sale have been spoken for before the issue date. An issue may be **undersubscribed** if the sales agents have been unable to generate sufficient interest among their customers to sell all of the securities by the issue date. An issue may also be **oversubscribed,** in which case there are more offers to buy than there are securities available.

It is tempting to assume that the best alternative is for an issue to be oversubscribed, but in fact this will alienate the investment banker's customers.

New Securities Issues

Information about new securities being issued is presented in distinctive advertisements published in the *Wall Street Journal* and other newspapers. These advertisements, called "tombstones" because of their appearance, are typically found in the "Money and Investing" section of the *Journal*.

The tombstone shown here indicates the number of shares of stock being issued (2,862,907 shares for Marquette Medical Systems, Inc.) and the investment banks involved in selling them. Three of the most important investment banks (listed in the middle of the advertisement) are involved in underwriting these securities.

This announcement is not an offer of securities for sale or a solicitation of an offer to buy securities.

March 17, 1997

2,862,907 Shares

Marquette Medical Systems, Inc.

Common Stock

Price $18.375 per share

———

Copies of the prospectus may be obtained from such of the undersigned (who are among the underwriters named in the prospectus) as may legally offer these securities under applicable securities laws.

Dillon, Read & Co. Inc.

Bear, Stearns & Co. Inc.

Robert W. Baird & Co.
Incorporated

Alex. Brown & Sons Incorporated	**Credit Suisse First Boston**	**Dean Witter Reynolds Inc.**
Donaldson, Lufkin & Jenrette Securities Corporation	**Goldman, Sachs & Co.**	**Hambrecht & Quist**
Lazard Frères & Co. LLC	**Merrill Lynch & Co.**	**J.P. Morgan & Co.**
Oppenheimer & Co., Inc.		**Prudential Securities Incorporated**
Robertson, Stephens & Company LLC		**Schroder Wertheim & Co.**
Smith Barney Inc.		**Wasserstein Perella Securities, Inc.**
Cowen & Company	**Fahnestock & Co. Inc.**	**Gerard Klauer Mattison & Co., Inc.**
Needham & Company, Inc.	**Brean Murray & Co., Inc.**	**C.L. King & Associates, Inc.**
Pennsylvania Merchant Group Ltd		**H.G. Wellington & Co. Inc.**

Suppose that you were issuing a security for the first time and had negotiated with your investment banker to sell the issue of 500,000 shares of stock at $20. Now you find out that the issue is oversubscribed. You would feel that the investment banker had set the price too low and that you had lost money as a result. Maybe the stock could have sold for $25 and you could have collected an extra $2.5 million ([$25 − $20] × 500,000 = $2,500,000). You, as well as other issuing firms, would be unlikely to use this investment banker in the future.

It is equally serious for an issue to be undersubscribed, if, to sell all of the securities to the public, it becomes necessary to lower the price below the price the investment bankers paid to the issuer. The investment banking firm stands to lose extremely large amounts of money because of the volume of securities involved. For example, review the tombstone shown in the "Following the Financial News" box once more. A total of 2,862,907 shares are being offered for sale at $18.375 a share. If the price must be lowered by even 25 cents per share, almost $716,000 would be lost. The high risk taken by investment bankers explains why they tend to be the most elite and highest-paid professionals on Wall Street.

Best Efforts An alternative to underwriting securities offerings is to offer them under a *best-efforts agreement*. In a best-efforts agreement, the investment banker sells the securities on a commission basis with no guarantee regarding the price the issuing firm will receive. The advantage to the investment banker of a best-efforts transaction is that there is no risk of mispricing the security. There is also no need for the time-consuming task of establishing the market value of the security. The investment banker simply markets the security at the price the customer asks. If the security fails to sell, the offering can be canceled.

Private Placements

In Chapter 11 we discussed an alternative method of selling securities called the *private placement*. In a private placement, securities are sold to a limited number of investors rather than to the public at large. The advantage of the private placement is that the security does not need to be registered with the SEC as long as certain restrictive requirements are met. Investment bankers are also often involved in private placement transactions. Although investment bankers are not required for a private placement, they often facilitate the transaction by advising the issuing firm on the appropriate terms for the issue and by identifying potential purchasers.

The buyers of private placements must be big enough to purchase large amounts of securities at one time. This means that the usual buyers are insurance companies, commercial banks, pension funds, and mutual funds. Private placements are more common for the sale of bonds than for stocks. Goldman, Sachs is the most active investment banking firm in the private placement market.

Mergers and Acquisitions

Investment banks have been active in the **mergers and acquisitions market** since the 1960s. Mergers and acquisitions refers to the process where two firms are combined to form one. Often this process is friendly, and the firms agree that certain economies can be captured by combining resources. At other times, the firm being purchased may resist. Resisted takeovers are called *hostile*. In these cases, the acquirer attempts to purchase sufficient shares of the target firm to gain a majority of the seats on the board of directors. Board members are then able to vote to merge the target firm with the acquiring firm.

Investment bankers serve both acquirers and target firms. Acquiring firms require help locating attractive firms to pursue, soliciting shareholders to sell their shares in a process called a *tender offer,* and raising the required capital to complete the transaction. Target firms may hire investment bankers to help ward off undesired takeover attempts.

The mergers and acquisitions market requires very specialized knowledge and expertise. Investment bankers involved in this market are highly trained (and, not incidentally, highly paid). The best-known investment banker involved in mergers and acquisitions is Michael R. Milken, who worked at Drexel Burnham Lambert, Inc. Milken is credited with inventing the junk bond market, which we discussed in Chapter 10. *Junk bonds* are high-risk, high-return debt securities that were used primarily to finance takeover attempts. By allowing companies to raise large amounts of capital, even small firms could pursue and take over large ones. During the 1980s, when Milken was most active in this market, merger and acquisition activity peaked. On February 13, 1990, Drexel Burnham Lambert filed for bankruptcy due to rising default rates on its portfolio of junk bonds, a slow economy, and regulations that forced the savings and loan industry out of the junk bond market. Milken pleaded guilty to securities fraud and was sent to prison.

As a result of the collapse of Drexel Burnham Lambert and the junk bond market, merger and acquisition activity slowed during the early 1990s. More recently, a healthy economy and regulatory changes have caused a resurgence, especially among commercial banks.

■ SECURITIES BROKERS AND DEALERS

Securities brokers and dealers conduct trading in secondary markets. *Brokers* are pure middlemen who act as agents for investors in the purchase or sale of securities. Their function is to match buyers with sellers, a function for which they are paid brokerage commissions.

In contrast to brokers, dealers link buyers and sellers by standing ready to buy and sell securities at given prices. Therefore, dealers hold inventories of securities and make their living by selling these securities for a slightly higher price than they paid for them—that is, on the *spread* between the *bid price,* the price that the broker pays for securities they buy for their inventory, and the *asked price,* the price they receive when they sell the securities. This is a high-risk business because dealers hold securities that can rise or fall in price; in recent years, several firms specializing in bonds have collapsed. Brokers, by contrast, are not as exposed to risk because they do not own the securities involved in their business dealings.[1]

Brokerage Services

Securities brokers offer several types of services.

Securities Orders If you call a securities brokerage house to buy a stock, you will speak with a broker who will take your order. You have three primary types of transactions available: market orders, limit orders, and short sells.

The two most common types of securities orders are the market order and the limit order. When you place a **market order,** you are instructing your agent to buy or sell the security at the current market price. When placing a market order,

---

[1]It is easy to remember the distinction between dealers and brokers if you relate to auto dealers and real estate brokers. Auto *dealers* take ownership of the cars and resell them to the public. Real estate *brokers* do not take ownership of the property; they just act as go-betweens.

there is a risk that the price of the security may have changed significantly from what it was when you made your investment decision. If you are buying a stock and the price falls, no harm is done, but if the price goes up, you may regret your decision. The most notable occasion when prices changed between when orders were placed and when they were filled was during the October 19, 1987 stock crash. Panicked investors told their brokers to sell their stocks, but the transaction volume was so great that day that many orders were not filled until hours after they were placed. By the time they were filled, the price of the stocks had often fallen far below what they were at the time the original orders were placed.

An alternative to the market order is the **limit order.** Here buy orders specify a *maximum* acceptable price and sell orders specify a *minimum* acceptable price. For example, you could place a limit order to sell your 100 shares of IBM at $100. If the current market price of IBM is less than $100, the order will not be filled. Unfilled limit orders are reported to the stock specialist, who works that particular stock on the exchange. When the stock price moves in such a way that limit orders are activated, the stock specialist initiates the trade.

When investors believe that the price of a stock will rise in the future, they buy that stock and hold it until the increase occurs. They can then sell at a profit and capture a gain for their effort. What can be done if an investor is convinced that a stock will *fall* in the future? The solution is to sell short. A **short sell** requires that the investor borrow stocks from a brokerage house and sell them today, with the promise of replacing the borrowed stocks by buying them in the future. Suppose that you just tried out the new Apple notebook computer and decided that it would sell poorly (in fact, in 1995, Apple had to recall all of its Powerbook computers to fix problems). You might believe that as the rest of the market learned of the poor product, the price of Apple's stock could decline. To take advantage of this situation, you might instruct your broker to short Apple 100 shares. The broker would then borrow 100 shares from another investor on your behalf and sell them at current market prices. You do not own those shares, of course. They are borrowed and at some point in the future, you would be required to purchase those 100 shares at the new market price to replace them. If you were right and the price of Apple declined, you would buy the shares at a lower price than you received for their earlier sale and would earn a profit. Market and limit orders allow you to take advantage of stock price *increases,* and short sells allow you to take advantage of stock price *decreases.* Analysts track the number of short positions taken on a stock as an indicator of the number of investors who feel that a stock's price is likely to fall in the future.

Other Services In addition to trading in securities, stockbrokers provide a variety of other services. Investors typically leave their securities in storage with the broker for safekeeping. If the securities are left with the broker, they are insured against loss by the Securities Investor Protection Corporation (SIPC), an agency of the federal government. This guarantee is not against loss in value, only against loss of the securities themselves.

Brokers also provide **margin credit.** Margin credit refers to loans advanced by the brokerage house to help investors buy securities. For example, if you are certain that Intel Corporation stock was going to rise rapidly when its latest computer chip is introduced, you could increase the amount of stock you can buy by borrowing from the brokerage house. If you had $5,000 and borrowed an additional $5,000, you could buy $10,000 worth of stock. Then if the price goes up as you predict, you could earn nearly twice as much as without the loan. The Federal Reserve sets the percentage of the stock purchase price that brokerage houses can lend. Interest rates on margin loans are usually 1 or 2 percentage points above the prime interest rate (the rate charged large, creditworthy corporate borrowers).

The forces of competition have led brokerage firms to offer services and engage in activities traditionally conducted by commercial banks. In 1977, Merrill Lynch developed the cash management account (CMA), which provides a package of financial services that includes credit cards, immediate loans, check-writing privileges, automatic investment of proceeds from the sale of securities in a money market mutual fund, and unified record keeping. CMAs were adopted by other brokerage firms and spread rapidly. Many of these accounts allow check-writing privileges and offer ATM and debit cards. In these ways, they compete directly with banks.

As a result of CMAs, the distinction between banking activities and the activities of nonbank financial institutions has become blurred. Walter Wriston, former head of Citicorp (the largest bank holding company in the country), has been quoted as saying, "The bank of the future already exists, and it's called Merrill Lynch."[2]

The advantage of brokerage-based cash management accounts is that they make it easier to buy and sell securities. The stockbroker can take funds out of the account when an investor buys a security and put the money into the account when the investor sells securities.

Full-Service Versus Discount Brokers   Prior to May 1, 1975, virtually all brokerage houses charged the same commissions on trades. Brokerage houses distinguished themselves primarily on the basis of their research and customer relations. In May 1975, Congress determined that fixed commissions were anticompetitive and passed the Securities Acts Amendment of 1975, which abolished fixed commissions. Now brokerage houses may charge whatever fees they choose. This has resulted in two distinct types of brokerage firms: full-service and discount.

Full-service brokers provide research and investment advice to their customers. Full-service brokers will often mail weekly and monthly market reports and recommendations to their customers in an effort to encourage them to invest in certain securities. For example, when the investment banking department of the brokerage house has an initial public offering available, brokers will contact customers they feel may be interested and offer to send a prospectus. Full-service brokers attempt to establish a long-term relationship with their customers and to help them assemble portfolios that are consistent with their financial needs and risk preferences. Of course, this extra attention is costly and must be paid for by requiring higher fees for initiating trades. Merrill Lynch is the biggest of the full-service brokers.

---

[2]Banking Takes a Beating. *Time,* December 3, 1984, p. 50.

Discount brokers simply execute trades on request. If you want to buy a particular security, you call the discount broker and place your request. No advice or research is typically provided. Because the cost of operating a discount brokerage firm is significantly less than the cost of operating a full-service firm, lower transaction costs are charged. These fees may be as little as half the fees charged by a full-service broker. Charles Schwab & Company is the best-known discount broker. Many discount brokerage firms are owned by large commercial banks, which have historically been prohibited from offering full-service brokerage services.

Securities Dealers

Securities dealers hold inventories of securities, which they sell to customers who want to buy. They also hold securities purchased from customers who want to sell.

It is impossible to overemphasize the importance of dealers to the smooth functioning of the U.S. financial markets. Consider what an investor demands before buying a security. In addition to requiring a fair return, the investor wants to know that the investment is *liquid*—that it can be sold quickly if it no longer fits into the investor's portfolio. Consider a small, relatively unknown firm that is trying to sell securities to the public. An investor may be tempted to buy the firm's securities, but if these securities cannot be resold easily, it is unlikely that the investor will take a chance on them. This is where the dealers become crucial. They stand ready to make a market in the security at any time—that is, they make sure that an investor can always sell or buy a security. For this reason, dealers are also called **market makers.** When an investor wishes to sell a thinly traded stock (one without an active secondary market), it is unlikely that another investor is simultaneously seeking to buy that security. This nonsynchronous trading problem is solved when the dealer buys the security from the investor and holds it in inventory until another investor is ready to buy it. The knowledge that dealers will provide this service encourages investors to buy securities that would be otherwise unacceptable. In countries with less well developed financial markets, where dealers will not make a market for less popular securities, it is extremely difficult for small, new, or regional firms to raise funds. Securities market dealers are largely responsible for the health and growth of small businesses in the United States.

■ REGULATION OF SECURITIES FIRMS

Many financial firms engage in all three securities market activities, acting as brokers, dealers, and investment bankers. The largest in the United States is Merrill Lynch; other well-known firms include PaineWebber, Dean Witter Reynolds, and Smith Barney. The SEC not only regulates the firms' investment banking operations but also restricts brokers and dealers from misrepresenting securities and from trading on *insider information,* unpublicized facts known only to the management of a corporation.

Two acts passed in 1933 and 1934 provide the primary basis for regulation of today's securities markets. These acts were passed shortly after the Great Depression and were largely responding to abuses that many people at the time felt were partly responsible for the economic troubles the country was suffering.

When discussing regulation, it is important to recognize that the public's confidence in the integrity of the financial markets is critical to the growth of our economy and the ability of firms to continue using the markets to raise new capital. If the public believes that there are other powerful players with superior information who can take advantage of smaller investors, the market will be unable to attract funds from these smaller investors. Ultimately, the markets could fail entirely.

The securities acts were designed with two goals: to protect the integrity of the markets and to restrict competition among securities firms so that they would be less likely to fail. The principal provisions of the acts are these:

- To establish the Securities and Exchange Commission (SEC), which is charged with administering securities laws
- To require that issuers register new securities offerings and that they disclose all relevant information to potential investors
- To require that all publicly held corporations file annual and semiannual reports with the SEC; publicly held corporations must also file a report whenever any event occurs of "significant interest" to investors
- To require that insiders file reports whenever shares are bought or sold
- To prohibit any form of market manipulation

Prior to the passage of these acts, the market was subject to much abuse. For example, a study conducted in 1933 showed evidence of 127 "investment pools" operating during 1932 alone. An investment pool is formed to manipulate the market. A group of investors band together and spread false but damaging rumors about the health of a firm. These rumors drive the price of the firm's stock down. When the price is depressed, the members of the pool buy the stock. Once they all hold shares purchased at artificially low prices, the members of the pool release good news about the company so that the price of the stock rises. Obviously, the members of the pool stand to earn huge profits. Small, uninformed investors lose. Practices such as these were outlawed by the securities acts of 1933 and 1934.

As noted in our discussion of private placements, not all securities issues are subject to SEC oversight. SEC registration is not required if less than $1.5 million in securities are issued per year, if the securities mature in less than 270 days, or if the securities are issued by the U.S. government or most municipalities.

Other legislation of significance to securities firms include the Glass-Steagall Act of 1933, which separated commercial and investment banking; the Investment Advisors Act of 1940, which required investment advisers to register with the SEC; and the Securities Protection Corporation Act of 1970, which established the Securities Investor Protection Corporation, which insures customers of securities firms from losses to their cash accounts up to $100,000 and from losses of securities documents up to $500,000. Other regulations related specifically to banks but of interest to securities firms are discussed in Chapter 13.

■ RELATIONSHIP BETWEEN SECURITIES FIRMS AND COMMERCIAL BANKS

For many years, commercial banks have lobbied for legislative relief to enable them to compete with securities firms. Consider how the business of banking has been eroded. Prior to the introduction of cash management accounts at Merrill Lynch, the only source of checking accounts was a bank. The Merrill Lynch account not only provided low-cost checking but also paid interest that was higher than the law permitted banks to pay. Securities firms were allowed to make loans, offer credit and debit cards, provide ATM access, and, most important, sell securities. In addition, securities firms could sell some types of insurance. It is not hard to understand why bankers were frustrated. Regulations prevented them from competing with securities firms, but no laws restricted securities firms from competing with banks.

Commercial banks clamored on Capitol Hill for a "level playing field." As noted in Chapter 16, regulatory relief in 1980 and 1982 substantially slowed the movement of funds from commercial banks to securities firms; however, banks were still not permitted to sell securities. This is gradually changing.

Recent legislation, court rulings, and regulatory decisions have provided commercial banks with limited authority to engage in investment banking activities. In the 1980s, court rulings granted commercial banks opportunities to act as investment advisers and provide brokerage services. The Supreme Court ruled in 1981 that bank holding companies could serve as advisers to investment companies. In 1984, the Supreme Court ruled that as long as a bank does not offer investment advice, it can provide discount brokerage services. Appeals courts subsequently ruled that a bank subsidiary could offer advice. In November 1986, the Federal Reserve ruled that Sumitomo Bank, a Japanese bank, could invest $500 million in Goldman, Sachs, a U.S. investment banking firm. And in June 1987, the Fed granted approval to three bank holding companies—Citicorp, Bankers Trust, and J. P. Morgan Guaranty—to underwrite certain securities that were prohibited by the 1933 act: commercial paper, certain municipal revenue bonds, mortgage-backed securities, and asset-backed securities. The holding companies were required to set up separate fully capitalized subsidiaries. In 1988, the U.S. Supreme Court upheld this approval, ruling that the wording of the Glass-Steagall Act permits limited underwriting and sales activities.

Many banks have been aggressively expanding their brokerage service activities in light of these changes. The most common new service is the marketing of mutual funds to bank customers. As of June 30, 1994, banks managed $227 billion in mutual fund assets. Though this is still a small percentage of the $2,086 billion in total funds under management, it represents a growing trend.

As a result of this regulatory forbearance, banks are also acquiring interest in brokerage houses and establishing relationships that are so close that customers may not even be aware that they are not dealing directly with the bank. This trend is likely to continue and poses a serious competitive threat to securities firms. Commercial banks have already established a relationship with millions of customers, many of whom would be happy to deal with one financial institution for their financial investments.

■ INVESTMENT FUNDS

The major brokerage houses, independent securities firms, and banks all offer a wide variety of mutual funds. *Mutual funds* pool the resources of many small investors by selling these investors shares and using the proceeds to buy securities. Through the asset transformation process of issuing shares in small denominations and buying large blocks of securities, mutual funds can take advantage of volume discounts on brokerage commissions and can purchase diversified portfolios of securities. Mutual funds allow the small investor to obtain the benefits of lower transaction costs in purchasing securities and to take advantage of the reduction of risk by diversifying the portfolio of securities held.

Mutual funds have greatly increased their holdings of stocks since 1980. The primary source of this growth has been the booming stock market; another has been the appearance of mutual funds that specialize in debt instruments (which first appeared in the 1970s). Before 1970, mutual funds invested almost solely in common stocks. Funds that purchase common stocks may specialize even further and invest solely in foreign securities or in specialized industries, such as energy or high technology. Funds that purchase debt instruments may specialize further in corporate, U.S. government, or tax-exempt municipal bonds or in long-term or short-term securities.[3] Currently, more than 5700 separate mutual funds are available to investors. This means that there are more distinct funds than there are stocks listed on the New York Stock Exchange and the American Stock Exchange combined. Figure 2 traces the increase in the number of separate mutual funds after 1960.

Types of Investment Funds

As the popularity of mutual funds has grown, so has the competition among them for investment dollars. Since most funds charge fees based on the dollars they manage, the greater the amount managed, the greater the fees earned. To attract investors, funds are established to appeal to a wide variety of investment strategies and goals. The major types of funds are summarized here.

Balanced Funds Balanced funds hold both stocks and bonds. These funds are often less risky than other types of funds. They provide more income each period but less capital appreciation. They tend to be popular with retired investors.

Bond Funds Bond funds hold only bonds. Since bonds have regular fixed payments, investors in bond funds receive a constant flow of income.

Value Funds These funds attempt to locate stocks with low price-earnings ratios and low market-to-book ratios. They represent an investment strategy that claims greater returns are possible from securities that are relatively less popular with other investors, as indicated by these ratios.

---

[3]Tax-exempt bond funds did not appear until after 1976, when a change in the tax law allowed mutual funds to pass through to shareholders the tax exemption on the interest income from municipal bonds.

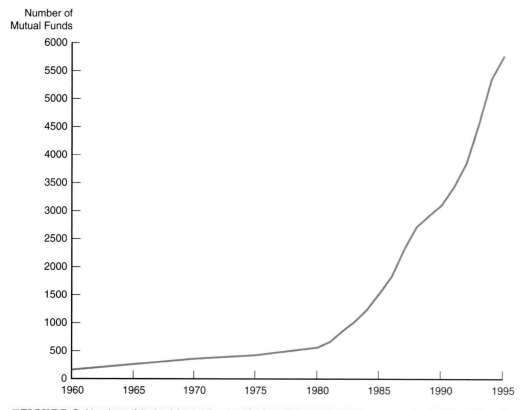

■FIGURE 2 Number of Active Mutual Funds, 1960–1995

Source: Investment Company Institute.

Growth Funds These funds attempt to locate stocks that will experience unusually rapid growth in the future. Because the firms in these funds are usually in a growth stage of their development, they seldom pay dividends. These funds are often more risky than other types of investment funds because it has proved difficult to identify firms that will continue to experience rapid growth.

Growth and Income Funds These funds seek to balance the risk of identifying growth stocks with the more stable income provided by mature firms that pay dividends.

Index Funds Index funds are rapidly becoming among the most popular type of investment funds. The managers of index funds simply buy the securities that are included in some popular stock index, such as the S&P 500. The only buying or selling is when a stock enters or leaves the index or when price changes require that the fund be re-balanced. Since no research or aggressive management is required of these funds, lower fees are charged. Research suggests that due to the lower fees, these funds outperform the more actively managed funds.

Money Market Mutual Funds These funds invest only in money market securities. There is very low risk and very low returns. (Money market mutual funds are discussed in more detail in Chapter 9.)

Figure 3 shows the distribution of assets by type of fund in 1986 and 1995. We can observe that the proportion of funds invested in equities has dramatically increased while the proportion invested in bonds and money market securities has decreased. This shift is due to the relatively low rates available on money market and bond securities in 1995.

Fee Structure of Investment Funds

Mutual funds are structured in two ways. The most common structure is an **open-end fund,** from which shares can be redeemed at any time at a price that is tied to the asset value of the fund. A mutual fund can also be structured as a **closed-end fund,** in which a fixed number of nonredeemable shares are sold at an initial offering and are then traded in the over-the-counter market like common stock. The market price of these shares fluctuates with the value of the assets held by the fund. In contrast to the open-end fund, however, the price of the shares may be above or below the value of the assets held by the fund, depending on factors such as the liquidity of the shares or the quality of the management. The greater popularity of the open-end funds is explained by the greater liquidity of their redeemable shares relative to the nonredeemable shares of closed-end funds.

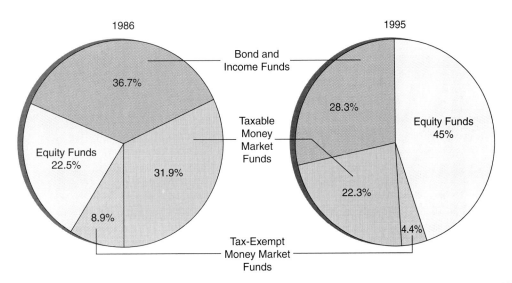

■FIGURE 3 Distribution of Mutual Fund Net Assets, by Type of Fund

Source: Investment Company Institute.

Originally, shares of most open-end mutual funds were sold by salespeople (usually brokers) who were paid a commission. Because this commission is paid at the time of purchase and is immediately subtracted from the redemption value of the shares, these funds are called **load funds.** Most mutual funds are currently **no-load funds;** the funds sell directly to the public (bypassing brokers) with no sales commissions. In both types of funds, the managers earn their living from management fees paid by the shareholders. These fees amount to 0.5% to 2% of the asset value of the fund per year. One important element in evaluating mutual funds is reviewing their fee structure.

APPLICATION   CALCULATING A MUTUAL FUND'S NET ASSET VALUE

If you invest in a mutual fund, you will receive periodic statements summarizing the activity in your account. The statement will show funds that were added to your investment balance, funds that were withdrawn, and any earnings that have accrued. One term on the statement that is critical to understanding the invest-ment's performance is the **net asset value** *(NAV)*. The net asset value is the total value of the mutual fund's stocks, bonds, cash, and other assets minus any liabili-ties such as accrued fees, divided by the number of shares outstanding. An exam-ple will make this clear.

Suppose that a mutual fund has the following assets and liabilities:

Stock (at current market value)	$20,000,000
Bonds (at current market value)	$10,000,000
Cash	$ 500,000
Total value of assets	$30,500,000
Liabilities	−$ 300,000
Net worth	$30,200,000

The net asset value is computed by dividing the net worth by the number of shares outstanding. If 10 million shares are outstanding, the net asset value is $3.02 ($30,200,000/10,000,000 = $3.02).

The net asset value rises and falls as the value of the underlying assets change. For example, suppose that the value of the stock portfolio held by the mutual fund rises by 10% and the value of the bond portfolio falls by 2% over the course of a year. If the cash and liabilities are unchanged, the new net asset value will be

Stock (at current market value)	$22,000,000
Bonds (at current market value)	$ 9,800,000
Cash	$ 500,000
Total value of assets	$32,300,000
Liabilities	−$ 300,000
Net worth	$32,000,000

$$NAV = \frac{\$32,000,000}{10,000,000} = \$3.20$$

The yield on your investment in the mutual fund is then

$$\text{Yield} = \frac{\$3.20 - \$3.02}{\$3.02} = \frac{\$0.18}{\$3.02} = 5.96\%$$

When you buy and sell shares in the mutual fund, you do so at the current *NAV.*

Regulation of Mutual Funds

Mutual funds are regulated by the Securities and Exchange Commission, which was given the ability to exercise almost complete control over investment companies in the Investment Company Act of 1940. Regulations require periodic disclosure of information on these funds to the public and restrictions on the methods of soliciting business.

Investment funds are run by brokerage houses and by institutional investors who now control over 50% of the outstanding stock in the United States. Over 70% of the total daily volume in stocks is due to institutions initiating trades. Many of the mutual funds are run by brokerage houses; others are run by independent investment advisers. Because of the volume of stock controlled by these investors, there is tremendous competition for their business. This has led to significant cost cutting and to the proliferation of alternative methods of trading. For example, computerized trading that eliminates the broker from the transaction accounts for a growing percentage of the activity in stocks.

SUMMARY

1. Investment banks are firms that assist in the initial sale of securities in the primary market and, as securities brokers and dealers, assist in the trading of securities in the secondary markets, some of which are organized into exchanges. The Securities and Exchange Commission regulates the financial institutions in the securities markets and ensures that adequate information reaches prospective investors.

2. Underwriting involves the investment banking firm's taking ownership of the stock issue by purchasing all of the shares from the issuer and then reselling them in the market. Issues may be oversubscribed, undersubscribed, or fully subscribed, depending on whether the price is set correctly.

3. Investment bankers assist issuing firms by providing advice, filing documents, and marketing issues. Investment bankers often assist in mergers and acquisitions and in private placements as well.

4. Securities brokers act as go-betweens and do not usually own securities. Securities dealers do buy and sell securities and by doing so make a market. By always having securities to sell and by always being willing to purchase securities, dealers guarantee the liquidity of the market.

5. Investors may place an order, called a *market order,* to buy a security at the current market price. They may also set limits to the lowest price at which they will sell their security or the highest price they will pay for a security. Orders of this type are called *limit orders.*

6. Some brokerage houses provide research and investment advice in addition to conducting trades on behalf of customers. These are called *full-service brokers. Discount brokers* simply place orders. Brokerage houses also store securities, advance loans to buy securities, and offer cash management accounts.

7. Investment funds pool the funds of many small investors and purchase large quantities of securities. These funds offer a wide variety of funds designed to appeal to most investment strategies.

KEY TERMS

QUESTIONS AND PROBLEMS

*1. What was the motivation behind legislation separating commercial banking from investment banking?

2. What law separated investment banking from commercial banking?

*3. What does it mean to say that investment bankers *underwrite* a security offering? How is this different from a best-efforts offering?

4. What are the primary services that an investment banker will provide a firm issuing securities?

*5. Does the fact that a security has passed an SEC review mean that investors can buy the security without having to worry about taking a loss on the investment?

6. Why do investment banking firms often form syndicates for selling securities to the public?

*7. Is it better for a security issue to be fully subscribed or oversubscribed?

8. Why would an investment banker advise a firm to issue a security using best efforts rather than underwriting?

*9. What is the difference between a hostile takeover and a merger?

10. What valuable service do dealers provide that facilitates transaction trading and keeping the markets liquid?

*11. What is the difference between a market order and a limit order?

12. Is it possible to make money if you know that the price of a security will *fall* in the future? How?

*13. Why do commercial banks object to brokerage houses' being allowed to offer many of the same services traditionally reserved for banks?

14. What is an index fund? Why are index funds increasingly popular?

*15. What is the difference between a load fund and a no-load fund?

PART V

The Management of Financial Institutions

CHAPTER 20

RISK MANAGEMENT IN FINANCIAL INSTITUTIONS

PREVIEW Managing financial institutions has never been an easy task, but in recent years it has become even more difficult because of greater uncertainty in the economic environment. Interest rates have become much more volatile, resulting in substantial fluctuations in profits and in the value of assets and liabilities held by financial institutions. Furthermore, as we have seen in Chapter 6, defaults on loans and other debt instruments have also climbed dramatically, leading to large losses at financial institutions. In light of these developments, it is not surprising that financial institution managers have become more concerned about managing the risk their institutions face as a result of greater interest-rate fluctuations and defaults by borrowers.

In this chapter we examine how managers of financial institutions cope with credit risk, the risk arising because borrowers may default on their obligations, and with interest-rate risk, the risk arising from fluctuations in interest rates. We will look at the tools that these managers use to measure risk and the strategies that they employ to reduce it.

MANAGING CREDIT RISK

A major part of the business of financial institutions such as banks, insurance companies, pension funds, and finance companies is making loans. In order for these institutions to earn high profits, they must make successful loans that are paid back in full (and so have low credit risk). The concepts of adverse selection and moral hazard (introduced in Chapter 2) provide a framework for understanding the principles that financial institution managers must follow to minimize credit risk and make successful loans.

Adverse selection is problematic in loan markets because bad credit risks (borrowers most likely to default) are the ones who usually line up for loans—in other words, those who are most likely to produce an *adverse* outcome are the most likely to be *selected*. Borrowers with very risky investment projects in mind have much to gain if their projects are successful, and so they are the most eager to obtain loans. Clearly, however, they are the least desirable borrowers because of the greater possibility that they will be unable to pay back their loans.

Moral hazard is a problem in loan markets because borrowers may have incentives to engage in activities that are undesirable from the lender's point of view. In such situations, it is more likely that the lender will be exposed to the *hazard* of default. Once borrowers have obtained a loan, they are more likely to invest in high-risk investment projects—projects that pay high returns to the borrowers if successful. The high risk, however, makes it less likely that the loan will be paid back.

To be profitable, financial institutions must overcome the adverse selection and moral hazard problems that make loan defaults more likely. The attempts of financial institutions to solve these problems help explain a number of principles for managing credit risk: screening and monitoring, establishment of long-term customer relationships, loan commitments, collateral, compensating balance requirements, and credit rationing.

Screening and Monitoring

Asymmetric information is present in loan markets because lenders have less information about the investment opportunities and activities of borrowers than borrowers do. This situation leads to two information-producing activities by financial institutions: screening and monitoring.

Screening Adverse selection in loan markets requires that financial institutions screen out the bad credit risks from the good ones so that loans will be profitable. To accomplish effective screening, financial institutions must collect reliable information from prospective borrowers. Effective screening and information collection together form an important principle of credit risk management.

When you go into a bank or a finance company to apply for a consumer loan (such as a car loan or a mortgage to purchase a house), the first thing you are asked to do is fill out forms that elicit a great deal of information about your personal finances. You are asked about your salary, bank accounts, other assets (such as cars, insurance policies, and furnishings), and outstanding loans; your record of loan, credit card, and charge account repayments; and the number of years you've worked and who your employers have been. You also are asked personal questions such as your age, marital status, and number of children. The bank or finance company uses this information to evaluate how good a credit risk you are by calculating your "credit score," a statistical measure derived from your answers that predicts whether you are likely to have trouble making your loan payments. Deciding on how good a risk you are cannot be entirely scientific, so the bank or finance company must also use judgment. A loan officer, whose job is to decide whether you should be given the loan, might call your employer or talk to some of the personal references you supplied. The officer might even make a judgment based on your demeanor or your appearance.

The process of screening and collecting information is similar when a financial institution makes a business loan. The loan officer needs to collect information about the company's profits and losses (income) and about its assets and liabilities. The officer also has to evaluate the likely future success of the business. So in addition to obtaining information such as sales figures, the loan officer might ask questions about the company's future plans, how the loan will be used, and the competition in the industry and might even visit the company to obtain a firsthand look at its operations. The bottom line is that, be it for personal or business loans, financial institutions need to be nosy.

One puzzling feature of lending by financial institutions is that they often specialize in lending to local firms or to firms in particular industries, such as energy. In one sense, this behavior appears surprising because it means that the financial institution is not diversifying its portfolio of loans and is therefore exposing itself to more risk. But from another perspective, such specialization makes perfect sense. Recall that the adverse selection problem requires that financial institutions screen out bad credit risks. It is easier for a financial institution to collect information about local firms and determine their creditworthiness than to collect similar information on firms that are far away. Similarly, by specializing in lending to firms in specific industries, the financial institution becomes more knowledgeable about these industries and is therefore better able to predict whether the firms it lends to will be able to make timely payments on their debt.

Monitoring   After a loan has been obtained, the borrower may have an incentive to take on risky activities that make it less likely that the loan will be paid off. To reduce this moral hazard, financial institution managers must adhere to the principle for managing credit risk of writing provisions (restrictive covenants) into loan contracts that prevent borrowers from engaging in overly risky activities. By monitoring borrowers' activities to see whether they are complying with the restrictive covenants and by enforcing the covenants if they are not, financial institution managers can make sure that borrowers are not taking on risks at the institution's expense. The need for financial institutions to engage in screening and monitoring explains why successful financial institutions spend so much money on auditing and information-collecting activities.

Long-Term Customer Relationships

An additional way for financial institution managers to obtain information about borrowers is to establish long-term customer relationships, another important principle of credit risk management.

If a prospective borrower has had a checking or savings account or loans with the financial institution over a long period of time, a loan officer can look at past activity in the accounts and learn quite a bit about the borrower. The balances in the checking and savings accounts tell the loan officer how liquid the potential borrower is and at what times of the year the borrower has a strong need for cash.

A review of the checks the borrower has written reveals the borrower's suppliers. If the borrower has borrowed previously from the financial institution, the institution has a record of the loan payments. Thus long-term customer relationships reduce the costs of information collection and make it easier to screen out bad credit risks.

The need for monitoring by financial institutions adds to the importance of long-term customer relationships. If the borrower has borrowed from the financial institution before, the institution has already established procedures for monitoring that customer. Therefore, the costs of monitoring long-term customers are lower than those for new customers.

Long-term relationships benefit the customers as well as the financial institution. A firm with a previous relationship will find it easier to obtain a loan at a low interest rate because the financial institution has an easier time determining if the prospective borrower is a good credit risk and incurs fewer costs in monitoring the borrower.

A long-term customer relationship has another advantage for the financial institution. No financial institution manager can think of every contingency when the institution writes restrictive covenants into a loan contract; there will always be risky borrower activities that are not ruled out. However, what if a borrower wants to preserve a long-term relationship with the financial institution to make it easier to get future loans at low interest rates? The borrower then has the incentive to avoid risky activities that would upset the financial institution, even if these risky activities are not specifically addressed in the loan contract. Indeed, if the financial institution manager doesn't like what a borrower is doing even when the borrower isn't violating any restrictive covenants, the manager has some power to discourage the borrower from such activity by threatening to refuse new loans in the future. Long-term customer relationships therefore enable financial institution managers to deal with even unanticipated moral hazard contingencies.

The advantages of establishing long-term customer relationships suggest that closer ties between corporations and financial institutions such as banks might be beneficial to both. One way to create these ties is for financial institutions to hold equity stakes in companies they lend to and for the institutions to have members on the boards of directors of these companies. Such financial arrangements do not exist between banks and corporations in the United States because they were outlawed by the Glass-Steagall Act in the 1930s. They are, however, an important feature of the Japanese and German financial systems. Box 1 discusses how financial ties work in these countries to help banks cope with asymmetric information.

Loan Commitments

Banks have a special vehicle for institutionalizing long-term relationships called a **loan commitment.** A loan commitment is a bank's commitment (for a specified future period of time) to provide a firm with loans up to a given amount at a fixed interest rate or, more commonly, at a rate that is tied to some market interest rate. The majority of commercial and industrial loans from banks are made under the loan commitment arrangement. The advantage for the firm is that it has a source

BOX 1   A GLOBAL PERSPECTIVE

Japanese and German Banking Arrangements
A Better Way to Deal with Asymmetric Information?

 An important feature of the Japanese economic system is the *keiretsu,* or industrial group. Each *keiretsu* is made up of a core group of banks and other financial intermediaries that are linked to a group of industrial firms, many of which trade with each other. Linkages between firms and banks are cemented by each group member's holding equity shares in the other members. Because of their equity holdings, banks have memberships on their *keiretsu* firms' supervisory boards (boards of directors), and former bank executives are often placed in top managerial positions at these firms. Not surprisingly, banks favor firms of their *keiretsu* when making loans and hold a large fraction of these firms' debt.

Although nothing as formal or extensive as the *keiretsu* exists in Germany, German banks also have very close ties with industry through the so-called *Hausbank* system. Bank customers keep equity shares "on deposit" at the bank and give the bank proxies to vote these shares for them. With these voting rights and their own holdings of shares, German banks control the votes of a large share of equity in German corporations and have representation on boards of directors of the majority of the largest German corporations.

The Japanese and German banking arrangements give banks tremendous advantages in collecting information and monitoring activities. Long-term customer relationships are strengthened because banks have ownership rights in firms to which they lend. For the reasons discussed in the text, these stronger long-term relationships make it easier for banks to collect information and monitor firms, thus enabling banks to reduce adverse selection and moral hazard problems. In addition, because the banks have a role in the management of firms, they have timely access to information and the ability to influence management to act in the banks' interest by not investing in projects deemed too risky.

You can see that Japanese and German banking arrangements give their banks an advantage that American banks do not have, which may enable the financial systems in these countries to channel funds more easily to firms with the most productive investment opportunities. However, these advantages do not mean that banks in these countries do not make mistakes and get into serious trouble, as has occurred recently in Japan (see Chapter 16). This raises the interesting issue of whether similar banking arrangements should be allowed in the United States.

of credit when it needs it. The advantage for the bank is that the loan commitment promotes a long-term relationship, which in turn facilitates information collection. In addition, provisions in the loan commitment agreement require that the firm continually supply the bank with information about the firm's income, asset and liability position, business activities, and so on. A loan commitment arrangement is a powerful method for reducing the bank's costs for screening and information collection.

Collateral

Collateral requirements for loans are important credit risk management tools. Loans with these collateral requirements are often referred to as **secured loans.** Collateral, which is property promised to the lender as compensation if the borrower defaults, lessens the consequences of adverse selection because it reduces the lender's losses in the case of a loan default. If a borrower defaults on a loan with collateral, the lender can sell the collateral and use the proceeds to make up for its losses on the loan. Collateral requirements thus offer important protection for financial institutions making loans, and that is why they are extremely common in loans made by financial institutions.

Compensating Balances

One particular form of collateral required when a bank makes commercial loans is called **compensating balances:** A firm receiving a loan must keep a required minimum amount of funds in a checking account at the bank. For example, a business getting a $10 million loan may be required to keep compensating balances of at least $1 million in its checking account at the bank. If the borrower defaults, this $1 million in compensating balances can be taken by the bank to make up some of the losses on the loan.

Besides serving as collateral, compensating balances help increase the likelihood that a loan will be paid off. They do this by helping the bank monitor the borrower and consequently minimize moral hazard. Specifically, by requiring the borrower to use a checking account at the bank, the bank can observe the firm's check payment practices, which may yield a great deal of information about the borrower's financial condition. For example, a sustained drop in the borrower's checking account balance may signal that the borrower is having financial trouble, or account activity may suggest that the borrower is engaging in risky activities; perhaps a change in suppliers means that the borrower is pursuing new lines of business. Any significant change in the borrower's payment procedures is a signal to the bank that it should make inquiries. Compensating balances therefore make it easier for banks to monitor borrowers more effectively and are consequently another important credit risk management tool.

Credit Rationing

Another way in which successful financial institution managers deal with adverse selection and moral hazard is through **credit rationing:** Lenders refuse to make loans even though borrowers are willing to pay the stated interest rate or even a higher rate. Credit rationing takes two forms. The first occurs when a financial institution refuses to make a loan of *any amount* to a borrower, even if the borrower is willing to pay a higher interest rate. The second occurs when the financial institution is willing to make a loan but restricts the size of the loan to less than the borrower would like.

At first you might be puzzled by the first type of credit rationing. After all, even if the potential borrower is a credit risk, why doesn't the financial institution just extend the loan but at a higher interest rate? The answer is that adverse selection rules out this solution. Individuals and firms with the riskiest investment projects are precisely the ones that are willing to pay the highest interest rates. If a borrower took on a high-risk investment and succeeded, the borrower would become extremely rich. But a financial institution wouldn't want to make such a loan precisely because the investment risk is high; the likely outcome is that the borrower will *not* succeed and the financial institution will not be paid back.

Charging a higher interest rate just makes adverse selection worse for the financial institution; that is, it increases the likelihood that the financial institution is lending to a bad credit risk. The financial institution would therefore rather not make any loans at a higher interest rate; instead, it would engage in the first type of credit rationing and would turn down loans.

Financial institutions engage in a second type of credit rationing to guard against moral hazard: They grant loans to borrowers, but not loans as large as the borrowers want. Such credit rationing is necessary because the larger the loan, the greater the benefits from moral hazard. For example, if a financial institution gives you a $1000 loan, you are likely to take actions that enable you to pay it back because you don't want to hurt your credit rating for the future. However, if the financial institution lends you $10 million, you are more likely to fly off to Rio to celebrate. The larger your loan, the greater your incentives to engage in activities that make it less likely that you will repay the loan. Because more borrowers repay their loans if the loan amounts are small, financial institutions ration credit by providing borrowers with smaller loans than they seek.

■ MANAGING INTEREST-RATE RISK

As the volatility of interest rates increased in the 1980s, financial institution managers became more concerned about their exposure to interest-rate risk, the riskiness of earnings and returns that is associated with changes in interest rates. To see what interest-rate risk is all about, let's take a look at the balance sheet of the First National Bank:

First National Bank			
Assets		Liabilities	
Reserves and cash items	$5 million	Checkable deposits	$15 million
Securities		Money market deposit	
Less than 1 year	$5 million	accounts	$5 million
1 to 2 years	$5 million	Savings deposits	$15 million
Greater than 2 years	$10 million	CDs	
Residential mortgages		Variable-rate	$10 million
Variable-rate	$10 million	Less than 1 year	$15 million
Fixed-rate (30-year)	$10 million	1 to 2 years	$5 million
Commercial loans		Greater than 2 years	$5 million
Less than 1 year	$15 million	Fed funds	$5 million
1 to 2 years	$10 million	Borrowings	
Greater than 2 years	$25 million	Less than 1 year	$10 million
Physical capital	$5 million	1 to 2 years	$5 million
		Greater than 2 years	$5 million
		Bank capital	$5 million

The first step in assessing interest-rate risk is for the bank manager to decide which assets and liabilities are rate-sensitive, that is, which have interest rates that will be reset (repriced) within the year. Note that rate-sensitive assets or liabilities can have interest rates repriced within the year either because the debt instrument matures within the year or because the repricing is done automatically, as with variable-rate mortgages.

For many assets and liabilities, deciding whether they are rate-sensitive is straightforward. In our example, the obviously rate-sensitive assets are securities with maturities of less than one year ($5 million), variable-rate mortgages ($10 million), and commercial loans with maturities less than one year ($15 million), for a total of $30 million. However, some assets that look like fixed-rate assets whose interest rates are not repriced within the year actually have a component that is rate-sensitive. For example, although fixed-rate residential mortgages may have a maturity of 30 years, homeowners can repay their mortgages early by selling their homes or repaying the mortgage in some other way. This means that within the year, a certain percentage of these fixed-rate mortgages will be paid off, and interest rates on this amount will be repriced. From past experience the bank manager knows that 20% of the fixed-rate residential mortgages are repaid within a year, which means that $2 million of these mortgages (20% of $10 million) must be considered rate-sensitive. The bank manager adds this $2 million to the $30 million of rate-sensitive assets already calculated, for a total of $32 million in rate-sensitive assets.

The bank manager now goes through a similar procedure to determine the total amount of rate-sensitive liabilities. The obviously rate-sensitive liabilities are money market deposit accounts ($5 million), variable-rate CDs and CDs with less than one year to maturity ($25 million), federal funds ($5 million), and borrowings with maturities of less than one year ($10 million), for a total of $45 million. Checkable deposits and savings deposits often have interest rates that can be changed at any time by the bank, although banks often like to keep their rates fixed for substantial periods. Thus these liabilities are partially but not fully rate-sensitive. The bank manager estimates that 10% of checkable deposits ($1.5 million) and 20% of savings deposits ($3 million) should be considered rate-sensitive. Adding the $1.5 million and $3 million to the $45 million figure yields a total for rate-sensitive liabilities of $49.5 million.

Now the bank manager can analyze what will happen if interest rates rise by 5 percentage points, say, on average from 10% to 15%. The income on the assets rises by $1.6 million (= 5% × $32 million of rate-sensitive assets), while the payments on the liabilities rise by $2.5 million (= 5% × $49.5 million of rate-sensitive liabilities). The First National Bank's profits now decline by $0.9 million (= $1.6 million − $2.5 million). Another way of thinking about this situation is with the net interest margin concept described in Chapter 13, which is interest income minus interest expense divided by bank assets. In this case, the 5% rise in interest rates has resulted in a decline of the net interest margin by 0.9% (= − $0.9 million/$100 million). Conversely, if interest rates fall by 5%, similar reasoning tells us that the First National Bank's income rises by $0.9 million and its net interest margin rises by 0.9%. This example illustrates the following point: ***If a financial institution has more rate-sensitive liabilities than assets, a rise in interest rates will reduce the net interest margin and income and a decline in interest rates will raise the net interest margin and income.***

Income Gap Analysis

The sensitivity of bank income to changes in interest rates can be measured more directly using **gap analysis** (also called **income gap analysis**), in which the amount of rate-sensitive liabilities is subtracted from the amount of rate-sensitive assets. This calculation, called the *gap,* can be written as

$$GAP = RSA - RSL \qquad (1)$$

where $\qquad\qquad\qquad\qquad RSA$ = rate-sensitive assets
$\qquad\qquad\qquad\qquad\qquad\quad RSL$ = rate-sensitive liabilities

In our example, the bank manager calculates GAP to be

$$GAP = \$32 \text{ million} - \$49.5 \text{ million} = -\$17.5 \text{ million}$$

Multiplying GAP times the change in the interest rate immediately reveals the effect on bank income:

$$\Delta I = GAP \times \Delta i \qquad (2)$$

where $\qquad\qquad\qquad\qquad \Delta I$ = change in bank income
$\qquad\qquad\qquad\qquad\qquad\quad \Delta i$ = change in interest rates

For example, when interest rates rise by 5%, the change in income is

$$\Delta I = -\$17.5 \text{ million} \times 5\% = -\$0.9 \text{ million}$$

This $0.9 million decline in bank income is the same as we found earlier.

The analysis we just conducted is known as *basic gap analysis,* and it suffers from the problem that many of the assets and liabilities that are not classified as rate-sensitive have different maturities. One refinement to deal with this problem, the *maturity bucket approach,* is to measure the gap for several maturity subintervals, called *maturity buckets,* so that effects of interest-rate changes over a multiyear period can be calculated.

Looking at the balance sheet for the First National Bank, the bank manager produces a more refined maturity bucket, not only by calculating the gap for less than one year as before, but also by estimating an income gap for the subinterval from one to two years. Rate-sensitive assets in this period consist of $5 million of securities maturing in one to two years, $10 million of commercial loans maturing in one to two years, and an additional $2 million (20% of fixed-rate mortgages) that the bank manager expects to be repaid in that period. Rate-sensitive assets in the one- to two-year maturity bucket are thus estimated at $17 million. Rate-sensitive liabilities in this period consist of $5 million of one- to two-year CDs, $5 million of one- to two-year borrowings, an additional $1.5 million of checkable deposits (the 10% of checkable deposits that the bank manager estimates are rate-sensitive in this period), and an additional $3 million of savings deposits (the 20% estimate of savings deposits). So the bank manager estimates the rate-sensitive liabilities at $14.5 million. The gap calculation for the one- to two-year period is thus $2.5 million (= $17 million − $14.5 million). If interest rates remain 5% higher, then in the second year, income will improve by $125,000 (= 5% × $2.5

million). By using the more refined maturity bucket approach, the bank manager can figure out what will happen to bank income over the next several years when there is a change in interest rates.

Duration Gap Analysis

The gap analysis we have examined so far focuses only on the effect of interest-rate changes on income. Clearly, owners and managers of financial institutions care not only about the effect of changes in interest rates on income but also about the effect of changes in interest rates on the market value of the net worth of the financial institution.[1]

An alternative method for measuring interest-rate risk, called **duration gap analysis,** examines the sensitivity of the market value of the financial institution's net worth to changes in interest rates. Duration analysis is based on Macaulay's concept of *duration,* which measures the average lifetime of a security's stream of payments (described in Chapter 3). Recall that duration is a useful concept because it provides a good approximation of the sensitivity of a security's market value to a change in its interest rate using the following formula:

$$\% \Delta P \approx -DUR \times \frac{\Delta i}{1 + i} \qquad (3)$$

where $\% \Delta P = (P_{t+1} - P_t)/P_t$ = percent change in market value of the security
DUR = duration
i = interest rate

After having determined the duration of all assets and liabilities on the bank's balance sheet, the bank manager could use this formula to calculate how the market value of each asset and liability changes when there is a change in interest rates and then calculate the effect on net worth. There is, however, an easier way to go about doing this, derived from the basic fact about duration we learned in Chapter 3: Duration is additive; that is, the duration of a portfolio of securities is the weighted average of the durations of the individual securities, with the weights reflecting the proportion of the portfolio invested in each. What this means is that the bank manager can figure out the effect that interest-rate changes will have on the market value of net worth by calculating the average duration for assets and for liabilities and then using those figures to estimate the effects of interest-rate changes.

To see how a bank manager would do this, let's return to the balance sheet of the First National Bank. The bank manager has already used the procedures outlined in Chapter 3 to calculate the duration of each asset and liability, as listed in

---

[1]Note that accounting net worth is calculated on a historical-cost (book-value) basis, meaning that the value of assets and liabilities is based on their initial price. However, book-value net worth does not give a complete picture of the true worth of the firm; the market value of net worth provides a more accurate measure. This is why duration gap analysis focuses on what happens to the market value of net worth, and not on book value, when interest rates change.

Table 1. For each asset, the manager then calculates the weighted duration by multiplying the duration times the amount of the asset divided by total assets, which in this case is $100 million. For example, in the case of securities with maturities less than one year, the manager multiplies the 0.4 year of duration times $5 million divided by $100 million to get a weighted duration of 0.02. (Note that physical assets have no cash payments, so they have a duration of zero years.) Doing this for all the assets and adding them up, the bank manager gets a figure for the average duration of the assets of 2.70 years.

The manager follows a similar procedure for the liabilities, noting that total liabilities excluding capital are $95 million. For example, the weighted duration for checkable deposits is determined by multiplying the 2.0-year duration by $15 million divided by $95 million to get 0.32. Adding up these weighted durations, the manager obtains an average duration of liabilities of 1.03 years.

■ TABLE 1 Duration of the First National Bank's Assets and Liabilities

	Amount ($ millions)	Duration (years)	Weighted Duration (years)
Assets			
Reserves and cash items	5	0.0	0.00
Securities			
Less than 1 year	5	0.4	0.02
1 to 2 years	5	1.6	0.08
Greater than 2 years	10	7.0	0.70
Residential mortgages			
Variable-rate	10	0.5	0.05
Fixed-rate (30-year)	10	6.0	0.60
Commercial loans			
Less than 1 year	15	0.7	0.11
1 to 2 years	10	1.4	0.14
Greater than 2 years	25	4.0	1.00
Physical capital	5	0.0	<u>0.00</u>
Average duration			2.70
Liabilities			
Checkable deposits	15	2.0	0.32
Money market deposit accounts	5	0.1	0.01
Savings deposits	15	1.0	0.16
CDs			
Variable-rate	10	0.5	0.05
Less than 1 year	15	0.2	0.03
1 to 2 years	5	1.2	0.06
Greater than 2 years	5	2.7	0.14
Fed funds	5	0.0	0.00
Borrowings			
Less than 1 year	10	0.3	0.03
1 to 2 years	5	1.3	0.07
Greater than 2 years	5	3.1	<u>0.16</u>
Average duration			1.03

Now the bank manager can use the formula in Equation 3 to figure out what happens if interest rates rise from 10% to 15%. Using Equation 3, the market value of the assets falls as follows:

$$\%\Delta P \approx -2.70 \times \frac{0.05}{1 + 0.10} = -0.123 = -12.3\%$$

With a total asset value of $100 million, this means that the market value of assets falls by $12.3 million. Again using Equation 3, the bank manager calculates the fall in the value of liabilities as

$$\%\Delta P \approx -1.03 \times \frac{0.05}{1 + 0.10} = -0.047 = -4.7\%$$

With total liabilities of $95 million, the market value of liabilities will fall by $4.5 million. The net result is that the net worth of the bank (the market value of assets minus the liabilities) has declined by $7.8 million ($= -\$12.3$ million $+ \$4.5$ million).

The bank manager could have gotten to this answer even more quickly by calculating what is called a *duration gap*, which is defined as follows:

$$DUR_{GAP} = DUR_A - \left(\frac{L}{A} \times DUR_L\right) \tag{4}$$

where
$$DUR_A = \text{average duration of assets}$$
$$DUR_L = \text{average duration of liabilities}$$
$$L = \text{market value of liabilities}$$
$$A = \text{market value of assets}$$

For the First National Bank, the duration gap is

$$DUR_{GAP} = 2.70 - \left(\frac{95}{100} \times 1.03\right) = 1.72 \text{ years}$$

To estimate what will happen if interest rates rise from 10% to 15%, the bank manager uses the DUR_{GAP} calculation in Equation 3 to obtain the change in the market value of net worth as a percentage of total assets. In other words, the change in the market value of net worth as a percentage of assets is calculated as

$$\%\Delta NW = -DUR_{GAP} \times \frac{\Delta i}{1 + i} \tag{5}$$

The result of this calculation is that the rise in interest rates from 10% to 15% would lead to a change in the market value of net worth as a percentage of assets of

$$\%\Delta NW = -1.72 \times \frac{0.05}{1 + 0.10} = -0.078 = -7.8\%$$

With assets totaling $100 million, this indicates a fall in the market value of net worth of $7.8 million, which is the same figure that we found before.

As our example makes clear, both income gap analysis and duration gap analysis indicate that the First National Bank will suffer from a rise in interest rates. Indeed, in this example, we have seen that a rise in interest rates from 10% to 15% will cause the market value of net worth to fall by $7.8 million, which is more than the initial amount of bank capital and so would cause the bank to be insolvent. Thus the bank manager realizes that the bank faces substantial interest-rate risk because a rise in interest rates could bankrupt the bank. Clearly, income gap analysis and duration gap analysis are useful tools for telling a financial institution manager the institution's degree of exposure to interest-rate risk.

■ **STUDY GUIDE** To make sure that you understand income gap and duration gap analysis, you should be able to verify that if interest rates fall from 10% to 5%, the First National Bank will find its income increasing and the market value of its net worth rising. For even more practice with these concepts, do some of the problems at the end of this chapter.

Example of a Nonbanking Financial Institution

So far we have focused on an example involving a banking institution that has borrowed short and lent long so that when interest rates rise, both income and the net worth of the institution fall. It is important to recognize that income and duration gap analysis applies equally to other financial institutions. Furthermore, it is important for you to see that some financial institutions have income and duration gaps that are opposite in sign to those of banks, so that when interest rates rise, both income and net worth rise rather than fall. To get a more complete picture of income and duration gap analysis, let us look at a nonbank financial institution, the Friendly Finance Company, which specializes in making consumer loans.

The Friendly Finance Company has the following balance sheet:

Friendly Finance Company			
Assets		Liabilities	
Cash and deposits	$3 million	Commercial paper	$40 million
Securities		Bank loans	
Less than 1 year	$5 million	Less than 1 year	$3 million
1 to 2 years	$1 million	1 to 2 years	$2 million
Greater than 2 years	$1 million	Greater than 2 years	$5 million
Consumer loans		Long-term bonds and	
Less than 1 year	$50 million	other long-term debt	$40 million
1 to 2 years	$20 million	Capital	$10 million
Greater than 2 years	$15 million		
Physical capital	$5 million		

The manager of the Friendly Finance Company calculates the rate-sensitive assets to be equal to the $5 million of securities with maturities less than one year plus the $50 million of consumer loans with maturities of less than one year, for a total of $55 million of rate-sensitive assets. The manager then calculates the rate-sensitive liabilities to be equal to the $40 million of commercial paper, all of which has a maturity of less than one year, plus the $3 million of bank loans maturing in less than a year, for a total of $43 million. The calculation of the income gap is then

$$GAP = RSA - RSL = \$55 \text{ million} - \$43 \text{ million} = \$12 \text{ million}$$

To calculate the effect on income if interest rates rise by 5%, the manager multiplies the GAP of $12 million times the change in the interest rate to get the following:

$$\Delta I = GAP \times \Delta i = \$12 \text{ million} \times 5\% = \$0.6 \text{ million}$$

Thus the manager finds that the finance company's income will rise by $0.6 million when interest rates rise by 5%. The reason that the company has benefited from the interest-rate rise, in contrast to the First National Bank, whose profits suffer from the rise in interest rates, is that the Friendly Finance Company has a positive income gap because it has more rate-sensitive assets than liabilities.

Like the bank manager, the manager of the Friendly Finance Company is also interested in what happens to the market value of the net worth of the company when interest rates rise by 5%. So the manager calculates the weighted duration of each item in the balance sheet, adds them up as in Table 2, and obtains a duration for the assets of 1.16 years and for the liabilities, 2.77 years. The duration gap is then calculated to be

$$DUR_{GAP} = DUR_A - \left(\frac{L}{A} \times DUR_L\right) = 1.16 - \left(\frac{90}{100} \times 2.77\right) = -1.33 \text{ years}$$

■ TABLE 2 Duration of the Friendly Finance Company's Assets and Liabilities

	Amount ($ millions)	Duration (years)	Weighted Duration (years)
Assets			
Cash and deposits	3	0.0	0.00
Securities			
Less than 1 year	5	0.5	0.05
1 to 2 years	1	1.7	0.02
Greater than 2 years	1	9.0	0.09
Consumer loans			
Less than 1 year	50	0.5	0.25
1 to 2 years	20	1.5	0.30
Greater than 2 years	15	3.0	0.45
Physical capital	5	0.0	0.00
Average duration			1.16
Liabilities			
Commercial paper	40	0.2	0.09
Bank loans			
Less than 1 year	3	0.3	0.01
1 to 2 years	2	1.6	0.04
Greater than 2 years	5	3.5	0.19
Long-term bonds and other long-term debt	40	5.5	2.44
Average duration			2.77

Since the Friendly Finance Company has a negative duration gap, the manager realizes that a rise in interest rates by 5 percentage points from 10% to 15% will increase the market value of net worth of the firm. The manager checks this by calculating the change in the market value of net worth as a percentage of assets:

$$\%\Delta NW = -DUR_{GAP} \times \frac{\Delta i}{1 + i} = -(-1.33) \times \frac{0.05}{1 + 0.10} = 0.061 = 6.1\%$$

With assets of \$100 million, this calculation indicates that net worth will rise in market value by \$6.1 million.

Even though the income and duration gap analysis indicates that the Friendly Finance Company gains from a rise in interest rates, the manager realizes that if interest rates go in the other direction, the company will suffer a fall in income and market value of net worth. Thus the finance company manager, like the bank manager, realizes that the institution is subject to substantial interest-rate risk.

Some Problems with Income and Duration Gap Analysis

Although you might think that income and duration gap analysis is complicated enough, further complications make a financial institution manager's job even harder.

One assumption that we have been using in our discussion of income and duration gap analysis is that when the level of interest rates change, interest rates on all maturities change by exactly the same amount. That is the same as saying that we conducted our analysis under the assumption that the slope of the yield curve remains unchanged. Indeed, the situation is even worse for duration gap analysis because the duration gap is calculated assuming that interest rates for all maturities are the same—in other words, the yield curve is assumed to be flat. As our discussion of the term structure of interest rates in Chapter 6 indicated, however, the yield curve is not flat, and the slope of the yield curve fluctuates and has a tendency to change when the level of the interest rate changes. Thus to get a truly accurate assessment of interest-rate risk, a financial institution manager has to assess what might happen to the slope of the yield curve when the level of the interest rate changes and then take this information into account when assessing interest-rate risk.

An additional problem with income gap analysis is that as we have seen, the financial institution manager must make estimates of the proportion of supposedly fixed-rate assets and liabilities that may be rate-sensitive. This involves estimates of the likelihood of prepayment of loans or customer shifts out of deposits when interest rates change. Such guesses are not easy to make, and as a result, the financial institution manager's estimates of income gaps may not be very accurate. A similar problem occurs in calculating durations of assets and liabilities because many of the cash payments are uncertain. Thus the estimate of the duration gap might not be accurate either.

Do these problems mean that managers of banks and other financial institutions should give up on measuring interest-rate risk? Of course, the answer is no.

Although income gap analysis and duration gap analysis are not infallible, they are nevertheless valuable tools for helping financial institution managers assess interest-rate risk.

■ THE PRACTICING FINANCIAL INSTITUTION MANAGER
Strategies for Managing Interest-Rate Risk

Once financial institution managers have done the duration and income gap analysis for their institutions, they must decide which alternative strategies to pursue. If the manager of the First National Bank firmly believes that interest rates will fall in the future, he or she may be willing to take no action knowing that the bank has more rate-sensitive liabilities than rate-sensitive assets and so will benefit from the expected interest-rate decline. However, the bank manager also realizes that the First National Bank is subject to substantial interest-rate risk because there is always a possibility that interest rates will rise rather than fall, and as we have seen, this outcome could bankrupt the bank. The manager might try to shorten the duration of the bank's assets to increase their rate sensitivity either by purchasing assets of shorter maturity or by converting fixed-rate loans into adjustable-rate loans. Alternatively, the bank manager could lengthen the duration of the liabilities. With these adjustments to the bank's assets and liabilities, the bank would be less affected by interest-rate swings.

For example, the bank manager might decide to eliminate the income gap by increasing the amount of rate-sensitive assets to $49.5 million to equal the $49.5 million of rate-sensitive liabilities. Or the manager could reduce rate-sensitive liabilities to $32 million so that they equal rate-sensitive assets. In either case, the income gap would now be zero, so a change in interest rates would have no effect on bank profits in the coming year.

Alternatively, the bank manager might decide to immunize the market value of the bank's net worth completely from interest-rate risk by adjusting assets and liabilities so that the duration gap is equal to zero. To do this, the manager can set DUR_{GAP} equal to zero in Equation 4 and solve for DUR_A:

$$DUR_A = \frac{L}{A} \times DUR_L = \frac{95}{100} \times 1.03 = 0.98$$

These calculations reveal that the manager should reduce the average duration of the bank's assets to 0.98 year. To check that the duration gap is set equal to zero, the calculation is

$$DUR_{GAP} = 0.98 - \left(\frac{95}{100} \times 1.03 \right) = 0$$

In this case, as in Equation 5, the market value of net worth would remain unchanged when interest rates change. Alternatively, the bank manager could calculate the value of the duration of the liabilities that would produce a duration gap of zero. To do this would involve setting DUR_{GAP} equal to zero in Equation 4 and solving for DUR_L:

$$DUR_L = DUR_A \times \frac{A}{L} = 2.70 \times \frac{100}{95} = 2.84$$

This calculation reveals that the interest-rate risk could also be eliminated by increasing the average duration of the bank's liabilities to 2.84 years. The manager again checks that the duration gap is set equal to zero by calculating

$$DUR_{GAP} = 2.70 - \left(\frac{95}{100} \times 2.84\right) = 0$$

■ **STUDY GUIDE** To see if you understand how a financial institution manager can protect income and net worth from interest-rate risk, first calculate how the Friendly Finance Company might change the amount of its rate-sensitive assets or its rate-sensitive liabilities to eliminate the income gap. You should find that the income gap can be eliminated either by reducing the amount of rate-sensitive assets to $43 million or by raising the amount of rate-sensitive liabilities to $55 million. Also do the calculations to determine what modifications to the duration of the assets or liabilities would immunize the market value of Friendly Finance's net worth from interest-rate risk. You should find that interest-rate risk would be eliminated if the duration of the assets were set to 2.49 years or if the duration of the liabilities were set to 1.29 years.

One problem with eliminating a financial institution's interest-rate risk by altering the balance sheet is that doing so might be very costly in the short run. The financial institution may be locked into assets and liabilities of particular durations because of its field of expertise. Fortunately, recently developed financial instruments, such as financial futures, options, and interest-rate swaps, help financial institutions manage their interest-rate risk without requiring them to rearrange their balance sheets. We discuss these instruments and how they can be used to manage interest-rate risk in the next two chapters. ■

SUMMARY

1. The concepts of adverse selection and moral hazard explain the origin of many credit risk management principles involving loan activities, including screening and monitoring, development of long-term customer relationships, loan commitments, collateral, compensating balances, and credit rationing.

2. With the increased volatility of interest rates that occurred in recent years, financial institutions became more concerned about their exposure to interest-rate risk. Income gap and duration gap analyses tell a financial institution if it has fewer rate-sensitive assets than liabilities (in which case a rise in interest rates will reduce income and a fall in interest rates will raise it) or more rate-sensitive assets than liabilities (in which case a rise in interest rates will raise income and a fall in interest rates will reduce it). Financial institutions can manage interest-rate risk by modifying their balance sheets and by making use of new financial instruments.

KEY TERMS

QUESTIONS AND PROBLEMS

1. Can a financial institution keep borrowers from engaging in risky activities if there are no restrictive covenants written into the loan agreement?

*2. Why are secured loans an important method of lending for financial institutions?

3. "If more customers want to borrow funds at the prevailing interest rate, a financial institution can increase its profits by raising interest rates on its loans." Is this statement true, false, or uncertain? Explain your answer.

*4. Why is being nosy a desirable trait for a banker?

5. Banks almost always insist that the firms it lends to keep compensating balances at the bank. Why?

*6. "Because diversification is a desirable strategy for avoiding risk, it never makes sense for a financial institution to specialize in making specific types of loans." Is this statement true, false, or uncertain? Explain your answer.

For Problems 7–14, assume that the First National Bank initially has the balance sheet shown on page 513 and that interest rates are initially at 10%.

7. If the First National Bank sells $10 million of its securities with maturities greater than two years and replaces them with securities maturing in less than one year, what is the income gap for the bank? What will happen to profits next year if interest rates fall by 3 percentage points?

*8. If the First National Bank decides to convert $5 million of its fixed-rate mortgages into variable-rate mortgages, what happens to its interest-rate risk? Explain with gap analysis.

9. If the manager of the First National Bank revises the estimate of the percentage of fixed-rate mortgages that are repaid within a year from 20% to 10%, what will be the revised estimate of the interest-rate risk the bank faces? What will happen to profits next year if interest rates fall by 2 percentage points?

*10. If the manager of the First National Bank revises the estimate of the percentage of checkable deposits that are rate-sensitive from 10% to 25%, what will be the revised estimate of the interest-rate risk the bank faces? What will happen to profits next year if interest rates rise by 5 percentage points?

11. Given the estimates of duration in Table 1, what will happen to the bank's net worth if interest rates rise by 10 percentage points? Will the bank stay in business? Why or why not?

*12. If the manager of the First National Bank revises the estimates of the duration of the bank's assets to four years and liabilities to two years, what is the effect on net worth if interest rates rise by 2 percentage points?

13. Given the estimates of duration in Problem 12, how should the bank alter the duration of its assets to immunize its net worth from interest-rate risk?

*14. Given the estimates of duration in Problem 12, how should the bank alter the duration of its liabilities to immunize its net worth from interest-rate risk?

For Problems 15–20, assume that the Friendly Finance Company initially has the balance sheet shown on page 519 and that interest rates are initially at 8%.

15. If the manager of the Friendly Finance Company decides to sell off $10 million of the company's consumer loans, half maturing within one year and half maturing in greater than two years, and uses the resulting funds to buy $10 million of Treasury bills, what is the income gap for the company? What will happen to profits next year if interest rates fall by 5 percentage points? How could the Friendly Finance Company alter its balance sheet to immunize its income from this change in interest rates?

*16. If the Friendly Finance Company raises an additional $20 million with commercial paper and uses the funds to make $20 million of consumer loans that mature in less than one year, what happens to its interest-rate risk? In this situation, what additional changes could it make in its balance sheet to eliminate the income gap?

17. Given the estimates of duration in Table 2, what will happen to the Friendly Finance Company's net worth if interest rates rise by 3 percentage points? Will the company stay in business? Why or why not?

*18. If the manager of the Friendly Finance Company revises the estimates of the duration of the company's assets to two years and liabilities to four years, what is the effect on net worth if interest rates rise by 3 percentage points?

19. Given the estimates of duration found in Problem 18, how should the Friendly Finance Company alter the duration of its assets to immunize its net worth from interest-rate risk?

*20. Given the estimates of duration in Problem 18, how should the Friendly Finance Company alter the duration of its liabilities to immunize its net worth from interest-rate risk?

CASE STUDY

Calculating and Comparing Gap, Duration, and Risk Management Alternatives

CONCEPTS IN THIS CASE

interest-rate risk
duration gap analysis
income gap analysis
minimizing risk of market value
interest-rate sensitive assets and liabilities

Your employer has asked you to examine the interest-rate risk of your bank relative to your direct competition.

Management is concerned that interest rates will fall by the end of the year and wants to see what would happen to the relative profitability of the firm if the decline actually occurs.

Interest-rate risk depends on each bank's relative position of interest-sensitive assets and liabilities. You begin the analysis by collecting the information and estimates.

Bank Balance Sheet

	Your Firm		Competition	
	Amount ($millions)	Duration (years)	Amount ($millions)	Duration (years)
Assets				
Reserves and cash items	3	0.0	4	0.0
Securities				
Less than 1 year	4	0.6	5	0.3
1–2 years	3	1.6	7	1.2
Greater than 2 years	7	5.0	9	4.0
Residential mortgages				
Variable-rate	9	0.4	21	0.9
Fixed-rate (30 years)	15	5.5	17	4.4
Commercial loans				
Less than 1 year	13	0.9	30	0.6
1–2 years	31	1.8	22	1.4
Greater than 2 years	55	6.0	30	5.4
Physical capital	10	0.0	25	0.0
Liabilities				
Checkable deposits	10	1.0	14	1.0
Money market deposit accounts	5	0.6	9	0.5
Savings deposits	12	1.0	16	1.0

continued

Bank Balance Sheet (*continued*)

	Your Firm		Competition	
	Amount ($millions)	Duration (years)	Amount ($millions)	Duration (years)
CDs				
Variable-rate	6	0.4	12	0.6
Less than 1 year	19	0.3	14	0.5
1–2 years	8	1.1	10	1.8
Greater than 2 years	15	2.9	10	2.2
Fed funds	10	0.0	14	0.0
Borrowings				
Less than 1 year	12	0.4	18	0.7
1–2 years	9	1.2	12	1.8
Greater than 2 years	39	2.9	31	3.8

To prepare your presentation for the bank officers, you anticipate and answer the following questions:

1. What is the total for interest-rate-sensitive assets for
   a. Your firm?
   b. Your competition?

2. What is the total for interest-rate-sensitive liabilities for
   a. Your firm?
   b. Your competition?

3. If interest rates decline by 3%
   a. What will be the estimated net interest margin for your firm?
   b. What will be the estimated net interest margin for your competition?

4. Compare the estimated relative success of your bank and your competition if interest rates
   a. Decline by 3%
   b. Increase by 3%

5. What is the gap of
   a. Your firm?
   b. Your competition?

6. Using the Macaulay concept of duration, calculate the weighted duration of each asset and liability for both your firm and your competition.

7. What is the average duration for
   a. Assets for your firm?
   b. Assets for your competition?
   c. Liabilities for your firm?
   d. Liabilities for your competition?

8. What is the duration gap for
   a. Your firm?
   b. Your competition?

9. Using the net worth formula if interest rates decline by 3%, what will be the expected change in the market value of net worth for
   a. Your firm?
   b. Your competition?

10. Using the net worth formula, if interest rates rise by 3%, what will be the expected change in the market value of net worth for
    a. Your firm?
    b. Your competition?

11. What would your firm need to do
    a. To eliminate the income gap using adjustments to rate-sensitive assets?
    b. To immunize the market value of net worth from interest-rate risk using duration?

CHAPTER 21

HEDGING WITH FINANCIAL DERIVATIVES I: FORWARDS AND FUTURES

■ **PREVIEW** Starting in the 1970s and increasingly in the 1980s and 1990s, the world became a riskier place for financial institutions. Swings in interest rates widened, and the bond and stock markets went through some episodes of increased volatility. As a result of these developments, managers of financial institutions have become more concerned with reducing the risk their institutions face. Given the greater demand for risk reduction, the process of financial innovation described in Chapter 13 came to the rescue by producing new financial instruments that help financial institution managers manage risk better. These instruments, called **financial derivatives,** have payoffs that are linked to previously issued securities and are extremely useful risk reduction tools.

In this chapter we look at two of the most important financial derivatives that managers of financial institutions use to reduce risk, forward contracts and financial futures. We examine not only how markets for each of these financial derivatives work but also how each can be used by financial institution managers to reduce risk.

■ FORWARD MARKETS

Forward contracts are agreements by two parties to engage in a financial transaction at a future (forward) point in time. Here we focus on forward contracts that are linked to debt instruments, called **interest-rate forward contracts;** later in the chapter we discuss forward contracts for foreign currencies.

Interest-Rate Forward Contracts

Interest-rate forward contracts involve the future sale of a debt instrument and have several dimensions: (1) specification of the actual debt instrument that will be delivered at a future date, (2) amount of the debt instrument to be delivered, (3) price (interest rate) on the debt instrument when it is delivered, and (4) date on which delivery will take place. An example of an interest-rate forward contract might be an agreement for the First National Bank to sell to the Rock Solid Insurance Company, one year from today, $5 million face value of the 8s of 2015 Treasury bonds (coupon bonds with an 8% coupon rate that mature in 2015) at a price that yields the same interest rate on these bonds as today's, say, 8%. Because Rock Solid will buy the securities at a future date, it is said to have taken a **long position,** while the First National Bank, which will sell the securities, is said to have taken a **short position.**

Hedging with Interest-Rate Forward Contracts

Why would the First National Bank want to enter into this forward contract with Rock Solid Insurance Company in the first place? The reason is that the First National Bank is able to **hedge** (protect itself) against interest-rate risk in case it wants to sell the bonds before they mature. For its part, the First National Bank, which is currently holding the $5 million of the 8s of 2015, may worry that if interest rates rise in the future, the price of these bonds will fall and expose it to a capital loss if they are sold. When it enters into the forward contract, it locks in the future price and so also eliminates the price risk it faces from interest-rate changes. We thus see that interest-rate forward contracts can allow financial institution managers to reduce (hedge against) interest-rate risk.

Why would the Rock Solid Insurance Company want to enter into the futures contract with the First National Bank? Rock Solid expects to receive premiums of $5 million in one year's time that it will want to invest in the 8s of 2015 but worries that interest rates on these bonds will decline between now and next year. By using the forward contract, it is able to lock in the 8% interest rate on the Treasury bonds (which will be sold to it by the First National Bank).

Pros and Cons of Forward Contracts

The advantage of forward contracts is that they can be as flexible as the parties involved want them to be. This means that an institution like the First National Bank may be able to hedge completely the interest-rate risk for the exact security it is holding in its portfolio, just as it has in our example.

However, forward contracts suffer from two problems that severely limit their usefulness. The first is that it may be very hard for an institution like the First National Bank to find another party (called a *counterparty*) to make the contract with. There are brokers to facilitate the matching up of parties like the First National Bank with the Rock Solid Insurance Company, but there may be few institutions that want to engage in a forward contract specifically for the 8s of 2015. This means that it may prove impossible to find a counterparty when a financial institution like the First National Bank wants to make a specific type of forward contract. Furthermore, even if the First National Bank finds a counterparty, it may have to sell for a price lower than it thinks it should for the bonds it wants to sell because there may not be anyone else to make the deal with. A serious problem for the market in interest-rate forward contracts, then, is that it may be difficult to make the financial transaction or that it will have to be made at a disadvantageous price; in the parlance of the financial world, this market suffers from a *lack of liquidity*. (Note that this use of the term *liquidity* when it is applied to a market is somewhat broader than its use when it is applied to an asset. For an asset, liquidity refers to the ease with which the asset can be turned into cash, whereas for a market, liquidity refers to the ease of carrying out financial transactions.)

The second problem with forward contracts is that they are subject to default risk. Suppose that in one year's time, interest rates rise so that the price of the 8s of 2015 falls. The Rock Solid Insurance Company might then decide that it would like to default on the forward contract with the First National Bank because it can now buy the bonds at a price lower than the agreed price in the forward contract. Or perhaps Rock Solid may not have been rock solid and will have gone bust during the year and so is no longer available to complete the terms of the forward contract. Because there is no outside organization guaranteeing the contract, the only recourse is for the First National Bank to go to the courts to sue Rock Solid, but this process will be costly. Furthermore, if Rock Solid is already bankrupt, the First National Bank will suffer a loss; the bank can no longer sell the 8s of 2015 at the price it had agreed with Rock Solid but instead will have to sell at a price well below that because the price of these bonds has fallen.

The presence of default risk in forward contracts means that parties to these contracts must check each other out to be sure that the counterparty is both financially sound and likely to be honest and live up to its contractual obligations. Because this is a costly process and because all the adverse selection and moral hazard problems discussed in earlier chapters apply, default risk is a major barrier to the use of interest-rate forward contracts. When the default risk problem is combined with a lack of liquidity, we see that these contracts may be of limited usefulness to financial institutions. Although there is a market for interest-rate forward contracts, particularly in Treasury and mortgage-backed securities, it is not nearly as large as the financial futures market, to which we turn next.

■ FINANCIAL FUTURES MARKETS

Given the default risk and liquidity problems in the interest-rate forward market, another solution to hedging interest-rate risk was needed. This solution was provided by the development of financial futures contracts by the Chicago Board of Trade starting in 1975.

Financial Futures Contracts

A **financial futures contract** is similar to an interest-rate forward contract in that it specifies that a debt instrument must be delivered by one party to another on a stated future date. However, it differs from an interest-rate forward contract in several ways that overcome some of the liquidity and default problems of forward markets.

To understand what financial futures contracts are all about, let's look at one of the most widely traded futures contracts, that for Treasury bonds, which are traded on the Chicago Board of Trade. (An illustration of how prices on these contracts are quoted can be found in the "Following the Financial News" box.) The contract value is for $100,000 face value of bonds. Prices are quoted in points, with each point equal to $1000, and the smallest change in price is one thirty-second of a point ($31.25). This contract specifies that the bonds to be delivered must have at least 15 years to maturity at the delivery date (and must also not be callable, that is, redeemable by the Treasury at its option, in less than 15 years). If the Treasury bonds delivered to settle the futures contract have a coupon rate different from the 8% specified in the futures contract, the amount of bonds to be delivered is adjusted to reflect the difference in value between the delivered bonds and the 8% coupon bond. In line with the terminology used for forward

---

FOLLOWING THE FINANCIAL NEWS

Financial Futures

The prices for financial futures contracts are published daily. In the *Wall Street Journal,* these prices are found in the "Commodities" section under the "Interest Rate" heading of the "Futures Prices" columns. An excerpt is reproduced here.

Interest Rate

TREASURY BONDS (CBT)-$100,000; PTS. 32NDS OF 100%.

	Open	High	Low	Settle	Change	Lifetime High	Lifetime Low	Open Interest
Mar	110-07	110-24	110-04	110-18	+ 10	120-00	99-26	493,083
June	109-24	110-07	109-21	110-02	+ 10	118-21	99-16	32,303
Sept	109-11	109-20	109-11	109-20	+ 10	117-21	100-18	5,821
Dec	108-26	109-06	108-26	109-06	+ 10	118-08	100-08	4,439

Est vol 475,000; vol Wed 560,366; open int 535,705, + 10,484.

Information for each contract is presented in columns, as follows. (The Chicago Board of Trade's contract for delivery of long-term Treasury bonds in March 1997, is used as an example.)

Open: Opening price; each point corresponds to $1000 of face value—110 7/32 is $110,219 for the March contract

High: Highest traded price that day—110 24/32 is $110,750 for the March contract

Low: Lowest traded price that day—110 4/32 is $110,125 for the March contract

Settle: Settlement price, the closing price that day—110 18/32 is $110,253 for the March contract

Chg: Change in the settlement price from the previous trading day— + 10/32 is + $313 for the March contract

Lifetime High: Highest price ever—120 is $120,000 for the March contract

Lifetime Low: Lowest price ever—99 26/32 is $99,813 for the March contract

Open Interest: Number of contracts outstanding—493,083 for the March contract, with a face value of $49 billion (493,083 × $100,000)

Source: Wall Street Journal, January 31, 1997, p. C14.

contracts, parties who have bought a futures contract and thereby agreed to buy (take delivery) of the bonds are said to have taken a *long position*, and parties who have sold a futures contract and thereby agreed to sell (deliver) the bonds have taken a *short position*.

To make our understanding of this contract more concrete, let's consider what happens when you buy or sell one of these Treasury bond futures contracts. Let's say that on February 1, you sell one $100,000 June contract at a price of 115 (that is, $115,000). By selling this contract, you agree to deliver $100,000 face value of the long-term Treasury bonds to the contract's counterparty at the end of June for $115,000. By buying the contract at a price of 115, the buyer has agreed to pay $115,000 for the $100,000 face value of bonds when you deliver them at the end of June. If interest rates on long-term bonds rise so that when the contract matures at the end of June the price of these bonds has fallen to 110 ($110,000 per $100,000 of face value), the buyer of the contract will have lost $5000 because he or she paid $115,000 for the bonds but can sell them only for the market price of $110,000. But you, the seller of the contract, will have gained $5000 because you can now sell the bonds to the buyer for $115,000 but have to pay only $110,000 for them in the market.

It is even easier to describe what happens to the parties who have purchased futures contracts and those who have sold futures contracts if we recognize the following fact: ***At the expiration date of a futures contract, the price of the contract is the same as the price of the underlying asset to be delivered.*** To see why this is the case, consider what happens on the expiration date of the June contract at the end of June when the price of the underlying $100,000-face-value Treasury bond is 110 ($110,000). If the futures contract is selling below 110, say, at 109, a trader can buy the contract for $109,000, take delivery of the bond, and immediately sell it for $110,000, thereby earning a quick profit of $1000. Because earning this profit involves no risk, it is a great deal that everyone would like to get in on. That means that everyone will try to buy the contract, and as a result, its price will rise. Only when the price rises to 110 will the profit opportunity cease to exist and the buying pressure disappear. Conversely, if the price of the futures contract is above 110, say, at 111, everyone will want to sell the contract. Now the sellers get $111,000 from selling the futures contract but have to pay only $110,000 for the Treasury bonds that they must deliver to the buyer of the contract, and the $1000 difference is their profit. Because this profit involves no risk, traders will continue to sell the futures contract until its price falls back down to 110, at which price there are no longer any profits to be made. The elimination of riskless profit opportunities in the futures market is referred to as **arbitrage,** and it guarantees that the price of a futures contract at expiration equals the price of the underlying asset to be delivered.[1]

Armed with the fact that a futures contract at expiration equals the price of the underlying asset makes it even easier to see who profits and loses from such

---

[1]In actuality, futures contracts sometimes set conditions for delivery of the underlying assets that cause the price of the contract at expiration to differ slightly from the price of the underlying assets. Because the difference in price is extremely small, we ignore it in this chapter.

a contract when interest rates change. When interest rates have risen so that the price of the Treasury bond is 110 on the expiration day at the end of June, the June Treasury bond futures contract will also have a price of 110. Thus if you bought the contract for 115 in February, you have a loss of 5 points, or $5000 (5% of $100,000). But if you sold the futures contract at 115 in February, the decline in price to 110 means that you have a profit of 5 points, or $5000.

Organization of Trading in Financial Futures Markets

Financial futures contracts are traded in the United States on organized exchanges such as the Chicago Board of Trade, the Chicago Mercantile Exchange, the New York Futures Exchange, the MidAmerica Commodity Exchange, and the Kansas City Board of Trade. These exchanges are highly competitive with one another, and each organization tries to design contracts and set rules that will increase the amount of futures trading on its exchange.

The futures exchanges and all trades in financial futures in the United States are regulated by the Commodity Futures Trading Commission (CFTC), which was created in 1974 to take over the regulatory responsibilities for futures markets from the Department of Agriculture. The CFTC oversees futures trading and the futures exchanges to ensure that prices in the market are not being manipulated, and it also registers and audits the brokers, traders, and exchanges to prevent fraud and to ensure the financial soundness of the exchanges. In addition, the CFTC approves proposed futures contracts to make sure that they serve the public interest. The most widely traded financial futures contracts listed in the *Wall Street Journal* and the exchanges where they are traded (along with the number of contracts outstanding, called **open interest,** on March 5, 1997) are listed in Table 1.[2]

Given the globalization of other financial markets in recent years, it is not surprising that increased competition from abroad has been occurring in financial futures markets as well.

 ## Globalization of Financial Futures Markets

Because American futures exchanges were the first to develop financial futures, they dominated the trading of financial futures in the early 1980s. For example, in 1985, all of the top ten futures contracts were traded on exchanges in the United States. With the rapid growth of financial futures markets and the resulting high profits made by the American exchanges, foreign exchanges saw a profit opportunity and began to enter this business. By the 1990s, Eurodollar contracts traded on the London International Financial Futures Exchange, Japanese government bond contracts and Euroyen contracts traded on the Tokyo Stock Exchange, French government bond contracts traded on the Marché à Terme International de France, and Nikkei 225 contracts traded on the Osaka Securities Exchange all became among the most widely traded futures contracts in the world. Even devel-

---

[2]For a more detailed treatment of financial futures and option markets, see Franklin R. Edwards and Cindy W. Ma, *Futures and Options* (New York: McGraw-Hill, 1992).

■ **TABLE 1**   Widely Traded Financial Futures Contracts

Type of Contract	Contract Size	Exchange*	Open Interest (March 5, 1997)
Interest-Rate Contracts			
Treasury bonds	$100,000	CBT	531,833
Treasury bonds	$50,000	MCE	11,213
Treasury notes	$100,000	CBT	312,442
Five-year Treasury notes	$100,000	CBT	217,587
Two-year Treasury notes	$200,000	CBT	26,512
Thirty-day Fed funds	$5 million	CBT	20,172
Treasury bills	$1 million	CME	9,970
One-month LIBOR	$3 million	CME	34,044
Municipal Bond Index	$1000	CBT	17,934
Eurodollar	$1 million	CME	2,388,907
Euroyen	100 million	CME	27,439
Euroyen	100 million	SIMEX	369,666
Sterling	£500,000	LIFFE	523,575
Long Gilt	£50,000	LIFFE	260,656
Euromark	DM 1 million	LIFFE	1,250,658
Euroswiss franc	SF 1 million	LIFFE	111,320
German government bonds	DM 250,000	LIFFE	290,276
Ten-year French govt. bonds	500,000 francs	MATIF	154,440
Italian government bonds	Lit 200 billion	LIFFE	127,539
Canadian banker's acceptance	C$1,000,000	ME	110,419
Ten-year Canadian government bonds	C$100,000	ME	29,965
Stock Index Contracts			
Standard & Poor's 500 Index	$500 × index	CME	204,656
Standard & Poor's MIDCAP 400	$500 × index	CME	11,415
NASDAQ 100	$100 × index	CME	7,548
Nikkei 225 Stock Average	$5 × index	CME	19,263
Financial Times–Stock Exchange 100-Share Index Composite Index	£25 per index point	LIFFE	71,816
Currency Contracts			
Yen	12,500,000 yen	CME	78,819
Deutschemark	125,000 marks	CME	112,867
Canadian dollar	100,000 Canadian $	CME	62,862
British pound	62,500 pounds	CME	38,791
Swiss Franc	125,000 francs	CME	52,904
Mexican peso	500,000 new pesos	CME	40,166

*Exchange abbreviations: CBT, Chicago Board of Trade; CME, Chicago Mercantile Exchange; LIFFE, London International Financial Futures Exchange; MATIF, Marché à Terme International de France; MCE, MidAmerica Commodity Exchange; ME, Montreal Exchange; NYFE, New York Futures Exchange; SIMEX, Singapore International Monetary Exchange.

Source: Wall Street Journal, March 5, 1997, p. C14.

oping countries are getting into the act. In 1996, seven developing countries (also referred to as *emerging-market countries*) established futures exchanges, and this number is expected to double within a few years.

Foreign competition has also spurred knockoffs of the most popular financial futures contracts initially developed in the United States. These contracts traded on foreign exchanges are virtually identical to those traded in the United States and have the advantage that they can be traded when the American exchanges are closed. The movement to 24-hour-a-day trading in financial futures has been further stimulated by the development of the Globex electronic trading system, which allows traders throughout the world to trade futures even when the exchanges are not officially open. Financial futures trading is thus well on the way to being completely internationalized, and competition between U.S. and foreign exchanges will continue to be intense in the future.

Explaining the Success of Futures Markets

The tremendous success of the financial futures market in Treasury bonds is evident from the fact that the total open interest of Treasury bond contracts was over 531,000 on March 5, 1997, for a total value of over $53 billion (531,833 × $100,000). There are several differences between financial futures and forward contracts and in the organization of their markets that help explain why financial futures markets like those for Treasury bonds have been so successful.

Several features of futures contracts were designed to overcome the liquidity problem inherent in forward contracts. The first feature is that, in contrast to forward contracts, the quantities delivered and the delivery dates of futures contracts are standardized, making it more likely that different parties can be matched up in the futures market, thereby increasing the liquidity of the market. In the case of the Treasury bond contract, the quantity delivered is $100,000 face value of bonds, and the delivery dates are set to be the last business day of March, June, September, and December. The second feature is that after the futures contract has been bought or sold, it can be traded (bought or sold) again at any time until the delivery date. In contrast, once a forward contract is agreed on, it typically cannot be traded. The third feature is that in a futures contract, not just one specific type of Treasury bond is deliverable on the delivery date, as in a forward contract. Instead, any Treasury bond that matures in more than 15 years and is not callable for 15 years is eligible for delivery. Allowing continuous trading also increases the liquidity of the futures market, as does the ability to deliver a range of Treasury bonds rather than one specific bond.

Another reason why futures contracts specify that more than one bond is eligible for delivery is to limit the possibility that someone might corner the market and "squeeze" traders who have sold contracts. To corner the market, someone buys up all the deliverable securities so that investors with a short position cannot obtain from anyone else the securities that they contractually must deliver on the delivery date. As a result, the person who has cornered the market can set exorbitant prices for the securities that investors with a short position must buy to fulfill their obligations under the futures contract. The person who has cornered the market makes a fortune, but investors with a short position take a terrific loss. Clearly, the possibility that corners might occur in the market will discourage people from taking a short position and might therefore decrease the size of the market. By allowing many different securities to be delivered, the futures contract makes it harder for anyone to corner the market because a much larger

---

■ BOX 1

The Hunt Brothers and the Silver Crash

In early 1979, two Texas billionaires, W. Herbert Hunt and his brother, Nelson Bunker Hunt, decided that they were going to get into the silver market in a big way. Herbert stated his reasoning for purchasing silver as follows: "I became convinced that the economy of the United States was in a weakening condition. This reinforced my belief that investment in precious metals was wise . . . because of rampant inflation." Although the Hunts' stated reason for purchasing silver was that it was a good investment, others felt that their real motive was to establish a corner in the silver market. Along with other associates, several of them from the Saudi royal family, the Hunts purchased close to 300 million ounces of silver in the form of either actual bullion or silver futures contracts. The result was that the price of silver rose from $6 an ounce to over $50 an ounce by January 1980.

Once the regulators and the futures exchanges got wind of what the Hunts were up to, they decided to take action to eliminate the possibility of a corner by limiting to 2000 the number of contracts that any single trader could hold. This limit, which was equivalent to 10 million ounces, was only a small fraction of what the Hunts were holding, and so they were forced to sell. The silver market collapsed soon afterward, with the price of silver declining back to below $10 an ounce. The losses to the Hunts were estimated to be in excess of $1 billion, and they soon found themselves in financial difficulty. They had to go into debt to the tune of $1.1 billion, mortgaging not only the family's holdings in the Placid Oil Company but also 75,000 head of cattle, a stable of Thoroughbred horses, paintings, jewelry, and even such mundane items as irrigation pumps and lawn mowers. Eventually both Hunt brothers were forced into declaring personal bankruptcy, earning them the dubious distinction of declaring the largest personal bankruptcies ever in the United States.

Nelson and Herbert Hunt paid a heavy price for their excursion into the silver market, but at least Nelson retained his sense of humor. When asked right after the collapse of the silver market how he felt about his losses, he said, "A billion dollars isn't what it used to be."

Source: G. Christian Hill, "Dynasty's Decline: The Current Question About the Hunts of Dallas: How Poor Are They?" *Wall Street Journal,* November 14, 1984, p. C28.

---

amount of securities would have to be purchased to establish the corner. Corners are more than a theoretical possibility, as Box 1 indicates, and are a concern to both regulators and the organized exchanges that design futures contracts.

Trading in the futures market has been organized differently from trading in forward markets to overcome the default risk problems arising in forward contracts. In both types, for every contract there must be a buyer who is taking a long position and a seller who is taking a short position. However, the buyer and seller of a futures contract make their contract not with each other but with the clearinghouse associated with the futures exchange. This setup means that the buyer of the futures contract does not need to worry about the financial health or trustworthiness of the seller, or vice versa, as in the forward market. As long as the clearinghouse is financially solid, buyers and sellers of futures contract do not have to worry about default risk.

To make sure that the clearinghouse is financially sound and does not run into financial difficulties that might jeopardize its contracts, buyers or sellers of futures contracts must put an initial deposit, called a **margin requirement,** of perhaps $2000 per Treasury bond contract into a margin account kept at their brokerage firm. Futures contracts are then **marked to market** every day. What this means is that at the end of every trading day, the change in the value of the futures contract is added to or subtracted from the margin account. Suppose that after buying the Treasury bond contract at a price of 115 on Wednesday morning, its closing price at the end of the day, the *settlement price*, falls to 114. You now have a loss of 1 point, or $1000, on the contract, and the seller who sold you the contract has a gain of 1 point, or $1000. The $1000 gain is added to the seller's margin account, making a total of $3000 in that account, and the $1000 loss is subtracted from your account, so you now only have $1000 in your account. If the amount in this margin account falls below the maintenance margin requirement (which can be the same as the initial requirement but is usually a little less), the trader is required to add money to the account. For example, if the maintenance margin requirement is also $2000, you would have to add $1000 to your account to bring it up to $2000. Margin requirements and marking to market make it far less likely that a trader will default on a contract, thus protecting the futures exchange from losses.

A final advantage that futures markets have over forward markets is that most futures contracts do not result in delivery of the underlying asset on the expiration date, whereas forward contracts do. A trader who sold a futures contract is allowed to avoid delivery on the expiration date by making an offsetting purchase of a futures contract. Because the simultaneous holding of the long and short positions means that the trader would in effect be delivering the bonds to itself, under the exchange rules the trader is allowed to cancel both contracts. Allowing traders to cancel their contracts in this way lowers the cost of conducting trades in the futures market relative to the forward market in that a futures trader can avoid the costs of physical delivery, which is not so easy with forward contracts.

■ THE PRACTICING FINANCIAL INSTITUTION MANAGER
Hedging Interest-Rate Risk with Financial Futures

Managers of financial institutions such as banks, insurance companies, pension funds, finance companies, and mutual funds make use of two basic kinds of hedging strategies involving forward markets and futures markets to reduce interest-rate risk: the micro hedge and the macro hedge. When a financial institution hedges the interest-rate risk for a specific asset it is holding, it is conducting a **micro hedge.** When the financial institution is hedging interest-rate risk on its overall portfolio, it is conducting a **macro hedge.** To illustrate these hedging strategies, let's look at how a financial institution manager—say, the manager of the First National Bank—can use futures markets to engage in both a micro and a macro hedge.[3]

Micro Hedge

Suppose that in March 1999, the First National Bank is holding $10 million face value of 10%-coupon-rate Treasury bonds selling at par that mature in the year 2010, referred to as the "10s of 2010." We have already seen that fluctuations

---

[3]Financial institutions also use financial futures to guarantee the cost of funds when they anticipate that they will make additional loans in the future.

in interest rates on these long-term bonds can cause major price fluctuations that result in large capital gains or losses in the coming year. One way that this risk could be hedged over the coming year is with the forward contract that was described earlier in the chapter in which the bank agrees to sell, at today's price and interest rate, $10 million of this bond to another party one year in the future, that is, in March 2000. However, as we have seen, finding a counterparty for this transaction might be difficult, so Mona, the manager of the First National Bank, decides to use the financial futures market instead.

Mona's problem is that there is no financial futures contract that corresponds exactly to the 10s of 2010 Treasury bond whose price she would like to lock in for next year. So she looks for a widely traded futures contract whose underlying asset price moves closely with the price of the asset her bank is holding. She decides that the Treasury bond contract traded at the Chicago Board of Trade is the best one for her hedge. This hedge is called a **cross hedge** because the underlying asset in the futures contract is not the same as the asset being hedged.

Mona knows that she needs to take a short position and sell Treasury bond futures contracts to hedge the interest-rate risk on the Treasury bonds. She figures this out by recognizing that if there is a fall in bond prices that would cause her bank to suffer losses on the bonds it is holding, the bank needs an equal offsetting gain on futures contracts. If the bank has taken a short position, then when the bond price falls, the bank can buy the bonds in the market at a lower price than the price at which it agreed to deliver the securities, thereby making the profit needed to offset the losses on the bonds it is holding.

Although the bank manager knows that she needs to take a short position, she still has to decide how many Treasury bond contracts she must sell to make sure that the change in the value of these futures contracts over the coming year is likely to offset the change in the value of the Treasury bonds she is hedging. Her first step in this process is to calculate the so-called **hedge ratio,** which tells her how many points the price of the hedged asset moves on average for a 1-point change in the futures contract used for the hedge. For example, if, when the price of the futures contract increases by 1 point, the price of the Treasury 10s of 2010 on average were to increase by 1.1 points, the hedge ratio would be 1.1.

The hedge ratio is important because it tells the bank manager the par dollar amount of futures contract needed per par dollar of the asset being hedged in order to provide the best hedge. Thus with a hedge ratio of 1.1, Mona should sell $1.10 face value of the futures contract for every dollar of face value of the Treasury 10s of 2010; that is, she should sell $11 million face value (= 1.1 × $10 million) of Treasury bond futures contracts. Doing this makes intuitive sense because a good hedge is one in which on average any fall in the value of the hedged assets is offset by the gains on the futures contract. The hedge ratio indicates that if the $10 million of Treasury 10s of 2010 fall in price by 1.1 points, for a loss of $110,000 (1.1% of $10 million), she wants to have a gain on average of $110,000 on the Treasury bond futures contract she has sold. Since the hedge ratio indicates that when the Treasury 10s of 2010 have a price decline of 1.1

points, the Treasury bond futures contract on average has a decline of 1 point, she will have a profit of $110,000 on the futures contract (1% of $11 million).

The hedge ratio is calculated in two steps, as is indicated by the formula given by Equation 1:

$$HR = \frac{\Delta P_a}{\Delta P_f} \times \beta_{af} \tag{1}$$

where HR = hedge ratio
ΔP_a = change in the price of the hedged asset as a percentage of par in response to a 1% change in the interest rate
ΔP_f = change in the price of the futures contract as a percentage of par in response to a 1% change in the interest rate
β_{af} = average change in the interest rate of the hedged asset for a given change in the interest rate of the futures contract

The first step is to calculate the first term in the formula, $\Delta P_a/\Delta P_f$, which tells us how much the value of the hedged asset changes relative to the futures contract when there is a change in interest rates. The hedge ratio formula gives the intuitive result that when there is a greater change in the hedged asset's value relative to the futures contract for a given change in the interest rate— that is, when $\Delta P_a/\Delta P_f$ is higher, meaning that HR is higher—more Treasury bond futures contracts are needed to complete the hedge.

The change in the values of the hedged asset and the futures contract when interest rates change by, say, 1 percentage point can be calculated using the duration concept described in Chapter 3 or by other methods. Let's say that Mona finds that when the interest rate rises from 10% to 11% in March 2000, the 10s of 2010 Treasury bonds her bank is holding would decline by 6.58% of par (that is, by 6.58 points), while the Treasury bond futures contract would decline by 5.98% of par (5.98 points). The relative change in the value of the hedged asset relative to the futures contract would then equal 6.58/5.98 = 1.10.

The second step is to calculate the second term in the formula, β_{af}, which tells us how the interest rates for the hedged asset and the financial futures contract move together. When $\beta_{af} = 0$, for example, the interest rate on the hedged asset does not tend to move at all with changes in the interest rate on the futures contract. When $\beta_{af} = 1$, the interest rate on the hedged asset rises 1 percentage point on average when the interest rate on the futures contract rises by 1 percentage point; that is, on average they move in tandem. If $\beta_{af} = 2$, the interest rate on the hedged asset on average rises by 2 percentage points when there is a 1-percentage-point rise in the interest rate on the futures contract.

As the formula indicates, when β_{af} is lower, HR is lower, yielding the intuitive result that if the interest rate on the hedged assets does not on average change much with a change in the interest rate on the futures contract, a smaller amount of futures contracts should be used in the hedge. For example, if the interest rates on the hedged asset and the futures contract did not move together at all ($\beta_{af} = 0$), the futures contract would not be at all helpful in constructing a hedge and so should not be used. That is exactly what the hedge ratio formula indicates because when the interest rates on the hedged asset and the futures contract do not move together, plugging $\beta_{af} = 0$ into the formula yields $HR = 0$.

The β_{af} term is calculated by means of a statistical analysis of past data that determines how much interest rates on the hedged asset change on average for a given change in the interest rate of the futures contract. The bank manager calculates that when the interest rate on the futures contract changes by 1 percentage point, the interest rate on the Treasury 10s of 2010 changes on average by 1 percentage point, meaning that $\beta_{af} = 1$. Plugging the estimates of $\beta_{af} = 1$ and $\Delta P_a / \Delta P_f = 1.10$ into the formula in Equation 1, she calculates the hedge ratio to be

$$ HR = \frac{\Delta P_a}{\Delta P_f} \times \beta_{af} = 1.10 \times 1 = 1.10 $$

Now Mona is almost done with her calculation of how many Treasury bond contracts she needs to sell to hedge the 10s of 2010 bonds her bank is holding. Recall that the hedge ratio is the par dollar amount of futures contract per par dollar of the asset being hedged, so to calculate the number of contracts, Mona just has to multiply the hedge ratio by the face value of the amount of bonds she is hedging and divide through by the face value of the futures contract. Expressed as a formula, the number of contracts she needs to sell is

$$ \text{Contracts} = HR \times \frac{PV_a}{PV_f} \qquad (2) $$

where HR = hedge ratio (1.10 in our example)

$\quad PV_a$ = par (face) value of the asset hedged ($10 million of Treasury 10s of 2010)

$\quad PV_f$ = par (face) value of the futures contract ($100,000 per Treasury bond futures contract)

In our example,

$$ \text{Contracts} = 1.10 \times \frac{\$10,000,000}{\$100,000} = 1.10 \times 100 = 110 $$

After calculating that she needs to sell 110 futures contracts, Mona now calls her broker and puts in an order to sell 110 of the March 2000 Treasury bond futures contracts at the Chicago Board of Trade.

To see that the bank manager has indeed hedged the interest-rate risk on the $10 million of Treasury 10s of 2010 her bank is holding, let's see what happens if interest rates on both the futures contract and the 10s of 2010 Treasury bonds rise from 10% in March 1999 to 11% in March 2000. As we have seen, the rise in the interest rate from 10% to 11% would result in a decline in the price of the Treasury 10s of 2010 by 6.58% of par. Thus on the $10 million face value of bonds that the bank is holding, it would have a loss of $658,000 over the course of the year. Conversely, as we have seen, the rise in the interest rate for the futures contract from 10% to 11% would result in a decline in the futures contract's price by 5.98% of par, which is $5980 per $100,000 contract. Since the bank manager has sold 110 of these contracts short, the decline in price results in a profit of $657,800 (110 × $5980), which almost exactly offsets the loss on the bonds the bank is holding. (The hedge is not perfect—that is, the loss is slightly higher than the gain—because the manager can sell only a whole number of contracts.)

Macro Hedge

Instead of just hedging the Treasury bonds and other individual assets and liabilities of the First National Bank, the bank manager might decide that it would be better to try to hedge the entire balance sheet of the bank in one fell swoop. Recall from Chapter 20 that the First National Bank, which has $100 million of assets, calculated that it had a duration gap of 1.72 years. If in March 1999 the bank manager sells $100 million of March 2000 futures contracts whose underlying bonds also have an average duration of 1.72 years, then a rise in interest rates over the coming year, which would cause the value of the bank's net worth to fall, would be offset by the profits earned on the short position from selling the futures contracts. In other words, the macro hedge would be such that

$$V_F \times DUR_F = -V_A \times DUR_{GAP} \qquad (3)$$

where V_F = value of the futures contracts
V_A = value of total bank assets
DUR_F = average duration of the underlying bonds in the futures contracts
DUR_{GAP} = duration gap measurement for the bank

If the duration of the deliverable bonds in the five-year $100,000 Treasury note futures contract equaled 1.72 years, the bank manager's task would be pretty easy. She would just need to sell $100 million of these futures contracts. (The sale of the futures contracts means that V_F is −$100 million, and this multiplied by the duration of 1.72 years equals the −$100 million × 1.72 on the right-hand side of Equation 3.) If these contracts were selling at the face value of $100,000, Mona would call her broker and put in an order to sell 1000 March 2000 five-year Treasury note contracts.

To see that Mona has correctly hedged the interest-rate risk of the bank's portfolio, let's again look at what happens if interest rates rise from 10% to 11% from March 1999 to March 2000. Using the Equation 5 formula from Chapter 20, the change in the bank's net worth as a percentage of its assets is

$$\% \Delta NW = -DUR_{GAP} \times \frac{\Delta i}{1 + i} = -1.72 \times \frac{0.01}{1.10} = 0.016 = 1.6\%$$

That is, when the interest rate rises by 1% from 10% to 11%, the First National Bank's net worth declines by $1.6 million (1.6% of $100 million of assets) to $98.4 million. But we can calculate the percentage change in the price of the futures contract using the Equation 3 formula from Chapter 20 as follows:

$$\% \Delta P = -DUR_F \times \frac{\Delta i}{1 + i} = -\left(1.72 \times \frac{0.01}{1 + 0.10}\right) = -0.016 = -1.6\%$$

So when the interest rate rises by 1% from 10% to 11%, the price of the futures contract falls by 1.6%. Because the bank manager sold $100 million of these contracts, the 1.6% decline in price results in a profit for the First National Bank of $1.6 million (1.6% of $100 million). The $1.6 million gain on the futures contract exactly offsets the $1.6 million decline in the bank's net worth from the rise in interest rates.

Unfortunately, the bank manager's job is not this easy because it is unlikely that she would find a futures contract whose underlying securities had a duration exactly equal to the bank's duration gap. To overcome this problem, the bank manager can mix futures contracts for bonds of different maturities into a $100 million portfolio of futures contracts, making sure that the portfolio's duration exactly equals the bank's duration gap of 1.72 years.

Alternatively, the bank manager can use a futures contract with a different duration, say, of 3.44 years, but sell a different amount of the contract. Using Equation 3 from this chapter,

$$V_F = -\frac{V_A \times DUR_{GAP}}{DUR_F} = -\frac{\$100 \text{ million} \times 1.72}{3.44} = -\$50 \text{ million}$$

Thus she would put in an order to sell $50 million of this contract. In this case, when interest rates rise from 10% to 11%, the percentage change in the price of the futures contract would be

$$\%\Delta P = -DUR_F \times \frac{\Delta i}{1 + i} = -3.44 \times \frac{0.01}{1 + 0.10} = -0.031 = -3.1\%$$

With the sale of $50 million of these contracts, the 3.1% decline in value results in a profit of $1.6 million ($0.0313 \times \$50$ million), which again exactly offsets the decline in the bank's net worth from the rise in interest rates.

Some Problems with Financial Futures Market Hedges

Although financial futures market hedges can help financial institutions reduce interest-rate risk, managers of these institutions can run into two basic problems when they try to hedge with financial futures.

Basis Risk   The first problem is associated with **basis risk,** the risk associated with the possibility that the prices of the hedged asset and the asset underlying the futures contract do not move together over time. In our discussion of the micro hedge, we recognized that this might happen by including the term β_{af} in the hedge ratio formula. However, this term tells us only how the interest rates for the hedged asset and the financial futures contract move together *on average.* Even if *on average* the interest rates on the hedged asset and the futures contract move in tandem such that $\beta_{af} = 1$, that does not mean that they *always* move in perfect unison.

For the bank manager's micro hedge, there is a high but not perfect correlation between the interest rates on the 10s of 2010 Treasury bonds and the long-term bonds deliverable in the Treasury bond futures contract. So even though there will be some basis risk, there will probably not be much. Indeed, to minimize basis risk, the financial institution manager should choose a futures contract whose underlying securities have interest-rate movements that are highly correlated with those on the asset to be hedged.

However, there are cases where substantial basis risk cannot be avoided. For example, suppose that the bank manager was attempting to hedge long-term municipal bonds by taking a short position in the Treasury bond futures contract and that sometime before the delivery date, a major default occurred in this market. (Such a default occurred in 1983 when the Washington State Public Power Supply System defaulted on $2.25 billion of its municipal bonds.) Such a default might cause a sharp upward movement in interest rates on municipal bonds because perceptions of higher default risk would shrink demand for them, while demand for default-free Treasury bonds would increase, possibly lowering their interest rates. The result could then be that interest rates on municipal bonds and on the Treasury bond futures contract would move in opposite directions. The rise in interest rates on municipal bonds would produce a loss on the municipal bonds the bank is holding, but the fall in interest rates on the Treasury bonds would result in an additional loss on the bank's short position in the futures contract. In this case, the futures hedge could make the situation even worse for the bank. The example here is extreme, but it does show that the dangers of basis risk are real.

Accounting Problems A second problem with futures hedges arises from the system of accounting that financial institutions use. Under generally accepted accounting principles, when a macro hedge is made that hedges not a specific financial asset but a financial institution's entire portfolio, profits or losses the institution makes on the hedge cannot be offset by the unrealized gains or losses on the institution's portfolio (so-called paper gains or losses that are not realized because sales of the items in the portfolio have not yet occurred). To see what this could mean, suppose that the bank manager's macro hedge works out perfectly, so when interest rates rise from 10% to 11%, the $1.6 million decrease in the value of assets relative to liabilities is exactly offset by a $1.6 million gain on the financial futures contracts. Although the bank has been completely immunized against the change in interest rates, the bank is required to show an increase in profits of the $1.6 million it makes on the hedge but is not allowed to offset this profit with the losses it suffered on the rest of its portfolio. This example illustrates that hedging with financial futures might result in apparent (but not real) fluctuations in income that could be misinterpreted by the markets or have adverse tax consequences.

■ STOCK INDEX FUTURES

As we have seen, financial futures markets can be useful in hedging interest-rate risk. However, financial institution managers, particularly those who manage mutual funds, pension funds, and insurance companies, also worry about **stock market risk,** the risk that occurs because stock prices fluctuate. Stock index futures were developed in 1982 to meet the need to manage stock market risk, and they have become among the most widely traded of all futures contracts.

Stock Index Futures

The prices for stock index futures contracts are published daily. In the *Wall Street Journal,* these prices are found in the section "Futures Prices" under the "Index" heading. An excerpt from this listing is reproduced here.

Index

S&P 500 INDEX (CME) $500 times index.

	Open	High	Low	Settle	Change	High	Low	Open Interest
June	738.25	748.20	736.70	747.30	+8.80	827.80	629.05	182,840
Sept	747.50	755.60	745.40	754.85	+8.85	835.70	707.50	5,468
Dec	754.00	763.90	753.00	763.05	+8.90	843.70	753.00	3,119
Mr98	765.00	772.50	762.20	772.15	+9.30	831.40	762.20	313

Est vol 78,945; vol Fr Wed 91,101; open int 191,740, + 3.606.
Indx prelim High 743,73; Low 733.54; Close 743.73 + 6.08

Information for each contract is given in columns, as follows. (The June S&P 500 Index contract is used as an example.)

Open: Opening price; each point corresponds to $500 times the index—738.25; that is, 738.25 × $500 = $369,125 per contract

High: Highest traded price that day—748.20, or $374,100 per contract

Low: Lowest traded price that day—736.70, or $368,350 per contract

Settle: Settlement price, the closing price that day—747.30, or $373,650 per contract

Chg: Change in the settlement price from the previous trading day—+8.80 points, or $4,400 per contract

High: High price for the year—827.80, or $413,900 per contract

Low: Low price for the year—629.05, or $314,525 per contract

Open Interest: Number of contracts outstanding—182,840, or a total value of $68 billion (= 182,840 × $373,650).

Source: Wall Street Journal, April 15, 1997, p. C16.

Stock Index Futures Contracts

To understand stock index futures contracts, let's look at the Standard & Poor's 500 Index futures contract (shown in the "Following the Financial News" box), the most widely traded stock index futures contract in the United States. (The S&P 500 Index measures the value of 500 of the most widely traded stocks.) Stock index futures contracts differ from most other financial futures contracts in that they are settled with a cash delivery rather than with the delivery of a security. Cash settlement gives these contracts the advantage of a high degree of liquidity and also rules out the possibility of anyone's cornering the market. In the case of the S&P 500 Index contract, at the final settlement date, the cash delivery due is $500 times the index, so if the index is at 400 on the final settlement date, $200,000 would be the amount due. The price quotes for this contract are also quoted in terms of index points, so a change of 1 point represents a change of $500 in the contract's value.

To understand what all this means, let's look at what happens when you buy or sell this futures contract. Suppose that on February 1, you sell one June contract at a price of 400 (that is, $200,000). By selling the contract, you agree to a delivery amount due of $500 times the S&P 500 Index on the expiration date at the end of June. By buying the contract at a price of 400, the buyer has agreed to pay $200,000 for the delivery amount due of $500 times the S&P 500 Index at the expiration date at the end of June. If the stock market falls so that the S&P 500 Index declines to 360 on the expiration date, the buyer of the contract will have lost $20,000 because he or she has agreed to pay $200,000 for the contract but has a delivery amount due of the $180,000 (360 × $500). But you, the seller of the contract, will have a profit of $20,000 because you agreed to receive a $200,000 purchase price for the contract but have a delivery amount due of only $180,000. Because the amount payable and due are netted out, only $20,000 will change hands; you, the seller of the contract, receive $20,000 from the buyer.

■ THE PRACTICING FINANCIAL INSTITUTION MANAGER
Using Stock Index Futures

Financial institution managers use stock index futures contracts to cope with stock market risk in two principal ways: to reduce systematic risk and to lock in stock prices. Let's first look at how the portfolio manager for the Rock Solid Insurance Company would go about hedging against systematic risk in the company's portfolio.

Reducing Systematic Risk

In Chapter 4 we learned that portfolios of assets have *systematic risk*, risk that cannot be eliminated through diversification. We also saw that systematic risk can be measured by beta, β, a variable that tells us the sensitivity of the portfolio's returns to a change in the value of the entire market. If we take the market to be represented by the S&P 500 Index, a broad measure of how well the market is doing, then the beta of a portfolio can be measured using statistical methods to determine how much on average the portfolio's value changes for a 1-percentage-point change in the S&P index.

Suppose that in March 1999, Mort, the portfolio manager, does this statistical calculation and finds that Rock Solid's portfolio of $100 million of stocks on average moves percentagewise one-for-one with the S&P index and so has a beta of 1; that is, if the value of the S&P index changes by 10%, the portfolio value changes by 10%. Suppose also that the March 2000 S&P 500 Index contracts are currently selling at a price of 400. How many of these contracts should Mort sell so that the beta of the combined portfolio, including the stock portfolio and the futures contracts, is equal to zero and hence Rock Solid is not exposed to any systematic risk over the coming year?

Because the beta of his stock portfolio is 1 (its value changes in exact proportion to the change in the S&P 500 Index), this calculation is quite easy. To immunize his portfolio against systematic risk, Mort must sell $100 million of S&P index futures, thereby agreeing to a delivery amount due of $500 times the S&P index in March 2000. At a price of 400 ($200,000 per contract), Mort sells $100 million/$200,000 = 500 contracts. If the S&P index falls 10% to 360, on average the $100 million portfolio will suffer a $10 million loss. At the same time, however, Mort makes a profit of 40 × $500 = $20,000 per contract because he agreed to receive $200,000 for each contract when the price was originally at 400, but at a price of 360 on the expiration date he has a delivery amount due of only $180,000 (360 × $500). Multiplied by the 500 contracts, the $20,000 profit per contract yields a total profit of $10 million. The $10 million profit on the futures contracts exactly offsets the loss on Rock Solid's stock portfolio, so the portfolio manager has been successful in hedging the stock market risk due to overall market swings.

If Mort's calculations reveal that Rock Solid's portfolio has a beta of 2—meaning that it has twice as much systematic risk as the market—then selling 500 contracts of the S&P stock index futures will not eliminate the systematic risk of the portfolio. With a beta of 2, if the S&P index goes down by 10% to 360, then on average the $100 million portfolio would suffer a 20% ($20 million) loss. As before, the 500 futures contracts would yield a profit of $10 million, but this profit would offset only half of the $20 million loss on the portfolio, for a net loss of $10 million.

Because Mort is a smart guy, he realizes that all he has to do to prevent this loss is sell twice as many futures contracts. In other words, if he sells 1000 futures contracts, when the S&P index goes down by 10% to 360, Rock Solid will have a profit of 40 × $500 = $20,000 per contract, which multiplied by the 1000 contracts yields a total profit of $20 million. Once again, the hedge position in S&P 500 Index futures provides a profit that exactly offsets the average loss on the portfolio due to overall market swings.

The portfolio manager has discovered that to hedge the systematic risk of a stock portfolio, the number of futures contracts sold must be adjusted proportionally to the beta of the portfolio. The following formula reveals the number of contracts that must to be sold to hedge systematic risk:

$$\text{Contracts} = \beta \times \frac{\text{value of portfolio}}{\text{value of contract}} \qquad (4)$$

We have now seen how hedging with stock index futures can immunize a portfolio from a decline in the overall market, but one consequence is that when the overall market rises, the company will not reap the profits. A rise in the overall market by 10% will on average produce a 20% increase in Rock Solid's portfolio if its beta is 2, for a profit of $20 million, but the $20 million loss on the 1000 futures contracts the portfolio manager has sold (= 1000 × $20,000 loss per contract) will yield a net profit of zero.

Why would the portfolio manager be willing to forgo profits when the stock market rises? The first reason is that he might be worried that a bear market was imminent and so wants to protect Rock Solid's portfolio from the coming decline. This feature of the stock index futures hedge is one reason why this type of hedging has been dubbed **portfolio insurance.** The second reason is that the portfolio manager may feel that he is particularly good at picking individual stocks that will do well but wants to minimize the risk due to overall swings in the market. With a stock index futures hedge, if he has been successful at picking good stocks that perform better than the market, his results will still look good even if there has been a sharp decline in the overall market.

Locking In Stock Prices

Suppose that the portfolio manager knows that his company will receive an inflow of funds in the future that have to be invested and believes that a stock market boom is imminent. In this case, he would like to be able to lock in the stock prices at which he will invest these funds in the future at current levels. Although he cannot do this for individual stocks, he can use stock index futures to do this for the overall market.

To understand this use of stock index futures, let us suppose that in January, Mort is informed by his boss that Rock Solid's insurance agents have been doing such a great job selling insurance recently that an additional $20 million of cash payments from insurance premiums will arrive at the firm in March. If the price of the March S&P index contract is 400 and the portfolio manager expects that the S&P index will rise by 5% to 420 by March, he can lock in the price of 400 on the $20 million by taking a long position and purchasing $20 million of S&P 500 Index futures. Since each contract is selling for $200,000 (400 × $500), the portfolio manager will put in an order to purchase 100 contracts (= $20 million/$200,000). With this purchase of futures contracts, the portfolio manager has in effect assured his company that he can buy the same number of shares with the $20 million coming in March that he could when the overall market was at the level represented by an S&P index price of 400. If stock prices go up 5% as expected with the S&P 500 Index rising to 420, the portfolio manager has a profit of $10,000 per contract because he has agreed to pay $200,000 per contract but has a cash payment due of $210,000 (420 × $500). Multiplying the $10,000 profit per contract times the 1000 contracts he bought yields a total profit of $1 million. When the $20 million in premiums arrives in March, Mort now has $21 million to invest—the $20 million in premiums plus the $1 million in profit. Even though the same amount of shares that Mort would have bought for $20 million will now cost 5% more, or $21 million, he is able to buy them because he has $21 million as a result of his futures contract purchase.

Although, as we have seen, the market in stock index futures has important benefits because it can be used to reduce risk, it is now quite controversial (see Box 2). Critics of this market assert that it has led to substantial increases in market volatility, especially in such episodes as 1987's Black Monday crash. ■

■ **THE PRACTICING FINANCIAL INSTITUTION MANAGER**

Hedging Foreign Exchange Risk with Forward and Futures Contracts

As we discussed in Chapter 9, foreign exchange rates have been highly volatile in recent years. The large fluctuations in exchange rates subject financial institutions and other businesses to significant foreign exchange risk because they

BOX 2

Program Trading and Portfolio Insurance

Were They to Blame for the Stock Market Crash of 1987?

In the aftermath of the Black Monday crash on October 19, 1987, in which the stock market declined by over 20% in one day, trading strategies involving stock price index futures markets have been accused (especially by the Brady Commission, which was appointed by President Reagan to study the stock market) of being culprits in the market collapse. One such strategy, called program trading, involves computer-directed trading between the stock index futures and the stocks whose prices are reflected in the stock price index. Program traders are a form of arbitrage conducted to keep stock index futures and stock prices in line with each other. For example, when the price of the stock index futures contract is far below the prices of the underlying stocks in the index, program traders buy index futures, thereby increasing their price, and sell the stocks, thereby lowering their price. Critics of program trading assert that the sharp fall in stock index futures prices on Black Monday led to massive selling in the stock market to keep stock prices in line with the stock index futures prices.

Some experts also blame portfolio insurance for amplifying the crash because they feel that when the stock market started to fall, uncertainty in the market increased, and the resulting increased desire to hedge stocks led to massive selling of stock index futures. The resulting large price declines in stock index futures contracts then led to massive selling of stocks by program traders to keep prices in line.

Because they view program trading and portfolio insurance as causes of the October 1987 market collapse, critics of stock index futures have advocated restrictions on their trading. In response, certain brokerage firms, as well as organized exchanges, have placed limits on program trading. For example, the New York Stock Exchange has curbed computerized program trading when the Dow Jones Industrial Average moves by more than 50 points in one day. However, some prominent finance scholars (among them Nobel laureate Merton Miller of the University of Chicago) do not accept the hypothesis that program trading and portfolio insurance provoked the stock market crash. They believe that the prices of stock index futures primarily reflect the same economic forces that move stock prices—changes in the market's underlying assessment of the value of stocks.

generate substantial gains and losses. Luckily for financial institution managers, the financial derivatives discussed in this chapter—forward and financial futures contracts—can be used to hedge foreign exchange risk.

Financial institution managers need to know how to manage foreign exchange risk for two reasons. First, financial institutions often act on behalf of their customers to reduce the foreign exchange risk they face by conducting foreign exchange transactions for them. Second, financial institutions are often exposed to foreign exchange risk themselves if they operate in more than one country.

To understand how financial institution managers manage foreign exchange risk, let's suppose that in January, the First National Bank's customer, Frivolous Luxuries, Inc., is due a payment of 20 million deutsche marks (DM) in two months for $10 million worth of goods it has just sold in Germany. Frivolous Luxuries is concerned that if the value of the deutsche mark falls substantially from its current value of 50 cents, the company might suffer a large loss because the DM 20 million payment will no longer be worth $10 million. So Sam, the CEO of Frivolous Luxuries, calls up his friend Mona, the manager of the First National Bank, and asks her to hedge this foreign exchange risk for his company. Let's see how the bank manager does this using forward and financial futures contracts.

Hedging Foreign Exchange Risk with Forward Contracts

Forward markets in foreign exchange have been highly developed by commercial banks and investment banking operations that engage in extensive foreign exchange trading and so are widely used to hedge foreign exchange risk. Mona knows that she can use this market to hedge the foreign exchange risk for Frivolous Luxuries. Such a hedge is quite straightforward for her to execute. She just enters a forward contract that obligates her to sell DM 20 million two months from now in exchange for dollars at the current forward rate of $0.50 per mark.[4]

In two months, when her customer receives the DM 20 million, the forward contract ensures that it is exchanged for dollars at an exchange rate of $0.50 per mark, thus yielding $10 million. No matter what happens to future exchange rates, Frivolous Luxuries will be guaranteed $10 million for the goods it sold in Germany. Mona calls up her friend Sam to let him know that his company is now protected from any foreign exchange movements, and he thanks her for her help.

Hedging Foreign Exchange Risk with Futures Contracts

As an alternative, Mona could have used the currency futures market to hedge the foreign exchange risk. In this case, she would see that the Chicago Mercantile Exchange has a March deutsche mark contract with a contract amount of DM 125,000 and a price of $0.50 per mark. To do the hedge, Mona must sell DM 20 million of the March futures, and since the contract size is DM 125,000, she sells 20 million/125,000 = 160 contracts. Given the $0.50-per-mark price, the sale of the contracts yields 160 × DM 125,000 × $0.50 = $10 million. The futures hedge thus again enables her to lock in the exchange rate for Frivolous Luxuries so that it gets its payment of $10 million.

One advantage of using the futures market is that the contract size of DM 125,000, worth $62,500, is quite a bit smaller than the minimum size of a forward contract, which is usually $1 million or more. However, in this case, the bank manager is making a large enough transaction that she can use either the forward or the futures market. Her choice depends on whether the transaction costs are lower in one market than in the other. If the First National Bank is active in the forward market, that market would probably have the lower transaction costs, but if First National rarely deals in foreign exchange forward contracts, the bank manager may do better by sticking with the futures market. ■

---

[4]The forward exchange rate will probably differ slightly from the current spot rate of 50 cents per mark because the interest rates in Germany and the United States may not be equal. In that case, as we saw in Equation 2 in Chapter 9, the future expected exchange rate will not equal the current spot rate and neither will the forward rate. However, since interest differentials have typically been less than 6% at an annual rate (1% at a bimonthly rate), the expected appreciation or depreciation of the mark over a two-month period has always been less than 1%. Thus the forward rate is always close to the current spot rate, and so our assumption in the example that the forward rate and the spot rate are the same is a reasonable one.

SUMMARY

1. Interest-rate forward contracts, which are agreements to sell a debt instrument at a future (forward) point in time, can be used to hedge interest-rate risk. The advantage of forward contracts is that they are flexible, but the disadvantages are that they are subject to default risk and their market is illiquid.

2. A financial futures contract is similar to an interest-rate forward contract in that it specifies that a debt instrument must be delivered by one party to another on a stated future date. However, it has advantages over a forward contract in that it is not subject to default risk and is more liquid.

3. A financial institution can use financial futures to hedge interest-rate risk for a specific asset that it is holding, known as a micro hedge, or to hedge the interest-rate risk on its overall portfolio, known as a macro hedge. Hedges with financial futures suffer from basis risk and accounting problems.

4. Stock index futures are financial futures whose underlying financial instrument is a stock market index like the Standard & Poor's 500 Index. Stock index futures can be used to hedge stock market risk by reducing systematic risk in portfolios or by locking in stock prices.

5. Financial institutions use forward and futures contracts to hedge foreign exchange risk. Futures contracts have the advantage that the size of the contract is typically smaller than for forward contracts. However, for large transactions, forward contracts can sometimes have smaller transaction costs, making them more advantageous.

KEY TERMS

arbitrage, p. 531
basis risk, p. 541
cross hedge, p. 537
financial derivatives, p. 527
financial futures contract, p. 529
forward contract, p. 527
hedge, p. 528

hedge ratio, p. 537
interest-rate forward contract, p. 527
long position, p. 528
macro hedge, p. 536
margin requirement, p. 535
marked to market, p. 535

micro hedge, p. 536
open interest, p. 532
portfolio insurance, p. 545
short position, p. 528
stock market risk, p. 542

QUESTIONS AND PROBLEMS

1. If the pension fund you manage expects to have an inflow of $120 million six months from now, what forward contract would you like to enter into to lock in current interest rates?

*2. If the portfolio you manage is holding $25 million of 10s of 2010 Treasury bonds with a price of 110, what forward contract would you enter into to hedge the interest-rate risk on these bonds over the coming year?

3. What are the major advantages that interest-rate forward contracts have over interest-rate futures contracts?

*4. Why do parties to a forward contract require more information about each other than parties to a futures contract?

5. If you have bought a $100,000 June Treasury bond futures contract at a price of 98 and the price rises to 101 at settlement, what will happen to your margin account?

*6. Suppose that you have $3000 in your margin account, which has a margin requirement of $2000, and you have sold a $100,000 June Treasury bond contract that has gone from a settlement price of 98 yesterday to a settlement price of 101 today. What will happen to the amount in your margin account, and what will the futures exchange require you to do?

7. If at the expiration date, the deliverable Treasury bond is selling for 101 but the Treasury bond futures contract is selling for 102, what will happen to the futures price? Explain.

*8. If you buy a $100,000 June Treasury bond contract for 108 and the price of the deliverable Treasury bond at the expiration date is 102, what is your profit or loss on the contract?

9. What is a corner in a futures market, and how can a futures exchange help prevent corners from occurring?

*10. Suppose that the pension you are managing is holding $15 million of six-year bonds, and if their interest rate rises by 1%, the bonds fall in price by 7 points. Suppose also that when its interest rate rises by 1%, the five-year Treasury bond contract falls by 6 points and when the T-bond futures contract interest rate rises by 1%, on average the interest rate on the six-year Treasury bonds rises by 1.2%. What should you do in the futures market to hedge the interest-rate risk on the $15 million of six-year bonds?

11. Suppose that the bank you are managing is holding $5 million of 13-year bonds, and if their interest rate rises by 1%, the bonds fall in price by 9 points. Suppose also that when its interest rate rises by 1%, the long-term Treasury bond contract falls by 10 points and when the T-bond futures contract interest rate rises by 1%, on average the interest rate on the 13-year Treasury bonds rises by 0.8%. What should you do in the futures market to hedge the interest-rate risk on the $5 million of 13-year bonds?

*12. Suppose that your bank, with $200 million of assets, has a duration gap of three years and the underlying deliverable bond for the five-year Treasury bond futures contract has a duration of 3.5 years. What kind of hedge should your bank do to protect its net worth against interest-rate risk?

13. Suppose that the finance company you manage has $500 million of assets and a duration gap of −4 years and the underlying deliverable bond for the five-year Treasury bond futures contract has a duration of three years. What kind of hedge should you do to protect the finance company's net worth against interest-rate risk?

*14. Suppose that the pension fund you are managing has a $300 million stock portfolio with a beta of 1.2.

If the S&P 500 Index futures contract is currently selling for 450, how many of these contracts would you have to sell to hedge the systematic risk of your portfolio?

15. Suppose that the pension fund you are managing has a $2 billion stock portfolio with a beta of 0.6. If the S&P 500 Index futures contract is currently selling for 400, how many of these contracts would you have to sell to hedge the systematic risk of your portfolio?

*16. If your pension fund will be receiving $100 million of payments in six months' time and you want to be able to lock in the 500 price of the S&P 500 Index with a futures contract, what should you do?

17. If the life insurance company you manage will be receiving $5 million of payments in one year's time and you want to be able to lock in the 400 price of the S&P 500 Index with a futures contract, what should you do?

*18. Suppose that your company will be receiving 30 million French francs six months from now and the franc is currently selling for 10 francs per dollar. If you want to hedge the foreign exchange risk in this payment, what kind of forward contract would you want to enter into?

19. If your company has a payment of 200 million deutsche marks due in March, one year from now, how would you hedge the foreign exchange risk in this payment with DM 125,000 futures contracts?

*20. If your company has to make a DM 10 million payment to a German company in June, three months from now, how would you hedge the foreign exchange risk in this payment with a DM 125,000 futures contract?

Micro Hedge, Macro Hedge, Managing Interest-Rate Risk, Market Value

CONCEPTS IN THIS CASE

forward contracts
long position
short position
hedge

financial futures contract
arbitrage
micro hedge
macro hedge

cross hedge
hedge ratio
basis risk

stock market risk
portfolio insurance

Your company president is concerned about the effect of interest-rate changes on rate-sensitive assets and liabilities. You have presented an analysis of both the income and the duration gap of the firm and how this would result in changes in the market value of the bank's net worth. This presentation made it clear that the bank needs to hedge against an adverse change in the market value of net worth. Based on economic forecasts, it is most likely that interest rates will rise in the next six months.

As a result of the excellent work you presented to management regarding gap analysis, you have been called on again to present alternatives that will manage this inherent risk. You see this as a way to learn more about the key management concerns of banks and to hone a fine presentation. However, you are not sure about these "hedging" concepts, so you seek out professionals in the area and begin to focus entirely on how these tools work.

Your professional "coach" in this area is Bob R. Smart. He has worked for many years setting up and managing hedging strategies. You are not intimidated by his experience, but you are interested in making a good first impression. With this in mind, you create a glossary for basic hedging methods, including forward contracts, interest-rate forward contracts, long position, short position, hedge, financial futures contract, arbitrage, micro hedge, macro hedge, cross hedge, hedge ratio, basis risk, stock market risk, and portfolio insurance.

Bob has asked you to bring your bank's current list of assets and liabilities to the study session to use in setting up both a micro and a macro hedge. A summary of your bank's position is as follows:

Total assets: $150 million
Duration gap: 2.20 years
Primary holdings of concern: $7 million in 6% Treasury
   bonds selling at par that will mature in 5 years; $12
   million in stocks with an average beta of 0.90

Your assignment after the first study session is to set up a micro hedge for the Treasury bonds that will help the bank offset the adverse effect of interest-rate increases on the bonds being held and to set up a macro hedge that will minimize any negative effect on the market value of net worth when interest rates rise.

You gather information from the most recent financial press regarding Treasury bond contracts with a maturity of about one year. Historical relationships between Treasury bond futures contracts and Treasury bonds indicate that the change in the value of the hedged asset relative to the futures contract would be about 1.3 and that interest rates on the hedged asset change on average for a given change in the interest rate on the futures contract by about 0.90. A 1% increase in interest rates results in a decline in value for Treasury bonds held at 8% on par.

1. If you expect interest rates to rise, what type of hedge should you set up, long or short?

2. What is the hedge ratio for the micro hedge?

3. How many futures contracts are needed to set up a complete hedge?

4. If interest rates rise by 1%, what would be the change in the value of the bank's
   a. Treasury bonds?
   b. Treasury bond futures contracts?

5. If the bank can set up $150 million in futures contracts whose underlying bonds have an average duration of 2.20 years, what would be the change in the value of the bank's
   a. Market value of net worth (without the futures contracts)?
   b. Macro hedge position?
   c. Market value of net worth (including the effects of the futures contracts)?

6. If the bank cannot find a set of futures contracts with the same duration as the bank (2.20 years) but has found enough contracts with a duration of 4.40 years,
   a. How much of this contract would the bank sell?
   b. For a 1% increase in interest rates, what would be the percentage change in the price of the futures contract?
   c. What would be the decline in the market value of the bank's net worth without the futures contract in place?
   d. What would be the change in the market value of the bank's net worth with the futures contract in place?

7. How could basis risk result in eliminating the forecasted success of the hedge positions described above?

8. Identify the generally accepted accounting principles that would influence your decision to use hedging strategies.

9. If on January 5 you see June S&P 500 Index contracts selling for 800, how many contracts must the bank sell to immunize its portfolio against systematic (market) risk?

10. If the S&P 500 falls by 10% between January 5 and June, what will be the change in
a. The market value of the bank's stocks?

b. The market value of the bank's index contracts described in Question 9?
c. The market value of the firm's net worth?

11. Explain how the bank would make use of forward contracts to hedge foreign exchange rate risk if they anticipate an increase in the value of the dollar relative to a foreign currency over the next six months.

12. Explain how the bank would make use of futures contracts to hedge foreign exchange rate risk if they anticipate a decrease in the value of the dollar relative to a foreign currency over the next six months.

CHAPTER 22

Hedging with Financial Derivatives II: Options and Swaps

■ **PREVIEW** In Chapter 21 we saw how managers of financial institutions use forward and futures contracts to reduce the risk their institutions face. Although forwards and futures are useful risk management tools, we have seen that they are not without problems. Forward markets often suffer from a lack of liquidity, and hedges using futures contracts are subject to basis risk and accounting problems. The desire to avoid these problems has spawned two other financial derivatives widely used to manage risk: options and swaps. In this chapter we examine how markets in options and swaps work and how they can be used by financial institution managers to reduce risk.

■ OPTIONS

Another vehicle for hedging interest-rate and stock market risk involves the use of options on financial instruments. **Options** are contracts that give the purchaser the option, or *right*, to buy or sell the underlying financial instrument at a specified price, called the **exercise price** or **strike price,** within a specific period of time (the *term to expiration*). The seller (sometimes called the *writer*) of the option is *obligated* to buy or sell the financial instrument to the purchaser if the owner of the option exercises the right to sell or buy. These option contract features are important enough to be emphasized: The *owner* or buyer of an option does not have to exercise the option; he or she can let the option expire without using it. Hence the *owner* of an option is *not obligated* to take any action but rather has the *right* to exercise the contract if he or she so chooses. The *seller* of an option, by contrast, has no choice in the matter; he or she *must* buy or sell the financial instrument if the owner exercises the option.

Because the right to buy or sell a financial instrument at a specified price has value, the owner of an option is willing to pay an amount for it called a **premium.** There are two types of option contracts: **American options** can be exercised *at any time up to* the expiration date of the contract, and **European options** can be exercised only *on* the expiration date.

Option contracts are written on a number of financial instruments (an example of which is shown in the "Following the Financial News" box). Options on individual stocks are called **stock options,** and such options have existed for a long time. Option contracts on financial futures called **financial futures options,** or, more commonly, **futures options,** were developed in 1982 and have become the most widely traded option contracts.

You might wonder why option contracts are more likely to be written on financial futures than on underlying debt instruments such as bonds or certificates of deposit. As you saw in Chapter 21, at the expiration date, the price of the futures contract and of the deliverable debt instrument will be the same because of arbitrage. So it would seem that investors should be indifferent about having the option written on the debt instrument or on the futures contract. However, financial futures contracts have been so well designed that their markets are often more liquid than the markets in the underlying debt instruments. Investors would rather have the option contract written on the more liquid instrument, in this case the futures contract. That explains why the most popular futures options, listed in Table 1, are written on many of the same futures contracts listed in Table 1 of Chapter 21.

FOLLOWING THE FINANCIAL NEWS

Futures Options

The prices for financial futures options are published daily. In the *Wall Street Journal*, they are found in the section "Futures Options Prices" under the "Interest Rate" heading. An excerpt from this listing is reproduced here.

Interest Rate

T-Bonds (CBT)

$100,000; points and 64ths of 100%

Strike Price	Calls-Settle			Puts-Settle		
	Mar	Jun	Sep	Mar	Jun	Sep
109	2-09	....	....	0-37	....	....
110	1-31	2-28	3-03	0-59	2-23	3-26
111	0-62	....	....	1-26	....	....
112	0-37	1-36	2-14	2-01	3-30	4-35
113	0-20	....	....	2-48	....	....
114	0-10	0-60	1-34	3-38	4-52	....

Est. vol. 125,000;

Wd vol. 108,679 calls; 67,341 puts

Op. Int. Wed 426,350 calls; 266,623 puts

Information for each contract is reported in columns, as follows. (The Chicago Board of Trade's

option on its Treasury bonds futures contract is used as an example.)

Strike Price: Strike (exercise) price of each contract, which runs from 109 to 114

Calls–Settle: Premium (price) at settlement for call options on the Treasury bond futures expiring in the month listed, with each full point representing $1000 and sixty-fourths of a point listed to the right of the hyphen; at a strike price of 110, the March call option's premium is 1 31/64, or $1,484 per contract

Puts–Settle: Premium (price) at settlement for put options on the Treasury bond futures expiring in the month listed, with each full point representing $1000 and sixty-fourths of a point listed to the right of the hyphen; at a strike price of 110, the March put option's premium is 59/64, or $922 per contract

Source: Wall Street Journal, January 31, 1997, p. C14.

■ TABLE 1 Widely Traded Financial Options Contracts

Type of Contract	Contract Size	Exchange*	Open Interest (April 14, 1997)	
			Calls	Puts
Interest-Rate Contracts				
Treasury bonds	$100,000	CBT	470,972	344,396
Treasury notes	$100,000	CBT	174,798	164,803
Five-year Treasury notes	$100,000	CBT	71,240	48,729
Municipal Bond Index	$1000	CBT	8,315	16,545
Eurodollar	$1 million	CME	955,373	959,715
Two-year Mid-curve Eurodollar	$1 million	CME	34,094	19,055
Long Gilt	£50,000	LIFFE	69,853	34,017
Euromark	DM 1 million	LIFFE	457,064	258,375
German government bonds	DM 250,000	LIFFE	227,927	260,983
Stock Index Contracts				
Standard & Poor's 500 Index	$500 × index	CME	94,974	127,431
Nasdaq 100	$100 times index	CME	640	1,409
New York Stock Exchange	$500 × index	NYFE	4,201	3,091
Currency Contracts				
Yen	12,500,000 yen	CME	51,707	50,394
Deutsche mark	125,000 marks	CME	45,368	40,946
Canadian dollar	100,000 Canadian $	CME	14,785	8,720
British pound	62,500 pounds	CME	30,874	32,000
Swiss Franc	125,000 francs	CME	23,542	20,890
Brazilian Real	100,000 reals	CME	0	15,631

*Exchange abbreviations: CBT, Chicago Board of Trade; CME, Chicago Mercantile Exchange; LIFFE, London International Financial Futures Exchange; NYFE, New York Futures Exchange.

Source: Wall Street Journal, April 15, 1997, p. C17.

The regulation of option markets is split between the Securities and Exchange Commission (SEC), which regulates stock options, and the Commodity Futures Trading Commission (CFTC), which regulates futures options. Regulation focuses on ensuring that writers of options have enough capital to make good on their contractual obligations and on overseeing traders and exchanges to prevent fraud and ensure that the market is not being manipulated.

Option Contracts

A **call option** is a contract that gives the owner the right to *buy* a financial instrument at the exercise price within a specific period of time. A **put option** is a contract that gives the owner the right to *sell* a financial instrument at the exercise price within a specific period of time.

■ STUDY GUIDE Remembering which is a call option and which is a put option is not always easy. To keep them straight, just remember that having a *call* option to *buy* a financial instrument is the same as having the option to *call in* the instrument for delivery at a specified price. Having a *put* option to *sell* a financial instrument is the same as having the option to *put up* an instrument for the other party to buy.

Profits and Losses on Option and Futures Contracts

To understand option contracts more fully, let's first examine the option on the June Treasury bond futures contract that we looked at in Chapter 21. Recall that if you buy this futures contract at a price of 115 (that is, $115,000), you have agreed to pay $115,000 for $100,000 face value of long-term Treasury bonds when they are delivered to you at the end of June. If you sold this futures contract at a price of 115, you agreed, in exchange for $115,000, to deliver $100,000 face value of the long-term Treasury bonds at the end of June. An option contract on the Treasury bond futures contract has several key features: (1) It has the same expiration date as the underlying futures contract, (2) it is an American option and so can be exercised at any time before the expiration date, and (3) the premium (price) of the option is quoted in points that are the same as in the futures contract, so each point corresponds to $1000. If, for a premium of $2000, you buy one call option contract on the June Treasury bond contract with an exercise price of 115, you have purchased the right to buy (call in) the June Treasury bond futures contract for a price of 115 ($115,000 per contract) at any time through the expiration date of this contract at the end of June. Similarly, when for $2000 you buy a put option on the June Treasury bond contract with an exercise price of 115, you have the right to sell (put up) the June Treasury bond futures contract for a price of 115 ($115,000 per contract) at any time until the end of June.

Futures option contracts are somewhat complicated, so to explore how they work and how they can be used to hedge risk, let's first examine how profits and losses on the call option on the June Treasury bond futures contract occur. In February, our old friend Irving the Investor buys, for a $2000 premium, a call option on the $100,000 June Treasury bond futures contract with a strike price of 115. (We assume that if Irving exercises the option, it is on the expiration date at the end of June and not before.) On the expiration date at the end of June, suppose that the underlying Treasury bond for the futures contract has a price of 110. Recall from Chapter 21 that on the expiration date, arbitrage forces the price of the futures contract to be the same as the price of the underlying bond, so it too has a price of 110 on the expiration date at the end of June. If Irving exercises the call option and buys the futures contract at an exercise price of 115, he will lose money by buying at 115 and selling at the lower market price of 110. Because Irving is smart, he will not exercise the option, but he will be out the $2000 premium he paid. In such a situation, in which the price of the underlying financial instrument is below the exercise price, a call option is said to be "out of the money." At the price of 110 (less than the exercise price), Irving thus suffers a loss on the option contract of the $2000 premium he paid. This loss is plotted as point A in panel (a) of Figure 1.

On the expiration date, if the price of the futures contract is 115, the call option is "at the money," and Irving is indifferent whether he exercises his option to buy the futures contract or not, since exercising the option at 115 when the market price is also at 115 produces no gain or loss. Because he has paid the $2000 premium, at the price of 115 his contract again has a net loss of $2000, plotted as point B.

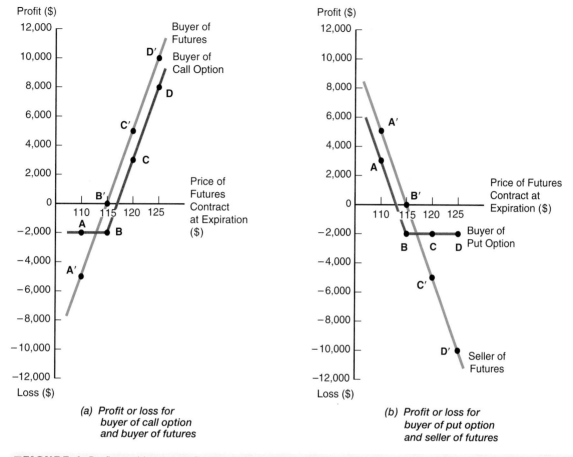

■FIGURE 1 Profits and Losses on Options Versus Futures Contracts

The futures contract is the $100,000 June Treasury bond contract, and the option contracts are written on this futures contract with an exercise price of 115. Panel (a) shows the profits and losses for the buyer of the call option and the buyer of the futures contract, and panel (b) shows the profits and losses for the buyer of the put option and the seller of the futures contract.

If the futures contract instead has a price of 120 on the expiration day, the option is "in the money," and Irving benefits from exercising the option: He would buy the futures contract at the exercise price of 115 and then sell it for 120, thereby earning a 5% gain ($5000 profit) on the $100,000 Treasury bond contract. Because Irving paid a $2000 premium for the option contract, however, his net profit is $3000 ($5000 − $2000). The $3000 profit at a price of 120 is plotted as point C. Similarly, if the price of the futures contract rose to 125, the option contract would yield a net profit of $8000 ($10,000 from exercising the option minus the $2000 premium), plotted as point D. Plotting these points, we get the kinked profit curve for the call option that we see in panel (a).

Suppose that instead of purchasing the futures *option* contract in February, Irving decides instead to buy the $100,000 June Treasury bond *futures* contract at the price of 115. If the price of the bond on the expiration day at the end of June declines to 110, meaning that the price of the futures contract also falls to 110, Irving suffers a loss of 5 percentage points, or $5000. The loss of $5000 on the futures contract at a price of 110 is plotted as point A′ in panel (a). At a price of 115 on the expiration date, Irving would have a zero profit on the futures contract, plotted as point B′. At a price of 120, Irving would have a profit on the contract of 5 percentage points, or $5000 (point C′), and at a price of 125, the profit would be 10 percentage points, or $10,000 (point D′). Plotting these points, we get the linear (straight-line) profit curve for the futures contract that appears in panel (a).

Now we can see the major difference between a futures contract and an option contract. As the profit curve for the futures contract in panel (a) indicates, the futures contract has a linear profit function: Profits grow by an equal dollar amount for every point increase in the price of the underlying financial instrument. By contrast, the kinked profit curve for the option contract is highly nonlinear, meaning that profits do not always grow by the same amount for a given change in the price of the underlying financial instrument. The reason for this nonlinearity is that the call option protects Irving from having losses that are greater than the amount of the $2000 premium. In contrast, Irving's loss on the futures contract is $5000 if the price on the expiration day falls to 110, and if the price falls even further, Irving's loss will be even greater. This insurance-like feature of option contracts explains why their purchase price is referred to as a premium. Once the underlying financial instrument's price rises above the exercise price, however, Irving's profits grow linearly. Irving has given up something by buying an option rather than a futures contract. As we see in panel (a), when the price of the underlying financial instrument rises above the exercise price, Irving's profits are always less than that on the futures contract by exactly the $2000 premium he paid.

Panel (b) plots the results of the same profit calculations if Irving buys not a call but a put option (an option to sell) with an exercise price of 115 for a premium of $2000 and if he sells the futures contract rather than buying one. In this case, if on the expiration date the Treasury bond futures have a price above the 115 exercise price, the put option is "out of the money." Irving would not want to exercise the put option and then have to sell the futures contract he owns as a result of exercising the put option at a price below the market price and lose money. He would not exercise his option, and he would be out only the $2000 premium he paid. Once the price of the futures contract falls below the 115 exercise price, Irving benefits from exercising the put option because he can sell the futures contract at a price of 115 but can buy it at a price below this. In such a situation, in which the price of the underlying instrument is below the exercise price, the put option is "in the money," and profits rise linearly as the price of the futures contract falls. The profit function for the put option illustrated in panel (b) of Figure 1 is kinked, indicating that Irving is protected from losses greater than the amount of the premium he paid. The profit curve for the sale of the futures contract is just the negative of the profit for the futures contract in panel (a) and is therefore linear.

Panel (b) of Figure 1 confirms the conclusion from panel (a) that profits on option contracts are nonlinear but profits on futures contracts are linear.

■ S T U D Y   G U I D E To make sure you understand how profits and losses on option and futures contracts are generated, calculate the net profits on the put option and the short position in the futures contract at prices on the expiration day of 110, 115, 120, and 125. Then verify that your calculations correspond to the points plotted in panel (b) of Figure 1.

Two other differences between futures and option contracts must be mentioned. The first is that the initial investment on the contracts differs. As we saw in Chapter 21, when a futures contract is purchased, the investor must put up a fixed amount, the margin requirement, in a margin account. But when an option contract is purchased, the initial investment is the premium that must be paid for the contract. The second important difference between the contracts is that the futures contract requires money to change hands daily when the contract is marked to market, whereas the option contract requires money to change hands only when it is exercised.

Factors Affecting the Prices of Option Premiums

If we again look closely at the *Wall Street Journal* entry for Treasury bond futures options in the "Following the Financial News" box, we learn several interesting facts about how the premiums on option contracts are priced. The first thing you might have noticed is that when the strike (exercise) price is higher, the premium for the call option is lower and the premium for the put option is higher. For example, when the strike price rises from 109 to 114, the premium for the March call option falls from 2 9/64 to 10/64, and the premium for the March put option rises from 37/64 to 3 38/64.

Our understanding of the profit function for option contracts illustrated in Figure 1 helps explain this fact. As we saw in panel (a), a higher price for the underlying financial instrument (in this case a Treasury bond futures contract) relative to the option's exercise price results in higher profits on the call (buy) option. Thus the lower the strike price, the higher the profits on the call option contract and the greater the premium that investors like Irving are willing to pay. Similarly, we saw in panel (b) that a higher price for the underlying financial instrument relative to the exercise price lowers profits on the put (sell) option, so that a higher strike price increases profits and thus causes the premium to increase.

The second thing you might have noticed in the *Wall Street Journal* entry is that as the period of time over which the option can be exercised (the term to expiration) gets longer, the premiums for both call and put options rise. For example, at a strike price of 110, the premium on the call option increases from 1 31/64 in March to 2 28/64 in June and to 3 3/64 in September. Similarly, the premium on the put option increases from 59/64 in March to 2 23/64 in June and to 3 26/64 in September. The fact that premiums increase with the term to expiration is also explained by the nonlinear profit function for option contracts. As the term to expiration lengthens, there is a greater chance that the price of the underlying financial instrument will be very high or very low by the expiration date. If the price becomes very high and goes well above the exercise price, the call (buy) option will yield a high profit, but if the price becomes very low and goes well below the exercise price, the losses will be small because the owner of the call option will simply decide not to exercise the option. The possibility of greater variability of the underlying financial instrument as the term to expiration lengthens raises profits on average for the call option.

Similar reasoning tells us that the put (sell) option will become more valuable as the term to expiration increases because the possibility of greater price variability of the underlying financial instrument increases as the term to expiration increases. The greater chance of a low price increases the chance that profits on the put option will be very high. But the greater chance of a high price does not produce substantial losses for the put option because the owner will again just decide not to exercise the option.

Another way of thinking about this reasoning is to recognize that option contracts have an element of "heads, I win; tails, I don't lose too badly." The greater variability of where the prices might be by the expiration date increases the value of both kinds of options. Since a longer term to the expiration date leads to greater variability of where the prices might be by the expiration date, a longer term to expiration raises the value of the option contract.

The reasoning that we have just developed also explains another important fact about option premiums. When the volatility of the price of the underlying instrument is great, the premiums for both call and put options will be higher. Higher volatility of prices means that for a given expiration date, there will again be greater variability of where the prices might be by the expiration date. The "heads, I win; tails, I don't lose too badly" property of options then means that the greater variability of possible prices by the expiration date increases average profits for the option and thus increases the premium that investors are willing to pay.

Summary

Our analysis of how profits on options are affected by price movements for the underlying financial instrument leads to the following conclusions about the factors that determine the premium on an option contract:

1. The higher the strike price, everything else being equal, the lower the premium on call (buy) options and the higher the premium on put (sell) options.
2. The greater the term to expiration, everything else being equal, the higher the premiums for both call and put options.
3. The greater the volatility of prices of the underlying financial instrument, everything else being equal, the higher the premiums for both call and put options.

The results we have derived here appear in more formal models, such as the Black-Scholes model, which analyze how the premiums on options are priced. You might study such models in other finance courses.

■ **THE PRACTICING FINANCIAL INSTITUTION MANAGER**
Hedging Interest-Rate Risk with Futures Options

In Chapter 21 we saw how a financial institution manager like Mona, the manager of the First National Bank, could use financial futures to hedge interest-rate risk. She could also do her hedging with futures options. Recall that Mona is concerned about the possible losses on $10 million of Treasury bonds that the First National Bank is holding if interest rates rise (and bond prices decline). We saw in Chapter 21 that the bank manager could conduct a micro hedge in which the bank sells 110 contracts of Treasury bond futures. A rise in interest rates and the resulting fall in bond prices and bond futures contracts would lead to profits on the bank's sale of the 110 futures contracts that would offset the losses on the $10 million of bonds the bank is holding.

As panel (b) of Figure 1 suggests, an alternative way for the manager to protect against a rise in interest rates and hence a decline in bond prices is to buy 110 contracts of put options written on the same Treasury bond futures. As long as the exercise price is not too far from the current price as in panel (b), the rise in interest rates and decline in bond prices will lead to profits on the futures and the futures put options, profits that will offset any losses on the $10 million of Treasury bonds.

The one problem with using options rather than futures is that the First National Bank will have to pay premiums on these 110 contracts, thereby lowering the bank's profits in order to hedge the interest-rate risk. Why might the bank manager be willing to use options rather than futures to conduct the hedge? The answer is that the option contract, unlike the futures contract, allows the First National Bank to gain if interest rates decline and bond prices rise. With the hedge using futures contracts, the First National Bank does not gain from increases in bond prices because the profits on the bonds it is holding are offset by the losses from the futures contracts it has sold. However, as panel (b) of Figure 1 indicates, the situation when the hedge is conducted with put options is quite different: Once bond prices rise above the exercise price, the bank does not suffer additional losses on the option contracts. At the same time, the value of the Treasury bonds the bank is holding will increase, thereby leading to a profit for the bank. Thus using options rather than futures to conduct the micro hedge allows the bank to protect itself from rises in interest rates but still allows the bank to benefit from interest-rate declines (although the profit is reduced by the amount of the premium).

Similar reasoning indicates that the bank manager might prefer to use options to conduct the macro hedge to immunize the entire bank portfolio from interest-rate risk. For example, Mona could conduct the $100 million macro hedge by selling 1000 five-year Treasury note futures contracts, or she could conduct the hedge by buying 1000 put options on the Treasury note futures. Again, the strategy of using options rather than futures has the disadvantage that the First National Bank has to pay the premiums on these 1000 contracts up front. By contrast, using options allows the bank to keep the gains from a decline in interest rates (which will raise the value of the bank's assets relative to its liabilities) because these gains will not be offset by large losses on the option contracts.

In the case of a macro hedge, there is another reason why the bank might prefer option contracts to futures contracts. Recall that profits and losses on futures contracts can cause accounting problems for banks because such profits and losses are not allowed to be offset by unrealized changes in the value of the rest of the bank's portfolio. Consider the case when interest rates fall. If Mona sells futures contracts to conduct the macro hedge, then when interest rates fall and the prices of the Treasury note futures contracts rise, she will have large losses. Of course, these losses are offset by unrealized profits in the rest of the bank's portfolio, but the bank is not allowed to offset these losses in its accounting statements. So even though the macro hedge is serving its intended purpose of immunizing the bank's portfolio from interest-rate risk, the bank would experience large accounting losses when interest rates fall. Indeed, bank managers have lost their jobs when perfectly sound hedges with interest-rate futures have led to large accounting losses. Not surprisingly, bank managers might shrink from using financial futures to conduct macro hedges for this reason.

Futures options, however, can come to the rescue of the managers of banks and other financial institutions. Suppose that Mona conducted the macro hedge by buying put options instead of selling Treasury note futures. Now if interest rates fall and bond prices rise well above the exercise price, the bank will not have large losses on the option contracts because it will just decide not to exercise its options. The bank will not suffer the accounting problems produced by hedging with financial futures. Because of the accounting advantages of using futures options to conduct macro hedges, option contracts have become important interest-rate-risk-hedging tools for financial institution managers.

Futures options are also particularly useful for offsetting risk created when the bank extends option-like commitments to certain bank customers. Banks sometimes make fixed-rate loan commitments to their customers, allowing customers to decide at their own discretion whether to borrow up to a certain amount from the bank at the specified fixed interest rate.[1] In effect, each such customer has been given the option to sell a bond to (borrow from) the bank at a given interest rate. Thus a loan commitment with a set interest rate is very similar to the bank's selling the customer a put option on bonds (an option to sell bonds). Because selling put options on bonds can expose the bank (the seller of the option) to substantial risk, the bank would like to hedge this risk by *buying* a put option that will cancel out the put option it has *sold*.

---

[1]Banks can also hedge loan commitments by having the interest rate on the loan tied to a market interest rate like the CD or T-bill rate. Variable-rate loan commitments of this type do not expose the bank to the interest-rate risk described in the text because the interest rate on the loan will move with the bank's cost of acquiring funds. Understandably, variable-rate loan commitments are more common than fixed-rate loan commitments.

To see how this could be done, let's see how the bank manager might want to offset the risk created by a loan commitment to the First National Bank's good customer, Frivolous Luxuries, Inc. Suppose that in January, First National extends a $2 million loan commitment to Frivolous Luxuries for a four-year loan at an interest rate of 7% and the commitment lasts for two months. Mona the Bank Manager knows that the four-year CD rate is currently 6%, which represents the cost of funds for the loan, so she figures that if interest rates remain the same as today's, the bank will have a comfortable profit margin of 1 percentage point on the loan. The problem is that Frivolous Luxuries is very likely to exercise the option provided by the loan commitment and take the loan if interest rates rise but is unlikely to take the loan if interest rates fall. If within the next two months interest rates rose by 2 percentage points, Frivolous Luxuries would almost surely take out the loan, and the First National Bank would be suffering a big loss because its cost of funds would be 1 percentage point higher than the interest rate on the loan.

Mona knows that to hedge this risk, she has to buy put options on a financial instrument whose interest rate moves closely with the rate on four-year CDs and whose expiration date is close to that on the loan commitment. She decides that March put options written on five-year Treasury note futures are her best bet. To decide on the number of put option contracts to buy, she goes through the same analysis she conducted when she carried out a micro hedge using futures. First she calculates the hedge ratio:

$$HR = \frac{\Delta P_a}{\Delta P_f} \times \beta_{af}$$

where HR = hedge ratio
ΔP_a = change in the price of the hedged asset as a percentage of par in response to a 1% change in the interest rate
ΔP_f = change in the price of the futures contract as a percentage of par in response to a 1% change in the interest rate
β_{af} = average change in the interest rate of the hedged asset for a given change in the interest rate of the futures contract

She finds that the change in the price of four-year CDs in response to a 1% rise in the interest rate is 3.80% of par, and the change in the price of the five-year Treasury bond is 4.40% of par, giving a value for $\Delta P_a/\Delta P_f$ of 0.86 (= 3.80/4.40). Mona then estimates that the interest rate on four-year CDs on average changes by 1.05 percentage points when the interest rate on the Treasury notes futures contract changes by 1 percentage point. Her calculation of the hedge ratio is thus

$$HR = \frac{\Delta P_a}{\Delta P_f} \times \beta_{af} = 0.86 \times 1.05 = 0.90$$

To calculate the number of contracts, she again uses the formula

$$\text{Contracts} = HR \times \frac{PV_a}{PV_f}$$

where HR = hedge ratio (0.90 in our example)
   PV_a = par value of the asset hedged ($2 million of the four-year CDs)
   PV_f = par value of the futures contract ($100,000 per five-year Treasury note futures contract)

In our example,

$$\text{Contracts} = 0.90 \times \frac{\$2,000,000}{\$100,000} = 0.90 \times 20 = 18$$

Choosing the strike price to be close to the current price, Mona completes the hedge by purchasing 18 put option contracts on five-year Treasury notes with a premium of, say, $2000 per contract. Thus for a total cost of $36,000 (= 18 × $2000), she has hedged the First National Bank's loan commitment. If interest rates rise and the loan commitment is exercised, the profits on the put option the bank manager has bought will offset the loss on the loan.

   If interest rates fall, the bank manager will not exercise the options, and so the bank will not be exposed to any additional losses. Here we can see the advantage of hedging the loan commitment with put option contracts rather than selling futures contracts. If Mona had sold futures contracts to hedge the loan commitment, the decline in interest rates would have produced losses on the futures contracts. However, because interest rates have fallen, it is likely that Frivolous Luxuries will decide not to take the loan offered under the commitment because it will not want to pay the high 7% interest rate. In this case, the First National Bank would have a loss on the futures but would not have an offsetting gain in profits from making the loan. Clearly, if the bank manager put the bank into this unhappy situation, she might get fired. Using futures options rather than futures contracts prevents this situation from occurring and is another reason why financial institution managers find hedging with futures options so attractive.

■ INTEREST-RATE SWAPS

In addition to forwards, futures, and options, financial institutions use one other important financial derivative to manage risk. **Swaps** are financial contracts that obligate one party to exchange (swap) a set of payments it owns for another set of payments owned by another party. There are two basic kinds of swaps: **Currency swaps** involve the exchange of a set of payments in one currency for a set of payments in another currency. **Interest-rate swaps** involve the exchange of one set of interest payments for another set of interest payments, all denominated in the same currency. We first focus on interest-rate swaps; later in the chapter we discuss currency swaps.

Interest-Rate Swap Contracts

Interest-rate swaps are an important tool for managing interest-rate risk, and they first appeared in the United States in 1982 when, as we have seen, there was an increase in the demand for financial instruments that could be used to reduce interest-rate risk. The most common type of interest-rate swap (called the *plain vanilla swap*) specifies (1) the interest rate on the payments that are being exchanged; (2) the type of interest payments (variable or fixed-rate); (3) the amount of **notional principal,** which is the amount on which the interest is being paid; and (4) the time period over which the exchanges continue to be made. There are many other more complicated versions of swaps, including forward swaps and swap options (called *swaptions*), but here we will look only at the plain vanilla swap. Figure 2 illustrates an interest-rate swap between the Midwest Savings Bank and the Friendly Finance Company. Midwest Savings agrees to pay Friendly Finance a fixed rate of 7% on $1 million of notional principal for the next ten years, and Friendly Finance agrees to pay Midwest Savings the one-year Treasury bill rate plus 1% on $1 million of notional principal for the same period. Thus as shown in Figure 2, every year, the Midwest Savings Bank would be paying the Friendly Finance Company 7% on $1 million while Friendly Finance would be paying Midwest Savings the one-year T-bill rate plus 1% on $1 million.

You might wonder why these two parties find it advantageous to enter into this swap agreement. The answer is that it may help both of them hedge interest-rate risk. Suppose that the Midwest Savings Bank, which tends to borrow short-term and then lend long-term in the mortgage market, has $1 million less of rate-sensitive assets than it has rate-sensitive liabilities. As we learned in Chapter 20, this situation means that as interest rates rise, the rise in the cost of funds (liabilities) is greater than the rise in interest payments it receives on its assets, many of which are fixed-rate. The result of rising interest rates is thus a shrinking of Midwest Savings' net interest margin and a decline in its profitability. As we saw in Chapter 20, to avoid this interest-rate risk, Midwest Savings would like to convert $1 million of its fixed-rate assets into $1 million of rate-sensitive assets, in effect making rate-sensitive assets equal rate-sensitive liabilities, thereby eliminating the gap. This is exactly what happens when it engages in the interest-rate swap. By taking $1 million of its fixed-rate income and exchanging it for $1 million of rate-sensitive Treasury bill income, it has converted income on $1 million of fixed-rate assets into income on $1 million of rate-sensitive assets. Now when

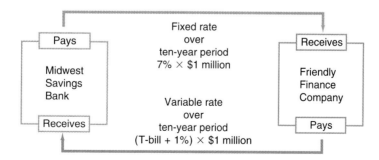

■FIGURE 2 Interest-Rate Swap Payments

In this swap arrangement with a notional principal of $1 million and a term of ten years, the Midwest Savings Bank pays a fixed rate of 7% × $1 million to the Friendly Finance Company, which in turn agrees to pay the one-year Treasury bill rate plus 1% × $1 million to the Midwest Savings Bank.

interest rates increase, the rise in rate-sensitive income on its assets exactly matches the rise in the rate-sensitive cost of funds on its liabilities, leaving the net interest margin and bank profitability unchanged.

The Friendly Finance Company, which issues long-term bonds to raise funds and uses them to make short-term loans, finds that it is in exactly the opposite situation to Midwest Savings: It has $1 million more of rate-sensitive assets than rate-sensitive liabilities. It is therefore concerned that a fall in interest rates, which will result in a larger drop in income from its assets than the decline in the cost of funds on its liabilities, will cause a decline in profits. By doing the interest-rate swap, it eliminates this interest-rate risk because it has converted $1 million of rate-sensitive income into $1 million of fixed-rate income. Now the Friendly Finance Company finds that when interest rates fall, the decline in rate-sensitive income is smaller and so is matched by the decline in the rate-sensitive cost of funds on its liabilities, leaving its profitability unchanged.

Advantages of Interest-Rate Swaps

To eliminate interest-rate risk, both the Midwest Savings Bank and the Friendly Finance Company could have rearranged their balance sheets by converting fixed-rate assets into rate-sensitive assets, and vice versa, instead of engaging in an interest-rate swap. However, this strategy would have been costly for both financial institutions for several reasons. The first is that financial institutions incur substantial transaction costs when they rearrange their balance sheets. Second, different financial institutions have informational advantages in making loans to certain customers who may prefer certain maturities. Thus, adjusting the balance sheet to eliminate interest-rate risk may result in a loss of these informational advantages, which the financial institution is unwilling to give up. Interest-rate swaps solve these problems for financial institutions because in effect they allow the institutions to convert fixed-rate assets into rate-sensitive assets without affecting the balance sheet. Large transaction costs are avoided, and the financial institutions can continue to make loans where they have an informational advantage.

We have seen that financial institutions can also hedge interest-rate risk with other financial derivatives such as futures contracts and futures options. Interest-rate swaps have one big advantage over hedging with these other derivatives: They can be written for very long horizons, sometimes as long as 20 years, whereas financial futures and futures options typically have much shorter horizons, not much more than a year. If a financial institution needs to hedge interest-rate risk for a long horizon, financial futures and option markets may not do it much good. Instead it can turn to the swap market.

Another advantage of interest-rate swaps is that they can allow two corporations to exploit their comparative advantages in borrowing in variable versus fixed-rate debt markets. For example, suppose that the Big Boy Corporation has a better credit rating and so can borrow $1 million either at a variable rate of the prime rate, assumed equal to the T-bill rate plus 2%, or issue bonds with a fixed rate of 7%, while the Little Guy Corporation can borrow $1 million at the prime rate plus 0.5% or borrow at a fixed rate of 9%. The Big Boy Corporation has a comparative advantage in borrowing with fixed-rate debt, while the Little Guy Corporation has a comparative advantage in borrowing with variable-rate debt. If Big Boy and Little Guy can arrange the swap between them shown in Figure 3, both lower their borrowing costs. Big Boy can issue bonds at the 7% rate and agree to pay to Little Guy a variable rate of the prime rate. Little Guy can borrow at prime plus 0.5% and agree to pay Big Boy a fixed rate of 8%. The result of this swap is that Little Guy has borrowed at an 8.5% fixed rate—the 8% it is paying to

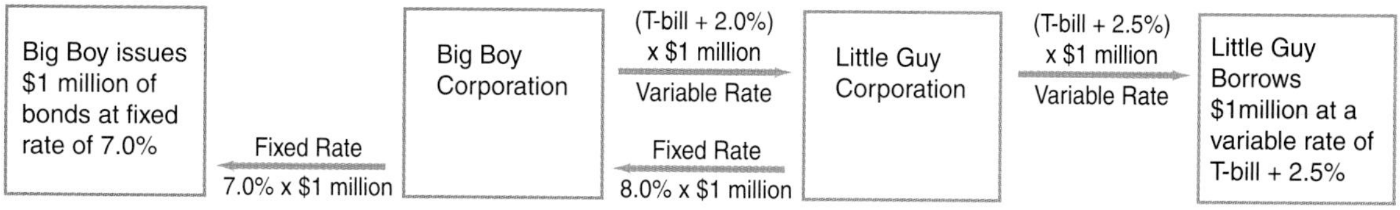

Per Year Borrowing Costs with and without Swaps

		Big Boy Corporation	Little Guy Corporation
With Swap	Payments	(T-bill + 2.0%) x $1 million (to Little Guy)	(T-bill + 2.5%) x $1 million (to variable rate lender)
		7.0% x $1 million (to bond holders)	8.0% x $1 million (to Big Boy)
	Receipts	8.0% x $1 million (from Little Guy)	(T-bill +2.0%) x $1 million (from Big Boy)
With Swap	Total Borrowing Costs = Payments – Receipts	(T-bill + 2.0% + 7.0% – 8.0%) x $1 million = (T-bill + 1.0%) x $1 million	[T-bill + 2.5% + 8.0% – (T-bill + 2.0%)] x $1 million = 8.5% x $1 million
Without Swap	Total Borrowing Cost	(T-bill + 2.0%) x $1 million	9.0% x $1 million
Savings with Swap	= Total Borrowing Cost without Swap – Total Borrowing Cost with Swap	1.0% x $1 million	0.5% x $1 million

■FIGURE 3 An Interest-Rate Swap Between Two Corporations

Big Boy Corporation borrows at a 7% fixed rate and pays Little Guy Corporation a variable-rate payment of the prime rate. Little Guy borrows at a variable rate of the prime rate plus 0.5% and pays Big Boy an 8% fixed-rate payment. Little Guy has a borrowing cost of 8.5%—the 8% it pays to Big Boy plus the 0.5% difference between its variable-rate loan payment of prime +0.5% and the prime rate it receives from Big Boy. Big Boy has a borrowing cost of the prime rate minus 1%—the prime rate it pays Little Guy minus the 1% profit it gets each year because the 8% it receives from Little Guy is 1% greater than its 7% fixed-rate payment. Both corporations are better off: Little Guy has reduced its borrowing cost from 9% to 8.5%, and Big Boy has reduced its borrowing cost from the prime rate to 1% below the prime rate.

Big Boy plus the 0.5% difference between what it pays out on the variable-rate loan (prime + 0.5%) and the variable-rate payment of the prime rate that it receives from Big Boy every year. Little Guy's borrowing costs have thus been lowered from a 9% to a 8.5% fixed rate. Big Boy, for its part, has been able to borrow at 1% below the prime rate—the prime rate it has to pay Little Guy minus the 1.0% profit it gets each year because the 8% fixed payment it gets from Little Guy is greater by 1 percentage point than the 7% fixed payment Big Boy makes on its bonds every year. Big Boy is also better off because it has lowered the borrowing cost from prime to 1% below prime. The ability to use the swap market to exploit corporations' comparative advantage in borrowing at variable-rate versus fixed-rate debt is an important advantage that has helped make this market so successful.

Disadvantages of Interest-Rate Swaps

Although interest-rate swaps have important advantages that make them very popular with financial institutions, they also have disadvantages that limit their usefulness. Swap markets, like forward markets, can suffer from a lack of liquidity. Let's return to looking at the swap between the Midwest Savings Bank and the Friendly Finance Company. As with a forward contract, it might be difficult for the Midwest Savings Bank to link up with the Friendly Finance Company to arrange the swap. In addition, even if the Midwest Savings Bank could find a counterparty like the Friendly Finance Company, it might not be able to negotiate a good deal because it couldn't find any other institution to negotiate with.

Swap contracts also are subject to the same default risk that we encountered for forward contracts. If interest rates rise, the Friendly Finance Company would love to get out of the swap contract because the fixed-rate interest payments it receives are less than it could get in the open market. It might then default on the contract, exposing Midwest Savings to a loss. Alternatively, the Friendly Finance Company could go bust, meaning that the terms of the swap contract would not be fulfilled.

It is important to note that the default risk of swaps is not the same as the default risk on the full amount of the notional principal because the notional principal is never exchanged. If the Friendly Finance Company goes broke because $1 million of its one-year loans default and it cannot make its interest payment to Midwest Savings, Midwest Savings will stop sending its payment to Friendly Finance. If interest rates have declined, this will suit Midwest Savings just fine because it would rather keep the 7% fixed-rate interest payment, which is at a higher rate, than receive the rate-sensitive payment, which has declined. Thus a default on a swap contract does not necessarily mean that there is a loss to the other party. Midwest Savings will suffer losses from a default only if interest rates have risen when the default occurs. Even then, the loss will be far smaller than the amount of the notional principal because interest payments are far smaller than the amount of the notional principal.[2]

---

[2]The actual loss will equal the present value of the difference in the interest payments that the bank would have received if the swap were still in force as compared to interest payments it receives otherwise.

Financial Intermediaries in Interest-Rate Swaps

As we have just seen, financial institutions do have to be aware of the possibility of losses from a default on swaps. As with a forward contract, each party to a swap must have a lot of information about the other party to make sure that the contract is likely to be fulfilled. The need for information about counterparties and the liquidity problems in swap markets could limit the usefulness of these markets. However, as we saw in Chapter 8, when informational and liquidity problems crop up in a market, financial intermediaries come to the rescue. That is exactly what happens in swap markets. Intermediaries such as investment banks and especially large commercial banks have the ability to acquire information cheaply about the creditworthiness and reliability of parties to swap contracts and are also able to match up parties to a swap. Hence large commercial banks and investment banks have set up swap markets in which they act as intermediaries.

Figure 4 shows how a swap contract works in a more realistic setting in which a commercial bank such as Citibank acts as the intermediary between Midwest Savings and Friendly Finance. Now both Midwest Savings and Friendly Finance make their swap contracts directly with Citibank rather than with each other. Midwest Savings agrees to exchange with Citibank a 7.05% fixed-rate interest payment for the one-year Treasury bill rate payment plus 0.95%. As we see in the figure, Citibank makes the counterpart swap agreement with the Friendly Finance Company, in which it exchanges a 6.95% fixed-rate payment for the one-year Treasury bill rate payment plus 1.05%. As in Figure 2, the notional amount of principal is $1 million, and the term of the swap agreement is ten years. Citibank makes a profit because it receives 7.05% from Midwest Savings but passes on only 6.95% to Friendly Finance, earning a spread of 0.1%. Citibank earns an additional spread of 0.1% by receiving the one-year T-bill rate plus 1.05% from Friendly Finance while paying out only the one-year T-bill rate plus 0.95% to Midwest Savings. The result is that Citibank makes a total of 0.2% × $1 million = $2000 from acting as an intermediary in this interest-rate swap.

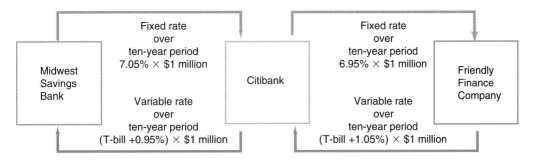

■FIGURE 4 Interest-Rate Swap Payments with an Intermediary

In the swap arrangement with an intermediary (Citibank), the Midwest Savings Bank agrees to pay a fixed rate of 7.05% × $1 million to Citibank, which in turn pays the one-year Treasury bill rate plus 0.95% × $1 million to the Midwest Savings Bank. At the same time, Citibank agrees to pay a fixed rate of 6.95% × $1 million to the Friendly Finance Company, which in turn pays the one-year Treasury bill rate plus 1.05% × $1 million. The result is that Citibank earns a spread of 0.1% on the Treasury bill payments and 0.1% on the fixed-rate payments, for a total of 0.2% × $1 million = $2000.

Comparing Figures 2 and 4, we see that both Midwest Savings and Friendly Finance give up a little bit by entering into the swap agreement with Citibank—they each receive an interest payment that is 0.05% less and pay an interest payment that is 0.05% more—but this arrangement has two major advantages for them. First, Citibank has been able to match up both parties, which probably would not have been possible without Citibank's help. Second, both parties know Citibank well and are confident that there will be no default risk on the swap contract. Because the Midwest Savings Bank and the Friendly Finance Company do not know each other well, their concerns about default risk might have prevented them from entering directly into the swap with each other. These two advantages of dealing with Citibank rather than with each other are why Midwest Savings and Friendly Finance are more likely to use Citibank as an intermediary when they conduct swaps and must be willing to pay for the right to do so.

Clearly, interest-rate swaps do pose some risk to commercial banks acting as intermediaries such as Citibank in our example. As we have seen in Chapter 16, concerns about the risks posed to banks by interest-rate swaps have led to regulations that force banks to hold more capital when they engage in the intermediation process in the swap market.

THE PRACTICING FINANCIAL INSTITUTION MANAGER
Hedging Interest-Rate Risk with Interest-Rate Swaps

We have already seen how the Midwest Savings Bank and the Friendly Finance Company can hedge interest-rate risk using interest-rate swaps, but to make our understanding of hedging with interest-rate swaps even more concrete, let's return again to the bank manager's hedging problem. Recall from Chapter 20 that the First National Bank has $32 million of rate-sensitive assets and $49.5 million of rate-sensitive liabilities. The bank thus has a gap of $-\$17.5$ million, and, as we saw in Chapter 20, if interest rates rise by 5 percentage points, the change in bank income is 5% $\times$ $-\$17.5$ million = $-\$0.9$ million.

How large an interest-rate swap does Mona the Bank Manager have to arrange to hedge this interest-rate risk and prevent the decline in profits when interest rates rise? The answer is straightforward: Mona has to arrange an interest-rate swap in which she exchanges income on $17.5 million of rate-insensitive assets for income on $17.5 million of rate-sensitive assets. Then the rate-sensitive income will in effect be on $49.5 million of rate-sensitive assets (= $32 million + $17.5 million), which exactly matches the $49.5 million of rate-sensitive liabilities, so $GAP = 0$. Now when interest rates rise by 5 percentage points, the income on the rate-sensitive assets will rise by 5% $\times$ $49.5 million = $2.5 million while the cost on the rate-sensitive liabilities will rise by the same 5% $\times$ $49.5 million = $2.5 million. The net result is that profits and the net interest margin do not change, and the hedge is successful.

Instead of using interest-rate swaps to eliminate interest-rate risk for the bank's income, the bank manager could have decided to hedge interest-rate risk for the bank's net worth. Suppose that the Friendly Finance Company offers Mona's bank the same interest-rate swap it offered Midwest Savings: The First National Bank would receive interest payments of 1% plus the one-year

Treasury bill rate over the next ten years in exchange for a 7% fixed-rate payment. How much notional principal of this swap should the bank manager agree to if she wants fully to hedge the interest-rate risk on the bank's net worth?

Mona's first step is to calculate the effective duration of the interest-rate swap she is being offered. Because the one-year Treasury bill is a pure discount bond, she knows that its duration is simply one year regardless of the interest rate. Thus the duration of the 1% plus the one-year Treasury bill rate interest payment is one year. She calculates the duration of the 7% fixed-rate payment made over the next ten years to be 8.1 years. Since the interest payments are made on the same notional principal, the duration of the swap is simply the duration of the payments her bank receives (the asset) minus the duration of the payments her bank makes (the liability), which in this case equals $1 - 8.1 = -7.1$.

Just as in the macro hedge she conducted using futures, Mona knows that she wants a rise in interest rates to cause the value of the interest-rate swap to rise by exactly the same amount as the bank's net worth would fall, thereby offsetting this decline. That will occur when the notional principal of the swap multiplied by the swap's duration is the same as the bank's assets multiplied by the duration gap:

$$V_S \times DUR_S = -V_A \times DUR_{GAP} \tag{5}$$

where
$$V_S = \text{notional principal of the swap}$$
$$V_A = \text{value of total bank assets}$$
$$DUR_S = \text{duration of the swap}$$
$$DUR_{GAP} = \text{duration gap measure for the bank}$$

Dividing both sides by DUR_S gives the formula for V_S, the notional principal of the swap:

$$V_S = \frac{-V_A \times DUR_{GAP}}{DUR_S} \tag{6}$$

Since the bank manager's earlier duration gap analysis revealed that the bank's duration gap is 1.72 years on $100 million of assets and she has calculated the duration of the swap to be -7.1 years, Mona plugs these numbers into the formula in Equation 6 to get

$$V_S = \frac{-V_A \times DUR_{GAP}}{DUR_S} = \frac{-\$100 \text{ million} \times 1.72}{-7.1} = \$24.2 \text{ million}$$

She contacts the Friendly Finance Company, and they agree to the swap for $24.2 million of notional principal.

To check that she has done her calculations correctly, Mona now goes through the thought experiment that we went through earlier in the chapter for assessing what happens if interest rates rise by 1 percentage point, from 7% to 8%. Recall that the change in net worth as a percentage of assets would be

$$\%\Delta NW = -DUR_{GAP} \times \frac{\Delta i}{1 + i} = -1.72 \times \frac{0.01}{1 + 0.07} = -0.016 = -1.6\%$$

The 1.6% decline in net worth on the $100 million of assets thus translates into a $1.6 million decline in net worth. Using the Equation 3 formula from Chapter 20, Mona determines that the percentage change in the value of the swaps is

$$\%\Delta P = -DUR \times \frac{\Delta i}{1 + i} = -(-7.1) \times \frac{0.01}{1 + 0.07} = 0.066 = 6.6\%$$

When this gain of 6.6% is multiplied by the $24.2 million notional principal of the swaps, Mona sees that she will have a gain of $1.6 million in the value of the swaps. Knowing that the decline in the bank's assets minus its liabilities is exactly matched by the increase in the value of the swaps, Mona now takes comfort in her knowledge that the value of the bank is fully protected from changes in interest rates.

THE PRACTICING FINANCIAL INSTITUTION MANAGER
Hedging Foreign Exchange Risk with Currency Options and Currency Swaps

As we discussed in Chapter 21, foreign exchange rates have been highly volatile in recent years, and so financial institution managers need tools to be able to hedge foreign exchange risk. Options and swaps enable managers to hedge not only interest-rate risk but foreign exchange risk as well.

To understand how financial institution managers manage foreign exchange risk, let's return to the example we used in Chapter 21 in which in January, the First National Bank's customer, Frivolous Luxuries, Inc., is due a payment of 20 million deutsche marks (DM) in two months for $10 million worth of goods it has just sold in Germany. Frivolous Luxuries wants to make sure that if the value of the mark falls substantially from its current value of 50 cents, the company will not suffer a large loss because the DM 20 million payment will no longer be worth $10 million. Mona the Bank Manager is asked to hedge this foreign exchange risk for Frivolous Luxuries. Let's see how she does this using options and swap contracts.

Hedging Foreign Exchange Risk with Currency Options

In Chapter 21 we saw that the bank manager could sell 160 March deutsche mark futures contracts with a contract amount of DM 125,000 and a price of $0.50 per mark. To do the hedge with options, the bank manager needs to buy 160 put options written on the same March deutsche mark futures contract, with an exercise price of $0.50 per mark. Then if the deutsche mark falls in value, she will exercise the contract and sell the DM 20 million at the $0.50 exercise price, again guaranteeing Frivolous Luxuries its $10 million. To do this, however, the bank manager has to pay a premium for the options, say, 1 cent per mark, for a cost of $1250 per contract and a total cost of $200,000 (= 160 × $1250).

The advantage of hedging with options is that if the deutsche mark rises in value, say, to $0.60, the bank manager will not exercise the option, but the DM 20 million payment will rise in value to $12 million, giving Frivolous Luxuries a net profit of $1.8 million ($2 million minus the $200,000 premium). Thus Frivolous Luxuries is protected from any losses due to a depreciation of the deutsche mark but will gain from any appreciation of the mark. If Sam, the CEO of Frivolous Luxuries, thinks that there is a good possibility that the deutsche mark might appreciate in the next two months to $0.60 but still wants to protect his company from any loss arising from a depreciation of the mark, he will prefer to have the bank manager hedge the foreign exchange risk with options. The $200,000 premium is a small cost to pay for the hedge when he believes that Frivolous Luxuries has a good possibility of making $1.8 million from the appreciation.

Hedging Foreign Exchange Risk with Currency Swaps

Suppose that Frivolous Luxuries expects to sell DM 20 million of goods not just this year but every year for the next seven years. Since futures markets do not offer contracts that far in the future, the bank manager can't use them to hedge Frivolous Luxuries' foreign exchange risk. She might be able to use a set of forward contracts to hedge the risk, but another, possibly cheaper, alternative is to use a currency swap. A currency swap involves an exchange of a periodic set of payments in one currency for a periodic set of payments in another currency.

To see how a currency swap works in a simple example, suppose that the exchange rate is expected to stay at $0.50 per deutsche mark in the future.[3] To hedge the DM 20 million payment that Frivolous Luxuries receives over the next seven years, the bank manager needs to arrange a seven-year swap in which Frivolous Luxuries exchanges DM 20 million each year for $10 million. By making this swap arrangement, Mona has protected Frivolous Luxuries' DM 20 million cash flow from any foreign exchange risk for the next seven years.   ■

APPLICATION | **ARE FINANCIAL DERIVATIVES A WORLDWIDE TIME BOMB?**

With the bankruptcies of Orange County in 1994 (see Box 1) and the Barings bank in 1995 (discussed in Chapter 13)—both of which involved trades in financial derivatives—politicians, the media, and regulators have become very concerned about the dangers of derivatives. This concern is international and has spawned a slew of reports issued by such organizations as the Bank for International

---

[3]If the interest rates in the two countries differ, then as we saw from the interest parity condition in Chapter 8, there is an expected change in the exchange rate. Now for interest parity to hold, the party receiving the currency from the country with the higher interest rate must continually increase the payments in the other currency to reflect the expected exchange rate change and the interest-rate differential. In other words, if German interest rates are higher by 2 percentage points than U.S. interest rates, meaning that there is an expected appreciation of the dollar of 2% per year, the party receiving the German marks would have to pay 2% more in dollars at the end of the first year, 4% more at the end of the second year, and so on.

▌ BOX 1

The Orange County Bankruptcy

Orange County, California, one of the richest counties in the United States, was forced to declare bankruptcy on December 6, 1994, in the largest municipal bankruptcy filing ever. Orange County's downfall were the investment activities of its treasurer, Robert Citron, who was in charge of the $7.8 billion investment fund, which had not only $4.7 billion of funds from Orange County agencies but also $3.1 billion from 180 other municipalities and local government agencies. For years, the Orange County fund looked like a good investment, with the annual returns averaging 10% over the 15-year period to 1994. Unfortunately, these high returns were obtained with a highly leveraged strategy in which the fund purchased amounts of medium- to long-term bonds several times the value of the fund by borrowing with repurchase agreements. Everything was fine until interest rates began to rise in late 1993 and early 1994 and bond prices declined, leaving the fund with large losses.

We have already seen in our discussion of the Barings collapse how the principal-agent problem becomes especially severe once a trader or a manager of a fund starts to experience sizable losses. Once in the hole, the manager of the fund knows that his or her future depends on reversing these losses promptly. In this situation, the fund manager has a strong moral hazard incentive to take excessive risks. This is exactly what Citron did in late 1993 and early 1994 when he began buying large amounts of "inverse floaters," highly risky derivative securities that have high payoffs if long-term bond rates decline. Unfortunately for Citron, interest rates continued to rise, and the fund slipped deeper in the hole. When Peter Swan, the president of the Irvine Ranch Water District, became suspicious about the financial situation of the fund in November 1994 and asked to redeem $400 million, the jig was up for Citron because the fund did not have the cash to meet this redemption. Finally, on December 5, Citron was forced to resign, and the following day, Orange County declared bankruptcy. When bankruptcy was declared, the fund had estimated losses of $1.5 billion, and was found to have $20 billion of securities, $8.5 billion of which were derivatives, a risky portfolio indeed.

Although the role of derivatives in the Orange County debacle has often been emphasized, the problem here was really one of leverage and the principal-agent problem at work. Indeed, an important reason that Citron was able to get away with such a risky strategy, particularly after the fund sustained large losses, was that disclosure requirements were not as strong as they could be for municipal investment funds in the state of California. In contrast to other states, which require monthly or even daily disclosure of the market value of their municipal investment funds, California required this disclosure only once a year. If California had stricter disclosure requirements, investors in Citron's fund would have found out more quickly the risks he was taking, making it more likely that they would have pulled out their funds. This might have prevented Citron from taking on the risks that he did, and the Orange County bankruptcy would have been avoided.

Settlements (BIS), the Bank of England, the Group of Thirty, the Office of the U.S. Comptroller of the Currency (OCC), the Commodity Futures Trading Commission (CFTC), and the Government Accounting Office (GAO). Particularly scary are the notional amounts of derivatives contracts—tens of trillions of dollars worldwide—and the fact that banks, which are subject to bank panics, are major players in the derivatives markets. As a result of these fears, some politicians have called for restrictions on banks' involvement in the derivatives markets. Are financial derivatives a time bomb that could bring down the world financial system?

There are three major concerns about financial derivatives. First is that financial derivatives allow financial institutions to increase their leverage; that is, they can in effect hold an amount of the underlying asset that is many times greater than the amount of money they have had to put up. Increasing their leverage enables them to take huge bets on currency and interest-rate movements, which if they are wrong can bring down the bank, as was the case for Barings in 1995. This concern is valid. As we saw earlier in the chapter, the amount of money placed in margin accounts is only a small fraction of the price of the futures contract, meaning that small movements in the price of a contract can produce losses that are many times the size of the initial amount put in the margin account. Thus although financial derivatives can be used to hedge risk, they can also be used by financial institutions to take on excessive risk.

The second concern is that financial derivatives are too sophisticated for managers of financial institutions because they are so complicated. Although it is true that some financial derivatives can be so complex that some financial managers are not sophisticated enough to use them—a possibility in the Orange County case—this seems unlikely to apply to the big international financial institutions that are the major players in the derivatives markets. Indeed, in the Barings case, the bank was brought down not by trades in complex derivatives but rather by trades in one of the simplest of derivatives, stock index futures. (Recall from Chapter 13 that Barings's problem was more a lack of internal controls at the bank than a problem with derivatives per se.)

A third concern is that banks have holdings of huge notional amounts of financial derivatives, particularly swaps, that greatly exceed the amount of bank capital, and so these derivatives expose the banks to serious risk of failure. Banks are indeed major players in the financial derivatives markets, particularly the swaps market, where our earlier analysis has shown that they are the natural market-makers because they can act as intermediaries between two counterparties who would not make the swap without their involvement. However, looking at the notional amount of swaps at banks gives a very misleading picture of their risk exposure. First is that because banks act as intermediaries in the swap markets, as in the swap in Figure 3, they are typically exposed only to credit risk—a default by one of their counterparties. Furthermore, swaps, unlike loans, do not involve payments of the notional amount but rather the much smaller interest payments based on the notional amounts. For example, in the swaps that Citibank arranges in Figure 3, the payments on each of the swaps are only the interest rate times the $1 million notional amount. In the case of a 7% interest rate, the payment is only $70,000 for the $1 million swap. Estimates of the credit exposure from swap contracts indicate that they are on the order of only 1% of the notional value of the contracts and that credit exposure at banks from derivatives is generally less than a quarter of their total credit exposure from loans. Banks' credit exposure from their derivatives activities are thus not out of line with other credit exposures they face. Furthermore, an analysis by the GAO indicates that actual credit losses incurred by banks in their derivatives contracts have been very small, on the order of 0.2% of their gross credit exposure.

The conclusion is that financial derivatives do have their dangers for financial institutions, but some of these dangers have been overplayed. The biggest danger occurs in trading activities of financial institutions, and as discussed in Chapter 16, regulators have been paying increased attention to this danger and have issued new disclosure requirements and regulatory guidelines for how derivatives trading should be done. The credit risk exposure posed by derivatives, by contrast, seems to be manageable with standard methods of dealing with credit risk, both by managers of financial institutions and their regulators.

SUMMARY

1. An option contract gives the purchaser the right to buy (call option) or sell (put option) a security at the exercise (strike) price within a specific period of time. The profit function for options is nonlinear— profits do not always grow by the same amount for a given change in the price of the underlying financial instrument. The nonlinear profit function for options explains why their value (as reflected by the premium paid for them) is negatively related to the exercise price for call options, positively related to the exercise price for put options, positively related to the term to expiration for both call and put options, and positively related to the volatility of the prices of the underlying financial instrument for both call and put options.

2. Financial institution managers use futures options to hedge interest-rate risk in a similar fashion to the way they use financial futures. Futures options may be preferred for macro hedges because they suffer from fewer accounting problems than financial futures.

3. Interest-rate swaps involve the exchange of one set of interest payments for another set of interest payments and have default risk and liquidity problems

similar to those of forward contracts. As a result, interest-rate swaps often involve intermediaries such as large commercial banks and investment banks that make a market in swaps.

4. Managers of financial institutions find that interest-rate swaps are useful ways to hedge interest-rate risk. Interest-rate swaps have one big advantage over financial futures and options: They can be written for very long horizons.

5. Options and swaps are useful for hedging not only interest-rate risk but also foreign exchange risk.

6. There are three concerns about the dangers of derivatives: They make it easier for financial institutions to increase their leverage and take big bets, they are too complex for managers of financial institutions to understand, and they expose financial institutions to large credit risks because the huge notional amounts of derivative contracts greatly exceed the capital of these institutions. The second two dangers seem to be overplayed, but the danger from increased leverage using derivatives is real.

KEY TERMS

American option, p. 554
call option, p. 555
currency swaps, p. 564
European option, p. 554
exercise price (strike price),
    p. 553

financial futures option
    (futures option), p. 554
interest-rate swap, p. 564
notional principal, p. 565
option, p. 553
premium, p. 554

put option, p. 555
stock option, p. 554
swap, p. 564

QUESTIONS AND PROBLEMS

1. Why is one of the most widely traded option contracts the one that has the five-year Treasury bond futures contract as its underlying instrument rather than the five-year Treasury bond itself?

*2. Suppose that you buy a call option on a $100,000 Treasury bond futures contract with an exercise

price of 110 for a premium of $1500. If on expiration the futures contract has a price of 111, what is your profit or loss on the contract?

3. If you buy a put option on a $100,000 Treasury bond futures contract with an exercise price of 95 and the price of the Treasury bond is 120 at expiration, is the contract in the money, out of the

money, or at the money? What is your profit or loss on the contract if the premium was $4000?

*4. If you buy a put option on a $100,000 Treasury bond futures contract with an exercise price of 125 and the price of the Treasury bond is 120 at expiration, is the contract in the money, out of the money, or at the money? What is your profit or loss on the contract if the premium was $2500?

5. Why is the profit function for an option contract nonlinear but the profit function for a futures contract linear?

*6. Why does a lower strike price imply that a call option will have a higher premium and a put option a lower premium?

7. Explain why greater volatility or a longer term to maturity leads to a higher premium on both call and put options.

*8. Suppose that the pension fund you are managing is holding $75 million of four-year bonds, and if their interest rate rises by 1%, the bonds fall in price by 3 points. Suppose also that when its interest rate rises by 1%, the five-year Treasury bond contract falls by 4 points. Also when the T-bond futures contract interest rate rises by 1%, on average the interest rate on the four-year Treasury bond rises by 1.5%. What should you do in the option market to hedge the interest-rate risk on the $75 million of four-year bonds?

9. Would you rather do the hedge in Problem 8 with futures contracts or with option contracts if you think it is more likely that interest rates will rise in the future rather than fall?

*10. Suppose the bank you are managing is holding $1 million of 20-year bonds, and if their interest rate rises by 1%, the bonds fall in price by 11 points. Suppose also that when its interest rate rises by 1%, the long-term Treasury bond contract falls by 8 points. Also, when the T-bond futures contract interest rate rises by 1%, on average the interest rate on the 20-year Treasury bonds rises by 0.95%. What should you do in the futures market to hedge the interest-rate risk on the $1 million of 20-year bonds?

11. Would you rather do the hedge in Problem 10 with futures contracts or with option contracts if you think it is more likely that interest rates will fall in the future rather than rise?

*12. Why are option contracts typically more desirable for hedging than futures contracts when a financial institution is conducting a macro hedge?

13. Why does it make better sense to hedge a fixed-interest-rate loan commitment with an option contract rather than with a futures contract?

*14. What are the advantages and disadvantages of using an interest-rate swap to hedge interest-rate risk relative to using futures contracts?

15. Why are financial intermediaries usually needed to help two parties make an interest-rate swap?

*16. If the savings and loan you manage has an income gap of −$42 million, describe an interest-rate swap that would eliminate the S&L's income risk from changes in interest rates.

17. If the finance company you manage has an income gap of +$5 million, describe an interest-rate swap that would eliminate the company's income gap.

*18. Suppose that you are offered a swap of a 10% fixed-interest-rate payment over the next 25 years that has a duration of 11 years for payments that are tied to the two-year zero-coupon rate. If the institution you are managing has a duration gap of −2 years and has $1 billion of assets, how much notional principal would you want the swap to have?

19. If your company has to make a DM 125 million payment to a German company three months from now, how would you hedge the foreign exchange risk in this payment with option contracts on DM 125,000 futures contracts?

*20. Suppose that interest rates in the United States and Great Britain are equal, the exchange rate is $1.50 per pound sterling, and your company is due a payment of £200,000 every year for the next five years. What currency swap would you make to hedge the foreign exchange risk on these payments?

CASE STUDY

Using Option Contracts and Currency Swaps to Manage Interest-Rate Risk

CONCEPTS IN THIS CASE

options
strike price
premium
American option
European option
stock option
futures option
call option
put option
swaps
currency swaps

Your previous presentations on risk management and hedging with financial derivatives and your recent promotion to senior risk manager have made you very happy. The senior management team considers you one of the most valuable assets of the firm, and you are seeking a new opportunity to demonstrate your potential for even greater responsibilities. As designated risk manager for the firm's portfolio, you are continually trying to find ways to manage risk without the problems of futures contracts (liquidity, basis risk, accounting requirements). Bob R. Smart continues to be your outside consultant on such matters, and he is now suggesting that the firm consider other financial derivatives being used by larger banks: options and swaps. He has set up a meeting to discuss these alternatives, and he hopes you are as successful as you were under his previous coaching. You recognize that your success started with a lot of hard work, creating definition sheets, setting up scenarios, and answering anticipated questions in advance. You decide to continue your previous success by repeating the same process in the study of options and swaps.

You begin by defining the terminology commonly used in trading options and swaps: option contract, call option, put option, exercise or strike price, option premium, American and European option contracts, stock options, swaps, currency swaps, and interest-rate swaps. Once you understand these terms, you gather information that would be useful in the practical testing of these new strategies.

Total assets: $150 million
Interest-rate-sensitive assets: $90 million
Interest-rate-sensitive liabilities: $120 million
Duration gap: 2.20 years
Primary holdings of concern: $7 million in 6% Treasury bonds at par with 5 years to maturity; $12 million in stock, with an average beta of 0.90

Obtain information from the financial press on the most recent call and put contracts on Treasury bond futures options (six-month maturity). The response of Treasury bonds to a 1% rise in interest rates is 7% of par, while the change in the price of the futures option contract is 6%. The interest rate on Treasury bonds on average changes by 1.10 percentage points when the interest rate on the Treasury notes futures contract changes by 1%.

1. To protect against a rise in interest rates and a decline in the value of bonds held, how many Treasury bond futures put options (where the exercise price is near the option price) must the firm purchase?

2. If the forecasted rise in interest rates does not occur, can the bank still profit from its position in the Treasury bond futures options purchased in Question 1?

3. How would the bank create a substitute for a macro hedge if it forecasted rising interest rates?
   a. What is the hedge ratio?
   b. How many contracts would be needed?

4. What is the most significant accounting principles difference between futures and options?

5. Given the gap of the bank, how large an interest-rate swap does the bank need to arrange to hedge interest-rate risk and prevent a decline in profits when interest rates increase?

6. You are offered an interest-rate swap in which you would receive interest payments of 1% over the one-year Treasury bill rate for the next five years in exchange for a 7% fixed-rate payment.
   a. If the effective duration of the 7% fixed-rate payment over the next five years is 6.3, what is the duration of the swap?

b. What is the notional principal of the swap?

c. What will be the change in net worth as a percentage of assets?

d. What will be the percentage change in the value of the swap if interest rates rise 1%?

e. What will be the net change in the value of the firm as a result of a 1% increase in interest rates?

7. Explain the difference between hedging foreign exchange risk with currency options and currency swaps and doing so using futures contracts.

PART VI

Central Banking and the Conduct of Monetary Policy

CHAPTER 23

STRUCTURE OF CENTRAL BANKS AND THE FEDERAL RESERVE SYSTEM

■ **PREVIEW** The most important player in financial markets throughout the world are central banks, the government authorities in charge of monetary policy. Central banks' actions affect interest rates, the amount of credit, and the money supply, all of which have direct impacts not only on financial markets but also on aggregate output and inflation. To understand the role that central banks play in financial markets and the overall economy, we need to understand how these organizations work. Who controls central banks and determines their actions? What motivates their behavior? Who holds the reins of power?

In this chapter we look at the institutional structure of major central banks and particularly focus on the Federal Reserve System, the most important central bank in the world. We start by focusing on the formal institutional structure of the Fed and then examine the more relevant informal structure that determines where the true power within the Federal Reserve System lies. By understanding who makes the decisions, we will have a better idea of how they are made. We then look at several other major central banks and see how they are organized. With this information, we will be more able to comprehend the actual conduct of monetary policy described in the following chapters.

■ ORIGINS OF THE FEDERAL RESERVE SYSTEM

Of all the central banks in the world, the Federal Reserve System probably has the most unusual structure. To understand why this structure arose, we must go back before 1913, when the Federal Reserve System was created.

Before the twentieth century, a major characteristic of American politics was the fear of centralized power, as seen in the checks and balances of the

Constitution and the preservation of states' rights. This fear of centralized power was one source of the American resistance to the establishment of a central bank (see Chapter 14). Another source was the traditional American distrust of moneyed interests, the most prominent symbol of which was a central bank. The open hostility of the American public to the existence of a central bank resulted in the demise of the first two experiments in central banking, whose function was to police the banking system: The First Bank of the United States was disbanded in 1811, and the national charter of the Second Bank of the United States expired in 1836 after its renewal was vetoed in 1832 by President Andrew Jackson.

The termination of the Second Bank's national charter in 1836 created a severe problem for American financial markets because there was no lender of last resort who could provide reserves to the banking system to avert a bank panic. Hence in the nineteenth and early twentieth centuries, nationwide bank panics became a regular event, occurring every 20 years or so, culminating in the panic of 1907. The 1907 panic resulted in such widespread bank failures and such substantial losses to depositors that the public was finally convinced that a central bank was needed to prevent future panics.

The hostility of the American public to banks and centralized authority created great opposition to the establishment of a single central bank like the Bank of England. Fear was rampant that the moneyed interests on Wall Street (including the largest corporations and banks) would be able to manipulate such an institution to gain control over the economy and that federal operation of the central bank might result in too much government intervention in the affairs of private banks. Serious disagreements existed over whether the central bank should be a private bank or a government institution. Because of the heated debates on these issues, a compromise was struck. In the great American tradition, Congress wrote an elaborate system of checks and balances into the Federal Reserve Act of 1913, which created the Federal Reserve System with its 12 regional Federal Reserve banks (see Box 1).

BOX 1   INSIDE THE FED

The Political Genius of the Founders of the Federal Reserve System

 The history of the United States has been one of public hostility to banks and especially to a central bank. How were the politicians who founded the Federal Reserve able to design a system that has become one of the most prestigious institutions in the United States?

The answer is that the founders recognized that if power was too concentrated in either Washington or New York, cities that Americans love to hate, an American central bank might not have enough public support to operate effectively. They thus decided to set up a decentralized system with 12 Federal Reserve banks spread throughout the country to make sure that all regions of the country were represented in monetary policy deliberations. In addition, they made the Federal Reserve banks quasi-private institutions overseen by directors from the private sector living in that district who represent views from that region and are in close contact with the president of the Federal Reserve bank. The unusual structure of the Federal Reserve System has promoted a concern in the Fed with regional issues as is evident in Federal Reserve bank publications. Without this unusual structure, the Federal Reserve System might have been far less popular with the public, making the institution far less effective.

■ FORMAL STRUCTURE OF THE FEDERAL RESERVE SYSTEM

The formal structure of the Federal Reserve System was intended by writers of the Federal Reserve Act to diffuse power along regional lines, between the private sector and the government, and among bankers, businesspeople, and the public. This initial diffusion of power has resulted in the evolution of the Federal Reserve System to include the following entities: the **Federal Reserve banks,** the **Board of Governors of the Federal Reserve System,** the **Federal Open Market Committee (FOMC),** the Federal Advisory Council, and around 4000 member commercial banks. Figure 1 outlines the relationships of these entities to one another and to the three policy tools of the Fed (open market operations, the discount rate, and reserve requirements) discussed in Chapter 24.

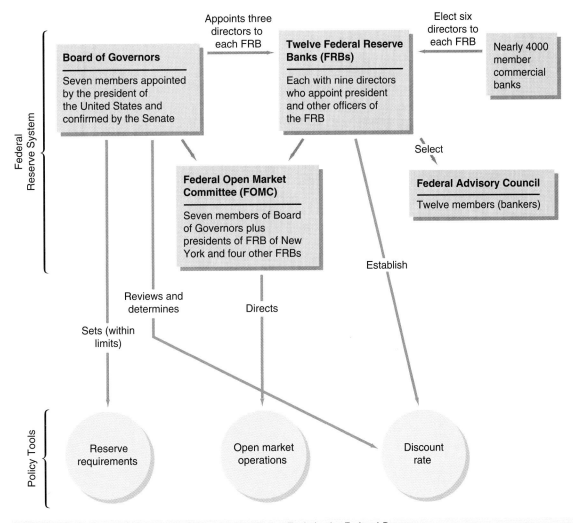

■FIGURE 1 Formal Structure and Allocation of Policy Tools in the Federal Reserve

Federal Reserve Banks

Each of the 12 Federal Reserve districts has one main Federal Reserve bank, which may have branches in other cities in the district. The locations of these districts, the Federal Reserve banks, and their branches are shown in Figure 2. The three largest Federal Reserve banks in terms of assets are those of New York, Chicago, and San Francisco—combined they hold over 50% of the assets (discount loans, securities, and other holdings) of the Federal Reserve System. The New York bank, with around one-quarter of the assets, is the most important of the Federal Reserve banks (see Box 2).

Each of the Federal Reserve banks is a quasi-public (part private, part government) institution owned by the private commercial banks in the district who are members of the Federal Reserve System. These member banks have purchased stock in their district Federal Reserve bank (a requirement of membership), and the dividends paid by that stock are limited by law to 6% annually. The member banks elect six directors for each district bank; three more are appointed by the Board of Governors. Together, these nine directors appoint the president of the bank (subject to the approval of the Board of Governors).

The directors of a district bank are classified into three categories, A, B, and C: The three A directors (elected by the member banks) are professional bankers,

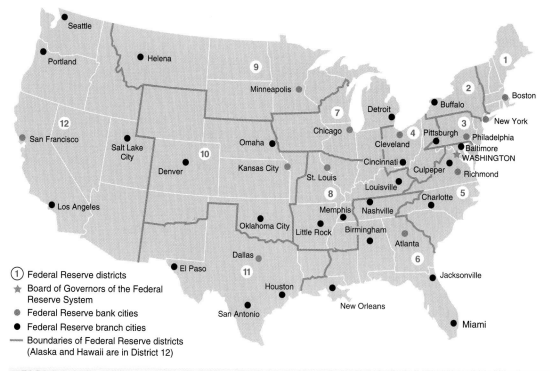

① Federal Reserve districts
★ Board of Governors of the Federal
   Reserve System
◉ Federal Reserve bank cities
● Federal Reserve branch cities
— Boundaries of Federal Reserve districts
   (Alaska and Hawaii are in District 12)

■**FIGURE 2** Federal Reserve System

Source: Federal Reserve *Bulletin.*

BOX 2   INSIDE THE FED

Special Role of the Federal Reserve Bank of New York

 The Federal Reserve Bank of New York plays a special role in the Federal Reserve System for several reasons. First, its district contains many of the largest commercial banks in the United States, the safety and soundness of which are paramount to the health of the U.S. financial system. The Federal Reserve Bank of New York conducts examinations of bank holding companies and state-chartered banks in its district, making it the supervisor of some of the most important financial institutions in our financial system. Not surprisingly, given this responsibility, the Bank Supervision group is one of the largest units of the New York Fed and is by far the largest bank supervision group in the Federal Reserve System.

The second reason for the New York Fed's special role is its active involvement in the bond and foreign exchange markets. The New York Fed houses the open market desk, which conducts open market operations—the purchase and sale of bonds—that determine the amount of reserves in the banking system. Because of this involvement in the Treasury securities market, as well as its walking-distance location near the New York and American Stock Exchanges, the officials at the Federal Reserve Bank of New York are in constant contact with the major domestic financial markets in the United States. In addition, the Federal Reserve Bank of New York also houses the foreign exchange desk, which conducts foreign exchange interventions on behalf of the Federal Reserve System and the U.S. Treasury. Its involvement in these financial markets means that the New York Fed is an important source of information on what is happening in domestic and foreign financial markets, particularly during crisis periods, as well as a liaison between officials in the Federal Reserve System and private participants in the markets.

The third reason for the Federal Reserve Bank of New York's prominence is that it is the only Federal Reserve bank to be a member of the Bank for International Settlements (BIS). Thus the president of the New York Fed, along with the chairman of the Board of Governors, represent the Federal Reserve System in its regular monthly meetings with other major central bankers at the BIS. This close contact with foreign central bankers and interaction with foreign exchange markets means that the New York Fed has a special role in international relations, both with other central bankers and with private market participants. Adding to its prominence in international circles is that the New York Fed is the repository for over $100 billion of the world's gold, an amount greater than the gold at Fort Knox.

Finally, the president of the Federal Reserve Bank of New York, currently William McDonough, is the only permanent member of the FOMC among the Federal Reserve bank presidents, serving as the vice chairman of the committee. Thus he, the chairman, and the vice chairman of the Board of Governors are the three most important officials in the Federal Reserve System.

and the three B directors (also elected by the member banks) are prominent leaders from industry, labor, agriculture, or the consumer sector. The three C directors, who are appointed by the Board of Governors to represent the public interest, are not allowed to be officers, employees, or stockholders of banks. This design for choosing directors was intended by the framers of the Federal Reserve Act to ensure that the directors of each Federal Reserve bank would reflect all constituencies of the American public.

The 12 Federal Reserve banks perform the following functions:

- Clear checks
- Issue new currency
- Withdraw damaged currency from circulation
- Evaluate proposed mergers and applications for banks to expand their activities

- Administer and make discount loans to banks in their districts
- Act as liaisons between the business community and the Federal Reserve System
- Examine bank holding companies and state-chartered member banks
- Collect data on local business conditions
- Use their staffs of professional economists to research topics related to the conduct of monetary policy

The conduct of monetary policy by the Federal Reserve involves actions that affect its balance sheet (holdings of assets and liabilities). Here we discuss the following simplified balance sheet:

Federal Reserve System	
Assets	Liabilities
Government securities	Currency in circulation
Discount loans	Reserves

Liabilities The two liabilities on the balance sheet, currency in circulation and reserves, are often referred to as the *monetary liabilities* of the Fed. They are an important part of the money supply story because increases in either or both will lead to an increase in the money supply (everything else being constant). The sum of the Fed's monetary liabilities (currency in circulation and reserves) and the U.S. Treasury's monetary liabilities (Treasury currency in circulation, primarily coins) is called the **monetary base.** When discussing the monetary base, we will focus only on the monetary liabilities of the Fed because the monetary liabilities of the Treasury account for less than 10% of the base.[1]

1. *Currency in circulation.* The Fed issues currency (those green-and-gray pieces of paper in your wallet that say "Federal Reserve note" at the top). Currency in circulation is the amount of currency in the hands of the public (outside of banks)—an important component of the money supply. (Currency held by depository institutions is also a liability of the Fed but is counted as part of reserves.)

Federal Reserve notes are IOUs from the Fed to the bearer and are also liabilities, but unlike most, they promise to pay back the bearer solely with Federal Reserve notes; that is, they pay off IOUs with other IOUs. Accordingly, if you bring a $100 bill to the Federal Reserve and demand payment, you will receive two $50s, five $20s, ten $10s, or one hundred $1 bills.

People are more willing to accept IOUs from the Fed than from you or me because Federal Reserve notes are a recognized medium of exchange; that is, they are accepted as a means of payment and so function as money.

---

[1]It is also safe to ignore the Treasury's monetary liabilities when discussing the monetary base because the Treasury cannot actively supply its monetary liabilities to the economy due to legal restrictions.

Unfortunately, neither you nor I can convince people that our own IOUs are worth anything more than the paper they are written on.[2]

2. *Reserves.* All banks have an account at the Fed in which they hold deposits. **Reserves** consist of deposits at the Fed plus currency that is physically held by banks (called vault cash because it is stored in bank vaults). Reserves are assets for the banks but liabilities for the Fed because the banks can demand payment on them at any time and the Fed is obliged to satisfy its obligation by paying Federal Reserve notes. As you will see, an increase in reserves leads to an increase in the level of deposits and hence in the money supply.

Total reserves can be divided into two categories: reserves that the Fed requires banks to hold (**required reserves**) and any additional reserves the banks choose to hold (**excess reserves**). For example, the Fed might require that for every dollar of deposits at a depository institution, a certain fraction (say, 10 cents) must be held as reserves. This fraction (10%) is called the **required reserve ratio**. Currently, the Fed pays no interest on reserves.

Assets The two assets on the Fed's balance sheet are important for two reasons. First, changes in the asset items lead to changes in reserves and consequently to changes in the money supply. Second, because these assets (government securities and discount loans) earn interest while the liabilities (currency in circulation and reserves) do not, the Fed makes billions of dollars every year—its assets earn income, and its liabilities cost nothing. Although it returns most of its earnings to the federal government, the Fed does spend some of it on "worthy causes," such as supporting economic research.

1. *Government securities.* This category of assets covers the Fed's holdings of securities issued by the U.S. Treasury. As you will see, the Fed provides reserves to the banking system by purchasing securities, thereby increasing its holdings of these assets. An increase in government securities held by the Fed leads to an increase in the money supply.

2. *Discount loans.* The Fed can provide reserves to the banking system by making discount loans to banks. An increase in discount loans can also be the source of an increase in the money supply. The interest rate charged banks for these loans is called the **discount rate.**

---

[2]The currency item on the Fed's balance sheet refers only to currency in circulation, that is, the amount in the hands of the public. Currency that has been printed by the U.S. Bureau of Engraving and Printing is not automatically a liability of the Fed. For example, consider the importance of having $1 million of your own IOUs printed up. You give out $100 worth to other people and keep the other $999,900 in your pocket. The $999,900 of IOUs does not make you richer or poorer and does not affect your indebtedness. You care only about the $100 of liabilities from the $100 of circulated IOUs. The same reasoning applies for the Fed in regard to its Federal Reserve notes.

For similar reasons, the currency component of the money supply, no matter how it is defined, includes only currency in circulation. It does not include any additional currency that is not yet in the hands of the public. The fact that currency has been printed but is not circulating means that it is not anyone's asset or liability and thus cannot affect anyone's behavior. Therefore, it makes sense not to include it in the money supply.

The 12 Federal Reserve banks are involved in monetary policy in several ways:

1. Their directors "establish" the discount rate (although the discount rate in each district is reviewed and determined by the Board of Governors).
2. They decide which banks, member and nonmember alike, can obtain discount loans from the Federal Reserve bank.
3. Their directors select one commercial banker from each bank's district to serve on the Federal Advisory Council, which consults with the Board of Governors and provides information that helps in the conduct of monetary policy.
4. Five of the 12 bank presidents each have a vote in the Federal Open Market Committee, which directs **open market operations** (the purchase and sale of government securities that affect both interest rates and the amount of reserves in the banking system). As explained in Box 2, the president of the New York Fed always has a vote in the FOMC, making it the most important of the banks; the other four votes allocated to the district banks rotate annually among the remaining 11 presidents.

Member Banks

All *national banks* (commercial banks chartered by the Office of the Comptroller of the Currency) are required to be members of the Federal Reserve System. Commercial banks chartered by the states are not required to be members, but they can choose to join. Currently, around one-third of the commercial banks in the United States are members of the Federal Reserve System, having declined from a peak figure of 49% in 1947.

Before 1980, only member banks were required to keep reserves as deposits at the Federal Reserve banks. Nonmember banks were subject to reserve requirements determined by their states, which typically allowed them to hold much of their reserves in interest-bearing securities. Because no interest is paid on reserves deposited at the Federal Reserve banks, it was costly to be a member of the system, and as interest rates rose, the relative cost of membership rose, and more and more banks left the system.

This decline in Fed membership was a major concern of the Board of Governors (one reason was that it lessened the Fed's control over the money supply, making it more difficult for the Fed to conduct monetary policy). The chairman of the Board of Governors repeatedly called for new legislation that required all commercial banks to be members of the Federal Reserve System. One result of the Fed's pressure on Congress was a provision in the Depository Institutions Deregulation and Monetary Control Act of 1980: All depository institutions became subject (by 1987) to the same requirements to keep deposits at the Fed, so member and nonmember banks would be on an equal footing in terms of reserve requirements. In addition, all depository institutions were given access to the Federal Reserve facilities, such as the discount window (discussed in Chapter 24) and Fed check clearing, on an equal basis. These provisions ended the decline in Fed membership and reduced the distinction between member and nonmember banks.

Board of Governors of the Federal Reserve System

At the head of the Federal Reserve System is the seven-member Board of Governors, headquartered in Washington, D.C. Each governor is appointed by the president of the United States and confirmed by the Senate. To limit the president's control over the Fed and insulate the Fed from other political pressures, the governors serve one nonrenewable 14-year term, with one governor's term expiring every other January.[3] The governors (many are professional economists) are required to come from different Federal Reserve districts to prevent the interests of one region of the country from being overrepresented. The chairman of the Board of Governors is chosen from among the seven governors and serves a four-year term. It is expected that once a new chairman is chosen, the old chairman resigns from the Board of Governors, even if there are many years left to his or her term as a governor.

The Board of Governors is actively involved in decisions concerning the conduct of monetary policy. All seven governors are members of the FOMC and vote on the conduct of open market operations. Because there are only 12 voting members on this committee (seven governors and five presidents of the district banks), the board has the majority of the votes. The board also sets reserve requirements (within limits imposed by legislation) and effectively controls the discount rate by the "review and determination" process, whereby it approves or disapproves the discount rate "established" by the Federal Reserve banks. The chairman of the board advises the president of the United States on economic policy, testifies in Congress, and speaks for the Federal Reserve System to the media. The chairman and other governors may also represent the United States in negotiations with foreign governments on economic matters. The board has a staff of professional economists (larger than those of individual Federal Reserve banks), which provides economic analysis that the board uses in making its decisions. (Box 3 discusses the role of the research staff.)

Through legislation, the Board of Governors has often been given duties not directly related to the conduct of monetary policy. In the past, for example, the board set the maximum interest rates payable on certain types of time deposits under Regulation Q. (Since Regulation Q was eliminated in 1986, the board no longer has this authority.) Under the Credit Control Act of 1969 (which expired in 1982), the board had the ability to regulate and control credit once the president of the United States approved. The Board of Governors also sets margin requirements, the fraction of the purchase price of the securities that has to be paid for with cash rather than borrowed funds. It also sets the salary of the president and

---

[3]Although technically the governor's term is nonrenewable, a governor can resign just before the term expires and then be reappointed by the president. This explains how one governor, William McChesney Martin Jr., served for 28 years. Since Martin, the chairman from 1951 to 1970, retired from the board in 1970, the practice of extending a governor's term beyond 14 years has become a rarity.

BOX 3   INSIDE THE FED

Role of the Research Staff

 The Federal Reserve System is the largest employer of economists not just in the United States but in the world. The system's research staff has around 1000 people, half of whom are economists. Of these 500 economists, 250 are at the Board of Governors, 100 are at the Federal Reserve Bank of New York, and the remainder are at the other Federal Reserve banks. What do all these economists do?

The most important task of the Fed's economists is to follow the incoming data from government agencies and private sector organizations on the economy and provide guidance to the policymakers on where the economy may be heading and what the impact of monetary policy actions on the economy might be. Before each FOMC meeting, the research staff at each Federal Reserve bank briefs its president and the senior management of the bank on its forecast for the U.S. economy and the issues that are likely to be discussed at the meeting. The research staff also provides briefing materials or a formal briefing on the economic outlook for the bank's region, something that each president discusses at the FOMC meeting. Meanwhile, at the Board of Governors, economists maintain a large econometric model (a model whose equations are estimated with statistical procedures) that helps them produce their forecasts of the national economy, and they too brief the governors on the national economic outlook.

The research staffers at the banks and the board also provide support for the bank supervisory staff, tracking developments in the banking sector and other financial markets and institutions and providing bank examiners with technical advice that they might need in the course of their examinations. Because the Board of Governors has to decide on whether to approve bank mergers, the research staff at both the board and the bank in whose district the merger is to take place prepare information on what effect the proposed merger might have on the competitive environment. To assure compliance with the Community Reinvestment Act, economists also analyze a bank's performance in its lending activities in different communities.

Because of the increased influence of developments in foreign countries on the U.S. economy, the research staff, particularly at the New York Fed and the board, produce reports on the major foreign economies. They also conduct research on developments in the foreign exchange market because of its growing importance in the monetary policy process and to support the activities of the foreign exchange desk. Economists also help support the operation of the open market desk by projecting reserve growth and the growth of the monetary aggregates.

Staff economists also engage in basic research on the effects of monetary policy on output and inflation, developments in the labor markets, international trade, international capital markets, banking and other financial institutions, financial markets, and the regional economy, among other topics. This research is published widely in academic journals and in Reserve bank publications. (Federal Reserve bank reviews are a good source of supplemental material for money and banking students.)

Another important activity of the research staff primarily at the Reserve banks is in the public education area. Staff economists are called on frequently to make presentations to the board of directors at their banks or to make speeches to the public in their district.

all officers of each Federal Reserve bank and reviews each bank's budget. Finally, the board has substantial bank regulatory functions: It approves bank mergers and applications for new activities, specifies the permissible activities of bank holding companies, and supervises the activities of foreign banks in the United States.

Federal Open Market Committee (FOMC)

The FOMC usually meets eight times a year (about every six weeks) and makes decisions regarding the conduct of open market operations, which influence the monetary base. The committee consists of the seven members of the Board of Governors, the president of the Federal Reserve Bank of New York, and presidents of four other Federal Reserve banks. The chairman of the Board of Governors also presides as the chairman of the FOMC. Even though only presidents of five of the Federal Reserve banks are voting members of the FOMC, the other seven presidents of the district banks attend FOMC meetings and participate in discussions. Hence they have some input into the committee's decisions.

Because open market operations are the most important policy tool that the Fed has for controlling the money supply, the FOMC is necessarily the focal point for policymaking in the Federal Reserve System. Although reserve requirements and the discount rate are not actually set by the FOMC, decisions in regard to these policy tools are effectively made there. The FOMC does not actually carry out securities purchases or sales. Rather it issues directives to the trading desk at the Federal Reserve Bank of New York, where the manager for domestic open market operations supervises a roomful of people who execute the purchases and sales of the government or agency securities. The manager communicates daily with the FOMC members and their staffs concerning the activities of the trading desk.

The FOMC Meeting

The FOMC meeting takes place in the boardroom on the second floor of the main building of the Board of Governors in Washington. The seven governors and the 12 Reserve Bank presidents, along with the secretary of the FOMC, the board's director of the Research and Statistics Division and his deputy, and the directors of the Monetary Affairs and International Finance Divisions, sit around a massive conference table. Although only five of the Reserve Bank presidents have voting rights on the FOMC at any given time, all actively participate in the deliberations. Seated around the sides of the room are the directors of research at each of the Reserve banks and other senior board and Reserve Bank officials, who, by tradition, do not speak at the meeting.

Except for the meetings before the February and July testimony by the chairman of the Board of Governors before Congress, the meeting starts on Tuesday at 9:00 A.M. sharp with a quick approval of the minutes of the previous meeting of the FOMC. The first substantive agenda item is the reports by the manager of system open market operations on foreign currency and domestic open market operations and other issues related to these topics. After the governors and Reserve Bank presidents finish asking questions and discussing these reports, a vote is taken to ratify them.

The next stage in the meeting is a presentation of the board staff's national economic forecast, which is referred to as the "green book" forecast (see Box 4), by the director of the Research and Statistics Division at the board. After the governors and Reserve Bank presidents have queried the division director about the forecast, the so-called *go-round* occurs: Each bank president presents an overview of economic conditions in his or her district and the bank's assessment of the national outlook, and each governor, except for the chairman, gives a view of the national outlook. By tradition, remarks avoid the topic of monetary policy at this time.

BOX 4   INSIDE THE FED

Green, Blue, and Beige
What Do These Colors Mean at the Fed?

Three research documents play an important role in the monetary policy process and at Federal Open Market Committee meetings. The national forecast for the next two years, generated by the Federal Reserve Board of Governors' Research and Statistics Division, is placed between green covers and is thus known as the "green book." It is provided to all who attend the FOMC meeting. The "blue book," in blue covers, is also provided to all participants at the FOMC meeting. It contains the projections for the monetary aggregates prepared by the

Monetary Affairs Division at the Board of Governors and contains typically three alternative scenarios for monetary policy (labeled A, B, and C). The "beige book," with beige covers, is produced by the Reserve banks and details evidence gleaned either from surveys or from talks with key businesses and financial institutions on the state of the economy in each of the Federal Reserve districts. This is the only one of the three books that is distributed publicly, and it often receives a lot of attention in the press.

After a coffee break, everyone returns to the boardroom and the agenda turns to current monetary policy and the domestic policy directive. The board's director of the Monetary Affairs Division then leads off the discussion by outlining the different scenarios for monetary policy actions outlined in the blue book (see Box 4) and may describe an issue relating to how monetary policy should be conducted. After a question-and-answer period, the chairman (currently Alan Greenspan) sets the stage for the following discussion by presenting his views on the state of the economy and then typically makes a recommendation for what monetary policy action should be taken. Then each of the FOMC members as well as the nonvoting bank presidents expresses his or her views on monetary policy, and the chairman summarizes the discussion and proposes specific wording for the directive to the open market desk (see Box 5). The secretary of the FOMC formally reads the proposed directive, and the members of the FOMC vote.[4]

Then there is an informal buffet lunch, and while eating, the participants hear a presentation on the latest developments in Congress on banking legislation and other legislation relevant to the Federal Reserve. Around 2:15 P.M. the meeting breaks up and the public announcement is made about the outcome of the meeting: whether the federal funds rate and discount rate have been raised, lowered, or left unchanged.[5] The postmeeting announcement is an innovation initiated in 1994. Before then, no such announcement was made, and the markets had to guess what policy action was taken. The decision to announce this information was a step in the direction of greater openness by the Fed.

[4]The decisions expressed in the directive may not be unanimous, and the dissenting views are made public. However, except in rare cases, the chairman's vote is always on the winning side.

[5]The meetings before the February and July chairman's testimony before Congress, required by the Humphrey-Hawkins legislation, have a somewhat different format. Rather than start Tuesday morning at 9 A.M. like the other meetings, they start at 2:30 on Tuesday and go over to Wednesday, with the usual announcement around 2:15 P.M. These longer meetings have the additional agenda item of a discussion and vote on the ranges for the monetary aggregates, which are transmitted to Congress, a requirement of the Humphrey-Hawkins Act. Because, as we will see in Chapter 24, monetary aggregates have been deemphasized in the conduct of monetary policy, this agenda item is not as important as it once was.

BOX 5   INSIDE THE FED

Decoding the FOMC Directive

The FOMC directive to the open market desk is released to the public immediately after the following FOMC meeting. Thus it usually appears six weeks or so after the policy action was taken and is published in the Federal Reserve *Bulletin*. The final operational paragraph of the directive provides a lot of information about the stance of monetary policy, but unfortunately it has nuances that require a magic decoder ring to unscramble its meaning. The first sentence of the operational paragraph reads as follows, with the italics indicating where the alternative words in parentheses fit in.

> In the implementation of policy for the immediate future, the Committee seeks to *(increase, decrease, maintain)* *(slightly, somewhat, significantly)* the existing degree of pressure on reserve positions.

"Increase" implies that the federal funds rate is to be raised, "decrease" means that the rate is to be lowered, and "maintain" means that the rate is to remain unchanged. The modifying word following indicates the extent of the change: "slightly" means one-quarter of a percentage point, "somewhat" means one-half of a percentage point, and "significantly" means three-fourths of a percentage point. Thus if the phrase "decrease somewhat" is used, this means that the federal funds rate is to be lowered by 0.5 percent.

A directive can also be described in the jargon of the FOMC as "symmetric" or "asymmetric." A *symmetric directive* means that the committee has no bias as to what should happen to the monetary policy stance between meetings. In this case, the chairman has the discretion to change the federal funds rate by a quarter of a percentage point without consulting the committee but is unlikely to do so without consultation. An *asymmetric directive* means that the FOMC has a preference regarding how monetary policy should be changed. If the directive is asymmetric, the chairman has the ability to direct the open market desk to conduct operations to change the federal funds rate in the direction specified by up to half a percentage point without consultation with the committee. However, even with an asymmetric directive, the current chairman, Alan Greenspan, prefers to consult with the committee if he believes a federal funds rate change is warranted. Whether a directive is symmetric or asymmetric can be discerned from the second sentence in the operational paragraph.

If the second sentence reads "somewhat greater or somewhat lesser reserve restraint would be acceptable in the intermeeting period," the directive is symmetric, and there is no bias to the monetary policy stance. If, however, the directive says "somewhat greater reserve restraint would or slightly less reserve restraint might be acceptable in the intermeeting period," it is asymmetric in the direction of raising interest rates, and if it is worded "slightly greater reserve restraint might or somewhat lesser reserve restraint would be acceptable in the intermeeting period," it is asymmetric with a bias toward lowering rates.

Now let's use our magic decoder ring to interpret the final operational paragraph of the directive from the FOMC meeting held on Tuesday, August 20, 1996. (The italicized phrases are the ones that change from directive to directive and tell us the stance of policy.)

> In the implementation of policy for the immediate future, the Committee seeks to *maintain* the existing degree of pressure on reserve positions. In the context of the Committee's long-run objectives for price stability and sustainable economic growth, and giving careful consideration to economic, financial, and monetary developments, *somewhat greater reserve restraint would or slightly lesser reserve restraint might* be acceptable in the intermeeting period. The contemplated reserve conditions are expected to be consistent with moderate growth in M2 and M3 over the coming months.

The first sentence indicates that the stance on monetary policy was unchanged at the August 20 meeting, leaving the federal funds rate as it was. However, the second sentence indicates that the directive was asymmetric, with a bias toward raising the federal funds rate in the intermeeting period.

■ INFORMAL STRUCTURE OF THE FEDERAL RESERVE SYSTEM

The Federal Reserve Act and other legislation give us some idea of the formal structure of the Federal Reserve System and who makes decisions at the Fed. What is written in black and white, however, does not necessarily reflect the reality of the power and decision-making structure.

As envisioned in 1913, the Federal Reserve System was to be a highly decentralized system designed to function as 12 separate, cooperating central banks. In the original plan, the Fed was not responsible for the health of the economy through its control of the money supply and its ability to affect interest rates. Over time, it has acquired the responsibility for promoting a stable economy, and this responsibility has caused the Federal Reserve System to evolve slowly into a more unified central bank.

The framers of the Federal Reserve Act of 1913 intended the Fed to have only one basic tool of monetary policy, the control of discount loans to member banks. The use of open market operations as a tool for monetary control was not yet well understood, and reserve requirements were fixed by the Federal Reserve Act. The discount tool was to be controlled by the joint decision of the Federal Reserve banks and the Federal Reserve Board (which later became the Board of Governors), so that both would share equally in the determination of monetary policy. However, the board's ability to "review and determine" the discount rate effectively allowed it to dominate the district banks in setting this policy.

Banking legislation during the Great Depression years centralized power within the newly created Board of Governors by giving it effective control over the remaining two tools of monetary policy, open market operations and changes in reserve requirements. The Banking Act of 1933 granted the FOMC authority to determine open market operations, and the Banking Act of 1935 gave the board the majority of votes in the FOMC. The Banking Act of 1935 also gave the board authority to change reserve requirements.

Since the 1930s, then, the Board of Governors has acquired the reins of control over the tools for conducting monetary policy. In recent years, the power of the board has become even greater. Although the directors of a Federal Reserve bank choose its president with the approval of the board, the board sometimes suggests a choice (often a professional economist) for president of a Federal Reserve bank to the directors of the bank, who then often follow the board's suggestions. Since the board sets the salary of the bank's president and reviews the budget of each Federal Reserve bank, it has further influence over the district banks' activities.

If the Board of Governors has so much power, what power do the Federal Advisory Council and the "owners" of the Federal Reserve banks—the member banks—actually have within the Federal Reserve System? The answer is almost none. Although member banks own stock in the Federal Reserve banks, they have none of the usual benefits of ownership. First, they have no claim on the earnings of the Fed and get paid only a 6% annual dividend, regardless of how much the Fed earns. Second, they have no say over how their property is used by the Federal Reserve System, in contrast to stockholders of private corporations. Third, there is usually only a single candidate for each of the six A and B directorships "elected" by the member banks, and this candidate is frequently suggested by the president of the Federal Reserve bank (who, in turn, is approved by the Board of Governors). The net result is that member banks are essentially frozen out of the political process at the Fed and have little effective power. Fourth, as its name implies, the Federal Advisory Council has only an advisory capacity and has no authority over Federal Reserve policymaking. Although the member bank "owners" do not have the usual power associated with being a stockholder, they do play an important but subtle role in the Federal Reserve System (see Box 6).

A fair characterization of the Federal Reserve System as it has evolved is that it functions as a central bank, headquartered in Washington, D.C., with branches in 12 cities. Because all aspects of the Federal Reserve System are essentially controlled by the Board of Governors, who controls the board? Although the chairman of the Board of Governors does not have legal authority to exercise control over this body, he effectively does so through his ability to act as spokesperson for the Fed and negotiate with Congress and the president of the United States. He also exercises control by setting the agenda of board and FOMC meetings. For example, the fact that the agenda at the FOMC has the chairman speak first about monetary policy enables him to have greater influence over what the policy action will be. The chairman also influences the board through the force of stature and personality. Chairmen of the Board of Governors (including Marriner S. Eccles, William McChesney Martin Jr., Arthur Burns, Paul A. Volcker, and Alan Greenspan) have typically had strong personalities and have wielded great power.

The chairman also exercises power by supervising the board's staff of professional economists and advisers. Because the staff gathers information for the board and conducts the analyses that the board uses in its decisions, it also has some influence over monetary policy. In addition, in the past, several appoint-

BOX 6   INSIDE THE FED

Role of Member Banks in the Federal Reserve System

 Although the member bank stockholders in each Federal Reserve bank have little direct power in the Federal Reserve System, they do play an important role. Their six representatives on the board of directors of each bank have a major oversight function. Along with the three public interest directors, they oversee the audit process for the Federal Reserve bank, making sure it is being run properly, and also share their management expertise with the senior management of the bank. Because they vote on recommendations by each bank to raise, lower, or maintain the discount rate at its current level, they engage in discussions about monetary policy and transmit their private sector views to the president and senior management of the bank. They also get to understand the inner workings of the Federal Reserve banks and the system so that they can help explain the position of the Federal Reserve to their contacts in the private and political sectors. Advisory councils like the Federal Advisory Council and others that are often set up by the district banks—for example, the Small Business and Agriculture Advisory Council and the Thrift Advisory Council at the New York Fed—are a conduit for the private sector to express views on both the economy and the state of the banking system.

So even though the owners of the Reserve banks do not have the usual voting rights, they are important to the Federal Reserve System because they make sure it does not get out of touch with the needs and opinions of the private sector.

ments to the board itself have come from within the ranks of its professional staff, making the chairman's influence even farther-reaching and longer-lasting than a four-year term.

The informal power structure of the Fed, in which power is centralized in the chairman of the Board of Governors, is summarized in Figure 3.

■ HOW INDEPENDENT IS THE FED?

When we look, in the next chapter, at how the Federal Reserve conducts monetary policy, we will want to know why it decides to take certain policy actions but not others. To understand its actions, we must understand the incentives that motivate the Fed's behavior. How free is the Fed from presidential and congres-

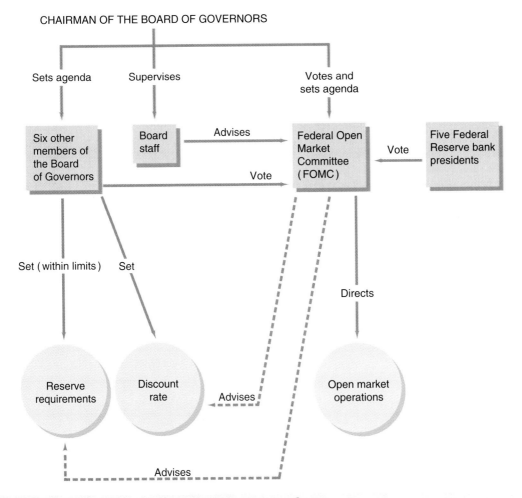

■**FIGURE 3** Informal Power Structure of the Federal Reserve System

sional pressures? Do economic, bureaucratic, or political considerations guide it? Is the Fed truly independent of outside pressures?

The Federal Reserve appears to be remarkably free of the political pressures that influence other government agencies. Not only are the members of the Board of Governors appointed for a 14-year term (and so cannot be ousted from office), but also the term is technically not renewable, eliminating some of the incentive for the governors to curry favor with the president and Congress.

Probably even more important to its independence from the whims of Congress is the Fed's independent and substantial source of revenue from its holdings of securities and, to a lesser extent, from its loans to banks. In recent years, for example, the Fed has had net earnings after expenses of around $20 billion per year—not a bad living if you can find it! Because it returns the bulk of these earnings to the Treasury, it does not get rich from its activities, but this income gives the Fed an important advantage over other government agencies: It is not subject to the appropriations process usually controlled by Congress. Indeed, the General Accounting Office, the auditing agency of the federal government, cannot audit the monetary policy or foreign exchange market functions of the Federal Reserve. Because the power to control the purse strings is usually synonymous with the power of overall control, this feature of the Federal Reserve System contributes to its independence more than any other factor.

Yet the Federal Reserve is still subject to the influence of Congress because the legislation that structures it is written by Congress and is subject to change at any time. When legislators are upset with the Fed's conduct of monetary policy, they frequently threaten to take control of the Fed's finances and force it to submit a budget request like other government agencies. A recent example is the call by Senators Dorgan and Reid in 1996 for Congress to have budgetary authority over the nonmonetary activities of the Federal Reserve. This is a powerful club to wave, and it certainly has some effect in keeping the Fed from straying too far from congressional wishes.

Congress has also passed legislation to make the Federal Reserve more accountable for its actions. In 1975, Congress passed House Concurrent Resolution 133, which requires the Fed to announce its objectives for the growth rates of the monetary aggregates. In the Full Employment and Balanced Growth Act of 1978 (the Humphrey-Hawkins Act), the Fed is required to explain how these objectives are consistent with the economic plans of the president of the United States. In recent years, Representative Henry Gonzalez, the former chairman of the House Banking Committee, has pressured the Fed to be less secretive in its deliberations about monetary policy—with some success, as the Fed's move to a post-FOMC announcement testifies.

The president can also influence the Federal Reserve. Because congressional legislation can affect the Fed directly or affect its ability to conduct monetary policy, the president can be a powerful ally through his influence on Congress. Second, although ostensibly a president might be able to appoint only one or two members to the Board of Governors during each presidential term, in actual practice the president appoints members far more often. One reason is that most governors do not serve out a full 14-year term. (Governors' salaries are substantially below what they can earn in the private sector, thus providing an incentive for them to take private sector jobs before their term expires.) In addition, the president is able to appoint a new chairman of the Board of Governors every four years, and a chairman who is not reappointed is expected to resign from the board so that a new member can be appointed.

The power that the president enjoys through his appointments to the Board of Governors is limited, however. Because the term of the chairman is not necessarily concurrent with that of the president, a president may have to deal with a chairman of the Board of Governors appointed by a previous administration. Alan Greenspan, for example, was appointed chairman in 1987 by President Ronald Reagan and was reappointed to another term by another Republican president, George Bush. When Bill Clinton, a Democrat, became president in 1993, Greenspan had several years left to his term. Clinton was put under tremendous pressure to reappoint Greenspan when his term expired and did so in 1996, even though Greenspan is a Republican.[6]

You can see that the Federal Reserve has extraordinary independence for a government agency and is one of the most independent central banks in the world. Nonetheless, the Fed is not free from political pressures. Indeed, to understand the Fed's behavior, we must recognize that public support for the actions of the Federal Reserve plays a very important role.

 ## STRUCTURE AND INDEPENDENCE OF FOREIGN CENTRAL BANKS

In contrast to the Federal Reserve System, which is decentralized into 12 district banks, which are privately owned, central banks in other industrialized countries consist of one centralized unit that is owned by the government. Here we examine the structure and degree of independence of four of the most important foreign central banks: the Bank of England, the Bundesbank in Germany, the Bank of Canada, and the Bank of Japan.

Bank of England

The Bank of England is the oldest central bank, having been founded in 1694. The Bank Act of 1946 gave the government statutory authority over the Bank of England. The governor of the Bank of England, currently Eddie George, is appointed by the government for a four-year term, as are the 16 directors.

Because the government has statutory power over the bank, it is the least independent of the central banks examined in this chapter. Indeed, the Bank of England can only make recommendations as to what monetary policy should be, as the decision to raise or lower interest rates resides not with the governor of the Bank of England but with the chancellor of the Exchequer (the equivalent of the

---

[6]Similarly, William McChesney Martin Jr., the chairman from 1951 to 1970, was appointed by President Truman (Dem.) but was reappointed by Presidents Eisenhower (Rep.), Kennedy (Dem.), and Nixon (Rep.). Also Paul Volcker, the chairman from 1979 to 1987, was appointed by President Carter (Dem.) but was reappointed by President Reagan (Rep.).

U.S. secretary of the Treasury). Recently, the government has made three major institutional changes that have increased somewhat the independence of the Bank of England. First, in February 1993, the monthly meeting between the chancellor and the governor to set monetary policy was formalized. Second, beginning in November 1993, the bank has been given more discretion to decide the timing of any interest-rate change decided by the chancellor, as long as the change is made before the next meeting. Third, since April 1994, the minutes of the meeting between the chancellor and the governor have been released two weeks after the next monthly meeting, a lag of six weeks. (Previously, the lag was 30 years—quite a change.) These measures have given the Bank of England a more public role in the setting of interest rates. However, several recent examples where the government has overruled the governor on interest-rate changes indicate that the Bank of England is still subservient to the government.

Deutsche Bundesbank

The Deutsche Bundesbank, more commonly referred to as the Bundesbank or as Buba by financial market participants, was founded in 1957 but had its predecessor in the Prussian Bank, founded in 1846. Like the Federal Reserve, the Bundesbank has a mix of national and regional appointees on the Direktorium, the monetary policymaking body of the bank. The state governments appoint heads of their state central banks, who are also directors of the Bundesbank. National directors, all of whom serve six-year terms, are appointed by the parliament. The governor of the Bundesbank, currently Hans Tietmayer, is appointed by the directors for an eight-year term.

The Bundesbank, along with the Swiss National Bank, is considered the most independent central bank in the world. Monetary policy is determined by the Bundesbank on its own authority, and there is no obligation for the bank to provide credit to the government. Furthermore, in contrast to the Federal Reserve, whose chairman is required to testify before Congress, the Bundesbank is not required to report to parliament or any other part of the federal government. In addition, the Bundesbank is the only central bank of the five discussed here who has the pursuit of price stability as its sole, formally stated primary mission.

Bank of Canada

Canada was late in establishing a central bank: The Bank of Canada was founded in 1934. Its directors are appointed by the government to three-year terms, and they appoint the governor, currently Gordon Thiesen, who has a seven-year term. The directors oversee a governing council of the four deputy governors and the governor.

The Bank Act was amended in 1967 to give the ultimate responsibility for monetary policy to the government. So on paper, the Bank of Canada is not as independent as the Federal Reserve. In practice, however, the Bank of Canada does essentially control monetary policy. In the event of a disagreement between the bank and the government, the minister of finance can issue a directive that the bank must follow. However, because the directive must be in writing and specific and applicable for a specified period, it is unlikely that such a directive would be issued, and none has been to date.

Bank of Japan

The Bank of Japan (Nippon Ginko) was founded in 1882 during the Meiji Restoration. Monetary policy is determined by the seven-member Policy Board, composed of the governor, currently Yasuo Matsushita, who is appointed by the government to a five-year term, and four members taken from the banking, commercial, or industrial sector appointed by the cabinet to three-year terms. Two nonvoting government representatives also sit on the Policy Board.

The Bank of Japan is not formally independent of the government, with the ultimate power residing with the Ministry of Finance. In addition, Ministry of Finance bureaucrats alternate with officials from the Bank of Japan as governor of the bank. However, by tradition it is understood that the government should not override the Bank of Japan's decisions about monetary policy, and the government has never invoked the provisions allowing it to override the bank. Therefore, the Bank of Japan, although not independent on paper, has a fair degree of independence in practice. Legislation is currently pending that would further increase the Bank of Japan's independence from the Ministry of Finance.

The Trend Toward Greater Independence

Our survey of the structure and independence of these major central banks indicates that the Bundesbank (and also the Swiss National Bank) are the most independent, followed closely by the Federal Reserve. The European Central Bank, which will come into being if European monetary union occurs in 1999 as planned, will have a structure like the Federal Reserve System in which central banks for each country would have a role similar to that of the Reserve banks. The European Central Bank would be highly independent, on a par with the Bundesbank; it would be independent of both the European Union (EU) and the national governments and would have complete control over monetary policy. In addition, like the Bundesbank, the European Central Bank's primary mission would be the pursuit of price stability. A trend in recent years is that more and more governments have been granting greater independence to their central banks; recent examples have been France and Spain. Both theory and experience suggest that more independent central banks produce better monetary policy, thus providing an impetus for this trend.

■ EXPLAINING CENTRAL BANK BEHAVIOR

One view of government bureaucratic behavior is that bureaucracies serve the public interest (this is the *public interest view*). Yet some economists have developed a theory of bureaucratic behavior that suggests other factors that influence how bureaucracies operate. The *theory of bureaucratic behavior* suggests that the objective of a bureaucracy is to maximize its own welfare, just as a consumer's behavior is motivated by the maximization of personal welfare and a firm's behavior is motivated by the maximization of profits. The welfare of a bureaucracy is related to its power and prestige. Thus this theory suggests that an important factor affecting a central bank's behavior is its attempt to increase its power and prestige.

What predictions does this view of a central bank like the Fed suggest? One is that the Federal Reserve will fight vigorously to preserve its autonomy, a prediction verified time and time again as the Fed has continually counterattacked congressional attempts to control its budget. In fact, it is extraordinary how effectively the Fed has been able to mobilize a lobby of bankers and businesspeople to preserve its independence when threatened.

Another prediction is that the Federal Reserve will try to avoid conflict with powerful groups that may threaten to curtail its power and reduce its autonomy. The Fed's behavior may take several forms. One possible factor explaining why the Fed is sometimes slow to increase interest rates and so smooths out their fluctuations is that it wishes to avoid a conflict with the president and Congress over increases in interest rates. The desire to avoid conflict with Congress and the president may also explain why in the past the Fed (particularly the chairman of the Board of Governors) devised clever stratagems to avoid blame for its past mistakes (see Box 7).

The desire of the Fed to hold as much power as possible also explains why it vigorously pursued a campaign to gain control over more banks. The campaign culminated in legislation that expanded jurisdiction of the Fed's reserve requirements to *all* banks (not just the member commercial banks) by 1987.

The theory of bureaucratic behavior seems applicable to the Federal Reserve's actions, but we must recognize that this view of the Fed as being solely concerned with its own self-interest is too extreme. Maximizing one's welfare does not rule out altruism. (You might give generously to a charity because it makes you feel good about yourself, but in the process you are helping a worthy cause.) The Fed is surely concerned that it conduct monetary policy in the public interest. However, much uncertainty and disagreement exist over what monetary policy should be. When it is unclear what is in the public interest, other motives may influence the Fed's behavior. In these situations, the theory of bureaucratic behavior may be a useful guide to predicting what motivates the Fed.

■ SHOULD THE FED BE INDEPENDENT?

As we have seen, the Federal Reserve is probably the most independent government agency in the United States. Every few years, the question arises in Congress as to whether the independence of the Fed should be curtailed. Politicians who strongly oppose a Fed policy often want to bring it under their supervision in order to impose a policy more to their liking. Should the Fed be independent, or would we be better off with a central bank under the control of the president or Congress?

BOX 7   INSIDE THE FED

Games the Fed Plays

 As the theory of bureaucratic behavior predicts, the Fed may play games to obscure its actions in order to avoid congressional interference in its activities. In 1975, Congress passed House Concurrent Resolution 133, which instructed the Fed to report quarterly to the banking committees of the House and the Senate its target ranges for the growth in the monetary aggregates over the next 12 months and how successful it had been in achieving its previous targets. One game that the Fed played was to report on several monetary aggregates (such as M1, M2, and M3) rather than on one: When the Fed testified to Congress on its success in achieving its past targets, it would focus on the particular monetary aggregate whose growth rate was closest to the target range.

In addition to this clever tactic, the Fed devised a procedure for setting its target for monetary aggregates (called *base drift*) that made it more likely that it would hit its targets, thereby avoiding conflict with Congress. Every quarter, the Fed would revise the target values for monetary aggregates by applying target growth rates to the amount at which the aggregate had ended up (a new base). When the Fed overshot its targets, as frequently occurred after 1975, it revised future target values upward, making it less likely that the monetary aggregates would exceed target ranges in the future. Similarly, if the Fed undershot its targets, it revised future target values downward, making it less likely that the monetary aggregates would fall below the target ranges in the future. Subsequent legislation now restricts the Fed to changing the base for its target ranges only once a year, reducing the extent of base drift.

Another indication that the Fed actively wanted to obscure its actions was its desire for secrecy, as reflected in the active defense of its delay in releasing FOMC directives to Congress or to the public. A former Fed official has stated that "a lot of staffers would concede that [secrecy] is designed to shield the Fed from political oversight." However, this official also stated that this was not a bad thing because "most politicians have a shorter time horizon than is optimal for monetary policy."* However, as discussed earlier, the Fed has provided more information about its monetary policy decisions in recent years.

---

*Quoted in "Monetary Zeal: How Federal Reserve Under Volcker Finally Slowed Down Inflation," *Wall Street Journal*, December 7, 1984, p. 23.

The Case for Independence

The strongest argument for an independent Federal Reserve rests on the view that subjecting the Fed to more political pressures would impart an inflationary bias to monetary policy. In the view of many observers, politicians in a democratic society are shortsighted because they are driven by the need to win their next election. With this as the primary goal, they are unlikely to focus on long-run objectives, such as promoting a stable price level. Instead, they will seek short-run solutions to problems, like high unemployment and high interest rates, even if the short-run solutions have undesirable long-run consequences. For example, we saw in Chapter 5 that high money growth might lead initially to a drop in interest rates but might cause an increase later as inflation heats up. Would a Federal Reserve under the control of Congress or the president be more likely to pursue a policy of excessive money growth when interest rates are high, even though it would eventually lead to inflation and even higher interest rates in the future? The advocates of an independent Federal Reserve say yes. They believe that a politically insulated Fed is more likely to be concerned with long-run objectives and thus be a defender of a sound dollar and a stable price level.

A variation on the preceding argument is that the political process in America leads to the so-called **political business cycle,** in which just before an election, expansionary policies are pursued to lower unemployment and interest rates. After the election, the bad effects of these policies—high inflation and high interest rates—come home to roost, requiring contractionary policies that politicians hope the public will forget before the next election. There is some evidence that such a political business cycle exists in the United States, and a Federal Reserve under the control of Congress or the president might make the cycle even more pronounced.

Putting the Fed under the control of the president (making it more subject to influence by the Treasury) is also considered dangerous because the Fed can be used to facilitate Treasury financing of large budget deficits by its purchases of Treasury bonds.[7] Treasury pressure on the Fed to "help out" might lead to a more inflationary bias in the economy. An independent Fed is better able to resist this pressure from the Treasury.

Another argument for Fed independence is that control of monetary policy is too important to leave to politicians, a group that has repeatedly demonstrated a lack of expertise at making hard decisions on issues of great economic importance, such as reducing the budget deficit or reforming the banking system. Another way to state this argument is in terms of the principal-agent problem discussed in Chapters 12 and 15. Both the Federal Reserve and politicians are agents of the public (the principals), and as we have seen, both politicians and the Fed have incentives to act in their own interest rather than in the interest of the public. The argument supporting Federal Reserve independence is that the principal-agent problem is worse for politicians than for the Fed because politicians have fewer incentives to act in the public interest.

Indeed, some politicians may prefer to have an independent Fed, which can be used as a public "whipping boy" to take some of the heat off their shoulders. It is possible that a politician who in private opposes an inflationary monetary policy will be forced to support such a policy in public for fear of not being reelected. An independent Fed can pursue policies that are politically unpopular yet in the public interest.

The Case Against Independence

Proponents of a Fed under the control of the president or Congress argue that it is undemocratic to have monetary policy (which affects almost everyone in the economy) controlled by an elite group responsible to no one. The current lack of accountability of the Federal Reserve has serious consequences: If the Fed performs badly, there is no provision for replacing members (as there is with politicians). True, the Fed needs to pursue long-run objectives, but elected officials of Congress vote on long-run issues also (foreign policy, for example). If we push the argument further that policy is always performed better by elite groups

---

[7]The Federal Reserve Act prohibited the Fed from buying Treasury bonds directly from the Treasury (except to roll over maturing securities); instead the Fed buys Treasury bonds on the open market. One possible reason for this prohibition is consistent with the foregoing argument: The Fed would find it harder to facilitate Treasury financing of large budget deficits.

like the Fed, we end up with such conclusions as the Joint Chiefs of Staff should determine military budgets or the IRS should set tax policies with no oversight from the president or Congress. Would you advocate this degree of independence for the Joint Chiefs or the IRS?

The public holds the president and Congress responsible for the economic well-being of the country, yet they lack control over the government agency that may well be the most important factor in determining the health of the economy. In addition, to achieve a cohesive program that will promote economic stability, monetary policy must be coordinated with fiscal policy (management of government spending and taxation). Only by placing monetary policy under the control of the politicians who also control fiscal policy can these two policies be prevented from working at cross-purposes.

Another argument against Federal Reserve independence is that an independent Fed has not always used its freedom successfully. The Fed failed miserably in its stated role as lender of last resort during the Great Depression, and its independence certainly didn't prevent it from pursuing an overly expansionary monetary policy in the 1960s and 1970s that contributed to rapid inflation in this period.

Our earlier discussion also suggests that the Federal Reserve is not immune from political pressures.[8] Its independence may encourage it to pursue a course of narrow self-interest rather than the public interest.

There is yet no consensus on whether Federal Reserve independence is a good thing, although public support for independence of the central bank seems to have grown in both the United States and abroad. As you might expect, people who like the Fed's policies are more likely to support its independence, while those who dislike its policies advocate a less independent Fed.

Central Bank Independence and Macroeconomic Performance in Seventeen Countries

We have seen that advocates of an independent central bank believe that macroeconomic performance will be improved by making the central bank more independent. Recent research seems to support this conjecture: When central banks are ranked from 1 (least independent) to 4 (most independent), inflation performance is found to be the best for countries with the most independent central banks.[9] As you can see in Figure 4, Germany and Switzerland, with the two most independent central banks, were also the countries with the lowest inflation rates in the 1973–1988 period. By contrast, the countries with the highest inflation in those years—Spain, New Zealand, Australia, and Italy—were also the countries

---

[8]For evidence on this issue, see Robert E. Weintraub, "Congressional Supervision of Monetary Policy," *Journal of Monetary Economics* 4 (1978): 341–362. Some economists suggest that lessening the independence of the Fed might even reduce the incentive for politically motivated monetary policy; see Milton Friedman, "Monetary Policy: Theory and Practice," *Journal of Money, Credit and Banking* 14 (1982): 98–118.

[9]Alberto Alesina and Lawrence H. Summers, "Central Bank Independence and Macroeconomic Performance: Some Comparative Evidence," *Journal of Money, Credit and Banking* 25 (1993): 151–162. However, Adam Posen, "Central Bank Independence and Disinflationary Credibility: A Missing Link," Federal Reserve Bank of New York Staff Report No. 1, May 1995, has cast some doubt on whether the causality runs from central bank independence to improved inflation performance.

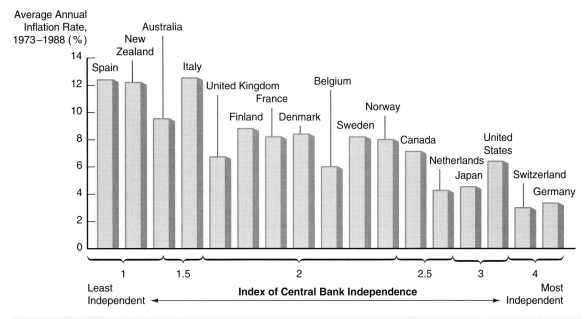

■FIGURE 4 Central Bank Independence and Macroeconomic Performance in Seventeen Countries

On the horizontal axis, the 17 central banks are rated from least independent, 1, to most independent, 4. More independent banks have generally produced lower inflation than less independent central banks. *Source:* Alberto Alesina and Lawrence H. Summers, "Central Bank Independence and Macroeconomic Performance: Some Comparative Evidence," *Journal of Money, Credit and Banking* 25 (1993): 151–162

with the least independent central banks. (The Spanish and New Zealand central banks have since gained greater independence.) Although a more independent central bank appears to lead to a lower inflation rate, this is not achieved at the expense of poorer real economic performance. Countries with independent central banks are no more likely to have high unemployment or greater output fluctuations than countries with less independent central banks.

SUMMARY

1. The Federal Reserve System was created in 1913 to lessen the frequency of bank panics. Because of public hostility to central banks and the centralization of power, the Federal Reserve System was created with many checks and balances to diffuse power.

2. The formal structure of the Federal Reserve System consists of 12 regional Federal Reserve banks, around 4000 member commercial banks, the Board of Governors of the Federal Reserve System, the Federal Open Market Committee, and the Federal Advisory Council.

3. Although on paper the Federal Reserve System appears to be decentralized, in practice it has come to function as a unified central bank controlled by the Board of Governors, especially the board's chairman.

4. The Federal Reserve is more independent than most agencies of the U.S. government, but it is still subject to political pressures because the legislation that structures the Fed is written by Congress and can be changed at any time. The theory of bureaucratic behavior indicates that one factor driving the Fed's behavior is its attempt to increase its power and prestige. This view explains many of the Fed's actions, although the agency may also try to act in the public interest.

5. The case for an independent Federal Reserve rests on the view that curtailing the Fed's independence and subjecting it to more political pressures would impart an inflationary bias to monetary policy. An independent Fed can afford to take the long view and not respond to short-run problems that will result in expansionary monetary policy and a political busi- ness cycle. The case against an independent Fed holds that it is undemocratic to have monetary policy (so important to the public) controlled by an elite that is not accountable to the public. An independent Fed also makes the coordination of monetary and fis- cal policy difficult.

KEY TERMS

Board of Governors of the Federal Reserve System, p. 585

discount rate, p. 589

excess reserves, p. 589

Federal Open Market Committee (FOMC), p. 585

Federal Reserve banks, p. 585

monetary base, p. 588

open market operations, p. 590

political business cycle, p. 605

required reserve ratio, p. 589

required reserves, p. 589

reserves, p. 589

QUESTIONS AND PROBLEMS

*1. Why was the Federal Reserve System set up with 12 regional Federal Reserve banks rather than one central bank, as in other countries?

2. What political realities might explain why the Federal Reserve Act of 1913 placed two Federal Reserve banks in Missouri?

*3. "The Federal Reserve System resembles the U.S. Constitution in that it was designed with many checks and balances." Discuss.

4. In what ways can the regional Federal Reserve banks influence the conduct of monetary policy?

*5. Which entities in the Federal Reserve System con- trol the discount rate? Reserve requirements? Open market operations?

6. Do you think that the 14-year nonrenewable terms for governors effectively insulate the Board of Governors from political pressure?

*7. Over time, which entities have gained power in the Federal Reserve System and which have lost power? Why do you think this has happened?

8. The Fed is the most independent of all U.S. gov- ernment agencies. What is the main difference between it and other government agencies that explains its greater independence?

*9. What is the primary tool that Congress uses to exercise some control over the Fed?

10. In the 1960s and 1970s, the Federal Reserve System lost member banks at a rapid rate. How can the theory of bureaucratic behavior explain the Fed's campaign for legislation to require all com- mercial banks to become members? Was the Fed successful in this campaign?

*11. "The theory of bureaucratic behavior indicates that the Fed never operates in the public interest." Is this statement true, false, or uncertain? Explain your answer.

12. Why might eliminating the Fed's independence lead to a more pronounced political business cycle?

*13. "The independence of the Fed leaves it completely unaccountable for its actions." Is this statement true, false, or uncertain? Explain your answer.

14. "The independence of the Fed has meant that it takes the long view and not the short view." Is this statement true, false, or uncertain? Explain your answer.

*15. The Fed promotes secrecy by not releasing FOMC directives to Congress or the public immediately. Discuss the pros and cons of this policy.

CHAPTER 24

CONDUCT OF MONETARY POLICY: TOOLS, GOALS, AND TARGETS

■ **PREVIEW** Understanding the conduct of monetary policy is important because it affects not only the money supply and interest rates but also the level of economic activity and hence our well-being. To explore this subject, we look first at the tools used to conduct monetary policy and then at the goals the Fed and other countries' central banks establish for monetary policy. After examining strategies for conducting monetary policy, we can evaluate central banks' conduct of monetary policy in the past, with the hope that it will give us some clues to where monetary policy may head in the future.

■ TOOLS OF MONETARY POLICY

Three basic tools of monetary policy are used to conduct monetary policy: open market operations, discount policy, and reserve requirements. We look at each of them in turn to see how the Fed wields them in practice and how relatively useful each tool is.

Open Market Operations

Open market operations, the central bank's purchase or sale of bonds in the open market, are the most important monetary policy tool because they are the primary determinant of changes in reserves in the banking system and interest rates. To see how they work, let's use T-accounts to examine what happens when the Fed conducts an open market purchase in which $100 of bonds are bought from the public.

When the person or corporation that sells the $100 of bonds to the Fed deposits the Fed's check in the local bank, the nonbank public's T-account after this transaction is

Nonbank Public		
Assets		Liabilities
Securities	−$100	
Checkable deposits	+$100	

When the bank receives the check, it credits the depositor's account with the $100 and then deposits the check in its account with the Fed, thereby adding to its reserves. The banking system's T-account becomes

Banking System			
Assets		Liabilities	
Reserves	+$100	Checkable deposits	+$100

The effect on the Fed's balance sheet is that it has gained $100 of securities in its assets column, while reserves have increased by $100, as shown in its liabilities column:

Federal Reserve System			
Assets		Liabilities	
Securities	+$100	Reserves	+$100

As you can see, the result of the Fed's open market purchase is an expansion of reserves and deposits in the banking system. Another way of seeing this is to recognize that open market purchases of bonds expand reserves because the central bank pays for the bonds with reserves. Because the monetary base equals currency plus reserves, we have shown that an open market purchase increases the monetary base by an equal amount. Also because deposits are an important component of the money supply, another result of the open market purchase is an increase in the money supply. This leads to the following important conclusion: ***An open market purchase leads to an expansion of reserves and deposits in the banking system and hence to an expansion of the monetary base and the money supply.***

Similar reasoning indicates that when a central bank conducts an open market sale, the public pays for the bonds by writing a check that causes deposits and reserves in the banking system to fall. Thus ***an open market sale leads to a contraction of reserves and deposits in the banking system and hence to a decline in the monetary base and the money supply.***

There are two types of open market operations: **Dynamic open market operations** are intended to change the level of reserves, and **defensive open market operations** are intended to offset movements in other factors that affect reserves, such as changes in Treasury deposits with the Fed or float. The Fed conducts open market operations in U.S. Treasury and government agency securities, especially U.S. Treasury bills.[1] The Fed conducts most of its open market operations in Treasury securities because the market for these securities is the most liquid and has the largest trading volume. It has the capacity to absorb the Fed's substantial volume of transactions without experiencing excessive price fluctuations that would disrupt the market.

As we saw in Chapter 23, the decision-making authority for open market operations is the Federal Open Market Committee (FOMC). The actual execution of these operations, however, is conducted by the trading desk at the Federal Reserve Bank of New York. The best way to see how these transactions are executed is to look at a typical day at the trading desk, located in a newly built trading room on the ninth floor of the Federal Reserve Bank of New York.

A Day at the Trading Desk

The head of domestic open market operations, currently Sandy Krieger, supervises the analysts and traders who execute the purchases and sales of securities. To get a grip on what might happen in the federal funds market that day, her workday and her staff's begins with a review of developments in the federal funds market the previous day and with an update on the actual amount of reserves in the banking system the day before. Later in the morning, Sandy's staff issues updated reports that contain detailed forecasts of what will be happening to some of the short-term factors affecting the supply and demand of reserves.

This information will help Sandy and her staff decide how large a change in reserves is needed to obtain a desired level of the federal funds rate. If the amount of reserves in the banking system is too large, many banks will have excess reserves to lend that other banks may have little desire to hold, and the federal funds rate will probably fall. If the level of reserves is too low, banks seeking to borrow reserves from the few banks that have excess reserves to lend may push the funds rate higher than the desired level. Also during the morning, the staff will monitor the behavior of the federal funds rate and contact some of the major participants in the funds market, which may provide independent information about whether a change in reserves is needed to achieve the desired level of the federal funds rate.

Early in the morning, members of Sandy's staff contact several representatives of the so-called **primary dealers,** government securities dealers (who operate out of private firms or commercial banks) that the open market desk trades with. Her staff finds out how the dealers view market conditions to get a feel for what may happen to the prices of the securities they trade in over the course of the day. They also call the Treasury to get updated information on the expected level of Treasury balances at the Fed in order to refine their estimates of the supply of reserves.

---

[1]To avoid conflicts of interest, the Fed does not conduct open market operations in privately issued securities. (For example, think of the conflict if the Federal Reserve purchased bonds issued by a company owned by the chairman's brother-in-law.)

Afterward, members of the Monetary Affairs Division at the Board of Governors are contacted, and the New York Fed's forecasts of reserve supply and demand are compared with the Board's. On the basis of these projections and the observed behavior of the federal funds market, the desk will formulate and propose a course of action to be taken that day, which may involve plans to add reserves to or drain reserves from the banking system through open market operations. If an operation is contemplated, the type, size, and maturity will be discussed.

The whole process is currently completed by midmorning, at which time a daily conference call is arranged linking the desk with the Office of the Director of Monetary Affairs at the Board and with one of the four voting Reserve Bank presidents outside of New York. During the call, a member of Sandy's unit will outline the desk's proposed reserve management strategy for the day. After the plan is approved, the desk is instructed to execute immediately any temporary open market operations that were planned for that day. (Outright operations, to be described shortly, may be conducted at other times of the day.)

The desk is linked electronically with its domestic open market trading counterparties by a computer system called TRAPS (Trading Room Automated Processing System), and all open market operations are now performed over this system. A message will be electronically transmitted simultaneously to all the primary dealers over TRAPS indicating the type and maturity of the operation being arranged. The dealers are given several minutes to respond via TRAPS with their propositions. The propositions are then assembled and displayed on a computer screen for evaluation. The desk will select all propositions, beginning with the most attractively priced, up to the point where the desired amount is purchased or sold, and it will then notify each dealer via TRAPS which of its propositions have been chosen. The entire selection process is typically completed in a matter of minutes.

These temporary transactions are of two basic types. In a **repurchase agreement** (often called a **repo**), the Fed purchases securities with an agreement that the seller will repurchase them in a short period of time, anywhere from 1 to 15 days from the original date of purchase. Because the effects on reserves of a repo are reversed on the day the agreement matures, a repo is actually a temporary open market purchase and is an especially desirable way of conducting a defensive open market purchase that will be reversed shortly. When the Fed wants to conduct a temporary open market sale, it engages in a **matched sale-purchase transaction** (sometimes called a **reverse repo**) in which the Fed sells securities and the buyer agrees to sell them back to the Fed in the near future.

At times, the desk may see the need to address a persistent reserve shortage or surplus and wish to arrange an operation that will have a permanent impact on the supply of reserves. Outright transactions, which involve a purchase or sale of securities that is not self-reversing, are also conducted over TRAPS. These operations are traditionally executed at times of day when temporary operations are not being conducted.

Discount Policy

Recall from Chapter 23 that discount loans are loans from the central bank to depository institutions and that the discount rate is the interest rate charged on these loans. Discount policy, which primarily involves changes in the discount rate, affects reserves in the banking system because when a discount loan is extended, the central bank increases a bank's reserves by an equal amount. The Federal Reserve facility at which discount loans are made to banks is called the **discount window.** It is easiest to understand how the Fed affects the volume of discount loans by looking at how the discount window operates.

Operation of the Discount Window

The Fed can affect the volume of discount loans in two ways: by affecting the *price* of the loans (the discount rate) or by affecting the *quantity* of the loans through its administration of the discount window.[2]

The mechanism through which the Fed's discount rate affects the volume of discount loans is straightforward: A higher discount rate raises the cost of borrowing from the Fed, so banks will take out fewer discount loans; a lower discount rate makes discount loans more attractive to banks, and loan volume will increase.

To examine how the Fed affects the quantity of discount loans through its administration of the discount window, we have to examine more closely how these loans are made.

The Fed's discount loans to the banks are of three types: adjustment credit, seasonal credit, and extended credit. *Adjustment credit loans* are the discount loans that play the most important role in monetary policy. They are intended to be used by banks to help them with short-term liquidity problems that may result from a temporary deposit outflow, and the rate charged on them is the basic discount rate established by the Federal Reserve banks and approved by the Board of Governors. Adjustment credit, which can be obtained with a phone call, is expected to be repaid fairly quickly—by the end of the next business day for the larger banks. In the 1990s, adjustment credit has shrunk to very low levels, with the result that discount lending has been playing a less important role in monetary policy (see Box 1).

Seasonal credit is given to meet the needs of a limited number of banks in vacation and agricultural areas that have a seasonal pattern. Since 1992, the interest rate charged on seasonal credit is tied to the monthly average federal funds and certificate of deposit rates, with the basic discount rate as a floor. *Extended credit*, given to banks that have experienced severe liquidity problems because of deposit outflows, is not expected to be repaid quickly. The interest rate on these loans is set at one-half of a percentage point above the interest rate charged on seasonal credit. Banks obtaining extended credit have to submit a proposal outlining the need for extended credit and a plan for restoring the liquidity of the bank. The most important example of extended credit to a bank was the Fed's loans to Continental Illinois in 1984, which exceeded $5 billion.

A bank faces three costs when it borrows from the discount window: the interest cost represented by the discount rate, the cost of concerns that might be

---

[2]Each Federal Reserve bank administers its own discount window facility. In our discussion here of discount policy, when we discuss the Fed's administration of the discount window, we are actually referring to the district banks' administration of their discount window facilities.

BOX 1   INSIDE THE FED

Why Has Adjustment Credit Borrowing Shrunk to Such Low Levels in the 1990s?

In recent years, adjustment credit borrowing has declined to very low levels, averaging below $100 million, making discount lending less important to the monetary policy process. Why has this occurred?

The Federal Reserve has not changed its rules on this kind of lending or discouraged its use, so the answer must lie with choices made by the borrowing banks. The problems in the banking industry in the late 1980s and early 1990s described in Chapter 16 provide a likely explanation for the decline in adjustment credit borrowing. Banks became reluctant to go to the discount window to borrow because often market par-

ticipants are able to guess who had done so. In an environment of concern about the health of banks, some banks fear that if they are perceived as seeking increased liquidity from the discount window, market participants will become concerned that the bank is in trouble and may begin pulling funds out of the bank. Consequently, even though perfectly healthy banks may need short-term liquidity, they have been reluctant to come to the discount window. With the return to health of the banking industry in recent years, these fears may diminish, and adjustment credit lending may increase again.

raised about the health of the bank if the market guesses that the bank has gone to the discount window, and the cost of being more likely to be turned down for a discount loan in the future because of too frequent trips to the discount window. The Fed's setting of rules for use of the discount window is frequently referred to as *moral suasion*.

Lender of Last Resort

In addition to its use as a tool to influence reserves in the banking system and the money supply, discounting is important in preventing financial panics. When the Federal Reserve System was created, its most important role was intended to be as the **lender of last resort;** it was to provide reserves to banks when no one else would in order to prevent bank failures from spinning out of control, thereby preventing bank and financial panics. Discounting is a particularly effective way to provide reserves to the banking system during a banking crisis because reserves are immediately channeled to the banks that need them most.

Using the discount tool to avoid financial panics by performing the role of lender of last resort is an extremely important requirement of successful monetary policymaking. Financial panics can also severely damage the economy because they interfere with the ability of these markets to move funds to people with productive investment opportunities (see Chapter 12).

Unfortunately, the discount tool has not always been used by the Fed to prevent financial panics, as the massive failures during the Great Depression attest. The Fed learned from its mistakes of that period and has performed admirably in its role of lender of last resort in the post–World War II period. Two examples of the use of the Fed's discount weapon to avoid bank panics are the provisions of huge loans to Franklin National Bank in 1974 and to Continental Illinois ten years later (see Box 2).

At first glance, it might appear as though the presence of the FDIC, which insures depositors from losses due to a bank's failure up to a limit of $100,000 per

▉ BOX 2   INSIDE THE FED

Discounting to Troubled Banks

Franklin National and Continental Illinois

 In May 1974, the public learned that Franklin National Bank, the twentieth-largest bank in the United States, with deposits close to $3 billion, had suffered large losses in foreign exchange trading and had made many bad loans. Large depositors, whose accounts exceeded the $100,000 limit insured by the FDIC, began to withdraw their deposits, and the failure of the bank was imminent. Because the immediate failure of Franklin National would have had repercussions on other vulnerable banks, possibly leading to more bank failures, the Fed announced that discount loans would be made available to Franklin National so that depositors, including the largest, would not suffer any losses. By the time Franklin National was merged into the European-American Bank in October 1974, the Fed had lent Franklin National the sum of $1.75 billion, nearly 5% of the total amount of reserves in the banking system. The quick Fed action was completely successful in preventing any other bank failures, and a possible bank panic was avoided.

A 1984 episode involved Continental Illinois National Bank and the Fed in a similar action. Continental Illinois had made many bad loans (primarily to businesses in the energy industry and to foreign countries), and rumors of financial trouble in early May 1984 caused large depositors to withdraw over $10 billion of deposits from the bank. The FDIC arranged a rescue effort in July 1984 that culminated in a $4.5 billion commitment of funds to save the bank; still, the Fed had to lend Continental Illinois over $5 billion—making its $1.75 billion loan to Franklin National look like small potatoes! The Fed's action prevented further bank failures, and again a potential bank panic was averted. ▉

---

account, would make the lender-of-last-resort function of the Fed superfluous. (The FDIC is described in detail in Chapter 16.) There are two reasons why this is not the case. First, it is important to recognize that the FDIC's insurance fund amounts to around 1% of the amount of these deposits outstanding. If a large number of bank failures occurred, the FDIC would not be able to cover all the depositors' losses. Indeed, the large number of bank failures in the 1980s and early 1990s, described in Chapter 16, led to large losses and a shrinkage in the FDIC's insurance fund, which reduced the FDIC's ability to cover depositors' losses. This fact has not weakened the confidence of small depositors in the banking system because the Fed has been ready to stand behind the banks to provide whatever reserves are needed to prevent bank panics. Second, the nearly $500 billion of large-denomination deposits in the banking system are not guaranteed by the FDIC because they exceed the $100,000 limit. A loss of confidence in the banking system could still lead to runs on banks from the large-denomination depositors, and bank panics could still occur despite the existence of the FDIC. The importance of the Federal Reserve's role as lender of last resort is, if anything, more important today because of the high number of bank failures experienced in the 1980s and early 1990s.

Not only can the Fed be a lender of last resort to banks, but it can also play the same role for the financial system as a whole. The existence of the Fed's discount window can help prevent financial panics that are not triggered by bank failures, as was the case during the Black Monday stock market crash of 1987 (see Box 3).

BOX 3 INSIDE THE FED

Discounting to Prevent a Financial Panic

The Black Monday Stock Market Crash of 1987

 Although October 19, 1987, dubbed "Black Monday," will go down in the history books as the largest one-day decline in stock prices to date (the Dow Jones Industrial Average declined by more than 500 points), it was on Tuesday, October 20, 1987, that financial markets almost stopped functioning. Felix Rohatyn, one of the most prominent men on Wall Street, stated flatly: "Tuesday was the most dangerous day we had in 50 years."* Much of the credit for prevention of a market meltdown after Black Monday must be given to the Federal Reserve System and the chairman of the Board of Governors, Alan Greenspan.

The stress of keeping markets functioning during the sharp decline in stock prices on Monday, October 19, meant that many brokerage houses and specialists (dealer-brokers who maintain orderly trading on the stock exchanges) were severely in need of additional funds to finance their activities. However, understandably enough, New York banks, as well as foreign and regional U.S. banks, growing very nervous about the financial health of securities firms, began to cut back credit to the securities industry at the very time when it was most needed. Panic was in the air. One chairman of a large specialist firm commented that on Monday, "from 2 P.M. on, there was total despair. The entire investment community fled the market. We were left alone on the field." It was time for the Fed, like the cavalry, to come to the rescue.

Upon learning of the plight of the securities industry, Alan Greenspan and E. Gerald Corrigan, then president of the Federal Reserve Bank of New York and the Fed official most closely in touch with Wall Street, became fearful of a spreading collapse of securities firms. To prevent this from occurring, Greenspan announced before the market opened on Tuesday, October 20, the Federal Reserve System's "readiness to serve as a source of liquidity to support the economic and financial system." In addition to this extraordinary announcement, the Fed made it clear that it would provide discount loans to any bank that would make loans to the securities industry, although this did not prove to be necessary. As one New York banker said, the Fed's message was, "We're here. Whatever you need, we'll give you."

The outcome of the Fed's timely action was that a financial panic was averted. The markets kept functioning on Tuesday, and a market rally ensued that day, with the Dow Jones Industrial Average climbing over 100 points.

---

*"Terrible Tuesday: How the Stock Market Almost Disintegrated a Day After the Crash," *Wall Street Journal,* November 20, 1987, p. 1. This article provides a fascinating and more detailed view of the events described here and is the source of all the quotations cited.

Although the Fed's role as the lender of last resort has the benefit of preventing bank and financial panics, it does have a cost. If a bank expects that the Fed will provide it with discount loans when it gets into trouble, as occurred with Continental Illinois, it will be willing to take on more risk knowing that the Fed will come to the rescue. The Fed's lender-of-last-resort role has thus created a moral hazard problem similar to the one created by deposit insurance (discussed in Chapter 16): Banks take on more risk, thus exposing the deposit insurance agency, and hence taxpayers, to greater losses. The moral hazard problem is most severe for large banks, which may believe that the Fed and the FDIC view them as "too big to fail"; that is, they will always receive Fed loans when they are in trouble because their failure would be likely to precipitate a bank panic.

Similarly, Federal Reserve actions to prevent financial panic, as occurred after the October 1987 stock market crash, may encourage financial institutions other than banks to take on greater risk. They, too, expect the Fed to ensure that they could get loans if a financial panic seemed imminent. When the Fed considers using the discount weapon to prevent panics, it therefore needs to consider the trade-off between the moral hazard cost of its role as lender of last resort and the benefit of preventing financial panics. This trade-off explains why the Fed must be careful not to perform its role as lender of last resort too frequently.

Announcement Effect

Discount policy serves another function for the Federal Reserve: It can be used to signal the Fed's intentions about future monetary policy. Hence if the Fed decides to slow the expansion of the economy by increasing the federal funds rate, it can amplify the announcement that it makes after the FOMC meeting by also raising the discount rate. This signal alone may rein in economic expansion because the public will expect monetary policy to be less expansionary in the future.

The problem with the announcement effect is that it is subject to misinterpretation. If the federal funds rate is rising relative to the discount rate, the volume of discount loans will rise because banks will find it advantageous to borrow more with discount loans and then lend the proceeds out in the federal funds market. In such a situation, the Fed may have no intention of amplifying the announcement of a federal funds rate increase, but to keep the amount of discounting from becoming excessive, it may raise the discount rate to keep it more in line with market interest rates. When the discount rate rises, the market may interpret this as a signal that the Fed is moving to a more contractionary policy, even if that is not the case. The announcement effect may be a hindrance rather than a help. Another approach is for the Fed to communicate directly with the public by announcing its intentions about monetary policy outright and then carrying them out. Fed announcements would be believed, and the market would respond accordingly.

Reserve Requirements

Changes in reserve requirements affect the demand for reserves: A rise in reserve requirements means that banks must hold more reserves, and a reduction means that they are required to hold less. The Depository Institutions Deregulation and Monetary Control Act of 1980 provided a simple scheme for setting reserve requirements. All depository institutions, including commercial banks, savings and loan associations, mutual savings banks, and credit unions, are now subject to the same reserve requirements, as follows: Required reserves on all checkable deposits—including non-interest-bearing checking accounts, NOW accounts, super-NOW accounts, and ATS (automatic transfer savings) accounts—are equal to 3% of the bank's first $49.3 million of checkable deposits[3] and 10% of the checkable deposits over $49.3 million, and the percentage set initially at 10% can be varied between 8% and 14% at the Fed's discretion. In extraordinary circumstances, the percentage can be raised as high as 18%.

Reserve requirements have been rarely used as a monetary policy tool because raising them can cause immediate liquidity problems for banks with low

---

[3]The $49.3 million figure is as of the beginning of 1997. Each year, the figure is adjusted upward by 80% of the percentage increase in checkable deposits in the United States.

excess reserves. When the Fed has raised these requirements in the past, it has usually softened the blow by conducting open market purchases or by making the discount window more available, thus providing reserves to banks that needed them. Continually fluctuating reserve requirements would also create more uncertainty for banks and make their liquidity management more difficult.

Advantages of Open Market Operations over the Other Tools

Of the three tools of monetary policy available to the Fed, the primary tool used is open market operations. This is because open market operations have several advantages over the other tools of monetary policy.

First, open market operations occur at the initiative of the Fed, which has complete control over their volume. This control is not found, for example, in discount operations, in which the Fed can encourage or discourage banks to take out discount loans by altering the discount rate but cannot directly control the volume of discount loans.

Second, open market operations are flexible and precise; they can be used to any extent. No matter how small a change in reserves is desired, open market operations can achieve it with a small purchase or sale of securities. Conversely, if the desired change in reserves or the monetary base is very large, the open market operations tool is strong enough to do the job through a very large purchase or sale of securities.

Third, open market operations are easily reversed. If a mistake is made in conducting an open market operation, the Fed can immediately reverse it. If the Fed decides that the federal funds rate is too low because it has made too many open market purchases, it can immediately make a correction by conducting open market sales.

Fourth, open market operations can be implemented quickly; they involve no administrative delays. When the Fed decides that it wants to change reserves, it just places orders with securities dealers, and the trades are executed immediately.

■ GOALS OF MONETARY POLICY

Six basic goals are continually mentioned by personnel at the Federal Reserve and other central banks when they discuss the objectives of monetary policy: (1) high employment, (2) economic growth, (3) price stability, (4) interest-rate stability, (5) stability of financial markets, and (6) stability in foreign exchange markets.

High Employment

The Employment Act of 1946 and the Full Employment and Balanced Growth Act of 1978 (more commonly called the Humphrey-Hawkins Act) commit the U.S. government to promoting high employment consistent with a stable price level. High employment is a worthy goal for two main reasons: (1) the alternative situation, high unemployment, causes much human misery, with families suffering financial distress, loss of personal self-respect, and increase in crime (though this last conclusion is highly controversial), and (2) when unemployment is high, the economy has not only idle workers but also idle resources (closed factories and unused equipment), resulting in a loss of output (lower GDP).

Although it is clear that high employment is desirable, how high should it be? At what point can we say that the economy is at full employment? At first, it might seem that full employment is the point at which no worker is out of a job, that is, when unemployment is zero. But this definition ignores the fact that some unemployment, called *frictional unemployment*, which involves searches by workers and firms to find suitable matchups, is beneficial to the economy. For example, a worker who decides to look for a better job might be unemployed for a while during the job search. Workers often decide to leave work temporarily to pursue other activities (raising a family, travel, returning to school), and when they decide to reenter the job market, it may take some time for them to find the right job. The benefit of having some unemployment is similar to the benefit of having a nonzero vacancy rate in the market for rental apartments. As many of you who have looked for an apartment have discovered, when the vacancy rate in the rental market is too low, you will have a difficult time finding the right apartment.

Another reason that unemployment is not zero when the economy is at full employment is due to what is called *structural unemployment*, a mismatch between job requirements and the skills or availability of local workers. Clearly, this kind of unemployment is undesirable. Nonetheless, it is something that monetary policy can do little about.

The goal for high employment should therefore not seek an unemployment level of zero but rather a level above zero consistent with full employment at which the demand for labor equals the supply of labor. This level is called the **natural rate of unemployment.**

Although this definition sounds neat and authoritative, it isn't because it leaves a troublesome question unanswered: What unemployment rate is consistent with full employment? On the one hand, in some cases, it is obvious that the unemployment rate is too high: The unemployment rate in excess of 20% during the Great Depression, for example, was clearly far too high. In the early 1960s, on the other hand, policymakers thought that a reasonable goal was 4%, a level that was probably too low because it led to accelerating inflation. Current estimates of the natural rate of unemployment place it between 5% and 6%, but even this estimate is subject to a great deal of uncertainty and disagreement. In addition, it is possible that appropriate government policy, such as the provision of better information about job vacancies or job training programs, might decrease the natural rate of unemployment.

Economic Growth

The goal of steady economic growth is closely related to the high-employment goal because businesses are more likely to invest in capital equipment to increase productivity and economic growth when unemployment is low. Conversely, if unemployment is high and factories are idle, it does not pay for a firm to invest in additional plants and equipment. Although the two goals are closely related, policies can be specifically aimed at promoting economic growth by directly encouraging firms to invest or by encouraging people to save, which provides more funds

BOX 4   A GLOBAL PERSPECTIVE

The Growing European Commitment to Price Stability

 Not surprisingly, given Germany's experience with hyperinflation in the 1920s, its central bank has the strongest commitment to price stability. In contrast to statutes for the German central bank, the statutes of other central banks in Europe set various objectives for policy, including all the goals outlined here in the text. However, European policymakers have been coming around to the view that the primary objective for a central bank should be price stability. The increased importance of this goal is reflected in the December 1991 Treaty of European Union, known as the Maastricht Treaty, which proposed the creation of the European System of Central Banks, which would function very much like the Federal Reserve System. The statute of the European System of Central Banks sets price stability as the primary objective of this system and indicates that the general economic policies of the European Union are to be supported only if they are not in conflict with price stability.

for firms to invest. In fact, this is the stated purpose of so-called supply-side economics policies, which are intended to spur economic growth by providing tax incentives for businesses to invest in factories and equipment and for taxpayers to save more. The public, politicians, and the media in the United States have become much more concerned about economic growth in recent years because of the dramatic slowdown since the early 1970s. In the 1950s and 1960s, real GDP grew in excess of $3\frac{1}{2}$% per year on average, whereas since 1973, it has grown at only 2 to $2\frac{1}{2}$%. This has generated an active debate over what can be done to increase our growth rate and whether monetary policy can play a role in boosting growth.

Price Stability

Over the past two decades, policymakers in the United States have become more aware of the social and economic costs of inflation and more concerned with a stable price level as a goal of economic policy. (The growing commitment to price stability is also evident in Europe—see Box 4.) Price stability is desirable because a rising price level (inflation) creates uncertainty in the economy, and that may hamper economic growth. For example, the information conveyed by the prices of goods and services is harder to interpret when the overall level of prices is changing, which complicates decision making for consumers, businesses, and government. Not only do public opinion surveys indicate that the public is very hostile to inflation, but also a growing body of evidence suggests that inflation leads to lower economic growth.[4] The most extreme example of unstable prices is *hyperinflation*, such as Argentina and Brazil experienced until recently. Many economists attribute the slower growth that these countries have experienced to their problems with hyperinflation.

Inflation also makes it hard to plan for the future. For example, it is more difficult to decide how much funds should be put aside to provide for a child's col-

---

[4]For example, see Stanley Fischer, "The Role of Macroeconomic Factors in Growth," *Journal of Monetary Economics* 32 (1993): pp. 485–512.

lege education in an inflationary environment. Further, inflation may strain a country's social fabric: Conflict may result because each group in the society may compete with other groups to make sure that its income keeps up with the rising level of prices.

Interest-Rate Stability

Interest-rate stability is desirable because fluctuations in interest rates can create uncertainty in the economy and make it harder to plan for the future. Fluctuations in interest rates that affect consumers' willingness to buy houses, for example, make it more difficult for consumers to decide when to purchase a house and for construction firms to plan how many houses to build. A central bank may also want to reduce upward movements in interest rates for the reasons we discussed in Chapter 23: Upward movements in interest rates generate hostility toward central banks like the Fed and lead to demands that their power be curtailed.

Stability of Financial Markets

As our analysis in Chapter 8 showed, financial crises can interfere with the ability of financial markets to channel funds to people with productive investment opportunities, thereby leading to a sharp contraction in economic activity. The promotion of a more stable financial system in which financial crises are avoided is thus an important goal for a central bank. Indeed, as discussed in Chapter 23, the Federal Reserve System was created in response to the bank panic of 1907 to promote financial stability.

The stability of financial markets is also fostered by interest-rate stability because fluctuations in interest rates create great uncertainty for financial institutions. An increase in interest rates produces large capital losses on long-term bonds and mortgages, losses that can cause the failure of the financial institutions holding them. In recent years, more pronounced interest-rate fluctuations have been a particularly severe problem for savings and loan associations and mutual savings banks, many of which got into serious financial trouble in the 1980s and early 1990s (as we have seen in Chapter 15).

Stability in Foreign Exchange Markets

With the increasing importance of international trade to the U.S. economy, the value of the dollar relative to other currencies has become a major consideration for the Fed. As we saw in Chapter 8, a rise in the value of the dollar makes American industries less competitive with those abroad, and declines in the value of the dollar stimulate inflation in the United States. In addition, preventing large changes in the value of the dollar makes it easier for firms and individuals purchasing or selling goods abroad to plan ahead. Stabilizing extreme movements in the value of the dollar in foreign exchange markets is thus viewed as a worthy goal of monetary policy. In other countries, which are even more dependent on foreign trade, stability in foreign exchange markets takes on even greater importance.

Conflict Among Goals

Although many of the goals mentioned are consistent with each other—high employment with economic growth, interest-rate stability with financial market stability—this is not always the case. The goal of price stability often conflicts with the goals of interest-rate stability and high employment in the short run (but probably not in the long run). For example, when the economy is expanding and unemployment is falling, both inflation and interest rates may start to rise. If the central bank tries to prevent a rise in interest rates, this may cause the economy to overheat and stimulate inflation. But if a central bank raises interest rates to prevent inflation, in the short run unemployment may rise. The conflict among goals may thus present central banks like the Federal Reserve with some hard choices.

■ CENTRAL BANK STRATEGY: USE OF TARGETS

The central bank's problem is that it wishes to achieve certain goals, such as price stability with high employment, but it does not directly influence the goals. It has a set of tools to employ (open market operations, changes in the discount rate, and changes in reserve requirements) that can affect the goals indirectly after a period of time (typically more than a year). If the central bank waits to see what the price level and employment will be one year later, it will be too late to make any corrections to its policy—mistakes will be irreversible.

All central banks consequently pursue a different strategy for conducting monetary policy by aiming at variables that lie between its tools and the achievement of its goals. The strategy is as follows: After deciding on its goals for employment and the price level, the central bank chooses a set of variables to aim for, called **intermediate targets,** such as the monetary aggregates (M1, M2, or M3) or interest rates (short- or long-term), which have a direct effect on employment and the price level. However, even these intermediate targets are not directly affected by the central bank's policy tools. Therefore, it chooses another set of variables to aim for, called **operating targets,** or alternatively called *instruments*, such as reserve aggregates (reserves, nonborrowed reserves, monetary base, or nonborrowed base) or interest rates (federal funds rate or Treasury bill rate), which are more responsive to its policy tools. (Nonborrowed reserves are total reserves minus borrowed reserves, which are the amount of discount loans; the monetary base is the sum of currency plus reserves in the banking system; the nonborrowed base is the monetary base minus borrowed reserves; and the federal funds rate is the interest rate on funds loaned overnight between banks.)[5]

The central bank pursues this strategy because it is easier to hit a goal by aiming at targets than by aiming at the goal directly. Specifically, by using intermediate and operating targets, it can more quickly judge whether its policies are on the right track, rather than waiting until it sees the final outcome of its policies on

---

[5]There is some ambiguity as to whether to call a particular variable an operating target or an intermediate target. The monetary base and the Treasury bill rate are often viewed as possible intermediate targets, even though they may function as operating targets as well. In addition, if the Fed wants to pursue a goal of interest-rate stability, an interest rate can be both a goal and a target.

employment and the price level.[6] By analogy, NASA employs the strategy of using targets when it is trying to send a spaceship to the moon. It will check to see whether the spaceship is positioned correctly as it leaves the atmosphere (we can think of this as NASA's "operating target"). If the spaceship is off course at this stage, NASA engineers will adjust its thrust (a policy tool) to get it back on target. NASA may check the position of the spaceship again when it is halfway to the moon (NASA's "intermediate target") and can make further midcourse corrections if necessary.

The central bank's strategy works in a similar way. Suppose that the central bank's employment and price-level goals are consistent with a nominal GDP growth rate of 5%. If the central bank feels that the 5% nominal GDP growth rate will be achieved by a 4% growth rate for M2 (its intermediate target), which will in turn be achieved by a growth rate of $3\frac{1}{2}$% for the monetary base (its operating target), it will carry out open market operations (its tool) to achieve the $3\frac{1}{2}$% growth in the monetary base. After implementing this policy, the central bank may find that the monetary base is growing too slowly, say, at a 2% rate; then it can correct this too slow growth by increasing the amount of its open market purchases. Somewhat later, the central bank will begin to see how its policy is affecting the growth rate of the money supply. If M2 is growing too fast, say, at a 7% rate, the central bank may decide to reduce its open market purchases or make open market sales to reduce the M2 growth rate.

One way of thinking about this strategy (illustrated in Figure 1) is that the central bank is using its operating and intermediate targets to direct monetary policy (the spaceship) toward the achievement of its goals. After the initial setting of the policy tools (the liftoff), an operating target such as the monetary base, which the central bank can control fairly directly, is used to reset the tools so that monetary policy is channeled toward achieving the intermediate target of a certain rate of money supply growth. Midcourse corrections in the policy tools can be made again when the central bank sees what is happening to its intermediate target, thus directing monetary policy so that it will achieve its goals of high employment and price stability (the spaceship reaches the moon).

■ CHOOSING THE TARGETS

As we see in Figure 1, there are two different types of target variables: interest rates and aggregates (monetary aggregates and reserve aggregates). In our example, the central bank chose a 4% growth rate for M2 to achieve a 5% rate of growth for nominal GDP. It could have chosen to lower the interest rate on the three-month Treasury bills to, say, 3% to achieve the same goal. Can the central bank choose to pursue both of these targets at the same time? The answer is no. The application of the supply and demand analysis of the money market that we covered in Chapter 5 explains why a central bank must choose one or the other.

---

[6]This reasoning for the use of monetary targets has come under attack because information on employment and the price level can be useful in evaluating policy. See Benjamin M. Friedman, "The Inefficiency of Short-Run Monetary Targets for Monetary Policy," *Brookings Papers on Economic Activity* 2 (1977): 292–346.

Tools of the Central Bank

Open market operations
Discount policy
Reserve requirements

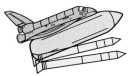
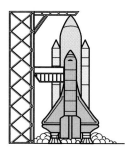

Operating Targets

Reserve aggregates
(reserves, nonborrowed
reserves, monetary base,
nonborrowed base)
Interest rates (short-term
such as federal funds rate)

Intermediate Targets

Monetary aggregates
(M1, M2, M3)
Interest rates (short-
and long-term)

Goals

High employment,
price stability,
financial market
stability and so on.

∎FIGURE 1 Central Bank Strategy

Let's first see why a monetary aggregate target involves losing control of the interest rate. Figure 2 contains a supply and demand diagram for the money market. Although the central bank expects the demand curve for money to be at M^{d*}, it fluctuates between $M^{d'}$ and $M^{d''}$ because of unexpected increases or decreases in output or changes in the price level. The money demand curve might also shift unexpectedly because the public's preferences about holding bonds versus money may change. If the central bank's monetary aggregate target of a 4% growth rate

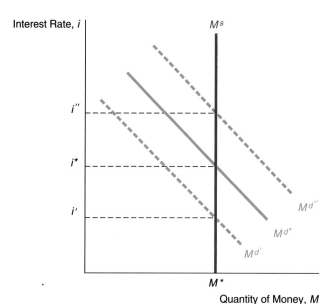

∎FIGURE 2 Result of Targeting on the Money Supply

Targeting on the money supply at $M*$ will lead to fluctuations in the interest rate between i' and i'' because of fluctuations in the money demand curve between $M^{d'}$ and $M^{d''}$.

in M2 results in a money supply of M^*, it expects that the interest rate will be i^*. However, as the figure indicates, the fluctuations in the money demand curve between $M^{d'}$ and $M^{d''}$ will result in an interest rate fluctuating between i' and i''. Pursuing a monetary aggregate target implies that interest rates will fluctuate.

The supply and demand diagram in Figure 3 shows the consequences of an interest-rate target set at i^*. Again, the central bank expects the money demand curve to be at M^{d*}, but it fluctuates between $M^{d'}$ and $M^{d''}$ due to unexpected changes in output, the price level, or the public's preferences toward holding money. If the demand curve rises to $M^{d''}$, the interest rate will begin to rise above i^*, and the price of bonds will fall. With an interest-rate target, the central bank will prevent the interest rate from rising by buying bonds to drive their price back up and the interest rate back down to its former level. The central bank open market purchase of bonds will mean that reserves and deposits in the banking system will rise because the central bank pays for these bonds with reserves, thus raising the money supply. The central bank will continue to make open market purchases until the money supply rises to $M^{s''}$, at which point the equilibrium interest rate is again i^*. Conversely, if the demand curve falls to $M^{d'}$ and lowers the interest rate, the central bank would keep interest rates from falling by selling bonds to keep their prices from rising. The central bank will make open market sales until the money supply falls to $M^{s'}$ and the equilibrium interest rate is i^*. The central bank's adherence to the interest-rate target thus leads to a fluctuating money supply as well as fluctuations in reserve aggregates.

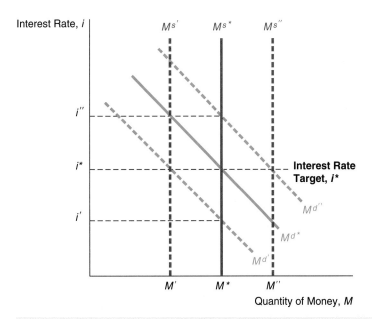

■FIGURE 3 Result of Targeting on the Interest Rate

Targeting the interest rate at i^* will lead to fluctuations of the money supply between M' and M'' because of fluctuations in the money demand curve between $M^{d'}$ and $M^{d''}$.

The conclusion from the supply and demand analysis is that interest-rate and monetary aggregate targets are incompatible: A central bank can hit one or the other but not both. Because a choice between them has to be made, we need to examine what criteria should be used to decide on the target variable.

Criteria for Choosing Intermediate Targets

The rationale behind a central bank's strategy of using targets suggests three criteria for choosing an intermediate target: It must be measurable, it must be controllable by the central bank, and it must have a predictable effect on the goal.

Measurability Quick and accurate measurement of an intermediate-target variable is necessary because the intermediate target will be useful only if it signals when policy is off track more rapidly than the goal. What good does it do for the central bank to plan to hit a 4% growth rate for M2 if it has no way of quickly and accurately measuring M2? Data on the monetary aggregates are obtained after a two-week delay, and interest-rate data are available almost immediately. Data on a variable like GDP that serves as a goal, by contrast, are compiled quarterly and are made available with a month's delay. In addition, the GDP data are less accurate than data on the monetary aggregates or interest rates. On these grounds alone, focusing on interest rates and monetary aggregates as intermediate targets rather than on a goal like GDP can provide clearer signals about the status of the central bank's policy.

At first glance, interest rates seem to be more measurable than monetary aggregates and hence more useful as intermediate targets. Not only are the data on interest rates available more quickly than on monetary aggregates, but they are also measured more precisely and are rarely revised, in contrast to the monetary aggregates, which are subject to a fair amount of revision. However, as we learned in Chapter 3, the interest rate that is quickly and accurately measured, the nominal interest rate, is typically a poor measure of the real cost of borrowing, which indicates with more certainty what will happen to GDP. This real cost of borrowing is more accurately measured by the real interest rate—the interest rate adjusted for expected inflation $(i_r = i - \pi^e)$. Unfortunately, the real interest rate is extremely hard to measure because we have no direct way to measure expected inflation. Since both interest rate and monetary aggregates have measurability problems, it is not clear whether one should be preferred to the other as an intermediate target.

Controllability A central bank must be able to exercise effective control over a variable if it is to function as a useful target. If the central bank cannot control an intermediate target, knowing that it is off track does little good because the bank has no way of getting back on track. Some economists have suggested that nominal GDP should be used as an intermediate target, but since the central bank has little direct control over nominal GDP, it will not provide much guidance on how the Fed should set its policy tools. A central bank does, however, have a good deal of control over the monetary aggregates and interest rates.

Our discussion of the money supply process and the central bank's policy tools indicates that a central bank does have the ability to exercise a powerful effect on the money supply, although its control is not perfect. We have also seen that open market operations can be used to set interest rates by directly affecting the price of bonds. Because a central bank can set interest rates directly whereas it cannot completely control the money supply, it might appear that interest rates dominate the monetary aggregates on the controllability criterion. However, a central bank cannot set real interest rates because it does not have control over expectations of inflation. So again, a clear-cut case cannot be made that interest rates are preferable to monetary aggregates as an intermediate target or vice versa.

Predictable Effect on Goals   The most important characteristic a variable must have to be useful as an intermediate target is that it must have a predictable impact on a goal. If a central bank can accurately and quickly measure the price of tea in China and can completely control its price, what good will it do? The central bank cannot use the price of tea in China to affect unemployment or the price level in its country. Because the ability to affect goals is so critical to the usefulness of an intermediate-target variable, the linkage of the money supply and interest rates with the goals—output, employment, and the price level—is a matter of much debate.

Criteria for Choosing Operating Targets

The choice of an operating target can be based on the same criteria used to evaluate intermediate targets. Both the federal funds rate and reserve aggregates are measured accurately and are available daily with almost no delay; both are easily controllable using the policy tools that we discussed earlier in the chapter. When we look at the third criterion, however, we can think of the intermediate target as the goal for the operating target. An operating target that has a more predictable impact on the most desirable intermediate target is preferred. If the desired intermediate target is an interest rate, the preferred operating target will be an interest-rate variable like the federal funds rate because interest rates are closely tied to each other (as we saw in Chapter 6). However, if the desired intermediate target is a monetary aggregate, a reserve aggregate operating target such as the monetary base will be preferred. Because there does not seem to be much reason to choose an interest rate over a reserve aggregate on the basis of measurability or controllability, the choice of which operating target is better rests on the choice of the intermediate target (the goal of the operating target).

■ FED POLICY PROCEDURES: HISTORICAL PERSPECTIVE

The well-known adage "The road to hell is paved with good intentions" applies as much to the Federal Reserve as it does to human beings. Understanding a central bank's goals and the strategies it can use to pursue them cannot tell us how monetary policy is actually conducted. To understand the practical results of the theoretical underpinnings, we have to look at how central banks have actually conducted policy in the past. First we will look at the Federal Reserve's past policy procedures: its choice of goals, policy tools, operating targets, and inter-mediate targets. This historical perspective will not only show us how our central bank carries out its duties but will also help us interpret the Fed's activities and see where U.S. monetary policy may be heading in the future. Once we are done study-ing the Fed, we will then examine central banks' experiences in other countries.

The Early Years: Discount Policy as the Primary Tool

When the Fed was created, changing the discount rate was the primary tool of monetary policy—the Fed had not yet discovered that open market operations were a more powerful tool for influencing the money supply, and the Federal Reserve Act made no provisions for changes in reserve requirements. The guiding principle for the conduct of monetary policy was that as long as loans were being made for "productive" purposes—that is, to support the production of goods and services—providing reserves to the banking system to make these loans would not be inflationary.[7] This theory, now thoroughly discredited, became known as the **real bills doctrine.** In practice, it meant that the Fed would make loans to mem-ber commercial banks when they showed up at the discount window with *eligible paper*, loans to facilitate the production and sale of goods and services. (Note that since the 1920s, the Fed has not conducted discount operations in this way.) The Fed's act of making loans to member banks was initially called *rediscounting* because the original bank loans to businesses were made by discounting (loaning less than) the face value of the loan, and the Fed would be discounting them again. (Over time, when the Fed's emphasis on eligible paper diminished, the Fed's loans to banks became known as *discounts*, and the interest rate on these loans the *dis-count rate*, which is the terminology we use today.)

By the end of World War I, the Fed's policy of rediscounting eligible paper and keeping interest rates low to help the Treasury finance the war had led to a raging inflation; in 1919 and 1920, the inflation rate averaged 14%. The Fed decided that it could no longer follow the passive policy prescribed by the real bills doctrine because it was inconsistent with the goal of price stability, and for the first time the Fed accepted the responsibility of playing an active role in influencing the econ-omy. In January 1920, the Fed raised the discount rate from $4\frac{3}{4}$% to 6%, the largest jump in its history, and eventually raised it further to 7% in June 1920, where it remained for nearly a year. The result of this policy was a sharp decline in the money supply and an especially sharp recession in 1920–1921. Although the blame for this severe recession can clearly be laid at the Fed's doorstep, in one sense the Fed's policy was very successful: After an initial decline in the price level, the infla-tion rate went to zero, paving the way for the prosperous Roaring Twenties.

Discovery of Open Market Operations

In the early 1920s, a particularly important event occurred: The Fed accidentally discovered open market operations. When the Fed was created, its revenue came

---

[7]Another guiding principle was the maintenance of the gold standard, which we will discuss in Chapter 25.

exclusively from the interest it received on the discount loans that it made to member banks. After the 1920–1921 recession, the volume of discount loans shrank dramatically, and the Fed was pressed for income. It solved this problem by purchasing income-earning securities. In doing so, the Fed noticed that reserves in the banking system grew and interest rates fell. A new monetary policy tool was born, and by the end of the 1920s, it was the most important weapon in the Fed's arsenal.

The Great Depression

The stock market boom in 1928 and 1929 created a dilemma for the Fed. It wanted to temper the boom by raising the discount rate, but it was reluctant to do so because that would mean raising interest rates to businesses and individuals who had legitimate needs for credit. Finally, in August 1929, the Fed raised the discount rate, but by then it was too late; the speculative excesses of the market boom had already occurred, and the Fed's action only hastened the stock market crash and pushed the economy into recession.

The weakness of the economy, particularly in the agricultural sector, led to a "contagion of fear" that triggered substantial withdrawals from banks, building to a full-fledged bank panic in November and December 1930. For the next two years, the Fed sat idly by while one bank panic after another occurred, culminating in the final panic in March 1933, at which point the new president, Franklin Delano Roosevelt, declared a bank holiday. (Why the Fed failed to engage in its lender-of-last-resort role during this period is discussed in Box 5.) The spate of bank panics from 1930 to 1933 were the most severe in U.S. history, and Roosevelt aptly summed up the problem in his statement, "The only thing we have to fear is fear itself." By the time the panics were over in March 1933, more than one-third of the commercial banks in the United States had failed.

War Finance and the Pegging of Interest Rates: 1942–1951

With the entrance of the United States into World War II in late 1941, government spending skyrocketed, and to finance it, the Treasury issued huge amounts of bonds. The Fed agreed to help the Treasury finance the war cheaply by pegging interest rates at the low levels that had prevailed before the war: $\frac{3}{8}$% on Treasury bills and $2\frac{1}{2}$% on long-term Treasury bonds. Whenever interest rates would rise above these levels and the price of bonds would begin to fall, the Fed would make open market purchases, thereby bidding up bond prices and driving interest rates down again. The result was a rapid growth in the monetary base and the money supply. The Fed had thus in effect relinquished its control of monetary policy to meet the financing needs of the government.

When the war ended, the Fed continued to peg interest rates, and because there was little pressure on them to rise, this policy did not result in an explosive growth in the money supply. When the Korean War broke out in 1950, however, interest rates began to climb, and the Fed found that it was again forced to expand the money supply at a rapid rate. Because inflation began to heat up (the consumer price index rose 8% between 1950 and 1951), the Fed decided that it was

BOX 5   INSIDE THE FED

Bank Panics of 1930–1933

Why Did the Fed Let Them Happen?

 The Federal Reserve System was totally passive during the bank panics of the Great Depression period and did not perform its intended role of lender of last resort to prevent them. In retrospect, the Fed's behavior seems quite extraordinary, but hindsight is always clearer than foresight.

The primary reason for the Fed's inaction was that Federal Reserve officials did not understand the negative impact bank failures could have on the money supply and economic activity. Friedman and Schwartz report that the Federal Reserve officials "tended to regard bank failures as regrettable consequences of bank management or bad banking practices, or as inevitable reactions to prior speculative excesses, or as a consequence but hardly a cause of the financial and economic collapse in process." In addition, bank failures in the early stages of the bank panics "were concentrated among smaller banks and, since the most influential figures in the system were big-city bankers who deplored the existence of smaller banks, their disappearance may have been viewed with complacency."*

Friedman and Schwartz also point out that political infighting may have played an important role in the passivity of the Fed during this period. The Federal Reserve Bank of New York, which until 1928 was the dominant force in the Federal Reserve System, strongly advocated an active program of open market purchases to provide reserves to the banking system during the bank panics. However, other powerful figures in the Federal Reserve System opposed the New York bank's position, and the bank was outvoted. (Friedman and Schwartz's discussion of the politics of the Federal Reserve System during this period makes for fascinating reading, and you might enjoy their highly readable book.)

*Milton Friedman and Anna Jacobson Schwartz, *A Monetary History of the United States, 1867–1960* (Princeton, N.J.: Princeton University Press, 1963), p. 358.

time to reassert its control over monetary policy by abandoning the interest-rate peg. An often bitter debate ensued between the Fed and the Treasury, which wanted to keep its interest costs down and so favored a continued pegging of interest rates at low levels. In March 1951, the Fed and the Treasury came to an agreement known as the Accord, in which pegging was abandoned but the Fed promised that it would not allow interest rates to rise precipitously. After Eisenhower's election as president in 1952, the Fed was given complete freedom to pursue its monetary policy objectives.

Targeting Money Market Conditions: The 1950s and 1960s

With its freedom restored, the Federal Reserve, then under the chairmanship of William McChesney Martin Jr., took the view that monetary policy should be grounded in intuitive judgment based on a feel for the money market. The policy procedure that resulted can be described as one in which the Fed targeted on money market conditions, a vague collection of variables that were supposed to describe supply and demand conditions in the money market. Included among these variables were short-term interest rates and **free reserves,** equal to excess reserves in the banking system minus the volume of discount loans.

The Fed considered free reserves a particularly good indicator of money market conditions because it thought that they represented the amount of slack in the banking system. The Fed viewed banks as having a first priority in using their excess reserves to repay their discount loans, so only the excess reserves not borrowed from the Fed represented the *free* reserves that could be used to make loans and create deposits. The Fed interpreted an increase in free reserves as an easing of money market conditions and used open market sales to withdraw reserves from the banking system. A fall in free reserves meant a tightening of money market conditions, and the Fed made open market purchases.

By the late 1960s, the rising chorus of criticism from monetarists who advocated an increased focus on monetary aggregates in the conduct of monetary policy and concerns about inflation finally led the Fed to abandon its focus on money market conditions.

Targeting Monetary Aggregates: The 1970s

In 1970, Arthur Burns was appointed chairman of the Board of Governors, and soon thereafter the Fed stated that it was committing itself to the use of monetary aggregates as intermediate targets.

Every six weeks, the Federal Open Market Committee would set target ranges for the growth rate of various monetary aggregates and would determine what federal funds rate (the interest rate on funds loaned overnight between banks) it thought consistent with these aims. The target ranges for the growth in monetary aggregates were fairly broad—a typical range for M1 growth might be 3% to 6%; for M2, 4% to 7%—while the range for the federal funds rate was a narrow band, say, from $7\frac{1}{2}\%$ to $8\frac{1}{4}\%$. The trading desk at the Federal Reserve Bank of New York was then instructed to meet both sets of targets, but as we saw earlier, interest-rate targets and monetary aggregate targets might not be compatible. If the two targets were incompatible—say, the federal funds rate began to climb higher than the top of its target band when M1 was growing too rapidly—the trading desk was instructed to give precedence to the federal funds rate target. In the situation just described, this would mean that although M1 growth was too high, the trading desk would make open market purchases to keep the federal funds rate within its target range.

The Fed was actually using the federal funds rate as its operating target. During the six-week period between FOMC meetings, an unexpected rise in income (which would cause the federal funds rate to hit the top of its target band) would then induce open market purchases and a too rapid growth of the money supply. When the FOMC met again, it would try to bring money supply growth back on track by raising the target range on the federal funds rate. However, if income continued to rise unexpectedly, money growth would overshoot again. This is exactly what occurred from June 1972 to June 1973, when the economy boomed unexpectedly: M1 growth greatly exceeded its target, increasing at approximately an 8% rate, while the federal funds rate climbed from $4\frac{1}{2}\%$ to $8\frac{1}{2}\%$. The economy soon became overheated, and inflationary pressures began to mount.

The opposite chain of events occurred at the end of 1974, when the economic contraction was far more severe than anyone had predicted. The federal funds rate fell dramatically from over 12% to 5% and persistently bumped against the bottom of its target range. The trading desk conducted open market sales to keep the federal funds rate from falling, and money growth dropped precipitously, actually turning negative by the beginning of 1975. Clearly, this sharp drop in money growth when the United States was experiencing one of the worst economic contractions of the postwar era was a serious mistake.

Using the federal funds rate as an operating target promoted a procyclical monetary policy despite the Fed's lip service to monetary aggregate targets. If the Federal Reserve really intended to pursue monetary aggregate targets, it seems peculiar that it would have chosen an interest rate for an operating target rather than a reserve aggregate. (However, as the discussion of the conduct of Japanese monetary policy later in this chapter makes clear, more effective monetary control can be achieved even when an interest rate is used as an operating target.) The explanation for why the Fed chose an interest rate as an operating target is that it was still very concerned with achieving interest-rate stability and was reluctant to relinquish control over interest-rate movements. The incompatibility of the Fed's policy procedure with its stated intent of targeting on the monetary aggregates had become very clear by October 1979, when the Fed's policy procedures underwent drastic revision.

New Fed Operating Procedures: October 1979–October 1982

In October 1979, two months after Paul Volcker became chairman of the Board of Governors, the Fed finally deemphasized the federal funds rate as an operating target by widening its target range more than fivefold: A typical range might be from 10% to 15%. The primary operating target became nonborrowed reserves which the Fed would set after estimating the volume of discount loans the banks would borrow. Figure 4 shows what happened to the federal funds rate and the growth rate of the M1 money supply both before and after October 1979. Not surprisingly, the federal funds rate underwent much greater fluctuations after it was deemphasized as an operating target. What is surprising, however, is that the deemphasis of the federal funds target did not result in improved monetary control: After October 1979, the fluctuations in the rate of money supply growth *increased* rather than decreased as would have been expected. In addition, the Fed missed its M1 growth target ranges in all three years of the 1979–1982 period.[8] What went wrong?

There are several possible answers to this question. The first is that the economy was exposed to several shocks during this period that made monetary control more difficult: the acceleration of financial innovation and deregulation, which added new categories of deposits such as NOW accounts to the measures of monetary aggregates; the imposition by the Fed of credit controls from March

---

[8]The M1 target ranges and actual growth rates for 1980–1982 were as follows:

Year	Target Range (%)	Actual Growth (%)
1980	4.5–7.0	7.5
1981	6.0–8.5	5.1
1982	2.5–5.5	8.8

Source: Board of Governors of the Federal Reserve System, *Monetary Policy Objectives, 1981–1983.*

Federal Reserve
Funds Rate (%)

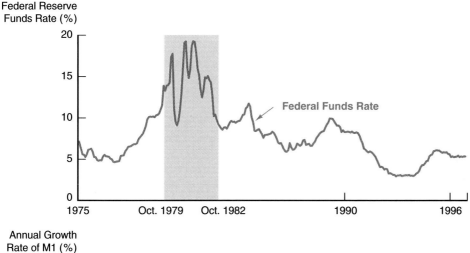

Annual Growth
Rate of M1 (%)

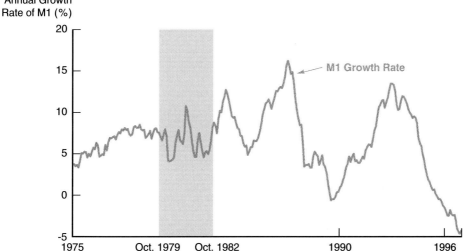

■FIGURE 4 Federal Funds Rate and Growth Rate of the Money Supply: Before and After October 1979

Sources: Federal Reserve *Bulletin;* Board of Governors of the Federal Reserve System.

to July 1980, which restricted the growth of consumer and business loans; and the back-to-back recessions of 1980 and 1981–1982.[9]

A more persuasive explanation for poor monetary control, however, is that controlling the money supply was never really the intent of Volcker's policy shift. Despite Volcker's statements about the need to target monetary aggregates, he was not committed to these targets. Rather, he was far more concerned with using interest-rate movements to wring inflation out of the economy. Volcker's primary

---

[9]Another explanation focuses on the technical difficulties of monetary control when using a nonborrowed reserves operating target under a system of lagged reserve requirements, in which required reserves for a given week are calculated on the basis of the level of deposits two weeks earlier. See David Lindsey, "Nonborrowed Reserve Targeting and Monetary Control," in *Improving Money Stock Control*, ed. Laurence Meyer (Boston: Kluwer-Nijhoff, 1983), pp. 3–41.

reason for changing the Fed's operating procedure was to free his hand to manipulate interest rates in order to fight inflation. It was necessary to abandon interest-rate targets if Volcker were to be able to raise interest rates sharply when a slowdown in the economy was required to dampen inflation. This view of Volcker's strategy suggests that the Fed's announced attachment to monetary aggregate targets may have been a smokescreen to keep the Fed from being blamed for the high interest rates that would result from the new policy.

The interest-rate movements in Figure 4 support this interpretation of Fed strategy. After the October 1979 announcement, short-term interest rates were driven up by nearly 5% until in March 1980 they exceeded 15%. With the imposition of credit controls in March 1980 and the rapid decline in real GDP in the second quarter of 1980, the Fed eased up on its policy and allowed interest rates to decline sharply. When recovery began in July 1980, inflation remained persistent, still exceeding 10%. Because the inflation fight was not yet won, the Fed tightened the screws again, sending short-term rates above the 15% level for a second time. The 1981–1982 recession and its large decline in output and high unemployment began to bring inflation down. The inflationary psychology apparently broken, interest rates were allowed to fall.

The Fed's anti-inflation strategy during the October 1979–October 1982 period was neither intended nor likely to produce smooth growth in the monetary aggregates. Indeed, the large fluctuations in interest rates and the business cycle, along with financial innovation, helped generate volatile money growth.

Deemphasis of Monetary Aggregates: October 1982–Early 1990s

In October 1982, with inflation in check, the Fed returned, in effect, to a policy of smoothing interest rates. It did this by placing less emphasis on monetary aggregate targets and shifting to borrowed reserves (discount loan borrowings) as an operating target. To see how a borrowed reserves target produces interest-rate smoothing, let's consider what happens when the economy expands so that interest rates are driven up. The rise in interest rates increases the incentives for banks to borrow more from the Fed, so borrowed reserves rise. To prevent the resulting rise in borrowed reserves from exceeding the target level, the Fed must lower interest rates by bidding up the price of bonds through open market purchases. The outcome of targeting on borrowed reserves, then, is that the Fed prevents a rise in interest rates.

The deemphasis of monetary aggregates and the change to a borrowed reserves target are visible in Figure 4, where we see much smaller fluctuations in the federal funds rate after October 1982 but continue to have large fluctuations in money supply growth. Finally, in February 1987, the Fed announced that it would no longer even set M1 targets. The abandonment of M1 targets was defended on two grounds. The first was that the rapid pace of financial innovation and deregulation had made the definition and measurement of money very difficult. The second is that there had been a breakdown in the stable relationship between M1 and economic activity. These two arguments suggested that a monetary aggregate such as M1 might no longer be a reliable guide for monetary policy. As a result, the Fed switched its focus to the broader monetary aggregate M2, which it felt had a more stable relationship with economic activity. However, in the early 1990s, this relationship also broke down, and in July 1993, Board of Governors Chairman Alan Greenspan testified before Congress that the Fed would no longer use any monetary targets, including M2, as a guide for conducting monetary policy.

Federal Funds Targeting Again: Early 1990s and Beyond

Having abandoned monetary aggregates as a guide for monetary policy, the Federal Reserve returned to using a federal funds target in the early 1990s. Indeed, from late 1992 until February 1994, a period of a year and a half, the Fed kept the federal funds rate targeted at the constant rate of 3%, a low level last seen in the 1960s. The explanation for this unusual period of keeping the federal funds rate pegged so low for such a long period of time was fear on the part of the Federal Reserve that the credit crunch mentioned in Chapter 13 was putting a drag on the economy (the "headwinds" referred to by Greenspan) that was producing a sluggish recovery from the 1990–1991 recession. Starting in February 1994, after the economy had returned to rapid growth, the Fed began to raise the federal funds rate in order to head off any future inflationary pressures, but with a new policy procedure. Instead of keeping the federal funds rate target secret, as it had done previously, the Fed now announced any federal funds target change. As mentioned in Chapter 23, around 2:15 P.M. after every FOMC meeting, the Fed now announces whether the federal funds rate target has been raised, lowered, or kept the same. As a result of this announcement, the outcome of the FOMC meeting is now big news, and the media devote much more attention to FOMC meetings because an announced change in the federal funds rate feeds into changes in other interest rates that affect consumers and businesses.

 ## International Considerations

The increasing importance of international trade to the American economy has brought international considerations to the forefront of Federal Reserve policy-making in recent years. By 1985, the strength of the dollar had contributed to a deterioration in American competitiveness with foreign businesses. In public pronouncements, Chairman Volcker and other Fed officials made it clear that the dollar was at too high a value and needed to come down. Because, as we saw in Chapter 8, expansionary monetary policy is one way to lower the value of the dollar, it is no surprise that the Fed engineered an acceleration in the growth rates of the monetary aggregates in 1985 and 1986 and that the value of the dollar declined. By 1987, policymakers at the Fed agreed that the dollar had fallen sufficiently, and sure enough, monetary growth in the United States slowed. These monetary policy actions by the Fed were encouraged by the process of **international policy coordination** (agreements among countries to enact policies cooperatively) that led to the Plaza Agreement in 1985 and the Louvre Accord in 1987 (see Box 6). International considerations, although not the primary focus of the Federal Reserve, are likely to be a major factor in the conduct of American monetary policy in the future.

BOX 6

International Policy Coordination

The Plaza Agreement and the Louvre Accord

By 1985, the decrease in the competitiveness of American corporations as a result of the strong dollar was raising strong sentiment in Congress for restricting imports. This protectionist threat to the international trading system stimulated finance ministers and the heads of central banks from the Group of Five (G-5) industrial countries—the United States, the United Kingdom, France, West Germany, and Japan—to reach an agreement at New York's Plaza Hotel in September 1985 to bring down the value of the dollar. From September 1985 until the beginning of 1987, the value of the dollar did indeed undergo a substantial decline, falling by 35% on average relative to foreign currencies. At this point, there was growing controversy over the decline in the dollar, and another meeting of policymakers from the G-5 countries plus Canada took place in February 1987 at the Louvre Museum in Paris. There the policymakers agreed that exchange rates should be stabilized around the levels currently prevailing. Although the value of the dollar did continue to fluctuate relative to foreign currencies after the Louvre Accord, its downward trend had been checked as intended.

Because subsequent exchange rate movements were pretty much in line with the Plaza Agreement and the Louvre Accord, these attempts at international policy coordination have been considered successful. However, other aspects of the agreements were not adhered to by all signatories. For example, West German and Japanese policymakers agreed that their countries should pursue more expansionary policies by increasing government spending and cutting taxes, and the United States agreed to try to bring down its budget deficit. At that time, the United States was not particularly successful in lowering its deficit, and the Germans were reluctant to pursue expansionary policies because of their concerns about inflation.

MONETARY TARGETING IN OTHER COUNTRIES

To understand more about how monetary policy is conducted, we must compare our experiences with those of other nations. Here we examine how central banks in other countries have conducted monetary policy. Note that many of their experiences parallel those in the United States.

As we noted in our study of the conduct of U.S. monetary policy, the Federal Reserve has flirted with monetary targeting as its basic monetary policy strategy. And the Fed was not alone in adopting a monetary targeting framework in the 1970s; many other central banks did as well. Why did monetary targeting become so popular in the 1970s?[10]

The primary reason was the rise in inflation throughout the industrialized world. Central banks realized that using nominal interest rates as a target variable could lead to rising inflationary pressures. They believed that monetary aggregates could serve as a guidepost, or *nominal anchor*, that could promote a less inflationary monetary policy. Of probably even more importance, central banks believed that monetary targets could help send almost immediate signals to both the public and markets about the stance of monetary policy and the intentions of the policymakers to keep inflation in check. These signals might then help fix

[10]The discussion here is based on Ben Bernanke and Frederic S. Mishkin, "Central Bank Behavior and the Strategy of Monetary Policy: Observations from Six Industrialized Countries," in *NBER Macroeconomics Annual*, 1992, ed. Oliver Blanchard and Stanley Fischer (Cambridge, Mass.: MIT Press, 1992), pp. 183–228.

inflation expectations and help produce lower wage and price increases and thus less actual inflation.

We examine the experiences of four foreign countries—the United Kingdom, Canada, Germany, and Japan—to evaluate the extent to which monetary targeting has been a successful strategy for monetary policy.

United Kingdom

As in the United States, the British introduced monetary targeting in late 1973 in response to mounting concerns about inflation. The Bank of England targeted M3, a broader monetary target than the Fed used, but did not pursue it seriously: Announced targets were consistently overshot, and the Bank of England frequently revised its targets midstream or abandoned them entirely. The outcome was greater volatility of British monetary aggregates compared to American ones. After inflation accelerated in the late 1970s, Prime Minister Margaret Thatcher in 1980 introduced the Medium-Term Financial Strategy, which proposed a gradual deceleration of M3 growth. Unfortunately, the M3 targets ran into problems similar to those of the M1 targets in the United States: They were not reliable indicators of the tightness of monetary policy. After 1983, arguing that financial innovation was wreaking havoc with the relationship between M3 and national income, the Bank of England began to deemphasize M3 in favor of a narrower monetary aggregate, M0 (the monetary base). The target for M3 was temporarily suspended in October 1985 and was completely dropped in 1987, and monetary targets were abandoned altogether when the nation tied its exchange rate to the deutsche mark and became part of the European Monetary System (EMS) in October 1990.

Canada

The Canadian experience with monetary policy closely parallels that of the United States. This is not surprising given the strong ties between the two economies and the fact that the value of the Canadian dollar has been closely linked to the U.S dollar.

In response to rising inflation in the early 1970s, the Bank of Canada introduced a program of "monetary gradualism" under which M1 growth would be controlled within a gradually falling target range. Monetary gradualism was no more successful in Canada than the initial attempts at monetary targeting in the United States and the United Kingdom. By 1978, only three years after monetary targeting had begun, the Bank of Canada began to distance itself from this strategy out of concern for the exchange rate. Because of the conflict with exchange rate goals, as well as the uncertainty about M1 as a reliable guide to monetary policy, the M1 targets were abandoned in November 1982. From November 1982 to January 1988, the Bank of Canada pursued a monetary policy strategy without an explicit nominal anchor, but in January 1988, John Crow, the governor (head) of the Bank of Canada, announced that the bank would subsequently pursue an objective of price stability.

Germany

Germany's central bank, the Bundesbank, also responded to rising inflation in the early 1970s by adopting monetary targets in 1975. The monetary aggregate chosen was a narrow one known as *central bank money*, the sum of currency in circulation and bank deposits weighted by the 1974 required reserve ratios. The Bundesbank has allowed growth outside of its target ranges for periods of two to three years, and overshoots of its targets have subsequently been reversed. The primary reason for allowing deviations from its targets has been exchange rate considerations, which have been important to international agreements such as the European Monetary System, the Plaza Agreement, and the Louvre Accord. In 1988, the Bundesbank switched targets from central bank money to M3. German monetary policy using monetary targeting has been quite successful in maintaining a low and stable inflation rate.

The reunification of Germany in 1990 created some difficult problems for monetary policy. The Bundesbank was torn between trying to restrain the inflationary pressures created by reunification and keeping its exchange rate in line with those in other European countries. These strains contributed to an exchange rate crisis in Europe in September 1992, which will be discussed further in Chapter 25. The Bundesbank continues to subscribe to monetary targeting, but recent research suggests that its commitment may be weaker than its rhetoric suggests.[11]

Japan

The increase in oil prices in late 1973 was a major shock for Japan, which experienced a huge jump in the inflation rate to greater than 20% in 1974—a surge facilitated by money growth in 1973 in excess of 20%. The Bank of Japan, like the other central banks discussed here, began to pay more attention to money growth rates. In 1978, the Bank of Japan began to announce "forecasts" at the beginning of each quarter for M2 + CDs. Although the Bank of Japan was not officially committed to monetary targeting, monetary policy appeared to be more money-focused after 1978. For example, after the second oil price shock in 1979, the Bank of Japan quickly reduced M2 + CDs growth, rather than allowing it to shoot up as occurred after the first oil shock. The Bank of Japan conducted monetary policy with operating procedures that are similar in many ways to those that the Federal Reserve has used in the United States. The Bank of Japan uses the interest rate in the Japanese interbank market (which has a function similar to that of the federal funds market in the United States) as its daily operating target, just as the Fed has done.

The Bank of Japan's monetary policy performance during the 1978–1987 period was much better than the Fed's. Money growth in Japan slowed gradually, beginning in the mid-1970s, and was much less variable than in the United States. The outcome was a more rapid braking of inflation and an average inflation rate

---

[11]See Richard Clarida and Mark Gertler, "How the Bundesbank Conducts Monetary Policy," National Bureau of Economic Research Working Paper No. 5581, May 1996.

that was lower in Japan. In addition, these excellent results on inflation were achieved with lower variability in real output in Japan than in the United States. The success of Japanese monetary policy in the 1978–1987 period using an interest rate as an operating target, in contrast to the lack of success in the 1970–1979 period in the United States when the Fed used a similar operating procedure, suggests that using an interest rate as an operating target is not necessarily a barrier to successful monetary policy. More important might be a commitment to a low inflation rate, something that was true for the Bank of Japan in this period.

In parallel with the United States, financial innovation and deregulation in Japan began to reduce the usefulness of the M2 + CDs monetary aggregate as an indicator of monetary policy. Because of concerns about the appreciation of the yen, the Bank of Japan significantly increased the rate of money growth from 1987 to 1989. Many observers blame speculation in Japanese land and stock prices (the so-called bubble economy) on the increase in money growth, and to reduce this speculation, in 1989 the Bank of Japan switched to a tighter monetary policy aimed at slower money growth. The aftermath has been a substantial decline in land and stock prices and the collapse of the bubble economy.

Lessons from Monetary Targeting Experiences

There are several lessons to be drawn from the experience with monetary targeting in the four countries and the United States. First, successful use of monetary targeting seems to require that the central bank pursue its targeting strategy seriously. Countries like the United States, Canada, and especially the United Kingdom were unable to use monetary targeting to bring inflation under control because the procedures they used to implement the targets did not imply a strong commitment to the strategy and they consistently overshot their monetary targets. Germany and Japan, by contrast, were more successful in using monetary aggregates to keep inflation in check. This did not mean that the Bundesbank and the Bank of Japan always met their targets; more critical to their success was that they subsequently reversed overshoots of the targets. A further lesson from the Japanese experience is that the success of monetary targeting can be achieved with operating procedures that focus on interest rates as the operating target. The final lesson is that the breakdown in the relationship between monetary aggregates and the goal variables, nominal GDP and inflation, in many countries made the monetary targeting strategy untenable. As the former governor of the Bank of Canada, John Crow, is said to have stated, "We didn't abandon monetary aggregates; they abandoned us."

THE NEW INTERNATIONAL TREND IN MONETARY POLICY STRATEGY: INFLATION TARGETING

Although central banks have abandoned monetary targeting, the reasons they adopted it in the first place remain. Central banks still see the need to have a nominal anchor that will promote price stability. Another nominal anchor for monetary policy can be the foreign exchange rate. As we will see in Chapter 25, some countries have achieved low inflation by tying the value of their currency to the currency of a country with a good inflation record. However, the problem with this strategy is that, as shown in Chapter 25, with a fixed exchange rate, a country no longer exercises control over its own monetary policy and so cannot use monetary policy to respond to domestic shocks.

The search for a nominal anchor has led many countries to pursue inflation targeting as their basic monetary strategy. To understand what inflation targeting is all about, we look at the experience in three countries, New Zealand, which was the first to adopt this strategy; Canada; and the United Kingdom.

New Zealand

As part of a general reform of the government's role in the economy, the New Zealand parliament in 1989 passed the Reserve Bank of New Zealand Act, which became effective on February 1, 1990. Besides increasing the independence of the central bank, the Reserve Bank of New Zealand, transforming it from one of the least independent to one of the most independent among the developed countries, the act also committed the Reserve Bank to the sole objective of price stability. The act stipulated that the minister of finance and the governor of the Reserve Bank should negotiate and make public a "policy targets agreement" that sets out the targets against which monetary policy performance will be evaluated. These agreements have specified numerical target ranges for inflation and the dates by which they were to be reached. An unusual feature of the New Zealand legislation is that the governor of the Reserve Bank is held personally accountable for the success of monetary policy. If the goals set forth in the policy targets agreement are not met, the governor is subject to dismissal.

The first policy targets agreement, signed by the minister of finance and the governor of the Reserve Bank on March 2, 1990, directed the Reserve Bank to achieve an annual inflation rate within the 0% to 2% range, and subsequent agreements stuck with this range until November 1996, when the upper limit was increased to 3%. As a result of tight monetary policy, the inflation rate was brought down from above 5% to below 2% by the end of 1992, but at the cost of a deep recession and a sharp rise in unemployment. Through 1996, inflation typically remained within the 0% to 2% range, with the exception of a brief period in 1995, when it exceeded the upper limit by a few tenths of a percentage point. (Under the Reserve Bank Act, the governor, Don Brash, could have been dismissed, but after parliamentary debate, he was retained in his job.) Since 1992, New Zealand's growth rate has been very high, with some years exceeding 5%, and unemployment has dropped significantly.

Canada

On February 26, 1991, a joint announcement by the minister of finance and the governor of the Bank of Canada established formal inflation targets. The target ranges were 2% to 4% by the end of 1992, 1.5% to 3.5% by June 1994, and 1% to 3% by December 1996. After the new government took office in late 1993, the target range was set at 1% to 3% from December 1995 until December 1998. Canadian inflation has also fallen dramatically since the adoption of inflation targets, from above the 5% level in 1991 to a 0% rate in 1995, well below the target range of 1% to 3%. However, as was the case in New Zealand, this decline was not without cost: Unemployment soared beyond the 10% level from 1991 until 1994 but has since fallen.

United Kingdom

When the United Kingdom left the European Monetary System after the speculative attack on the pound in September 1992 (more on this in Chapter 25), the British decided to turn to inflation targets to replace the exchange rate as the nominal anchor. As you may recall from Chapter 23, the central bank in the United Kingdom, the Bank of England, does not have statutory authority over monetary policy; it can only make recommendations. Thus it was the chancellor of the Exchequer (the equivalent of the U.S. Treasury secretary) who announced an inflation target for the nation on October 8, 1992. Three weeks later, he "invited" the governor of the Bank of England to issue on a quarterly basis a report on the progress being made in achieving the target—an invitation that the governor accepted. The inflation target range was set at 1% to 4% until the next election (May 1997), with the intent that the inflation rate should settle down to the lower half of the range (below 2.5%). Along with this inflation target, the government implemented the three institutional changes mentioned in Chapter 23, which, along with the governor's report, gave the Bank of England a more independent voice on monetary policy.

Before the adoption of inflation targets, inflation had already been falling in the United Kingdom, from a peak of 9% at the beginning of 1991 to 4% at the time of adoption. After a small upward movement in early 1993, inflation continued to fall until by the third quarter of 1994, it was at 2.2%, within the intended range articulated by the Chancellor. Subsequently inflation rose, climbing above the 2.5% level by 1996. Meanwhile growth of the U.K. economy was strong, causing a reduction in the unemployment rate.

Lessons from Inflation Targeting Experiences

Several lessons can be drawn from the inflation targeting experiences in these three countries. First, as the New Zealand and Canadian experience indicates, inflation targets have not been able to produce a decline in inflation without a substantial decline in output and a rise in unemployment. Hopes that inflation targets would lead to disinflation at a lower cost have not been realized. Second, inflation targets have so far worked well in keeping inflation at moderate levels. One important advantage of inflation targets is that they keep the goal of price stability in the public's eye, thus making the central bank more accountable for keeping inflation low, which can also help reduce political pressures on the central bank to pursue inflationary monetary policy.

How successful will inflation targeting be at keeping inflation low in the countries examined here? It is still too early to tell. Nonetheless, many other countries have followed New Zealand, Canada, and the United Kingdom in adopting inflation targets, including Australia, Finland, Israel, Spain, and Sweden. The growing popularity of inflation targeting indicates that it might become the wave of the future for central bank strategy.

THE PRACTICING FINANCIAL INSTITUTION MANAGER
Using a Fed Watcher

As we have seen, the most important player in the determination of the U.S. money supply and interest rates is the Federal Reserve. When the Fed wants to inject reserves into the system, it conducts open market purchases of bonds, which cause their prices to increase and their interest rates to fall, at least in the short term. If the Fed withdraws reserves from the system, it sells bonds, thereby depressing their price and raising their interest rates. From a longer-run perspective, if the Fed pursues an expansionary monetary policy with high money growth, inflation will rise and, as we saw in Chapter 5, interest rates will rise as well. Contractionary monetary policy is likely to lower inflation in the long run and lead to lower interest rates.

Knowing what actions the Fed might be taking can thus help financial institution managers predict the future course of interest rates with greater accuracy. Because, as we have seen, changes in interest rates have a major impact on a financial institution's profitability, the managers of these institutions are particularly interested in scrutinizing the Fed's behavior. To help in this task, managers hire so-called Fed watchers, experts on Federal Reserve behavior who may have worked in the Federal Reserve System and so have an insider's view of Federal Reserve operations.

Divining what the Fed is up to is by no means easy. Box 2 in Chapter 23 suggests that the Fed has a penchant for secrecy. The Fed does not disclose the content of the minutes of FOMC meetings at which it decides the course of monetary policy until six weeks after each meeting. In addition, the Fed does not provide information on the amount of certain transactions and frequently tries to obscure from the market whether it is injecting reserves into the banking system by making open market purchases and sales simultaneously.

Fed watchers, with their specialized knowledge of the ins and outs of the Fed, scrutinize the public pronouncements of Federal Reserve officials to get a feel for where monetary policy is heading. They also carefully study the data on past Federal Reserve actions and current events in the bond markets to determine what the Fed is up to.

If a Fed watcher tells a financial institution manager that Federal Reserve concerns about inflation are high and the Fed will pursue a tight monetary policy and raise short-term interest rates in the near future, the manager may decide immediately to acquire funds at the currently low interest rates in order to keep the cost of funds from rising. If the financial institution trades foreign exchange, the rise in interest rates and the attempt by the Fed to keep inflation down might lead the manager to instruct traders to purchase dollars in the foreign exchange market. As we saw in Chapter 8, these actions by the Fed would be likely to cause the value of the dollar to appreciate, so the purchase of dollars by the financial institution should lead to substantial profits.

If, conversely, the Fed watcher thinks that the Fed is worried about a weak economy and will thus pursue an expansionary policy and lower interest rates, the financial institution manager will take very different actions. Now the manager might instruct loan officers to make as many loans as possible so as to lock in the higher interest rates that the financial institution can earn currently. Or the manager might buy bonds, anticipating that interest rates will fall and their prices will rise, giving the institution a nice profit. The more expansionary policy is also likely to lower the value of the dollar in the foreign exchange market, so the financial institution manager might tell foreign exchange traders to buy foreign currencies and sell dollars in order to make a profit when the dollar falls in the future.

A Fed watcher who is right is a very valuable commodity to a financial institution. Successful Fed watchers are actively sought out by financial institutions and often earn high salaries, well into the six-figure range.

SUMMARY

1. The three basic tools of monetary policy are open market operations, discount policy, and reserve requirements. Open market operations are the primary tool used by the Fed to control the money supply because they occur at the initiative of the Fed, are flexible, are easily reversed, and can be implemented quickly.

2. The six basic goals of monetary policy are high employment, economic growth, price stability, interest-rate stability, stability of financial markets, and stability in foreign exchange markets.

3. By using intermediate and operating targets, a central bank like the Fed can more quickly judge whether its policies are on the right track and make midcourse corrections, rather than waiting to see the final outcome of its policies on such goals as employment and the price level. The Fed's policy tools directly affect its operating targets, which in turn affect the intermediate targets, which in turn affect the goals.

4. Because interest-rate and monetary aggregate targets are incompatible, a central bank must choose between them on the basis of three criteria: measurability, controllability, and the ability to affect goal variables predictably. Unfortunately, these criteria do not establish an overwhelming case for one set of targets over another.

5. The historical record of the Fed's conduct of monetary policy reveals that the Fed has switched its operating targets many times, returning to a federal funds rate target in recent years.

6. In response to the rise in inflation in the early 1970s, central banks around the world also began to target monetary aggregates. Monetary targeting seems to have been most effective when it has been pursued seriously, which does not mean that targets are always met; more critical to success was a reversal of overshoots of the targets. Unfortunately, the breakdown in many countries of the relationship between monetary aggregates and the goal variables, nominal GDP and inflation, made the monetary targeting strategy untenable.

7. After disappointments with monetary targeting, the search for a nominal anchor has lead several countries to pursue inflation targeting as their basic monetary strategy. Although inflation targeting so far has been successful in keeping inflation rates low in countries that have adopted it, hopes that inflation targets would lead to disinflation at a lower cost have not been realized.

8. Because predicting the Federal Reserve's actions can help managers of financial institutions predict the course of future interest rates, which has a major impact on the financial institutions' profitability, such managers value the services of Fed watchers, experts on Federal Reserve behavior.

KEY TERMS

defensive open market operations, p. 610

discount window, p. 613

dynamic open market operations, p. 610

free reserves, p. 630

intermediate target, p. 622

international policy coordination, p. 635

lender of last resort, p. 614

matched sale-purchase transaction (reverse repo), p. 612

natural rate of unemployment, p. 619

open market operations, p. 609

operating target, p. 622

primary dealer, p. 611

real bills doctrine, p. 628

repurchase agreement (repo), p. 612

QUESTIONS AND PROBLEMS

*1. "Unemployment is a bad thing, and the government should make every effort to eliminate it." Do you agree or disagree? Explain your answer.

2. Which goals of the Fed frequently conflict?

*3. "If the demand for money did not fluctuate, the Fed could pursue both a money supply target and an interest-rate target at the same time." Is this statement true, false, or uncertain? Explain your answer.

4. Classify each of the following as either an operating target or an intermediate target, and explain why.
   a. The three-month Treasury bill rate
   b. The monetary base
   c. M2

*5. What procedures can the Fed use to control the three-month Treasury bill rate? Why does control of this interest rate imply that the Fed will lose control of the money supply?

6. If the Fed has an interest-rate target, why will an increase in money demand lead to a rise in the money supply?

*7. "Interest rates can be measured more accurately and more quickly than the money supply. Hence an interest rate is preferred over the money supply as an intermediate target." Do you agree or disagree? Explain your answer.

8. Compare the monetary base to M2 on the grounds of controllability and measurability. Which do you prefer as an intermediate target? Why?

*9. "Discounting is no longer needed because the presence of the FDIC eliminates the possibility of bank panics." Is this statement true, false, or uncertain? Explain your answer.

10. The benefits of using Fed discount operations to prevent bank panics are straightforward. What are the costs?

*11. Explain why the rise in the discount rate in 1920 led to a sharp decline in the money supply.

12. Excess reserves are frequently called idle reserves, suggesting that they are not useful. Does the episode of the rise in reserve requirements in 1936–1937 bear out this view?

*13. How did the Fed's failure to perform its role as the lender of last resort contribute to the decline of the money supply in the 1930–1933 period?

14. Why is pegging the nominal interest rate problematic for a central bank?

*15. How have the Federal Reserve's concerns about the value of the U.S. exchange rate affected monetary policy?

16. "The failure of the Fed to control the money supply in the 1970s and 1980s suggests that the Fed is not able to control the money supply." Do you agree or disagree? Explain your answer.

*17. "When the economy enters a recession, either a free reserve target or an interest-rate target will lead to a slower rate of growth for the money supply." Explain why this statement is true. What does it say about the use of free reserves or interest rates as targets?

18. How can bank behavior and the Fed's behavior cause money supply growth to be procyclical (rising in booms and falling in recessions)?

*19. Which is more likely to produce smaller fluctuations in the federal funds rate, a nonborrowed reserves target or a borrowed reserves target? Why?

20. Why might the Fed say that it wants to control the money supply but in reality not be serious about doing so?

CHAPTER 25

THE INTERNATIONAL FINANCIAL SYSTEM AND MONETARY POLICY

■ PREVIEW Thanks to the growing interdependence between the U.S. economy and the economies of the rest of the world, the international financial system now plays a more prominent role in economic events in the United States. In this chapter we examine the evolution of the international financial system during the past half century and where it may be heading in the future. In addition, we see how international financial transactions and the structure of the international financial system affect monetary policy in the United States and provide substantial profit opportunities for financial institutions.

■ INTERVENTION IN THE FOREIGN EXCHANGE MARKET

In Chapter 8 we analyzed the foreign exchange market as if it were a completely free market that responds to all market pressures. However, the foreign exchange market, like many others, is not free of government intervention; central banks regularly engage in international financial transactions called **foreign exchange interventions** in order to influence exchange rates. In our current international financial arrangement, called a **managed float regime** (or a **dirty float**), exchange rates fluctuate from day to day, but central banks attempt to influence their countries' exchange rates by buying and selling currencies. The exchange rate analysis we developed in Chapter 8 is used here to explain the impact that central bank intervention has on the foreign exchange market.

Foreign Exchange Intervention and the Money Supply

The first step in understanding how central bank intervention in the foreign exchange market affects exchange rates is to see the impact on the monetary base and the money supply from a central bank sale in the foreign exchange market of some of its holdings of assets denominated in a foreign currency (called **international reserves**). Suppose that the Fed decides to sell $1 billion of its foreign assets in exchange for $1 billion of U.S. currency. (This transaction is done at the foreign exchange desk at the Federal Reserve Bank of New York—see Box 1.) The Fed's purchase of dollars has two effects. First, it reduces the Fed's holding of international reserves by $1 billion. Second, because its purchase of currency removes it from the hands of the public, currency in circulation falls by $1 billion. We can see this in the following T-account for the Federal Reserve:

Federal Reserve System		
Assets	Liabilities	
Foreign assets (international reserves) −$1 billion	Currency in circulation	−$1 billion

Because the monetary base is made up of currency in circulation plus reserves, this decline in currency implies that the monetary base has fallen by $1 billion.

BOX 1 INSIDE THE FED

A Day at the Federal Reserve Bank of New York's Foreign Exchange Desk

 Although the U.S. Treasury is primarily responsible for foreign exchange policy, decisions to intervene in the foreign exchange market are made jointly by the U.S. Treasury and the Federal Reserve as represented by the FOMC (Federal Open Market Committee). The actual conduct of foreign exchange intervention is the responsibility of the foreign exchange desk at the Federal Reserve Bank of New York, which is right next to the open market desk.

Dino Kos, the head of foreign exchange operations at the New York Fed, supervises the traders and analysts who follow developments in the foreign exchange market. Every morning at 7:30, a trader on Kos's staff who has arrived at the New York Fed in the predawn hours speaks on the telephone with counterparts at the U.S. Treasury and provides an update on overnight activity in overseas financial and foreign exchange markets. Later in the morning, at 9:30, Kos and his staff hold a conference call with senior staff at the Board of Governors of the Federal Reserve in Washington. In the afternoon, at 2:30, they have a second conference call, which is a joint briefing of officials at the board and the Treasury. Although by statute the Treasury has the lead role in setting foreign exchange policy, it strives to reach a consensus among all three parties—the Treasury, the Board of Governors, and the Federal Reserve Bank of New York. If they decide that a foreign exchange intervention is necessary that day—an unusual occurrence, as a year may go by without a U.S. foreign exchange intervention—Kos instructs his traders to carry out the agreed-on purchase or sale of foreign currencies. Because funds for exchange rate intervention are held separately by the Treasury (in its Exchange Stabilization Fund) and the Federal Reserve, Kos and his staff are not trading the funds of the Federal Reserve Bank of New York; rather they act as an agent for the Treasury and the FOMC in conducting these transactions.

As part of their duties, before every FOMC meeting, Kos and his staff help prepare a lengthy document full of data for the FOMC members, other Reserve Bank presidents, and Treasury officials that describes developments in the domestic and foreign markets over the previous five or six weeks, a task that keeps them especially busy right before the FOMC meeting.

If instead of paying for the foreign assets sold by the Fed with currency, the persons buying the foreign assets pay for them by checks written on accounts at domestic banks, then the Fed deducts the $1 billion from the deposit accounts these banks have with the Fed. The result is that deposits with the Fed (reserves) decline by $1 billion, as shown in the following T-account:

Federal Reserve System		
Assets	Liabilities	
Foreign assets (international reserves) −$1 billion	Deposits with the Fed (reserves)	−$1 billion

In this case, the outcome of the Fed sale of foreign assets and the purchase of dollar deposits is a $1 billion decline in reserves and a $1 billion decline in the monetary base because reserves are also a component of the monetary base.

We now see that the outcome for the monetary base is exactly the same when a central bank sells foreign assets to purchase domestic bank deposits or domestic currency. This is why when we say that a central bank has purchased its domestic currency, we do not have to distinguish whether it actually purchased currency or bank deposits denominated in the domestic currency. We have thus reached an important conclusion: *A central bank's purchase of domestic currency and corresponding sale of foreign assets in the foreign exchange market leads to an equal decline in its international reserves and the monetary base.*

We could have reached the same conclusion by a more direct route. A central bank sale of a foreign asset is no different from an open market sale of a government bond. We learned in Chapter 24 that an open market sale leads to an equal decline in the monetary base; therefore, a sale of foreign assets also leads to an equal decline in the monetary base. By similar reasoning, a central bank purchase of foreign assets paid for by selling domestic currency, like an open market purchase, leads to an equal rise in the monetary base. Thus we reach the following conclusion: *A central bank's sale of domestic currency to purchase foreign assets in the foreign exchange market results in an equal rise in its international reserves and the monetary base.*

The intervention we have just described, in which a central bank allows the purchase or sale of domestic currency to have an effect on the monetary base and hence on the money supply, is called an **unsterilized foreign exchange intervention.** But what if the central bank does not want the purchase or sale of domestic currency to affect the monetary base and the money supply? All it has to do is to counter the effect of the foreign exchange intervention by conducting an offsetting open market operation in the government bond market. For example, in the case of a $1 billion purchase of dollars by the Fed and a corresponding $1 billion sale of foreign assets, which we have seen would decrease the monetary base by $1 billion, the Fed can conduct an open market purchase of $1 billion of government bonds, which would increase the monetary base by $1 billion. The resulting T-account for the foreign exchange intervention and the offsetting open market operation leaves the monetary base unchanged:

Federal Reserve System		
Assets	Liabilities	
Foreign assets (international reserves) −$1 billion	Monetary base (reserves)	0
Government bonds +$1 billion		

A foreign exchange intervention with an offsetting open market operation that leaves the monetary base unchanged is called a **sterilized foreign exchange intervention.**

Now that we understand that there are two types of foreign exchange interventions, unsterilized and sterilized, let's look at how each affects the exchange rate.

Unsterilized Intervention

Your intuition might lead you to suspect that if a central bank wants to lower the value of the domestic currency, it should sell its currency in the foreign exchange market and purchase foreign assets. Indeed, this intuition is correct for the case of an unsterilized intervention.

Recall that in an unsterilized intervention, if the Federal Reserve decides to sell dollars in order to buy foreign assets in the foreign exchange market, this works just like an open market purchase of bonds that increases the monetary base and the money supply. Hence we find ourselves analyzing exactly the situation described in Figure 7 of Chapter 8, which is reproduced here as Figure 1. The higher money supply leads to a higher U.S. price level in the long run and so to a lower expected future exchange rate. The resulting decline in the expected appreciation of the dollar increases the expected return on foreign deposits and shifts the RET^F schedule to the right. In addition, the increase in the money supply will lead to a higher real money supply in the short run, which causes the interest rate on dollar deposits to fall. The resulting lower expected return on dollar deposits translates as a leftward shift in the RET^D schedule. The fall in the expected return on dollar deposits and the increase in the expected return on foreign deposits means that foreign assets have a higher expected return than dollar deposits at the old equilibrium exchange rate. Hence people will try to sell their dollar deposits, and the exchange rate will fall. Indeed, as we saw in Chapter 8, the increase in the money supply will lead to exchange rate overshooting, whereby the exchange rate falls by more in the short run than it does in the long run.

Our analysis leads us to the following conclusion about unsterilized interventions in the foreign exchange market: *An unsterilized intervention in which domestic currency is sold to purchase foreign assets leads to a gain in international reserves, an increase in the money supply, and a depreciation of the domestic currency.*

The reverse result is found for an unsterilized intervention in which domestic currency is purchased by selling foreign assets. The purchase of domestic currency by selling foreign assets (reducing international reserves) works like an open market sale to reduce the monetary base and the money supply. The

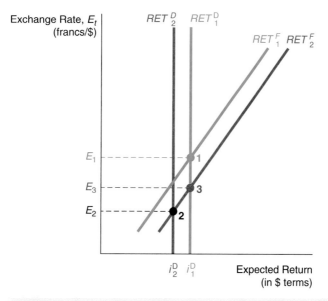

■FIGURE 1 Effect of a Sale of Dollars and a Purchase of Foreign Assets

A sale of dollars and the consequent open market purchase of foreign assets increase the monetary base. The resulting rise in the money supply leads to a higher domestic price level in the long run, which leads to a lower expected future exchange rate. The resulting decline in the expected appreciation of the dollar raises the expected return on foreign deposits, shifting the RET^F schedule rightward from RET^F_1 to RET^F_2. In the short run, the domestic interest rate i^D falls, shifting RET^D from RET^D_1 to RET^D_2. The short-run outcome is that the exchange rate falls from E_1 to E_2. In the long run, however, the interest rate returns to i^D_1, and RET^D returns to RET^D_1. The exchange rate therefore rises from E_2 to E_3 in the long run.

decrease in the money supply raises the interest rate on dollar deposits and shifts RET^D rightward while causing RET^F to shift leftward because it leads to a lower U.S. price level in the long run and thus to a higher expected appreciation of the dollar and hence a lower expected return on foreign deposits. The increase in the expected return on dollar deposits relative to foreign deposits will mean that people will want to buy more dollar deposits, and the exchange rate will rise. ***An unsterilized intervention in which domestic currency is purchased by selling foreign assets leads to a drop in international reserves, a decrease in the money supply, and an appreciation of the domestic currency.***

Sterilized Intervention

The key point to remember about a sterilized intervention is that the central bank engages in offsetting open market operations so that there is no impact on the monetary base and the money supply. In the context of the model of exchange rate determination we have developed here, it is straightforward to show that a sterilized intervention has *no effect* on the exchange rate. Remember that in our model, foreign and domestic deposits are perfect substitutes, so equilibrium in the foreign exchange market occurs when the expected returns on foreign and domestic deposits are equal. A sterilized intervention leaves the money supply unchanged and so has no way of directly affecting interest rates or the expected future exchange rate.[1] Because the expected returns on dollar and foreign deposits are unaffected, the expected return schedules remain at RET^D_1 and RET^F_1 in Figure 1, and the exchange rate remains unchanged at E_1.

At first it might seem puzzling that a central bank purchase or sale of domestic currency that is sterilized does not lead to a change in the exchange rate. A central bank purchase of domestic currency cannot raise the exchange rate because with no effect on the domestic money supply or interest rates, any resulting rise in the exchange rate would mean that the expected return on foreign deposits would be greater than the expected return on domestic deposits. Given our assumption that foreign and domestic deposits are perfect substitutes (equally desirable), this would mean that no one would want to hold domestic deposits.[2] So the exchange rate would have to fall back to its previous level, where the expected returns on domestic and foreign deposits were equal.

◼ BALANCE OF PAYMENTS

Because international financial transactions such as foreign exchange interventions have considerable effect on monetary policy, it is worth knowing how these transactions are measured. The **balance of payments** is a bookkeeping system for recording all payments that have a direct bearing on the movement of funds between a nation (private sector and government) and foreign countries.

The balance-of-payments account in the accompanying "Following the Financial News" box uses a standard double-entry bookkeeping system much like one that you or I might use to keep a record of payments and receipts. All transactions involving payments from foreigners to Americans are entered in the "Receipts" column with a plus sign (+) to reflect that they are credits; that is, they result in a flow of funds to Americans. Receipts include foreign purchases of American products such as computers and wheat (exports), purchases from foreign tourists (services), income earned from American investment abroad

---

[1]Note that a sterilized intervention could indicate what central banks want to happen to the future exchange rate and so might provide a signal about the course of future monetary policy. In this way, a sterilized intervention could lead to shifts in the RET^F schedule, but in reality it is the future change in monetary policy, not the sterilized intervention, that is the ultimate source of exchange rate effects. For a discussion of the signaling effect, see Maurice Obstfeld, "The Effectiveness of Foreign Exchange Intervention: Recent Experience, 1985–1988," in *International Policy Coordination and Exchange Rate Fluctuations,* ed. William H. Branson, Jacob A. Frenkel, and Morris Goldstein (Chicago: University of Chicago Press, 1990), pp. 197–237.

[2]If domestic and foreign deposits are not perfect substitutes, a sterilized intervention can affect the exchange rate. However, most studies find little evidence to support the position that sterilized intervention has a significant impact on foreign exchange rates. For a further discussion of the effects of sterilized versus unsterilized intervention, see Paul Krugman and Maurice Obstfeld, *International Economics,* 4th ed. (Reading, Mass.: Addison Wesley Longman, 1997).

(investment income), foreign gifts and pensions paid to Americans (unilateral transfers), and foreign payments for American assets (capital inflows).

All payments to foreigners are entered in the "Payments" column with a minus sign (−) to reflect that they are debits because they result in flows of funds to other countries. Payments include American purchases of foreign products such as French wine and Japanese cars (imports), American travel abroad (services), income earned by foreigners from investments in the United States (investment income), foreign aid and gifts and pensions paid to foreigners (unilateral transfers), and American payments for foreign assets (capital outflows).

FOLLOWING THE FINANCIAL NEWS

The Balance of Payments

Newspapers periodically report information on the balance of payments. Balance-of-trade figures (merchandise exports minus imports) are reported monthly in the last week of the month. The complete set of items in the balance of payments is published on a quarterly basis, with the previous quarter's figures published between the eighteenth and twentieth day of the last month of the following quarter. An example of the balance-of-payments accounts for the United States appears here.

U.S. Balance of Payments, 1995 ($ billions)

	Receipts (+)	Payments (−)	Balance
Current Account			
(1) Merchandise exports	+575		
(2) Merchandise imports		−750	
Trade balance			−175
(3) Net investment income		−11	
(4) Net services	+63		
(5) Net unilateral transfers		−30	
Current account balance:			
(1) + (2) + (3) + (4) + (5)			−153
Capital Account			
(6) Capital outflows		−270	
(7) Capital inflows	+316		
(8) Statistical discrepancy	+7		
Official reserve transactions balance:			
(1) + (2) + (3) + (4) + (5) + (6) + (7) + (8)			−100
Method of Financing			
(9) Increase in U.S. official reserve assets		−10	
(10) Increase in foreign official reserve assets	+110		
Total financing of surplus: (9) + (10)			+100
Balance of Payments			
Sum: (1) through (10)			0

Source: Survey of Current Business, April 1996.

Current Account

The **current account** shows international transactions that involve currently produced goods and services. The difference between merchandise exports (line 1) and imports (line 2) is called the **trade balance.** When merchandise imports are greater than exports (here by $175 billion), we have a trade balance deficit; if exports are greater than imports, we have a trade balance surplus.

The next three items in the current account are the net payments or receipts that arise from investment income, the purchase and sale of services, and unilateral transfers (gifts, pensions, and foreign aid). In 1995, for example, net investment income was minus $11 billion (in line 3) for the United States because Americans received less investment income from abroad than they paid out. Americans bought less in services from foreigners than foreigners bought from Americans, so net services generated $63 billion in receipts (line 4). Since Americans made more unilateral transfers to foreign countries (especially foreign aid) than foreigners made to the United States, a $30 billion payment is shown in line 5.

The sum of the items in lines 1 through 5 is the current account balance, which in 1995 showed a deficit of $153 billion. The current account balance is an important balance-of-payments concept for several reasons. As we can see from the balance-of-payments account, any surplus or deficit in the current account must be balanced either by capital account transactions (lending or borrowing abroad) or by changes in government reserve asset items:

Current account + capital account = change in government reserve assets

The current account balance tells us whether the United States (private sector and government combined) is increasing or decreasing its claims on foreign wealth. A surplus indicates that America is increasing its claims on foreign wealth, and a deficit, as in 1995, indicates that the country is reducing its claims on foreign wealth.[3]

Financial analysts follow the current account balance closely because they believe that it can provide information on the future movement of exchange rates. The current account balance provides some indication of what is happening to the demand for imports and exports, which, as we saw in Chapter 8, can affect the exchange rate. In addition, the current account balance provides information about what will be happening to U.S. claims on foreign wealth in the long run. Because a movement of foreign wealth to American residents can affect the demand for dollar assets, changes in U.S. claims on foreign wealth, reflected in the current account balance, can affect the exchange rate over time.[4]

---

[3]The current account balance can also be viewed as showing by how much total saving exceeds private sector and government investment in the United States. We can see this by noting that total U.S. saving equals the increase in total wealth held by the U.S. private sector and government. Total investment equals the increase in the U.S. capital stock (wealth physically in the United States). The difference between them is the increase in U.S. claims on foreign wealth.

[4]If American residents have a greater preference for dollar assets than foreigners do, a movement of foreign wealth to American residents when there is a balance-of-payments surplus will increase the demand for dollar assets over time and will cause the dollar to appreciate.

Capital Account

The **capital account** describes the flow of capital between the United States and other countries. Capital outflows are American purchases of foreign assets (a "Payments" item), and capital inflows are foreign purchases of American assets (a "Receipts" item). The capital outflows (line 6) are less than the capital inflows (line 7), resulting in a net flow of $46 billion in funds from foreigners in exchange for claims against American individuals and corporations.

The statistical discrepancy (line 8) represents errors due to unrecorded transactions involving smuggling and other capital flows. The statistical discrepancy, which keeps the balance-of-payments account in balance, is +$7 billion, which suggests that some of the other items in the balance of payments may not be measured very accurately. Many experts believe that the statistical discrepancy is primarily the result of large hidden capital flows, and so the item has been placed in the capital account part of the balance of payments.

Official Reserve Transactions Balance

The sum of lines 1 through 8, called the **official reserve transactions balance,** equals the current account balance plus the items in the capital account. When we refer to a surplus or a deficit in the balance of payments, we actually mean a surplus or deficit in the official reserve transactions balance. Because the balance-of-payments account must balance, the official reserve transactions balance tells us the net amount of international reserves that must move between central banks to finance international transactions. One reason we are particularly interested in the movements of international reserves is that, as we saw earlier in the chapter, these movements can have an important impact on the money supply and exchange rates.

Methods of Financing the Balance of Payments

Because most countries' currencies are not held by other countries as international reserves, these countries must finance an excess of payments over receipts (a deficit in the balance of payments) by providing international reserves to foreign governments and central banks. A balance-of-payments deficit is associated with a loss of international reserves; likewise, a balance-of-payments surplus is associated with a gain.

In contrast to other countries' currencies, the U.S. dollar and dollar-denominated assets are the major component of international reserves held by other countries. Thus a U.S. balance-of-payments deficit can be financed by a decrease in U.S. international reserves, an increase in foreign central banks' holdings of international reserves (dollar assets), or both. Conversely, a U.S. balance-of-payments surplus can be financed by an increase in U.S. international reserves, a decrease in foreign central banks' international reserves, or both.

For the United States in 1995, the official reserve transactions deficit of $100 billion was financed by a $10 billion increase in U.S. international reserves (-10 in the "Payments" column of line 9) and a $110 billion increase of foreign holdings of dollars (in the "Receipts" column of line 10).[5] On net, the United States' indebtedness to foreign governments (central banks) increased by $100 billion (the $110 billion foreign increase in holdings of U.S. dollars minus the $10 billion increase in U.S. holdings of international reserves). This $100 billion increase in net U.S. government indebtedness just matches the $100 billion official reserve transactions deficit, so the sum of lines 1 through 10 is zero, and the account balances.

■ EVOLUTION OF THE INTERNATIONAL FINANCIAL SYSTEM

Before examining the impact of international financial transactions on monetary policy, we need to understand the past and current structure of the international financial system.

Gold Standard

Before World War I, the world economy operated under the **gold standard,** meaning that the currency of most countries was convertible directly into gold. American dollar bills, for example, could be turned in to the U.S. Treasury and exchanged for approximately $\frac{1}{20}$ ounce of gold. Likewise, the British Treasury would exchange $\frac{1}{4}$ ounce of gold for £1 sterling. Because an American could convert $20 into 1 ounce of gold, which could be used to buy £4, the exchange rate between the pound and the dollar was effectively fixed at $5 to the pound. Tying currencies to gold resulted in an international financial system with fixed exchange rates between currencies. The fixed exchange rates under the gold standard had the important advantage of encouraging world trade by eliminating the uncertainty that occurs when exchange rates fluctuate.

To see how the gold standard operated in practice, let us see what occurs if, under the gold standard, the British pound begins to appreciate above the $5 par value. If an American importer of £100 of English tweed tries to pay for the tweed with dollars, it costs more than the $500 it cost before. Nevertheless, the importer has another option involving the purchase of gold that can reduce the cost of the tweed. Instead of using dollars to pay for the tweed, the American importer can exchange the $500 for gold, ship the gold to Britain, and convert it into £100. The shipment of gold to Britain is cheaper as long as the British pound is above the $5 par value (plus a small amount to pay for the cost of shipping the gold).

The appreciation of the pound leads to a British gain of international reserves (gold) and an equal U.S. loss. Because a change in a country's holdings of international reserves (gold) leads to an equal change in its monetary base, the movement of gold from the United States to Britain causes the British monetary base to rise and the American monetary base to fall. The resulting rise in the British money supply raises the British price level, while the fall in the U.S. money sup-

---

[5]At first it may seem strange that when the United States gains $10 billion of international reserves, it is entered in the balance of payments as a payment with a negative sign. Recall, however, that when a central bank loses international reserves, it has sold foreign assets. Thus a decrease in international reserves is just like an inflow of capital in the capital account and appears as a payment with a negative sign.

ply lowers the U.S. price level. The resulting increase in the British price level relative to the United States then causes the pound to depreciate. This process will continue until the value of the pound falls back down to its $5 par value.

A depreciation of the pound below the $5 par value, on the contrary, stimulates gold shipments from Britain to the United States. These shipments raise the American money supply and lower the British money supply, causing the pound to appreciate back toward the $5 par value. We thus see that under the gold standard, a rise or fall in the exchange rate sets in motion forces that return it to the par value.

As long as countries abided by the rules under the gold standard and kept their currencies backed by and convertible into gold, exchange rates remained fixed. However, adherence to the gold standard meant that a country had no control over its monetary policy because its money supply was determined by gold flows between countries. Furthermore, monetary policy throughout the world was greatly influenced by the production of gold and gold discoveries. When gold production was low in the 1870s and 1880s, the money supply throughout the world grew slowly and did not keep pace with the growth of the world economy. The result was deflation (falling price levels). Gold discoveries in Alaska and South Africa in the 1890s then greatly expanded gold production, which caused money supplies to increase rapidly and price levels to rise (inflation) until World War I.

Bretton Woods System and the IMF

World War I caused massive trade disruptions. Countries could no longer convert their currencies into gold, and the gold standard collapsed. Despite attempts to revive it in the interwar period, the worldwide depression, beginning in 1929, led to its permanent demise. As the Allied victory in World War II was becoming certain in 1944, the Allies met in Bretton Woods, New Hampshire, to develop a new international monetary system to promote world trade and prosperity after the war. In the agreement worked out among the Allies, central banks bought and sold their own currencies to keep their exchange rates fixed at a certain level (called a **fixed exchange rate regime**). The agreement lasted from 1945 to 1971 and was known as the **Bretton Woods system.**

The Bretton Woods agreement created the **International Monetary Fund (IMF),** headquartered in Washington, D.C., which had 30 original member countries in 1945 and currently has over 150. The IMF was given the task of promoting the growth of world trade by setting rules for the maintenance of fixed exchange rates and by making loans to countries that were experiencing balance-of-payments difficulties.[6] As part of its role of monitoring the compliance of member countries with its rules, the IMF also took on the job of collecting and standardizing international economic data.

---

[6]Rules for the conduct of trade between countries (the setting of tariffs and quotas) were given to the General Agreement on Tariffs and Trade (GATT), headquartered in Geneva. For a discussion of how this agency operates, see John Williamson, *The Open Economy and the World Economy* (New York: Basic Books, 1983).

The Bretton Woods agreement also set up the International Bank for Reconstruction and Development, commonly referred to as the **World Bank,** also headquartered in Washington, which provides long-term loans to help developing countries build dams, roads, and other physical capital that would contribute to their economic development. The funds for these loans are obtained primarily by issuing World Bank bonds, which are sold in the capital markets of the developed countries.[7]

Because the United States emerged from World War II as the world's largest economic power, with over half of the world's manufacturing capacity and the greater part of the world's gold, the Bretton Woods system of fixed exchange rates was based on the convertibility of U.S. dollars into gold (for foreign governments and central banks only) at $35 per ounce. The fixed exchange rates were to be maintained by intervention in the foreign exchange market by central banks in countries besides the United States who bought and sold dollar assets, which they held as international reserves. The U.S. dollar, which was used by other countries to denominate the assets that they held as international reserves, was called the **reserve currency.** Thus an important feature of the Bretton Woods system was the establishment of the United States as the reserve currency country.

How a Fixed Exchange Rate Regime Works The most important feature of the Bretton Woods system was that it set up a fixed exchange rate regime. Figure 2 shows how a fixed exchange rate regime works in practice using the model of exchange rate determination we learned in Chapter 8. Panel (a) describes a situation in which the domestic currency is initially overvalued: The schedule for the expected return on foreign deposits RET_1^F intersects the schedule for the expected return on domestic deposits RET_1^D at exchange rate E_1, which is lower than the par (fixed) value of the exchange rate E_{par}. To keep the exchange rate at E_{par}, the central bank must intervene in the foreign exchange market to purchase domestic currency by selling foreign assets, and this action, like an open market sale, means that the monetary base and the money supply decline. Because the exchange rate will continue to be fixed at E_{par}, the expected future exchange rate remains unchanged, and so the schedule for the expected return on foreign deposits remains at RET_1^F. However, the purchase of domestic currency, which leads to a fall in the money supply, also causes the interest rate on domestic deposits i^D to rise. This increase in turn shifts the expected return on domestic deposits RET^D to the right. The central bank will continue purchasing domestic currency and selling foreign assets until the RET^D curve reaches RET_2^D and the equilibrium exchange rate is at E_{par} at point 2 in panel (a).

We have thus come to the conclusion that *when the domestic currency is overvalued, the central bank must purchase domestic currency to keep the exchange rate fixed, but as a result it loses international reserves.*

Panel (b) in Figure 2 shows how a central bank intervention keeps the exchange rate fixed at E_{par} when the exchange rate is initially undervalued, that

---

[7]In 1960, the World Bank established an affiliate, the International Development Association (IDA), which provides particularly attractive loans to third-world countries (with 50-year maturities and zero interest rates, for example). Funds for these loans are obtained by direct contributions of member countries.

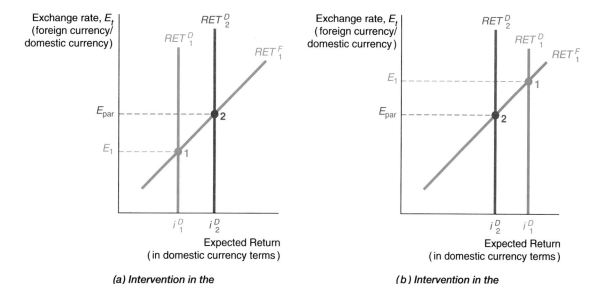

■FIGURE 2 Intervention in the Foreign Exchange Market Under a Fixed Exchange Rate Regime

In panel (a), the exchange rate at E_{par} is overvalued. To keep the exchange rate at E_{par} (point 2), the central bank must purchase domestic currency to shift the schedule for the expected return on domestic deposits to RET_2^D. In panel (b), the exchange rate at E_{par} is undervalued, so a central bank sale of domestic currency is needed to shift RET^D to RET_2^D to keep the exchange rate at E_{par} (point 2).

is, when RET_1^F and the initial RET_1^D intersect at exchange rate E_1, which is above E_{par}. Here the central bank must sell domestic currency and purchase foreign assets, and this works like an open market purchase to raise the money supply and to lower the interest rate on domestic deposits i^D. The central bank keeps selling domestic currency and lowers i^D until RET^D shifts all the way to RET_2^D, where the equilibrium exchange rate is at E_{par}—point 2 in panel (b). Our analysis thus leads us to the following result: ***When the domestic currency is undervalued, the central bank must sell domestic currency to keep the exchange rate fixed, but as a result it gains international reserves.***

As we have seen, if a country's currency has an overvalued exchange rate, its central bank's attempts to keep the currency from depreciating will result in a loss of international reserves. If the country's central bank eventually runs out of international reserves, it cannot keep its currency from depreciating, and a **devaluation** must occur, meaning that the par exchange rate is reset at a lower level.

If, by contrast, a country's currency has an undervalued exchange rate, its central bank's intervention to keep the currency from appreciating leads to a gain of international reserves. Because, as we will see shortly, the central bank might not want to acquire these international reserves, it might want to reset the par value of its exchange rate at a higher level (a **revaluation**).

Note that if domestic and foreign deposits are perfect substitutes, as is assumed in the model of exchange rate determination used here, a sterilized exchange rate intervention would not be able to keep the exchange rate at E_{par} because, as we have seen in Chapter 8, neither RET^F nor RET^D will shift. For example, if the exchange rate is overvalued, a sterilized purchase of domestic currency will still leave the expected return on domestic deposits below the expected return on foreign deposits at the par exchange rate—so pressure for a depreciation of the domestic currency is not removed. If the central bank keeps on purchasing its domestic currency but continues to sterilize, it will just keep on losing international reserves until it finally runs out of them and is forced to let the value of the currency seek a lower level.

One implication of the foregoing analysis is that a country that ties its exchange rate to a larger country's currency loses control of its monetary policy. If the larger country pursues a more contractionary monetary policy and decreases its money supply, this would lead to lower expected inflation in the larger country, thus causing an appreciation of the larger country's currency and a depreciation of the smaller country's currency. The smaller country, having locked its exchange rate, will now find its currency overvalued and will therefore have to sell the larger country's currency and buy its own to keep its currency from depreciating. The result of this foreign exchange intervention will then be a decline in the smaller country's international reserves, a contraction of the monetary base, and thus a decline in its money supply. Sterilization of this foreign exchange intervention is not an option because this would just lead to a continuing loss of international reserves until the smaller country was forced to devalue. The smaller country no longer controls its monetary policy because movements in its money supply are completely determined by movements in the larger country's money supply.

Smaller countries are often willing to tie their exchange rate to that of a larger country in order to inherit the more disciplined monetary policy of their bigger neighbor, thus ensuring a lower inflation rate. An extreme example of such a strategy is the currency board, which has been used by Hong Kong and has recently been adopted by countries such as Argentina (see Box 2), Latvia, and Estonia.

Bretton Woods System of Fixed Exchange Rates Under the Bretton Woods system, exchange rates were supposed to change only when a country was experiencing a "fundamental disequilibrium," that is, large persistent deficits or surpluses in its balance of payments. To maintain fixed exchange rates when countries had balance-of-payments deficits and were losing international reserves, the IMF would loan deficit countries international reserves contributed by other members. As a result of its power to dictate loan terms to borrowing countries, the IMF could encourage deficit countries to pursue contractionary monetary policies that would strengthen their currency or eliminate their balance-of-payment deficits. If the IMF loans were not sufficient to prevent depreciation of a currency, the country was allowed to devalue its currency by setting a new, lower exchange rate.

A notable weakness of the Bretton Woods system was that although deficit countries losing international reserves could be pressured into devaluing their currency or pursuing contractionary policies, the IMF had no way to force surplus countries to revise their exchange rates upward or pursue more expansionary

▉ **BOX 2**

Argentina's Currency Board

Argentina has a long history of monetary instability, with inflation rates fluctuating dramatically and sometimes surging beyond 1,000% a year. To end this cycle of inflationary surges, Argentina decided to adopt a currency board in April 1991. A *currency board system* is one in which the domestic currency has 100% backing in foreign reserves and in which the note-issuing authority, whether the central bank or the government, adopts a fixed exchange rate against a particular foreign currency and then stands ready to exchange domestic currency for foreign currency at that rate whenever the public requests it.

The Argentine currency board works as follows. Under Argentina's convertibility law, the peso/dollar exchange rate is fixed at one to one, and a member of the public can go to the Argentine central bank and exchange a peso for a dollar, or vice versa, at any time. A currency board is just a variant of a fixed exchange rate regime in which the commitment to the fixed exchange rate is especially strong because the conduct of monetary policy is in effect put on autopilot and is completely taken out of the hands of the central bank and the government. The money supply can expand only when dollars are exchanged for pesos at the central bank, meaning that the increased amount of pesos is matched by an equal increase in foreign exchange reserves. The central bank therefore no longer has the ability to print money and thereby cause inflation.

The early years of Argentina's currency board looked stunningly successful. Inflation, which had been running at an 800% rate in 1990, fell below 5% by the end of 1994, and economic growth was rapid, averaging almost 8% annually from 1991 to 1994. However, a currency board is not without problems. In the aftermath of the Mexican peso crisis, concern about the health of the Argentine economy resulted in the public's pulling money out of the banks (deposits fell by 18%) and exchanging pesos for dollars, thus causing a contraction of the Argentine money supply. The result was a sharp decline in Argentine economic activity, with real GDP down more than 5% in 1995 and the unemployment rate jumping above 15%. Only in 1996 did the economy begin to recover. Because the Central Bank of Argentina has no control over monetary policy under the currency board system, it was relatively helpless to counteract the contractionary monetary policy stemming from the public's behavior. Furthermore, because the currency board does not allow the central bank to create pesos and lend them to the banks, it has very little capability to act as a lender of last resort. With help from international agencies, such as the IMF, the World Bank, and the Interamerican Development Bank, who lent Argentina over $5 billion to help shore up its banking system, the currency board still survives. However, the Argentine public is not as enamored with the currency board as it once was.

policies. Particularly troublesome in this regard was the fact that the reserve currency country, the United States, could not devalue its currency under the Bretton Woods system even if the dollar was overvalued. When the United States attempted to reduce domestic unemployment in the 1960s by pursuing an inflationary monetary policy, a fundamental disequilibrium of an overvalued dollar developed. Because surplus countries were not willing to revise their exchange rates upward, adjustment in the Bretton Woods system did not take place, and the system collapsed in 1971. Attempts to patch up the Bretton Woods system with the Smithsonian Agreement in December 1971 proved unsuccessful, and by 1973, America and its trading partners had agreed to allow exchange rates to float.

Managed Float

Although exchange rates are currently allowed to change daily in response to market forces, central banks have not been willing to give up their option of intervening in the foreign exchange market. Preventing large changes in exchange rates makes it easier for firms and individuals purchasing or selling goods abroad to plan into the future. Furthermore, countries with surpluses in their balance of payments frequently do not want to see their currencies appreciate because it makes their goods more expensive abroad and foreign goods cheaper in their country. Because an appreciation might hurt sales for domestic businesses and increase unemployment, surplus countries have often sold their currency in the foreign exchange market and acquired international reserves.

Countries with balance-of-payments deficits do not want to see their currency lose value because it makes foreign goods more expensive for domestic consumers and can stimulate inflation. To keep the value of the domestic currency high, deficit countries have often bought their own currency in the foreign exchange market and given up international reserves.

The current international financial system is a hybrid of a fixed and a flexible exchange rate system. Rates fluctuate in response to market forces but are not determined solely by them. Furthermore, many countries continue to keep the value of their currency fixed against other currencies, as in the European Monetary System (to be described shortly).

The IMF continues to function as a data collector and international lender but does not attempt to encourage fixed exchange rates. The IMF's role of international lender has also become important recently because of situations like the third-world debt crisis of the 1980s and the more recent Mexican peso crisis (discussed later in the chapter). The IMF has been directly involved in helping developing countries with difficulties in repaying their loans and provided large loans to Mexico and other countries in the aftermath of the Mexican peso crisis.

Another important feature of the current system is the continuing de-emphasis of gold in international financial transactions. Not only has the United States suspended convertibility of dollars into gold for foreign central banks, but since 1970 the IMF has been issuing a paper substitute for gold, called **special drawing rights (SDRs)**. Like gold in the Bretton Woods system, SDRs function as international reserves. Unlike gold, whose quantity is determined by gold discoveries and the rate of production, SDRs can be created by the IMF whenever it decides that there is a need for additional international reserves to promote world trade and economic growth.

The use of gold in international transactions was further deemphasized by the IMF's elimination of the official gold price in 1975 and by the sale of gold by the U.S. Treasury and the IMF to private interests in order to demonetize it. Currently, the price of gold is determined in a free market. Investors who want to speculate in it are able to purchase and sell at will, as are jewelers and dentists who use gold in their businesses.

European Monetary System (EMS)

In March 1979, eight members of the European Economic Community (Germany, France, Italy, the Netherlands, Belgium, Luxembourg, Denmark, and Ireland) set up the European Monetary System (EMS), in which they agreed to fix their exchange rates vis-à-vis one another and to float jointly against the U.S. dollar. Spain joined the EMS in June 1989, the United Kingdom in October 1990, and

Portugal in April 1992. The EMS created a new monetary unit, the *European currency unit* (ECU), whose value is tied to a basket of specified amounts of European currencies. Each member of the EMS is required to contribute 20% of its holdings of gold and dollars to the European Monetary Cooperation Fund and in return receives an equivalent amount of ECUs.

The exchange rate mechanism (ERM) of the European Monetary System works as follows. The exchange rate between every pair of currencies of the participating countries is not allowed to fluctuate outside narrow limits around a fixed exchange rate. (The limits were typically ±2.25% but were raised to ±15% after the September 1992 foreign exchange crisis.) When the exchange rate between two countries' currencies moves outside of these limits, the central banks of both countries are supposed to intervene in the foreign exchange market. If, for example, the French franc depreciates below its lower limit against the German mark, the Bank of France must buy francs and sell marks, thereby giving up international reserves. Similarly, the German central bank must also intervene to buy marks and sell francs and consequently increase its international reserves. The EMS thus requires that intervention be symmetric when a currency falls outside the limits, with the central bank with the weak currency giving up international reserves and the one with the strong currency gaining them. Central bank intervention is also very common even when the exchange rate is within the limits, but in this case, if one central bank intervenes, no others are required to intervene as well.

A serious shortcoming of fixed exchange rate systems such as the Bretton Woods system or the European Monetary System is that they can lead to foreign exchange crises involving a "speculative attack" on a currency—massive sales of a weak currency or purchases of a strong currency to cause a sharp change in the exchange rate. In the following application, we use our model of exchange rate determination to understand how the September 1992 exchange rate crisis that rocked the European Monetary System came about.

APPLICATION | SEPTEMBER 1992 FOREIGN EXCHANGE CRISIS

In the aftermath of German reunification in October 1990, the German central bank, the Bundesbank, faced rising inflationary pressures, with inflation having accelerated from below 3% in 1990 to near 5% by 1992. To get monetary growth under control and to dampen inflation, the Bundesbank raised German interest rates to near double-digit levels. Figure 3 shows the consequences of these actions by the Bundesbank in the foreign exchange market for sterling. Note that in the diagram, the pound sterling is the domestic currency and RET^D is the expected return on sterling deposits, while the foreign currency is the German mark (deutsche mark, DM), so RET^F is the expected return on mark deposits.

The increase in German interest rates i^F shifted the RET^F schedule rightward to RET^F_2 in Figure 3, so that the intersection of the RET^D_1 and the RET^F_2 schedules at point $1'$ was below the lower exchange rate limit (2.778 marks per pound, denoted E_{par}) under the exchange rate mechanism. To lower the value of the mark relative to the pound and restore the pound/mark exchange rate to within the

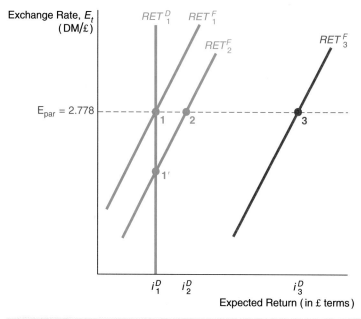

■FIGURE 3 Foreign Exchange Market for British Pounds in 1992

The realization by speculators that the United Kingdom would soon devalue the pound increased the expected return on foreign (German mark, DM) deposits and shifted RET_2^F rightward to RET_3^F. The result was the need for a much greater purchase of pounds by the British central bank to raise the interest rate to i_3^D to keep the exchange rate at DM 2.778 per pound.

ERM limits, either the Bank of England had to pursue a contractionary monetary policy, thereby raising British interest rates to i_2^D and shifting the RET^D schedule to the right to point 2, or the Bundesbank could pursue an expansionary monetary policy, thereby lowering German interest rates, which would shift the RET^F schedule to the left to move back to point 1. (The shifts in RET^D to point 2 or RET^F to point 1 are not shown in the figure.)

The catch was that the Bundesbank, whose primary goal is fighting inflation, was unwilling to pursue an expansionary monetary policy, while the British, who were facing their worst recession in the postwar period, were unwilling to pursue a contractionary monetary policy to prop up the pound. This impasse became clear when in response to great pressure from other members of the EMS, the Bundesbank was willing to lower its lending rates by only a token amount on September 14 after a speculative attack was mounted on the currencies of the Scandinavian countries. So at some point in the near future, the value of the pound would have to decline to point 1'. Speculators now knew that the appreciation of the mark was imminent and hence that the value of foreign (mark) deposits would rise in value relative to the pound. As a result, the expected return on mark deposits increased sharply, shifting the RET^F schedule to RET_3^F in Figure 3.

The huge potential losses on pound deposits and potential gains on mark deposits caused a massive sell-off of pounds (and purchases of marks) by speculators. The need for the British central bank to intervene to raise the value of the pound now became much greater and required a huge rise in British interest rates all the way to i_3^D. After a major intervention effort on the part of the Bank of England, which included a rise in its lending rate from 10% to 15% that still wasn't enough, the British were finally forced to give up on September 16: They pulled out of the ERM indefinitely, allowing the pound to depreciate by 10% against the mark.

Speculative attacks on other currencies forced devaluation of the Spanish peseta by 5% and the Italian lira by 15%. To defend its currency, the Swedish central bank was forced to raise its daily lending rate to the astronomical level of 500%! By the time the crisis was over, the British, French, Italian, Spanish, and Swedish central banks had intervened to the tune of $100 billion; the Bundesbank alone had laid out $50 billion for foreign exchange intervention. Because foreign exchange crises lead to large changes in central banks' holdings of international reserves and thus affect the official reserve asset items in the balance of payments, these crises are also referred to as **balance-of-payments crises.**

The attempt to prop up the European Monetary System was not cheap for these central banks. It is estimated that they lost $4 to $6 billion as a result of exchange rate intervention during the crisis.

■ **THE PRACTICING FINANCIAL INSTITUTION MANAGER**
Profiting from a Foreign Exchange Crisis

Large banks and other financial institutions often conduct foreign exchange trading operations that generate substantial profits for their parent institution. When a foreign exchange crisis like the one that occurred in September 1992 comes along, foreign exchange traders and speculators are presented with a golden opportunity. The foregoing analysis of this crisis helps explain why.

As we saw in Figure 3, the high German interest rates resulted in a situation in which the British pound was overvalued, in that the equilibrium exchange rate in the absence of intervention by the British and German central banks was below the lower exchange rate limit of 2.778 German marks per British pound. Once foreign exchange traders realized that the central banks would not be willing to intervene sufficiently or alter their policies to keep the value of the pound above the 2.778-mark-per-pound lower limit, the traders were presented with a "heads I win, tails you lose" bet. They knew that there was only one direction in which the exchange rate could go—down—and so they were almost sure to make money by buying marks and selling pounds. Our analysis of Figure 3 reflected this state of affairs; another way of looking at this one-sided bet is to recognize that it implies that the expected return on mark-denominated deposits increased sharply, shifting the RET^F schedule to RET_3^F in Figure 3.

Savvy foreign exchange traders, who read the writing on the wall early in September 1992, sold pounds and bought marks. When the pound depreciated 10% against the mark after September 16, they made huge profits because the marks they had bought could now be sold at a price 10% higher. Foreign exchange traders at Citibank are reported to have made $200 million in the week of the September 1992 exchange rate crisis—not bad for a week's work! But these profits pale in comparison to those made by George Soros, an investment fund manager whose funds are reported to have run up profits of $1 billion during the crisis. (However, Soros gave some of these profits back in 1994 when he acknowledged that he had suffered a $600 million loss from trades on the yen.) Clearly, foreign exchange trading can be a highly profitable enterprise for financial institutions, particularly during foreign exchange rate crises.

APPLICATION | MEXICAN PESO CRISIS OF DECEMBER 1994

As part of a reform plan initiated in 1987 to stabilize the Mexican economy, the Mexican government decided to put limits on the movements of the peso against the dollar. When the ruling party's presidential candidate was assassinated in March 1994, investors became concerned that the government might devalue the currency despite promises not to do so. The result was a speculative attack on the peso that not only brought down the peso but also threatened to bring down the currencies of other developing countries, particularly those in Latin America. Figure 3 can be used to understand the sequence of events during the Mexican peso crisis. We just need to recognize that RET^D is now the expected return on peso deposits and, since the foreign currency is the dollar, RET^F is the expected return on dollar deposits, with both denominated in the domestic currency, the peso.

Because of investors' concerns that the peso might be devalued after the March assassination, the expected return on dollar deposits rose, thus moving the RET^F schedule from RET^F_1 to RET^F_2 in Figure 3. The result was that the intersection of RET^D_1 and RET^F_2 was below the lower exchange limit E_{par} of around 30 cents per peso. To keep the peso from falling through this limit, the Mexican authorities needed to buy pesos and sell dollars, to raise interest rates to i^D_2 by shifting the RET^D curve to the right. This is exactly what they did, raising interest rates from around 10% to over 20% and losing close to half of their $30 billion in international reserves in the process. For the time being, the peso held, but more bad luck was to hit the Mexicans. An uprising in the southern state of Chiapas, the assassination of another high official in the ruling party, and concerns about the large current account deficit and the new untried president, who was inaugurated on December 1, led to further rumors of devaluation. Now the RET^F curve shifted even farther to the right, say, to RET^F_3, and the Mexican authorities intervened further, doubling interest rates again and almost completely exhausting the nation's foreign exchange reserves. Once speculators guessed that the Mexicans were running out of reserves, the game was up. With near certainty that the Mexican government would be forced to devalue, the expected return on dollar deposits increased sharply, shifting RET^F even farther to the right, making a devaluation inevitable. On December 20, Mexico's government had to devalue the peso; it had lost more than half its value by early 1995.

The aftermath of this crisis was not only speculative attacks on other developing countries' currencies but also a full-scale financial crisis in Mexico that, as we saw in Chapter 12, severely damaged the nation's economy. The foreign exchange rate crisis that shocked the European Monetary System in September 1992 cost central banks a lot of money, but the public in European countries was not seriously affected. The Mexican public was not so lucky; as described in Chapter 12, the speculative attack that caused the collapse of the peso produced a severe depression that cost all Mexicans dearly.

■ INTERNATIONAL CONSIDERATIONS AND MONETARY POLICY

Our analysis in this chapter so far has suggested several ways in which monetary policy can be affected by international events. And these occurrences can have significant implications for the way monetary policy is conducted.

Direct Effects of the Foreign Exchange Market on the Money Supply

When central banks intervene in the foreign exchange market, they acquire or sell off international reserves, and their monetary base is affected. When a central bank intervenes in the foreign exchange market, it gives up some control of its money supply. For example, in the early 1970s, the German central bank faced a dilemma. In attempting to keep the German mark from appreciating too much against the U.S. dollar, the Germans acquired huge quantities of international reserves, leading to a rapid rate of money growth that the German central bank considered inflationary.

The Bundesbank could have tried to halt the growth of the money supply by stopping its intervention in the foreign exchange market and reasserting control over its own money supply. Such a strategy has a major drawback when the central bank is under pressure not to allow its currency to appreciate: The lower price of imports and higher price of exports as a result of an appreciation in its currency will hurt domestic producers and increase unemployment.

Because the U.S. dollar has been a reserve currency, the U.S. monetary base and money supply have been less affected by developments in the foreign exchange market. As long as foreign central banks, rather than the Fed, intervene to keep the value of the dollar from changing, American holdings of international reserves are unaffected. The ability to conduct monetary policy is typically easier when a country's currency is a reserve currency.[8]

Balance-of-Payments Considerations

Under the Bretton Woods system, balance-of-payments considerations were more important than they are under the current managed float regime. When a nonreserve currency country is running balance-of-payments deficits, it necessarily gives up international reserves. To keep from running out of these reserves, under the Bretton Woods system it had to implement contractionary monetary policy to strengthen its currency. Exactly that occurred in the United Kingdom before its

---

[8]However, the central bank of a reserve currency country must worry about a shift away from the use of its currency for international reserves.

devaluation of the pound in 1967. When policy became expansionary, the balance of payments deteriorated, and the British were forced to "slam on the brakes" by implementing a contractionary policy. Once the balance of payments improved, policy became more expansionary until the deteriorating balance of payments again forced the British to pursue a contractionary policy. Such on-again, off-again actions became known as a "stop-go" policy, and the domestic instability it created was criticized severely.

Because the United States is a major reserve currency country, it can run large balance-of-payments deficits without losing huge amounts of international reserves. This does not mean, however, that the Federal Reserve is never influenced by developments in the U.S. balance of payments. Current account deficits in the United States suggest that American businesses may be losing some of their ability to compete because the value of the dollar is too high. In addition, large U.S. balance-of-payments deficits lead to balance-of-payments surpluses in other countries, which can in turn lead to large increases in their holdings of international reserves (that was especially true under the Bretton Woods system). Because such increases put a strain on the international financial system and may stimulate world inflation, the Fed worries about U.S. balance-of-payments and current account deficits. To help shrink these deficits, the Fed might pursue a more contractionary monetary policy.

Exchange Rate Considerations

Unlike balance-of-payments considerations, which have become less important under the current managed float system, exchange rate considerations now play a greater role in the conduct of monetary policy. If a central bank does not want to see its currency fall in value, it may pursue a more contractionary monetary policy of reducing the money supply to raise the domestic interest rate, thereby strengthening its currency. Similarly, if a country experiences an appreciation in its currency, domestic industry may suffer from increased foreign competition and may pressure the central bank to pursue a higher rate of money growth in order to lower the exchange rate.

The pressure to manipulate exchange rates seems to be greater for central banks in countries other than the United States, but even the Federal Reserve is not completely immune. The growing tide of protectionism stemming from the inability of American firms to compete with foreign firms because of the strengthening dollar from 1980 to early 1985 stimulated congressional critics of the Fed to call for a more expansionary monetary policy to lower the value of the dollar. As we saw in Chapter 24, the Fed then did let money growth surge to very high levels. A policy to bring the dollar down was confirmed in the Plaza Agreement of September 1985, in which the finance ministers from the five most important industrial nations in the free world (the United States, Japan, West Germany, the United Kingdom, and France) agreed to intervene in foreign exchange markets to achieve a decline in the dollar. The dollar continued to fall rapidly after the Plaza Agreement, and the Fed played an important role in this decline by continuing to expand the money supply at a rapid rate.

SUMMARY

1. An unsterilized central bank intervention in which the domestic currency is sold to purchase foreign assets leads to a gain in international reserves, an increase in the money supply, and a depreciation of the domestic currency. Available evidence suggests, however, that sterilized central bank interventions have little long-term effect on the exchange rate.

2. The balance of payments is a bookkeeping system for recording all payments between a country and foreign countries that have a direct bearing on the movement of funds between them. The official reserve transactions balance is the sum of the current account balance plus the items in the capital account. It indicates the amount of international reserves that must be moved between countries to finance international transactions.

3. Before World War I, the gold standard was predominant. Currencies were convertible into gold, thus fixing exchange rates between countries. After World War II, the Bretton Woods system and the IMF were established to promote a fixed exchange rate system

in which the U.S. dollar was convertible into gold. The Bretton Woods system collapsed in 1971. We now have an international financial system that has elements of a managed float and a fixed exchange rate system. Some exchange rates fluctuate from day to day, although central banks intervene in the foreign exchange market, while other exchange rates are fixed, as in the European Monetary System.

4. Three international considerations affect the conduct of monetary policy: direct effects of the foreign exchange market on the money supply, balance-of-payments considerations, and exchange rate considerations. Inasmuch as the United States has been a reserve currency country in the post–World War II period, U.S. monetary policy has been less affected by developments in the foreign exchange market and its balance of payments than is true for other countries. However, in recent years, exchange rate considerations have been playing a more prominent role in influencing U.S. monetary policy.

KEY TERMS

balance of payments, p. 650
balance-of-payments crisis, p. 663
Bretton Woods system, p. 655
capital account, p. 653
current account, p. 652
devaluation, p. 657
fixed exchange rate regime, p. 655
foreign exchange intervention, p. 645

gold standard, p. 654
International Monetary Fund (IMF), p. 655
international reserves, p. 646
managed float regime (dirty float), p. 645
official reserve transactions balance, p. 653
reserve currency, p. 656
revaluation, p. 657

special drawing rights (SDRs), p. 660
sterilized foreign exchange intervention, p. 648
trade balance, p. 652
unsterilized foreign exchange intervention, p. 647
World Bank, p. 656

QUESTIONS AND PROBLEMS

1. If the Federal Reserve buys dollars in the foreign exchange market but conducts an offsetting open market operation to sterilize the intervention, what will be the impact on international reserves, the money supply, and the exchange rate?

*2. If the Federal Reserve buys dollars in the foreign exchange market but does not sterilize the intervention, what will be the impact on international reserves, the money supply, and the exchange rate?

3. For each of the following, identify in which part of the balance-of-payments account it appears (current account, capital account, or method of financing) and whether it is a receipt or a payment.
   a. A British subject's purchase of a share of Johnson & Johnson stock
   b. An American's purchase of an airline ticket from Air France
   c. The Swiss government's purchase of U.S. Treasury bills

d. A Japanese's purchase of California oranges

e. $50 million of foreign aid to Honduras

f. A loan by an American bank to Mexico

g. An American bank's borrowing of Eurodollars

*4. Why does a balance-of-payments deficit for the United States have a different effect on its international reserves than a balance-of-payments deficit for the Netherlands?

5. Under the gold standard, if Britain became more productive relative to the United States, what would happen to the money supply in the two countries? Why would the changes in the money supply help preserve a fixed exchange rate between the United States and Britain?

*6. What is the exchange rate between dollars and francs if one dollar is convertible into $\frac{1}{20}$ ounce of gold and one franc is convertible into $\frac{1}{40}$ ounce of gold?

7. If a country's par exchange rate was undervalued during the Bretton Woods fixed exchange rate regime, what kind of intervention would that country's central bank be forced to undertake, and what effect would it have on its international reserves and the money supply?

*8. How can a large balance-of-payments surplus contribute to the country's inflation rate?

9. "If a country wants to keep its exchange rate from changing, it must give up some control over its money supply." Is this statement true, false, or uncertain? Explain your answer.

*10. Why can balance-of-payments deficits force some countries to implement a contractionary monetary policy?

11. "Balance-of-payments deficits always cause a country to lose international reserves." Is this statement true, false, or uncertain? Explain your answer.

*12. How can persistent U.S. balance-of-payments deficits stimulate world inflation?

13. "Inflation is not possible under the gold standard." Is this statement true, false, or uncertain? Explain your answer.

*14. Why is it that in a pure flexible exchange rate system, the foreign exchange market has no direct effects on the money supply? Does this mean that the foreign exchange market has no effect on monetary policy?

15. "The abandonment of fixed exchange rates after 1973 has meant that countries have pursued more independent monetary policies." Is this statement true, false, or uncertain? Explain your answer.

Glossary

adaptive expectations: Expectations of a variable based on an average of past values of the variable. 165

advances: See *discount loans*.

adverse selection: The problem created by asymmetric information before a transaction occurs: the people who are the most undesirable from the other party's point of view are the ones who are most likely to want to engage in the financial transaction. 27

all-risk policy: Insurance that insures against all perils except those specifically named in the policy. 457

American depository receipts (ADR): A receipt for foreign stocks held by a trustee. The receipts trade on U.S. stock exchanges instead of the actual stock. 264

American option: An option that can be exercised at any time up to the expiration date of the contract. 554

amortized: The principal amount due is paid in stages over a period of time. Each payment includes the accrued interest and an amount which is applied to repay the principal. When all of the payments have been made the loan is paid off. 270

annuity: An insurance product that pays a fixed stream of payments. 451

appreciation: Increase in a currency's value. 189

arbitrage: Elimination of a riskless profit opportunity in a market. 531

asset: A financial claim or piece of property that is a store of value. 4, 73

asset management: The acquisition of assets that have a low rate of default and diversification of asset holdings to increase profits. 330

asset market approach: Determining asset prices using stocks of assets rather than flows. 102

asymmetric information: The inequality of knowledge that each party to a transaction has about the other party. 27

balance of payments: A bookkeeping system for recording all payments that have a direct bearing on the movement of funds between a country and foreign countries. 650

balance of payments crisis: A foreign exchange crisis stemming from problems in a country's balance of payments. 663

balance sheet: A list of the assets and liabilities of a bank (or firm) that balances-total assets equal total liabilities plus capital. 322

balloon loan: A loan where the payments do not fully pay off the principal balance such that the final payment must be larger than the rest. 270, 471

bank failure: A situation in which a bank cannot satisfy its obligations to pay its depositors and other creditors and thus goes out of business. 415

bank holding companies: Companies that own one or more banks. 363

bank panic: The simultaneous failure of many banks, as during a financial crisis. 313

banks: Financial institutions that accept deposits and make loans (such as commercial banks, savings and loan associations, and credit unions). 8

bank supervision: Overseeing who operates banks and how they are operated. 420

banker's acceptance: A short-term promissory note drawn by a company to pay for goods on which a bank guarantees payment at maturity. Usually used in international trade. 20, 233

basis point: One one-hundredth of a percentage point. 56

basis risk: The risk associated with the possibility that the prices of a hedged asset and the asset underlying the futures contract do not move closely together over time. 541

bearer instrument: A security payable to the holder or "bearer" when presented. No proof of ownership is required. 230

best-effort underwriting: The underwriter does not take ownership of the security issue nor commit to selling the issue at a given price. Instead the underwriter solicits, offers and attempts to market the security for the best price possible. 265

beta: A measure of sensitivity of an asset's return to changes in the value of the market portfolio, which is also a measure of the asset's marginal contribution to the risk of the market portfolio. 77

Board of Governors of the Federal Reserve System: A board with seven governors (including the chairman) that plays an essential role in decision making within the Federal Reserve System. 585

bond: A debt security that promises to make payments periodically for a specified period of time. 4

bond indenture: A document which accompanies a bond which spells out the details of the bond issue, such as the covenants, sinking fund provisions and so forth. It states the lender's rights and privileges, and the borrower's obligations. 253

book entry: A system of tracking securities ownership where no certificate is issued. Instead the security issuer keeps records, usually electronically, of who holds outstanding securities. 226

branches: Additional offices of banks that conduct banking operations. 364

Bretton Woods system: The international monetary system in use from 1945 to 1971 in which exchange rates were fixed and the U.S. dollar was freely convertible into gold (by foreign governments and central banks only). 655

brokered deposits: Deposits that enable depositors to circumvent the $100,000 limit at each bank so the total amount deposited is fully insured. 430

brokers: Agents for investors who match buyers with sellers. 17

bubble: A situation in which the price of an asset differs from its fundamental market value. 181

call option: An option contract that provides the right to buy a security at a specified price. 555

call provision: A right usually included in the terms of a bond which gives the issuer the ability to repurchase outstanding bonds before they mature. 254

capital account: An account that describes the flow of capital between the United States and other countries. 653

capital adequacy management: Managing the amount of capital the bank should maintain and then acquire the needed capital. 330

capital market: A financial market in which longer-term debt (maturity of greater than one year) and equity instruments are traded. 18

capital mobility: A situation in which foreigners can easily purchase a country's assets and the country's residents can easily purchase foreign assets. 198

captive finance company: A finance company which is owned by a retailer and which makes loans to finance the purchase of goods from the retailer. 478

cash flow: The difference between cash receipts and cash expenditures. 313

casualty (liability) insurance: Protects against financial losses because of a claim of negligence. 456

central bank: The government agency that oversees the banking system and is responsible for the amount of money and credit supplied in the economy; in the United States, the Federal Reserve System. 9, 361

Central Liquidity Facility (CLF): The lender of last resort for credit unions that was created in 1978 by the Financial Institutions Reform Act. 409

certainty equivalent: An amount that will be received or spent with certainty. An insurance payment is a certainty equivalent since it removes the risk that unexpected amounts will need to be spent. 445

closed-end fund: A fund that sells a fixed number of shares of stock and which does not continue to accept investments. 501

coinsurance: When a policyholder shares a percentage of the losses along with the insurance company. 433, 461

collateral: Property that is pledged to the lender to guarantee payment in the event that the borrower should be unable to make debt payments. 295

collateralized mortgage obligation (CMO): Securities classified by when prepayment is likely to occur. Investors may buy a group of CMOs which are likely to mature at a time that meets the investors needs. 284

common bond membership: A requirement that all members of credit unions share some common bond such as working for the same employer. 406

common stock: A security which gives the holder an ownership interest in the firm. This ownership interest includes the right to any residual cash flows and the right to vote on major corporate issues. 259

compensating balance: A required minimum amount of funds that a firm receiving a loan must keep in a checking account at the bank. 512

competitive bidding: Treasury securities are sold either competitively or noncompetitively. In a competitive auction those bidders submitting the highest price are awarded the securities. 225

consol: A perpetual bond with no maturity date and no repayment of principal that periodically makes fixed coupon payments. 49

conventional mortgages: Mortgage contract originated by banks and other mortgage lenders that are not guaranteed by the FHA or VA. They are often insured by private mortgage insurance. 277

costly state verification: Monitoring a firm's activities, an expensive process in both time and money. 305

coupon bond: A credit market instrument that pays the owner a fixed interest payment every year until the maturity date, when a specified final amount is repaid. 42

coupon rate: The dollar amount of the yearly coupon payment expressed as a percentage of the face value of a coupon bond. 42

creditor: A holder of debt. 310

credit rationing: A lender's refusing to make loans even though borrowers are willing to pay the stated interest rate or even a higher rate or restricting the size of loans to less than the amount being sought. 512

credit risk: The risk arising from the possibility that the borrower will default. 330

credit union: A financial institution that focuses on servicing the banking and lending needs of its members who must be linked by a common bond. 407

Credit Union National Association (CUNA): A central credit union facility which encourages establishing credit unions and provides information to its members. 406

Credit Union National Extension Bureau (CUNEB): A central credit union facility established in 1921 that was later replaced by the Credit Union National Association. 406

cross hedge: A hedge in which the asset underlying the futures or options contract is not the same as the asset being hedged. 537

currency: Paper money (such as dollar bills) and coins. 19

currency swap: A swap that involves the exchange of a set of payments in another currency. 564

current account: An account that shows international transactions involving currently produced goods and services. 652

current yield: An approximation of the yield to maturity that equals the yearly coupon payment divided by the price of a coupon bond. 51

dealers: People who link buyers with sellers by buying and selling securities at stated prices. 17

debt deflation: A situation in which a substantial decline in the price level sets in, leading to a further deterioration in firms' net worth because of the increased burden of indebtedness. 315

deductible: An amount of any loss that must be paid by the insured before the insurance company will pay anything. 447

deep markets: A market where there are many participants and a great deal of activity thus assuring that securities can be sold rapidly at fair prices. 225

default: A situation in which the party issuing a debt instrument is unable to make interest payments or pay off the amount owed when the instrument matures. 19

default-free bonds: Bonds with no default risk, such as U.S. government bonds. 139

default risk: The risk that a loan customer may fail to pay a loan as promised. 139, 473

defined-benefit plan: A pension plan where the benefits are stated up front and are paid regardless how the investments perform. 462

defined-contribution plan: A pension plan where the contributions are stated up front, but the benefits paid depend on the performance of the investments. 463

demand curve: A curve depicting the relationship between quantity demanded and price when all other economic variables are held constant. 96

demand deposit: A deposit held by a bank which must be paid to the depositor on demand. Demand deposits are more commonly called checking accounts. 229

deposit outflows: Losses of deposits when depositors make withdrawals or demand payment. 330

deposit rate ceilings: Restrictions on the maximum interest rates payable on deposits. 351

depreciation: Decrease in a currency's value. 189

devaluation: Resetting of the par value of a currency at a lower level. 657

direct placement: The issuer bypasses the dealer and sells the security directly to the end investor. 233

discount bond: A credit market instrument that is bought at a price below its face value and whose face value is repaid at the maturity date; it does not make any interest payments. Also known as a *zero-coupon bond*. 42

discount loans: A bank's borrowing from the Federal Reserve System. Also known as *advances*. 324

discount points: Points paid when a mortgage loan is obtained which lower the annual interest rate on the debt. 271

discount rate: The interest rate that the Federal Reserve charges banks on discount loans. 332, 589

discount window: The Federal Reserve facility at which discount loans are made to banks. 613

discount yield: See *yield on a discount basis*.

discounting: The reduction in the value of a security at purchase such that when it matures at full value, the investor receives a fair return. 224

disintermediation: A reduction in the flow of funds into the banking system that causes the amount of financial intermediation to decline. 351

diversification: The holding of many risky assets. 77

dividends: Periodic payments made by equities to shareholders. 16

down payment: A portion of the original purchase price that is paid by the borrower so that the borrower will have equity in the asset pledged as collateral. 274

dual banking system: The system in the United States in which banks supervised by the federal government and banks supervised by the states operate side by side. 362

duration: The average lifetime of a debt security's stream of payments. 61

duration gap analysis: A measurement of the sensitivity of the market value of a bank's assets and liabilities to changes in interest rates. 516

econometric model: A model whose equations are estimated using statistical procedures. 126

economies of scale: Reflects the savings that can be achieved through increased size. 26, 481

economies of scope: Reflects the increased business that can be achieved by offering many products in one easy-to-reach location. 482

Edge Act corporation: A special subsidiary of a U.S. bank that is engaged primarily in international banking. 376

effective exchange rate index: An index reflecting the value of a basket of representative foreign currencies. 210

efficient markets theory: The application of the theory of rational expectations to financial markets. 167

Employee Retirement Income Security Act (ERISA): A comprehensive act passed in 1994 which set standards that must be followed by all pension plans. 467

equities: Claims to share in the net income and assets of a corporation (such as common stock). 16

equity capital: see *net worth*.

equity multiplier: The amount of assets per dollar of equity capital. 336

Eurobonds: Bonds denominated in a currency other than that of the country in which they are sold. 24

Eurodollars: U.S. dollars that are deposited in foreign banks outside of the United States or in foreign branches of U.S. banks. 21

European option: An option that can be exercised only at the expiration date of the contract. 554

excess demand: A situation in which quantity demanded is greater than quantity supplied. 99

excess reserves: Reserves in excess of required reserves. 325, 589

excess supply: A situation in which quantity supplied is greater than quantity demanded. 99

exchange rate: The price of one currency in terms of another. 187

exchange rate overshooting: A phenomenon whereby the exchange rate changes by more in the short run than it does in the long run when the money supply changes. 209

exchanges: Secondary markets in which buyers and sellers of securities (or their agents or brokers) meet in one central location to conduct trades. 17

exercise price: The price at which the purchaser of an option has the right to buy or sell the underlying financial instrument. Also known as the *strike price*. 553

expectations hypothesis: The proposition that the interest rate on a long-term bond will equal the average of the short-term interest rates that people expect to occur over the life of the long-term bond. 148

expected return: The return on an asset expected over the next period. 74

factoring: The sale of accounts receivable to another firm which takes responsibility for collections. 475

Federal Credit Union Act: An act passed in 1934 which allowed federal charting of credit unions in all states. 406

federal funds: Short-term deposits bought or sold between banks. 20

federal funds rate: The interest rate on overnight loans of deposits at the Federal Reserve. 21

Federal Home Loan Bank Act of 1932: An act of Congress that created the Federal Home Loan Bank Board and a network of regional home loan banks. 392

Federal Home Loan Bank Board (FHLBB): An agency responsible for regulating and controlling savings and loan institutions. It was eliminated by FIRREA in 1989. 392

Federal Open Market Committee (FOMC): The committee that makes decisions regarding the conduct of open market operations; composed of the seven members of the Board of Governors of the Federal Reserve System, the president of the Federal Reserve Bank of New York, and the president of four other Federal Reserve banks on a rotating basis. 585

Federal Reserve banks: The 12 district banks in the Federal Reserve system. 585

Federal Reserve System (the Fed): The central banking authority responsible for monetary policy in the United States. 9

Federal Savings and Loan Insurance Corporation (FSLIC): An agency that provided deposit insurance to savings and loan similar to the Federal Deposit Insurance Corporation which insured banks. FSLIC was eliminated in 1989. 392

financial crisis: A major disruption in financial markets that is characterized by sharp declines in asset prices and the failures of many financial and non-financial firms. 311

financial derivatives: Instruments that have payoffs that are linked to previously issued securities and are extremely useful risk reduction tools. 527

financial engineering: The process of researching and developing new financial products and services that would meet customer needs and prove profitable. 347

financial futures contract: A futures contract in which the standardized commodity is a particular type of financial instrument. 529

financial futures options: Options in which the underlying instrument is a futures contract. Also called *futures options*. 554

financial guarantee: A contract that guarantees that the bond purchases will be paid both the principal and interest in the event the issuer defaults on the obligation. 257

Financial Institutions Reform Act: Passed in 1978, the act created the Central Liquidity Facility as the lender of last resort for credit unions. 209

Financial Institutions Reform Recovery and Enforcement Act: An act passed in 1989 to stop the losses which were building in the savings and loan industry. It reversed much of the deregulation included in the Garn St Germain Act of 1982. 409

financial instrument: See *security*.

financial intermediaries: Institutions (such as banks, insurance companies, mutual funds, pension funds, and finance companies) that borrow funds from people who have saved and then make loans to others. 8

financial intermediation: The process of indirect finance whereby financial intermediaries link lender-savers and borrower-spenders. 25

financial markets: Markets in which funds are transferred from people who have a surplus of available funds to people who have a shortage of available funds. 3

financial panic: The widespread collapse of financial markets and intermediaries in an economy. 34

firm-commitment underwriting: The underwriter agrees to buy the entire security issue at a pre-specified price, then to resell it. This method of issuing securities assures the issuer that the whole issue will be marketed. 265

Fisher effect: The outcome that when expected inflation occurs, interest rates will rise; named after economist Irving Fisher. 109

fixed exchange rate regime: A regime in which central banks buy and sell their own currencies to keep their exchange rates fixed at a certain level. 655

fixed-payment loan: A credit market instrument that provides a borrower with an amount of money that is repaid by making a fixed payment periodically (usually a month) for a set number of years. 42

floor plan: A type of loan where inventory is pledged as security and a portion of the loan is paid each time as an item of inventory is sold. 476

foreign bonds: Bonds sold in a foreign country and denominated in that country's currency. 23

foreign exchange intervention: An international financial transaction in which a central bank buys or sells currency to influence foreign exchange rates. 645

foreign exchange market: The market in which exchange rates are determined. 7, 187

foreign exchange rate: see *exchange rate*.

forward contract: An agreement by two parties to engage in a financial transaction at a future (forward) point in time. 527

forward exchange rate: The exchange rate for a forward transaction. 189

forward rate: The interest rate predicted by the expectations hypothesis of the term structure of interest rates to prevail in the future. 158

forward transaction: An exchange rate transaction that involves the exchange of bank deposits denominated in different currencies at some specified future date. 189

free reserves: Excess reserves in the banking system minus the volume of discount loans. 630

free-rider problem: The problem that occurs when people who do not pay for information take advantage of the information that other people have paid for. 299

fully funded: Describing a pension plan in which the contributions to the plan and their earnings over the years are sufficient to pay out the defined benefits when they come due. 463

fully funded pension plan: A defined benefit plan that has the assets available to make its projected benefit payments. 463

fully subscribed: A security issue for which all of the securities available have been spoken for before the issue date. 490

futures options: See *financial futures options*.

gap analysis: A measurement of the sensitivity of bank profits to changes in interest rates, calculated by subtracting the amount of rate-sensitive assets. Also called *income gap analysis*. 515

general obligation bonds: Bonds that are secured by the full faith and credit of the issuer, which includes the taxing authority of municipalities. 251

Glass-Steagall Act: An act which made it illegal for commercial banks to underwrite securities for sale to the public. 486

gold standard: A regime under which a currency is directly convertible into gold. 654

hedge: To protect oneself against risk. 528

hedge ratio: A ratio that indicates how many points the price of the hedged asset moves on average for a 1-point change in the futures contract used for the hedge. 537

incentive-compatible: Aligning the incentives of both parties to a contract. 308

income gap analysis: See *gap analysis*.

indexed bonds: Bonds whose interest and principal payments are adjusted for changes in the price level, and whose interest rate thus provides a direct measure of a real interest rate. 69

individual retirement account: Retirement accounts where pre tax dollars can be invested by individuals not covered by an alternative retirement plan. 468

initial public offering (IPO): The first time a corporation sells securities to the public. 246

insolvent: A situation in which the value of a firm's or bank's assets have fallen below its liabilities; bankrupt. 314

installment credit: A loan that requires the borrower to make a series of equal payments over some fixed length of time. 471

insured mortgage: Mortgages guaranteed by either the Federal Housing Administration or the Veterans Administration. These agencies guarantee that the bank making the loan will not suffer any losses if the borrower defaults. 277

interest parity condition: The observation that the domestic interest rate equals the foreign interest rate plus the expected appreciation in the foreign currency. 199

interest rate: The cost of borrowing or the price paid for the rental of funds (usually expressed as a percentage per year). 4

interest-rate forward contracts: Forward contracts that are linked to debt instruments. 527

interest-rate risk: The possible reduction in returns that is associated with changes in interest rates. 59, 330

interest-rate swap: A financial contract that allows one party to exchange (swap) a set of interest payments for another set of interest payments owned by another party. 564

intermediate target: Any number of variables, such as monetary aggregates or interest rates, that have a direct effect on employment and the price level and that the Fed seeks to influence. 622

intermediate-term: With reference to a debt instrument, having a maturity of between one and ten years. 16

international banking facilities (IBFs): Banking establishments in the United States that can accept time deposits from foreigners but are not subject to either reserve requirements or restrictions on interest payments. 376

International Monetary Fund (IMF): The international organization created by the Bretton Woods agreement whose objective is to promote the growth of world trade by making loans to countries experiencing balance-of-payments difficulties. 655

international policy coordination: Agreements among countries to enact policies cooperatively. 635

international reserves: Central bank holdings of assets denominated in foreign currencies. 646

inverted yield curve: a yield curve that is downward sloping. 146

investment banker: A securities dealer who facilitates the transfer of securities from the original issuer to the public. 264

investment banks: Firms that assist in the initial sale of securities in the primary market. 17

January effect: An abnormal rise in stock prices from December to January. 175

junk bonds: Bonds which are rated as lower then BBB by bond rating agencies. Junk bonds are not investment grade, rather are considered speculative. They usually have a high yield to compensate investors for their high risk. 141, 256

law of large numbers: The law says that when many people are insured the probability distribution of the losses will assume a normal probability distribution. 451

law of one price: The principle that if two countries produce an identical good, the price of this good should be the same throughout the world no matter which country produces it. 192

leasing: An arrangement where one party obtains the right to use an asset for a fee paid to another party for a predetermined length of time. 476

leveraged buyout (LBO): When managers of a firm borrow heavily to finance the purchase of a firm. 257

leverage ratio: A bank's capital divided by its assets. 419

liabilities: IOUs or debts. 14

liability management: The acquisition of funds at low cost to increase profits. 330

lien: A legal document which becomes part of the record attached to a piece of property. It gives the lender a right to foreclose or seize the property if the loan is not paid as promised. 273

limit order: An order placed by a customer to buy stock that specifies a maximum price or an order to sell stock that places a minimum acceptable price. 494

liquid: Easily converted into cash. 17

liquidity: The relative ease and speed with which an asset can be converted into cash. 74

liquidity management: The decision made by a bank to maintain sufficient liquid assets to meet the bank's obligations to depositors. 330

liquidity preference framework: A model developed by John Maynard Keynes that predicts the equilibrium interest rate on the basis of the supply of and demand for money. 114

liquidity premium theory: The theory that the interest rate on a long-term bond will equal an average of short-term interest rates expected to occur over the life of the long-term bond plus a positive term (liquidity) premium. 153

liquidity risk: The risk that a firm may run out of cash to pay bills and to keep the firm operating. 473

load fund: A mutual fund that charges a fee either when money is added or withdrawn from the fund. 502

loan commitment: A bank's commitment (for a specified future period of time) to provide a firm with loans up to a given amount at an interest rate that is tied to some market interest rate. 340, 510

loan sale: The sale under a contract (also called a *secondary loan participation*) of all or part of the cash stream from a specific loan, thereby removing the loan from the bank's balance sheet. 339

loanable funds: The quantity of loans. 101

loanable funds framework: Determining the equilibrium interest rate by analyzing the supply of and demand for bonds (loanable funds). 101

London interbank bid rate (LIBID): The rate of interest large international banks charge on overnight loans among themselves. 235

London interbank offer rate: The interest rate charged on short-term funds bought or sold between large international banks. Often abbreviated as LIBOR. 235

long position: A contractual obligation to take delivery of an underlying financial instrument. 528

long-term: With reference to a debt instrument, having a maturity of ten years or more. 16

luxury: An asset for which the wealth elasticity of demand is greater than 1. 74

macro hedge: A hedge of interest-rate risk for a financial institution's entire portfolio. 536

managed float regime: The current international financial environment in which exchange rates fluctuate from day to day, but central banks attempt to influence their countries' exchange rates by buying and selling currencies. Also known as a *dirty float*. 645

margin credit: Loans advanced by a brokerage house to help investors buy securities. 494

margin requirement: A sum of money that must be kept in an account (the margin account) at a brokerage firm. 535

marked to market: Repriced and settled in the margin account at the end of every trading day to reflect any change in the value of the futures contract. 535

market equilibrium: A situation occurring when the quantity that people are willing to buy (demand) equals the quantity that people are willing to sell (supply). 99

market fundamentals: Items that have a direct impact on future income streams of the security. 171

market maker: Dealers who buy or sell securities from their own inventories so that they ensure that there is always a market in which investors can buy or sell their securities. 496

market order: An order placed by a customer to buy stock that has the broker buy at the current market price. 493

maturity: Time to the expiration date (maturity date) of a debt instrument. 16

mean reversion: The phenomenon that stocks with low returns today tends to have high returns in the future, and vice versa. 176

mergers and acquisitions market: An informal and unorganized market where firms are bought, sold, or merged with other firms. 492

micro hedge: A hedge for a specific asset. 536

monetary base: The sum of the Fed's monetary liabilities (currency in circulation and reserves) and the U.S. Treasury's monetary liabilities (Treasury currency in circulation, primarily coins). 588

monetary neutrality: A proposition that in the long run, a percentage rise in the money supply is matched by the same percentage rise in the price level, leaving unchanged the real money supply and all other economic variables such as interest rates. 208

monetary policy: The management of the money supply and interest rates. 9

money: Anything that is generally accepted in payment for goods or services or in the repayment of debts. Also called *money supply.* 9

money center banks: Large banks in key financial centers. 334

money market: A financial market in which only short-term debt instruments (maturity of less than one year) are traded. 18

money market mutual funds: Funds which accumulate investment dollars from a large group of people and then invest in short-term securities such as Treasury bills and commercial paper. 501

money market securities: Securities which have an original maturity of less than one year, such as Treasury bill, commercial paper, banker's

acceptances, and negotiable certificates of deposit. 18, 223

money supply: See *money.*

moral hazard: The risk that one party to a transaction will engage in behavior that is undesirable from the other party's point of view. 28

mortgage: A long-term loan secured by real estate. 270

mortgage pass-through: A security that has the multiple borrower's mortgage payments pass-through a trustee before being disbursed to the investors. 283

mortgage-backed security (securitized mortgage): A security which is secured (collateralized) by a pool of mortgage loans. 282, 285

mutual bank: A bank owned by the depositors. 393

mutual insurance company: An insurance company that is owned by the policyholders and has the objective of providing insurance for the lowest possible price. 448

named-peril policy: Insures against loss from perils that are specifically named in the policy. 457

National Association of Securities Dealers Automated Quotation System (NASDAQ): A computerized network which links dealers around the country together and provides price quotes on over-the-counter securities. 247

national banks: Federally chartered banks. 362

National Credit Union Act of 1970: The act which established the National Credit Union Administration (NCUA)/National Credit Union Administration (NCUA) An independent agency charged with the task of regulating and supervising federally chartered credit unions and state chartered credit unions that receive federal deposit insurance. 408

National Credit Union Share Insurance Fund (NCUSIF): An agency established by the National Credit Union Act of 1970 that is controlled by the NCUA and insures the deposits in credit unions for $100,000 per account. 408

natural rate of unemployment: The rate of unemployment consistent with full employment at which the demand for labor equals the supply of labor. 619

necessity: An asset for which as wealth grows, the percentage increase in demand is less than the percentage increase in wealth—in other words, an asset with a wealth elasticity less than 1. 74

negotiable certificates of deposit: A bank issued a short-term security that documents a deposit and specifies the interest rate and the maturity date. 229

net asset value: The total value of a mutual fund's assets minus any liabilities divided by the number of shares outstanding. 502

net interest margin (NIM): The difference between interest income and interest expense as a percentage of assets. 345

net worth: The difference between a firm's assets (what it owns or is owed) and its liabilities (what it owes). Also called *equity capital*. 302

net worth certificates: Debt certificates issued by the FSLIC to troubled savings and loans that could be booked as capital rather than as a liability. 392

no-load fund: A mutual fund which does not charge a fee when funds are added to or withdrawn from the fund. 502

nominal interest rate: An interest rate that does not take inflation into account. 67

non-bank banks: Limited-service banks that either do not make commercial loans or do not take in deposits. 366

noncompetitive bidding: Treasury securities are sold either competitively or noncompetitively. In a noncompetitive bid the securities are awarded at the weighted average of the competitive bids accepted. 225

nonsystematic risk: The component of an asset's risk that is unique to the asset and so can be eliminated by diversification. 77

notional principle: The amount on which interest is being paid in a swap arrangement. 565

off-balance-sheet activities: Bank activities that involve trading financial instruments and the generation of income from fees and loan sales, all of which affect bank profits but are not visible on bank balance sheets. 339, 419

official reserve transactions balance: The current account balance plus items in the capital account. 653

open-end fund: A mutual fund that continues to accept investments and allows investors to redeem shares at any time. The value of the shares is tied to the value of investment assets of the fund. 501

open interest: The number of contracts outstanding. 532

operating expenses: The expenses incurred from a bank's ongoing operations. 343

operating income: The income earned on bank's ongoing operations. 342

operating target: Any of a set of variables, such as reserve aggregates or interest rates, that the Fed seeks to influence and that are responsive to its policy tools. 622

opportunity cost: The amount of interest (expected return) sacrificed by not holding an alternative asset. 115

options: Contracts that give the purchaser the option (right) to buy or sell the underlying financial instrument at a specified price, called the *exercise price* or *strike price*, within a specific period of time (the *term to expiration*). 553

overfunded pension plan: A plan which has assets greater than needed to make the projected benefit payments owed by the plan. 490

oversubscribed: A security issue where there are more offers to buy than there are securities available for sale. 490

over-the-counter (OTC) market: A secondary market in which dealers at different locations who have an inventory of securities stand ready to buy and sell securities "over the counter" to anyone who comes to them and is willing to accept their prices. 17

passbook savings account: Interest bearing savings accounts held at commercial banks. 402

Penny Benny: The Pension Benefit Guarantee Corporation, which is the government pension insurance agency. 467

Pension Benefit Guarantee Corporation (Penny Benny): A government agency that performs a role similar to that of the FDIC in that it insures pension benefits up to a limit if the company with an underfunded pension plan goes bankrupt. 467

pension plan: An asset pool that accumulates over an individual's working years and is paid out during the nonworking years. 462

political business cycle: A business cycle caused by expansion policies before an election. 605

portfolio insurance: A hedge with stock index futures that protects a portfolio from stock market risk. 545

preferred habitat theory: The theory that the interest rate on a long-term bond will equal the average of the short-term interest rates expected to occur over the life of the long-term bond plus a term premium that responds to supply and demand conditions for that bond. 153

preferred stock: Stock which has a fixed dividend that must be paid before common dividends. It often does not mature and usually does not provide the holder voting rights in the company. 259

premium: The amount paid for an option contract. 554

present discounted value: See *present value*.

present value: Today's value of a payment to be received in the future when the interest rate is *i*. Also called *present discounted value*. 43

primary market: A financial market in which new issues of a security are sold to initial buyers. 16

principal-agent problem: A moral hazard problem that occurs when the managers in control (the agents) act in their own interest rather than in the interest of the owners (the principals) due to differing sets of incentives. 303

private mortgage insurance (PMI): Insurance that protects the lender against losses from defaults on mortgage loans. 274

private pension plan: Pension plans sponsored by employers, groups and individuals. 464

property insurance: Insurance that protects against losses from fire, theft, storm, explosion, and neglect. 456

prospectus: A portion of the registration that is filed with the SEC and made available to the public before they buy a security. 488

public pension plan: A pension plan sponsored by a governmental body. 464

put option: An option contract that provides the right to sell a security at a specified price. 555

quotas: Restrictions on the quantity of foreign goods that can be imported. 194

random walk: The movements of a variable whose future changes cannot be predicted (are random) because, given today's value, the variable is just as likely to fall as to rise. 173

rate of capital gain: The change in a security's price relative to the initial purchase price. 58

rate of return: See *return*.

rational expectations: Expectations that reflect optimal forecasts (the best guess of the future) using all available information. 165

real bills doctrine: A guiding principle (now discredited) for the conduct of monetary policy that states that as long as loans are made to support the production of goods and services, providing reserves to the banking system to make these loans will not be inflationary. 628

real interest rate: The interest rate adjusted for expected changes in the price level (inflation) so that it more accurately reflects the true cost of borrowing. 67

real terms: Terms reflecting actual goods and services one can buy. 67

registered bonds: Require the owner of the bonds to register with the company to receive interest payments. Registered bonds have largely replaced bearer bonds which did not require registration. 253

registration statement: A statement that must be filed with the SEC on the sale of securities with over a 270-day maturity to the public. It contains information about the firm's financial condition, management, competition, industry, and experience. 488

Regulation Q: The regulation under which the Federal Reserve System has the power to set maximum interest rates that banks can pay on savings and time deposits. 36

Regulation Z: Also known as the truth in lending bill, it requires that lenders disclose the full cost of a loan to the borrower. 479

regulatory forbearance: Regulators refraining from exercising their regulatory right to put insolvent S&Ls out of business. 394

reinsurance: Allocates a portion of the risk to another company in exchange for a portion of the premium. 457

reinvestment risk: The interest-rate risk associated with the fact that the proceeds of short-term investments must be reinvested at a future interest rate that is uncertain. 60

repossession: The taking of an asset that has been pledged as collateral for a loan when that loan defaults. 476

Repurchase agreement: A form of loan where the borrower simultaneously contracts to sell securities and contracts to repurchase them, either on demand or on a specified date. 612

required reserve ratio: The fraction of deposits that the Fed requires be kept as reserves. 325, 589

required reserves: Reserves that are held to meet Fed requirements that a certain fraction of bank deposits be kept as reserves. 325, 589

reserve account: An account used to make insurance and tax payments due on property securing a mortgage loan. A portion of each monthly loan payment goes into the reserve account. 281

reserve currency: A currency such as the U.S. dollar, that is used by other countries to denominate the assets they hold as international reserves. 656

reserve for loan losses: An account which offsets the loan accounts on a lender's books that reflects the lender's project losses due to default. 479

reserve requirements: Regulation making it obligatory for depository institutions to keep a certain fraction of their deposits in accounts with the Fed. 36

reserves: Banks' holding of deposits in accounts with the Fed, plus currency that is physically held by banks (vault cash). 325, 589

Resolution Trust Corporation (RTC): A temporary agency created by FIRREA which was responsible for liquidating the assets of failed savings and loans. 399

restrictive covenants: Provisions that restrict and specify certain activities that a borrower can engage in. 254, 295

return: The payments to the owner of a security plus the change in the security's value, expressed as a fraction of its purchase price; or precisely called the *rate of return*. 57

return on assets (ROA): Net profit after taxes per dollar of assets. 336

return on equity (ROE): Net profit after taxes per dollar of equity capital. 336

revaluation: Resetting of the par value of a currency at a higher level. 657

revenue bonds: The source of income that is used to pay the interest and to retire revenue bonds is from a specific source, such as a toll road or the income from an electric generating plant. If this revenue source is unable to make the payments, the bonds can default, despite the issuing municipality being otherwise healthy. 251

risk: The degree of uncertainty associated with the return on an asset. 74

risk premium: The spread between the interest rate on bonds with default risk and the interest rate on default-free bonds. 139

risk structure of interest rates: The relationship among the various interest rates on bonds with the same term to maturity. 138

roll over: Renewing a debt when it matures. 473

Savings Association Insurance Fund (SAIF): A new deposit insurance fund created by FIRREA that replaces FSLIC and is administered by the FDIC. 399

seasoned issues: Securities that have been trading publicly for long enough to have let the market clearly establish the securities value. 487

secondary market: A financial market in which securities that have previously been issued (and are thus secondhand) can be resold. 17

secondary reserves: U.S. government and agency securities held by banks. 326

secured debt: Debt guaranteed by collateral. 295

secured loan: A loan guaranteed by collateral. 512

securitization: The process of transforming illiquid financial assets into marketable capital market instruments. 380

security: A claim on the borrower's future income that is sold by the borrower to the lender. Also called a *financial instrument*. 4

segmented markets theory: A theory of term structure that sees markets for different-maturity bonds as completely separated and segmented such that the interest rate for bonds of a given maturity is determined solely by supply of and demand for bonds of that maturity. 151

Separate Trading of Registered Interest and Principal Securities (STRIPS): A security that has the periodic interest payments separated from the final maturity payment and the two cash flows are sold to different investors. 249-250

share draft account: Accounts at credit unions that are similar to NOW accounts. 352

shelf registration: An arrangement with the Securities and Exchange Commission that allows a single registration document to be filed that permits multiple securities issues. 266

short position: A contractual obligation to deliver an underlying financial instrument. 528

short-term: With reference to a debt instrument, having a maturity of one year or less. 16

short sell: An arrangement with a broker where securities are borrowed and sold. The borrowed securities are replaced with securities purchased later. Short sells let investors earn profits from falling securities prices. 494

simple loan: A credit market instrument providing the borrower with an amount of funds that must be repaid to the lender at the maturity date along with an additional payment (interest). 42

sinking fund: A provision of many bond contracts that requires the issuer to set aside each year a portion of the final maturity payment so that investors can be certain the funds will be available at maturity. 254

special drawing rights (SDRs): An IMF-issued paper substitute for gold that functions as international reserves. 660

spot rate: The exchange rate at a given moment. 158, 189

spot transaction: The predominant type of exchange rate transaction, involving the immediate exchange of bank deposits denominated in different currencies. 189

state banks: State-chartered banks. 362

sterilized foreign exchange intervention: A foreign exchange intervention with an offsetting open market operation that leaves the monetary base unchanged. 647

stock: A security that is a claim on the earnings and assets of a corporation. 5

stock company: A firm that issue stock and has the objective of making a profit for its shareholders. 448

stock market risk: The risk associated with fluctuations in stock prices. 542

stock option: An option on an individual stock. 554

strike price: See *exercise price*.

superregional banks: Bank holding companies similar in size to money center banks, but whose head-quarters are not based in one of the money center cities (New York, Chicago, San Francisco). 368

supply curve: A curve depicting the relationship between quantity supplied and price when all other economic variables are held constant. 98

swap: A financial contract that obligates one party to exchange (swap) a set of payments it owns for a set of payments owned by another party. 564

syndicate: A group of investment banks which come together for the purpose of issuing a security. The syndicate spreads the risk of the issue among the members. Each participant attempts to market the security and shares in losses. 265, 490

systematic risk: The component of an asset's risk that cannot be eliminated by diversification . 77

T-account: A simplified balance sheet with lines in the form of a T that lists only the exchanges that occur in balance sheet times starting from some initial balance sheet position. 327

tariffs: Taxes on imported goods. 194

term security: A security with a specified maturity date. 229

term structure of interest rates: The relationship among interest rates on bonds with different terms to maturity. 138

theory of portfolio choice: The theory that the quantity demanded of an asset is (1) usually positively related to wealth, (2) positively related to its expected return relative to alternative assets, (3) negatively related to the risk of its return relative to alternative assets, and (4) positively related to its liquidity relative to alternative assets. 76

theory of purchasing power parity (PPP): The theory that exchange rates between any two currencies will adjust to reflect changes in the price levels of the two countries. 192

thrift institutions (thrifts): Savings and loan associations, mutual savings banks, and credit unions. 30

trade association: Groups of credit unions that have organized to provide a variety of services to a large number of credit unions. 409

trade balance: The difference between merchandise exports and imports. 652

transactions costs: The time and money spent trying to exchange financial assets, goods, or services. 25

Treasury bills: Securities sold by the federal government with initial maturities of less than one year. They are often considered the lowest risk security available. 19

tombstone: A large block ad placed in financial newspapers advertising that a security will be offered for sale by an underwriter or group of underwriters. 490

underfunded: Describing a pension plan in which the contributions and their earnings are insufficient to pay out the defined benefits when they come due. 463

underfunded pension plan: A plan which does not have the assets available to make the benefit payments project owned by the plan. 463

undersubscribed: A securities issue which has fewer offers to buy than there are securities available for sale. 490

underwriters: Investment banks that guarantee prices on securities to corporations and then sell the securities to the public. 448

underwriting: Guaranteeing prices on securities to corporations and then selling the securities to the public. 264

unexploited profit opportunity: A situation in which an investor can earn a higher than normal return. 170

unsecured debt: Debt not guaranteed by collateral. 295

unsterilized foreign exchange intervention: A foreign exchange intervention in which a central bank allows the purchase or sale of domestic currency to affect the monetary base. 647

U.S. Central Credit Union: A central bank for credit unions that was organized in 1974 and provides banking services to the state central credit unions. 408

usury: Charging an excessive or inordinate interest rate on a loan. 479

wealth: All resources owned by an individual, including all assets. 74

wealth elasticity of demand: The measure of how much, with everything else unchanged, demand for an asset changes in percentage terms in response to a percentage change in wealth. 74

wholesale market: Markets where extremely large transactions occur such as for money market funds or foreign currency. 218

World Bank: The International Bank for Reconstruction and Redevelopment, an international organization that provides long-term loans to assist developing countries in building dams, roads, and other physical capital that would contribute to their economic development. 656

vault cash: Currency that is physically held by banks and stored in vaults overnight. 325

venture capital firm: A financial intermediary that pools the resources of its partners and uses the funds to help entrepreneurs start up new businesses. 306

yield curve: A plot of the interest rates for particular types of bonds with different terms to maturity. 146

yield on a discount basis: The measure of interest rates by which dealers in bill markets quote the interest rate on U.S. Treasury bills. Also known as the *discount yield.* 52

yield to maturity: The interest rate that equates the present value of payments received from a credit market instrument with its value today. 44

zero-coupon bond: See *discount bond.*

Answers to Selected Questions and Problems

CHAPTER 1

2. Businesses would cut investment spending because the cost of financing this spending is now higher, and consumers would be less likely to purchase a house or a car because the cost of financing their purchase is higher.

4. No. People who borrow to purchase a house or a car are worse off because it costs them more to finance their purchase; however, savers benefit because they can earn higher interest rates on their savings.

6. Higher stock prices mean that consumers' wealth is higher and so they will be more likely to increase their spending.

8. It makes British goods more expensive relative to American goods. American businesses will find it easier to sell their goods in the United States and abroad, and the demand for their products will rise.

10. In the mid- to late 1970s and the late 1980s and early 1990s, the value of the dollar was low, making travel abroad relatively more expensive; that would have been a good time to vacation in the United States and see the Grand Canyon. As the dollar's value rose in the early 1980s, travel abroad became relatively cheaper, making it a good time to visit the Tower of London.

12. Savings and loan associations, mutual savings banks, credit unions, insurance companies, mutual funds, pension funds, and finance companies.

14. The profitability of financial institutions is affected by changes in interest rates, stock prices, and foreign exchange rates; fluctuations in these variables expose these institutions to risk.

CHAPTER 2

1. The share of IBM stock is an asset for its owner because it entitles the owner to a share of the earnings and assets of IBM. The share is a liability for IBM because it is a claim on its earnings and assets by the owner of the share.

3. Yes, because the absence of financial markets means that funds cannot be channeled to people who have the most productive use for them. Entrepreneurs then cannot acquire funds to set up businesses that would help the economy grow rapidly.

5. This statement is false. Prices in secondary markets determine the prices that firms issuing securities receive in primary markets. In addition, secondary markets make securities more liquid and thus easier to sell in the primary markets. Therefore, secondary markets are, if anything, more important than primary markets.

7. Because you know your family member better than a stranger, you know more about the borrower's honesty, propensity for risk taking, and other traits. There is less asymmetric information than with a stranger and less likelihood of an adverse selection problem, with the result that you are more likely to lend to the family member.

9. Loan sharks can threaten their borrowers with bodily harm if borrowers take actions that might jeopardize paying off the loan. Hence borrowers from a loan shark are less likely to engage in moral hazard.

11. Yes, because even if you know that a borrower is taking actions that might jeopardize paying off the loan, you must still stop the borrower from doing so. Because that may be costly, you may not spend the time and effort to reduce moral hazard, and so moral hazard remains a problem.

13. Because the costs of making the loan to your neighbor are high (legal fees, fees for a credit check, and so on), you will probably not be able to earn 5% on the loan after your expenses even though it has a 10% interest rate. You are better off depositing your savings with a financial intermediary and earning 5% interest. In addition, you are likely to bear less risk by depositing your savings at the bank rather than lending them to your neighbor.

15. Increased discussion of foreign financial markets in the U.S. press and the growth in markets for international financial instruments such as Eurodollars and Eurobonds.

CHAPTER 3

1. Less. It would be worth $1/(1 + 0.20) = \$0.83$ when the interest rate is 20%, rather than $1/(1 + 0.10) = \$0.91$ when the interest rate is 10%.

3. $\$1100/(1 + 0.10) + \$1210/(1 + 0.10)^2 + \$1331/(1 + 0.10)^3 = \$3000$.

5. $\$2000 = \$100/(1 + i) + \$100/(1 + i)^2 + \cdots + \$100/(1 + i)^{20} + \$1000/(1 + i)^{20}$.

7. 14.9%, derived as follows: The present value of the $2 million payment five years from now is $\$2/(1 + i)^5$ million which equals the $1 million loan. Thus $1 = 2/(1 + i)^5$. Solving for i, $(1 + i)^5 = 2$, so that $i = \sqrt[5]{2} - 1 = 0.149 = 14.9\%$.

9. If the one-year bond did not have a coupon payment, its yield to maturity would be ($1000 − $800)/$800 = $200/$800 = 0.25 = 25%. Since it does have a coupon payment, its yield to maturity must be greater than 25%. On the other hand, because the current yield is a good approximation of the yield to maturity for a twenty-year bond, we know that the yield to maturity on this bond is approximately 15%. Therefore, the one-year bond has a higher yield to maturity.

11. You would rather own the Treasury bill because it has a higher yield to maturity. As the example in the text indicates, the discount yield's understatement of the yield to maturity for a one-year bond is substantial, exceeding one percentage point. Thus the yield to maturity on the one-year bill would be greater than 9%, the yield to maturity on the one-year Treasury bond.

13. No. If interest rates rise sharply in the future, long-term bonds may suffer such a sharp fall in price that their return might be quite low, possibly even negative.

15. The observers are right. They reason that nominal interest rates were below expected rates of inflation in the late 1970s, making real interest rates negative. The expected inflation rate, however, fell much faster than nominal interest rates in the mid-1980s, so nominal interest rates were above the expected inflation rate and real rates became positive.

17. The present value of the five $80 coupon payments plus the $1000 face value of the bond are, respectively, $77.67, $75.41, $73.21, $71.08, $69.01, and $862.61, which sum to a total present value of $1228.99. The weights for these payments are, respectively, 0.0631982, 0.0613593, 0.0595692, 0.0578361, 0.0561518, and 0.7018853. The duration is then the sum of the weighted maturities: (1 × 0.0631982) + (2 × 0.0613593) + (3 × 0.0595692) + (4 × 0.0578361) + (5 × 0.0561518 + (5 × 0.7018853) = 4.3861543 years.

19. The approximate percentage change in the price is $-DUR \times \Delta i/(1 + i) = -8 \times 0.01/1.07 = -0.075 = -7.5\%$.

CHAPTER 4

2. (a) More, because your wealth has increased; (b) more, because it has become more liquid; (c) less, because its expected return has fallen relative to Polaroid stock; (d) more, because it has become less risky relative to stocks; (e) less, because its expected return has fallen.

4. (a) More, because they have become more liquid; (b) more, because their expected return has risen relative to stocks; (c) less, because they have become less liquid relative to stocks; (d) less, because their expected return has fallen; (e) more, because they have become more liquid.

6. Purchasing shares in the pharmaceutical company is more likely to reduce my overall risk because the correlation of returns on my investment in a football team with the returns on the pharmaceutical company should be low. By contrast, the correlation of returns on an investment in a football team and an investment in a basketball team are probably pretty high, so in this case there would be little risk reduction if I invested in both.

8. True. When an asset's beta is higher, its systematic risk is higher. Since this systematic risk cannot be diversified away, the asset is less desirable, everything else being equal, and the demand for the asset will be lower. (Note that we assume that investors are risk-averse and hence do not like risk.)

10. It wouldn't matter from a risk point of view because both stocks have a beta of 0.5 and have the same amount of systematic risk.

12. Risk premium = $R^e - R_f = \beta(R^e_m - R_f) = 3(8\% - 5\%) = 9\%$.

14. The expected returns of Security 2 and Security 3 are both equal to 7.5%, and the expected return on the portfolio is 0.5(7.5%) + 0.5(7.5%) = 7.5%. The standard deviation of the return on Security 2 and Security 3 are also both equal to 7.5%. The covariance of returns on Security 2 and Security 3 = σ_{23} = 0.1(20% − 7.5%)(−5% − 7.5%) + 0.2(5% − 7.5%)(10% − 7.5%) + 0.2 (15% − 7.5%)(15% − 7.5%) + 0.2 (10% − 7.5%)(5% − 7.5%) + 0.2 (0% − 7.5%)(0% − 7.5%) + 0.1(−5% − 7.5%) (20% − 7.5%) = −11.25%. The standard deviation of the portfolio is then $\sqrt{(0.5)^2(7.5\%)^2 + (0.5)^2(7.5\%)^2 + 2(0.5)(0.5)(-11.25\%}$ = $\sqrt{22.5\%}$ = 4.7%. Since the expected return on this portfolio is the same as that made up equally of Securities 1 and 2 but the standard deviation of the return on the portfolio made up equally of Securities 1 and 2 is lower than that of this portfolio (2.7% versus 4.7%), you would prefer to hold the portfolio made up equally of Securities 1 and 2.

CHAPTER 5

1. When the Fed sells bonds to the public, it increases the supply of bonds, thus shifting the supply curve B^s to the right. The result is that the intersection of the supply and demand curves B^s and B^d occurs at a higher equilibrium interest rate, and the interest rate rises. With the liquidity preference framework, the decrease in the money supply shifts the money supply curve M^s to the left, and the equilibrium interest rate rises. The answer from the loanable funds framework is consistent with the answer from the liquidity preference framework.

3. When the price level rises, the quantity of money in real terms falls (holding the nominal supply of money constant); to restore their holdings of money in real terms to their former level, people will want to hold a greater nominal quantity of money. Thus the money demand curve M^d shifts to the right, and the interest rate rises.

6. Interest rates would rise. A sudden increase in people's expectations of future real estate prices raises the expected return on real estate relative to bonds, so the demand for bonds falls. The demand curve B^d shifts to the left, and the equilibrium interest rate rises.

8. In the loanable funds framework, the increased riskiness of bonds lowers the demand for bonds. The demand curve B^d shifts to the left, and the equilib-

rium interest rate rises. The same answer is found in the liquidity preference framework. The increased riskiness of bonds relative to money increases the demand for money. The money demand curve M^d shifts to the right, and the equilibrium interest rate rises.

10. Yes, interest rates will rise. The lower commission on stocks makes them more liquid than bonds, and the demand for bonds will fall. The demand curve B^d will therefore shift to the left, and the equilibrium interest rate will rise.

12. The interest rate on the AT&T bonds will rise. Because people now expect interest rates to rise, the expected return on long-term bonds such as the $8\frac{1}{8}$s of 2022 will fall, and the demand for these bonds will decline. The demand curve B^d will therefore shift to the left, and the equilibrium interest rate will rise.

14. Interest rates will rise. When bond prices become volatile and bonds become riskier, the demand for bonds will fall. The demand curve B^d will shift to the left, and the equilibrium interest rate will rise.

CHAPTER 6

2. U.S. Treasury bills have lower default risk and more liquidity than negotiable CDs. Consequently, the demand for Treasury bills is higher, and they have a lower interest rate.

4. True. When bonds of different maturities are close substitutes, a rise in interest rates for one bond causes the interest rates for others to rise because the expected returns on bonds of different maturities cannot get too far out of line.

6. (a) The yield to maturity would be 5% for a one-year bond, 6% for a two-year bond, 6.33% for a three-year bond, 6.5% for a four-year bond, and 6.6% for a five-year bond. (b) The yield to maturity would be 5% for a one-year bond, 4.5% for a two-year bond, 4.33% for a three-year bond, 4.25% for a four-year bond, and 4.2% for a five-year bond. The upward-sloping yield curve in (a) would be even steeper if people preferred short-term bonds over long-term bonds because long-term bonds would then have a positive risk premium. The downward-sloping yield curve in (b) would be less steep and might even have a slight positive upward slope if the long-term bonds have a positive risk premium.

8. The flat yield curve at shorter maturities suggests that short-term interest rates are expected to fall moderately in the near future, while the steep upward slope of the yield curve at longer maturities indicates that interest rates further into the future are expected to rise. Because interest rates and expected inflation move together, the yield curve suggests that the market expects inflation to fall moderately in the near future but to rise later on.

10. The reduction in income tax rates would make the tax-exempt privilege for municipal bonds less valuable, and they would be less desirable than taxable Treasury bonds. The resulting decline in the demand for municipal bonds and increase in demand for Treasury bonds would raise interest rates on municipal bonds while causing interest rates on Treasury bonds to fall.

12. Lower brokerage commissions for corporate bonds would make them more liquid and thus increase their demand, which would lower their risk premium.

14. The expected one-year interest rate two years from now is $i^{e}_{t+2} = [(1 + i_{3t} - k_{3t})^{3}/(1 + i_{2t} - k_{2t})^{2}] - 1 = [(1 + 0.06 - 0.0035)^{3}/(1 + 0.05 - 0.0025)^{2}] - 1 = 0.075 = 7.5\%$.

CHAPTER 7

1. False. Expectations can be highly inaccurate and still be rational because optimal forecasts are not necessarily accurate: A forecast is optimal if it is the best possible even if the forecast errors are large.

3. No, because he could improve the accuracy of his forecasts by predicting that tomorrow's interest rates will be identical to today's. His forecasts are therefore not optimal, and he does not have rational expectations.

5. No, you shouldn't buy stocks because the rise in the money supply is publicly available information that will be already incorporated into stock prices. Hence you cannot expect to earn more than the equilibrium return on stocks by acting on the money supply information.

7. No, because this is publicly available information and is already reflected in stock prices. The optimal forecast of stock returns will equal the equilibrium return, so there is no benefit from selling your stocks.

9. No, if the person has no better information than the rest of the market. An expected price rise of 10% over the next month implies over a 100% annual return on IBM stock, which certainly exceeds its equilibrium return. This would mean that there is an

unexploited profit opportunity in the market, which would have been eliminated in an efficient market. The only time that the person's expectations could be rational is if the person had information unavailable to the market that allowed him or her to beat the market.

11. False. The people with better information are exactly those who make the market more efficient by eliminating unexploited profit opportunities. These people can profit from their better information.

13. True in principle. Foreign exchange rates are a random walk over a short interval such as a week because changes in the exchange rate are unpredictable. If a change were predictable, large unexploited profit opportunities would exist in the foreign exchange market. If the foreign exchange market is efficient, these unexploited profit opportunities cannot exist and so the foreign exchange rate will approximately follow a random walk.

15. False. Although human fear may be the source of stock market crashes, that does not imply that there are unexploited profit opportunities in the market. Nothing in rational expectations theory rules out large changes in stock prices as a result of fears on the part of the investing public.

CHAPTER 8

2. False. Although a weak currency has the negative effect of making it more expensive to buy foreign goods or to travel abroad, it may help domestic industry. Domestic goods become cheaper relative to foreign goods, and the demand for domestically produced goods increases. The resulting higher sales of domestic products may lead to higher employment, a beneficial effect on the economy.

4. It predicts that the value of the French franc will fall 5% in terms of dollars.

6. Even though the Japanese price level rose relative to the American, the yen appreciated because the increase in Japanese productivity relative to American productivity made it possible for the Japanese to continue to sell their goods at a profit at a high value of the yen.

8. The pound depreciates but overshoots, declining by more in the short run than in the long run. Consider Britain the domestic country. The rise in the money supply leads to a higher domestic price level in the long run, which leads to a higher expected future exchange rate. The resulting expected depreciation

of the pound raises the expected return on foreign deposits, shifting RET^F to the right. The rise in the money supply lowers the interest rate on pound deposits in the short run, which shifts RET^D to the left. The short-run outcome is a lower equilibrium exchange rate. However, in the long run, the domestic interest rate returns to its previous value, and RET^D shifts back to its original position. The exchange rate rises to some extent, although it still remains below its initial position.

10. The dollar will depreciate. A rise in nominal interest rates but a decline in real interest rates implies a rise in expected inflation that produces an expected depreciation of the dollar that is larger than the increase in the domestic interest rate. As a result, the expected return on foreign deposits rises by more than the expected return on domestic deposits. RET^F shifts rightward more than RET^D, so the equilibrium exchange rate falls.

12. The dollar will depreciate. An increased demand for imports would lower the expected future exchange rate and result in an expected appreciation of the foreign currency. The higher resulting expected return on foreign deposits shifts the RET^F schedule to the right, and the equilibrium exchange rate falls.

14. The contraction of the German money supply will increase German interest rates and raise the future value of the mark, both of which will shift RET^F (with Germany as the foreign country) to the right. The result is a decline in the value of the dollar.

CHAPTER 9

1. The money markets can be characterized as having securities that trade in one year or less, are of large denomination, and are very liquid.

3. Banks have higher costs than the money markets owing to the need to maintain reserve requirements. The lower cost structure of the money markets, coupled with the economies of scale resulting from high volume and large-denomination securities, allows for higher interest rates.

5. Following the Great Depression, regulators were primarily concerned with stopping banks from failing. By removing interest-rate competition, bank risk was substantially reduced. The problem with these regulations was that when market interest rates rose above the established interest-rate ceiling, investors withdrew their funds from banks.

7. Businesses both invest and borrow in the money markets. They borrow to meet short-term cash flow needs, often by issuing commercial paper. They invest in all types of money market securities as an alternative to holding idle cash balances.

9. Life insurance companies can invest for the long term because the timing for their liabilities is known with reasonable accuracy. Property and casualty insurance companies cannot predict the natural disasters that cause large payouts on policies.

11. In competitive bidding for securities, buyers submit bids. A noncompetitive bidder accepts the average of the rate paid by the competitive bidders.

13. The Federal Reserve cannot directly set the federal funds rate of interest. It can influence the interest rate by adding funds to or withdrawing reserves from the economy.

15. Banker's acceptances substitute the creditworthiness of a bank for that of a business. When a company sells a product to a company it is unfamiliar with, it often prefers to have the promise of a bank that payment will be made.

CHAPTER 10

1. Investors use capital markets for long-term investment purposes. They use money markets, which have lower yields, primarily for temporary or transaction purposes.

3. The primary market is for securities being issued for the very first time, and the issuer receives the funds paid for the security. The secondary market is for securities that have been issued previously but are being trading among investors.

5. NASDAQ is a computer network that allows traders to monitor stocks traded on the over-the-counter market. It provides current bid and ask prices on about 4500 actively traded securities.

7. Treasury bills mature in less than 1 year, Treasury notes mature in 1 to 10 years, and Treasury bonds mature in 10 to 30 years.

9. Agencies that issue securities include the Ginnie Mae (formerly the Government National Mortgage Association), the Federal Housing Administration, the Veterans Administration, the Federal National Mortgage Association, and the Student Loan Marketing Association. The first four fund mortgage loans and the last funds college student loans.

11. A sinking fund contains funds set aside by the issuer of a bond to pay for the redemption of the bond when it matures. Because a sinking fund increases the likelihood that a firm will have the funds to pay off the bonds as required, investors like the feature.

As a result, interest rates are lower on securities with sinking funds.

13. Stocks do not mature, do not pay a fixed amount every period, and often give holders the right to vote on management issues.

15. By forming a syndicate, the risk of issuing a security is spread among many different firms.

CHAPTER 11

1. Securities in the mortgage markets are collateralized by real estate.

3. The global market for loans results in competition that keeps the rates low.

5. A lien is a publicly recorded notice that a piece of real property has been pledged as collateral. Mortgage lenders file liens to secure loans.

7. Lenders may require private mortgage insurance.

9. The Veterans Administration and the Federal Housing Administration guarantee lenders against losses from loans insured by them. Conventional loans do not have this guarantee, so the lender usually requires private mortgage insurance.

11. The goal of the graduated-payment loan is to let the borrower qualify by reducing the first few years' payments, whereas the goal of the growing-equity loan is to let the borrower pay off early.

13. The bank accepts the home as security and advances money each month. When the borrower dies, the borrower's estate sells the property to retire the debt.

15. The payments on a pool of mortgages are sent by the borrowers to a trustee, who then passes the payments through to holders of securities that are backed by the pass-through.

CHAPTER 12

2. Financial intermediaries develop expertise in such areas as computer technology so that they can inexpensively provide liquidity services such as checking accounts that lower transactions costs for depositors. Financial intermediaries can also take advantage of economies of scale and engage in large transactions that have a lower cost per dollar per transaction.

4. Standard accounting principles make profit verification easier, thereby reducing adverse selection and moral hazard problems in financial markets and hence making them operate better. Standard accounting principles make it easier for investors to screen out good firms from bad firms, thereby reducing the adverse selection problem in financial markets. In addition, they make it harder for managers to understate profits, thereby reducing the principal-agent (moral hazard) problem.

6. Smaller firms that are not well known are the most likely to use bank financing. Since it is harder for investors to acquire information about these firms, it will be hard for the firms to sell securities in the financial markets. Banks that specialize in collecting information about smaller firms will then be the only outlet these firms have for financing their activities.

8. Yes. The person who is putting her life savings into her business has more to lose if she takes on too much risk or engages in personally beneficial activities that don't lead to higher profits. So she will act more in the interest of the lender, making it more likely that the loan will be paid off.

10. True. If the borrower turns out to be a bad credit risk and goes broke, the lender loses less because the collateral can be sold to make up any losses on the loan. Thus adverse selection is not as severe a problem.

12. The separation of ownership and control creates a principal-agent problem. The managers (the agents) do not have as strong an incentive to maximize profits as the owners (the principals). Thus the managers might not work hard, might engage in wasteful spending on personal perks, or might pursue business strategies that enhance their personal power but do not increase profits.

14. A stock market crash reduces the net worth of firms and so increases the moral hazard problem. With less of an equity stake, owners have a greater incentive to take on risky projects and spend corporate funds on items that benefit them personally. A stock market crash, which increases the moral hazard problem, thus makes it less likely that lenders will be paid back. So lending and investment will decline, creating a financial crisis in which financial markets do not work well and the economy suffers.

CHAPTER 13

2. The rank from most to least liquid is (c), (b), (a), (d).

4. Reserves drop by $500. The T-account for the First National Bank is as follows:

First National Bank

Assets		Liabilities	
Reserves	−$500	Checkable deposits	−$500

6. The bank would rather have the balance sheet shown in this problem because after it loses $50 million due to deposit outflow, the bank would still have excess reserves of $5 million: $50 million in reserves minus required reserves of $45 million (10% of the $450 million of deposits). Thus the bank would not have to alter its balance sheet further and would not incur any costs as a result of the deposit outflow. By contrast, with the balance sheet in Problem 5, the bank would have a shortfall of reserves of $20 million ($25 million in reserves minus the required reserves of $45 million). In this case the bank will incur costs when it raises the necessary reserves through the methods described in the text.

8. No. When you turn a customer down, you may lose that customer's business forever, which is extremely costly. Instead, you might go out and borrow from other banks, corporations, or the Fed to obtain funds so that you can make the customer's loan. Alternatively, you might sell negotiable CDs or some of your securities to acquire the necessary funds.

10. You would want to make short-term loans. Then, when these loans mature, you will be able to make loans at higher interest rates, which will generate more income for the bank.

12. True. Banks can now pursue new loan business much more aggressively than in the past because when they see profitable loan opportunities, they can use liability management to acquire new funds and expand the bank's business.

14. Interest expenses have large fluctuations because interest rates fluctuate so much; provisions for loan losses fluctuate a lot because when the economy turns down or a particular sector of the economy deteriorates, the potential for loan losses rises dramatically.

16. The net interest margin measures the difference between interest income and expenses. It is important because it indicates whether asset and liability management is being done properly so that the bank earns substantial income on its assets and has low costs on its liabilities.

18. To lower capital and raise *ROE,* holding its assets constant, it can pay out more dividends or buy back some of its shares. Alternatively, it can keep its capital constant but increase the amount of its assets by acquiring new funds and then seeking out new loan business or purchasing more securities with these new funds.

20. It can raise $1 million of capital by issuing new stock. It can cut its dividend payments by $1 million, thereby increasing its retained earnings by $1 million. It can decrease the amount of its assets so that the amount of its capital relative to its assets increases, thereby meeting the capital requirements.

CHAPTER 14

2. (a) Office of the Controller of the Currency; (b) the Federal Reserve; (c) state banking authorities and the FDIC; (d) the Federal Reserve.

4. New technologies such as electronic banking facilities are frequently shared by several banks, so these facilities are not classified as branches. Thus they can be used by banks to escape limitations to offering services in other states and, in effect, to escape limitations from restrictions on branching.

6. International banking has been encouraged by giving special tax treatment and relaxed branching regulations to Edge Act corporations and to international banking facilities (IBFs); this was done to make American banks more competitive with foreign banks. The hope is that it will create more banking jobs in the United States.

8. No, because the Saudi-owned bank is subject to the same regulations as the American-owned bank.

10. The rise of inflation and the resulting higher interest rates on alternatives to checkable deposits meant that banks had a big shrinkage in this low-cost way of raising funds. The innovation of money market mutual funds also meant that the banks lost checking account business. The abolishment of Regulation Q and the appearance of NOW accounts did help decrease disintermediation but raised the cost of funds for American banks, which now had to pay higher interest rates on checkable and other deposits. Foreign banks were also able to tap a large pool of domestic savings, thereby lowering their cost of funds relative to American banks.

12. The growth of the commercial paper market and the development of the junk bond market meant that corporations were now able to issue securities

rather than borrow from banks, thus eroding the competitive advantage of banks on the lending side. Securitization has enabled other financial institutions to originate loans, again taking away some of the banks' loan business.

CHAPTER 15

1. All of the depositors at a mutual bank are owners of the firm. Instead of receiving interest payments, they receive dividend income.

3. The primary assets of S&Ls are loans, for the most part mortgage loans.

5. Because depositors were insured by the government against losses, they had no incentive to monitor bank management.

7. The net worth ratio is the most common measure of capital adequacy.

9. Credit unions are mandated to provide financial services to consumers rather than corporate customers.

11. Only people living in a certain geographic area or employed in a specific business or by a particular employer are eligible for membership in a credit union.

13. The common bond membership rule restricts membership in any particular credit union so that the average size of credit unions is substantially lower than for commercial banks.

15. The main advantages of credit unions are employer support, tax-exempt status, and strong trade associations.

CHAPTER 16

2. There would be adverse selection because people who might want to burn their property for some personal gain would actively try to obtain substantial fire insurance policies. Moral hazard could also be a problem because a person with a fire insurance policy has less incentive to take measures to prevent a fire.

4. Regulations that restrict banks from holding risky assets directly decrease the moral hazard of risk taking by the bank. Requirements that force banks to have a large amount of capital also decrease the banks' incentives for risk taking because banks now have more to lose if they fail. Such regulations will not completely eliminate the moral hazard problem because bankers have incentives to hide their holdings of risky assets from the regulators and to overstate the amount of their capital.

6. The S&L crisis did not occur until the 1980s because interest rates stayed low before then, so S&Ls were not subjected to losses from high interest rates. Also, the opportunities for risk taking were not available until the 1980s, when legislation and financial innovation made it easier for S&Ls to take on more risk, thus greatly increasing the adverse selection and moral hazard problems.

8. FIRREA provided funds for the S&L bailout, created the Resolution Trust Corporation to manage the resolution of insolvent thrifts, eliminated the Federal Home Loan Bank Board and gave its regulatory role to the Office of Thrift Supervision, eliminated the FSLIC and turned its insurance role and regulatory responsibilities over to the FDIC, imposed restrictions on thrift activities similar to those in effect before 1982, increased the capital requirements to those adhered to by commercial banks, and increased the enforcement powers of thrift regulators.

10. If political candidates receive campaign funds from the government and are restricted in the amount they spend, they will have less need to satisfy lobbyists to win elections. As a result, they may have greater incentives to act in the interest of taxpayers (the principals), and so the political process might improve.

12. Eliminating or limiting the amount of deposit insurance would help reduce the moral hazard of excessive risk taking on the part of banks. It would, however, make bank failures and panics more likely, so it might not be a very good idea.

14. The economy would benefit from reduced moral hazard; that is, banks would not want to take on too much risk because doing so would increase their deposit insurance premiums. The problem is, however, that it is difficult to monitor the degree of risk in bank assets because often only the bank making the loans knows how risky they are.

CHAPTER 17

1. People carry insurance because they are risk-averse and prefer to know their wealth with certainty.

3. Information asymmetry exists when one party to a transaction knows more about the situation than the other does. Often the person buying insurance knows more about the risk than the insurance company knows.

5. Insurance companies protect themselves by requiring inspections and medical examinations, insuring groups rather than individuals, and insisting on a deductible.

7. Most are stock companies.

9. Term life insurance pays a death benefit if the policyholder dies; no other benefit is paid. Whole policies pay a death benefit but also include a savings program that pays out if the policyholder lives.

11. Reinsurance allocates a portion of the risk to another company in exchange for a portion of the premium.

13. A more sophisticated public, greater awareness of providing for retirement, and a lack of confidence in Social Security have led to growth in private pension plans.

15. The demographics suggest that more people will be retiring than will be entering the workforce in the future. With fewer people paying into the plan and more taking out, it could go bankrupt.

CHAPTER 18

1. A balloon loan requires that a single large payment be made when the loan matures, whereas on an installment loan, the borrower makes a series of small, equal payments.

3. They often have poor credit records, low incomes, or inferior security. All of these factors make them unacceptable to banks.

5. Yes, because there is no well-established secondary market for their loans.

7. Factoring is selling accounts receivable to a finance company. The selling firm gets immediate cash for its sales and avoids having to go after its customers for collections.

9. Under a floor plan, the finance company holds the inventory as security and only releases its lien on the inventory when the items are sold and the loan is paid.

11. The tax code allows the interest paid on loans secured by homes to be deducted from taxes. This lowers the effective cost of the debt.

13. Regulation Z requires that the company disclose the annual percentage rate charged on loans in a prominent and understandable fashion.

15. No, consumers did not perceive any great benefit to dealing with a single firm for all of their financial needs.

CHAPTER 19

1. Regulators felt that investment banking was riskier and had led to bank failures during the Great Depression.

3. When an offering is underwritten, the investment banker purchases the issue at a prespecified price. In a best-efforts issue, the investment banker does not take ownership.

5. No, a SEC review simply determines if the proper documents have been filed.

7. It is better to be fully subscribed because oversubscription indicates that the investment bankers priced the security too low.

9. In a hostile takeover, the target firm does not want control to pass to the acquiring firm, and so its management makes every effort to prevent the takeover from happening. In a merger, both sides work together to expedite the union of the firms.

11. A market order has the broker buy the security at the current market price. A limit order sets a maximum price for buying the security and a minimum price for selling the security.

13. Banks object because legislation prevents banks from entering the brokerage business but does not prevent brokers from entering the banking business.

15. Load funds charge fees; no-load funds do not.

CHAPTER 20

2. Secured loans are an important method of lending for financial institutions because if the borrower defaults, the financial institution can take title to the collateral, sell it off, and use the proceeds to offset any losses on the loan. Thus the financial institution can worry less about the adverse selection problem because it has some protection even if the borrower was a bad credit risk.

4. To reduce adverse selection, a banker needs to screen out bad credit risks by learning as much as possible about potential borrowers. Similarly, to minimize moral hazard, the banker must continually monitor borrowers to see that they are complying with restrictive loan covenants. Hence it pays for the banker to be nosy.

6. False. Although diversification is a desirable strategy for a bank, it may still make sense for a bank to specialize in certain types of lending. For example, a bank may have developed expertise in screening and monitoring a particular kind of loan, thereby improving its ability to handle problems of adverse selection and moral hazard.

8. Rate-sensitive assets increase by $5 million, so *GAP* goes from −$17.5 million to −$12.5 million. Because *GAP* falls in absolute value, the effect of changes in interest rates on its profits and hence on its interest-rate risk is smaller.

10. The manager raises the estimate of rate-sensitive liabilities by $2.25 million so that *GAP* goes from −$17.5 million to −$19.75 million. Because *GAP* rises in absolute value, the effect of changes in interest-rates on its profits and hence its interest rate risk is larger. If interest rates rise by 5 percentage points, profits next year change by $\Delta I = GAP \times \Delta i = -\$19.75$ million $\times 0.05 = -\$0.9875$ million.

12. The duration gap is now $DUR_{GAP} = DUR_A - (L/A \times DUR_L) = 4 - (95/100 \times 2) = 2.1$ years. The percentage change in net worth as a percentage of assets is $\%\Delta NW = -DUR_{GAP} \times \Delta i /(1 + i) = -2.1 \times 0.02/(1 + 0.10) = -0.038 = -3.8\%$. With $100 million of assets, net worth declines by $3.8 million, from $5 million to $1.2 million.

14. It should solve the following equation: $0 = 4 - (95/100 \times DUR_L)$. This yields a duration of liabilities DUR_L of 4.2 years.

16. Interest-rate risk stays the same because rate-sensitive assets and rate-sensitive liabilities increase by an equal amount, leaving the income gap the same. The Friendly Finance Company still has an income gap of $12 million, and to eliminate it, it could either reduce its rate-sensitive assets to $43 million or increase its rate-sensitive liabilities to $55 million.

18. The duration gap is now $DUR_{GAP} = DUR_A - (L/A \times DUR_L) = 2 - (90/100 \times 4) = -1.6$ years. The percentage change in net worth as a percentage of assets is $\%\Delta NW = -DUR_{GAP} \times \Delta i/(1 + i) = -(-1.6) \times 0.03/(1 + 0.08) = 0.044 = 4.4\%$. With $100 million of assets, net worth increases by $4.4 million, from $10 million to $14.4 million.

20. It should solve the following equation: $0 = 2 - (90/100 \times DUR_L)$. This yields a duration of liabilities DUR_L of 2.22 years.

CHAPTER 21

2. You would enter into a contract that specifies that you will sell the $25 million of 7s of 2010 at a price of 110 one year from now.

4. Forward contracts are subject to default risk, so each party to the contract must have information about the honesty and financial health of the other party to the contract. This is not necessary with a futures contract because buyers and sellers sign the contract with the futures exchange, not with each other. All buyers and sellers need to know about is

the reliability of the exchange, and this requires much less information than knowing about each other.

6. The price rises by 3 points, which means that you have suffered a loss of $3000 on your contract. This amount is subtracted from your margin account, leaving you with no money in the account. To meet the margin requirement of $2000, you will be required to add $2000 to your account.

8. You have a loss of 6 points or, $6000 per contract.

10. The hedge ratio is $HR = (\Delta P_a/\Delta P_f) \times \beta_{af} = 7/6 \times 1.2 = 1.4$. So you should sell $HR \times (PV_a/PV_f) = 1.4 \times (\$15 \text{ million}/\$100{,}000) = 210$ contracts.

12. The value of the futures contracts is $V_F = -(V_A \times DUR_{GAP})/DUR_F = -(\$200 \text{ million} \times 3)/3.5 = -\$171.4$ million. With contract amounts of $100,000, you should sell 1714 contracts.

14. The number of contracts you should sell = beta × value of portfolio/value of contract = $1.2 \times \$300$ million/$(450 \times \$500) = 1600$ contracts.

16. You want to buy $100 million of S&P futures with a delivery date close to six months from now. At the price of 500, this amounts to $100 million/$(500 \times \$500) = 400$ contracts.

18. You would want to enter into a contract in which you agree to deliver 30 million French francs six months from now in exchange for U.S. $3 million.

20. You would want to buy DM 10 million worth of June deutsche mark futures contracts. Since the contract is DM 125,000, you should buy 80 contracts (= 10 million/125,000).

CHAPTER 22

2. You have a profit of 1 point = $1000 when you exercise the contract, but you have paid a premium of $1500 for the call option, so your net profit is −$500, a loss of $500.

4. The put option is in the money, and you would exercise the contract, selling the futures contract for 125 when it can be bought for 120, yielding a profit of 5 points, or $5000. Subtracting the $2500 premium gives a net profit of $2500.

6. Because for any given price at expiration, a lower strike price means a higher profit for a call option and a lower profit for a put option. A lower strike price makes a call option more desirable and raises its premium and makes a put option less desirable and lowers its premium.

8. The hedge ratio is $HR = (\Delta P_a/\Delta P_f) \times \beta_{af} = 3/4 \times 1.5 = 1.125$. You should buy put option contracts in the amount of $HR \times (PV_a/PV_f) = 1.125 \times \$75$ million/$\$100{,}000 = 844$ contracts.

10. You would rather do it by selling futures contracts because you expect their price to fall. Then the profit on the futures would be greater than that on the put options, which have a net profit that is reduced by the amount of the premium you paid.

12. Because they suffer fewer accounting problems than futures contracts. If interest rates fall, the losses on the futures contracts cannot be offset by the gains in the value of the bank's assets. Even though the hedge has worked, the manager of the institution will look bad and may get fired. But if put options are bought, the loss on these contracts will be limited to the premiums paid and hence will not look so bad.

14. The advantages are that such a swap is very flexible and so can be made for the exact type of rate sensitivity that a financial institution requires and can also be made for long periods of time. The disadvantages are that the swap market can suffer from a lack of liquidity and swaps are subject to the same default risk encountered with forward contracts.

16. It would swap interest on $42 million of fixed-rate assets for the interest on $42 million of variable-rate assets, thereby eliminating its income gap.

18. The duration of the swap is 11 years minus the duration of the two-year zero-coupon bond = 9 years. The notional principal of the swap is $V_S = (-V_A \times DUR_{GAP})/DUR_S = (-\$1 \text{ billion} \times -2)/9 = \$222$ million.

20. You would swap $200,000 every year for payments of $300,000 every year for five years.

CHAPTER 23

1. Because of traditional American hostility to a central bank and centralized authority, the system of 12 regional banks was set up to diffuse power along regional lines.

3. Like the U.S. Constitution, the Federal Reserve System, originally established by the Federal Reserve Act, has many checks and balances and is a peculiarly American institution. The ability of the 12 regional banks to affect discount policy was viewed as a check on the centralized power of the Board of Governors, just as states' rights are a check on the centralized power of the federal government. The provision that there be three types of directors (A, B, and C) representing different groups (professional bankers, businesspeople, and the public) was

again intended to prevent any group from dominating the Fed. The Fed's independence of the federal government and the setting up of the Federal Reserve banks as incorporated institutions were further intended to restrict government power over the banking industry.

5. The Board of Governors sets reserve requirements and the discount rate; the FOMC directs open market operations. In practice, however, the FOMC helps make decisions about reserve requirements and the discount rate.

7. The Board of Governors has clearly gained power at the expense of the regional Federal Reserve banks. This trend toward ever more centralized power is a general one in American government, but in the case of the Fed it was a natural outgrowth of the Fed having been given the responsibility for promoting a stable economy. This responsibility has required greater central direction of monetary policy, the role taken over the years by the Board of Governors and by the FOMC, which the board controls.

9. The threat that Congress will acquire greater control over the Fed's finances and budget.

11. False. Maximizing one's welfare does not rule out altruism. Operating in the public interest is clearly one objective of the Fed. The theory of bureaucratic behavior only points out that other objectives, such as maximizing power, also influence Fed decision making.

13. False. The Fed is still subject to political pressure because Congress can pass legislation limiting the Fed's power. If the Fed is performing badly, Congress can therefore make the Fed accountable by passing legislation that the Fed does not like.

15. The argument for not releasing the FOMC directives immediately is that it keeps Congress off the Fed's back, thus enabling the Fed to pursue an independent monetary policy that is less subject to inflation and political business cycles. The argument for releasing the directive immediately is that it would make the Fed more accountable.

CHAPTER 24

1. Disagree. Some unemployment is beneficial to the economy because the availability of vacant jobs makes it more likely that a worker will find the right job and that the employer will find the right worker for the job.

3. True. In such a world, hitting a monetary target would mean that the Fed would also hit its interest

target, or vice versa. Thus the Fed could pursue both a monetary target and an interest-rate target at the same time.

5. The Fed can control the interest rate on three-month Treasury bills by buying and selling them in the open market. When the bill rate rises above the target level, the Fed would buy bills, which would bid up their price and lower the interest rate to its target level. Similarly, when the bill rate falls below the target level, the Fed would sell bills to raise the interest rate to the target level. The resulting open market operations would of course affect the money supply and cause it to change. The Fed would be giving up control of the money supply to pursue an interest-rate target.

7. Disagree. Although nominal interest rates are measured more accurately and more quickly than the money supply, the interest rate variable that is of more concern to policymakers is the *real* interest rate. Because the measurement of real interest rates require estimates of inflation, it is not true that real interest rates are necessarily measured more accurately and more quickly than the money supply. Interest-rate targets are therefore not necessarily better than money supply targets.

9. False. The FDIC would not be effective in eliminating bank panics without Fed discounting to troubled banks in order to keep bank failures from spreading.

11. The rise in the discount rate caused a sharp drop in discount borrowing on the part of the banks. The resulting sharp drop in the monetary base then led to a sharp drop in the money supply.

13. Because the Fed did not lend to troubled banks during this period, massive bank failures occurred, leading to a decline in the money supply when depositors increased their holdings of currency relative to deposits and banks increased their excess reserves to protect themselves against runs. As our money supply model indicates, these decisions by banks and depositors led to a sharp contraction of the money supply.

15. When the Federal Reserve was concerned that the dollar had risen too much by the mid-1980s, it pursued expansionary monetary policy in the 1985–1987 period to bring the value of the dollar back down again. When it felt that the dollar had fallen far enough by 1987, it pursued more contractionary policy to keep the dollar from falling further.

17. When the economy enters a recession, interest rates usually fall. If the Fed is targeting interest rates, it tries to prevent a decline in interest rates by selling bonds, thereby lowering their prices and raising interest rates to the target level. The open market sale would then lead to a decline in the monetary base and in the money supply. The decline in interest rates would also cause excess reserves to rise and the volume of discount loans to fall, thereby raising free reserves. With a free reserve target, the Fed would find monetary policy easy and would pursue contractionary policy. Therefore, neither interest-rate nor free reserve targets are very satisfactory because both can lead to a slower rate of money supply growth during a recession, just when the Fed would not want to slow money supply growth.

19. A borrowed reserves target will produce smaller fluctuations in the federal funds rate. In contrast to when there is a nonborrowed reserves target, when the federal funds rate rises with a borrowed reserves target, the Fed prevents the tendency of discount borrowings to rise by buying bonds to lower interest rates. The result is smaller fluctuations in the federal funds rate with a borrowed reserves target.

CHAPTER 25

2. The purchase of dollars involves a sale of foreign assets, which means that international reserves fall and the monetary base falls. The resulting fall in the money supply causes interest rates to rise and $RET^\$$ to shift to the right while it lowers the future price level, thereby raising the future expected exchange rate, causing RET^F to shift to the left. The result is a rise in the exchange rate. However, in the long run, the $RET^\$$ curve returns to its original position, and so there is overshooting.

4. Because other countries often intervene in the foreign exchange market when the United States has a deficit so that U.S. holdings of international reserves do not change. By contrast, when the Netherlands has a deficit, it must intervene in the foreign exchange market and buy guilders, which results in a reduction of international reserves for the Netherlands.

6. Two francs per dollar.

8. A large balance-of-payments surplus may require a country to finance the surplus by selling its currency in the foreign exchange market, thereby gaining international reserves. The result is that the central bank will have supplied more of its currency to the public, and the monetary base will rise. The

resulting rise in the money supply can cause the price level to rise, leading to a higher inflation rate.

10. Countries may implement a contractionary monetary policy when they decide to intervene in the foreign exchange market and buy domestic currency to finance the deficit. The result is that they sell off international reserves and their monetary base falls, leading to a decline in the money supply.

12. When other countries buy U.S. dollars to keep their exchange rates from changing vis-à-vis the dollar because of the U.S. deficits, they gain international reserves and their monetary base increases. The outcome is that the money supply in these countries grows faster and leads to higher inflation throughout the world.

14. There are no direct effects on the money supply because there is no central bank intervention in a pure flexible exchange rate regime; therefore, changes in international reserves that affect the monetary base do not occur. However, monetary policy can be affected by the foreign exchange market because monetary authorities may want to manipulate exchange rates by changing the money supply and interest rates.

CREDITS

Page 26 : "Stock Market Indexes" from the *Wall Street Journal*, January 31, 1997, p. C12. Reprinted by permission of the *Wall Street Journal*, © 1997 Dow Jones & Company, Inc. All Rights Reserved Wordwide.

Page 54: "Bond Prices and Interest Rates" from the *Wall Street Journal*. October 8, 1996, p. C21. Reprinted by permission of the *Wall Street Journal*, © 1996 Dow Jones & Company, Inc. All Rights Reserved Wordwide.

Page 113: "Credit Markets" from the *Wall Street Journal*. October 2, 1996, p. C21. Reprinted by permission of the *Wall Street Journal*, © 1996 Dow Jones & Company, Inc. All Rights Reserved Wordwide.

Page 127: "Sampling of Interest-Rate, Economic and Currency Forecasts" from the *Wall Street Journal*, January 2, 1997, p. C2. Reprinted by permission of the *Wall Street Journal*, © 1997 Dow Jones & Company, Inc. All Rights Reserved Wordwide.

Page 137: "Commodities" from the *Wall Street Journal*, September 17, 1996, p. C19. Reprinted by permission of the *Wall Street Journal*, © 1996 Dow Jones & Company, Inc. All Rights Reserved Wordwide.

Page 147: "Yield Curves" from the *Wall Street Journal*, January 31, 1997, p. C17. Reprinted by permission of the *Wall Street Journal*, © 1997 Dow Jones & Company, Inc. All Rights Reserved Wordwide.

Page 190: "Currency Trading" from the *Wall Street Journal*, October 9, 1996, p. C15. Reprinted by permission of the *Wall Street Journal*, © 1996 Dow Jones & Company, Inc. All Rights Reserved Wordwide.

Page 212: "Foreign Exchange" from the *Wall Street Journal*, September 13, 1996, p. C17. Reprinted by permission of the *Wall Street Journal*, © 1996 Dow Jones & Company, Inc. All Rights Reserved Wordwide.

Page 238: "Money Rates" from the *Wall Street Journal*, January 31, 1997, p. C17. Reprinted by permission of the *Wall Street Journal*, © 1997 Dow Jones & Company, Inc. All Rights Reserved Wordwide.

Page 261: "Stock Prices" from the *Wall Street Journal*, January 30, 1997, p. C5. Reprinted by permission of the *Wall Street Journal*, © 1997 Dow Jones & Company, Inc. All Rights Reserved Wordwide.

Page 490: "Top Ten Underwriters of U.S. Debt and Equity Issues, 1994" from the *Wall Street Journal*, January 3, 1995, p. C1. Reprinted by permission of the *Wall Street Journal*, © 1995 Dow Jones & Company, Inc. All Rights Reserved Wordwide.

Page 491: "Tombstone" for Marquette Medical Systems, Reproduced with permission from Marquette Medical Systems, Inc.

Page 530: "Future Prices—Interest Rate" from the *Wall Street Journal*, January 31, 1997, p. C14. Reprinted by permission of the *Wall Street Journal*, © 1997 Dow Jones & Company, Inc. All Rights Reserved Wordwide.

Page 543: "Future Prices—Index" from the *Wall Street Journal*, April 15, 1997, p. C16. Reprinted by permission of the *Wall Street Journal*, © 1997 Dow Jones & Company, Inc. All Rights Reserved Wordwide.

Index